World War III
Unmasking The End Time Beast

By Rabbi Simon Altaf

Your Arms To Yisrael Publishing

North Miami Beach, Florida – 2006

ISBN: 1599160528

Contributions

My first praise is to YHWH Elohim of my salvation, Yahushua Adonai (my YHWH) my living Savior who called me out of Islam thirty-five years into my life. This was my time of calling because without this none of this would be possible. I am writing this seven years and 6 months into my salvation experience (saved September 17th 1998 – March 24th 2006). I give ALL THE GLORY and honor to my Master Yahushua. Yahushua is my Rabbi, my personal teacher, my personal Savior and Adonai (my YHWH). All that I have learned so far is through His direction because of His love for me. He is the Elohim of Israel, YHWH Elohim of grace, mercy and truth who has mercy unto a **thousand generations** of those that love Him and keep His commandments.

> Isaiah 12:2 Behold, YHWH is my salvation, I will trust and not be afraid;" For **YAH**, the Master, is my strength and my song; **He also has become my salvation.**"

My salvation was made possible by three people, one Yahushua Himself, another an Egyptian brother Timothy Ibrahim and the third person who had the vision to save Muslims for Messiah, Jochen Katz of www.answering-islam.org It was upon Jochen's insistence that Timothy wrote his testimony, which brought the truth into my life through the internet of all places. That is what Yahushua HaMashiach had ordained for me. Most people think that the internet is only a den of corruption. However they forget that YHWH works in mysterious ways and many good things also happen through this marvellous technology. I call this a congregation with wires, or wireless, as the case maybe. May the Master reward these individuals for their work for the kingdom of YHWH to reach out to those who may otherwise be lost forever.

I would like to extend my thanks to Ramon Baca of http://www.ezekiel33graphics.com who designed the front and back covers of this book. I recommend him for all your graphic needs and he has some excellent T-Shirts on his website for you also. I would also like to thank Walid Shoebat who is my Palestinian buddy and ex-terrorist friend, who is also a believer in Yahushua. He first challenged me to answer some very difficult questions that I could not answer pertaining to Europe as the location of the coming Anti-Messiah, as I had been taught incorrectly. He alerted me to Bible prophecies and the Islamic connection and why Islam fits. We spent many hours studying/arguing/debating prophecies, after which the first book entitled This is Our Eden was published, which is now out of print. I have spent much time on my knees in prayer to Yahweh to show/reveal His truths to me and He has been most faithful. He continues to teach me, as my education is by no means finished. The joy of now facing Jerusalem and bowing to Yahweh, as opposed to Allah and facing Mecca cannot be explained in words.

I am grateful to Robert Forsbach of www.prophecymaps.com who supplied the maps in this book that he has especially designed for this project upon my request and with my instructions. He worked so hard and so many hours late into the night to bring this project to fruition. Robert was directed to me by the Master Yahushua Himself, as I did not know him previously. They say a picture speaks a thousand words and Robert has used his extraordinary skills and talent to convey these words with the maps he produced for this book. It is a great privilege to work with Robert, and may the Master's blessings be upon him and his household.

I would like to thank my wife Aaliyah for her patience with me while the book was being written allowing me to concentrate on this important task. I consider it the utmost priority for our last generation, a calling that the Master had established for me even before my birth.

I am dedicating this book to all the martyred brothers and sisters, the true heroes of our faith, who were faithful to our Master Yahushua and who did not bow their knees to Baal. You are not forgotten you will shine like stars forever. You are not like Hollywood stars, they are only stars for a season, and then they fade away. You are going to have an eternal brightness ablaze in glory. One day I also look forward to meeting with you in the presence of our great Adonai Yahweh. I consider myself honored to serve the Master as you have served Him so faithfully.

Daniel 12:2-3: And many of those who sleep in the dust of the earth shall awake, **some to everlasting life**, some to shame and everlasting contempt. Those who are wise **shall shine like the brightness of the firmament**, and those who turn many to **righteousness like the stars forever and ever**.

To read my full testimony please visit:
http://www.abrahamic-faith.com/Testimony/Mohammed.html

You can e-mail me at: shimoun63@yahoo.com and I will respond to your e-mails with any further questions if you are unsure of anything. I welcome all mail.

Prologue

The purpose of this book is simply to illustrate where we are in YHWH's plan and to look at what has been written about Bible prophecy by helping the reader understand Bible prophecy. There are perhaps thousands of Bible prophecy books written by thousands of different authors all with good intentions. I do not have the time and resources to look at all of these writers, but I will mention a few key authors who are well known in Christian circles.

This book is for the body of Yahushua for this last generation, as well as to promote understanding about the faith of Islam and why it wants to dominate the world. The purpose is not hatred for Muslims since much of my own family remain Muslims and I do love the Muslim people, that there are good Muslims in the world. The first human was created in the image of the one true YHWH while the rest of humanity followed the image of Adam Genesis 5:3 thus inheriting sin. My prayer is that many Muslims will come to know Yahushua of Nazareth as their living and personal Savior as I myself have found.

All the quotes in this book are referenced from the King James Version (KJV) or the New King James Version Bible (NKJV) and where this differs it will be quoted as such. This has been done since most everyone is familiar with them and can get a copy of them, but I personally recommend the *Restoration Scriptures True Name Edition Study Bible* as the closest to preserving the original meanings of the Hebrew and Aramaic texts. My comments in the biblical verses are in square brackets, or parenthesis where appropriate.

When Yahushua the Messiah is used, I speak of the one commonly, but incorrectly known as Jesus. When YHWH, or Yahweh is used, I speak of the one commonly, but incorrectly known as simply God.

I

Table of Contents

III

Chapter 1

The Revival of Global Jihad

What we are seeing today in the world is clearly a revival of **FANATIC ISLAM** and the Bible puts it something like this.

> **Revelation 13:3** I saw <u>one</u> of his heads as if it had been **mortally wounded**, and his **deadly wound was healed**. And all the world marvelled and followed the beast.

The last Empire that was brought to a close by the British, French and with the help of the forgotten Australians in 1924 was Islamic, this was the beast that was MORTALLY WOUNDED but not eradicated completely, the Bible called this the **1ˢᵗ beast of Revelation** (Revelation 13:1a) and the Bible also calls this **"another beast"** (Revelation 13:11a) that is really the 1ˢᵗ beast and a literal revival of Islam out of the different parts of the earth. This 2ⁿᵈ beast is really the <u>same</u> 1ˢᵗ beast and carries ALL the hallmarks of the 1ˢᵗ beast, remembering that both of these BEASTS are the one and the same playing the same role, the only difference being the 1ˢᵗ beast was wounded and dormant, now it is resuscitated medically speaking and is fully healed actively killing and devouring in pieces across the world, this is a force truly to be reckoned with.

> **Revelation 13:11** Then I saw **another beast** coming up out of the earth; and he had **two** horns like a lamb, and he spake as a dragon.

> [rise of pure fundamentalist Islam from all over the world in every country, the two horns are the two major divisions of Islam, Sunni and Shiites]

How can it be two beasts yet the same one e.g. Islamic?

This can be seen easily in the fact that the beast was **wounded** and yet now has revived.

Remember the 1ˢᵗ beast was wounded <u>not</u> removed so it revives as a new beast yet exercising the authority of the <u>first</u> and making people worship the image e.g. the likeness of or the emblem of Islam that Allah is god. We are a likeness unto Yahweh yet we are not little replicas of Yahweh, but a likeness of Him i.e. we carry His personality, His attributes in some measure i.e. intelligence, love and the ability to communicate. We are created by His breath therefore we have eternal souls no matter whether we are Hindu, Jew or Muslim the soul is eternal therefore the punishment in hell is also eternal, or likewise the heavenly abode is eternal, as the soul never dies. That is an attribute of Yahweh that He is eternal and never dies. He does not want to send us to hell (Ezekiel 18:23), but for our unbelief in the shed blood of Yahushua, many people choose eternal damnation by their actions.

Sadly much of the human race will be in hell. We cannot say we are little Messiah's since that would be blasphemous and would point to polytheism, Hinduism, or some similar type of theology. I do believe that in times past, Yahweh in order to protect His name and not to unduly punish people, hid or concealed the sacred names of Yahweh and Yahushua, as even today we see people cursing God, cursing Jesus and using them as a swear words yet they do not know the true sacred name, even here I see the mercy of Yahweh over mankind.

How many comings of Yahushua according to Scripture? Two:

1st identified as the **Son of Joseph** the suffering servant King (Isaiah 42, 52, 53).
2nd identified as the **Son of David** as Messiah the King (Jeremiah 23:5).

We have two comings yet one and the **same** Messiah. So we have two beasts yet the same kingdom. Do you see the parallel? Interesting that the Messiah was wounded at His first coming and killed for our sins, yet rose from the dead, returned to the Father, and will return as glorious King at His 2nd coming. The beast was wounded and revived, but when the beast is killed it will not be able to revive itself.

In Daniel Yahushua is called **a Prince** (Daniel 8:25) while in Jeremiah **a King** (Jeremiah 23:5), and in Isaiah **a servant** (Isaiah 42:1). How come Christians never argue that these are three different people? Because they are all **one** person, yet some argue that the beasts have to be different people or kingdoms. These arguments are not consistent with Scripture. If the second beast was Roman Catholicism, then it by no means would agree to the people worshipping as Muslims, but would want the worship directed in its churches not in Mosques. There is no Scripture for the two uniting, or for Islam changing to accept the concept of Allah having a son. The Qur'an clearly dictates and proclaims that one cannot be a worshipper of Allah, if one confesses that Allah has a son. This is just wishful thinking for those who are not well versed in Islam.

Now my question is how can it be two comings yet one Messiah? Do we have two Yahushua's? No the same person comes twice. The same way the same beast comes **twice** here lays the answer to this mystery.

The beast of **Revelation 13:2** is a geographic composite that sits in the Middle East, but the beast in **Revelation 13:11** is the same beast. But this time rather than come out of the Middle East the revival is in the earth, we are not told which part of the earth it comes out of. Remember the reference in Hebrew whereby 'Ha-Eretz' can be the whole world, a geographic location, or even a country. Likewise for Yahushua He will not have to be born again as a baby to return a 2nd time. And in like manner the beast is already a conglomerate of peoples. They do not have to form a new kingdom, as the kingdom is already here. It was just dormant and it will grow to a full force, as we are experiencing today i.e. the revival of radical Islam across the world.

5

Revelation 13:11 And I beheld **another beast** coming up **out of the earth [Ha Eretz]**; and he had two horns like a lamb, and he spake as a dragon.

Remember how the dragon i.e. s.a.tan spoke with Chava (Eve) in the garden? Gently with deception "you shall surely not die" (Genesis 3:4), and so likewise does Islam. It speaks with the words of salvation, but s.a.tan deceives people.

At the same time we have many moderate Muslims making mention of Islam as peaceful. This has become the rhetoric of the 21st century. Unfortunately such rhetoric has no value in our society when we are constantly being hit by **homicide bombers** across the world, because actions speak louder than words. Someone needs to ask that million dollar question; "why are radical Muslims willing to blow themselves up to kill other innocent civilians if the religion is teaching peace?" People in the Muslim world are not doing a good job teaching that elusive peace, or that their religion really has nothing to do with peace, but rather with destruction and the mayhem that we are seeing across our cities.

Let us ask why from the inception of Islam every country that it seems to touch is torn apart with violence and destruction bringing chaos to the economy and subjection of its people!

Take a look at some examples of this phenomenon;

- ❖ Pakistan - has not had one stable government since its creation in 1947; it claims to be an Islamic nation, parts of the country are on Sha'ria [legal code of Islam].
- ❖ Iraq – Chaos for the last 30 years also claims to be Islamic.
- ❖ Jordan – faction and fighting amongst the Muslims. If it were not for the support of the west then Jordan would be forgotten in history. It was established with the help of the British as a thank you gift to King Abdullah of Jordan giving Israeli land away to the Muslims at least 75% in approximation.
- ❖ Iran – Islamists factions; it did see some stability during the days of the late Shah of Iran.
- ❖ Afghanistan – It was embroiled in bitter war with Russia, tribal warfare amongst its people that has been continuing for decades to this very day.
- ❖ Libya – Dictatorial regime.
- ❖ Sudan-Ethnic cleansing by Muslims of innocent Christians.
- ❖ Nigeria- Ethnic persecution by Muslims of innocent Christians.

The list of countries is way too exhaustive to detail here, but you get my point of what I am saying.

Teachings of the Qur'an;

What are the moderate Muslims going to do about the violent verses in the Qur'an that are active today according to Muslim scholarly opinion? If their excuse is that these are being misapplied today, then surely there being in the Qur'an in the first place, is the very reason why fanatics can apply them and are right in their thinking, when they have a majority backing from many Islamic scholars to these verses still being in force and active for ALL Muslims worldwide today. If the verses in question are not in force, then why are many Muslims in the world acting upon them to become human bombers? Surely the question should be asked. Are all the Islamic teachers wrong, or have their Muslim followers gone off the rail?

As I said before actions speak louder then words. If Muslims are honest and true then the verses of the sword are still incumbent on ALL Muslims. The only way Muslims can circumvent such verses is to reform the Qur'an, but unfortunately the reformation of the Qur'an is not up for negotiation. The bottom line is this. Islam has a violent past and a violent present and future and a lot more trouble is to come in the world. We should prepare to deal with the consequences of a violent present and future. I believe in the strategy of massive Muslim conversions to Yahushua, giving us less potential terrorists and Israel haters, plus precious souls saved. I also know that the possibility of this is fairly remote, but still we must try. The answer to the problem is not less but more Christian evangelism! The question is who is going to do it? Who wants to be killed by fanatic Muslims trying to reach them? The answer lies in people like me and others who have come out of Islam. We are the best candidates to enlighten the Muslim people with the truth of the saving knowledge of Yahushua the Messiah, because we are <u>not</u> afraid to die.

A lot of people would like to understand the reasons why would people from a distant land attack us with such brutality.
This reminded me of the 9/11 event and a verse from the book of Revelation came to my mind.

> **Revelation 9:11** And they had a **<u>king over them</u>, which is the angel of the bottomless pit,** whose name in the **Hebrew tongue is <u>Abaddon</u>,** but in the **Greek tongue hath his name <u>Apollyon</u>.**

It may come as a surprise for some to know that Allah has a beautiful name out of the 99 names that is described in the Arabic language as **Al-Mumit**. This is the 62nd name of Allah that means exactly as the book of Revelation described it as **"the one who can destroy."** Did we not see on 9/11 the wrath of Allah on the USA nation through the Muslims? Many were shown a glimpse of the "one who can destroy."

> **<u>Revelation 13:9</u>** If anyone has an ear let him hear.

Allah also has a name in the Arabic called **Al-Mutakabir** meaning the proud one. Now ask yourself, who is the **<u>proud one</u>** and why was s.a.tan thrown out of heaven?

Who deceives people in the world?

> **<u>Surat Al-Nisa 4:142</u>** *The Hypocrites - they seek to deceive Allah, <u>but it is Allah who deceives them</u>. When they stand up to prayer, they stand without earnestness, to be seen of men, but little do they hold Allah in remembrance.*

Who plots against people in the world?

> **<u>Surat Al-Anfal 8:30</u>** And when those who disbelieve plot against thee [O Mohammed] to wound thee fatally, or to kill thee or to drive thee forth; they plot, **but Allah [also] plotteth; and Allah is the best of plotters.**

In the UK we recently saw the evidence of something incredibly described in the book of **<u>Daniel 7:7</u>** as the fourth beast, this book was written nearly 2,555 years ago written in Aramaic by Daniel the prophet identifying events occurring today, this is incredible stuff;

7

Daniel 7:7-8 After this I saw in the night visions, and behold, a **fourth beast**, dreadful and **terrible**, **exceedingly strong**. It had **huge iron teeth**; it was **devouring**, **breaking in pieces**, and **trampling the residue with its feet**. It was **different from all the beasts** that were before it, and **it had ten horns**.

The attacks happened in the UK on 7/7, it is uncanny that the prophet Daniel described a beast that would rise up from the Great Sea (Mediterranean) and is **dreadful**, **terrible** and **exceedingly strong**, **devouring** and **breaking** in pieces.

Daniel 7:2-3 Daniel spoke, saying, "I saw in my vision by night, and behold, the four winds of heaven were stirring up the **Great Sea**. "And **four great beasts** came up from the sea, each different from the other.

Could this beast described by Daniel the prophet be the same beast that struck us in the UK? Is Yahweh trying to teach us something that we perhaps are blind to spiritually? Many in the churches who should know about this are totally unaware, because the book of Daniel, and in particular these verses, are hardly read and many fail to understand these as the people in the pulpit try to spiritualize these away.

It is taught in Islam to strive in the way of Allah that means in anyway possible and the clerics have decided that this includes homicide bombings to force people to accept the values of Islam and expel the enemy from Islamic lands. Where Islam dominates they want the west to stay out, if they are not willing to accept their values, because they see the west as a decadent society with empty spirituality and the Islamic people are trying to fill the void with the rhetoric of peaceful Islam in the lives of Western people.

Sura 5:35 O you who believe! Be careful of (your duty to) Allah and seek means of nearness to Him and strike hard in His way that you may be successful.

During May 17th, 2005, we heard of riots and trouble in Afghanistan, Pakistan, Uzbekistan and other Muslim nations because of an alleged claim that some Americans desecrated the Qur'anic passages in Guantanamo Bay by throwing them down the toilet. This riot in Pakistan was incited by the ubiquitous cricketer turned politician Imran Khan, the so called peace maker who saw this as an opportunity to kick back against General Pervez Musharraf and his regime in Pakistan. A similar event not so long ago occurred in Nigeria during 2002 when during a Miss world beauty pageant Muslims rioted, not because of what women were wearing, but because a newspaper made the comment that Muhammad the Muslim prophet would have probably married the winner had he been around. And it was this that sparked the Muslim outburst and even though the newspaper apologised three times, the Muslims still burned down the office.

The Muslims also want justice for Abu Ghraib Prison in Iraq over what some USA soldiers did. But the Muslim world should question their own ethics first and show justice in their own nations before asking for justice elsewhere. Have they asked for justice when Muslim women were raped in Abu Ghraib and their husbands tortured and killed there by Saddam and his evil men?

This has to stop in the Muslim world where they start rampaging and killing innocent people and usually it is the innocent Muslims who end up dead.

In Pakistan Qazi Hussain Ahmed another extremist Islamic leader incited groups across Turkey, Britain, Egypt and other nations to riot against what the USA did.

I am well acquainted with this double standard in the Islamic world. In October 2000 when the Israeli forces retreated from Nablus as a peace making gesture the Muslims rioted. They painted the biblical patriarch Joseph's tomb's dome green; they also urinated on the tomb even though they claim to revere the patriarch as the prophet Yousef, the great grandson of the prophet Abraham, who they claim was a Muslim. Later when Rabbi Hillel Lieberman went to save the remains of the desecrated Torah scrolls from the tomb he was killed by the Palestinians. His body was thrown into a cave. In April 2002 Palestinian gunmen entered the church of the nativity a site holy both to Christians and Muslims. Once inside, they urinated and defecated in the church destroying many ancient relics.

On the one hand the Muslims claim to acknowledge all the biblical patriarchs as prophets, but on the other hand we see this obscene behavior. Why did the Muslim world not protest these desecrations and the unnecessary murder of innocent Rabbi Lieberman? Why the double standards in the Muslim world? This is the hypocrisy that we need to understand.

Our politicians inform us that these are fringe groups, or Islamic extremists and that these fanatics do not represent the majority view of Islamic teachings. We saw Osama bin Laden waltz on our TV screens four days before the 2004 USA election. This should tell you something. A picture speaks a thousand words and it shows that the USA is struggling to keep the extremists at bay. This illustrates that the Muslims are fighting to establish the soon coming of "**The Last Caliph**" eagerly awaited in Islam and **the REVIVAL OF GLOBAL JIHAD** that the Islamic world has expected for a long time. It is not good to be hiding this fact that we are facing a global war, and the Bible stands as the testimony to all this. Islam is truly being REVIVED as it was in the 7th century. We are coming to the close of our history whether we

like it or not. For us as believers in Yahushua it should be a glorious time to expect our Master to return.

Revelation 13:3 I saw one of his heads as if it had been mortally wounded, and **his deadly wound was healed**. And ALL the world marvelled and followed the beast.

The beast that was wounded. The Islamic Empire that was brought to a close in 1924 is now being revived all over the world in its truest form. We are now seeing the revival of fanatic Islam, and we should expect much trouble in the world. I hope to unmask this person that the Bible refers to in various passages as "**The Assyrian**," "**Gog of the land of Magog**," "**The Little Horn**," "**The King of Babylon**" and the "**Prince of Tyre**." Believe it or not, the Book of Revelation has come alive and is now fully in force in our generation because we stand as the generation before the coming of Yahushua our Master the Messiah of Israel.

The Muslims are tenacious fighters and are not going away quietly; our technology can help, but cannot <u>eliminate</u> terrorism. This is a harsh reality so do not be fooled by the rhetoric that we will eliminate global terrorism without some major battles. Afghanistan proved to be a testing ground for Russia where the rag tag army of the Mujahideen gave Russia a humiliating defeat. This is also the place where Osama bin Laden planned his attack on the World Trade Center and brought down the twin towers collapsing to the ground. Who would have thought that they could achieve such a goal in a country like America?

These people not only did achieve their initial goal, but also continue to survive and inflict damage on the west. These are the foot soldiers of Allah and this is a fight that will continue until the end. The only person who will gain the final victory will be Yahushua Himself when He returns. In the meantime it is business as usual for these guys. Governments may change such as in Iraq where Zechariah's prophecy is being fulfilled where YHWH calls this **wickedness** (**Zechariah 5:11**); but under the bonnet it is the same old Islam disguised in different packages and governments.

In addition our leaders say that Islam is a religion of peace, but some adherents of Islam pursue terrorism for their own immoral purposes and carry out attacks against the civilized world. Therefore, our war is really against those promoting terror and destruction. However, the Muslims generally see this as an attack on Islam from the west, and are rising up to meet the West in an onslaught that the Bible tells us will end in **Armageddon**.

Are our leaders telling us the truth?

The simple answer is they <u>cannot</u> tell the truth because of the problems this would create. I was in the Muslim camp once. I know the facts better then reported by the media or our leadership. If Christians promote their faith by actively preaching in the world, the love of YHWH for mankind and the atoning death of Yahushua the Messiah for the salvation of men, should we view the Christians as extremists?

What about those Christian churches that are quite content to have homosexual Bishops ordained? Should they be viewed as living with the correct biblical doctrine when the Bible clearly teaches that this is an abomination before YHWH and a sin?

<u>Leviticus 18:22</u> You shall not lie with a male as with a woman. It is an **abomination**.

The same way we should not judge the Muslims by the 'do it yourself ' Islam in the West, but by the true form of Islam that was and is practiced in some eastern countries. We also need to measure them by the agreed doctrine of the Qur'an and Hadiths, not by people's conceived ideas of Islam.

The truth of the matter is that the ones who do not voice a concern about homosexual Bshops amongst Christian churches are the ones in the wrong camp, while the ones who take the message of the love of YHWH and the need of atonement for mans' sin are in the right camp. In the same manner, Muslims who hold strict adherence to the Qur'anic text and the Hadiths (sayings and deeds of their prophet Muhammad), are also following the strict teachings in accordance with Islam and therefore are in the <u>correct</u> camp. The majority Muslims who do not follow this practice are equally considered by the Muslims to be in the wrong camp and rightly so judged by the Qur'an. This means the ones in Osama's camp are correctly following the teachings of the Qur'an and the moderates are not! This is the reason why he is revered and people wear Osama bin Laden T-shirts in the Muslim world. You can kill Osama bin Laden, but ten more will stand up in his place, so the problem is not Osama alone.

The Qur'an clearly teaches to wage ACTIVE WAR against the Infidels, or those who occupy Muslim lands, or those who oppose the teachings of Muhammad. I will illustrate these things in this book to show that we are not up against a peaceful religion, but a force that is out to destroy all democratic values upon which the west functions. The two peoples (two houses) that fanatic Islam hates the most are evangelical Christians and Jews, because the evangelical Christians stand and pray for Israel and strongly support the rights of the existence of the Jews in Israel, without negotiating the surrender of their land to the Palestinians. We are not just dealing with demagogues, but a religion that is determined to take us back to a 7th century paradigm.

Let us examine a verse in the Qu'ran that is commonly known to be the verse of the sword. The following verse (Sura 9:29) is <u>universally</u> agreed to by all Islamic schools of thought to apply to our time. This is believed to be the last Sura of the Qu'ran, whereby Muslims have to actively conduct jihad (outer struggle by war), to bring about the Islamic government in ALL the world, and to establish the caliphate (one supreme caliph e.g. a leader). **This speaks volumes, while all the PEACEFUL verses (relating to co-existence with non-Muslims) in the Qu'ran before this verse are 'Naasikh' and 'Mansookh' (that means to be abolished, replaced and abrogated, made null and void completely).**

> **Sura 9.29** Fight those who do not believe in Allah [**Allah is not YHWH Elohim of the Bible**], nor in the latter day [**atheists, polytheists, humanists and animists**], nor do they prohibit what Allah and His Apostle have prohibited [**this includes all people who do not comply with food restrictions and general laws of Islam**], nor follow the <u>religion of truth</u> [**that means "Islam" and applies to all non-Muslim people**], out of those who have been given the Book [**includes Jews and Christians especially**], until they pay the tax in acknowledgment of superiority [**submission tax called jizzya for those who do not believe in Muhammad and Allah**] and they are in a state of subjection [**humiliate them in subjection, i.e. until they feel the only path for them is to become Muslims to avoid this over taxation and daily humiliation**].

The above verse has therefore abolished all 114 peaceful verses in the Qu'ran that were revealed to Muhammad before it. This verse was allegedly revealed to Muhammad in Medina by Allah (the Islamic god) through the angel Gabriel. Moderate Muslims wrongly cite peaceful verses in the Qu'ran in order to mislead other people into DIY (do it yourself), packaged Islam for western consumption. When Muhammad was in Mecca, he preached there for thirteen years with a peaceful form of Islam during which time the peaceful verses were used during Islam's weakness. But when he moved to Yathrib (Medina) he started to make followers and the Islamic calendar dating started there after the hijra (migration of the prophet). As his followers increased in Medina to his newfound religion, the Suras changed from being peaceful to hostility. These Medinan Suras abrogated ALL the peaceful verses revealed to him in Mecca. Since the Qu'ran is not in any chronological order, it is very difficult for any ordinary person to know which are Meccan Suras and which are Medinan without going into an in depth study of the Qu'ran and Islam. From that point in order to justify the Quraish merchant caravan raids, he advised his followers that they were serving Allah by attacking the enemy.

The people who live in Western nations do not really understand the nature of society/culture in Islamic nations, I encourage you to visit some Muslim nations and see for yourself how some of these people live and function.

The Western 'DIY' version of Islam is far removed from true Islam, but is rather an Islam especially packaged for the west. All the true teachings are removed so the new converts do not understand what Islam represents until they are indoctrinated into basic

Islam. At that point the Muslim Imams (religious clerics) can then introduce the other teachings, so these people will find them more palatable and also so that there will be no way out for them, because the fanatic Muslims will kill them for sure if they leave Islam, as they will be considered apostate.

We can read the famous Bukhari Hadith [sayings and deeds of Muhammad] on this topic, which states:

Hadith Sahih al Bukhari, Vol. 9 p 45

Narrated Ikrima: Some Zanadiqa (atheists) were brought to Ali and he burnt them. The news of this event reached Ibn Abbas who said, "If I had been in his place, I would not have burnt them, as Allah's apostle forbade it, saying 'do not punish anyone with Allah's punishment (fire).' **I would have killed them according to the statement of Allah's apostle: 'whoever changed his Islamic religion, *then kill him*.'** (Emphasis mine)

Hadith Sunan Abu Dawud, Vol. 3 p 1213

Abu Musa said: Mu'adh came to me when I was in the Yemen. A man who was a Jew embraced Islam and then retreated from Islam. When Mu'adh came, he said: 'I will not come down from my mount until he is killed.' He was then **killed**.

Therefore, generally most Muslim converts or otherwise remain in Islam out of fear and not because of the love for truth. Look at many western girls marrying Muslims, who convert out of love not out of conviction for Islam. A majority of such marriages end up in divorce. One prime example is that of Jemimah Goldsmith. It is very difficult for Western girls to adapt to Eastern Islamic values and culture, even though Jemimah went further then most learning the language and adapting to the society, but things still did not work out. The Muslim prophet Muhammad himself said **"kill them wherever you find them,"** this means anywhere in the world not just in an Islamic state. A lot of what has been happening in Iraq lately against the Muslims who have been captured and beheaded by radical Muslims themselves is a prime example that they are seen to be helping the west who are considered infidels. So these Muslim prisoners are considered by Islamists to be apostate Muslims to be killed. Daily there are Iraqi policemen captured and killed. Fanatics are killing the moderates because they consider them expendable and apostate in order to teach other Muslims a lesson not to side with the west.

Sahih Bukhari Hadith Volume 6, Book 61, Number 577:

I heard the Prophet saying, "In the last days (of the world) there will appear young people with foolish thoughts and ideas. They will give good talks, but they will go out of Islam as an arrow goes out of its game, their faith will not exceed their throats. **So, wherever you find them, kill them, for there will be a reward for their killers on the Day of Resurrection."** (underline mine)

Sura 4:89 They but wish that ye should reject faith, as they do, and thus be on the same footing (as they): so take not friends from their ranks until they flee in the way of Allah (from what is forbidden). But if they turn renegades, seize them and **slay them** [must be killed] wherever ye find them; and (in any case) take no friends or helpers from their ranks.

12

Sura 47:4 Therefore, when <u>ye meet the unbelievers</u> (in fight), <u>smite at their necks</u>; [behead the unbelievers] at length, when ye have thoroughly subdued them, bind a bond firmly (on them): thereafter (is the time for) either generosity or ransom: [or you can take a ransom] until the war lays down its burdens. Thus (are ye commanded): but if it had been Allah's Will, He could certainly have exacted retribution from them (Himself); but (He lets you fight) in order to test you, some with others. But those who are slain in the way of Allah, He will never let their deeds be lost.

Sura 8:12 I shall cast terror into the hearts of the infidels. Strike off their heads, [**behead them**] maim them in every limb.

Do you not see that the Islamists who kill these secular Muslims are fulfilling the Hadiths and Qu'ran for reward? Most Islamic Scholars know and argue that the peaceful verses have been replaced by the verses of the <u>sword</u> that are now incumbent upon all Muslims. Those that do not follow these are seen as apostate Muslims, i.e. they do not hold to the Qu'ran truthfully. Therefore their punishment by other strict Muslims is death, as we have seen that the strict observers of this faith have killed some of those Muslims who simply want to work with the West and do not follow the strict teachings of the Qu'ran, which mostly are unworkable in today's society. Consider this! Islam does not allow the taking of a photo, or listening to music. So if you took a photo, whether for a passport, or otherwise, then that would be breaking Islamic law, This is what I mean by unworkable laws of Islam. In Saudi Arabia it is haram (wrong) to celebrate the birthdays of Muslim saints even the birthday of the Muslim prophet is not allowed to be celebrated. My friend told me that while in Saudi Arabia he said to someone happy Christmas during December and he was told promptly not to utter these words of infidels. He promptly replied Jesus is considered a prophet in Islam and this is His birthday isn't it? He was told we do not celebrate birthdays!

It is readily apparent that moderate Muslims living in Islamic countries never oppose any action by the so-called extremists?

The Muslim goal is simply to overcome the non-Muslim world and mold it into an Islamic world/Empire. They make no secret about this. It is not some hidden agenda, or some secret mission; in fact in this regards the Muslims are very honest and sincere. The Islamic Scholar Maududi (1903 – 1979) and founder of the Jamaat-e-Islami (Party of Islam) had this to say in his book "Jihad in Islam"...

> "Islam wishes to **destroy all states and governments anywhere on the face of the earth, which is opposed to the ideology and program of Islam regardless of the country or the nation which rules it**. The purpose of Islam is to set up a state on the basis of its own ideology and program, regardless of which Nation assumes the role of the standard bearer of Islam, or the rule of which nation is undermined in the process of the establishment of an ideological Islamic State."
> --Sayeed Abul A'la Maududi, Jihad in Islam p 9

He further states:

> "It must be evident to you from this discussion that the objective of Islamic 'Jihad' is to **eliminate the rule** of an **un-Islamic system** and establish in its stead an Islamic system of state rule. **Islam does not intend to confine this revolution**

to a single state, or a few countries; the aim of Islam is to bring about a universal revolution."
--Sayeed Abul A'la Maududi, Jihad in Islam p 24 – (Underline emphasis mine)

Friday, July 23, 2004, the Barnabas Fund that investigates the plight of persecuted Christians reported that in Iraq an Assyrian Christian owner of the Al-Hanna restaurant in Mosul's Al-Dawasa district had been murdered by an Islamic group because he had American customers. His business partner a Muslim, had his hands cut off and eyes gouged out by the Islamists.[1] Indeed, this is a stark warning that they will not tolerate Muslims working with Christians, because they consider these Muslims to be apostate and not following Islam exactly as I stated earlier.

I am writing this book to show the world that in order to survive this onslaught by the Islamists whose only agenda is the destruction and plundering of the west, we need to take a critical look at the current trends. The Bible documented our problems along with the solutions many centuries earlier, in what we call Bible prophecies. The question is do we accept the Bible as authoritative, or a book too old to solve our problems and continue to waste time in dialogue with the terrorists.

Today, terrorists dominate our televisions screens. The media presents beheadings as regular events showing that innocent people are being killed "in the name of Allah" and the question on everyone's lips is why?

I will show that this is not a new trend but this is simply a revival of the old fundamentalist religion of Islam. We must warn our peaceful Muslim neighbors of the catastrophe this will lead into unless they reform and turn away from this ideology. They need to beware that their souls are headed into everlasting torment for following a lie that the Bible calls "THE LIE." The Bible is emphatic that this trouble would happen in the last days and I will examine prophetic passages to show why this only fits with Islam and no other group of people, or religion on the face of our planet, who can possibly tie into this equation. **If you have paid attention so far to the conflict in Israel then you will come to a realization that the end time battle is really between the twelve tribes of Israel and the twelve tribes of Ishmael. Consider this as the 12 princes of light verses the 12 princes of darkness.**

We aught to ask ourselves, how do we solve all these problems, what is the answer to this strife and contention?

These are some of the questions that many people ask and this book is written to try and address some of those questions of the 21st century. Interestingly enough, when YHWH Elohim of Abraham, Isaac and Jacob gave His oracles to the Hebrew nation in the wilderness, when Moses rescued the children of Israel from slavery in Egypt, YHWH gave the answers to these questions also. YHWH gave the answers to the prophets of old, but we must take a deeper look in order to see what YHWH had to say about the source of this conflict, and how our world will be brought to a close by a cataclysmic end following these events.

In this we are all together, the Hindus, the Christians, and the Jews, no matter who you are including moderate Muslims. You will all be affected, but the solution lies in one

---

[1] http://www.assistnews.net/Stories/s04070079.htm

person only, and that is the person of Yahushua the Messiah (Yahushua of Nazareth), who can really bridge the gap and bring true peace between Muslims and the rest of the world. Two thousand years ago He died on a Roman cross to vanquish death. Next, He rose from the dead to gain victory for those that call Him Master and Savior and love Him dearly and follow Him to do good in the world by giving life and not death. He truly changes lives and mine is one such life that He changed from the road of destruction to the road of everlasting peace and eternal life with YHWH my Father.

With YHWH our Creator all is possible, but He has given us free will and choice to choose the right or the wrong way. I can love and pray for the Muslims who seek the true YHWH and I can confirm that YHWH is love and seeks those that search for Him whether Muslim, Hindu or Jew. It is true that YHWH will save Muslims that seek Him out of the fanatic religion of Islam to His everlasting love, while those Muslims that are bent on destruction will face destruction in this life with everlasting eternal consequences in the next. They will not find the seventy-two houris (perpetual virgins, black-eyed with big bosoms) they think they will get, which is a mere deception of the adversary.

Chapter 2

Lets All Get On The Bandwagon?

Look at most prophecy books on the shelves and they are all stuck on the same page. Either it is the Roman Catholic Church that is going to give us the Anti-Messiah in the form of the Pope, or the Anti-Messiah will turn up waltzing from some part of Europe. The clock for most prophecy writers is stuck either in Europe, usually Germany or the Vatican in Italy, while for others it is a combination of the USA failing and falling and the EU rising. Nevertheless the majority view is stuck on the EU, or the Anti-Messiah being some shady papal figure about to be revealed. Well for most it was not Benedict the XVI. I am sure he would have been relieved to know that he is not the Anti-Messiah, though the evangelicals would love him to play the part, as that is what they are taught even though wrongly.

Hal Lindsay the famous prophecy writer puts it like this in his book "Late Great planet Earth";

> The United States will not hold its present position of leadership in the Western world; financially, the future leader will be Western Europe. Internal political chaos caused by student rebellion and Communist subversion will begin to erode the economy of our nation. Lack of moral principle by citizens and leaders will so weaken law and order that a state of anarchy will finally result. The military capability of the United States, though it is at present the most powerful in the world, has already been neutralized because no one has the courage to use it decisively. When the economy collapses so will the military. (Hal Lindsey, p.184. Late Great planet Earth)

My comments:
One should ask the question to Mr Lindsay where does he get the idea that the USA economy will fail and fall? What text of the Bible did he use to decide that Western Europe is going to rise and on what hermeneutics? This is the sort of prophecy teaching that is rampant in evangelical circles and without any biblical justification. I asked Hal for a discussion on his prophecy views, someone from his office replied that he does not have time and is busy.

1st prophecy writer comments:

"The Roman Empire never ceased to exist. The Revived Roman Empire is really just the old Roman Empire revived. The Roman Empire was not destroyed or conquered by another power. It fell from within. Before the Roman Empire decayed from within, it stretched all the way to Great Britain in Europe. So really the New World Order, is really the Old World Order, the 6th Kingdom that was, when John the Revelator wrote, 5 Kingdoms have fallen, one is. The 7th is the Revived Roman Empire."[2]

2nd prophecy writer comments:

John Walvoord who argues that the seven kings represent the seven Gentile kingdoms, which have followed one another in succession. Egypt, Assyria, Babylon, Persia, and Greece are the five past kingdoms. Rome, of John's day, is the sixth. "All six of these kingdoms persecuted the people of YHWH (Israel). The seventh brief kingdom that gives rise to the eighth kingdom of the Antichrist (17:11)."

3rd prophecy writer comments:

"In meditating for many years on what might be implied in "the image of the beast," I could never find the least satisfaction in all the theories that had ever been propounded, till I fell in with an unpretending but valuable work, which I have noticed already, entitled *An Original Interpretation of the Apocalypse*. That work, evidently the production of a penetrating mind deeply read in the history of the Papacy, furnished at once the solution of the difficulty. There the image of the beast is pronounced to be the Virgin Mother, or the Madonna.

This at first sight may appear a very unlikely solution. But when it is brought into comparison with the religious history of Chaldea, the unlikelihood entirely disappears. In old Babylonian paganism, there was an *image* of the Beast from the sea; and when it is known what that image was, the question will, I think, be fairly decided. When Dagon was first set up to be worshipped, while he was represented in many different ways, and exhibited in many different characters, the favorite form in which he was worshipped, as the reader well knows, was that of a child in his mother's arms. In the natural course of events, the mother came to be worshipped along with the child, yes, to be the favorite object of worship.

To justify this worship, as we have already seen, that mother, of course, must be raised to divinity, and divine powers and prerogatives ascribed to her. Whatever dignity, therefore, the son was believed to possess a like dignity that was ascribed to her. Whatever name of honor he bore, a similar name was bestowed upon her. He was called Belus, "the Master"; she, Beltis, "My Lady." He was called Dagon, "the Merman"; she, Derketo, "the Mermaid." He, as the World-king, wore the bull's horns; she, as we have already seen, on the authority of Sanchuniathon, put on her own head a *bull's* head, as the ensign of royalty." [3]

4th prophecy writer comments:

"The United States (the two horned beast), will cause all to worship the first beast by enforcing the "mark of the first beast by law! The word "cause" in the original Greek means "force.""

---

[2] http://www.tribulationalinstitute.com/new_page_7.htm
[3] http://philologos.org/__eb-ttb/sect74.htm

A national Sunday law will be enforced in our country. In chapter one we have already seen that it is coming and some of the reasons why. We've already learned that the "two horned beast' is the U.S. The first beast is the Papacy. The image of the beast is a religious power just like the beast in our country teaching many of the same false teachings - the majority of the Protestant world.

To say it plainly, Revelation 13 is revealing to us the astonishing fact that Protestant America will cause all to worship the Papacy and receive its "mark by passing a national - Sunday law, and that all who do not go along with it will suffer the consequences!

When man reaches the depth of spiritual decay and passes that law, it will not only make an "image" to the beast in our country - and copy the old papal principle of persecution, it will set up the procedure for all to receive the "mark of the beast!" String fellow, Bill ALL IN THE NAME OF THE LORD. (Clermont: Concerned Publications, 1981), p. 134-135.

It's coming clear! You see, it won't be the beast, which enforces its "mark" by law in our country; it will be its "image" Protestant America.[4]

5th theory:
"The Antichrist could well rise out of the current chaos in the former Soviet Union. The prophet Ezekiel names him as the ruler of "Magog," a name that biblical scholars agree denotes a country, or region of peoples to the north of Israel. Many have interpreted this to mean modern day Russia. His power base will include the leading nations of Europe, whose leaders, the Bible says, will "give their power & strength unto the beast."[5]

Phew! So many are stuck on the EU clock. You can pickup any book on the shelf and the theme is the same; the EU is corrupt, or the big bad USA is stomping around the world. You will also find sarcasm in people's writings the way they write it shows hatred towards the USA, its presidents, especially the current President George W. Bush (2005). Some writers even slam President George Bush as a harlot, or sold out to the Arabs. Unfortunately most of their data comes from the liberalists with their own agenda.

6th theory:
"Since the Roman Empire must be revived, the EU (European Union) is the only candidate."

My response:

These sorts of claims are made all the time but without any valid biblical basis. Let me show you the flaw in these sorts of theories above.

They use one line of text from Daniel the prophet;

> **Daniel 9:26** "And after the **sixty-two weeks Messiah** shall be **cut off**, but not for Himself; and the **people of the prince who is to come shall destroy the city and the sanctuary**. The end of it shall be with a flood, and till the end of the war desolations are determined.

---

[4] http://www.biblerevelations.org/sundaylaw/sundaylaw06.htm
[5] http://www.countdown.org/armageddon/antichrist.htm

The typical interpretation is that Yahushua will come after a certain calculated time and be killed on the cross (so far so good) and then the "people of the prince" aka Romans (Titus) would come and destroy the Temple to which they point to the history of the destruction of the Temple in 70 AD. "The end of it shall be with a flood."

They claim the flood was the symbolic overflowing of the army of the Romans.

Let me show you the problem in this view.

Yahushua certainly did come and die but not for Himself but for others sins. If the "**people of the prince**" are the Romans then there are two problems. First of all the Temple was destroyed, but the problem is that the flood is not symbolic but <u>literal water</u> and has been waiting to happen for 2000 years. That is flaw number 1. How do I know it is a literal flood? Whenever YHWH says in the Bible that it would be "like," or "as" something then the word "like," or "as" are used to explain, let me show you.

When the writers of the Bible want to show us that this is **"as a flood"** it is specified:

> <u>Isaiah 28:2</u> "Behold, the Master hath a mighty and strong one, [which] as a tempest of hail [and] a destroying storm, "**as a flood**" of mighty waters overflowing, shall cast down to the earth with the hand." "Behold, the Master hath a mighty and strong one, [which] as a tempest of hail [and] a destroying storm, **as a flood** of mighty waters overflowing, shall cast down to the earth with the hand."

Now in the passage of Isaiah the usage is "as a flood" or "like a flood."

However we read in Jeremiah:

> <u>Jeremiah 47:2</u> Thus saith the LORD; Behold, waters rise up out of the north, and shall be **an overflowing flood**, and shall overflow the land, and all that is therein; the city, and them that dwell therein: then the men shall cry, and all the inhabitants of the land shall howl.

The usage of the words in Jeremiah are <u>literal</u>; YHWH will make an utter end of them by a literal flood and this is the reason why Daniel's usage is <u>literal</u> not allegorical. Most of the Anti-Messiah's armies will be destroyed with a <u>literal</u> flood. YHWH's toilet system to flush the enemy. Did that happen in AD 70? The answer is no, not yet so it is yet future. *Daniel 9:26 ...The end of it shall be with a flood.*

The Hebrew word used in **Daniel 9:26** "sheteph" literally means **overflowing of water**, i.e. physical water not allegorical water.

Second let us read **Daniel 9:27** and see our biggest problem;

> <u>Daniel 9:27a</u> Then "he" [Anti-Messiah] shall **confirm a covenant** with many for **one** week;

If we accept for a minute that the army that was to come was Roman and the prince was Titus, then it also entails that it is the same "he" in verse 27 who <u>must</u> set-up the covenant. In other words Titus must set-up the covenant, but we find this is not the case.

18

Titus never set-up <u>any</u> agreement or peace treaty with Israel so this is flaw number two that breaks Scripture. There is nothing in verse 26 that suggests that there is a gap. We can have the fulfilment of verse 26 because in the Hebrew language there is no break between verse 26 and 27 and verse 26 must follow through to verse 27. Remember the numbering did not exist in the Bible, but was put later for ease of reading; you can thank the Roman Catholics for this. This is hard to understand and to explain.

However if we said ok, let us say verse 26 is partially fulfilled then who are the "people of the prince" to come?

If the people are Roman for a minute then the armies that helped to destroy Jerusalem were Legion X Fretensis composed of the following units.

-Thracum Syriaca E.
-IV Cohort Thracia
-Syria Ulpia Petraeorum
-IV Cohort Arabia

Note these are all Middle Eastern people not European, this still points to Islamic nations i.e. **people of the prince**, the descendents of the people who attacked Jerusalem.

The evidence that it's speaking of the ancestors of Anti-Messiah is the usage of the "he" in verse 27:

"And <u>he</u> shall confirm the covenant with many for one week." This "he" is referring to the same person in verse 26 "**the prince that shall come.**"

Therefore, this "he" cannot be Titus. This same rule applies to Daniel chapter 11.

In fact many have ridiculed the Bible for that specific reason - how could Titus be referred to here and way into the future? The Hebrew grammar is quite clear. Is Titus coming back from the dead? Maybe to help the prophecy writers he might, but it will not happen as he awaits his final fate in Sheol.
But the answer to this objection is simple - **the "prince" is the anti-Messiah of which his people, his ancestors (eastern legions of the Roman Empire) destroyed Jerusalem and the Temple. So it must follow that the coming prince is not from the west and in agreement with Daniel 11's "little horn."**

In fact, Messiah Himself ends the arguments. In **Matthew 24:15** we read *"When ye therefore shall see the abomination of desolation, spoken of by Daniel the prophet, standing in the holy place."*

This reference cannot be to **Daniel 9:26** but **Daniel 9:27**, since in **Daniel 9:26** <u>no</u> abomination took place but a <u>destruction</u>. This abomination also cannot be what Antiochus Epiphanies did since that was way before Yahushua time.

We need to examine the only references in Daniel regarding an abomination - **Daniel 11:31**, **Daniel 12:11**, **Daniel 9:27**, and **Daniel 8:13**.

In **Daniel 8:13**, it is clearly regarding <u>one</u> horn from the Grecian 4 divisions of Alexander's Grecian Empire:

19

Daniel 8:9 "And out of one of them came forth **a little horn**, which waxed exceeding great, toward the south, and toward the east, and toward the pleasant [land]."

Then an amazing verse after it states:

Daniel 8:10 "And it waxed great, [even] to the host of heaven; and it cast <u>down</u> [some] of the <u>host and of the stars to the ground</u>, and stamped upon them."

If this is Antiochus, then how did he "cast down [some] of the host of heaven to the ground (fallen angels)"? This is definitely end times terminology. Also, why would Yahushua refer to a man who was long dead before Yahushua' birth?

In **Daniel 11:21** the man who is a type of the Anti-Messiah comes on the scene from the <u>north</u> and this is believed to be Antiochus Epiphanies who came from the Seleucid division, one of the <u>four</u> divisions of the Grecian Empire.

But Yahushua in **Matthew 24:15** placed **Daniel 11:31** into the future pointing to the Anti-Messiah as this "abomination of desolation" before His second coming and <u>not</u> in the Maccabees period. **Daniel 11:5-20** is a broad sketch of post-Grecian Empire history (Daniel 11:2-4) which leads right up to the time of the Anti-Messiah ("Little Horn") in Daniel 11:21.

This shows, to a certain degree, that many prophecies of the Bible have a type of fulfilment, Antiochus being an excellent example. We must never assume that the Bible is all history.

So, the confirmation of Yahushua's simple scheme for the future is found in Daniel. Here we follow Yahushua's instructions carefully. The abomination of desolation is the one described by Daniel (**Matthew 24:15**). The precise expression "abomination of desolation" occurs in **Daniel 11:31** with a further reference to its appearance in the holy place in **Daniel 12:11**. **Daniel 9:27** contains a third reference and also **Daniel 8:13**.

To summarize, Daniel describes a final evil ruler, the **King of the North**, who sets "the abomination of desolation" and puts an end to Temple sacrifices (**Daniel 11:31**).

It is crucially important to see that in **Daniel 12:11** about three and a half years will elapse between the appearance of the abomination of desolation and the end of the age. Yahushua is merely elaborating, in Matthew 24, what was already laid out by Daniel's "abomination of desolation" (**Daniel 11:31**; **Matthew 24:15**); tribulation for 3 1/2 years (Daniel 12:1, 7, 11) and then the resurrection (**Daniel 12:2**). The whole of Daniel 11 and 12 must be read in its entirety and the Daniel passage must be kept in mind as the background to Yahushua's discourse in **Matthew 24:3**.

The connection between **Matthew 24:15** and **Daniel 11:31** (**12:11**) is established by Yahushua's own words: *"Let the reader understand that I am referring to the book of Daniel"* *(see Matt. 24:15).*

Remember the one key to **Matthew 24**, the tribulation of which Yahushua spoke is to be followed immediately by cosmic signs and the second coming. The tribulation is to be triggered by the "abomination of desolation" already prophesied by **Daniel 11:31**. When

20

these facts are held together, they build up a composite picture of events destined to happen just before Yahushua arrives.

So, in accordance with Matthew 24, we must conclude that the Anti-Messiah as the Bible states is **Middle Eastern** in **_Daniel 8:9_** is *"From one of the prominent horns came a **small horn** whose power grew very great. **It extended toward the south** and the east and **toward the glorious land of Israel**. "*

He must come from the Grecian part of this Roman Empire i.e. the Eastern part. Remember that the territories of future Empires superimpose the previous empires so they may govern some regions of the previous empire and may not rule other regions of the previous Empire. **Since he is going south, he must be coming from the north parts in relation to Israel, exactly as specified in Ezekiel 38, Joel 3 and many other places.**

Antiochus in Daniel 8 is the forerunner of a pre-figuring of the Anti-Messiah linking him to the Grecian Empire rather then the "Prince to come" in **Daniel 9:26**. Daniel 9:26's 69 weeks is completely fulfilled with no connection in the passage or chapter to this "prince to come" to the final remaining week since it was preserved by Messiah for the **"little horn"** referred to in Daniel 8 and 11. Also, in Daniel 11 and Matthew 24, they both agree that the Temple is desecrated not destroyed, yet in Daniel 9 it's completely destroyed. So the short-term fulfilment of the *destruction of the Temple in* Daniel 9 cannot be the same as the abomination of desolation by the *"little horn"* of Daniel 8 and 11.

The main current theory that has been making the rounds since at least the last two hundred years is that he will come out of the European Union and will be part of the Roman Catholic Church. This region is not limited to just one part of Europe. Some think Italy others point to Germany and France as likely candidates.

1. All the EU nations today (25 in total) of which fifteen are in Western Europe and ten in Eastern Europe.

The C.I.S Republics, south of Russia were a part of the Roman Empire. So are we to say that the C.I.S nations will join Europe in order to fit this theory? The C.I.S nations are not a part of the EU nations. Neither are Libya, Tunis, Morocco, Algeria and Mauritania, which were part of the Western Roman Empire. Turkey and much of the Middle East are also not part of this coalition of nations.

2. There were 10 toes, on January 1, 1995, Austria, Finland, and Sweden were added to the European Union, bringing the total to 15 and then in May 2004 another 10 Eastern European nations joined making this interpretation unlikely. So for this interpretation to fit, a major shuffle must occur to eliminate 10 nations from the west and five from the East.

This theory has an incredible problem since in the first argument we must have 5 nations on each leg, and in this case we have 15 toes in the Western leg and 10 toes in the Eastern one. Not to forget that 5 Islamic states (Libya, Tunisia, Morocco, Mauritania and Algeria) <u>must</u> be included since they were part of the Western Roman Empire (see map below). This alone is an issue for all prophecy students to ponder. Even if ten nations from the west and five from the East were removed the prophecy would still not fit because the clay spoken of is "red" and frankly speaking it is Middle Eastern clay not European clay.[6]

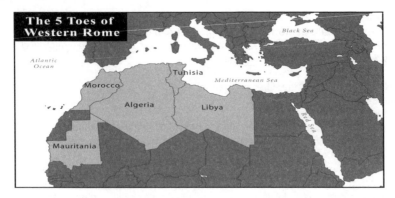

Turkey is currently having issues that need to be resolved in order to enter Europe. How does Turkey which was the seat of the Eastern Roman Empire and also the seat or throne of s.a.tan (**Revelation 2:12-13**; Pergamos in Turkey) fit in this equation? The fact is it doesn't. Turkey must resolve many internal and external human rights issues spanning for hundreds of years in order to join and it is highly unlikely that these issues will be resolved. Turkey might get some sort of watered down entry, but even if they make the EU entry it does not matter because it strengthens the case for Islam. How is Europe going to stop seventy two million Muslims from entering Europe?

While Europe cannot be the one from other passages in the Bible such as **Daniel 11:30** which speaks of Greece and not Rome. In **Daniel 11:30** the Anti-Messiah is attacked by Europe itself.

We have had ten more nations join in Eastern Europe so that gives us 15 toes sticking out of one leg and ten in the other. The proponents of this theory so far have not come out to admit that they could not find a shoe that fits. Maybe they can get one specially designed.

Let's analyze the Bible, as it should be.

The Bible is a book designed to be read in its cultural context and with the correct hermeneutics. We can see that many prophecy teachers apply very loose interpretations and dance all over the Bible to fit their view. What we must do is put the book back where it belongs and use the proper analysis that it deserves. I find myself rather fortunate that the Master called me out of a Muslim background and that I also have a key understanding of Middle Eastern culture. Some things come naturally to ex-Muslims, simply because of our background, while the Holy Spirit did indeed intervene in many areas of my life to reveal biblical knowledge and much needed correction.

Unnecessary attacks on President George W. Bush.

Whenever something happens in the White House these days then all the prophecy writers jump on the bandwagon paying little attention to the wider picture. I am sure I

---

[6] http:www.prophecymaps.com

stand amongst a few, but mostly we have seen that people like to knit pick. There is a herd mentality out there and this is sadly our human condition as unfortunately many Christians can also fall prey to the mass hysteria as well.

When someone professes to be a Christian and claims to pray daily before sitting in his office (President Bush) then why is it that some individuals from certain ministries are bent on ridiculing him, calling him a whore, sold out to the Arabs and so forth? You get my point? Such things only serve to strengthen the hands of those who are leftists and have a liberalist agenda. Unfortunately such talk only tickles ears for the glory of their name rather than Yahweh's name. These people do not realize what damage they are doing feeding into the leftist camps that lack the basic understanding of Bible prophecy. The things that George Bush has done are actually what the Master has already revealed in the Bible as part of His will and plan. So President George W. Bush is actually acting out the Master's will, even if it appears that he is doing the wrong thing.

President Bush may make statements about the Muslim god, but it is important to understand that these are political statements not facts. These statements are prepared by his aids who want to make it look good to the Islamic nations at a time the USA is at war in Afghanistan and Iraq. Sure I agree they border on blaspheme trying to equate Allah with Yahweh, since there is no comparison, but Mr Bush is not a missionary but a President. So let us not forget that if he were to openly declare that Allah is evil and that all Muslims following him are also evil, by definition then he would not have any support from any Islamic country left and it would make life very difficult for many American people. His credibility would be finished. This is the Master's way to bring Israel out of its slumber and to show the Muslims who the true Creator is because it is <u>not</u> Allah. Of course, the rest of the world needs to learn also because burying your head in sand and saying there is no YHWH is <u>not</u> only foolish but also detrimental to your eternal health.

Let me show you how he is doing the Master's will.

Israel's division of its land was prophesied and many of the people know that England was the nation that gave away 75% of mandated land to create Jordan. But again, Churchill followed YHWH's plan without even knowing about it. Yahweh Elohim certainly allowed England to do this, but in the process she lost many other areas of her empire that simply disappeared. Let me explain; if someone goes to hell tomorrow, can he blame Yahweh that he did not know? In fact, Yahweh may have sent people in this individual's direction to reveal His will, but the individual may have either simply ignored the advise, or was not concerned about it. Whose fault is it then?

It is the individual's fault because Yahweh would not leave anyone without a witness of some sort. But what the individual can do is exercise his free will. It does not mean that his free will choice is right or wrong, but it does have consequences. Those that reject Yahushua of Nazareth will be damned in hell forever, sadly so, but those who accept Him will have eternal life with Him. It is a matter of freewill and free choice and not about a YHWH who hates, or wants to punish people for pleasure. In fact just the opposite is true as He is our YHWH of love.

<u>John 3:16-17</u> "For YHWH <u>so</u> loved the world that He gave **His only** begotten [unique] Son, [Yahushua] that whoever believes in Him should not perish but have everlasting life. For YHWH did not send His Son into the world to condemn the world, but that the world through Him might be saved." (Yahushua is a Savior)

23

Now we are not just talking about a simple division of land but the creation of a Palestinian state without which the **alliance of the confederacy of nations** of <u>Psalm 83</u> <u>cannot</u> be fulfilled. In **Psalm 83:7** we are told in no uncertain terms that **Philistia** will come up <u>against</u> Israel. How will they come up against Israel unless they are a nation? This is why a Palestinian state is a <u>reality</u> that will happen and then we will see these prophecies coming to pass. We live in the last days and we have to be prepared. Note Tyre was destroyed as a nation by the Greeks, but the Bible prophecy is clear it is the "inhabitants of Tyre" i.e. people living in that region that are part of the end time confederacy.

> **Psalm 83:18** That men may know that You, whose **NAME** alone is the Master **YHWH** are the Most High over all the earth.

Yahweh is revealing His name to the nations even as we speak.

Quite frankly nothing is new under the sun. Being more technologically advanced does not change anything. We are six thousand years into our planet and we still struggle to supply clean water to many poor parts of the world, I know of many homes today that are in Pakistan, India and Africa that are without modern amenities like electric, water, gas, cars and TV, yet we see people in the overfed west whining all the time. Needless to say we should thank Yahushua our Messiah for His love and compassion on us to give us abundantly and we should strive to help those in need. The recent earthquakes in Pakistan showed how feeble its systems are to cope with disaster. Little do they realize that because of their mistakes, such as their hatred of Israel, unnecessary persecution and the killing of Christians had allowed YHWH to act His will, to show the people that these actions need to stop and that they must come to know that the true Creator's Name is not Allah, but Yahweh.

Now about Babylon let's get one thing straight, Babylon is a <u>literal</u> place in Scripture and it happens to be in the Middle East not in America or in Europe. Yes you read that correctly! It happens to be in the **Middle East**. This fact alone unfortunately causes a lot of prophecy writers to fall by the wayside, no matter how scholarly or how many PhDs they hold, which is totally irrelevant at this point. This alone poses a huge issue to all the theorists out there for the Anti-Messiah coming out of Europe, or the USA as not only unbiblical, but completely untrue and misleading to people.

Some think that prophecy can only be interpreted by PhD scholars. **Well if this was the case then why is it that for two millennia they have failed to identify the beast?** Yet others think that only the Jews can understand prophecy. Well if the Jews alone were only able to understand prophecy, then they would not have missed their Messiah when He came the first time. In YHWH's sphere He gives knowledge and wisdom to those He wills and those He chooses. He may choose to open up prophecy to some people a little at a time, while to others a lot faster. These prophecies were sealed so the earlier people could not properly interpret, or see the end time beast. But now the seal is off and these are being unveiled before your eyes right in front of you on TV, tabloids and magazines. But do you have the spiritual eyes to see it?

This is why Yahushua said in, ***Revelation 13:9*** *"If anyone has **an ear**, let him hear."*

Everybody is born with two ears and mostly good hearing, so Yahushua is not talking about two physical ears. He simply asks that if you have a spiritual desire for understanding, then understand the truth.

24

If you pickup the cover of a book and it says Anti-Messiah out of Europe, or the USA then to be honest the book is not worth spending money on. Quite clearly the writer most likely has tried to apply very loose hermeneutics, that for him almost everything is seen allegorically relating to the west. He will invariably interpret Babylon as Rome or the USA, and will interpret Edom as Europe. There are plenty of writers doing this today. Avoid these books altogether and save your money. In fact go get yourself a good concordance and some basic Hebrew education. These books err and lead into error and those people who have put their trust in such books will be disappointed when the time comes. So perhaps if you are reading this book then it is a wake up call to sound the alarm.

There is sufficient evidence in this book to prove why only Islam fits the bill of the end time beast. If there is something that you are not sure of then you are most welcome to e-mail me at shimound63@yahoo.com and ask questions that you need clarification on. I cannot put all the knowledge that I have in this book due to resource constraints. But there is enough in here to help you understand, and this should encourage you to study the Bible for yourself and pray to Yahushua the Messiah for understanding. I have been told reliably that the number to dial for YHWH is 00 yes that is zero zero i.e. on your knees. I myself ring that number often and also dial 333 while in zero zero position so that the international link can be established where He may open up your understanding;

> **Jeremiah 33:3**`Call to **Me**, and **I will answer you**, and **show you great and mighty things**, which you do not know.'

It is Yahweh who makes the foolish wise and the wise foolish; for the scholarly type I make an open invitation for a face-to-face discussion on this subject in any forum. I make a lot of information available on my website at http://www.abrahamic-faith.com on talks I did on the subject and I make them available freely on the pubic domain. Freely I receive and freely I give. Understand that I also give the book away free to some people who cannot afford it, while for others you would have to pay since it will cost money to print it. You can also catch me on the radio at http://www.yesumasih.com with a good program called "Christianity Answers" where I take on the Muslim apologists and their arguments live, here I also teach how to deal with the Islamic agenda.

> **Revelation 18:2** And he cried mightily with a loud voice, saying, "**Babylon the great is fallen**, is fallen, and has become a habitation of demons, a prison for every foul spirit, and a cage for every unclean and hated bird!

Now if Babylon is the **whole world system** as believed by some then the whole world will fall down and become a habitation of demons! But unfortunately this translation is not tenable because Babylon is a particular place marked for His wrath. The very next verse 3 marks this as a literal place with which the kings have committed fornication and also a city in verse 10. *Revelation 18:3* ... *"the kings of the earth have committed fornication with her."*

> **Revelation 18:10** "standing at a distance for fear of her torment, saying, `Alas, alas, **that great city** Babylon.

Scripture is written in black and white so that no one can deny that the **destruction of Babylon** has been prophesied in Isaiah chapter 13 and 14. Also read what Jeremiah Chapters 50 and 51 predict. Both Isaiah and Jeremiah agree to disagree with the world's view. Their view is that the destruction of Babylon is like Sodom and Gomorrah after which

25

it is **never** inhabited. **If this is simply the one-world system then where will the Christians live in the Millennium reign if the whole world is Babylon**? See the problems with this view?

We can see that in **Isaiah 13:17** something key that "the Medes" would participate in the destruction of Babylon. This is a key to unlock some of this prophecy.

> **Isaiah 13:17** "Behold, **I will stir up the Medes against them**, who will not regard silver; and as for gold, they will not delight in it.

Today the Kurds happen to be the descendents of the Medes, and it will be very difficult to see the Kurds coming up to destroy the USA, or Europe. That is completely out of focus and simply living in a fantasy land. Scholars seeing this destruction simply assumed that this took place in 539 BC. But the problem remains that the destruction is permanent, and we do not see that this has ever happened in history. So the climax remains to be fulfilled in the very near future. If you want to get insight into the Anti-Messiah I encourage you to read up on Salah din Ayubi the Kurd who fought King Richard the Lion. Then you may understand the part to be played by the Kurdi people.

It is very easy to fit prophecy accurately when we see that Iraq is the central location for Babylon. And guess what? The Kurds have been the persecuted minority in Iraq and Turkey. Now let us not forget it was Sadaam Hussain who gassed the Kurds of Halabja. Do we then see why YHWH showed us that it would be the Kurds who would help destroy Babylon? Could this be time for settling old scores?

This appears as a climactic event in the book of Revelation. Why would John write a prophecy in Revelation regarding a "Mystery Babylon" and its destruction, especially if John had lived way after the fall of Babylon in 539 B.C? This should make us ponder - what in the world is the Bible speaking of regarding all these Babylons? We have **"Babylon the great mother of harlots,"** **"Mystery Babylon,"** **"daughter of Babylon,"** **"Babylon the great mountain,"** and many others.

For the Catholic Church to be even considered as a candidate it must change **Times** and **Laws** (**Daniel 7:25**), **invoke <u>beheading</u> as a capital punishment for Christians**, establish "non separation between church and state." That amongst many things are things that the Pope is unlikely to be able to pull off easily. Also don't forget it has to have it's central headquarters relocated from Rome to the Middle East. I do not think that the Muslims will allow the Catholics to build a similar headquarters in their country anytime soon. So it's best we give up this daydreaming of Europe giving us the Anti-Messiah.

The Catholic Church on top of all these requirements must also deny that YHWH (Yahweh) is our Father and that Yahushua is the Son of YHWH - **I John 2:22** *"He is* ***<u>antichrist</u>*** *who denies* ***<u>the Father and the Son</u>***."

Yet, Islam meets all these requirements and hundreds more, yet is somehow rejected by the majority simply because it doesn't fit their traditional heritage and learning passed down from generation to generation.

Pinning our faith to the sleeves of the fathers is one of the features of this flawed method that remains. Just now, however, the world is waking up to the fact that error may live and thrive for a thousand years, and never be disturbed during that time.

What can anyone say? Tradition, tradition! It can even blind men to true bible prophecy.

A. Is the Anti-Messiah Jewish?

So are you saying that the Anti-Messiah will not be a Jew because I have been taught that he will be a messiah that the Jews have to accept, i.e. he must 'sell the goods?'

In a recent debate with a so-called scholar unfortunately he came out with the most absurd statement I have ever heard. He must sell the goods. Upon inquiring about what Scripture reference he was talking about "sell the goods" he could only come up with John 5:43.

> **John 5:43** I am come in My Father's name, and ye receive Me not: if another shall come in his own name, him ye will receive.

There are those who claim to be chasing after some man's ministry, but unfortunately sometimes they themselves end up teaching falsehood. But the irony is they cannot see the log in their own eyes, yet they can see the spec in their brothers. I did not realize that scholarly education has become so poor that verses such as John 5:43 are being used to prove that the Anti-Messiah will be Jewish. Things must be quite desperate for people to use these kinds of verses. First of all I have never heard of John 5:43 as evidence that the Anti-Messiah must be a Jew. The only Scripture I know of that is used in scholarly circles is Daniel 11:37 that appears to come close to prove or disprove his identity.

> **Daniel 11:37 Neither shall he regard the Elohim of his fathers, nor the desire of women, nor regard any god**: for he shall magnify himself above all.

First of all **John 5:43** is not a Scripture about the coming prince i.e. the Anti-Messiah. The Bible does not teach that he has to be Jewish, or come in his own name. The premise is a straw man in John 5:43. People who want to use this as an argument build up this straw man but it fails on many grounds.

Nowhere is there even <u>one</u> clear Scripture that the Anti-Messiah has to claim to be a Messiah of Israel or even be Jewish! In fact Scripture is quite clear he is a leader and has to sign an agreement (Daniel 9:27). This statement in itself has a huge significance. Let me explain, the person who is the Messiah he has to come in Yahweh's NAME, that is the NAME that Yahushua of Nazareth was talking about, "I come in my Father's NAME." So the Father has a NAME and likewise so does the Son or Yahushua, which in this case represents this same NAME; that is Yahweh. Why would a leader who simply has to sign a deal have to worry about what NAME he represents? There is no reason whatsoever. Second, if Christian scholars are falling head over heels to prove this Scripture is for the Anti-Messiah then what hope do the Jews have of ever finding their true Messiah? The Jews have in times past made mistakes of accepting many false Messiahs and have been wrong every time. In fact this Anti-Messiah will simply be just that i.e. he will be anti true Messiah and His people! In other words, **he will be against the "anointed" and His followers, not one from their midst**. To understand these just take a look at the Jews and Christians. Who hates the Jews and Christians today to the point of <u>beheading</u> them?

27

Do Hindus? No. Do Buddhists? No. Do Atheists? No. Do Muslims? Yes and they behead Jews and Christians plus anyone else (other secular Muslims) who disagrees with them.

If your answer is Islam then according to many scriptural references that I have pointed to and will be presenting in this book, then Islam is where we need to look for the Anti-Messiah. He is anti Christian and anti Jewish period. He's not a self-hating Jew! Why? Simple. He hates the true followers of Yahweh. Jews many not recognize the Messiah, but they still worship Yahweh (whom they call HaShem) the one true YHWH.

We have seen the Jews proclaim many a Messiah and I will only cite two such cases to prove the point:

Shimon Bar Cochba was also hailed as the Messiah in 132 AD in the Jewish rebellion. In fact all Bar Cochba needed was a leading Rabbi to rubber stamp him and away they went. But alas this was a disaster waiting to happen when the Romans killed many Jews.

Rabbi Akiva was quick to proclaim Bar Kokhba "a messianic king!" He applied a Bible verse directly to him "a star, kochav, has arisen out of Jacob (Num. 24:17)." So Simon became known as Bar Kochba, Son of the Star. His mission was clear and sanctioned by rabbinical authority. For a people starved for hope, the approval of Akiva was more than enough proof of Bar Kochba's authenticity.[7]

This kind of thing continued but it gets a bit more comical when another person Shabbetai Zvi comes on the scene who also proclaimed to be a Messiah, but the Muslims set him straight by 'making' him a Muslim. Yes that is right he became a Muslim, so much for his Messiahship.[8]

On September 15, 1666, Shabbetai Zvi, brought before the Sultan and given the choice of death or apostasy, prudently chose the latter, setting a turban on his head to signify **his conversion to Islam**, for which he was rewarded with the honorary title "Keeper of the Palace Gates" and a pension of 150 piasters a day. The apostasy shocked the Jewish world. Leaders and followers alike refused to believe it.

The Daniel 11:37 text however is the only proof text that could have come close to proving the coming of a Jewish Anti-Messiah. However it has one major flaw; the word used for Elohim is the **"Elohai"** of his fathers that translates to "gods" in the plural.

37 Neither shall he regard **the elohai of his ahvot**, nor the desire of women, nor regard any Eloah: for he shall magnify himself above all. (RSTNE)

---

[7] http://www.jasher.com/Messiahs.htm

[8] http://www.jewishvirtuallibrary.org/jsource/loc/False.html

So once again this cannot apply to any Messianic figure. We must read verse 38 that broadens our understanding.

> **Daniel 11:38** But in his estate shall he honor the Eloah of force [violence and jihad]: and an **Eloah whom his fathers knew not shall he honor** with **gold, and silver**, and with precious stones, and pleasant things.

It correctly falls in line with Muslims because the Muslim Anti-Messiah did not believe in the "gods" of his forefathers (polytheism), but he believed in the god of Muhammad i.e. Allah and honours this god with gold and silver just like the Muslims do today. Remembering before Muhammad came his forefathers were pagan Arabs worshipping many gods in Mecca. So this shows us clearly the prophecy cannot be fulfilled by anyone other than a Muslim. Also note that he does not regard the desires of women just like in the Islamic culture women are no more then housewives and cannot take up political positions. Even today in Saudi Arabia women are not allowed to drive alone, or in Afghanistan under the Taliban were not allowed to go to school.

Bar Cochba proclaimed himself as Messiah so the prophecy in John 5:43 is already fulfilled by him. Then several other people in history did likewise, all of them claiming to be Messiah, so again we see multiple fulfilment of this prophecy. The word "Messiah" simply means, "Anointed One." So what anointing did Bar Cochba have? None whatsoever! The bottom line is this. All it took for the entire Jewish people to proclaim a Messiah is one Rabbi and his vote.

We also see this pattern in the Lubavitch movement today where they proclaimed Rabbi Manachem Schneerson as a Messiah and his followers are still awaiting his resurrection. This is all man's vain imaginations since the one to rise after three days has arisen already, so why the need to proclaim another Messiah?

In Dr. Arnold Fruchtenbaum's work, " Nationality," p. 8 he writes:

Stated in a syllogism, this argument goes as follows:

- "Major Premise: The Jews will accept the Antichrist as the Messiah
- Minor Premise: The Jews will never accept a Gentile as the Messiah.
- Conclusion: The Antichrist will be a Jew."

This is quite a strange conclusion since it does not follow. First of all the major premise above is false since there are no Scriptures dictating this to be the case. Again the minor premise is just that i.e. minor. The Jews do not accept a gentile Messiah, but who said they ever need to, since there is no need scripturally for them to do this. Why even contend that this is a minor premise when there is no reference in the Bible dictating that this person proclaims himself as the Messiah of Israel or that the Jewish nation need to accept this?

In Dr. Arnold Fruchtenbaum's " Nationality" on p. 11 he offers a scriptural line; using the Scriptures of Revelation 7:4-8.

29

Stated in a syllogism, this argument goes as follows:

- Major Premise: The tribe from whom the Antichrist would come is not listed among the 144,000.
- Minor Premise: Dan is not among the 144,000.
- Conclusion: The Antichrist is from the tribe of Dan.

First of all Dr Arnold completely ignores the fact that the tribe of Dan is included in the divisions of land distribution in Ezekiel 48:2 in the millennium, this destroys the major premise.

> **Ezekiel 48:2** And by the border of Dan, from the east side unto the west side, a portion for Asher.

One could assume that the reason they are not listed in the Revelation account is simply because it was Dan that introduced idolatry in Israel and perhaps this is one of the reasons why they were excluded in the count. But nevertheless we can never really know the true reason since Yahweh did not tell us and only He knows better.

However we cannot fail to see that the Renewed Covenant is with all the twelve tribes of Israel in Jeremiah 31:31 and that included Dan.

> **Jeremiah 31:31** Behold, the days come, saith the Master, that I will make a new covenant with the house of Israel, and with the house of Judah:

Dan needs to be present in the land when the Messiah returns. One cannot overlook this fact, so this causes both the major and minor premises to disappear into thin air. Unfortunately sometimes the so-called scholars end up misleading rather than leading by building up straw man arguments from silence.

> **Jeremiah 31:27** Behold, the days come, saith the Master, that I will sow the **house of Israel** and the **house of Judah** with the seed of man, and with the seed of beast.

Therefore the only thing that reasonably follows is that the conclusion is actually in error by this assertion. Since the Anti-Messiah (one who opposes all taught and done by Messiah, including his Jewish heritage) is not proclaiming himself as The Messiah, then the conclusion that should follow is that he can and will in fact be a non-Jew. In fact most of the Jewish enemies have been non-Jews e.g. Amelekites, Midians, Philistines, Babylonians, Persians and the Romans.

Thus by Scripture references mentioned in this book it follows that Islam alone is not only THE BEAST of the end times according to the Bible, but also will give us the Anti-Messiah which is a correct conclusion born out of Scripture. Anyone and I mean anyone who claims to be a who's who in the world of eschatological scholarship needs to prove if they can an Anti-Messiah who must be Jewish, using clear scriptural references. We cannot take ambiguous references to prove his identity when we have clear references in the Bible such as Ezekiel 38:2, Daniel 7:7, 8:9 and Micah 5:6; these are ALL clearly

30

related to the Anti-Messiah and to the Middle East region. One could argue as to which part of the Middle East it is and that would be a valid argument. But to argue for Europe or the USA is clear and blatant error that should be avoided and the person teaching this should be examined most carefully. It does not matter if one saying it is Europe happens to be a great person, or someone who is known very well. A correct interpretation of all facts requires correct examination and avoidance of error as much as possible.

Chapter 3

Discovering the Beast of Daniel Seven

The Horns and the Little Horn

In this book we will look at who was Daniel the prophet speaking about, that 4th terrible beast that came up and was different from the previous three beasts. We will discuss why this beast is not Western Europe, as many believe because of the rules of interpretation and the requirements that are needed for the last Empire of the age, which does not fit with Western Europe. Daniel's apocalyptic book is the key to understanding the book of Revelation and the rest of the Bible must be in tune with these prophecies. We indeed find that this is the case. Remember that Daniel was a captive in what is referred to in the Bible as Babylon, which today is Iraq proper. Daniel the prophet was in the kingdom of the famous king Nebuchadnezzar, this was the 1st of the three deportations of Jews to Babylon.

This happened around about 605 BC, the king of Judah was Jehoiakim at that time. The 2nd deportation happened around 597 BC when he took most of Judah's leaders, including the young prophet Ezekiel and the rest of the national treasures (**2 Chronicles 36:10, 2 Kings 24:10-17**). The 3rd final deportation took place 11 years later around 586 BC. Daniel means "El is my judge" and Daniel's prophetic ministry was about 70 years, and he lived at least 85 years or more. Let us look at the verses concerned.

> **Daniel 7:7-8** After this I saw in the night visions, and behold, a **fourth beast, dreadful and terrible**, **exceedingly strong**. It had **huge iron teeth**; it was **devouring, breaking in pieces**, and **trampling the residue** with **its feet**. It was **different** from **all the beasts that were before it**, and it had **ten horns**. I was considering the horns, and there was **another horn, a little one, coming up among them**, before whom **three of the first horns were plucked out by the roots**. And there, in this horn, were eyes like the eyes of a man, and a mouth **speaking pompous words**.

Note these things;
- ❖ The beast is exceedingly strong yet weak (Daniel 2:41).
- ❖ Dreadful and terrible.
- ❖ It breaks/wears out governments.
- ❖ It is different from the previous three. (Was Rome different?)
- ❖ The little horn sprouting out from this is the Anti-Messiah.

Islam fits all the above and much more...

31

The ten horns are ten kings with nations and Daniel mentions a plucking that was to take place of three of these ten nations. These are the nations that represented these ten horns that were formed.

1. Turkey
2. Syria
3. Lebanon
4. Egypt
5. Jordan
6. Saudi Arabia
7. Iran (Persia)
8. **Mosul (Plucked)**
9. **Basrah (Plucked)**
10. **Baghdad** (Plucked)

Mosul, **Basrah** and **Baghdad** were carved out from the region of the Middle East by the British Government in 1922 but these three horns were not even able to establish their roots just as the Master said in the Bible, the biblical word in Aramaic is "akar" written in Hebrew as "akar," which means to pluck out i.e. not allow it to be established. This is the only place I have found this word in the Bible where it is used in such a sequence. There are other Hebrew words for "pluck" that could have been used in the Hebrew such as "nasach" or "kalah" but they are not used here because this word "akar" is very descriptive of the action that was to take place. Note that the three nations **Mosul**, **Basrah** and **Baghdad**, or the three horns that were plucked were made into a single State called Iraq.

In order to understand the 4th beast we must first look at the first three beasts.

Daniel 7:4 ...The first was like a lion

This is Iraq, the Babylonian Empire.

Daniel 7:5 And suddenly another beast, a second, like a bear...

The 2nd is Medo-Persia, today's Iran and the Kurds.

Daniel 7:6 "After this I looked, and there was another, like a leopard...

The 3rd is the Grecian Empire, from Turkey all the way to Pakistan today in our new borders.

Daniel 7:7 "After this I saw in the night visions, and behold, a **fourth beast, dreadful** and **terrible, exceedingly strong.**

The fourth beast is Islam that shares the region of the Eastern Roman leg not the European Roman leg.

Have you ever wondered why the two major battles after World War I and II were being fought in the Arab lands? This is because all the action of the end time battle is going to take place in the Middle East. So our eyes must be firmly focused on the Middle Eastern nations and especially Israel, which remains YHWH's ticking prophesy time clock. The Master Yahushua said to His disciples in the book of Matthew.

32

Matthew 24:34 Assuredly, I say to you, **THIS GENERATION** will by no means pass away till all these things are fulfilled.

Have you ever wondered what this meant that "this generation" would by no means pass away? This statement has confused some believers. Did Yahushua mean that the people standing there would not die, or was He talking of a truth that actually is fulfilled in our time? The clue is in the rendering of the word "generation." The Greek word "*ghen-eh-ah*" does give us somewhat of a clue; the word meaning "a nation." So Yahushua was speaking about the nation of Israel that would not pass away. But we know that the nation of Israel was dispersed across the world after Yahushua's death and resurrection. I believe the New Testament was written in Aramaic/Hebrew and later translated to Greek. This is why many Aramaic words exist in the New Testament and some of the translations of the words are not accurate through the Greek. But when you look at the Peshitta Aramaic things become a whole lot clearer.

When I looked at the Peshitta Aramaic text the dialect spoken by Yahushua I realised what this word actually meant, the word "generation" in the Aramaic is "sharbata" and is correctly translated in Peshitta as **TRIBE**. So we can see Yahushua was referring to the "**Tribe of Yahudah**" (Judah) that was in the land of Israel to be dispersed and re-gathered for the end times play.

If you know anything of Israel's history and have read the Hebrew Old Testament carefully then you will know that the ten tribes of Israel had been scattered to the east by the Assyrians prior to Yahushua' birth. When Yahushua was born the only tribe in the land of Israel were Judah, Benjamin and some of Levi, although there were also remnants of some of the other tribes because some of the other tribe's kinsmen had moved down south before the dispersal of Ephraim. An example is Anna the prophetess mentioned in Luke 2:36 from the tribe of Asher who served the Master in the Temple. But by and large the northern kingdom of Israel had been scattered and mixed with the nations during the times of the Assyrians. So Yahushua was correctly saying that the tribe of Judah would stand in the land once again before these things come to pass. That means Yahushua also prophesied the dispersal and re-gathering of Israel back to the land and that indeed happened in 1948. Yahushua said "THIS GENERATION" by no means will pass away or correctly "This TRIBE" will by no means pass away and we can see YHWH is faithful that no one has been able to eradicate the Jews, though many have tried including Hitler, but YHWH is faithfully protecting the Jewish people for His plan even though most reject Yahushua as their Messiah and live in plain and ignorant idolatry. Yahweh however has not rejected them.

So behind every word of Yahushua there is a fundamental truth that we have to grapple with and we cannot just discard His words as mere talk.

When Yahushua said: **_Matthew 9:6_** *"But that you may know that the **Son of Man** has power on earth to **forgive** sins"* then He said to the paralytic, *"Arise, take up your bed, and go to your house."*

Only YHWH can forgive sins, so Yahushua here demonstrated that He was not just any ordinary man, but an extraordinary human being who was eternally YHWH and who had taken on flesh to reveal Himself in order to come and redeem mankind. Salvation had come but the Jews failed to grasp that the first coming of Yahushua was as a Servant and it was the 2nd coming that was to see Him as the mighty King returning to subdue nations. Therefore they missed the boat because they were too busy following religion. YHWH in

His ultimate wisdom wanted a relationship not a religion. He wanted to deal with sin once and for all times and that had to be dealt by Yahushua's sacrifice to redeem men.

>Isaiah 42:1 "Behold! My Servant whom I uphold, My Elect One in whom My soul delights! I have put My Spirit upon Him; He will bring forth justice to the Gentiles.

Another look at that famous Statue of Nebuchadnezzar

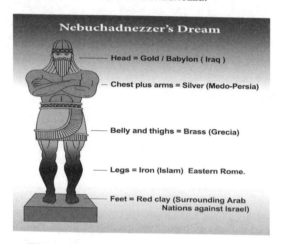

Nebuchadnezzer's Dream

Head = Gold / Babylon (Iraq)

Chest plus arms = Silver (Medo-Persia)

Belly and thighs = Brass (Grecia)

Legs = Iron (Islam) Eastern Rome.

Feet = Red clay (Surrounding Arab Nations against Israel)

>Daniel 2:37-45 "You, O king, are a king of kings. For the Eloah of heaven has **given you a kingdom, power, strength, and glory**; (38) "and wherever the children of men dwell, or the beasts of the field and the birds of the heaven, He has given them into your hand, and has made you ruler over them all you **are this head of gold.** (39) "But after you shall arise **another kingdom** inferior to yours; then another, **a third kingdom of bronze**, which shall rule over all the earth. (40) "And the **fourth kingdom shall be as strong as iron**, inasmuch as iron **breaks in pieces and shatters all things**; and **like iron that crushes, that kingdom will break in pieces and crush all the others**. (41) "Whereas you saw the **feet and toes, partly of potter's clay and partly of iron, the kingdom shall be divided**; yet the **strength of the iron shall be in it**, just as you saw the **iron mixed with ceramic clay**. (42) "And as the **toes of the feet were partly of iron and partly of clay**, so the kingdom shall be partly strong and partly fragile. (43) "As you saw iron mixed with ceramic clay, **they will mingle with the** seed of men; **but they will not adhere to one another, just as iron does not mix with clay. (44) "And in the days of these kings YHWH Elohim of heaven will set up a kingdom which shall never be destroyed; and the kingdom shall not be left to other people**; it shall break in pieces and consume all these kingdoms, and it shall stand forever. **(45) "Inasmuch as you saw that the** stone was cut out of the mountain without hands, and that **it broke in pieces** the **iron**, the **bronze**, the **clay**, the **silver**, and the **gold** the great YHWH has made known to the king what will come to pass after this. The dream is certain, and its interpretation is sure."

Did you read that in <u>Daniel 2:45</u> that ALL these kingdoms broke in pieces <u>together</u>? The **IRON**, the **BRONZE**, the **CLAY**, the **SILVER** and the **GOLD**, in other words though the Empires such as **Babylon**, **Medo-Persia** and **Greece**, came and went but these **three**

Empires continue in the 4th beast with the Eastern Roman leg that is **Islam** because Islam occupied ALL the Middle Eastern regions of these **Empires** that is why they can continue and so the final end happens when the Messiah returns to remove this last Empire. The next picture shows how these Empires have consolidated in the Middle East.

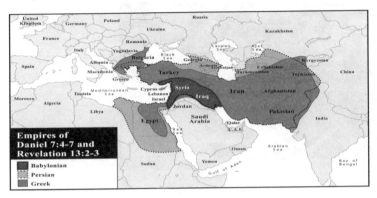

The Iron mixed with the clay, the clay here is RED clay and this is significant of Edom which is a play on words that means RED as it comes from the root word "dahm" meaning blood. The toes are Arab nations, while the metal or iron is an area that was shared by both the Roman and Grecian Empire, but is now occupied by the Muslim nations and it more closely resembles the Greco/Assyrian Empire.

> **Daniel 2:43** "As <u>you saw iron mixed with ceramic clay</u>, they will mingle <u>with the seed of men</u>; but they <u>will not adhere to one another</u>, just as <u>iron does not mix with clay</u>. (Red clay)

The legs of Iron are the Islamic Empire that continued from Rome in the Middle East. The ten toes partly weak and partly strong are the Arab nations, which have strength, but also have division amongst them. We can see the wars Muslims have been fighting with each other e.g. the Iran/Iraq war. The Bible gives it away describing how these nations "mingle" with the "seed of men" but do not "adhere" to each other. Even the Aramaic word for "mingle" is "Arab." So is the Master trying to tell us something? In my opinion these are clues to lead us to the correct conclusion they are not just there for allegory alone. I believe they are an Arab kingdom mingled with other seeds of different nations (Islamic nations) giving us the end-time army meaning they are ALL Muslim.

Ezekiel chapter 35 is all about the judgment of Islamic kingdoms/nations. YHWH describes them as **Mount Seir** and a mountain is an allegoric terminology for a kingdom. This is prophetically applied to this Empire.

> **Ezekiel 35:1-5**-Moreover the word of the Master came to me, saying, (2) "Son of man, <u>set your face against Mount Seir</u> and prophesy against it, (3) and say to it, `Thus says the Master YHWH: "**Behold, O Mount Seir, <u>I am against you</u>; <u>I will stretch out My hand against you</u>, and make you most desolate**; (4) I shall <u>lay your cities</u> waste, and you shall be desolate. <u>Then you shall know that I am the Master</u>. (5) Because you have had an <u>ancient hatred</u>, and <u>have</u>

shed the blood of the children of Israel by the **power of the sword** at the time **of their calamity**, when their **iniquity came to an end**.

Map of Psalm 83 – CLAY NATIONS

Note these things…

"O Mount Seir" - Allegoric for the entire Islamic world.

Mount Seir is the name of the fifty mile long mountain range south-southeast of the Dead Sea, Jordan today and happens to be ruled by the only Hashemite king (from the tribe of Muhammad). It is in the ancient land of Edom, where Esau settled as the Bible shows us;

> **Gen 36:8** So Esau dwelt in Mount Seir. (Esau is Edom and symbolic for All the Muslim nations).

Back to Ezekiel 35:3- "I will stretch out My hand" – It is Yahweh who is doing the judgement

"Then you shall know"– It's obvious they do <u>not</u> know Yahweh right now as they worship a foreign god Allah.

"Ancient Hatred" – The current Palestinian Muslim hatred has absolutely nothing to do with the Jews in Israel occupying a piece of land. This hatred started with Ishmael written about in the pages of Genesis and extends all the way in history to completion of the judgements in the book of Revelation. Esau hated Jacob because of the birthright (**Genesis 25:34**) and wanted to kill Jacob (**Genesis 27:41**). Later Esau married into the Ishmaelites so the two have now become <u>one</u> family. Therefore the distinction between the Arab and Egyptian is now difficult to understand. Remember the later Yasser Arafat was an Egyptian claiming to be a Palestinian.

"Have shed the blood of children of Israel" – After reading the Torah we find plenty of evidence to know that Israel fought these people to survive as a nation; the wars were not offensive in nature but defensive. I would need another book to explain the reasons, typologies and the climate around ancient Israel in the wilderness. However for that you will have to do the research yourselves. They were not even defending a land during Moses' time but more importantly personal survival and national identity was at stake.

"Power of the sword" – The enemy has always been stronger in number and weapons but Yahweh has been beside Israel. I remember a beautiful phrase in the Bible that King David used with Goliath and often when people say to me Simon are you not afraid of writing about or speaking about these people, I quote them this Scripture that I myself live by.

> **1 Samuel 17:45** Then **David said to the Philistine, "You come to me with a sword, with a spear, and with a javelin. But I come to you in the NAME of Yahweh of hosts, YHWH Elohim of the armies of Israel, whom you have defied.**

If the Elohim of Israel cannot protect me then no one can and I live under the shadow of His wings. He called me out and I came running. I was brought up in a very tough district in Pakistan amongst many gangs with constant shootings and battles, guns and knives do not scare me, I am a martial arts expert and spent time in the British reserve army. I was involved in a NATO led exercise in the 80s in Germany. YHWH primed me before He brought me into His kingdom. I know I have been called for this mission for this end time generation.

My situation is a bit like the British SAS, or the American special forces, I work behind the enemy lines this is the most dangerous place to work, I supply critical information like their strengths and their weaknesses up the chain of command to the body of believers who are on the front lines taking the gospel of Yahushua to the Muslims. Those that are missionaries to the Muslim world and those behind the missionaries are believers who I call the supply line. The women, the men the children who help in the effort to reach souls fill the supply lines and supply us with their prayers to our great YHWH. They pray all the time that the Master will make us successful to deliver the Good News of Yahushua to these people.

Two thousand years of Israel's punishment for the crime of the rejection of Yahushua of Nazareth, along with all their dispersal, heartache, homelessness, and refugee status is coming to an end. Now our Master Yahushua has brought the Jewish people back home because the time of their punishment is over. Now is the time for them to seek Yahweh their Elohim, as one day soon to come, many will recognize Yahushua as the Messiah and as their own YHWH revealed in flesh.

> **Ezekiel 11:17** "Therefore say, 'thus says the Master GOD: "**I will gather you from the peoples, assemble you from the countries** where you have been scattered, and **I will give you the land of Israel.**"

It is the Elohim of Israel who gives the land back to Israel, the British were simply doing what Yahushua intended them to do.

YHWH has punished the Jewish nation for the rejection of their Messiah by dispersing the nation around the world. At this time their punishment has come to an end in their Diaspora and YHWH has gathered them back in the land of Israel. The rest of the biblical promises can now be fulfilled one day soon, when they will have a national repentance and say "Baruch haba B'Shem YHWH (blessed is He who comes in the name of YHWH)." We are told in **Ezekiel 35:4-5** that YHWH will make this kingdom of Islamic nations desolation e.g. destroy them from being different governments because of the <u>ancient hatred</u> they have had against the Jews. These verses actually more fit our time then any other time period in history. It says when the punishment for sin comes to an end, the Islamists will kill the Jewish people. We see this in Israel today, with the first intifada in 2000, the series of suicide bombing attacks with over 100 suicide bombers and many innocent Jewish civilians being blown up in the name of Allah. Little children have been shot by the Palestinian terrorists simply because they are Jewish. Old women have been shot and they have spared no one. This will prevail from this time forward right thorough to the time of Jacob's Trouble, until Messiah comes to put an end to the final beast empire. Obviously it is Islam that troubles both houses of Jacob as no other entity on earth.

Then we have the "little horn" of **Daniel 7,** which is from the Eastern Region of Rome making scholars think that the Anti-Messiah is Roman.

We also have another "little horn" of **Daniel 8:9** that would appear to contradict **Daniel 7:8** because it arises out of the Grecian Empire of Alexander the great which was completely Middle East centric. Then we also have the "Gog" from the "land of Magog," who happens to be the same person (Anti-Messiah) described by a different name. **We know all this can be easily reconciled as this is an area shared by both the <u>Eastern</u> provinces of the Roman Empire and the Grecian Empire in general.**

The Iron Nations that do not mix with the clay nations.

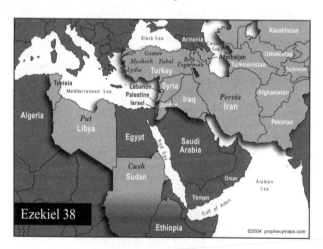

Remember Iraq fired scud missiles on Saudi soil because the clay does not mix with iron! Also Turkey battled with Saudi Arabian forces almost destroying Mecca.

For those who find it incredulous that Muslim's should attack the spiritual headquarters of Islam perhaps should read the following event in history during mid 1900's.

"**Hussein supervised the attack on Mecca**, while Faisel and Ali were in command of the force directed against Medina, the grand Shereef was successful at Mecca. The forts on the three hills overlooking that forbidden and sacred city were garrisoned by the Sultan's most faithful Circassian mercenaries and picked Turkish troops. On the day of the attack, the Arabs swept through the gates and captured the main bazaar, the residential section, the administration buildings, and the sacred mosque of the Holy Kaaba. For a fortnight the battle raged around the two smaller forts, which were finally taken; during all this fighting the aged Shereef remained in his palace directing operations in spite of **scores of Turkish three-inch shells that riddled his residence. The Turks might have been able to hang on for many months had it not been for their own folly. The Ottoman seems to be a Mohammedan in theory only, occasionally adhering to the ritual and even less frequently adhering to the spirit of the Qu'ran. Heedless of the deep-set religious feelings of their enemies and co-religionists, they suddenly began to bombard the mosque of the Kaaba, the most sacred shrine of all Islam. One shell actually hit the black stone burning a hole in the holy carpet and killing nine Arabs who were kneeling in prayer.** Hussein's followers were so enraged by this impious act that they swarmed over the walls of the great fort and captured it after desperate hand-to-hand fighting with knives and daggers."[9]

Notice Rome added government to its conquests, but Islam does not do this and notice the teeth of iron in Daniel's beast represent strength and it **breaks** and **devours, but does not set up government**. Islam fits this description perfectly.

Islam conquered many nations but did not add government. Islam in the world today usually has only dictatorial governments and no democracies. This is a different beast from the previous three and it has 10 horns (i.e. 10 kings). The beast is a whole kingdom not just one nation and it has 10 kings and the Bible talks about an 11th the little horn that comes up described in Daniel 7:8, Daniel 8:9 and as Gog of Ezekiel 38:2.

Egypt, Libya and North Africa were Christian nations before Islam invaded them; they had to learn the hard way not to appease Islam. Thousands of people irrespective of men women and children were massacred and nobody talks about this forgotten history. The bottom line **those that appease Islam will fall!**

According to the Syrian Orthodox patriarch, Michael the Syrian (1126–1199), Muslims conquered Cilicia and Caesarea of Cappadocia in the year 650 in this way: [my comments in square brackets]

They [the Taiyaye, or Muslim Arabs] moved into Cilicia and took prisoners and when **Mu'awiya** [ruthless Muslim Caliph] arrived he ordered all the inhabitants to be **put to the sword**; [including children] he placed guards so that no one escaped. After gathering up all the wealth of the town, they set to torturing the leaders to make them show them things [treasures] that had been hidden. The Taiyaye led everyone into slavery men and women, boys and girls, they committed much debauchery in that unfortunate town; they wickedly committed

---

[9] "With Lawrence of Arabia" by Lowell Thomas (Arrow Books 1962), Hutchinson & Co. (Publishers) Ltd 1925, pages 60-61

immoralities inside churches.[10] [It has been reported that even nuns were raped on the altars openly].

These are the very regions where Saul of Tarsus or Paul preached.

Here is a contemporary account of the Muslims' arrival in Nikiou, **an Egyptian** town, in the 640's:

> When the Muslims arrived in Nikiou, there was not one single soldier to resist them. They seized the town and **slaughtered everyone they met in the street** and in the churches men, women and children, sparing nobody. Then they went to other places, pillaged and killed all the inhabitants they found . . . But let us now say no more, for it is impossible to describe the horrors the Muslims committed when they occupied the island of Nikiou.[11]

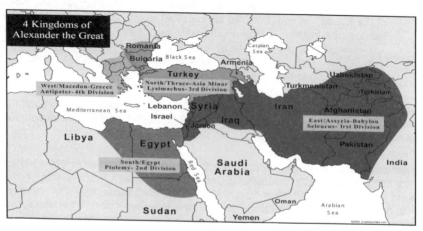

Identification of the "Little Horn"

In fact we are clearly told by <u>**Daniel 8:9**</u> pinpointing the "little horn" (Anti-Messiah) that arises from the Grecian division of the <u>four</u> regions (See map above) **from the Seleucid portion based in the Middle East. Again Alexander's Empire was all the way East to Pakistan and no portion of Western Europe was ever part of the Grecian Empire**. We also know that the "land of Magog" is Turkey with parts of Iraq/Syria so the area where the Antichrist will appear from is portions of Turkey with Northern Iraq that are today hotly contested by the Kurds.

Many prophecy teachers have wrongly concluded that the "little horn" of <u>**Daniel 8:9**</u> was Antiochus Epiphanies. However he can only be a type, but not the actual fulfilment of that passage because the Bible itself tells us in <u>**Daniel 8:17**</u> the following;

---

[10] http://www.frontpagemag.com/websat/Helper/editor/editor.asp?FormArea=divBody&HidArea=txtBody#_ftn6
[11] [11] "With Lawrence of Arabia" by Lowell Thomas (Arrow Books 1962), Hutchinson & Co. (Publishers) Ltd 1925, pages 60-61

Daniel 8:17 So he came near where I stood: and when he came, I was afraid, and fell upon my face: but he said unto me, Understand, O son of man: for at the **time of the end shall be the vision**.

This prophecy as indicated by the angel to Daniel is for the **time of the end,** not as believed by many for Antiochus in the past.

Let us briefly look at what Zechariah tells us;

Zechariah 9:13-17 For I have **bent Judah**, My bow, fitted the bow with Ephraim, and **raised up your sons, O Zion**, **against your sons, O Greece**, and made you like the sword of a mighty man."

Interesting, no mention of Rome here but it mentions the "tribe of Judah" that will fight in the end of days with "Grecia." This is not Greece of today, but the words in Hebrew for Greece are "Yawan." This place is confirmed by Josephus to be **Western Turkey**. This is surprising and yet still many are running to find the anti-Messiah nation in Europe. Is it not amazing what the Master YHWH is trying to show us? There is something else amazing in this passage that I must briefly explain.

Genesis 48:19 ...and his descendants [Ephraimites] shall become a **multitude of nations**. [Melo Ha Goyim]

When Joseph came back from Egypt with his two sons they were accepted into their rightful family by Jacob (Israel) and were blessed. The ecclesia/church is also accepted into the family of YHWH. Ephraim the younger got the greater blessing because he was going to become a "Melo ha Goyim," a multitude, or fullness of gentile nations. Ephraim also means, "double fruit," remember names are important.

This is the same Ephraim, the House of Israel (the 10 tribes) that Yahweh divorced. The prophet Hosea wrote about this event and Isaiah confirmed that the re-betrothal would take place in the future. We read in Genesis that the son Ephraim was to become a "Melo Ha Goyim," (**Genesis 48:19**) a "multitude of Gentile nations." So this is the way the Master has incorporated, or grafted in the Gentile nations. The same engrafting that He revealed to Abraham in **Genesis 12** and the same engrafting Paul correctly understood in **Romans 11:17**.

Revelations 19:7-8 "Let us be glad and rejoice and give Him glory, for the **marriage of the Lamb has come, and His wife has made herself ready**." And to her it was granted to be arrayed in fine linen, clean and bright, for the fine linen is the righteous acts of the saints.

Spiritually speaking the story of the prodigal son (**Luke 15:11-32**) is really the picture of our church today. No wonder when Jacob blessed the sons of Joseph into his household he gave the greater blessing to Ephraim the younger one and said that Ephraim would become **"Melo Ha Goyim,"** a multitude of gentile nations, or a "company of nations." The majority of the church today is in idolatry just like Ephraim was into idolatry. The northern tribes of Israel replaced YHWH's holy feasts with their own days, their own temple and their own priesthood. The church does the same today. The church today even ordains gay bishops contrary to the Bible, marries gays contrary to the Bible, and many in the

41

church teach that Allah is really just another name for YHWH, contrary to the Bible. And the list goes on and on.

They celebrate Christ-mass contrary to the Bible, they associate with Easter but in reality the two mentioned celebrations are the feast of Tabernacles and Passover. They also have changed His calendar to their own and not following the lunar calendar for the feasts and not even keeping the feasts as they should be kept. We see idolatry in our midst, but as the Ephraimites realize their mistakes they will come out of this idolatry and start to keep the feasts, keep the commandments and come into the rightful worship of Yahweh. We already see a growing movement where many people in the church are realizing that we should be keeping the feasts and should be honoring the Master and not associate with Pagan rites. Ephramites are having a spiritual awakening.

> **Jeremiah 16:19** O Master, my strength, and my fortress, and my refuge in the day of affliction, the Gentiles shall come unto thee from the ends of the earth, and shall say, surely our fathers have <u>inherited</u> lies, vanity, and things wherein there is no profit.

The salvation of the gentiles was revealed to Abraham many millennia ago when he was told:

> **Genesis 12:3** I will **bless** those **who bless you**, and I will **curse him who curses you**; and in you **ALL the families of the earth shall be blessed**.

Let's look at what this really means, that the Master is teaching us here that through Abraham ALL the families of the earth **will be blessed**.

In English it may not be so obvious but in Hebrew the verse for "In you ALL the families of the earth shall be blessed" reads "**Ve nivrechu becah kol mishpachot ha-adamah.**"

There is a deep profound truth here that is again hidden in the English translation and is usually not translated as the biblical Hebrew declares. The Hebrew word used here "**Nivrechu**" is translated as "be blessed," however the actual Hebrew word used for "be blessed" is not "Nivrechu" but "**Yivrechu.**" In the Jewish Rabbinic opinion this word is more correctly translated "**intermingled**," "mixed" or to be "**grafted in**" as Paul said.

In the Jewish *ArtScroll Bible Series*, Volume 1, page 432, it is written:

> There is an opinion shared by Rashbam [to Genesis 28:14], Chizkuni, Da'as Zekeinum, and quoted by Tur that the verb (ve nivrecu) in Genesis 12:3 is related to the root barak as in the Mishnaic term mavreek meaning to "intermingle or graft" [Kelaim 7:1, Sotah 43a]. As Heidenheim explains it, this interpretation is inspired by the fact that nowhere else besides here do we find barak in the sense of **blessing in the niphal conjugation**, while in the sense of "**grafting**" it is common in that form. [bold emphasis mine]

When we look at the underlining language and what the Jewish Rabbis have agreed we come to a very rich understanding of what YHWH was trying to teach us here, now let us read the text with this <u>proper</u> understanding.

42

> **Genesis 12:3b** And in <u>you</u> [Abraham] **ALL THE FAMILIES** of the earth **NIVRECHU [will be <u>grafted in</u>].**

Next time when you read Paul's epistles you will get a better understanding of what Paul was teaching by revelation when he wrote in **Romans 11:17**. This really was his understanding of **Genesis 12,** and how remarkable it is too.

> **Romans 11:17** And if some of the branches were <u>broken off,</u> [some of the Hebrews cut off but not ALL of them] and you, [Gentiles/nations] being a wild olive tree, were **grafted in among them,** and with them became a partaker of the root and fatness of the olive tree.

The olive tree is ISRAEL, so we become part of the tree of the Israel of YHWH. **We become one tree and not two trees growing separately.** If there is only one tree that is now growing up then that also means we are Hebrews, or Israelites by this very definition and YHWH sees us as His people, just as He seen Jewish Israel. Israel remains His original and eternal chosen.

So with this new understanding we can move forward to understand the following points:

Judah is the bow; Ephraim (spiritually the Christian church) is the one also doing the war that is why we see the European Alliance with the USA that will come up against the Anti-Messiah nations that we are clearly told about in **Jeremiah 51**. Ask yourself who fought the two gulf wars? Who were the driving force behind it and you will get an idea of the central nations playing their part.

> **Jeremiah 51:27** Set up a banner **in the land, blow the trumpet among the nations! Prepare the nations against her,** [the Anti-Messiah] **call the kingdoms together against her: Ararat, Minni,** and **Ashchenaz.** [Armenia and Europe] Appoint a marshal against her; cause the horses to come up like the bristling locusts.

Look where the armies come from;

> **Jeremiah 50:9** For behold, **I will raise and cause to come up** against Babylon **an assembly of great nations from the north country,** and they shall array themselves against her; from there **she shall be captured. Their arrows shall be like those of an expert warrior; none shall return in vain.**

YHWH is doing the raising; one of the "great nations" in the "north country" is the UK. This allied alliance is none other than the UK and the USA with her plus other European allied nations that will come up and their "arrows" i.e. precision bombs like of an expert warrior. None shall return in vain when they plunder Babylon with their laser guided bombs and missiles. This will be Yahweh's hand of judgment on Babylon. YHWH raised up the USA 250 years ago not only to become a helper nation to Israel that gets persecuted in our time, but also as a conduit and a channel of Yahweh's blessings on the Jewish people. So behind USA's rise as a superpower nation is Yahweh and His purposes are clearly lining up as the Bible dictates. In fact the USA was founded by Christopher Columbus who was a believing Jew.

43

The Bible is our best witness and the evidence is before us. This prophesy in **Jeremiah 50:9** along with several others rules out Western Europe as the empire from which Anti-Messiah emerges. s.a.tan would very much love for you to concentrate your efforts on Germany, Rome and Europe, while the real beast does its business. Who said that Christians could not be deceived, there are plenty of teachers misleading Christians into error, as error continues to reign in our churches with many wrong teachings. When we accept a lie we go in error and loose our true joy in the Master. Let me give you an example.

When we say abortion is ok and is the mother's choice, we have then accepted a lie to murder a child that is alive in the womb. The acceptance of this lie will not only be sin, but also living this lie will cause us immense pain. Sure many look for legitimate reasons for abortion, but murder is murder, even if you want to call it termination. Aborting a child because he is disabled, or malformed in some way is not a reason for termination.

This is all the more reason for us to have this child to show the child our true love. Love is not based on whether we are fully whole, or in part whole. Would you stop loving your wife or husband because they became disabled in some way, or would you look for another partner? Sadly in our society these things are rife, and we need to repent and return to the Master. Let me give you another example, in Iraq the people have been freed from a tyrant, although they are free now but they still want to be ruled by Islam and Sha'ria law, so what is the point in this freedom? Is this true freedom when Islam puts you in bondage and you have to live a lie? The lie <u>must</u> be replaced by truth, if you are to be truly free, and this Truth is the Master Yahushua the Messiah. When He sets you free you are free indeed *John 8:32*. *"And you shall know the truth, and the truth shall make you free."*

Yahushua referred to Himself as **The Truth**, the Hebrew word used is **emet**; the word stands for **truth, stable, trustworthy, tried and tested**. The Alef and the Taf is a reference to YHWH Elohim of Abraham, Isaac and Jacob i.e. I am the Alpha and the Omega (Revelation 1:8) or I am the First and the Last (Isaiah 44:6). The middle letter mem is symbolic for the tried and tested word of YHWH that is true and trustworthy. The mem has the value forty and this number represents trials and tests in the Bible such as Israel in the wilderness for 40 years, so that Yahweh's word is tried, tested and true.

Psalm 12:6 The words of the Master [Yahweh] are **pure** words: as silver tried in a furnace of earth, purified seven times.

The <u>middle</u> pillar represents the Messiah Yahushua; it is the second letter and middle letter for the Hebrew word "truth." This number two in order is representative of the Messiah, the 2nd person of the triune Godhead who was going to take on the form of a **man** and die for our sins to atone for our sins once and for all times.

The bottom line in this overall picture is this that **FREEDOM** <u>without</u> **TRUTH** is useless i.e. the Iraqi war and the rest since YHWH is **Truth**. The majority in Iraqi does not even believe in the Elohim of Israel, so how can they be free from the bondage and slavery of Islam?

s.a.tan wants people to be looking at the wrong things and argue over petty matters, looking at areas and issues that have no significance. In warfare this is called a diversion, creating a diversion, an explosion a feigned attack in one area, to mislead the opposition and to weaken their resolve in another area. So when the army gathers in that area to defend it, wham the forces hit the real area with little defence so as to overtake or subdue it. What did you think the struggle is? This is no game, as we are at war with s.a.tan. The only thing is we only see it and gain understanding when we look at it with our spiritual eyes. If we look at it with our physical sight then we do not gain the full understanding.

We are in open warfare with s.a.tan folks and our weapons are not guns, bullets or missiles, but our real weapon for warfare with s.a.tan is Yahushua the Messiah and His manual the Bible. How to fight s.a.tan and his cohorts is already written about in the Bible. We should be praying and casting off s.a.tan and his allies in the name of Yahushua. He is our defence, and we need to learn how to use the things that we have at our disposal to thwart this aerial enemy. s.a.tan has created a diversion. Remember s.a.tan is not the TV depicted red creature with two horns on his head. In fact s.a.tan is a very clever being, more so then you and I and has been around for a very long time. In reality however he is a defeated creature, and is living on borrowed time. We are winners in Yahushua the Messiah right now, as we are the sons and daughters of the Supreme King. But we need to know how to defend against s.a.tan's vile attacks, and use our weapons of warfare wisely, by consulting our manual the Bible, with guidance from the Holy Spirit.

1 John 2:22 Who is a liar but <u>he who denies that Yahushua is the Messiah</u>? <u>He is antichrist</u> <u>who denies the Father and the Son</u>.

No Roman Catholic would say that Yahushua is not the Messiah, or Master. However every Muslim will deny that Yahushua is YHWH and they believe He was only a prophet. Yet many want to waste time and energy making out that it is the Roman Catholics, or the Pope who is the Anti-Messiah. Will you believe YHWH about what He says in the Bible, or will you believe prophecy teachers who lack understanding in this area? Make this decision now and pick up your Bible and focus in on what He says? When it comes to religion, only Islam fits this category that denies Yahushua as the Son of YHWH, or YHWH high and enthroned above. **John had this revelation and has identified the mark of the Anti-Messiah people for us.** Disbelieve at your own peril. Some scholars believe that this chapter was simply speaking of people who were Christians who left the faith quoting **1 John 2:19**.

They went out from us, but they were not of us; for if they had been of us, they would no doubt have continued with us: but they went out, that they might be made manifest that they were not all of us.

If this is what these scholars claim then let them prove that the Anti-Messiah <u>must</u> be a Christian by their way of exegesis, which just cannot fit Scripture since the Anti-Messiah is neither a backslidden Christian nor a Jew.

1 John 2:23 Whoever <u>denies the Son does not have the Father</u> either; he who acknowledges the Son has the Father also.

The Bible is absolutely clear that those who do not acknowledge the Sonship of Yahushua do <u>not</u> know the Father either. Doctrinally this only fits the Muslims, who have **NO** eternal life in their present circumstances. Simply put, they need Yahushua in order to have eternal life. They are either in the camp with the wicked one, or in the camp with Yahushua. There is no middle ground. If a Muslim repents of his sins and accepts what Yahushua did on the cross, that He shed His blood for the Muslims' sins also, then the Muslims MUST also reject Allah as god. Then they also can be saved today and can have eternal life in Yahushua. Dear Muslim do not loose your chance to gain eternal life with Yahushua the Messiah of Israel and your Messiah and Master. The same is also true for the rest of the world and those who do not know Yahushua as their Savior. But here we are particularly dealing with Islam in prophecy.

> **Sura 2:116** "They say: [Christians] '**Allah hath begotten a son**.' glory be to Him. Nay, to Him belongs all that is in the heavens and on earth: everything readers worship to him."

Muslims will quite happily tell you why they reject Christianity. They are rather glad to tell you that "Allah is not the Father of Isa, their version of Yahushua," and that "Allah could never become flesh." They also insist that "Allah does not have a Son," and that "Isa was never crucified," in that it was someone else and that "Isa did not rise from the dead." The next Sura is quite clear of what they believe about Isa. That He is not the **Son of Allah**, and in this case Allah allegedly says, Isa is not eternal and that He is only a servant. Of course Isa is a fake, while Yahushua as described in the New Testament is the real beef.

> **Sura 19:88-93** And they say, The All-merciful has taken unto <u>Himself a son</u>. You have <u>indeed advanced something hideous</u>. As if the skies are about to burst, the earth to split asunder and its mountain to fall down in the utter ruin for that **they have attributed to the All-Merciful a son**; and behaves not the <u>All-Merciful to take a son</u>. None there in the heavens and earth but comes to **the All-Merciful, as a servant.**"

I will have to agree with the Muslims that Allah cannot become flesh and does not have a Son since <u>Allah is not the Elohim of Israel whose name alone is Yahweh.</u>

The prophecy teachers who want to play gymnastics with YHWH's written words and try to make out the 4th beast to be Rome err, as there is no biblical justification for any portion of Western Europe to be a part of this kingdom. It is imperative to understand that ALL four Empires of Daniel were not only <u>Middle East</u> centric, but they had to have been based **between the two rivers of Babylon,** that is the **River Euphrates and the River Tigris.** Rome never had a capital in Babylon, but ALL the previous Empires **did** including that of Alexander. Ask any of your favorite prophecy teachers to show you even <u>one</u> western European nation that is mentioned in the Bible as one that stands with the Anti-Messiah's kingdom. You will find none, nada, zero zilch.

Rome and Europe as the Anti-Messiah nations have passed their shelf lives and sell by dates. The prophecy writers should stop selling these theories. If we are to include western Empire as part of Rome, then we must include Northern African nations that were correctly the western part of Rome, e.g. nations such as **Libya**, **Tunis**, **Morocco**, **Mauritania** and **Algeria**. By what right do the prophecy teachers make Western Europe part of historic Rome? There is no biblical basis for such a conclusion and any such conclusion made is erroneous. What right do we have of removing the true former western Roman nations listed above in North Africa that were the power base of Rome? If Rome has Western Europe as part of its end time revival, then what about Turkey, Egypt and Morocco? The prophecy writers will still struggle because they cannot document one nation in Western Europe mentioned in the Bible. In fact it is just the opposite.

Let me help you so that you know that there are some key nations that will stand against the Anti-Messiah one of which is Great Britain.

> **Jeremiah 51:27** Set up a banner in the land, blow the trumpet among the nations! Prepare the nations against her, call the kingdoms together against her; **Ararat, Minni, and Ashchenaz.** [Europe allied to fight the Anti-Messiah] Appoint a marshal against her; cause the horses to come up like the bristling locusts.

Yahweh is going to punish Allah the god **Bel** through these Western European nations. This is the reason why the USA and UK are in coalition together who have fought two wars in Iraq. In the end Yahweh is going to stop the flow of people to Mecca the spiritual harlot capital of the world and no more souls will be swallowed up by Bel (Allah).

> **Jeremiah 51:44** I will punish **Bel in Babylon**, and **I will bring out of his mouth what he has swallowed**; and the nations shall **not** stream to him anymore. Yes, the wall of Babylon shall fall.

Now that we have some understanding let me set forth some clear proposals.

Where is Babylon?

The only place on earth that has ever been called Babylon has been Iraq and by extension Saudi Arabia has been referred to as the "daughter of Babylon." Sometimes Yahweh sees Babylon as the nation of Saudi Arabia, but the whole Islamic kingdom has been referred to as Mount Seir, Mount Esau, or even Edom, **but the Master has never called any western nation Babylon.** In fact it will be incredibly ignorant to place Babylon in Europe to believe that Babylon shifted 5000 miles to the North or even to the USA some 10000 miles away! This is only in the imagination of those who have no understanding of true Babylon and its end-time goals. In order to justify any such theory we must have proof from Scripture, but we have none.
Yahweh even names the location of end time Babylon so no one need be confused.

> **Jeremiah 51:24-25** And **I will render unto Babylon** and to all the inhabitants **of Chaldea** all their evil that they have **done in Zion** in your sight, saith the Master. Behold, I am against thee, **O destroying mountain**, saith the Master, which destroyest all the earth: and I will stretch out mine hand upon thee, and roll thee down from the rocks, and will make thee a **burnt mountain.**

A mountain is an allegoric kingdom. Is YHWH going to burn one mountain in Iraq, or destroy the **whole kingdom with people attached to it**? Think about that.

> **Jeremiah 51:4** Thus the slain shall fall in the **land of the Chaldeans**, and they that are thrust through, in her streets.

> **Jeremiah 51:6** Flee from the **midst of Babylon**, and every one save his life! Do not be cut off in **her** iniquity, for this is the time of the Master's vengeance; He shall **recompense** her.

Yahweh does not leave us guessing where is Babylon is;

> **Genesis 10:10** And the beginning of his kingdom was Babel, and Erech, and Accad, and Calneh, in the **land of Shinar**. [biblical name for Iraq.]

You will find these city names in Europe or in the Middle East? **In fact, you find them only in Iraq that has always and will always be called Babylon.**

Who is the Harlot of Babylon?

I propose Mecca in Saudi Arabia, which has full biblical support, as I shall demonstrate in this book.

Who is the daughter of Babylon?

I propose Saudi Arabia with biblical supported evidence in this book.

Which is the probable country of origin of the Anti-Messiah?

It is likely that Turkey, or Kurdistan reading the prophecy of **Ezekiel 38** and the little horn of **Daniel 7** and **Daniel 8:9**. The Muslims are also looking for the Mahdi in their eschatology, and this is the reason why the Anti-Messiah is called **The Assyrian (Micah 5:5-6**), also called "**O Pharaoh King of Egypt,**" and The **KING OF BABYLON** (**Isaiah 14:4**).

> **Micah 5:6** They shall waste with the sword the **land of Assyria**, and the **land of Nimrod** at **its entrances**; thus **He shall deliver us from The Assyrian**, when he comes into our land and when he treads within our borders.

Why would YHWH call the Anti-Messiah by these TITLES if he were to turn up in Italy? Do you see that in **Micah 5:6** above YHWH gives it to you on a silver plate? The Anti-Messiah is called "**The Assyrian**" in/from the "**land of Assyria**" and the "**land of Nimrod?**" The belief of Europe being the Anti-Messiah's ten toes, or kingdom is not only a gross contradiction, but certainly not-negotiable with the biblical text and cannot be reconciled with Scripture. It is not wise to assume any European Anti-Messiah on our part, considering the above TITLES belong to the same person out of the Middle East. YHWH points the land out for us.

48

Chapter 4

Saudi Arabia - A Nation At Ease and the Harlot of Babylon

First we have to see if Saudi Arabia is mentioned in the Bible, or are we reading this in to the text. There are plenty of prophecy teachers out there who read things into the text that are not there. This is what I would call eisegesis, whereas we need to do exegesis, i.e. extract information from the biblical text rather then putting information into the text. Recently I went to a prophecy sermon and there a leading prophecy writer who has been writing for some 40 years stated that the Anti-Messiah will make the world into ten separate zones. In this supposed new one-world order Europe would be one such zone. During question time, I only needed to ask one key question to highlight this error. Where does the Bible indicate that it is a "one-world government," or 10 zones? His answer was to look at the 10 kings in **Revelations 17:12** and the "ten horns which thou sawest are ten kings."

I spoke to him at length after his talk explaining how these 10 kings could not be called 10 divisions of the earth and how that this is a gross exaggeration of the text. The 10 kings in question are part of the Middle Eastern Empire not Western Europe or the USA. He agreed that it does not state the **obvious** and agreed with what I presented. In the same way you will find many prophecy teachers who write many books on the Anti-Messiahs coming out of Europe. Yet they fail to provide <u>one</u> reference to show where in the Bible YHWH has ordained wrath on Western Europe during the tribulation period, along with the Anti-Messiah allegedly coming from a <u>region</u> in Europe, or the USA. I asked another prophecy teacher to just show me <u>one</u> passage that says the Anti-Messiah is from the landmass of Europe or the USA. Again, he also never came back with a response and I am still waiting. Let us see if Saudi Arabia fits the picture of true Babylon in the Bible, or even more correctly as the "daughter of Babylon." I have been crying from the rooftops that the Anti-Messiah is from the Middle East, but so far only a few discernible people have paid attention. Now however the time is coming that you will see for yourself the evidence set before you. The seals are off and Daniel's text is no longer sealed as believed by some.

> **Daniel 12:9** And he said, Go thy way, Daniel: for the words are closed up and sealed till the time of the end.

> **Matthew 24:15** When ye therefore shall see the abomination of desolation, spoken of by Daniel the prophet, stand in the holy place, (whoso reads, let him understand:)

The abomination of desolation (Al-Aqsa Mosque) has been standing there since 688-705 when it was constructed, and we should know that the time has come to know about this last Empire.

> **Matthew 24:34** Verily I say unto you, this **generation** shall not pass, till all these things be fulfilled.

We are the last generation according to Yahushua's prophecy in Matthew 24:34, because the word for "generation" is the Aramaic "Sherbata" meaning tribe. Simply put Yahushua was saying that the tribe of Judah shall not perish. They had to be dispersed and gathered back into the land of Israel and we know the dispersal happened and the

49

gathering back also has begun. Israel stands as a nation since 1948 and Jerusalem was freed by Israel in 1967. Friends our grand finale has kicked in.

> **Isaiah 46:10** Declaring the **end from the beginning**, and from ancient times the things that are not yet done, saying, My counsel shall stand, and I will do all my pleasure:

If you understand the book of Genesis as I have highlighted some key passages, then you will understand the end times Empire. The truth actually lies back in Genesis.

> **Revelation1: 1** The Revelation of Yahushua Messiah, which YHWH gave unto him, to shew unto his servants things which must shortly come to pass; and he sent and signified it by his angel unto his servant John:

In fact when the book of Revelation was revealed it was to open up our understanding of the end to come, because the book's purpose was to reveal the end as it is going to be, even though the final Empire had not yet been established. However YHWH wanted to show Yochanan (John) the times to come in order to prepare all Israelites, which includes all **believers**.

A.   Babylon and The Daughter Of Babylon

In prophecy Babylon is mostly used for Iraq. But it is also used in conjunction for Saudi Arabia. The reason is simple. They share a common religion and ancestry; you will find some of Muhammad's closest followers settled in Iraq after his death. Have you ever heard of the Umayyad dynasty? I suggest you read up about it. You will also find both Iraq and Saudi Arabia have quite large reserves of oil and share much in common.

The fourth caliph Ali bin Abu Talib did move his capital to Iraq. He was the first cousin of the prophet of Islam. Recently in the Gulf war on our TV screens you would have seen the Imam Ali mosque that Muqtada Al-Sadr had occupied to fight the USA forces. This is the place of the first Martyr of Islam and the starting point of the Shiite sect of Islam, the second largest sect in Islam after Sunnis (the largest sect). (By the way, I was a Sunni Muslim myself, so I can give you a lot of the information first hand.)

Fighting here by the Mahdi militia (it is the Mahdi the Muslims are expecting to hail as their Messiah) brought many injuries to the surrounding people. They attacked the USA forces then hid in the mosque, playing a cat and mouse game where the cat did not go after the mouse into the hole. The USA forces could have blown the mosque to smithereens, but did not do this out of respect for their holy shrine, and yet the tactics of the Mahdi Army leave us with a bad taste in the mouth.

The Anti-Messiah nations were never Europe, or America at any point in time or history. Neither will they be. The whole scenario is around Israel in the Middle East. It is the twelve tribes of Ishmael (the twelve sons of Ishmael **Genesis 17:20**) versus the twelve sons of Israel (**Genesis 49:28**). This is an eternal battle between darkness verses light (Malachi 1:2-4-'Jacob have I loved; Esau have I hated'). If believers are redeemed Israel from both houses, and since house enter 'Jacob's Trouble,' it behoves us to know who is the enemy causing Jacob (us) his trouble. We MUST identify that enemy, if we are to prepare mentally, spiritually and physically to enter the time of OUR (BELIEVERS) Trouble! Its time to take that honest look for yourself!

How do we know if Saudi Arabia is in the biblical text? We look for biblical names for these places before they were changed to modern names. The name "Saudi" is from the "house of Saud," but the name Arabia is used in reference to this place many times. The Bible uses the name "Kedar" for Saudi Arabia. For adherents of prophecy readers, it also uses the term Midianites for Arabs generally and at times Arabia directly:

Tyre, Magog, Mount Seir, Babylon, Teman, **Mystery Babylon**, Edom and Dummah are all referred to in the Bible and are ALL Islamic nations today. One wonders why the prophecy writers today try to place these nations in Europe when in context they are all in the Middle East.

In later prophecy, Saudi Arabia is referred to as "the daughter of Babylon" because it came out of the false religions of Iraq.

In **Psalm 137:8** O **daughter of Babylon** [Saudi Arabia], who art to be **destroyed**; happy shall he be, that rewardeth thee as thou hast served us.

Why does the Bible call Saudi Arabia the "**daughter of Babylon**" here? It is because the religion that Saudi Arabia proclaims as holy truth came right out of Babylon in Iraq. The worship of Allah is taken from the one that was once known as the god Bel. Let me paint a picture of Iraq using King Nebuchadnezzar once in power. Remember Daniel and his three friends. They were renamed with Daniel becoming Belteshazzar. A name change means a nature change and this was what was effectively being done. Let me remind you why YHWH changed Abram's name to Abraham because Yahweh called him out of Ur of the Chaldees and so for Abraham crossing over the river means crossing over from death to life.

Av-ram = Exalted Father in himself
Av-Ra-**H-**am = Exalted Father with a Heh or with the Sprit of Yahweh.

Daniel = El is my Judge, or my Judge is El
Belteshazzar = Beltis protect the king

The names were meant to remove Yahweh from these lads and change their nature designed to distance them from the Elohim of Israel.

Let me explain some of the things that previous Empires did as this hides a spiritual truth that Islam has;

- ❖ **Assyrians**: They indoctrinated you to be absorbed in their culture, i.e. mix into their society.
- ❖ **Babylonian**: Name changes plus bowing to their god.
- ❖ **Grecian**: Banned Judaism.

Islam does all of these and more. You see converts to Islam, English, American and Caucasian peoples suddenly acquiring a **dress change,** wearing Arab style dresses, getting a **name change** to a Muslim name and no longer worshipping the true YHWH. All these traits exist in Islam and they are reflective of the Empires above. Reflective also of what the Anti-Messiah nations will do.

Note Islam is destined to be destroyed completely and utterly by the Elohim of Israel, but it has a time span before this destruction takes effect.

The Hastings' Encyclopaedia of Religion and Ethics (volume I, pg. 326) says it *"is a proper name applicable only to their peculiar god."* It further says: *"Allah is a pre-Islamic name...corresponding to the Babylonian god known as Bel."* 'Bel' simply means 'lord' and this is a title of reverence to the moon-god 'Sin'.

Jeremiah 50:42 They shall hold the **bow and the lance**; they are cruel and shall not show mercy. Their voice shall roar like the sea; they shall ride on horses, set in array, **like a man for the battle, against you**, O **daughter of Babylon** (Saudi Arabia).

This daughter of Babylon (Saudi Arabia) is mentioned which will be utterly destroyed.

Jeremiah 51:33 For thus says the Master of Hosts, the Elohim of Israel: **"the daughter of Babylon"** is like a threshing floor when it is time to thresh her; yet a little while and the time of her harvest will come."

The Master is giving time to the "**daughter of Babylon**" (Saudi Arabia) before the time of her destruction; perhaps some people there will certainly repent and come out.

Zechariah 2:7 "Up, Zion! Escape, you who dwell with the **daughter of Babylon** [Saudi Arabia]."

The Master is warning Zion/Israel for any Jews and Christians to escape this land before the destruction comes upon Saudi Arabia, and not to have anything to do with her in terms of commerce or habitation. The term "Zion" includes Christians, because YHWH sees Zion intrinsically as people who are His followers and that includes Bible believing Christians. I take it now you are confused, how can Zion be applied to Christians? Let me explain another Bible truth.

Jeremiah 4:16-17 "Make **mention to the nations, yes, proclaim against Jerusalem,** that **watchers [Christians] come from a far country and raise their voice against the cities of Judah**. (17) Like keepers of a field they are **against her all around**, because she has been **rebellious against Me**," says the Master.

There is a prophecy in Jeremiah that the "watchers" the Hebrew word "Notzar" come from a "far country." These Christians come from ALL over the world to proclaim Yahushua as their Messiah. These Notzars are Christians, because Yahushua the Messiah was called the one who is from the "**City of the Branch**" e.g. Natzer-eth, or Nazareth. It is actually Netzer, one of the titles given to the Messiah of being a Nazarene and ALL His early followers were called Nazarenes (Matthew 2:23/Acts 24:5), or as seen in the title above in Hebrew as "watchers." Be careful not all the words translated in the Bible as "watchers" apply to Christians as sometimes they apply to angels because the underlying Hebrew word is different e.g. in **Daniel 4:13** a "watcher" angel descended and the Aramaic word for this "watcher" is *"eer."*

In my opinion the far country is non other but the USA. For biblical writers the far country is furtherest west of Israel. Check your maps. What is furthest west on the map from Israel? The only nation that sticks out like a soar thumb is the USA.

Jeremiah 31:6 For there shall be a day, that the **watchmen** [Hebrew notzar] upon the **mount Ephraim** shall cry, **Arise ye, and let us go up to Zion unto the Master YHWH our Elohim.**

These watchmen in the Hebrew language "Notzar," or Notzarim (Christians) going up to Mount Zion are also referred to as "Mount Ephraim," and the symbolic Mount Ephraim are all of the worldwide community of Bible believing Christians in the Ephraimite church.

The prophecy in **Jeremiah 31:27** dictates that both the "House of Judah" and "House of Israel" have to be present in the land before the Messiah can return.

Jeremiah 31:27 "Behold, the days are coming," says the Master, "that I will sow the **house of Israel** and the **house of Judah** with the seed of man and the seed of beast.

Exactly as Jacob knew that the younger will be blessed and become in Hebrew the "Melo Ha Goyim"/fullness of the nations (**Genesis 48:19**). So we can see how both Judah and Ephraim are present in the land, though many Ephraimites do not recognize their identity, but YHWH will yet bring greater numbers back.

Jeremiah 23:5 "Behold, **the days are coming**," says the Master, "**That I will raise to David a Branch of righteousness; a King shall reign and prosper,** and **execute judgment and righteousness in the earth**.

Here in **Jeremiah 23:5** it is YHWH who declares that He will raise up a King who is given the title "Branch of righteousness." In this passage the branch is in the Hebrew word "Tzemach." This is applied by the Rabbis to the King Messiah, who we believe is Yahushua of Nazareth.

Isaiah 14:19 but you are cast out of your grave like an **abominable branch,** [Netzer] Like the garment of those who are slain, thrust through with a sword, who go down to the stones of the pit, like a corpse trodden under foot.

The Hebrew word "Netzer" is used in Isaiah 14 where s.a.tan is being described and suddenly the text switches over to the Anti-Messiah of the end-times as the "abominable branch." We could say these passages show us some real hidden meanings of the parallels between the true Messiah of Israel who is Yahushua of Nazareth and the "abominable branch," the false 'peaceful leader,' who will come to sign the peace deal with Israel and a security plan from the Muslim world.

Isaiah 11:1 There shall come forth a **Rod from the stem of Jesse**, and **a Branch [Netzer]** shall grow out of his roots.

Note in Isaiah 11:1 Yahushua is referred to as the Good Branch, the King Messiah while in **Isaiah 14:19** it is the evil wicked depiction of s.a.tan portrayed as the Anti-Messiah.

When the Arabs conquered this land they ruled it for less then 100 years and neglected the land and the indigenous Jewish population living there. The Jews who returned from Europe did not just simply take over the land, but had to purchase lands from the absentee Arab land owners at extortionate prices and then worked swamp infested lands, planting, and irrigating the land, working the land, to make it what it is today.

Jeremiah 31:3-7 (3) The Master has appeared of old to me, saying: "Yes, I have loved you with an **everlasting love**; [the nation of Israel reference to Jacob and his progeny] therefore with loving kindness I have drawn you. (4) Again **I will build you,** [YHWH does the building] and you shall be rebuilt, O virgin of Israel! You shall again be adorned with your tambourines, and shall go forth in the dances of those who rejoice. (5) **You shall yet plant vines on the mountains of Samaria**; the planters shall plant and eat them as ordinary food. (6) **For there shall be a day** when the **watchmen will cry on Mount Ephraim**, `Arise, and let us go up to Zion**, to the Master our YHWH Elohim.' (7) " For thus says the Master: "Sing with gladness for Jacob, and shout among **THE CHIEF OF NATIONS** [this is the USA]; proclaim, give praise, and say, `O Master, save Your people, the **remnant of Israel!**"

The Master planted Israel back in their land and no one could change that. He loves His covenant people and draws them to repentance and faith in Him through the person of Yahushua of Nazareth. How can they plant vines in Samaria if there is no Samaria? The division of Israel that has been worked out today under the so-called peace plan will not last. There is an amazing prophecy in these verses, "Watchmen will cry on Mount Ephraim." Who are these watchmen and who is Mount Ephraim?

The Hebrew gives it away for those who have spiritual eyes to see, for the word watchmen the Hebrew word is **Notzar.** These are the Christians who will proclaim and pray for Israel. What is Mt. Ephraim? And what who is referred to as the first-born son of Yahweh. Ephraim went into Idolatry and YHWH punished Ephraim and dispersed them. They were known as the "House of Israel," the northern kingdom, the ones who became the "Melo Ha Goyim," as given by the blessing of Jacob in **Genesis 48:19**. So Mount Ephraim is non other than the mixture of gentile nations, who have Israelite blood, and yet today many still do not know their identity. But YHWH does indeed know! The prodigal son (**Luke 15:11-32**) is really the story of Ephraim the long lost son who is found, who had left his Father and family and ended up in all sorts of problems until he returned to his Father. This is the symbolic picture of the church, also in all sorts of idolatry today.

Hosea 4:17 Ephraim is joined to idols; let him alone.

Who is singing in **Jeremiah 31:7** the "chief of nations" is non other but the USA and the Christians who will get up and go to Jerusalem. They will pray for their brothers the Jews. We know the Christian church is symbolically represented in this verse, because the northern kingdom of Israel changed the holy days and holy feasts and entered into idolatry. The church has also switched the days from Sabbath to Sun-day and the feasts from Passover to Easter (the goddess of springtime and fertility), the Feast of Tabernacles to Christ-Mass. The Mt. of Ephraim is symbolic for nations and kingdoms. This mountain is symbolic for the kingdom of Christians, or non Jewish Israel, who in the end of days are praying and for and rising up on behalf of Jewish Israel.

Jeremiah 4:17 - that watchers come from a FAR COUNTRY and raise their voice against the cities of Judah.

Did somebody forget about the USA Christians?

Here it is plainly evident that these people coming from "afar" are again the Christians from the USA, the nation due west of Israel, who go and prophetically proclaim the "feast of Tabernacles" in Jerusalem every year. This movement started in the 1980s. It is clear

54

these people are linked with **Jeremiah 31:7** and not only the USA is pictured here, but other nations join also. But right now in the end times, who is literally the "chief of nations?"

How about the USA, the superpower that YHWH predicted some 2605 years ago. The Bible prophecies are impressive, even if you look at them from a secular angle, as YHWH gets it right every time. Hallelu-Yah.

On the other hand, the violence by the Palestinian Muslims is predicted also and goes hand in hand to plant bombs and become suicide bombers to shed innocent blood in the name of their god Allah.

> **Isaiah 59:7** Their feet run to evil, and they make haste to shed innocent blood; their thoughts are thoughts of iniquity; **wasting** and **destruction** are in their paths.

Who are the homicide bombers in Iraq shedding innocent blood, as I write this week the 25th of June 2005, two suicide bombers blew themselves up in Iraq killing Iraqi policemen and in the second instance, killing USA soldiers?

Now to continue on in the Qu'ran, Sura 106 is a well-known early Meccan Sura i.e. it predates the hijrah (the flight) when Muhammad (the Muslim prophet) fled to Medina from the Quraish tribe in Mecca, upon initial persecution from his own tribe, who did not believe him to be a prophet. The Quraish tribe were Arabs from whom Muhammad descended. They were engrossed in pagan idolatrous worship in the Ka'ba and they were doing all the rites that the Muslims do today, minus the idols in the Ka'ba (cube).

> **Sura 106.1-4** For the protection of the Quraish (2) Their protection during their trading caravans in the winter and the summer (3) So let them serve the **lord of this house (This house is Ka'ba and the Master is Hu-bal or Ha-baal in Hebrew, referred to as the false god)** (4) Who feeds them against hunger and gives them security against fear (Note no mention of Yahweh).

The Quraish were willing to defend their religion against Muhammad and his claims of prophethood.

The Quraish who were unwilling to give up their pagan practices. They could only have understood the "**lord of this house**" to be the moon-god, 'the god' in Arabic, or Allah. It is only after this Sura was revealed that Muhammad came back to destroy the idols in the Ka'ba and fight the people that refused to accept his prophethood. Even then Muhammad told them to worship "**the lord of this house**" i.e. the Meccan god in Ka'ba who was still the god Hu-bal, or ha-Ba-al.

The Quraish wanted no part of Muhammad's theology, until he proclaimed the "lord of this [pagan] house," as god, and the Quraish knew this was already one of their gods, so they were quite happy to hear this revised version and accept this.

Interestingly Muhammad never spoke about the one true YHWH. He never knew His name and he never spoke about Abraham in any of the early Meccan Suras. He never had Abraham's monotheistic message as this name only starts to appear in the Qu'ran in later Medinan Suras where Muhammad tried to justify his faith to link it with Judaism. This clearly shows that he did not know any true biblical Judaism, or Christianity, or the mode of true revelation. He simply pasted all the pagan practices of Mecca into his new created religion of Islam, minus the idols in the cube at Mecca. Muslims today deny that Allah was the chief idol of Mecca known as the god of forces, or god of Jihad. Remember for the first thirteen years in Mecca Muhammad never proclaimed his message as the same one of Abraham, Isaac or Jacob.

> **Daniel 11:38** "But in their place **he shall honor a god of fortresses**; [god of jihad] and a god which his fathers did not know **he shall honor with gold and silver**, with precious stones and pleasant things.

A god that Muhammad's fathers did not know is the "god of jihad" because Muhammad's ancestors worshipped several gods in Mecca each one having his own god, whereas Muhammad only revered one god Allah, in whose name Muslims today wage war against the west. All Muslims are required to honor their god Allah by giving 2.5% out of their wealth and assets to this god of jihad as zakat (special tax of their wealth to Allah to help the poor) in gold, silver and cash.

It may be astonishing to learn that a reference to an Indian King, King Vikramadity's whose inscription was found in the Ka'ba in Mecca, quite possibly proving that the Arabian Peninsula formed a part of his Indian Empire." It is quite possible that this was indeed a Hindu Temple of some sort before Muhammad, as we know that Hindus worship many deities and the Ka'ba before Muhammad's time did house at least 360 deities if not more. Whether this was part of the Indian king's empire or not remains to be seen, but the Hindu Indians certainly have a similar worship circumambulation of a cube.

"This discovery changes the entire complexion of ancient history and to a great extent, the history of ancient India. For one thing we may have to revise our concepts about the king who had the largest empire in history. It could be that the expanse of King Vikramaditya's empire was larger than that of all others. [12]

"The text of the crucial Vikramaditya inscription, found inscribed on a gold dish hung inside the Ka'ba shrine in Mecca, is found recorded on page 315 of a volume known as "Sayar-ul-Okul" treasured in the Makhtab-e-sultania (library) in Istanbul, Turkey." (IBID)

> "Rendered in free English the inscription says "Fortunate are those who were born (and lived) during King Vikrama's reign. He was a noble, generous, dutiful ruler, devoted to the welfare of his subjects."

> "That the so-called Kutab Minar in Delhi could well be King Vikramaditya's tower commemorating his conquest of Arabia." (IBID)

> "The first modern edition of "Sayar-ul-Okul" was printed and published in Berlin in A.D. 1864. A subsequent one was published in Beirut in A.D. 1932." (IBID)

---

[12] Reproduced by Muslim Digest, July to Oct. 1986 pages. 23-24) (Article written by Mr P.N. Oak at N-128, Greater Kailas 1, New Delhi 14, India and distributed from Durban, South Africa)

Now let us go back to the pages of Genesis to trace some more answers for the origins of the Islamic nations.

> **Genesis 25:12-18** Now these are the generations of Ishmael, Abraham's son, whom **Hagar the Egyptian**, Sarah's handmaid, bare unto Abraham: And these are the **names of the sons of Ishmael**, by their names, according to their generations: the firstborn of Ishmael, Nebajoth; and **Kedar**, and Adbeel, and Mibsam, And Mishma, and <u>Dumah</u>, and Massa, Hadar, and **Tema**, Jetur, Naphish, and Kedemah: These are the sons of Ishmael, and these are their names, by their towns, and by their castles; <u>twelve princes according to their nations</u>. And these are the years of the life of Ishmael, a hundred and thirty and seven years: and he gave up the ghost and died; and was gathered unto his people. And they dwelt from **Havilah unto Shur**, that is **before Egypt**, as thou goest toward **Assyria**: and he died in the presence of all his brethren.

Note a few things from the verses above:

- ❖ Ishmael was born through an Egyptian woman.
- ❖ Ishmael had 12 sons/princes.
- ❖ These 12 princes became nations.
- ❖ They occupied parts of Egypt, Syria (modern Iraq and Syria) and southern parts of Jordan and Arabia.

> **Genesis 17:20** And as for Ishmael, **I have heard thee**: behold, **I have blessed him**, and will make him fruitful, and **will multiply him exceedingly**; <u>twelve princes shall he beget</u>, and **I will make him a great nation**.

YHWH said he would **bless** Ishmael and make him a **great nation**; the Arabs today are truly blessed and are a great nation just like YHWH said they would be. They have plenty of oil and wealth, this is part of the material blessing promised to them and it is Yahweh who gave them these blessings. They did not acquire them with their own strength, neither was it Allah the moon god who gave them these blessings.

Kedar was a son of Ishmael of the twelve princes; the Master has lot to say about these people, as they are important end-time players in prophecy.

People like to read "one-world government" into the text when we find no such reference.

Let's take a look at Psalm 120, which speaks about these people.

B.   Where is Babylon?

While some prophecy teachers cannot see a person called an Anti-Messiah other then in the epistle of 1 John 2, they contend that the Anti-Messiah is not a person. Just because different prophets do not call him the Anti-Messiah, does not invalidate the person of the Anti-Messiah.

In **Ezekiel 38:17** we read *"Thus saith the Master YHWH; Art thou he of whom I have spoken in old time by my servants the prophets of Israel."* We have to ask the question when did the other prophets speak about him as "Gog"? However we must understand that different prophets described the same person of the Anti-Messiah by different TITLES. So this is not only a real person, but also a leader as described, and he has been spoken about by many prophets. The following are just some of his titles.

- Gog (Ezekiel 38:2)
- The Assyrian (Micah 5:6)
- The Anti-Messiah (1 John 2:22) - which Messiah?
- Son of Perdition (2 Thessalonians 2:3)
- The Lawless One (2 Thessalonians 2:8)
- Man of Sin (2 Thessalonians 2:3)
- Lucifer (Isaiah 14:12)
- The House of The Wicked (Habakkuk 3:13)
- The Plunderer (Isaiah 21:2)
- "King of Babylon (Isaiah 14:4)
- Pharaoh (Jeremiah Ezekiel 29:2)
- King of Egypt (Ezekiel 29:3)

One such TITLE **The Assyrian** is given because he is from a particular region e.g. the Assyrian Empire. Abraham was also an Assyrian and a Babylonian from that region, and the Anti-Messiah is going to be given such a title as above because of his location and whereabouts.

> **Deuteronomy 26:5** And thou shalt speak and say before YHWH thy Elohim, A **Syrian ready to perish was my father**, and he went down into Egypt, and sojourned there with a few, and became there a nation, great, mighty, and populous:

Babylon was never called by the name Iraq in the Bible but by the term **Babylon** and the other biblical name for that landmass has been Shinar. *Genesis 10:10 And the beginning of his kingdom was Babel, and Erech, and Accad, and Calneh, in the land of Shinar.* This leaves us under no illusions of where Babylon was or is.

Notice the reason Yahweh calls the Anti-Messiah **"The ASSYRIAN"** which is his actual identity. Its like Yahushua's proper name Yahushua, that really Biblically means "He has become my personal salvation," or some say Yahweh saves, while others Yahu saves, as the word Yah could have been pronounced Yahu with the vowel markers. Why call His short name Yahushua if He could not save? This is why with in the NAME of Yahushua, or Yahushua is **salvation** and **redemption.** His identity as the **Elohim of Israel** and of course the location of His birthplace, plus the significance of Him being a Jew of a certain lineage, is very very important. Likewise Yahushua could never be a golden haired blue-eyed Swedish looking man. That is the error of the church that is propagated on church windows to confuse people and sideline the Hebrew people, the true people chosen by Yahweh, the flesh and blood descendants of Abraham our father. Likewise with the title of THE ASSYRIAN is the complete identity of the Anti-Messiah, the one who opposes Yahweh's eternal plan. The tile of **THE ASSYRIAN** identifies to us his location i.e. the Middle East and his fowl plan to annihilate the Hebrew people and kill the Christians, the ones who are grafted in to Israel.

58

The Assyrian Empire

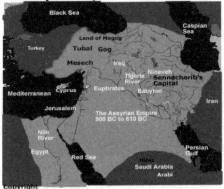

www.abrahamic-faith.com

When Yahweh attaches nations to Babylon, He does not mean Europe. It is the **SURROUNDING NATIONS** against Israel that are mainly Islamic and any other countries that form that empire are also Muslim, so that even nations like Pakistan are included and not excluded. Yahweh knew that Pakistan would form part of this empire and this is why He had to separate it from India and form the "Islamic Republic of Pakistan," one of the most hostile nations today against Israel. Pakistan has many terrorists and radical Muslims living in the very land of Pakistan, while the army of Pakistan pretends not to see them and the ISS (Pakistan Secret Service) funds them.

The Harlot of Babylon

Who can better fit this description than Saudi Arabia (Mecca) because the Muslim god Allah originated as **lil** from Sumer, again the Middle East, that later became **il** and then it was exported from Babylon by Nabonidus in the 6th century BC to Saudi Arabia, where the Arabs started worshipping Allah long before Muhammad was born. The god is known by different names in different regions, the root of which is **lil**, **enlil**, **Sin**, **il and Bel** etc. "The Controller of the Night," had the crescent moon as his emblem, which became the primary religious symbol of Islam and many other false religions. In Arabia he was also known as hu-bal or ha-baal. In 637AD, a new era began when the Saudi Arabians conquered Mesopotamia whereby "Babylon" then became part of the Arab-Islamic Empire. The worship of the Moon god "Sin" was widespread and common during the time of Abraham. In the Bible, Abraham was asked to leave Ur of the Chaldees, where the moon god Sin was worshipped and told to migrate to Canaan and worship Yahweh instead.

The term "Daughter of Babylon"

My proposal of Saudi Arabia as the candidate is based on solid scriptural argument and evidence because of what happened with Nabonidus earlier. This is dealt with in this book already. Babylon is a physical place with spiritual concepts and with borders and people. Babylon cannot be **Europe,** or the USA, since the borders do not match and city names are not USA names of cities or states.
Jeremiah confirms this view.

Jeremiah 51:24-25 And **I will render** <u>unto Babylon</u> and to all the inhabitants of <u>Chaldea all their evil</u> that they have **done in Zion** in **your sight**, saith the Master. Behold, I am against thee, **O destroying mountain**, saith the Master, **which destroyest all the earth**: and I will stretch out mine hand upon thee, and roll thee down from the rocks, and will make thee a **burnt mountain**.

A mountain is an allegoric kingdom, Yahweh's wrath is not going to burn just one mountain in Iraq, or else there would be little point in that wrath burning an empty mountain. He is going to destroy the **whole Islamic kingdom with Muslim people attached to it;** we do need to think about this.

Jeremiah 51:2 And I will send winnowers to Babylon, who shall winnow her and **empty her land**.

Jeremiah 51:6 Flee from the **midst of Babylon**, and <u>every one save his life</u>! Do not be cut off in **her** iniquity, for this is the time of the Master's vengeance; He shall **recompense** her.

Yahweh is an Elohim of order and not disorder and He does not leave us guessing where Babylon is contrary to people confusion. This is the same YHWH who in Moses time gave such precise instructions for constructing the priestly garments, the Ark of the Covenant and the articles of the Tabernacle such as the Menorah as one such important article. Have you read how precise He was and why He was so precise? Have you ever tried asking that question? There are reasons but this book is not going to discuss those reasons. But I'd like you to research those reasons, so you can enrich your knowledge.

Genesis 10:10 And the beginning of his kingdom was Babel, and Erech, and Accad, and Calneh, in the **land of Shinar**.

Therefore the biblical name for Iraq is as Scripture dictates is "the Land of Shinar" and or Babylon.

Burden of the desert
Isaiah 21:1 The burden of the <u>desert of the sea</u>. As whirlwinds in the south pass through; so it cometh **from the desert, from a terrible land**.

Saudi Arabia is literally the **DESERT OF THE SEA** i.e. nations around about it, and seas around about it. Look at the Middle East map below and identify the SEAS.

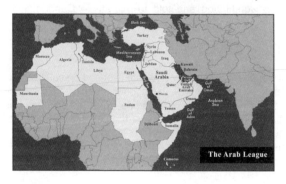

The only thing is here the prophets at times saw Babylon as one entity including Saudi Arabia, because although in Isaiah 21 **verse 9** "Babylon is fallen." But the cities mentioned are not in Iraq, but in Arabia i.e we do not see Erech, Accad and Calneh. It's like in Middle Eastern culture when you name a family instead of naming each individual person you just name one person that is the head and that includes all of them. We see that in the Bible with the tribes where just one person is named, that it includes thousands of descendents underneath them such as **Judah**.

In Jeremiah YHWH gives us another indication that Arabia is the nation with many seas;

> **Jeremiah 51:13** O you who dwell <u>by</u> **many waters**, abundant in treasures, your end has come, the measure of your covetousness.

Yahweh does not say O you who dwell <u>with</u> many waters so this is not allegoric for **people,** nations and tongues like in the Book of Revelation. This is a literal reference for seas. It fits Saudi Arabia much better than Rome.

> **Micah 5:5-6** And this **One shall be peace [The Messiah]**. When **the Assyrian** comes into **our land**, and when <u>he treads in our palaces [Temple Mount]</u>, then we will raise against him **seven shepherds** and **eight princely men**. They shall waste with the sword the <u>**land of Assyria**</u>, and the <u>**land of Nimrod**</u> at its entrances; thus He shall deliver us from **The Assyrian**, when he comes into **our land and when he treads within our borders**.

This is a prophecy concerning the Messiah Yahushua's second return upon this earth to the holy hill, or Mount Zion in Jerusalem. The Messiah will be **the peace**, in Hebrew "ha shalom," He will be the **tower of refuge** and strength in the last days against **The Assyrian** and therefore the "Assyrian" is clearly another title for the Anti-Messiah.

Remember Abraham being called the Assyrian and this person being called the Assyrian.

When did an Assyrian come into Judah where the palaces of Israel are located? Sennacherib was not allowed to enter into Jerusalem, **but this one <u>must</u> enter and WILL divide Jerusalem.**

Burden against the Sea (Saudi Arabia)
Isaiah 21:1-10 <u>The burden against the Wilderness of the Sea</u>. As whirlwinds in the South pass through, so it comes from the **desert, from a terrible land**. A distressing vision is declared to me; the treacherous dealer deals treacherously, and <u>the plunderer plunders</u>. Go up, **O Elam! Besiege, O Media!**

Iran is part of this confederacy and so are the Kurds (the Medes). They are not going to join Europe to attack Europe aka Germany, or Rome as that would be absurd, since the borders mentioned are in the Middle East.

Burden of Dumah (Arabia)
Isaiah 21:11-12 "The burden of **Dumah**. He calleth to me out of Seir, Watchman, what of the night? Watchman, what of the night? The watchman said, The morning cometh, and also the night: if ye will enquire, enquire ye: return, come."

Dumat el-Jandal is in Saudi Arabia mentioned here by Isaiah again a location in the Hijaz i.e. Arabia not Europe.

Burden against Arabia

Isaiah 21:13-17 "The burden upon Arabia. In the **forest in Arabia** shall ye lodge, O ye travelling companies of **Dedanim**. The inhabitants of the land of **Tema** brought water to him that was thirsty, they prevented with their bread him that fled. For they fled from the swords, from the drawn sword, and from the bent bow, and from the grievousness of war. For thus hath the Master said unto me, within a year, according to the years of an hireling, and **all the glory of Kedar shall fail**: And the residue of the number of archers, the mighty men of the children of Kedar, shall be diminished: for the Elohim of Israel hath spoken [it]."

The Bible talks about these things happening in the **end of days**, these things have not happened yet.

Ezekiel 38:15-16 And thou shalt come from thy place out of the **north parts**, thou, and many people with thee, all of them riding upon horses, a great company, and a mighty army: And thou shalt come up against My people of Israel, as a cloud to cover the land; it shall be in the latter days, and I will bring thee against **My land, that the heathen may know me**, when I shall be sanctified in thee, O Gog, before their eyes.

This "Gog" is the Anti-Messiah that will come from the north, this is the prophecy of the Anti-Messiah who will very likely come from Turkey and will be of the Turkic people. The **northern quarters** refers to Southern Russia, which are all Islamic nations and are mostly **Turkic people**. This person will have an alliance with the Islamic nations as described in **Psalm 83**. As one believer appropriately put it Turkey is the black horse that many have failed to recognize.

The Schaff-Herzog Encyclopaedia of Religious Knowledge, citing ancient Assyrian writings, places the location of the **land of Magog** in the landmass between **ancient Armenia and Media**, in short, the republics south of Russia and north of Israel, comprised of Azerbaijan, Afghanistan, Turkistan, Chechnya, **Turkey**, Tajikstan and Dagestan etc. Significantly, all of these nations are Muslim nations today.

This is the heart of the vast Islamic Ottoman Empire for many centuries. Hesiod, the father of Greek didactic poetry, identified Magog with the Scythians and southern Russia in the 7th century B.C. Hesiod was a contemporary of Ezekiel. Flavius Josephus records that the Greeks called the Magogians "Scythians." Philo, in the 1st century, identifies Magog with Turkey and southern Russia That entire northern region is described in Ezekiel 38 as the "remote parts of the north." The Bible does not say "farthest north," It simply says: "the house of Togarmah of the north quarters" (Ezekiel 38:6).

This Gog from Magog is another name for the Anti-Messiah.

Obadiah 1:9 Then your mighty men, O Teman, shall be dismayed, to the end that everyone from the **mountains of Esau** may be cut off by slaughter.

I have to ask this important question, why would Yahweh want to cut down and slaughter Teman if this is not Muslim lands being judged then what is?

> **Obadiah 1:10** "For **your violence** against **your brother Jacob**, **shame shall cover you**, and you shall **be cut off forever** [cast off into Hell].

Notice it says "brother," since Esau was Jacob's brother, Arabs or cousins from the wife of Abraham that was Hagar. In Middle Eastern culture a cousin is also considered a brother.

> **Daniel 8:9** And **out of one of them came forth a little horn**, which waxed exceeding great, toward the south, and toward the east, and toward the pleasant land [Israel].

The anti-Messiah is seen rising up in one of the four kingdoms formed by the splintering of Alexander's Greek Empire (little horn). These four kingdoms were:
1) **Egypt**
2) **Syrio-Babylonia**
3) **Macedonia**
4) **Asia Minor.**

Oh dear NO Europe!

In **Daniel 8:9** the Anti-Messiah comes from one of the four Greek factions "little horn," being that "the vision is **for the time of the end**" (8:17). That can't be Antiochus as the sole "little horn," while the "little horn" of chapter 7 is for sure the "end-time" anti-Messiah. The end time man mentioned here causes 1/3 of the angels to fall. Did Antiochus do that? No.

> **Daniel 8:10** And it waxed great, *even* to the host of heaven; and it cast down *some* of **the host and of the stars to the ground**, and stamped upon them.

Yet, how do we reconcile this with Daniel 9 (Roman)?

> **Daniel 9:27** says that the prince that is to come will also do the 7 yr. covenant. So if the prince is Titus of **Daniel 9:26,** then the prophecy fails, as he did not do any covenant with Israel. So it cannot be Titus, plus there was no literal flood. The verse is continuous with no pause.

The only plausible way is that the Anti-Messiah MUST come from an area neutral and shared by BOTH EMPIRES - THE GRECIAN EMPIRE AND THE ROMAN EMPIRES. **Daniel 9 does not reveal which part** of the Roman Empire he comes from, but **chapter 11 DOES**. He comes from the **Seleucid** kingdom. This is why he is called **THE ASSYRIAN**; look at the Assyrian map above.

> **Daniel 8:9** And **out of one of them [four divisions of Alexander's Empire] came forth a "little horn,"** which waxed exceeding great, toward the south, and toward the east, and toward the pleasant land [Israel].

The question we should be asking is why would Yahweh take John to A DESERT to show him this vision (Revelation 17:3)? The whole thing was in a DESERT - the woman

63

and the beast coming out of the waters was in a DESERT area. The question we need to answer is how does this fit with Rome better than Arabia? The answer I have already given above is that it fits much better with Arabia. **I could find nine references of Rome mentioned in the apostolic writings by name of "Rome" (New Testament) and not one of the Rome verses are about an end-time wrath to be poured out on future Rome. Now that is a problem if you ask me, since most prophecy teachers teach an end-time wrath on Rome and the Vatican, or the USA.**

I think we have a major problem with Europe!

> ➤ **This city in Revelation 18 burns literally (Revelation 18:10,16,18,19,21)!**
> ➤ **It is built around a Desert (Revelation 17:3).**
> ➤ **It stands besides 7 mountains (Revelation 17:9).**
> ➤ **The merchants sell it their merchandise, fast cars, planes, gold and other stuff mentioned in (Revelation 18:12-13).**
> ➤ **It is called Babylon (Revelation 18:10).**
> ➤ **The 10 Kings will burn the harlot (Revelation 17:16).**
> ➤ **The harlot must burn with oil according to Scripture (Isaiah 34:9).**

Thanks to Yahweh we have a SOLUTION.

> <u>Isaiah 34:9</u> **Its streams shall be turned into pitch, and its dust into brimstone; <u>its land shall become burning pitch.</u>**

This is where if scholars do not recognize that Islam plays a major end time role they will falter. In one such recent debate with a scholar I clearly demonstrated why only Islamic nations fit the bill like a glove on the hand. All he could come up with was attack my character, my book, and King James as a homosexual based on the lies of someone else. He also belittled one of the greatest scholars in history Sir Robert Anderson. Clearly such shoddy scholars are to be avoided in debates, since they cannot even tell you what city will burn in the end of days. On top of that, he made the biggest blunder by calling this end time city that burns Jerusalem.

The burning is with streams <u>of crude oil</u> that are turned into pitch (i.e. crude oil). The words in <u>Isaiah 34:9</u> signify pitch and tar.

Europe does not have the oil to burn in the way described by the Bible. The full force effect of burning for the Middle Eastern nations can only happen where there is **abundance of oil** and this only fits with the Middle East. One could argue that Russia has oil, or Canada has oil, but we cannot make Arabia to exist in Russia, neither we can say that Edom especially Bosrah is in Canada.

Here is a handy chart showing the most of the world's oil supplies come from the Middle East and not Europe, or America, thus making the Islamic confederated nations the target of YHWH's soon to be revealed destruction seen in Isaiah 34:9.

Greatest Oil Reserves by Country, 2005

Rank	Country	Proved reserves

		(billion barrels)
1.	Saudi Arabia	261.9
2.	Canada	178.8[1]
3.	Iran	125.8
4.	Iraq	115.0
5.	Kuwait	101.5
6.	United Arab Emirates	97.8
7.	Venezuela	77.2
8.	Russia	60.0
9.	Libya	39.0
10.	Nigeria	35.3

NOTES: Proved reserves are estimated with reasonable certainty to be recoverable with present technology and prices. 1. Includes 174.5 billion barrels of oil sands reserves. *Source: Oil & Gas Journal*, Vol. 102, No. 47 (Dec. 10, 2004). From: U.S. Energy Information Administration. Note Canadian oil is not that easy to drill into as the Arab oil.

We cannot break Scripture no matter how much some may try. So therefore we have to acknowledge that according to Scripture the place that will be smoldering will be in a desert. The names of these peoples are identified quite clearly, as has been suggested, by very strong scriptural references to the Middle East only. Although the whole world stands under the judgement and wrath of Yahweh, this particular wrath that we are dealing with is the end-time wrath. It is poured out specifically on the nations that are bent on the destruction of Israel. The bottom line is that, Rome, or New York is never mentioned as targeted for wrath and is not the candidate for the "great city" that burns in Revelation 18.

C. Psalms 120-Israel's Cry For Justice

1. In my distress I cried unto the Master, and He heard me.

When Israel is in distress they will cry out to the Master. Right now they trust in their strength, but this situation will change when they are at their lowest point.

2. Deliver my soul, O Master, from lying lips, and from a deceitful tongue.

All the Muslims who want to make peace do so based on lies and hypocrisy just to destroy Israel, kill the Jews and grab their land. Just take a look at the Arab people. They do not want to make peace, but desire the destruction of the Jewish state, at every opportunity given to them.

3. What shall be given unto thee? Or what shall be done unto thee, thou false tongue?

Their hearts store evil and tongues speak from the fullness of the heart. The Psalmist asks what can be done to such people.

4. Sharp arrows of the mighty, with coals of juniper.

The end shall be destruction by the Master Himself.

5. Woe is me, that I sojourn in Mesech [Turks], that I dwell in the tents of Kedar [Arabs]!

Hebrews who lived surrounded by Turkic nations in Asia Minor and Arab nations who surround the tiny State of Israel.

6. My soul hath long dwelt with him that hateth peace.

The Jews are long suffering dwelling amongst them to make peace to get rid of the daily violence, but no peace is in sight.

7. I am for peace: but when I speak, they are for war.

The Jews certainly want to make peace and live with their Islamic neighbors in love and harmony. But the Islamists are only preparing for one thing. You guessed it, WAR. Take a look at Iran; the nuclear missiles being produced are for war against the Jews and the west. They make no secret about this and have openly declared to wipe out the Jewish state if provoked. Pakistan is secretly behind Iran supplying them nuclear information. They refuse to accept the Jewish state and will be happy if Jews give up their land to the Palestinians.

If you look at Psalm 74 onwards each Psalm has an element pointing to these people. Psalm 120 indicates these people are deceitful; they are not interested in peace and always at war with the Jews. Their intention is destruction. Do we not see that all the Islamic lands around about Israel help the Palestinians with ammunition and finance? Egypt though has a peace deal with Israel, but secretly allows the building of underground tunnels in the Palestinian regions which link to Egypt to smuggle weapons. Hezbollah on the northern front are supplied with Kassam rockets, missiles, guns and bullets supplied by Syria and Iran to fire into Jewish villages, sporadically killing innocent Jewish civilians. Sometimes Arabs are killed also. Iran also helps Hezbollah and the Palestinians. Saudi Arabia arranges triathlons/telethons to raise funds to help the Palestinians in the ongoing war with Israel and makes no secret about this.

If you have the chance to watch any of the Asian Muslim channels in the UK on the Sky Satellite network, you will see that they raise funds by showing pictures of poor Palestinians being oppressed and killed by the alleged evil Israeli Jews. They then ask Muslims to send money to support the PA groups. This is propaganda that is allowed on British soil. It is a shame that the UK broadcasting authority does not crack down on this type of misinformation that is brainwashing Muslims in the UK. Then the government wonders where did the suicide bombers came from when the media is itself responsible for allowing this information that in turn allows these youths to take a stand against the west. One would wonder what is Hizbullah and Hamas doing in Britain? Our government has a lot of house cleaning to do.

Look at the following specially drawn "PA road map for peace." The Palestinians have drawn this map to settle the case for Israel to live in peace with them permanently. The only peace they want is the "**whole piece**" of the Jewish homeland for themselves, and to cut the Jews into pieces. Until that happens, the struggle will continue. But the Elohim of Israel has other plans in which the Palestinians will become bird fodder.

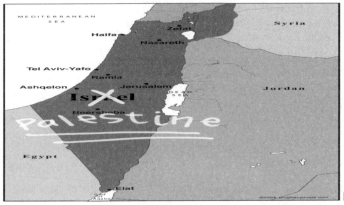

PA Flag [13]

Do we not see this pattern in the Middle East? This is the present situation that Israel faces with daily constant terror threats from the Islamic nations around about them. Iran has issued threats to Israel that they will destroy Israel's nuclear reactor, so that Israel does not get any ideas to destroy Iran's nuclear facility, whose sole purpose is to build nuclear missiles to destroy the Jews and to threaten the west. The Bible predicts at least two strikes of nuclear nature. **I can foresee that one day soon we in the west will be held hostage by radical Muslim terrorists threatening to strike us with these types of weapons**. Now you have been warned. I will explain the nature and threat and the nuclear attacks to come in my future book that will help to explain the bowls, seals and trumpet judgements to come from the book of Revelation, with the title to be announced in the future. While the world sleeps, we are fast moving to the end-times climax.

Even though Turkey has a peace treaty with Israel, secretly they hate the Jews. Recently, Turkey dropped all future contracts with Israel in favor of Syria as a partner. Things are turning around in Turkey for the worse, but will Israel realize it in time to wake up from its slumber?

Quite clearly the Mesech in Psalm 120 verse 5 above is the same as mentioned in **Ezekiel 38:2**:

> Son of man, set thy **face against Gog**, the **land of Magog**, the **chief prince of Meshech and Tubal**, and **prophesy against him,**

Today, these are Turkic peoples occupying southern Russia, better known as Commonwealth Independent States in Asia Minor. The CIS nations are all Islamic, and thus the "land of Magog" is none other than Turkey. So the land of the Anti-Messiah is <u>even</u> identified to leave us with no ambiguity.

The Schaff-Herzog Encyclopaedia of Religious Knowledge, citing ancient Assyrian writings, places the location of the **land of Magog** in the landmass between **ancient Armenia and Media**, in short, the republics south of Russia and north of Israel, comprised

---

of Azerbaijan, Afghanistan, Turkistan, Chechnya, **Turkey**, Iran and Dagestan. Significantly, all of these nations are Muslim nations today.

It is these people that are going to come up against Israel in the latter days together with the Islamic confederacy to war against Israel. That is quite clearly described in **Psalm 83** and also in **Ezekiel 35:3**. In short this person has a Turkic bloodline and if we read **Daniel chapter 11 carefully,** the Anti-Messiah is from the Seleucid kingdom that is parts of Turkey and old Assyria, or today's modern day Iraq, Syria and Lebanon. The chances are that "Gog" fits the typology of Salah din Ayubi the Muslim conqueror who was a Kurd, so we must watch this land mass between Southeastern Turkey, Northern Iraq (Kurdistan), Syria and Lebanon. The people likely to head this confederacy are going to be Turkic people with Turkey itself playing a major role. In fact the Anti-Messiah may well be a Turkic person right out of Turkey. But we should keep an eye on Kurdistan, modern Syria with Lebanon in the equation. Apparently Kurdistan seems to be the most flourished democratic region in the Arab Middle East, definitely one to watch.

The Macmillan Bible Atlas, Oxford Bible Atlas, The Moody Atlas of Bible Lands, and others, locate Magog, Meshech, Tubal, Gomer and Beth Togarmah in Asia Minor, not Russia as a whole. But this includes only portions of southern Russia, while northern Russians are Slavic people historically speaking. This region of Asia Minor includes the following:

-**Turkey**
-**Uzbekistan**
-**Azerbaijan**
-**Tajikistan**
-**Girgestan**
-**Uzbekistan**
-**Kyrgyzstan**
-**Turkmenistan**

Hesiod the contemporary of Ezekiel had also indicated in historical writings that the Magogians were Scythians and Southern-Russians in the 7th century BC who today would form the CIS nations.

Josephus Flavious a Jewish/Roman historian agrees with this, Philo agrees with this theory also.

We find that Ezekiel places these people in the same region and calls them "the House of Togarmah" in **Ezekiel 38:6**. Is it not amazing that YHWH showed us these are Turkic nations who all turn out to be Islamic? Wow. What an awesome YHWH we serve. Give Him praise. Hallelu-Yah.

Revelation 13:3 "And I saw one of his heads as it were wounded to death; and his deadly wound was healed: and all the world wondered after the beast."

Notice the head is wounded not "cut off" i.e. it is only injured, so it comes back to life later. This is in clear reference to the close of the Ottoman Empire in 1924. Islam did not die, but the Ottoman's were defeated in that their power was brought to a close. The above passage shows the revival of true Islam that was to take place was then yet future in our time and is happening as we speak. Have we not heard repeatedly how Islam is the fastest growing religion in the west? Did you know that in Great Britain alone about 14,000

68

of the elite (the Children of Lords) have converted into Islam? This will surely spell trouble for this nation in the latter days, as they try to influence the laws of this nation. In most of the world the Muslims are trying to revive true Islam. Is that not an indicator of the signs of our times? Are we going to ignore these signs? If that does not convince you then look at the beheadings, and incitement of violence against the Jews and the Western nations.

Of what atrocity did Yahushua warn us?

> **John 16:2** "They will put you <u>out of the synagogues</u>; yes, the time is coming that **whoever kills you will think that he offers YHWH service**.

Do Muslims not kill Christians and Jews in the world chanting 'Allah hu Akbar' (Allah is great)? They kill Jews, Christians and non-Muslims alike and they will even quite happily kill those they consider nominal Muslims, who they consider are on the side of the west. Only the radical Muslims offer Allah their god this service, the "he" in **John 16:2** more accurately are Islamic people, though loosely we can apply it to others, but the tightest glove fit is only with Islamic nations ***Revelation 13:9***. If anyone has an ear, let him hear.

The muttawa (religious police) in Saudi Arabia literally drag Christians out of their homes during prayer and lock them up in prisons, even beheading some for Bible study. Yes you got that right. People in Saudi Arabia can be beheaded for simply telling others about Yahushua the Messiah as Master. Why do you think the west does not report on this activity? It is because of the power of the petrodollar my friends. We need black gold in the west, so we ought not to call the Arabs, or Islam evil because it hurts our friendship with them. This is why Revelation 18 says:

> **Revelation 18:3**-"For **all the nations** have drunk of the **wine of the wrath of her fornication**, the **kings of the earth** have **committed fornication with her**, and the **merchants of the earth have become rich through** the **abundance of her luxury**."

Take a look at the big oil companies and how rich they are e.g. Shell, Texaco, BP, the Halliburton Corporation etc and you will realize they have shared in the abundance of her luxury [Saudi Arabia], which is oil. These companies make billions of dollars in profit through this black gold. What would happen to these companies if the oil stopped? What would happen to our economy?

Revelation helps us here too…

> **Revelation 18:9-11** "And the **kings of the earth** who **committed fornication** and **lived luxuriously with her will weep and lament for her**, when they see the **smoke of her burning**, "standing at a distance for **fear of her torment**, saying, `Alas, alas, that **great city Babylon**, that mighty city! For in one hour your judgment has come.' "And the merchants **of the earth will weep and mourn over her**, for **no one buys their merchandise anymore**:

The kings of the earth have committed fornication with the Arabs because they were involved in profiteering with this harlot (Mecca). They did not care about their people who were killed by this harlot (through terrorism perpetrated by Islamists based on Saudi teachings of Islam), and these merchants will weep and cry because when they see Saudi Arabia burning with the rest of Babylon, the smoke will be visible from all the seas that connect this Desert land mass. People from many miles will be able to see her smoke;

the merchants will weep, because they cannot sell fast cars, private jets, expensive diamonds and pearls to this nation anymore.

These were the merchants who laid lavish banquets for these Arabs to sell their merchandise. Could this possibly hurt the Western economy? The answer is most definitely yes, given what we saw during the 2nd Gulf War where Petrol prices soared to $70 a barrel and this at a time when no oil was lost. But what will occur when oil is burning in smoke and the West will have difficulty securing oil for themselves? You can calculate what can and will happen as a result. Some economies for sure will collapse, while others will struggle to survive. This is the plain truth unless we can get away from oil consumption, which seems unlikely in the short term.

History tells us that Islam controlled a large part of the world and is now attempting successfully to heal its wound and revive the Islamic Empire. In fact it is being revived as we speak; just take a look around you! The culture of beheading, shooting, murdering innocent people without trial is back. It almost feels like we are back in the 7th Century. Saudi Arabia has been exporting its ideology, the true values of Muhammad for the last two hundred years since Mohammad Abdul Wahab. It is on the forefront of this attempt to export Islamic ideology in order to achieve the goal of the revival of true Islam. Not the wishy washy Islam you see practiced by some Muslims, who themselves are apostate by true Islamic standards. The critical mass has been built in the last fifty-two years and there is no stopping this mass now.

Did you not see the beheadings of two Pakistani workers in Iraq July 2004, even though they were Muslims, yet were killed because they were considered to be apostate as they were working for the west? This is truly sad because a mother lost a son, a sister a brother, the wife a husband and the children a father, an important breadwinner in the Muslim household. This death was completely unnecessary. These two men were probably only out there to work for bettering their family's lives. The Muslim countries do not have a state benefit system, so when a tragic death like this happens the whole family can come under hardship. I really feel sorry for these people and what was their fault for this needless tragedy? Islamic extremism and jihad in Allah's namesake are a real hazard for even moderate Muslims. The only way to save yourself is to remove the lie and replace it with truth.

Saudi Arabia spends a great deal of petrodollars to do this every year to open Islamic centers, and mosques all over the world. They even pay Muslim organizations to prosecute anyone against Islam. The case of Daniel Scott from Australia is one such case. I met this person personally and he was brought to trial convicted of being guilty because he gave a seminar on Islam. The case against him was entirely funded by Saudi Arabia and we are seeing many similar cases today e.g. another one of Oriana Fallaci the Italian author against her book "The force of reason."

Revelation mentions this **nation, the harlot of Babylon,** time and time again who will persecute people.

D.　　Revelation 17 – Let Us Take Another Look

1. Then one of the seven angels who had the seven bowls came and talked with me, saying to me, "Come, I will show you the judgment of the **great harlot who sits on many waters**

70

Mecca the city that sits on <u>many</u> waters; this reference is to the seas around it: Does Rome sit on many waters? Rome has only one ocean, the Mediterranean! The prophecy fails with Rome.

THE TRUE HARLOT IS SURROUNDED BY THE waters:
- ❖ **Persian Gulf**
- ❖ **Arabian Sea**
- ❖ **Red Sea**
- ❖ **Gulf of Aden**
- ❖ **Gulf of Oman**
- ❖ **Mediterranean Sea**
- ❖ **Caspian Sea**
- ❖ **Black Sea.**

Does this <u>not</u> look like <u>many</u> waters? Just look at the map of the Arab league above? Here YHWH has been very descriptive so that we cannot miss this, yet still people do not pay attention to the text and try to spiritualize this.

The seven heads are explained in **Revelation 17:9** and we will discuss this there.
>   2. "With whom the <u>kings of the earth</u> committed fornication, and the inhabitants of the earth were <u>made</u> drunk with the <u>wine of her fornication</u>."

The kings of the earth refer to the merchants buying oil and the fornication represents that they have "sold Islam" as a peaceful good religion to their people. That is the "wine of her fornication," i.e. selling this as good when it is evil, leading people to hell permanently with no return. YHWH is not pleased with this situation at all. Why should Yahweh be pleased? Much of His creation is headed in the wrong direction in spite of the fact that He sent His <u>only</u> Son to die on the cross for His creation, so that they may have eternal life. People will see the love of Yahushua Messiah and come out of Babylon, but how many will come out before the end we just do not know. Our job is to tell them even if it offends them. Are you doing this job?

---

[14] www.prophecymaps.com

Is it any wonder why Yahushua said *in **Matthew 7:13** "Enter by the **narrow** gate; for **wide** is the gate and broad is the way that leads to destruction, and there are many who go in by it.*

Saudi Arabia not only sells oil, but also sells the Islamic religion to the world. Many people dare not question their governments because they know without the oil their economies would not survive. This is a vicious circle, and without oil we cannot drive our industry. We should have invented alternative methods of fuel, but the lack of progress and the high cost of development is what has deterred many governments. Plus the governments do make plenty of money from fuel sold, which they buy cheaply from the Gulf States. So the incentives for doing the development are outweighed by the income derived through oil revenues.

Compare these fuel duties (taxes) to understand how these nations are getting rich:

- ❖ $2.82 of every $4 gallon in France!
- ❖ $2.56 of every $4 gallon in Germany!
- ❖ $2.53 of every $4 gallon in Italy!
- ❖ 39 cents of every $2 gallon of gas fuel in the USA!
- ❖ $5.00 of every $6 gallon in the UK!

Note that these are old prices. A gallon of oil with the recent fuel hikes is running in the UK at almost £4.23 pence a gallon and fuel in the USA is at $3 a gallon and in some places has gone as high as $6, due to the crisis created by Hurricane Katrina in New Orleans and more by world oil supply demand plus not forgetting the war in Iraq and Afghanistan.

Do we seriously think that the nations that are getting tax revenue and getting rich would be interested in alternative fuels? You can decide the answer for that yourself.

Now ask yourself if Saudi Arabia was to be blown up tomorrow, will the kings of the nations weep and wail or not? How many economies will go bust?

Rev 17:3-So he carried me away **in the Spirit into the wilderness**. And I saw a woman sitting on a scarlet beast [city in control of an Empire], which was **full of names of blasphemy** [denying the true YHWH], having seven heads [**7 Mountains and 7 kings**] and ten horns [**10 kings in subsequence of time**].

The woman is the harlot city of Mecca, selling its whoredom to the world. The scarlet color represents the Islamic kingdom with blood on its hands. Now ask yourself; who is behind the bloodshed in Sudan for the last twenty years? If you said Saudi Arabia then you are intelligent enough to know the truth behind the scenes.

Who was funding the militants in Indonesia to kill the Christians?
Who was funding the terror attacks in Israel?
Who funded the attacks on the USA Embassies?
Who funded the blowing of the twin towers in New York?
Who supplied 19 of the 21 9/11/01 murderers?

If your answer is Saudi Arabia, then you are most intelligent and discerning to recognize this. Most who think that this happens by itself are only deluding themselves. Islam blasphemies the one true Elohim by replacing Him with Allah calling Muhammad the prophet of Allah and saying he is the greatest prophet. Is this not a blasphemy on the Master of Masters and King of Kings, the Master Yahushua the Messiah?

> 4. The woman was arrayed in **purple** and **scarlet**, and adorned with gold and precious stones and pearls, having in her hand a **golden cup full of abominations** and the **filthiness of her fornication**.

The woman is the city and purple represents riches, this is a very rich city. Scarlet represents a sinful city, which is living in sin killing the saints, and this is described with the following aspect.

> 5. And on her forehead a name was written: MYSTERY BABYLON THE GREAT, THE MOTHER OF HARLOTS and of THE ABOMINATIONS OF THE EARTH.

This is Islamic headquarters, "Mystery Babylon," which many people have failed to recognize. This place is the "**mother of harlots**" (YHWH calls ALL Islamic countries prostitutes). Would not YHWH call a nation that is taking 1.5 billion people straight to hell, the abominations of the earth? Today fifty-two official Islamic nations contain an Islamic majority, with the Muslim presence in all other nations of the world today increasing in alarming rates.

> 6. And I saw the woman, drunk with the **blood of the saints** and with the **blood of the martyrs of Yahushua**. And when I saw her, I marvelled with great amazement.

This Empire/Kingdom kills and devours Christians and Torah keeping disciples of Yahushua and thus has gotten the blood of saints on its hands.

> 7. But the angel said to me, "Why did you marvel? I will tell you the mystery of the woman [city or province] and **of the beast** [the Islamic Empire] that carries her, which has the **seven heads** and the **ten horns**.

The Angel wants to explain to John who this beast/kingdom and the woman are, this false kingdom arose from Babylon in Iraq and this harlot city is Mecca today in Saudi Arabia.

> 8. **The beast that you saw was, and "is not,"** [revival of radical Islam, not seen since the 7th century AD] and will ascend out of the bottomless pit and **go to perdition**. And those who dwell on the earth **will marvel, whose names are not written in the Book of Life from the foundation of the world, when they see the beast that was, and is not, and yet is.**

Those that marvel at this beast/Empire are the Muslims, as they will not be able to enter heaven because they ALL carry the mark and it is their names that are not written in the Book of Life.

John has been told two things and we will fully expound on these later. John is being told that this is not the Roman Empire of John's day ("**is not**" in above verse) and he is also told that this end time empire is from the pit of the grave/hell, i.e. it will take many people to hell with them. There are many people in this world not saved including Muslims and the Muslims will marvel at this beast/empire because when Islam goes to war with the west and Israel, the unsaved people in support of Islam will wonder with amazement. **Today many marvel at how great and how brave these Muslims are, because they have taken on the might of the USA and the west.**

E.   Symbols Associated With A Mountain?

Revelation 17:9 "Here is the mind which has wisdom: The **seven heads are seven mountains** on which the woman sits.

The reading of a mountain can be literal or figurative depending on the text in question and the context of the passage. In the case of **Revelation 17:9** the reading is literal of <u>real</u> mountains on which, (or around which) this woman [Mecca] sits.

Ezekiel 34:6 My sheep wandered through all the <u>mountains</u>, and upon every high hill: yea, my flock was scattered upon all the face of the earth, and none did search or seek [after them].

From Ezekiel it is quite clear that a mountain can be figuratively applied to nations, kingdoms, or peoples because in Ezekiel, YHWH shows how He scattered His people through out the world, i.e. nations, kingdoms and peoples. His people Israel wondered through <u>many</u> countries, but no Shepherd went after them to rescue them, or to seek for them in order to preach the Good News to them. Instead they were hated for being Jews, persecuted and killed by European Christians and Catholics alike. Even many so-called Christians have blood on their hands.

A mountain can be a literal mountain, or it can be applied to nations/Kingdoms. It is clear from **Revelation 17:15** "And he saith unto me, the <u>waters</u> which thou sawest, where the <u>whore sitteth</u>, **are peoples, and multitudes, and nations, and tongues**." This is the drash/allegoric reading and is the meaning of the text explained by the angel.

YHWH is telling us here that rivers and waters are the flow of nations, peoples and tongues and that is what is being taught in **Revelation 17:15**. Therefore, the city that YHWH calls a "whore" [Mecca in Saudi Arabia] sitteth on <u>many</u> waters between many people. Now look at the Saudi Arabian map above, as it sits right in the middle of the seas between many peoples and many nations. Is not the Master YHWH great to show us this and how it fits?

Yahushua said this: **Matthew 17:20** So Yahushua said to them, "Because of your unbelief; for assuredly, I say to you, <u>if you have faith</u> as <u>a mustard seed</u>, you will say <u>to this mountain</u>, `Move from here to there,' and it will move; and nothing will be impossible for you.

Now is Yahushua teaching us black magic? Some people will have you believe this is so, but Yahushua is not teaching us black magic, but is teaching us a very good principle. He is saying if you have faith as small as a mustard seed, you can have a great effect **on kingdoms/nations/peoples,** which is described as **the mountain** in this passage. Now as a Christian you have the power to influence many people to show them eternal life through Yahushua the Messiah. Now does that effect these people's destiny or not? It absolutely does. Let us go back in time; has not Yahushua's message affected so many

74

nations and changed their destiny? Yahushua's message did change the vast Roman Empire that was practicing pagan idolatry.

Now that we have the correct knowledge on a "**mountain**" we are well set to solve the mystery of the <u>seven</u> mountains of **Revelation 17:3, 9.**

The city discussed here sits near mountains and is Mecca. Its rule affects kingdoms and nations. Does Saudi Arabia not affect kingdoms and nations? Remember it controls 26% of the world oil supplies and the eternal destiny of 1.5 billion people?

Verse 17:9 "<u>Here is the mind which has wisdom</u>: The <u>seven heads</u> are <u>seven mountains</u> on which the woman [Mecca] sits. They are also **seven** kings.

Now many prophecy teachers have wrongly made out the seven mountains here to be **seven hills** in order to make prophecy line up with Rome. Unfortunately the Greek word used in this passage is "oros" which can only translate as a "**mountain**" and not into a "hill." Remember mountains have summits and hills do not. So it is no good pretending it is a small mountain. The text is pretty clear that here that mountain is a mountain with a summit.

There is only one passage in the Bible translated as a hill and even that passage is translated incorrectly as the word there used is again a "mountain" and not hill e.g. in Matthew chapter 5.

Matthew 5:14 "You are the <u>light of the world</u>. A city that is set on a hill cannot be hidden.

You will find that there are Bible versions that do translate this verse correctly e.g.

Matthew 5:14 Ye are the light of the world: a city situated on the top of a <u>mountain</u> cannot be hid. (Darby Translation)

Even the New Living Translation has a correct reading of the word for mountain.

Matthew 5:14 You are the light of the world--like a city on a <u>mountain</u>, glowing in the night for all to see.

The word above is "oros" and can only mean a mountain; it is obvious a light is more visible from a mountain than a hill.

Let us look at another example in the book of Luke, which is even clearer…

Luke 3:5 Every valley shall be filled and every **mountain [oros] and hill [bounos]** brought low; and the crooked places shall be made straight and the rough ways made smooth;

Note the word used for Hill in **Luke chapter 3** is "bounos" and for Mountain is "oros."

Strongs **[1015]** bounos - Greek for hill
Strongs **[3735]** oros - Greek for mountain

This is enough to show the **erroneous theory of Rome being on seven mountains** and remove it entirely from the picture.

F.   The Anti-Messiah Revealed

Revelation 17:10 There are also seven kings. **Five have fallen** [five past Empires], **one is** [6th being Rome itself] and the other has not yet come [Islam not yet revealed]. **And when he/it comes, he/it must continue a short time**.

Revelation 17:11 "**And the beast that was, and is not, is himself also the eighth, and is of the seven, and is going to perdition.**

Islam will have a brief closing i.e. the Ottoman Empire brought to a close, but not cut off, as Islam had to be revived again as predicted in **Revelation 13:11**.

Points to note:
- ❖ **FIVE HAVE FALLEN**; Five past Empires
- ❖ **ONE IS**; the current Roman Empire in John's day
- ❖ **The OTHER HAS NOT YET COME**; The 7th Islamic Empire that was still to come in the future.
- ❖ **IS HIMSELF/ITSELF ALSO THE EIGHTH AND IS OF/FROM THE SEVEN/SEVENTH**;

This is the Islamic that came and was the 7th and is also the 8th **in its future revived form**. Today we see this in the shape of revived radical Islam.

- ❖ **1st Empire** to rule the Middle East   Egyptian Empire
- ❖ **2nd Empire** to rule the Middle East   Assyrian Empire
- ❖ **3rd Empire** to rule the Middle East   Babylonian Empire
- ❖ **4th Empire** to rule the Middle East   Medo-Persian Empire
- ❖ **5th Empire** to rule the Middle East   Grecian Empire

We know that there were also Chinese dynasties that could classify as empires, but these are not part of prophecy, as they never ruled Israel, or the Middle East regions.

Figure 1[15]

Egypt can qualify as an Empire because they ruled the land of Israel in 1450 BC. Egypt conquered Canaan by Thutmose III in 1450 B.C. and this control lasted some four hundred years.

These five Empires are the "five (that) **have** fallen" in the past at the time of John. They are listed above.

The **6th Empire** to conquer the Middle East was the **Roman Empire** (as clearly identified by the angel in Revelation), which during John's time (approximately 100 AD) was at the height of its power. The Roman Empire had ceased to exist in the west after the defeat of the Western Roman Empire in 410 A.D. when the barbarians sacked the city of Rome. Zeno (**Tarasicodissa**) safely held the Roman imperial throne at Constantinople (modern day Istanbul) and moved to the east (Byzantium in Turkey). This was the seat of power, for our purposes we can call this the **Eastern leg of the Roman Empire**.

The **7th Empire** to control the area of the Middle East was the **Arab Muslim/Islamic Empire,** which the angel told John about, **"the other" that has NOT yet come.** At the time John wrote Revelation the Roman Empire was ruling, yet John specifically writes, *"is not."* **The 7th beast producing the 8th beast did not yet exist, thus ruling out Rome totally!** This quite clearly rules out any **revived Roman Empire theory** that people are shouting from the rooftops. This is not a revived Roman Empire at all. In order for the revived Roman Empire theory to work, we need Italy in power, and then all the western nations that were old Roman nations need to be revived and subject to Italy. Also, we cannot forget the major centers of Roman eastern power, such as Alexandria, Constantinople and North Africa. You cannot have one without the other.

The other problem with the Roman view is that it breaks Scripture.

> **Numbers 24:24** But ships shall come from the coasts of Cyprus, and they shall afflict Asshur and afflict Eber, and so shall Amalek, until he perishes."

Quite clearly the Hebrew word used for Cyprus is "**Kittim**." This prophecy has never been fulfilled and these nations that are classified as Cyprus here includes Spain and Italy, the very Roman/western nations that will fight the Anti-Messiah.

> **Daniel 11:30** states that Roman ships **[out of the west]** will come against the Anti-Messiah.

In **Daniel (11:30)** "the **Ships of Kittim comes against him**" (the Anti-Messiah). This is backed up with Numbers 24:24, and so the Bible agrees that these are Western nations.

But who are the "Ships of Kittim"? How did we conclude that they are western European nations?

Balaam foretold (**Numbers 24:24**) "**that ships shall come from the coast of Kittim, and afflict Eber.**" **Daniel prophesied (11:30) that the ships of Kittim would come against the king of the north**. Josephus identifies Cyprus as Kittim, whose ancient capital was called Kition by the Greeks,[16] and also extended to include lands west of Syria, all of Greece, as far as Illyricum and Italy. Note that these lands are not Muslim. The name originally designated the Phoenician port of **Citium in Cyprus**. The term

---

[16] New International Standard Bible Encyclopedia

appeared in the Dead Sea Scrolls, and was used of the Romans in the Septuagint for Daniel 11:30. So, if the Anti-Messiah is an individual who is western European (Roman), then this would mean that the supposed Anti-Messiah territory is in fact fighting itself, as most misled current theorists believe that the Anti-Messiah will be from Europe! This poses a major problem for these interpretations. Anti-Messiah cannot come from Europe, because then Europe would have to attack itself! **Rather as mentioned before, the attackers of the Anti-Messiah come FROM Europe!**

In general, Kittim (Chittim) is used of all the islands and various settlements on the seacoasts, which they had occupied, and later of the peoples who succeeded them, when Phoenician power declined. Hence it designates generally the islands and coasts of the Mediterranean and the races that inhabit them. The Dodanim who were leaders of a race that descended from Javan (Genesis 10:4), were known in history as the Dardani, originally inhabiting Illyricum and are ethnically related to Kittim. In **1 Chronicles 1:7**, they are referred to as Rodanim. The LXX and the Samaritan Version also read Rhodii, so some have concluded that the Rhodians are the inhabitants of the island of Rhodes.

In **Genesis 10:4**, the word "**Kittim**" is applied to the descendants of Yahvan/Javan, and indicates that the Greek-Latin races, whose territory extended along the coasts of the Mediterranean, dwelt on these islands. Kittim, Elisha, Tarshish, and Dodanim (Rodanim) are all ethnically related and inlcude modern day Sicily with Southern Italy, Spain and Rhodes respectively. Josephus, the Jewish historian states that "all islands, and the greatest part of the seacoast, are called Chethim (Kittim) by the Hebrews." And so, this must be taken as the testimony of one well acquainted with the opinions of the learned world in his time.

In summary, the question remains – Is there any mention of European nations, or peoples in the Bible? The answer is a resounding YES. The term "ships of Chittim" in the Septuagint/LXX is literally translated as "Romans," which included all the nations from Cyprus to Spain.

These nations attacked Antiochus historically according to prophecy in **Daniel 11**. And if we are correct regarding a double fulfilment, they will attack the Anti-Messiah in the end times. No European country is on the receiving end of YHWH's wrath in the prophecies of the end times. So why then do we see the majority of modern prophecy teachers of the Bible so fixated on Europe as the central point of end time prophecy? It appears to be s.a.tan's attempt to catch even the 'very elect' completely off guard, by looking the wrong way, so as to be blindsided by end time tribulation!

The Chittim nations are not the only European Union nations mentioned. In fact there are more in the Bible such as:

Romans 15:24-Spain
Acts 2:10-Rome
Acts 18:2-Italy

Yet, not even in one of these references do we read of a judgment, or an oracle, regarding the end-times wrath of YHWH. On the contrary. We see that the above nations are actually participating **against** the Anti-Messiah.

These seven heads are the head of s.a.tan that are described in Revelation 17:
1. **Egyptian**

78

2. **Assyrian**
3. **Babylonian**
4. **Medo-Persian**
5. **Grecian**
6. **Roman**
7. **Islamic**

Empires	Number Of Horns
Egyptian	1
Assyrian	1
Babylonian	1
Medo-Persian	2
Grecian	4 – Since Alexander's kingdom split into 4 areas of the Middle East.
Roman	1
Islamic	1–And then the Islamic Empire to be revived. This is the 11th and final horn being the Anti-Messiah.

Revelation 12:3 And another sign appeared in heaven: behold, a great, fiery **red dragon having seven heads.**

This would mean that the Anti-Messiah could come from any of these regions to qualify in this untenable theory. Fortunately YHWH does not leave us in the dark to work things out for ourselves. We are quite clearly shown in **Daniel 8:9** that the Anti-Messiah is from Alexander's 4th division of his Empire, based entirely in the Middle East, all the way to Pakistan.

> **Revelation 13:11-15** Then I saw **another beast** coming up out of the earth, (12a) And he exercises all the authority of the **first** beast [the 7th King was the Islamic Empire] (15) He was granted power to give **breath to the image of the beast**, that the **image of the beast** should **both speak and cause as many as would not worship** the image of the beast to be killed.

Note these points please:

-Another beast - Revival of radical Islam.
-Give breath to the Image of the beast – Give life to Islam, revive it fully.
-Image of the beast should speak – Islam is revived and starts to kill people and all peoples will see its actions.

Giving breath to the image does not mean giving breath to some statue, but it means giving life to the religion of Islam and resurrecting it back to its **former** glory. This is a literal for revival of Islam in the world and it is happening fast.

Sir Robert Anderson (Former Chief of London's Scotland Yard, famous apologist and Bible commentator 1841-1918) stated:

"In the history of Babylonia there is nothing to correspond with the predicted course of the first Beast, for it is scarcely legitimate to suppose that the vision was a prophecy of the career of Nebuchadnezzar."

"Neither is there in the history of Persia anything answering to the bear-like beast with that precision and fullness which prophecy demands. The language of the English version suggests a reference to Persia and Media but the true rendering appears to be: "It made for itself one dominion," instead of "It raised up itself on one side."

"While the symbolism of the sixth verse seems at first sight to point to the Grecian Empire, it will appear upon a closer examination that at its advent the leopard had four wings and four heads. This was its primary and normal condition, and it was in this condition that dominion was given to it." This surely is very different from what Dan. 8:8 described and what the history of Alexander's Empire realized, viz., the rise of a single power, which in its decadence continued to exist in a divided state."

Then, Sir Robert Anderson concludes: "Each of the three first Empires of the second chapter (Babylon, Persia, and Greece) were in turn destroyed and en-gulped by its successor; but the kingdoms of the seventh chapter all continued together upon the scene, though "the dominion, was with the fourth (Dan. 7:12). The verse seems to imply that the four beasts came up together, and at all events there is nothing to suggest a series of Empires, each destroying its predecessor, though the symbolism of the vision was (in contrast with that of chap. 2) admirably adapted to represent this. Compare the language of the next vision (Dan. 7: 3-6)."

Concerning the Roman Empire:

"While the fourth beast is **unquestionably** Rome, the language of the seventh and twenty-third verses leaves no doubt that it is the Roman Empire in its revived and <u>future</u> phase. Without endorsing the views of Maitland, Browne, etc., it must be owned that there was **nothing in the history of ancient Rome to correspond with the main characteristic of this beast unless the symbolism used is to be very loosely interpreted.** To **"<u>devour the earth</u>," "<u>tread it down and break it in pieces</u>,"** is fairly descriptive of other Empires, but Ancient Rome was precisely the one power which **added government to conquest**, and instead of treading down and breaking in pieces the nations it subdued, sought rather to mould them to its own civilization and polity. **All this-and more might be added-suggests that the entire vision of the seventh chapter may have a future reference."** (Emphasis mine)

He amazingly stated that the Middle East would be the area of the main conflict and that the whole vision and the revived Empire was future and doubtful to be Rome as seen in the past:

Sir Robert Anderson makes his conclusion that <u>**Daniel 7**</u> is strictly speaking of the end times Empires that come at once, this is not Roman in character because Romans added "government to conquest." This is the lynch pin. Islam does **not** add government to **conquest** and wherever Islam has ruled in history it has left that country in a state of turmoil because Islamic law just cannot cope with democracy, or the protocols that a civil society needs to live in. Islam today occupies the Middle Eastern Roman regions. This is what Winston Churchill had to say about the Islamic regions of his day:

Winston Churchill on Islam-
Sir Winston Churchill, from The River War, first edition, Vol. II,
Pages 248-50 (London: Longmans, Green & Co., 1899).

SOURCE: FrontPage Magazine
FrontPageMagazine.com | September 17, 2004

"How dreadful are the curses which Mohammedanism lays on its votaries!

Besides the fanatical frenzy, which is as dangerous in a man as hydrophobia in a dog, there is this fearful **fatalistic** apathy. The effects are apparent in many countries. Improvident habits, slovenly systems of agriculture, sluggish methods of commerce, and insecurity of property exist wherever the followers of the Prophet rule or live. A degraded sensualizm deprives this life of its grace and refinement; the next of its dignity and sanctity. The fact that in Mohammedan law every woman must belong to some man as his absolute property, **either as a child, a wife, or a concubine, must delay the final extinction of slavery until the faith of Islam has ceased to be a great power among men.** Individual Moslems may show splendid qualities...but the influence of the religion paralyses the social development of those who follow it. No stronger retrograde force exists in the world. Far from being moribund, Mohammedanism is a **militant** and **proselytizing** faith. It has already spread throughout Central Africa, raising fearless warriors at every step; and were it not that Christianity is sheltered in the strong arms of science, the science against which it had vainly struggled, the civilization of modern Europe might fall, as fell the **civilization of ancient Rome.**"

Note Sir Winston Churchill makes an interesting point that Christian civilization would have fallen, had it not been for the advancement of science. But to be 100% accurate and honest, it is more then science. How about YHWH's grace on the Christian world instead of science alone because these European nations were ALL Christian at one time and "obeyed" YHWH. What happened to Russia with all its best science, nuclear missiles and space programs? It was broken into many pieces because they did not believe in YHWH and also persecuted His chosen people the Jews.

Also make note that Rome was a Mediterranean Empire, not a Western European Empire as most think.

-- New Jerusalem with Apocrypha-
Psalms 33:12a How blessed is the nation whose Elohim is Yahweh.

Now **Daniel 7:2** expressly names the Mediterranean ("the Great Sea") as the scene of the conflict between the four beasts."

Now **the last Empire** is to do 3 things:

❖ Devour the Earth
❖ Tread it down
❖ Break in pieces

81

Islam is slowly **devouring** all the earth, making countries Islamic and it has a huge numbers of followers. Islam is treading down nations. It is coming with destruction not with government. Just take a look at Somalia, Lebanon, Sudan and now also Nigeria the north and south divide. Note Islam divides just like Daniel said.

Islam is good at breaking in pieces; some examples below will help:

- Destroyed the twin towers.
- Destroyed trains in the Spain bombing.
- Attack on the USA Naval ship.
- Attack on the USA compound in Khobar.
- Destroyed the USA helicopters shot down in Mogadishu.
- Destroyed the USA Embassy in Nairobi.
- Destroyed the Marriott Hotel in Indonesia
- Destroyed the Neve Shalom Synagogue and Beth Israel Synagogues in Turkey.
- Destroyed many buses and places killing civilians in Israel by suicide bombings.
- Destroyed a bus and the trains in London by bombing.
- More future attacks to come in London and Europe.

Note these are only some of the <u>many</u> examples of death and destruction caused by <u>this</u> rising Empire/Kingdom.

Daniel 8:8 Therefore the male goat grew very great; but when he became strong, the large horn was broken [Alexander dies from illness], and in place of it **four notable ones came up toward the four winds of heaven** [four kingdoms]. And out of one of them came **a little horn** [The Anti-Messiah], which grew exceedingly great toward the south, toward the east, and toward the Glorious Land.

The above verses spell it out very <u>clearly</u> that the male goat (Alexander the Great) grew great and then he died suddenly as we know just before his 33rd birthday due to a mysterious illness. After his death, his kingdom including all of the Middle East up to northern India was divided into <u>four</u> regions with four generals ruling it. The Anti-Messiah mentioned as the **"little horn"** comes out of one of these. There is no mistake about it. Europe is not even in the picture of the Anti-Messiah nations. Those that teach that Europe, or the USA is part of this end time empire are misleading people whether out of ignorance, or perhaps in sincerity. But they should stop this teaching and apologize to the body of Yahushua and open their eyes and minds to the real beef that is happening right here. I have politely asked a few of the best prophecy teachers around to prove their case and asked for discussions to bring this to the table. Each time they have either refused to discuss the issues, or simply failed to respond. They are not even interested in being open, even when the Bible verses themselves stare them in the face. They pretend not to notice them. **These four kingdoms were as follows:**

1. Greek/Macedonian region: Ruled by Cassander
Macedonia is an Islamic state presently.

2. Thracia/Turkey region:
Bulgaria and Turkey today. Ruled by Lysimachus and later called the Byzantine Empire (Islamic).

82

3. Babylonian/Persian region:

Southern Russia (Islamic)
Afghanistan (Islamic)
Iran (Islamic)
Syria (Islamic)
Lebanon (Islamic) and all the coastland to the city of Tyre.

This region was also known as the Seleucid Dynasty and ruled by Seleucus (These are All Islamic today).

4. Egypt region: which in prophecy includes Libya and the Nubians, is also an Islamic region today, ruled by Ptolemy. Ever wondered why Sudan went to Islamists?

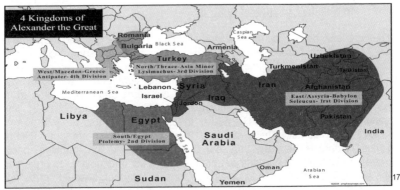

The Grecian Empire

Note the Anti-Messiah will rise out of **one** of the **four divisions** of the Grecian Empire, no prophecy expert can deny this. This is likely to be a Turkish Muslim as referred to by the "Gog" personality in Ezekiel 38, part of the Seleucid Empire also mentioned in Daniel 11.

> **Revelation 17:11** "And the **beast that was**, and **is not**, is himself also **the eighth**, and is **of the seven**, and is **going to perdition**.

The angel revealed the last Empire and its identity by showing us that the next Empire that is to come which we know was Islamic after the Roman Conquests. The Islamic Empire defeated the Roman Empire so the angel was talking about Islam. He says, "**is himself also the eighth**," and is **of the seven**, and is **going to perdition**. If we read above it says he "is not" i.e. he was not revealed yet and is not means "is not" Roman either.

This Muslim Empire is also returning as the **8th Empire** so we need to pay attention to the text and not go with the crowd who want to make this a Roman pope, or a Jewish Messiah. The 8th is of the 7th and is going to cause much trouble in the world. He will be judged to be cast into the Lake of Fire.

---

[17] http://www.prophecymaps.com

Revelation 17:12 "And the ten horns which you saw are ten kings who have received no kingdom as yet, but they receive authority for one hour as kings with the beast.

This indicates that there will be 10 kings involved who will give their allegiance to the Beast/Kingdom/Empire. Logically these will have to be Islamic nations who will support this empire, though it could incorporate a non-Islamic nation. But that seems hardly unlikely considering the number of Islamic nations that vehemently hate Israel. If we start adding up the official Arab/Muslim nations alone, we can find enough to qualify for this task.

V.13-"These are of **one mind**, and they will give their power and authority to the beast. "These will make war **with the Lamb**, and the **Lamb will overcome them**, for He is Master of lords and King of kings; and those who are with Him are called, **chosen, and faithful**."

They can only be of "one mind" if they all follow the same god and the same principles. There is no mixing here between Muslims and Catholics as some want to make it out, because Catholics and Muslims do not worship the same Elohim, which also means the two are not of "one mind." Interestingly this Islamic confederacy will make war with the Master Yahushua described as **"the Lamb,"** the same Lamb who came to die on the cross 2000 years ago. It is Yahushua the Messiah, who will bring this Islamic Empire/Kingdom to its end at His return. It says that those that are with Him are called "chosen" and "faithful." These are the true believers who are both "Hebrews" and "gentiles." Hebrews because they are the "chosen" and the "gentiles" because they showed utmost "faith" in carrying out the Messiah's commandments to preach the gospel to the world. The gentiles could be called "chosen," but then it would not be appropriate, as the ones whom YHWH chose above all the nations, were the Hebrew people as His representatives. The Messiah tells us in the story of the centurion that the gentiles **showed great faith,** more so then corporate Jewish Israel put together.

Matthew 8:10 When Yahushua heard it, He marvelled, and said to those who followed, "Assuredly, I say to you, I have not found **such great faith, not even in Israel!**"

When Yahushua uses the word "**assuredly,**" He is emphasizing a point as in this case. In the Hebrew language a word is usually used twice with reinforcement to emphasize a point e.g. the Hebrew word khar khar to mean, "it is cold," or "it is very cold." The same principle applies in the above verse.

Revelation 17:15 And he said to me, "The waters which you saw, where the **harlot sits, are peoples, multitudes, nations, and tongues.**

This is describing Saudi Arabia in detail, as its residents are made up of many nations and it sits between many peoples. It has plenty of foreign workers with different tongues, or peoples who go to work there e.g. from some of the following countries:

- India
- Pakistan
- Bangladesh
- Philippines

84

- Indonesia
- Sudan
- Egypt
- Morocco
- Yemen
- Afghanistan
- UK
- USA
- Emirates
- France
- Germany
- Many other nations...

These are only a few of the many countries that have workers in the kingdom of Saudi Arabia. Can we fit this truth to Rome? Rome has mainly tourists, but in Saudi Arabia foreign nationals reside and work; yet still, they are even treated like slaves. About 60% of the Saudi workforce are foreign nationals and over 90% of the workers in the private sector are non-Saudis. Saudi Arabia fits this verse much more then Rome. Unless you live in Saudi Arabia, you cannot understand the deprivation of their society and the form of treatment given to the foreign workers that is at times appalling, where e.g. Saudi maids usually from foreign lands are forcefully raped.

Jeremiah 51:9 "We would have healed Babylon, but she is not healed: forsake her, and **let us go every one into his own country**."

Furthermore, they have no right to obtain Saudi citizenship, so it is foreseeable why they will flee back to their own country.

Revelation 17:16 "And the **ten horns** which you saw on the beast, these **will hate the harlot**, make **her desolate** and **naked, eat her flesh and burn her with fire**.

Al-Qaeda wants to take over Saudi Arabia and destroy the House of Saud, because they do not consider the members of the House of Saud to be good Muslims. They do not care whether they bomb the holy city of Mecca, as long as their objectives are met.

Most people do not realize that Muhammad just before his death said to get rid of all polytheists, including Christians and Jews living in Arabia. This is why Osama ben Ladin does not like the Saudi Royals today.

Sahih Muslim Book 19 No. 4366 (Hadith)

It has been narrated by 'Umar b. al-Khattib that he heard the Messenger of Allah (may peace be upon him) say '**I will expel the Jews and Christians from the Arabian Peninsula and will not leave any but Muslims.**'

The Anti-Messiah himself who will attack Arabia and destroy Mecca will likely carry this out in the end-times as the Bible foresees.

The Muslim prophecies even talk about just such an event....

It is well known amongst the Muslims that they have to start the battles in order to bring the end. Muhammad said something, which is recorded in Muslim tradition as a prophecy.

Sunan Abu-Daawood, Book of Battles (Kitab Al-Malahim), Book 37, Number 4281:

"The flourishing state of Jerusalem will be when Yathrib (Medina in Arabia) is in ruins, the ruined state of Yathrib will be when the Great War comes (Mecca destroyed), the conquest of Constantinople when the Dajjal (Anti-Messiah) comes forth. **He (the Prophet) struck his thigh or his shoulder with his hand and said: 'This is as true as you are here or as you are sitting'** (translation by Mu'adh ibn Jabal).

Book 37, Number 4282:

Outbreak of the Great War will be at the conquest of Constantinople (Istanbul in Turkey) and the "The greatest war, the conquest of Constantinople and the coming forth of the Dajjal (Anti-Messiah) will take place within a period of seven months."

The old name for Medina in Saudi Arabia where Muhammad took refuge from his tribe the Quraish is called "Yathrib" and this is the place today where the green dome is (Muhammad's mosque). Medina as a name means a city probably used by the Jews in Arabia. From the above text it appears that the Muslims are lining up for a person of Turkic descent, who will destroy Medina and Mecca, because it was the Turks who tried to destroy Mecca in the past. They will most probably try again and this time the Bible indicates a complete destruction. From this, one can deduce that Anti-Messiah is from Turkey, but we also know that the Bible validates our theory that he is from Turkey, as it talks about Asia Minor. Yahushua the Messiah said the following to us in the Bible; was He trying to teach us a lesson?

Revelation 2-13A "And to the angel of the church in Pergamos write, these things says He who has the sharp two-edged sword: "I know your works, and where you dwell, where s.a.tan's throne is.

The "THRONE IS" is in the present tense as we speak and not merely a throne that was! Interestingly the church in "Pergamos" is in Turkey and s.a.tan's seat dwells there actively today. This means this place has a prophetic significance because this was not only the seat of the power of Eastern Roman Empire, but this was the seat of the power of the Islamic Ottoman Empire also. This is where the Ottoman Empire came from and once again this points us to a revival of this Islamic Empire. Yahushua was absolutely clear about this, but do we have the eyes to see it?

86

All 7 churches above are in Asia Minor, so that this gives us another picture that in the end-times the church will come under persecution. The symbolic picture points to the Islamic Empire that will carry out the worst persecution, which is already happening today. Just two days ago three young Indonesian Christian girls were beheaded in Poso. Earlier this year a pastor and his driver (an evangelist) were killed in Pakistan by the Muslims; one pastor was beheaded in Bangladesh for showing the Yahushua movie recently. Persecution is here whether we see it or not.

Some people like to make the "seat of s.a.tan" a physical object, which they believe moved to Berlin. But they fail to realize that this is a spiritual seat not a physical seat, and is there in the present tense of the text. Who can see s.a.tan's physical seat? If we named a city in England and called it Jerusalem, built a big temple there and then said this is the third temple of Jerusalem, would that be a viable option? Could England somehow become Israel? It could never be. Jerusalem is a physical place and just as much as we cannot move a physical place to another country, we cannot relocate a spiritual place. Some even believe that Israel no longer has any significance in YHWH's economy and that Yahweh has rejected Israel permanently and Israel as a nation has no worth. Yet the irony is that not only does Yahweh love Israel as His chosen people, but also He says that the law/Torah shall go forth from Zion. Since when did Zion move?

The daughter of Rome, protestant Christianity, has a lot to learn and needs to come out of its idolatry and let go of its ways. Yahweh wants true worship and an obedient heart that fulfils His commandments. We see that in Christianity there is a lack lustre attitude with anything goes; people do not keep YHWH's holy commandments, they do not adhere to His laws, His Sabbaths, or His feasts. They know very little about His chosen nation the Hebrews and the church thinks it has a covenant when it has no covenant outside of its being part of Israel. The covenants were with Israel, since the bride is Israel, the church either stands with Israel as part of Israel, or falls without Israel. The choices are clear.

The 'isms' in Christianity are driving the believers out of churches. The bottom line is either we stand with Israel as grafted in people, or we fall. The church did not begin in Acts 2 as is taught in theological seminaries. Yahushua was a Jew who came for the Hebrews. We the gentiles, the lost son **Ephraim**, are one with Israel and Yahweh rejoices when we return to our roots of biblical Hebrew Christianity. The church is present in Genesis, if only we have the eyes to see it. In YHWH's theology there are two houses, the House of Israel (The 10 tribes) and the House of Judah. You are either part of one house, or the other, but you cannot be part of a third house called a church because YHWH's vision does not incorporate it. We are ALL part of ONE olive tree, not two and we ALL share the same root.

Many Christians are going to get a rude awakening when Yahweh returns. There are also certain types of Christians of the variety of Sabeel. These are Palestinian Christians who love to hate the Jews and hate Israel to the point that they support homicide bombers and their ideology. Well I have something to say to this variety of Christians. Though you hate Israel, Yahushua did talk about a group of people who call Him 'Master, Master', but He says to them "I do not know you" (Matthew 7:22-23). Could this lot of Christians be these people, to whom the Master will say "away from Me you evil doers. I never knew you?"

Either you repent of your sins and return (teshuvah in the Hebrew), or face the music. You need to let go of your hate and recognize that you stand with Israel because Yahweh is building one nation on earth for Himself. The nation of true Bible believers who He promised to engraft into Abraham, the one new man. That is the same engrafting that Paul spoke about, which was the promise actually given to Abraham. That nation by the way is Israel, whom Yahweh fully intends to see fulfilling His plan. You cannot stand with the Muslim nations, the very ones who carry the "mark of the beast" and proclaim the land of Israel as your own. YHWH has given the Arabs a vast land mass 670 times more then the Jewish nation, and so there is no good reason for this fighting. But behind this evil is only one person and that is s.a.tan the master of deception and even Christians can be deceived by him. The only sure way to eliminate this deception and protect our understanding is both through the written word and the living word, Yahushua of Nazareth.

Continuing with the prophecies for the critics who think that the Muslims cannot destroy Mecca, or that this seems to be a preposterous theory, then please read the account below which is both true and historical.

> "Hussein supervised the attack on Mecca, while Faisel and Ali were in command of the force directed against Medina, the Grand Shereef was successful at Mecca. The forts on the three hills overlooking that forbidden and sacred city were garrisoned by the Sultan's most faithful Circassian mercenaries and by hand picked Turkish troops. On the day of the attack, the Arabs swept through the gates and captured the main bazaar, the residential section, the administration buildings, and the sacred mosque of the Holy Kaaba.

> For a fortnight the battle raged around the two smaller forts, which were finally taken, during this fighting the aged Shereef remained in his palace directing operations in spite of **scores of Turkish three-inch shells that riddled his residence**. The Turks might have been able to hang on for many months had it not been for their own folly. The Ottoman seems to be a Mohammedan in theory only, occasionally adhering to the ritual and even less frequently adhering to the spirit of the Qu'ran.

> Heedless of the deep-set religious feelings of their enemies and co-religionists, **they suddenly began to bombard the mosque of the Kaaba, the most sacred shrine of all Islam. One shell actually hit the black stone burning a hole in the holy carpet and killing nine Arabs who were kneeling in prayer.** Hussein's followers were so enraged by this impious act that they swarmed over

the walls of the great fort and captured it after desperate hand-to-hand fighting with knives and daggers."[19] (Emphasis mine)
This event is recorded in history so we can see that this is not impossible, but can and will happen in future.

The Turks bombed Mecca in the past where as Al-Hajjaj ben Yusef Al-Thaqafi catapulted it as well. Both attacks are a prefigurement of future destruction of Mecca, part of the "harlot" of Babylon. Yahweh put it in the minds of Muslims to carry out the destruction and it is matter of time before this takes place.

Revelation 17:17 "For YHWH has put it into their hearts to **fulfil His purpose**, to be of one mind, and to give their kingdom to the beast, until the words of YHWH are fulfilled.

YHWH will bring this about as He has put it in their hearts, Al-Qaeda is ready to destroy Saudi cities and there are many other Islamic nations who would like to take control of these places. The threat and destruction of Mecca is imminent.

Revelation 17:18 "And the woman whom you saw is that great city which reigns over the kings of the earth."

This great city (Mecca) has authority over the kings of the earth because of the power of the oil, which the kings of the earth need to further their wealth. Without oil nothing moves, whole economies can come to a standstill, because of our reliance on oil. So this is a very powerful leveraging tool that the Saudi's have and they have successfully used it to change world opinion in their favor. With this they can and have corrupted the nations (**Revelation** 17:2; 18:3; 19:2) with Islamic influence.

Ezekiel 38:21 And I will call for <u>a sword against him</u> throughout all my mountains, saith the Master YHWH: <u>every man's sword shall be against his brother</u>.

Although the verses in Ezekiel 38:21 happen at the battle of Armageddon, one thing is certain that there are 2 swords, one from outside (war with the UK/USA nations getting involved) and the other the Muslims will fight and kill each other (likely Sunni versus Shiite types of war). The beast [Islam] will destroy the "harlot" and "burn" it.

Isaiah 10:5 "Woe to Assyria, the rod of My anger and the staff in whose hand is My indignation.

It is YHWH who brings the Assyrian into the land of Israel.

Isaiah 10:6 I will send him against an ungodly nation, and against the people of My wrath I will give him charge, to seize the spoil, to take the prey, and to tread them down like the mire of the streets.

-New American Standard-

---
[19] "With Lawrence of Arabia" by Lowell Thomas (Arrow Books 1962), Hutchinson & Co. (Publishers) Ltd 1925, pages 60-61

Isaiah 10:6 I send it against a godless nation and commission it against the people of My fury, to capture booty and to seize plunder, and to trample them down like mud in the streets.

YHWH has sent him for His wrath against His people Israel who are in all sorts of idolatry and grave sins, there are many Jewish homosexuals and some Rabbis try to use the passage of Jonathan and David to justify the serious sin of homosexuality when no such thing existed between Jonathan and David, they also accept homosexuality and same sex marriages now can we say with 100% honesty that Yahweh will not punish these lot? Israel is in open rebellion and a Godless nation so let's not pretend Israel is holy today, just recently November 2006 we saw how an open gay parade was allowed in Jerusalem by the highest judges, the Assyrian comes for "booty and plunder" just like the "Gog" in Ezekiel 38:12a would.

Ezekiel 38:12a "to take **plunder** and to take **booty**,

This is a typical Islamic trait to "take booty and plunder." Muhammad used to get 20% from the booty that his followers would make raiding caravans and Jewish settlements.

These verses in **Isaiah 10** have not been fulfilled as traditionally believed. For this we need to take a look at the references Isaiah makes to the Assyrian King. This is not Sennacherib, as he never entered Jerusalem. We need to pay attention and read our Bibles carefully.

Isaiah 37:33-37 "Therefore thus says the Master concerning the king of Assyria: `He shall not come into this city, nor shoot an arrow there, nor come before it with shield, nor build a siege mound against it.

(34) By the way that he came, by the same shall he return; and he shall not come into this city,' says the Master.

(35) `For I will defend this city, to save it for My own sake and for My servant David's sake.' "

(36) Then the angel of the Master went out, and killed in the camp of the Assyrians one hundred and eighty-five thousand; and when people arose early in the morning, there were the corpses all dead.

(37) So Sennacherib king of Assyria departed and went away, returned home, and remained at Nineveh.

Note YHWH did not allow Sennacherib to come into and trample Jerusalem, but this future Assyrian King is allowed to do this. YHWH supernaturally destroyed Sennacherib's army and he went home with a sad face.

Isaiah 19:4 And the Egyptians I will give into the **hand of a cruel master, and a fierce king will rule over them**," says the Master, the Master of hosts.

90

Daniel 11:27 "Both these kings' hearts shall be bent on evil, and they shall speak lies at the same table; but it shall not prosper, for the end will still be at the appointed time.

Note that YHWH has given Egypt over to this **fierce** king (The Anti-Messiah). Egypt is deceived by Muslim leaders with whom they sit and eat at the same table yet they lie and switch sides. This ties in with what Daniel wrote. **Daniel 11:24** "He shall enter peaceably, even into the richest places of the province; and he shall do what his fathers have not done, nor his forefathers: he shall disperse among them the plunder, spoil, and riches; and **he shall devise his plans against the strongholds**, but only for a time [1 year].

This will last for a period of one year as specified above.

After Egypt's judgement (after the Day of the Master) YHWH heals Egypt and Assyria and calls them My people. This indicates a true revival in the Muslim world after Armageddon not before.

> **Isaiah 19:25** whom the Master of hosts shall bless, **saying, "Blessed is Egypt My people, and Assyria** the work of My hands, and **Israel My inheritance**."

A point on Hebrew being the language of Yahweh

Those people that think Hebrew is not important, or is not the language that YHWH chose to speak with His people, be careful, as Yahweh has brought this language back to His people Israel. In Acts 26:14 "And when we all had fallen to the ground, I heard a voice speaking to me and saying in the Hebrew/Aramaic language, [square script Hebrew] `Saul, Saul, why are you persecuting Me? It is hard for you to kick against the goads.' This is also one of the signs for Israel being back in the land and having their language back just before they will call on Yahweh. Zephaniah also makes mention of this as one of the signs before the **great Day of the Master**. This is the primary language that the Torah (five books of Moses) was written in. Notice s.a.tan tried to take this sign away via the Muslims, by saying Arabic is the perfect language of Allah, and so they believe the Qu'ran is revealed in Arabic for that reason. They also are taught that the Arabs are the best of peoples, so this way they tried to replace both the Jews and their language in one hit.

> **Zephaniah 3:9** "For then I will restore to the peoples **a pure language** [Hebrew], that they **all may call on the name of the Master**, to serve Him with one accord.

And Guess what? Five cities in Egypt will speak this language, but we find no mention of Arabic being spoken as a sign.

> **Isaiah 19:18** In that day five cities in the land of Egypt will speak the language of Canaan and swear by the Master of hosts; one will be called the City of Destruction.

91

This is very interesting that in **Acts 26:14** even when Yahushua spoke to Paul on the road to Damascus, He chose to speak to Paul who was multilingual in the language of Hebrew/Aramaic.

This does not mean that YHWH cannot speak, or hear us in other languages, but it seems that Hebrew has a great significance with Yahweh. He even put this language as a **sign (OT)** of the end of days, in that His people will speak it and other peoples will speak it, as in the Egyptians.

Some people ask would all the world's languages be restored to Hebrew because at the tower of Babel the languages were brought to confuse the people, when the world did in fact have one language. Namely Hebrew, before the other tongues came about. All I can tell you is that Hebrew is important. I cannot say whether YHWH will make the entire world speak one language, because the Bible, though alluding to nations speaking Hebrew, may only apply it to the believing community.

G.   Saudi Arabia - Other significant findings?

Isaiah 47:8 "Therefore hear now this, thou that art given to pleasures"

Many Saudi's with an abundant wealth engage in many expensive pursuits such as gambling in Vegas, Monte Carlo and specially designed top of the range cars for sports and outdoors.

Revelation 19:2 "For true and righteous are His judgments, because He has judged the great harlot who corrupted the earth with her fornication; and He has avenged on **her the blood of His servants shed by her.**"

Saudi Arabia has truly corrupted the world with its religion of Islam and its power base of oil. Because of the nature of Islam and its strong association with darkness, it has had many Christians killed in the name of the Islamic god Allah, because Christians would not submit to him. Remember the blood of His servants that has been shed is collective in all the Islamic nations, because of the influence of Saudi Islam. So the judgment is for the harlot first, followed by the rest of the Islamic nations that YHWH will destroy on the mountains of Israel. And He will send many judgements on the Islamic world as He sees fit. The Asian Tsunami is one such act.

The Bible also teaches us that the Muslims will kill Muslims and we see this in the world with brother against brother.

Ezekiel 38:21: "I will call for a sword against Gog throughout all My mountains," says the Master YHWH. **Every man's sword will be against his brother.**

❖ Turkey (Muslims) fought Arabia (Muslims) during Ottoman reign.
❖ Iraq (Muslims) and Iran's (Muslims) bitter war.
❖ Afghanistan's tribal wars against each other, all entirely Muslim, for the last twenty-five years and continuing even today.
❖ Sunni Muslims against Shiite Muslims and vice versa across the whole world. In Pakistan there is frequently grenades thrown in Shiite mosques to kill them.

❖ In Iraq the largest suicide bombing attack against the Shiite Muslims by the Sunnis first appeared in The New York Times as report appeared.

February 21, 2005
The New York Times

Six suicide bombers, including one on a bicycle, hurled themselves into Iraqi crowds and set off explosives on Saturday, killing as many as 39 people and wounding about 150 in a wave of mayhem intended to disrupt Ashura, the holiest day in Shiite Islam.

Judges 7:22 When the three hundred blew the trumpets, the **Master set every man's sword against his companion throughout the whole camp**; and the army fled to Beth Acacia, toward Zererah, as far as the border of Abel Meholah, by Tabbath.

Yahweh has declared it and we find that **this pattern** of what happened with Gideon's army fighting the Midianites. This is set to repeat in the future and throughout time, as when they ALL turned against each other i.e. brother against brother, that means Muslims will kill Muslims. You can prove this for yourself when the Muslims blew up the Samara Mosque the sacred shrine to the Shiites in Iraq and then in retaliation the Iraqi Shiites went around demolishing Sunni mosques and killing many Sunnis as a result, during the end of February 2006. This has resulted in countless deaths both in the Sunni and Shiite camps. Once again one brother's sword is against his other brother.

We can conclude that once again that THE BIBLE proves itself true because Yahweh is trustworthy (Amen).

H.   Discovering the city of the 7 Mountains

Revelations 17:18 "the woman which thou sawest is that **great city**, which reigneth over the kings of the earth."

Revelation chapter 19:2 continues to speak of Babylon as a real "city," not just an allegoric place that will be judged by YHWH and destroyed permanently. If we use the correct rules of biblical interpretation, we can see that Babylon is indeed the seat of power for the final empire of the Anti-Messiah in the Middle East.

In **Revelation 17:9** we are told in no uncertain terms that **this woman** (city) sits on, or more accurately "across" **seven** mountains," that in an allegorical sense always represents a kingdom, nation or empire. In its literal pashat reading it could just mean a mountain, but in the context of **Revelation 17:9** it represents the literal interpretation. The city sits near the mountains; the Greek word "epi" is correctly translated "by" or "across," rather than "on." The only qualification of this city I can find is **Mecca** and the reasons are given in this book, where the case is made that Mecca is the only city that has **seven** mountains surrounding it and the only one qualified to be the **harlot of Babylon,** because this religion came out from the mouth of Babylon (Iraq).

93

Mecca is a city surrounded around with **seven prominent mountains** that geographers cite as:

1) Jabal Quba
2) Jabal al Qinaa
3) Jabal Li Aali
4) Jabal Jifan
5) Jabal Jijad
6) Jabal Qubais
7) Jabal Hindi

The difference between a hill and a mountain is firstly mountains are more prominent and secondly they have a summit where as hills do not. Mecca also has the following **seven hills**, though the biblical text in Revelation does not speak about hills at all. But many prophecy writers have erroneously forced this view.

1) Jabal abu Siba
2) Jabal Safa
3) Jabal Marwah
4) Jabal abu Milhah
5) Jabal abu Ma'aya
6) Jabal abu Hulayah
7) Jabal abu Ghuzlan

Nevertheless in <u>my</u> opinion, we cannot say that the harlot city sits on seven hills; this is nothing but a straw man and a forced interpretation of prophecy, because the word that is used in the above passage is the Greek word **'OROS,'** which in its proper context only means a **MOUNTAIN**. This is distinct from **'BOUNOS,'** which is the Greek word for hill. Clearly, <u>seven</u> mountains do not surround Rome; yet, we see countless prophecy writers copying each other's errors by misinterpreting this passage. **Mecca is the only place in the world today that fits this prophecy much better then Rome. Mecca is the only place coupled with Mystery Babylon that fits this description.** In order to fit Rome, the prophecy teachers forget that nothing else matches with Rome, as the locations, cities, names, events, and places are ALL different and not European. What a real prophetic blunder! Yet ironically many call themselves prophets of today!

She is **"drunk with the blood of the saints and with the blood of the martyrs of Yahushua"** <u>Revelation (17:6)</u>. The people described as "saints" in the New Testament are seen to be gentile believers in Yahushua Messiah. But this description can very well be applied to Jews, or gentiles without a problem. This is an on going active persecution that will get worse. Do we see any persecution in Rome, or by Rome today? The answer is no. Now try applying this to Saudi Arabia, where Christians are "beheaded" for the witness of Yahushua the Messiah, exactly as **Revelation 20-4b** stated: "And I saw **the souls of those who had been beheaded** for their **witness of Yahushua** and for the word of YHWH."

This is the only nation that will not allow Christians to build a church; it will not even allow Jews to enter its land after Muhammad had them banished from Saudi Arabia in the 7th century AD. This country actively encourages intolerance towards non-Muslims all over the world; its adherents have no problem with labelling Jews as rats and monkeys and Christians as pigs.

In TV broadcasts Sheikh Abd Al-Rahman Al-Saudis quoted:

In his sermons, often broadcast by official Saudi state television and translated by the Middle East Media Research Institute (MEMRI), al-Saudis has called Jews "**the scum of the human race, accursed by Allah, who turned them into apes and pigs...an ongoing continuum of deceit, obstinacy, licentiousness, evil, and corruption**" (April 19, 2002).

In one of his sermons, Saudi sheikh Abd Al-Rahman Al-Sudayyis, imam and preacher at the Al-Haraam mosque — the most important mosque in Mecca — beseeched Allah to **annihilate** the Jews. He also urged the Arabs to give up peace initiatives with them because they are "**the scum of the human race, the rats of the world, the violators of pacts and agreements, the murderers of the prophets, and the offspring of apes and pigs.**"

Pick up any Western tabloid and you will see reports of beheadings in the Middle Eastern nations carried out by the Islamists. Also brutally beheaded in Iraq in June 2004 was Kim Sun Il, an evangelical Christian, whose fault was simply that he went out of love seeking to give the gospel to the Muslims and the radical Muslims gave him death! This is the tragic situation.

Saudi Arabia is even mentioned in **Jeremiah 49:33** by the name of Kedar, as Kedar was a descendant of Ishmael, the father of the Arabs. It may be of interest to note that the Muslims claim that Muhammad is a descendant of Ishmael.

There is an interesting prophecy for Elam (Iran) in the Bible that is also set for destruction.

Jeremiah 49:34-39 The word of the Master that came to Jeremiah the prophet **against Elam**, in the beginning of the reign of Zedekiah king of Judah, saying, "Thus says the Master of hosts: `Behold, I will break the bow of Elam, the foremost of their might. Against Elam I will bring the four winds from the four quarters of heaven, and scatter them **toward all those winds**; there shall be no nations where the outcasts of Elam will not go. For I will cause **Elam to be dismayed** before their enemies and before those who seek their life. I will bring disaster upon them, my fierce anger,' says the Master; `and I will send the sword after them until I have consumed them. I will set My throne in Elam, and will destroy from there the king and the princes,' says the Master. `But it shall come to pass in the latter days: I will bring back the captives of Elam,' says the Master.**"

Let us pick up some key elements in this prophecy. Iran has put itself in prime position to be attacked because it has openly declared to wipe out Israel and produce nuclear weapons. I do not think the judgement is immediate, but let us wait and see.

* Iran is one of the strengths of the Anti-Messiah's armies. Any wonder why there are nuclear missiles being build up in Iran as I write? Chances are that they will get away with it, given all the media hype, while everyone has debates over it. The Bible says Iran will succeed.
* Iran will be destroyed and its people scattered in the entire world in a war in which many countries will be involved. These are likely to include the USA, UK and Europe with other nations participating.

95

❖ Yahweh will personally judge Iran for her idolatries and sins. Ahmadnijad the current Iranian leader recently made a comment that "Israel should be wiped off the face of the earth."
❖ Yahweh will raise nations from all the <u>four quarters of the earth</u> to fight Iran.
❖ Iranians will be killed by other nations.
❖ Yahweh will remove kings or princes there to set up His throne.
❖ In the <u>latter days</u> Yahushua the Messiah will forgive the Iranians and bring them back to their land just like He did with Israel. Then they shall worship Yahweh the Elohim of Israel in Zion. Amen.

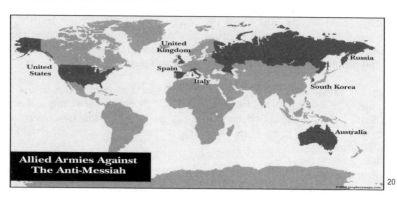

These prophecies fit with the Gog of **Ezekiel 38** since Persia [Iran] is included as well. Also **Isaiah 13** with Jeremiah's prophecies for the Ishmaelites (Arabs). The nations raised from the four quarters of heaven will most likely be the USA, Australia, Northern Russia and the Key Ally of the USA, which is <u>Great Britain</u>. The only nation that fits the description of the kings from the ends of the earth (Jeremiah 50:41) fits with the USA (look at the map above). The UK would form a key ally from the European side.

Remember Russia supplied key information to USA President (George W. Bush) during the war with Afghanistan. In fact it is well known that it was only with the intelligence of President Putin that President Bush attacked Afghanistan, so Russia will play a key role against the Anti-Messiah. Russia has been mourning its losses with the Al-Qaeda led attacks in Moscow and Beslan (Chechnya), where one incident of suicide bombing, two incidents of planes shot down, and the hostage taking of many school children were all enacted by these Islamists. The recent attacks in Nalchik by armed Islamists show the extent of the beast warring with Northern Russia. Australia is also at war with radical Islam, as their embassy was destroyed in Jakarta on 9th of September 2004. The Al-Qaeda linked group Jemaah Islamiya made this statement:

"We decided to settle accounts with Australia, one of the worst enemies of Allah and Islam ... and a Mujahideen brother succeeded in carrying out a martyr operation with a car bomb against the Australian embassy."

Jeremiah 51:6 Flee from the **midst of Babylon**, and <u>every one save his life</u>! Do not be cut off in **her** iniquity, for this is the time of the Master's vengeance; He shall **recompense** her.

---

[20] www.prophecymaps.com

If Rome was the beast, then the workers would have to leave. But consider that Rome has mainly tourists. Moreover, the destruction is for Babylon (Iraq), and we see that the daughter of Babylon (Saudi Arabia) is also involved in this judgement, because a switch is made in **_Jeremiah 51:33 from Babylon to her daughter!_**

For thus says the Master of hosts, the Elohim of Israel: "The daughter of Babylon is like a threshing floor when it is time to thresh her; yet a little while and the time of her harvest will come." We must remember that the term Babylon encompasses Arabia and here it certainly does where 60% of its workforce, which is foreign, will leave and return back to their own lands.

YHWH is warning everyone to leave Saudi Arabia because her time of destruction has come by bringing the nations together. These include the above, Great Britain plus the USA (the two brothers together), Northern Russia and Australia (the third brother, sharing a common blood and ancestry i.e. British blood), and in fact even Italy is amongst them. South Korea would also be included. Spain will turn around and also help, just like it did in the past when the Muslims invaded it. Later on the Spaniards expelled the Muslims. These will make up the **seven** shepherds of Israel in the end of days (Micah 5:5).

Jeremiah 51:9 - "We would have healed Babylon, but she is not healed: **forsake her**, and let us go every one into his own country."

All laborers in Saudi Arabia are foreigners, some from Arab lands and many from under developed Asian countries such as Pakistan, Bangladesh, Sri Lanka, the Philippines, Thailand and others. Foreign nationals are what constitute the Saudi labor force. There are approximately three million foreigners in Saudi Arabia's total population of 16.7 million. About 60% of the Saudi workforce is made up of foreign nationals, and over 90% of the workers in the private sector are non-Saudis. Furthermore, they have no right to obtain citizenship, so it is understandable why they will each flee each "into his own country."

Revelation 18:7 "How much **she hath glorified herself**, and lived in **luxury**."

Some could only dream of the very affluent lives and luxuries that the Saudis boast about with their great amount of wealth. Their homes are adorned with marble and artefacts, laden with gold and silver. Just look at their architecture to ascertain their prosperity; silver spoons, golden cups and plates are but few items to name.

Isaiah 47:10 "For thou hast trusted in **thy** wickedness: thou hast said, **none seeth me**."

Could we honestly say this is referring to New York or Rome? These cities do not sin secretly, but sin openly for all to see and judge. But this city Mecca sins secretly, believing that they are squeaky clean, the most righteous. How often have you heard of scandals coming out of Saudi Arabia? Now compare that with the sex scandals and love affairs that emerge out of New York and Rome. Currently there are so many lawsuits pending against the Catholic Church that it could almost bring the establishment down.

The Arabs have a male dominated culture. If you have read about Islam, the one thing that sticks out like a sore thumb is male chauvinism. All the rights are afforded to men who portray a kind of outward righteousness while inwardly they live sinful lives. They abuse their authority over women, beat them, sleep around with their slaves, and practice bigamy (It is usual to have up to four wives; some sheikhs have 25 wives at least if not

97

more). These practices lead one to wonder where the godliness is in their lives. Recently while speaking to a friend in Saudi Arabia he said that the people here are very sinful, they have affairs secretly, practice adultery with other's wives and for sexual liaisons, they go to Dubai the sex capital of the Arab world.

Another friend in Kuwait said to me there is so much lewdness here, no one's wife or daughter is safe, because the sheikhs could take the fancy of a girl and either try to purchase her or have her abducted. Now the Arabs are preying on poor young girls in India, in what is termed marriage, where a marriage with a rich sheikh is organized with a middleman and after 72 hours the marriage is annulled or a divorce given! This is all done in the name of Islam to satisfy the lusts of the rich sheikhs and what I call legal prostitution under the guise of marriage. The sheikhs are usually anywhere between 40 to 70 years old and the girls involved are 12 years and onwards. Usually the girls' parents are so poor that they want to marry their daughters off thinking that they are getting rid of a burden and that their daughters will settle in a richer family with a better lifestyle.

There is no such thing as freewill in an Islamic society and democracy is a word hated by most Arabs and Muslims in authority. There are no elections, or political parties in Saudi Arabia, as the House of Saud rules with the Sha'ria Law (Legal code of Islam) and with the Qu'ran being used as their guideline. Torture and inhumane activity is common in that land. Justice is hardly served, by cutting off people's hands and feet, and making them cripples for life with no disability allowance. Can you imagine the sort of society that this creates? My Saudi friend said it is an awful site seeing innocent peoples' heads rolling.

Isaiah 34:2 For the **indignation** of the Master is against all nations, [context is Islamic nations] and His fury **against all their armies** [the Islamic confederacy]; He has utterly destroyed them, He has given them over to the slaughter [judgment is set, they will be killed].

YHWH has set judgment for all the Islamic nations. YHWH used the word Edom (Jordan) symbolically and literally to indicate judgment on all these nations, including the Palestinian people who are really Jordanians. The amount of human rights violations that go on in the Islamic countries are enough to write ten books. It is sad that even moderate Muslims have to suffer such things and the poor Muslim has no chance of living in such a society. Standing together and praying in a mosque makes no difference, because giving a hand of charity to their poor Muslim neighbors is hardly even considered in an Islamic society.

Cheap oil expensive water?
In Arab lands oil is cheap and water is expensive. The oil literally gushes out in the Middle East because of its abundance and also it's cheap to drill oil in the Middle East in comparison to say the North Sea. No wonder many nations for decades have been reliant on it. Instead of doing research and development they have simply relied on Arab oil for their economic survival, acting as if it will never run out. When the time comes for this oil to burn then one thing is for sure. YHWH is not going to wait sixty-five years for the oil to run out. If it runs out according to the current estimate, then how can this prophecy of oil burning ever be fulfilled in the Arab lands? This means the time is now close for these fields to burn! It also means that we are close to the judgment and there has to be oil there for this to happen. One may ask, how close are we? Well time will tell, but you could take an educated guess and still be prepared for all eventualities. We cannot predict the date, or time, but we can see the signs for our personal preparation though. Armageddon is not

at all that far off as most think. We are looking at a lot less then sixty-five years i.e. before the oil runs out, or else the Bible prophecy would fail. But since we know that no Bible prophecy has ever failed, then this will likely occur in the lifetime of many and it will catch many unprepared.

Isaiah 34:6-10 The **sword of the Master is filled with blood**, it is made **overflowing with fatness**, and with the **blood of lambs and goats, with the fat of the kidneys of rams.** For the Master has a **sacrifice in Bozrah**, and a **great slaughter in the land of Edom.** (7) The **wild oxen shall come down with them**, and the **young bulls with the mighty bulls; their land shall be soaked with blood, and their dust saturated with fatness.**" (8) For it is the **day of the Master's vengeance**, the **year of recompense for the cause of Zion.** (9) Its **streams shall be turned into pitch**, and its **dust into brimstone**; its **land shall become burning pitch.** (10) It shall **not be quenched night or day**; its **smoke shall ascend forever. From generation to generation it shall lay waste; no one shall pass through it forever and ever.**

Note the symbols:

❖ Wild oxen, young bulls and mighty bulls, all figurative references to fighting men, both young and seasoned warriors, who will be killed.
❖ These men will be killed in Bozrah.
❖ Great slaughter in the land of Edom, or present day Jordan and its surrounding nations.
❖ Recompense for the cause of Zion i.e. Israel.
❖ Streams turned into pitch (referring to oil) that will burn in the Arab oil rich regions.

The same words are used, this time for judgement, with oil burning, smoke ascending in the land of Edom. Now a literal reading of the passage shows us destruction and oil wells burning in the Jordanian land and any other lands connected with Edom. The Bible is clear the land will lay waste just like Saudi Arabia and no one shall pass through it. This prophecy is yet to be fulfilled and will be fulfilled.

In **Isaiah 34:2-10** we are told some interesting facts.

Isaiah 34: 2-10 (2) For the **indignation of the Master** is against **ALL** [Islamic] nations, and His fury against all their armies; He has utterly destroyed them, He has **given them over to the slaughter.** (3) Also their **slain shall be thrown out**; their **stench shall rise from their corpses,** and the **mountains shall be melted with their blood.** (9) Its streams shall be turned into pitch and its dust into brimstone; its **land shall become burning pitch.** (10) **It shall not be quenched night or day; its smoke shall ascend forever.**"

The Master's wrath for the end-times battle is not against all nations e.g. every man, woman and child in the world, but specifically against all those nations that came up to fight Israel. **These are Islamic nations** and these references tie up with **Ezekiel 38, Zechariah 12:2 and Psalm 83.** The word "ALL" is a synecdoche and represents some of all. Many people try to apply ALL to ALL and unfortunately this is where that kind of conclusion will fail. It is evident even in **Isaiah 34** that the judgment is against ALL Islamic nations, but specifically the land mentioned is Edom. **That means the object of the**

wrath is specifically ALL the heathen surrounding nations that gather together to destroy Israel.

The description of **pitch** here clearly points to the Middle East region and is used here by YHWH leaving us in no doubt as to where the action will take place. Pitch is used for the substance of bitumen and tar and it is only related to oil. Unfortunately for some prophecy writers, there is no oil to be burned in the streets of Europe, or the USA, but there is plenty in the Gulf nations. We should make a special note that the land is not burning pitch now, but will become "**burning pitch**" in the future i.e. when the oil wells will burn. The smoke of this oil will ascend into the sky and darken the land, just like it did when the first Gulf War took place. This prophecy can only be fulfilled in an oil rich region and quite clearly the context of the passage is judgment on the rich Islamic nations that have oil. Saudi Arabia is believed to hold 25% of the world oil reserves and is a key exporter with 90% of its revenue from oil. Imagine when this oil starts to go up in smoke, how long do you think it will burn? All nations around about Saudi Arabia will be able to see this destruction and all the merchants will mourn at this once rich nation as described in *Revelation 18:11*. *"And the merchants of the earth will **weep and mourn over her,** for no one buys their merchandise anymore."* Have you realized that if the prophecy was for Rome, or the USA, that they simply do not have this type of oil rich region for this to occur?

Jeremiah 49:21 The earth shakes at the noise of their fall; at the cry its noise is heard at the **RED SEA (Mecca sits on the eastern part of the Sea of Reeds)**.

Did I read that correctly? The earth shakes at a particular region? Where? The whole world shakes at the news of Saudi Arabia's burning! The noise is heard at the "**Red Sea.**" YHWH is even gracious to pinpoint the location for those that still refuse to believe. We better open our eyes and switch on our antennas to pick the correct frequency for the big destruction that is coming in the land of Saudi Arabia, Iraq, Jordan and other oil rich Islamic states.

Revelation 18:11 "And the **merchants of the earth** will **weep** and **mourn** over her, for no one buys their merchandise anymore"

No rich man weeps unless his profits sink and his business is doomed. We have seen many rich men commit suicide when their businesses are going to become bankrupt. Well, these rich merchants will weep because their businesses are about to sink and go down under.

The Master tells us that this country is not only oil rich, but it relies on imports to feed its people. Saudi Arabia has a vast desert region and it looks like a desert island also. It imports livestock, grains and even water. Its gross domestic product (GDP) was estimated at 241 billion USD (USA dollars), with export trade estimated at 66.9 billion USD, with 90% of it being oil. Its import is estimated at around 29.7 billion USD. Not only are the western nations dependent on it's oil, but it is the oil that adds stability to our world today. If we have fluctuating oil prices as we did recently in the 2004/2005 Gulf War along with the instability in Iraq, we saw a panicking stock market yo-yoing up and down, effecting a lot of individuals worldwide.

When Saudi Arabia goes down, the reliance on its oil will cause heavy economic fallout around the world. The merchants of the world will truly weep, for no one buys their merchandise anymore. Many businesses will go bust, especially the ones who rely on

100

exporting goods to the Middle East region, because these are the merchants crying, because their goods are not selling anymore.

The European nations on the other hand import a wide range of goods and are not heavily dependent on their imports. Their gross GDP is much higher. Italy for example, has a well-established silk industry, stone industry and motorcar industry. Italy's export revenues stand at 259.2 billion USD and imports at 238.2 billion USD. If the city in revelation was the Vatican in Rome, then what does Italy have to offer the nations so they can bemoan her? I am sure not many people will be crying over the short supply of Fiats. The Vatican does not have any commercial concerns, or trade with ALL nations of the world. The Vatican is nothing more then a religious center that has no power in the world stage today. In fact, Roman Catholic bishops have been sued left, right and center in the USA for child molestation cases, and have struggled to meet their payout bills. The Catholic Church has been pleading for more donations from its followers because of its depleting cash reserves. How many Catholic priests have you seen recently flying in their own personal jets and driving fast expensive cars? Come to the land of Saudi Arabia and you will surely see plenty of oil rich sheikhs owning personal jets and owning very expensive top of the range prestigious cars that have been built to order.

Armed with the above information, one cannot conclude it is Italy, or that merchants will be wailing over it. Italy is with the alliance against the Anti-Messiah not with him. In fact, just recently I was speaking to a friend in Kuwait and he was telling me how there are so many foreign workers in Kuwait. He said that the oil rich people hate the west, yet want to live with the benefits of western capitalistic economic values. Yet they do not desire a change of mindset needed for freedom of speech and other liberties found in the west. He also said corruption is rife, everything is done with "vasta," i.e. influence.

Isaiah 47:15 Thus shall they be unto thee with whom thou hast labored, even thy merchants, from thy youth: they shall wander **every one to his quarter**; **none shall save thee**.

If we look back at the first Gulf War in 1991, we know that Iraq fired scud missiles in 1991 at Saudi Arabia, the alleged holy soil. Saddam could not care less, but still the Saudi's do have double standards by accepting Saddam as a brother after the war and were seen hugging and kissing him.

Even though the Americans came to save them and free Kuwait, the Arabs continue to view the USA as the great s.a.tan rather than a true friend.

Saudi Foreign Minister, Prince Saud al-Faisal, did not permit the USA to attack Iraq from Saudi territory in the previous Gulf War.

One day after the nomination of Henry Kissinger as chairman of the 9/11 investigation commission, Prince Nayif bin Abdul Aziz, Interior Minister of Saudi Arabia, was interviewed by the Kuwaiti newspaper 'Assiasa.' In the interview, which was republished in the Saudi daily 'Asharq Al-Awsat' on Nov. 28, Prince Nayif expressed his doubts about the official story that Al-Qaeda carried out the Sept. 11, 2001 attacks. Here are some excerpts:

"I am supposed to believe that 19 young men, of whom 15 are Saudis, managed to conduct this operation, and that bin Laden and the Al-Qaeda group did that independently. This is impossible. I will never believe that. If they have this capability, then they must be supermen, or probably have some heavenly power.

Yes, they are persons who are capable of killing people, blowing some shops, or become walking coffins taking themselves and others to death, but to carry out an operation with such precision, no.

I cannot believe it. I am a security man. I have lived with security matters for over 30 years. But we can say that they are either agents, or ignorant people. In both cases, their actions were against Islam and Muslims."[21]

The Arab people have always been good at denials and it would be very surprising if they came out telling the truth. They have a habit of lying and old habits die-hard. This is unfortunate to write, but it is true and they will also sell their services to the highest bidder. So it's business first, loyalty second. We find just a few Arab individuals who are honest, and so those few that are honest get a bad name because of the masses that are not.

Saudi Arabia- Imports the following merchandise mentioned in <u>Revelation 18:12-13</u>.

* **The merchandise of gold, silver and precious stones.**
* **Pearls.**
* **Fine linen, purple, silk and scarlet.**
* **Wood, ivory and brass.**
* **Iron and marble.**
* *Every kind of citron wood.*
* **All manner of vessels of ivory.**
* **All manner of vessels of most precious wood.**
* **Brass and Iron.**
* **Marble.**
* **Cinnamon and scents, ointments and frankincense.**
* **Wine.**
* **Beasts, sheep and horses.**
* **Chariots.**
* **Slaves.**
* **Souls of men.**

Now ask yourself this question, does Saudi Arabia import all those specific items listed above or not? The answer is absolutely YES. Now repeat the question again with Italy importing the items above. The answer is no, as Italy is self sufficient in some of the items above and so instead of importing, they actually <u>export</u> some of those items mentioned above.

Saudi Arabia purchases its slaves from the slavery houses of Sudan and this wholesale slave trade enabled the Saudis in the 18th century to rebuild their cities and re-establish the trade routes. This all happened under Sultan of Oman Seyyid Said. The land of Zanzibar was where the lucrative slave trade was taken over by the Saudis. Also ivory and spices were imported into the Saudi Kingdom from Zanzibar, while the slave trade was quite lucrative for the Arabs. Slavery is a part of Islam, accepted and practiced by the

[21] **Saudi Foreign Minister 'Will Never Believe' US 911 Story,** Rumor Mill News Reading Room Forum, Posted By Rosalinda 12-3-2, Source: Asharq Al-Awsat.com, Kuwait, Nov. 28 12-4-2

Muslims even though it was banned in the kingdom in 1968. However, I personally know from a friend in Saudi Arabia who became a Christian and told me that it was openly practiced until King Faisal's death in 1975. Even today they secretly buy slaves and keep them in their palaces. But who is to know and care for these desperate slaves who have no one to call upon but the Master YHWH, who will judge this nation for its sins. A new trend has started where these Sheikhs go to India and marry very young girls from poor Muslims families by paying middlemen who are Islamic clerics. This practice is nothing short of legal prostitution, under the guise of marriage to not just one young girl as young as 12 or 13, but to several girls at the same time. Islamic law allows these girls to be married and divorced. This practice is actually rife in India and other Islamic states. The rich Sheikhs benefit by paying off sums of money to middle men. The girl's parents are so poor that they willingly marry their daughters to get rid of the burden, not realizing the intent of the men involved.

The Arab culture is also well known for its gold, silver and precious stones consumption, as many people like to adorn themselves in these delicacies. These items attributed to the largest bulk of Saudi import estimated at $909 Million USD in 2001.

Saudi Arabia imports pearls from other nations and Japan. Saudis imported $2.459 Million USD worth of precious stones. Since fashion is not one of Islam's traits and is not practiced widely as in the west, and since Islam discourages these practices under Sha'ria law, this is thus a significant amount of import. It is clear that Babylon in its proper context is Iraq, and the **daughter of Babylon** is Saudi Arabia. Babylon is used interchangeably in the Bible at times to speak of Islam in general and Saudi Arabia as the harlot of Babylon.

Saudis are into their luxury wear of silk clothes due to the strict Islamic dress code and hot arid climate of that region. Saudis love to indulge in collecting expensive artefacts, collecting ivory swords and exquisite daggers. Islamic art woven on expensive materials is commonplace.

Iron is imported into the Saudi kingdom for construction of beautiful architecture and marble for floors and exterior design. Saudi Arabia does produce its own marble, but not in sufficient quantity to meet its needs, so it imports a lot more from Pakistan, Jordan, Turkey and Italy to fulfil its needs. The mosque in Medina is entirely constructed of marble with gold. The flooring and mosque in Mecca is predominantly made of marble also. Remember that it is Osama Bin Laden's family that manages all the construction needs of the holy sites.

The Saudis have a need to import livestock, cattle, sheep and poultry due to the desert conditions in which animal breeding is expensive and impossible. They also import very expensive luxury cars as one of their quieter pursuits. New York, or Italy does not import cattle. In fact wheat is sold by the USA, rather then importing it, since they have so much of it to give away free.

Saudi Arabia has been actively Islamizing the world and spent many billions of dollars doing just that by building mosques, Islamic centers worldwide and teaching the strict Sha'ria code of Islam as the way forward. Islam is the second most evangelical religion in the world, out to destroy the credibility of Judaeo-Christian values by denouncing the former as both corrupt and outdated. It makes the claim that is has the last testament with the correct mode of revelation. It's funny how Muhammad never knew the one true Elohim, or His name Yahweh, never spoke to Him face to face, never knew about Yahushua's true purpose on earth and His deity, and never knew why the Messiah had to

103

come to fulfil the Torah by dying on the cross and rising from the dead. Muhammad's whole Islamic concept is set in 7th century Arabian ignorance and superstition. Islam tries to deny every trait of true biblical Christianity. Islam promotes hate campaigns against the Jews and the west using the Qu'ran as its legitimate god given tool. How do we stop the hatred? The answer lies in how we stopped Hitler by defeating the ideology and showing it to be false. There is no need to wage war on Muslims; we simply need to show using our media, TV, radio, newspapers and active discussion and debate that Islamic ideology is false. We must present plenty of evidence so that common sense prevails amongst Muslims, so that they can see that they do not follow truth, but rather follow something created by Muhammad, that has no spiritual value.

This ideology is not much different than Hitler who indoctrinated 60 million Germans into hating the Jews; however, Hitler got most of his ideas from Islam. Are you surprised? It is a well-known fact that Hajji Amin Al-Hussaini met with Himmler and Hitler to devise the final solution for the Jews to exterminate all the Jews. Muslims have their hands full of Jewish blood as they helped Hitler condemn and persecute the Jews and Christians. **They recruited Bosnian Muslim troops called the Hanschar that were recruited by Hajji Amin Al-Hussaini into several divisions of the Waffen SS to help Hitler.**

Hajji Amin Al Hussaini inspecting the Hanschar troops. [22]

Himmler inspecting the Hanschar troops.

---

[22] http://www.srpska-mreza.com/bookstore/handschar/handschar.htm

Is it any surprise that the Muslims are indoctrinated theologically into hating the Jewish and Christian world the same way today? The only thing is now we have a bigger problem with 1.5 billion Muslims. When you claim this is by "Allah's will" then it is the most dangerous type of hatred. The Qu'ran is the handbook for today's modern radical Muslim terrorist. The reality is that if you give a Qu'ran to a Muslim, tell him to study it thoroughly and follow it, then you have a home made terrorist ready to blow himself up for Allah taking innocent lives. Allah desires sacrifice of Muslim children and Muslims have plenty of children to sacrifice in the Name of Allah. Who do you think desired sacrifice of humans in the Bible? Do Baal and Molech ring a bell? These were the ancient false gods desiring sacrifices of human children. Today Muslims will happily sacrifice their children in the name of Allah. One of my friends in Israel goes to a Muslim barber in Jerusalem and the Muslim barber gloats to my friend about his young son exclaiming 'one day my son will grow up to become a suicide bomber against the Jews.' What a tragic waste of human life!

There is a joke about a Muslim and a Christian. The Christian says I will die for my faith and the Muslims say "I must kill you for my faith; the Muslim says I will fulfil my obligation and you will fulfil yours, so get ready to die infidel." This is actually true, even though it is thrown around as a joke. This is what is happening to the Christians in the Muslim world today. They are being butchered for their faith, just like the Jews were butchered in the Muslim lands. Christian blood, like Jewish blood is also cheap.

Islam corrupts souls; no other nation fits the biblical description of the "**Harlot of Babylon**" other than Saudi Arabia. Saudi Arabia is the nerve center of Islam; this is where all this hatred originated from, behind this hatred is only one person: s.a.tan, that old deceiver and the one that puts doubt in people's minds. Paul rightly said we fight **spiritual** forces, **principals and principalities and this is it.**

Many nations commit harlotry with Islam and Saudi Arabia because of the vast oil reserves of the Arab nations. Even George W. Bush said to the world that "**Islam is peace**" and this was after the September 11 attacks. Was George W. Bush lying, or just misinformed?

Unfortunately the same statement was made by our Prime Minister Tony Blair. For our leaders the Qu'ran itself refutes them because it does not allow for dialogue between Muslims and non-Muslims;

<u>Sura 3.85</u> **If anyone desires a religion other than Islam (submission to Allah), never will it be accepted of him; and in the Hereafter He will be in the ranks of those who have lost (all spiritual good).**

The Qu'ran makes it clear that the Muslims are not to accept any other faith other than Islam. So this rules out any peace between Muslims and non-Muslims, so why the rhetoric? The peace initiatives need to come from the Islamists and they need to show it by their actions, as the current actions against the west only show hostility not peace.

<u>Sura 9:5</u> **But when the forbidden months are past, then fight and slay the pagans wherever ye find them, and seize them, beleaguer them, and lie in wait for them in every stratagem (of war); but if they repent, and establish regular prayers and practise regular charity, then open the way for them: for Allah is Oft-forgiving, Most Merciful.**

105

The only way a non-Muslim is allowed to live is by converting to Islam and then he may have peace. Otherwise he is to be fought until he submits to Islam, so making peace is virtually impossible according to the Qu'ran.

> **Sura 5:51** <u>O ye who believe! Take not the Jews and the Christians for your friends and protectors: They are but friends and protectors to each other. And he amongst you that turns to them (for friendship) is of them. Verily Allah guideth not a people unjust</u>.

Well the Qu'ran itself rules out any friendship, or peace initiative with Mr. Bush and Mr. Blair, which includes Ariel Sharon, because <u>according</u> to the Muslims, these are Christians and Jews. They must not be taken as friends, as they say hear it from Mohammed's own mouth. In my opinion Mr. Blair is not an evangelical Christian, but Muslims think he is. If he is then do not make any peace with him and if he isn't then still the edict in Sura 9:5 is to fight until they convert to Islam. You decide how it is possible to make peace under such terms. We only delude ourselves though we should try our best to love our Muslim neighbors and convince them to leave Islam as an untrue faith leading to eternal damnation. The truth stands to be seen in Yahushua of Nazareth, the One who could bridge this gap giving us a sure peace. That is the reality. If Muslims accept Him, then we can have lasting peace, all led by the same King/Savior. But I am doubtful if many will accept this solution, as the Bible itself stands testimony that the Islamic nations will form a confederacy to fight Israel and bring much destruction to the world through open warfare.

I believe the statement that George W. Bush made was a political statement, although he confesses to being a born again believer who seeks the Master daily and commits all decisions to Him. Nevertheless, people under his authority have questionable motives. This has absolutely no bearing on what true Islam is in reality, or what his stance is on the Muslim terrorists that he is pursuing. President Bush needs to realize until we deal with the <u>ideology</u>, the terrorists are not going away quietly. Yesterday it was the Twin Towers and tomorrow it will be a dirty bomb, so we better decide how to deal with the threat today.

The question is not can they strike but when, where and how. Killing a few radical Muslims here, or there will not eliminate terrorism, since its source is in the pages of the Qu'ran. We have to expose the ideology to be evil that stems from the Qu'ran and we have to win hearts and minds of the Muslims to show the truth. We have to take the love of Yahushua the Messiah that can change lives and save souls. Until we are prepared to deal with the **Islamic ideology,** we only deter ourselves from dealing with the greater threat that is about to come. Calling Islam peaceful only veils the threat and confuses people further who are looking for answers.

I understand that a president of such a superpower cannot make a blanket statement against a religion saying it is evil because he has different nationalities and faiths residing there. One wrong statement would not only have cost him the election, but also great problems at home, with people saying he is racist, or indifferent. Some Christians label George W. Bush as a prostitute sold out to the Arabs. I personally do not believe this to be true. Nowhere did Yahweh object to people doing business with non-Christians. In fact, one only needs to read the accounts of King David and King Solomon to realize that they had extensive business dealings with the surrounding nations.

I am not here to defend President George W. Bush, or his decisions, but we must remember that George W. Bush is a president, not a missionary. We must be careful not to make such statements like the one above which only make for unhealthy reading and do not cast a good light on a leader who is a professed believer. Not only this, but also this plays into the hands of those that will use this to ridicule him further. It is not wise. We should be praying for him to make wise decisions that affect our world, not slandering him. He has an immense responsibility in his hands and he needs our prayers and support.

We know that Islam means "submission" not peace. That is submission to the will of Allah who commands Muslims everywhere to die for his sake. No wonder we saw 15 of the 19 suicide hijackers coming from Saudi Arabia, who were and still are hailed as heroes, called the "magnificent 19 in the Muslim world." The origin of the suicide bombers was this country which the Bible calls "the daughter of Babylon!" Yahushua the Messiah told us that you will know them by their fruits (works) and we know that the fruits of Islam have been bitter to the nations 'round about' throughout history, and can never be sweet until the lie is replaced with the truth.

I. What is the image of the beast in Revelation 13:15?

We have already identified the beast, and in view of this, we will seek to exercise wisdom to identify, what is this image of the beast.

> **Revelation 13:15b** "…That the **image of the beast should both speak**, and cause that as many as would not worship the image of the beast should be killed."

"Image" means "likeness," just as in Genesis 1:26a when "YHWH said, Let us make man in our image." The sin caused Adam to fall and for all of us to be separated from YHWH. Our Designer created us to be in fellowship with Him. Why is YHWH a tri-unity one may ask? Well He is a personality and with in the tri-unity of the Godhead is the ability to communicate, express love and share wisdom/Intelligence. The monadic concept of a god e.g. Allah, does not have the ability to do this. So any Unitarian god with this monadic characteristic cannot be reasoned to exist. YHWH also made man a personality with the ability to share similar attributes. If you want to know more about the tri-unity of the Godhead then please visit my website http://www.abrahamic-faith.com to see the CDs/audio lectures that are produced to address this particular issue. I also address this issue in my other book "Yahushua Or Isa - The True Path For Salvation."

So the "image of the beast" means that it's the likeness of the first empire including the original kingdom (Babylon), which Arabia and Islam do resemble.

On that note, it is fascinating that the crescent moon was an emblem used by Babylon, Rome, and Islam as well. The crescent moon is also the emblem of s.a.tan (Hilal ben Shachar) as in **Isaiah 14** for the word "Lucifer." Hilal literally means 'crescent moon' and the sign of the "dawn" for s.a.tan. This is the unleashing of s.a.tan into a body of a man (Anti-Messiah) who will come from the north of Israel. He is referred to as the "little horn," which is also the shape of a crescent moon, another indication that he is a Muslim!

This is supported by **Revelation 2:12-13**-These are the words of Yahushua:

> And to the angel of the assembly in Pergamos write; These things saith he which hath the sharp sword with two edges; I know thy works, and where thou dwellest, even **where s.a.tan's seat is**: and thou holdest fast my name, and hast not

denied my faith, even in those days wherein Antipas was my faithful martyr, who was slain among you, **where s.a.tan dwelleth**.

Pergamos (Pergamon) is/was in Turkey, north of Israel.

This by itself paints s.a.tan's symbol as a crescent moon and star (Venus). This is also the symbol on the Turkish flag and an emblem on the Ottoman Turks uniform. A perfect symbol for s.a.tan as described in Isaiah 14 and matches the domain of the Anti-Messiah – Turkey. Not surprisingly, being the symbol that originated from Babylon and the Moon-god, other Islamic nations also have it as a national symbol.

How can the "image" of the beast speak?

It is very important to note the use of the word "image" in relation to kingdoms in the Bible has nothing to do with statues or idols as such.

An excellent example is found in **Hosea 3:4**

> "For the children of Israel shall abide many days without a king, and without a prince, and without a sacrifice, and without an **image**, and without an ephod, and [without] teraphim."

How could Israel be "without an image?" Obviously, this means that Israel will have no emblem if it has no kingdom. Image can also be designated as an emblem of a kingdom.

So in Revelation, the Anti-Messiah will revive **a kingdom** and **an emblem**, a banner. This makes the whole allegory clear, that the mark is also the emblem/image of the beast/empire. The Islamic emblem being imprinted on arms and foreheads is an excellent example of what is happening today all over the world especially in Islamic nations. So, to make an image of a kingdom is to revive it and give it life in that they should give life to the image of the beast, which had the wound by a sword, and did live.

To make and carry an image, an emblem of something is akin to expressing allegiance to whatever the image, or emblem represents and thus submitting to the will of the beast/Empire. The Bible says all those who worship this image are those people who have no name in the **Book of Life.** So even a moderate Muslim who does not want to commit homicide bombings, or jihad against the west, still carries the mark. He or she sadly cannot enter eternal life until he, or she repents and rejects the false worship in Islam and accepts the true Elohim of Israel, the Messiah Yahushua who died for our sins.

J.   The Iranian connection

Ahmadinejad: Wipe Israel off map

Wednesday 26 October 2005, 19:03 Makka Time, 16:03 GMT

Ahmadinejad addressed students at a conference

Iranian President Mahmoud Ahmadinejad has openly called for Israel to be wiped off the map.

"The establishment of the Zionist regime was a move by the world oppressor against the Islamic world," the president told a conference in Tehran on Wednesday, entitled The World without Zionism.

"The skirmishes in the occupied land are part of a war of destiny. The outcome of hundreds of years of war will be defined in Palestinian land," he said.

"As the Imam said, Israel must be wiped off the map," said Ahmadinejad, referring to Iran's revolutionary leader Ayat Allah Khomeini.

His comments were the first time in years that such a high-ranking Iranian official has called for Israel's eradication, even though such slogans are still regularly used at government
rallies.

First of all I would like to say that the people of Iran are beautiful and intelligent people and this call to wipe Israel off the map is a call by Mahmoud Ahmadinejad more to do with the spiritual powers that be rather than physical human feelings of individual people of Iran.   Mahmoud Ahamdinejad's name means "praise worthy Saviour" interesting interpretation of the name and in the Hebrew language and middle-east Bible culture name always is related to the nature of the person and we can see what part Mahmoud wants to play for his and the other radical Muslim people. Many good Iranian people are tired with the way they are being treated in Iran, the lack of freedom and treatment by the Mullahs (Muslim clerics) has dismayed many youngsters of Iran, many of these people are looking for a way out of Iran to the West so they could not care less what happens to Israel let alone the destruction of Israel. We must remember that Iran is the first country in the world where King Cyrus made an unprecedented decision to free the Jewish captives and let them go home and repair their Temple, he is the one who setup the first human rights charter and Persia was a lot bigger than today in the old days, in fact it even encompassed today's modern Pakistan. Pakistan's dialect or language of Urdu came from the Persian script and this is a dialect of Aramaic thus Urdu has many similar words to the Aramaic language.

> **2 Chronicles 36:22-23** Now in the first year of Cyrus king of Persia, that the word of the Lord spoken by the mouth of Jeremiah might be fulfilled, the Lord stirred up the spirit of Cyrus king of Persia, so that he made a proclamation throughout all his kingdom, and also put it in writing, saying, (23) "Thus says Cyrus king of Persia: `All the kingdoms of the earth the Lord God of heaven has given me. And He has commanded me to build Him a house at Jerusalem which is in Judah. Who is there among you of all His people? May the Lord his God be with him, and let him go up!' "

Daniel the prophet was alive in Babylon during the reign of King Cyrus in Persia. King Cyrus was called the anointed or Moshiach by Elohim as he became the deliverer of the Jewish people this shows he had some kind of vision or understanding from the Elohim of Israel since he was a worshipper of Marduk, Bel and Nebo. Many Christians don't realise Yahweh can use people both inside and outside the faith to bring about His divine will. He does not need to convert everyone to Christianity to bring about His will. King Cyrus was one such person used to do just that. Persia has a lot of connections with the end of days plan. For one Elam has to be the strength of the Anti-Messiah this means Iran could not be attacked as most people predicted wrongly two years ago. The time is not yet as I said this for at least two years back in 2004 that Iran will become the strength just as the Bible says. Since Pakistan was part of the Persian Empire thus it too reflects Bible prophecy fulfilment as it the only Islamic nation carrying a nuclear bomb that one day will be used against Israel.

> **Jeremiah 49:35-36** "Thus says the Lord of hosts: `Behold, I will break the bow of Elam, the **foremost of their might**. (36) Against Elam I will bring the **four winds from the four quarters of heaven**, and scatter them toward all those winds; there shall be no nations where the outcasts of Elam will not go.

Iran is the chief strength of the Anti-Messiah and will be broken down by nations coming up against her from all four corners of the world i.e. these will be the shepherd nations or coalition partners joining forces to smash Iran. In order for the break-up of Iran and for it to be scattered to the entire world it first has to acquire power which it is gaining and it will become strong with its missile and nuclear technology in the very near future. After the destruction and scattering of Elam Yahweh will have mercy on the people of Iran and will bring them back from their dispersal.

> **Jeremiah 49:39** `But it shall come to pass in the latter days: I will bring back the captives of Elam,' says the Lord."

He will gather the outcasts of Iran lovingly like a Father after her dispersal thus Iranian citizens will receive mercy and be able to enter the kingdom of Yahweh upon repentance.

Hostilities between Iran and Saudi Arabia

> **Isaiah 21:1-2** The burden against the **Wilderness of the Sea**. As whirlwinds in the South pass through, so it comes from the desert, from a terrible land. (2) a distressing vision is declared to me; the treacherous dealer deals treacherously, and the plunderer plunders. **Go up, O Elam! Besiege, O Media!** All its sighing I have made to cease.

The reference "wilderness of the sea" is for the nation of the Saudis who will get into hostility with Iran.

> **Jeremiah 51:11** Make the arrows bright! Gather the shields! The Lord has raised up the **spirit of the kings of the Medes**. For His plan is against Babylon to destroy it, because it is the vengeance of the Lord, the vengeance for His temple. .

Who are the Medes?

These are the Kurdi people in Northern Iraq these will likely join the coalition to attack both Iraq and Arabia. Most probably the Kurdis will join coalition with the US forces at some point in the near future.

Persia has been raised to attack Babylon that means both Iraq and Saudi Arabia the "daughter of Babylon". Iran had a war with Iraq for almost ten years. Now December 2006 Iran is sending fighters who are Shias and they are slaying the Sunnis of Iraq causing a bloody bath there, the only trouble is the Shias outnumber the Sunnis two to one so have a greater chance of succeeding in tit for tat killings to eradicate the Sunni minority which is causing an alarm in the Sunni world and Saudi circles. Nawaf Obaid, an adviser to the Saudi government, is managing director of the Saudi National Security Assessment Project in Riyadh and an adjunct fellow at the Center for Strategic and

International Studies in Washington who commented on this situation. Some excerpts from the article follow.

[23]Just a few months ago it was unthinkable that President Bush would prematurely withdraw a significant number of American troops from Iraq. But it seems possible today, and therefore the Saudi leadership is preparing to substantially revise its Iraq policy. Options now include providing Sunni military leaders (primarily ex-Baathist members of the former Iraqi officer corps, who make up the backbone of the insurgency) with the same types of assistance -- funding, arms and logistical support -- that Iran has been giving to Shiite armed groups for years.

Another possibility includes the establishment of new Sunni brigades to combat the Iranian-backed militias. Finally, Abdullah may decide to strangle Iranian funding of the militias through oil policy.

If Saudi Arabia boosted production and cut the price of oil in half, the kingdom could still finance its current spending. But it would be devastating to Iran, which is facing economic difficulties even with today's high prices. The result would be to limit Tehran's ability to continue funnelling hundreds of millions each year to Shiite militias in Iraq and elsewhere.

What's clear is that the Iraqi government won't be able to protect the Sunnis from Iranian-backed militias if American troops leave. Its army and police cannot be relied on to do so, as tens of thousands of Shiite militiamen have infiltrated their ranks. Worse, Iraq's prime minister, Nouri al-Maliki, cannot do anything about this because he depends on the backing of two major leaders of Shiite forces.

In this case, remaining on the sidelines would be unacceptable to Saudi Arabia. To turn a blind eye to the massacre of Iraqi Sunnis would be to abandon the principles upon which the kingdom was founded.

It would undermine Saudi Arabia's credibility in the Sunni world and would be a capitulation to Iran's militarist actions in the region.

To be sure, Saudi engagement in Iraq carries great risks -- it could spark a regional war. So be it: The consequences of inaction are far worse.

Iran has been meddling in Pakistani affairs when some Sunni militant group's leaders were slain and in retaliation Pakistan Sunnis killed the Iranian representatives in Pakistan. I grew up in a Shia neighbourhood in Pakistan and personally found the Shia people to be good people though I was always getting into fights with their kids usually outnumbering us 3 to 12 and we would beat the kids up with complaints coming to our home to restraint us though we never started the fight as they always attacked us first. I was born in Pakistan in one of the toughest gangster districts a place called Gowalmandi, to be honest that turned out to be a blessing making me somewhat of a street fighter, I came to England and became a Karate Expert gaining national and international champion titles able to handle myself anywhere in the world taking up after my dad who also I personally

---

witnessed beating 12 people up on his own with a belt after a local family ganged up and attacked my aunt's family.

Jeremiah 51:13 O you who dwell by **many waters**, abundant in treasures, your end has come, the measure of your covetousness.

This reference to "many waters" is only applicable in the narrower context to Saudi Arabia who will have enmity with Iran in some serious way.

Jeremiah 51:19 The Portion of Jacob is not like them, for He is the Maker of all things; and **Israel is the tribe of His inheritance**. The Lord of hosts is His name.

Now here come the reference to Jacob not just Judah but to the 12 tribes of Israel particularly, there is Judah but there is Jacob which is a reference to all the 12 tribes which means gentile nations formed by the Ephraimites will get involved in the fight against Iran. The only way Israel can come from all four corners of the world is the way to describe the Ephraimites.

Jeremiah 51:20 "You are **My battle-ax** and **weapons of war**: for with you I will break the nation in pieces; with you I will destroy kingdoms;

This reference does not fit Jewish Israel today but it does indeed fit the 12 tribes together because there are many Ephraimites in the US, UK and European nations which means they have been used especially the UK to destroy kingdoms together with the US while Jewish Israel has been used to bust Arab nations roundabout and will be doing so again soon thus the whole house of Jacob works in tangent as a club in Yahweh's hand to beat these countries like little balls being knocked all over the place. Can anyone argue that the US is a tame nation or the British Empire has not been conquering different territory in the past at times with brutal rule? Anybody knowing the history of India would have heard of the brutal massacres that were conducted by the British killing many innocent civilians, just check out the Jalianwala Bagh massacre below conducted by General Dwyer.

[24]Jalianwala Bagh massacre of April 13, 1919 was one of the most inhuman acts of the British rulers in India. The people of Punjab have gathered on the auspicious day of Baisakhi at Jalianwala Bagh, adjacent to Golden Temple (Amritsar), to lodge their protest peacefully against persecution by the British Indian Government. General Dwyer appeared suddenly with his armed police force and fired indiscriminately at innocent empty handed people leaving hundreds of people dead, including women and children. General Dwyer, the butcher of Jalianwala Bagh, was later murdered by Udham Singh to avenge this barbaric act.

In this war both Iraq and Saudi will be involved in receiving the death blows. The wider reference is to the Islamic kingdoms as in the following verse.

Jeremiah 51:25 Behold, I am against you, **O destroying mountain**, who destroys all the earth," says the Lord. And I will stretch out My hand against you, roll you down from the rocks, and make you a **burnt mountain**.

---

[24] http://www.indhistory.com/jallianwalla-bagh-massacre.html

The reference to the "destroying mountain" is not to a literal mountain but an allegory or drash to a kingdom that has strength and is one that is taking people to hell all over the earth, this is the strictest reference to Islam where it has no salvation for people, well Yahweh is not going to burn one mountain but destroy the whole Islamic kingdom and tear it down from Satan's hands.

Islam on the other hand is the hammer that strikes nations knocking them around, Yahweh allows it to be used as a judgement hammer. The countries that don't fall in line with His divine will or are backslidden then here comes the hammer thus you have no protection from Yahweh when this starts to happen just note they come out of the woodwork and strike different areas. The hammer has been active in both the US and UK for the last 2 years at least and for 26 years in the US.

Jeremiah 50:23a How the hammer of the whole earth has been cut apart and broken!

So when different bits of terrorism are taking place Yahweh has allowed this to happen by lifting His protection off from the affected nation for many good reasons such as backslidden Christians and Jewish people profaning the name of Yahweh by living in abominable sins in their life and relishing in it. Deliverance will come once repentance is made.

Jeremiah 51:26 They shall not take from you a stone for a corner nor a stone for a foundation, but you shall be desolate forever," says the Lord.

Islam may claim to give salvation and other goodies like hooris (72 virgin women times 72 in mansions – thus Muslims are attracted by lust of the flesh) but Yahweh makes it clear that this is not the "stone for a corner" referring to the allegory of the Messiah who became the "corner stone" and a strong foundation for us the believers.

Jeremiah 51:27 Set up a banner in the land, blow the trumpet among the nations! Prepare the nations against her, call the kingdoms together against her: **Ararat**, **Minni**, and **Ashchenaz**. Appoint a marshal against her; cause the horses to come up like the bristling locusts.

Yahweh will bring Ararat, Mini i.e. the Armenians who were butchered by the Muslims in great numbers up to 1.5 million or more and he will call the European nations alongside to fight and destroy Iraq (Babylon) will lie in ruins and the "daughter of Babylon" (Saudi Arabia) the harlot province will be hit very hard.

In fact the Medes will participate to destroy Babylon and the daughter of Babylon so that is Kurdis that will fight Iraq and will also attack Saudi Arabia in some way.

Jeremiah 51:28 Prepare against her the nations, with the **kings of the Medes**, its governors and all its rulers, All the land of his dominion.

One might ask the pretext for Iran to attack Iraq and Saudi Arabia? How about Shia and Sunni warfare for power struggle and the number two cause that is oil which has brought regional power and corruption in Islamic nations. This scripture teaches us that Kurdistan will have some type of autonomy and thus rule its own region.

113

We know these two horns will fight each other for control (Shia and Sunni).

> **Revelation 13:11** Then I saw another beast coming up out of the earth, and **he had two horns** like a lamb and spoke like a dragon.

The Bible also tells us that brother will kill brother i.e. referring to Muslims and the evidence is right in front of us.

> **Ezekiel 38:21** I will call for a sword against Gog throughout all My mountains," says the Lord God. Every man's sword will be against his brother.

Further elaboration in the book of Revelation

> **Revelation 6:4** And there went out another horse that was red: and power was given to him that sat thereon to take peace from the earth, and that they should kill one another: and there was given unto him a great sword.

This earth mentioned is the area of Babylon i.e. Iraq where the action starts and has already started. Where did we see the US and UK go to war? Iraq then we have our bearings straight. If you find it hard to understand then today is December 2006 as I write this piece please take a look at Iraq (Babylon) it perfectly fits the book of Revelation with the beheadings and bloodshed of Sunnis killing Shias and vice versa. Now we know the accuracy of the Bible is so incredible.

Chapter 5

Are Radical Muslims Trying to Revive Islam of 7th Century Arabia?

What the fanatic adherents of Islam are doing today is NOT hijacking the religion of Islam, but reviving the old fundamentalist religion of Islam into its correct 7th century paradigm. They are trying to impose the 7th century fundamentalist religion, unto a 21st century world. For this reason, they are trying to follow what Muhammad laid out for them in their holy text of the Qur'an and his life that is recorded in the Hadiths (deeds of Muhammad).

The Muslim agenda is clear and the Muslims do not hide it either; so at least we have to give them credibility here. See one such example:

[25]**PA TV Sermon: Subjugate Christians, Exterminate Jews!**
Arab Press May 13th, 2005
A sermon broadcast last Friday on PA (Palestinian Authority) television called for the subjugation of all Christian countries under Islam and the extermination of every Jew. This is an excerpt.

The Muslim cleric, Ibrahim Mudayris, told his Arab audience, "The day will come and we shall rule **America** and **Britain**, we shall rule the entire world, except the Jews." He explained that, unlike the Christian countries, Jews cannot be placed under subjugation. He told PA television viewers that the only **fate awaiting Jews is death by extermination**.

Both the Qur'an and the Hadiths deliver plenty of justification for what the radical Muslims do today. This is why we do not see mass protests by moderate Muslims for Islamic despots like Saddam Hussain, and the now deceased Yasser Arafat, both of whom killed their own people and ruled them with a rod of Iron. Saddam through brutal force, Arafat through a program of homicide bombings, to entice them to gain 72 virgin hooris (women) in heaven.

Have you noticed that there is not one staged demonstration by Muslims in the world to protest against killings, or beheadings by the fanatic adherents of Islam? The question must be asked why. The answer is simpler than we think. The ones who are doing the killings are in the correct Islamic camp and can prove their actions by their "holy texts." The others are shown to be wrong and only distance themselves since they do not hold to the full Sha'ria (law of Islam). There was a small demonstration held by some fifty Muslims in England after the July 7th 2005 London bombings against the radicals, but even there the fifty that showed up had their own agenda. This is what I call the two faces of Islam. Sources close to me revealed that behind the scenes these people were blaming England and America for the troubles and bombings and that this was a simple political ploy.

It's ironic that in a nation where at least 1.5 million Muslims live, that only fifty people could barely make a demonstration and even then the motive was entirely political and not because they felt genuine sadness over the events of 7th July 2005. Why would they since it was their own that were carrying out Allah's will? How can one believe that these young men were being trained in the UK under radical Islam, yet no one knew? It is high time

---

[25] http://www.israelnationalnews.com/news.php3?id=82128

that all the mosques in Britain and America should be monitored for this type of activity, since they have become the breeding ground for terrorism.

Here is part of a story of what happened to two moderate Muslims from Pakistan in Iraq, who were only there to earn money for their families, yet were considered to be apostate and thus brutally slain with decapitation.

ISLAMABAD, July 30, 2004 (Online): Foreign Minister Khursheed Mehmood Kasuri Thursday said that government is in touch with Pakistani embassy in Iraq for recovery of the dead bodies of two Kashmiris killed by Iraqi captors.

The government and people of Pakistan have heard this tragic news from Iraq with deep sorrow and anguish. "It is indeed sad that despite a unanimous resolution in the NA (national assembly) and appeals from the President of Pakistan, the Prime Minister and myself the Iraqi captors of two Pakistani hostages Raja Azad Khan and Sajid Naeem did not heed to the appeals and went ahead with killing two innocent Muslims from Pakistan who were there as workers and bread winners of their families and had no political agenda," he said.

It is painfully obvious that what the Muslims do today is completely compatible with the early Islam of Muhammad. Sadly, many innocent Muslims are also killed by the strict keepers of this faith, who see these other Muslims as apostates helping the infidels.

A. What is the cause of this relentless hatred by the Muslims?

Why do the Muslims hate Israel so much? Surely it is not a land issue alone!

This is true, it is not a land issue alone, as we shall examine. If it was just the land issue then the Arabs have at least six hundred and fifty times more land than Israel to give a little to the Palestinians. But it is a lot more than this.

How does YHWH see things?

> Joel 3:1-3 "For behold, **in those days** and at that time, when I bring back the **captives of Judah and Jerusalem,** (2) I will also gather all nations, and bring them down to the **Valley of Jehoshaphat**; and **I will enter into judgment** with them there **on account of My people, My heritage Israel,** whom they have **scattered among the nations; they have also divided up My land.** (3) They have cast lots **for My people,** have given a boy in exchange for a harlot, and sold a girl for wine, that they may drink.

In "those days" that means we are living in these days today because Judah is back in the land of Israel and since 1967 Jerusalem is also freed. But the struggle rages on between the Palestinians and other Muslim nations and Israel for this little piece of real estate.

Here is a graph of what the Arabs own to what the Israelis have.

Country	Area (sq km)	Israel
Sudan	2,505,810	
Algeria	2,381,740	
Saudi Arabia	1,960,582	
Libya	1,759,540	
Egypt	1,001,450	
Yemen	547,030	
Morocco	446,550	
Iraq	437,072	
Oman	212,460	
Syria	185,180	
Tunisia	163,610	
Jordan	92,300	
United Arab Emirates	82,880	
Kuwait	17,820	
Qatar	11,437	
Lebanon	10,400	
Total	11,805,461 (sq km)	20,770 (sq km)

The figures are staggering **11.8 million** Sq KM to **20.7 thousand** SQ KM and of course the Arabs have plenty of oil and money to accommodate a million Palestinians refugees. But they will not do this. If you travelled in a plane from Mauritania to UAE, it takes almost eight hours of flight time. This is how big a land- mass that is occupied by the Arabs. The Arabs own 650 times more land mass then the Israelites. This is the reality that many do not realize. When we come to GDP the Arab GDP is $3700 verses Israel's of $18000; the Arabs have an amazingly low GDP. The education rates in the Middle Eastern Islamic nations are appalling to say the least.

The Arabs today and in the past are using the Palestinian Arabs as pawns for their game of cat and mouse to bring down Israel. The Elohim of Israel says that He will bring judgement to those nations that will divide the land of Israel. So who are those nations?

Sure the west is certainly not helping, because they are giving Israel their marching orders, commanding them to make peace and give land to the Palestinian Authority. But who is really being judged other then the western nations, because the problem is not just the western nations, but in reality the Islamic nations are the problem.

Joel 3:12 "Let the nations be wakened, and come up to the Valley of Jehoshaphat; for there I will sit to **JUDGE ALL THE SURROUNDING NATIONS.**

So from the above verses, the judgement is clearly on the "**surrounding nations,**" which means judgement on the Islamic nations in the correct biblical context.

Isaiah 28:14-15 (14) Therefore hear the **word of the Master,** you scornful men, **who rule this people who are in Jerusalem,** (15) because you have said, "**We have made a covenant with death,** and with **Sheol we are in agreement. When the overflowing scourge passes through, it will not come to us, for**

we have made lies our refuge, and under falsehood we have hidden ourselves."

The core problem is with Israel's leadership that is corrupt and willing to sacrifice Jewish lives in order to appease the Edomites (Jordanians) and the Ishmaelites (Arabs) and of course the rest of the world, who are quite happy to let terrorism win by letting them have the land of Israel.

The problem with the west is they rely on Arab oil and have extensive business contracts with the Arab nations. So in order to accommodate they try to lean to a certain direction in favour of the Arab nations and thus they do not give Israel the same leverage that they tend to give to their Arab counterparts. The other problem is that in Europe during the 12th to the 18th century, the Jews were severely persecuted and they escaped to Muslim lands for safety. There they lived in safety, as long as they held to the Dhimma laws, where both the Jews and Christians were nothing more than second-class citizens. Today the Jews have a little piece of land they can call home and we all want to divide it in pieces. Very sad indeed.

So what is the fault of the Western world?

Could it possibly be appeasement of the radical elements?

The west's weak response and lack of a firm stand against radical Islamic elements along with our governments collusion with the Arabs, is due to their rich monopolies of oil for the sake of profit.

The Book of Revelation puts it like this.

> **Revelation 18:3** "For all the nations have drunk of the wine of the wrath of her fornication, **the kings of the earth have committed fornication with her**, and the merchants of the earth have become rich through the **abundance of her luxury**."

It is pretty clear that Israel will be divided; she has already been divided, while the communities of Yesha (Judea and Samaria) are being asked to be uprooted. The people have been told in no uncertain terms to get ready to get out, or be expelled forcefully. Gaza residents have been evacuated and Gaza has been handed over to the PA authority.

Someone has to fulfil YHWH's plan and Mr. Bush is it with Ariel Sharon.

So this means YHWH will not only judge the western nations who want to divide Israel, but also Israel's own corrupt leadership and those people who think giving land for peace will help in their cause.

Gaza belongs to the tribe of Judah, but is claimed by the Palestinians as their own when they <u>never</u> even lived there in the distant past.

> **Judges 1:18** Also **Judah took Gaza with its territory**, Ashkelon with its territory, and Ekron with its territory.

118

YHWH through the prophet Joel refers to all of Israel as "**My people**" and those who try to divide it will suffer. He does indeed give us the reasons and the real people behind the division also.

> **Joel 3:6** Also the people of Judah and the people of Jerusalem. You have sold to the **Greeks [Yavanee]**, that you may remove them far from their borders.

"You have sold people of Judah and people of Jerusalem" to the Greeks. The word used here for the "Greeks" is "Yavanee" and is not the same Greece we know of today. These "Yavanees" are the landmass of western Turkey according to the historian Josephus. So who is selling to whom?

The western alliance in collusion with Israel's leadership is giving the land away and trying to remove Judah from its border, in favour of the Muslim people, because Yavanee refers to the Islamic Empire not Greece. The theologians need to get their theology right and the Christians need to stop jumping on the bandwagon of the "judgment on America" crowd! If no one divides Israel, then who will fulfil Yahweh's plan? President Bush is only doing what YHWH intends him to do and the real dividers are the Islamic nations not the western. This is where common sense needs to prevail, seeing that this is meant to happen.

> **Joel 3:7** "Behold, **I will raise them out of the place to which you have sold them**, and will return your retaliation upon your own head.

Notice YHWH is going to raise Judah out of the place where they were sold and the retaliation will be returned to those who enacted the division. This should force us to re-examine our actions.

There are two elements to this problem of hatred between the Islamic nations and Israel.

1. Spiritual

2. Physical but more spiritual.

Let us look at the pages of Genesis to see where it all started:

When Adam and Eve fell they were given a very particular prophecy:

The Bible tells us in **Genesis 3:15**: And I will put enmity between **you** and the woman, and between **your seed** and her **Seed**; *(Zerah)* He shall crush *shuwph* your head (*ro'sh*), And you shall bruise His heel `aqeb."

Who is the "you" in **Genesis 3:15** – s.a.tan? "Your seed" is not only s.a.tan, but his followers also.

"Her seed" is pointing to the virgin birth of the Messiah and the collective group who are the ancestors of Yahushua, or his physical brethren who are the Jews, including the spiritual brethren e.g. gentile believers in Yahushua. s.a.tan cannot exactly persecute

119

Yahushua in heaven, but can bring problems in the life of believers on earth. In fact in front of Yahushua he is powerless.

The source of the <u>seed</u> is normally the man and not the woman. Therefore, this includes all of the physical brethren the Jews and the grafted in brethren who are the latter day gentiles (lost house of Israel). In Gen. 3:15, the word *seed* Hebrew *"zerah"* is singular, referring to Yahushua Himself, but its implication is both singular as well as a group of people. The Jews who are Yahushua's brothers are not all saved. They are simply the descendants of Abraham, Isaac and Jacob, just like Yahushua the Messiah, and thus part of the same group.

Paul also tells us the same thing in Romans chapter **16:20** that YHWH Elohim of Peace/Shalom, will "crush" s.a.tan. The Greek word used here is *"soon-tree-bo,"* which means literally "to crush."

The Hebrew word *"shuwph"* not only means to bruise, but also to "crush." Yahushua will crush s.a.tan, (the Hebrew word *shuwph* is used) and he [s.a.tan] will injure Yahushua, i.e. the sacrifice on the cross.

Is this tenable? Not quite. Can s.a.tan injure/crush Yahushua by killing Him, or crushing Him, because the same word **shuwph** is used for s.a.tan's acts towards Yahushua? Theologically and physically not so. s.a.tan a created being cannot injure the uncreated YHWH. In Aramaic *"the Memra"* (Active word), the Master Yahushua the Messiah Himself laid down His own life (**John 10:15**) without anyone forcing Him to do so. In my opinion what this text is saying is that s.a.tan and his followers will war with Yahushua's followers. Yahushua had no physical descendants (offspring), therefore His spiritual descendants (believers) and His physical brethren the Jews remain his target. s.a.tan cannot war against Yahushua and win, but he can try and war against Yahushua's followers and His physical brethren. s.a.tan can also sets up obstacles and doubts for believers in Yahushua, which he often does. s.a.tan can use his army to kill the physical brethren and the spiritual descendants literally by violence through other people.

YHWH is teaching something very significant in this as a future prophecy.

Let's take another look: [26]

<u>And I will put</u>	PHR.	[07896]	shiyth	TENSE
<u>enmity</u>		[0342]	'eybah	
<u>between thee ar d the woman</u>,	PHR.	[0802]	'ishshah	
<u>and between thy seed</u>	PHR.	[02233]	zera`	

---

[26] http://www.blueletterbible.org/kjv/Gen/Gen003.html#15

and her seed;	`PHR.`	[02233]	זֶרַע zera`	
it shall *bruise*	`PHR.`	[07779]	שׁוּף shuwph	`TENSE`
thy head,	`PHR.`	[07218]	רֹאשׁ ro'sh	
and thou shalt *bruise*	`PHR.`	[07779]	שׁוּף shuwph	`TENSE`
his heel.	`PHR.`	[06119]	עָקֵב `aqeb	

Genesis 3:15 And I will put enmity between <u>thee</u> and <u>the woman</u>, and between <u>thy seed</u> and <u>her seed</u>; it shall bruise <u>thy head</u>, ro'sh and thou shalt bruise **his heel/his Jacob**.

The traditional meaning accepted by all for **Genesis 3:15** is that this is for Yahushua dying on the cross i.e. physical suffering and He crushes s.a.tan. Now let me set forth another explanation to better understand this text, which may show us things we did not realize before.

First we must understand that s.a.tan is a spirit being, and so spirits cannot be killed, but only restrained. Have you ever wondered why the angels that rebelled against YHWH were bound in chains and <u>not</u> killed instantly? Because these are spirit beings that YHWH has created first in the order of creation, and when their time is up, they will be put in the Lake of Fire to suffer **eternal torment.** They will not perish out of existence, as some might believe. The same way YHWH has created humans and put His spirit in the human beings, this makes human souls potentially eternal, i.e. the physical body is nothing but dust. The spirit being i.e. soul of man/woman is not perishable. That is why the ones who disobey will go to eternal fire permanently and will not perish, but suffer eternal torment e.g. some believe that the sense of phasing out like a kind of battery discharging is not true.

We must realize that YHWH is eternal and when He creates a soul He has put something in the created human being of Himself and man cannot perish, or be destroyed. That is why we cannot have annihilation, but eternal torment for those that choose to disobey. Understand that the Anti-Messiah is going to be powered by s.a.tan he will need to control someone in order to act out his evil will on the people of the earth. The Muslims have accepted him who we know is s.a.tan disguised as Allah, though they do not truly know that they are following the one who deceives them. But if you try to tell a Muslim that this is the case, they are very hard hearted and very few will listen to you. This is why in order to redeem Muslims <u>prayer</u> is essential alongside common sense, because these spirits that are deceiving billions of Muslims are susceptible to prayer. Now since these Muslims have become s.a.tan's prime tools let us see how he intends to use them.

In my humble opinion this is how I would translate **Genesis 3:15**.

Genesis 3:15 And I will put enmity [**bloodshed and violence**] between you [**s.a.tan and his followers**] and the woman, [**figurative Messiah born by the virgin birth and His followers plus the physical descendents the Jews, that includes unbelieving Jews**], and between your seed [**s.a.tan's followers**

Islamic hatred against Jews and Christians through violence and bloodshed] and her Seed [Yahushua's followers]. He shall bruise your head, [Yahushua will crush s.a.tan and subdue him ready for the lake of sulphur] and you shall bruise His heel [s.a.tan and his cohorts will kill Yahushua's followers e.g. both spiritual and physical descendants through warfare and bloodshed]." (My comments are in bold)

The Hebrew word for "heel" **Akeb** is used in the sense of **an army lead by a commander**, i.e. Yahushua is leading the army of believers against s.a.tan's kingdom. The seed is used as a singular (Messiah) and also as a group when applied to the **nation of Israel**, since when we accept Yahushua as the Messiah, we become part of this nation/seed. Therefore, we are **grafted in** gentiles, after we accept Yahushua's offer of salvation (**Genesis 22:18** and **Galatians 3:18**).

Note: All four uses of the Hebrew word "*eybah*" [enmity] outside <u>Genesis 3:15</u> are **all associated with bloodshed**; YHWH was telling us what is to come and how to recognize it, what the Islamists do today was prophesied more than 3,400 years ago in the 3rd chapter of Genesis.

Uses of the word "*Eybah*"; <u>Numbers 35:21</u>, <u>Numbers 35:22</u> and <u>Ezekiel 25:15</u>

If s.a.tan had been crushed as the Hebrew word "*shuwph*" suggests simply by Yahushua's death on the cross, then why is he still alive and killing Christians and Jews today? If that is what Christians believe happened on the cross, then s.a.tan should have been finished long ago. But s.a.tan is pretty much alive and kicking today, deceiving the nations, so that the **crushing** is yet future at the return of Yahushua of Nazareth.

The two-part answer lies in this prophecy. Yahushua defeated s.a.tan's master <u>plan</u> of taking people to hell by sacrificing Himself on the cross by His shed blood. But his (s.a.tan's) physical crushing (**shuwph**) is yet future, including the crushing of his kingdom [his followers including both humans and angels] upon Yahushua's return. This is what the Master was trying to show us all along in Genesis. The real beef is here today building for the last 1,400 years and it is radical Islam that is truly showing the spirit of s.a.tan.

He that hath understanding let him understand!

<u>Psalm 49:3</u> My mouth shall speak wisdom, and the meditation of my heart shall bring understanding.

Remember the battle centres around Jerusalem, that the Muslims claim Jerusalem as their own? Have you ever wondered why Jerusalem is never ever mentioned in the Qur'an and yet the Muslims claim ownership?

B.   The battle for Jerusalem, the Law shall go forth from Zion?

History lesson for the battle of Jerusalem

<u>Genesis 2:8</u> The Master YHWH planted a garden **eastward in Eden**, and there He put the man whom He had formed.

122

It is a well-established fact through ancient inscriptions and tablets that the area of Iraq is the cradle of civilization that runs along the Euphrates and Tigris Rivers into the Nile River in Egypt. Iraq is central to the fact that ALL false religions were birthed there. Let me now explain the significance of Jerusalem and why we have the Islamic kingdom fighting to take over the whole area. It is believed by Jewish traditions and the Bible validates it as well, that Jerusalem is the **centre of the world**. Aerial and satellite pictures have been taken of Jerusalem and if you measure all four uttermost parts of the world from Jerusalem you will find Jerusalem is at the **"centre of the world."** Next, it is believed by Jewish tradition that the **Garden of Eden** was in Jerusalem and the **Temple Mount** is the **very place** where the **tree of life** was located. Even the Bible is a witness to this, that Jerusalem is the centre of the world.

Ezekiel 5:5 "Thus says the Master YHWH: "This is Jerusalem; I have set her in the **midst (tokh) of the nations** and the countries all around her."

The word "tokh" for "midst" can more correctly be referred to as the centre of a place. Yahushua confirms He will dwell in the middle, or centre of the world and that is Jerusalem, right at the Temple-Mount in the 3rd Temple.

Zechariah 2:10 "Sing and rejoice, O daughter of Zion! For behold, I am coming and I will **dwell in your midst**," says the Master.

Scholars say that the garden that the Master planted in the east can refer to the Middle East. The true Temple Mount was about 26 acres and today it is slightly larger. Elohim's name is YHWH in Hebrew and numerically it is equivalent to 26. YHWH said I am going to put **My NAME** there on the Temple Mount. YHWH literally has His "NAME" there. Old Egyptian stories talk about this garden in the land of Canaan (Israel). It was believed in tradition and also by the "church fathers" that YHWH put His **foundation** stone on the Temple Mount. The Jews, in Hebrew, refer to the bedrock on the Temple Mount as **"Even He-Shetivah,"** which means "the foundation stone." This spot is believed to be Solomon and Zerubbabel's Temple. The Muslims refer to this place in Arabic as **"Kubbat es-Sakhra,"** which means **"Stone of Foundation."** There is inscribed on the western side of the Dome of the Rock, **"The Rock of the Temple from the Garden of Eden."** This is why it is also believed by Jews that Adam was created here and this is the exact spot where YHWH created the "foundation of the world," as mentioned by Isaiah the prophet who writes about this.

Isaiah 28:16 Therefore thus saith the Master YHWH, **Behold I lay in Zion** for a **foundation a stone**, a **tried stone**, a **precious corner stone**, a **sure foundation**; he that believeth shall not make haste.

Christians believe this refers to Yahushua Messiah but actually not only does this refers symbolically to Yahushua the Messiah, but literally it is the place of Mount Moriah, where the first man Adam was created and fell into sin according to Jewish traditions.

The English word for "lay" is the Hebrew word "yasad" which means to "appoint" and to "establish." Yahushua was "appointed" and "established" for His mission and this place of the Temple Mount was also "appointed" for these things to happen.

The Hebrew word for "precious" **"yakar"** means "excellent," "costly," "honourable"; these are all terms applied to the Messiah of Israel.

Genesis 28:10-12 And Jacob went out from <u>Beersheba</u>, [Israel] and went toward **Haran**. [a place in Iraq] (11) And he lighted upon a **certain place**, [Temple Mount] and tarried there all night, because the sun was set; and he took of the stones of that place, and put *them for* his **pillows**, and lay down in that place to sleep. (12) And he dreamed, and **behold a ladder set up on the earth**, and the top of it reached to heaven: and behold the **angels of YHWH ascending and descending on it**.

17 And he was afraid, and said, How dreadful *is* <u>this place</u> Ha-Maqowm! This *is* none other but the **house of YHWH**, and this is the "<u>gate of heaven</u>."

Where was Jacob going? Iraq. Where did Jacob stay? The Hebrew word for "a place" is "**Ha Maqowm**" which is recognized as another name for YHWH by the Rabbis.

Exodus 3:5 Then He said, "Do not draw near this place. Take your sandals off your feet, for **THE PLACE [Ha-Maqowm]** where you stand is **holy ground**."

This is why the Rabbis recognize "**Ha-Maqowm**" to be another name for YHWH, because this is where YHWH met with Moses, or better this place is the "**throne of Yahweh**."

Jeremiah 17:12 A glorious high throne from the beginning is **the place [Ha-Maqowm]** of our sanctuary

This is the place of Yahweh's throne.

Genesis 22:9 Then they came to "the place" (Ha-Maqowm) of which YHWH had told him. And Abraham **built an altar** there and placed the wood in order; and he **bound Isaac his son** and laid him on the altar, upon the wood.

Abraham was also privy to this place, "**Ha-Maqowm**."

Where was Jacob resting at night? **The Temple Mount!**

17 And he was afraid, and said, How dreadful *is* **this place**! This *is* none other but the **house of YHWH**, (Beyt-Elohim) and this is the "**Gate of heaven**" (Shahar Shamayim).

Shahar Ha-Shamayim is another name for **Yahushua the Messiah** who is the **Gate of Heaven**.

Isaiah 14:12 How you are <u>fallen from heaven</u>, O Lucifer, son of the morning! [Hilal ben Shechar] How you are cut down to the ground, you who weakened the nations!

Hilal Ben Shachar = Son of perdition - refers to s.a.tan, and also a play on words, with Shahar and shachar. One being the **GATE of HEAVEN**-Yahushua the Messiah, and the other the **GATE of HELL**, being s.a.tan the deceiver.

Matthew 7:13 "Enter by the **narrow gate**; [Yahushua of Nazareth] for **wide is the gate (Shahar) and broad is the way** that leads to destruction, and there are many who go in by it.

Which GATE would you want to walk through?

This is why s.a.tan is fighting to keep the Temple Mount today. It was and is the literal place on earth for the "**House of Yahweh**," the place where **His NAME** is on the earth forever. Even today it exists there and is also referred to as the "**Gate of Heaven**."

1 Kings 5:5 "And behold, I propose to build a house for the name of the Master [Yahweh] my Elohim, as the Master spoke to my father David, saying, `Your son, whom I will set on **your throne** in **your place, he shall build the house for My name.**'

Back to King Solomon, It is estimated that the materials that King Solomon used to construct the Master's Temple on Mount Moriah were 100,000 talents of gold, one million talents of silver and the bronze was not measured, because an amount unable to be counted applies here. The estimated value of this material today would be around **32.5 billion pounds UK Sterling**. King Solomon employed 180,000 labourers for seven years to complete this delicate task.

1 Kings 6:38: So he was **seven years** in building it.

This is to give you an idea at not only how rich King Solomon was, but also his heart for the Elohim of Israel, leading him to spend that amount of money. This is incredible in itself. No man in history has spent so much money to build a "house for YHWH," with a desire like King Solomon had for YHWH that leaves most of us baffled at his love for Him. Businessmen today spend billons on projects that can return billions in profit. But they would be hesitant to spend money on something that would be returning nothing in monetary value. This is the difference between today's billionaires and yesterday's billionaire. King Solomon built his treasure in heaven. If you ask someone today to give a tithe to YHWH, they might cringe at the thought, thinking its something of an ancient age. Christians especially today need to examine themselves, because today it is the other way around. The ones who are following false gods give the most to build large mosques and Islamic centres, whereas Christians quarrel over whether they should pay tithes or not.

We spend lavishly on ourselves, but when it comes to doing anything for our mighty and precious Savoir Yahweh Elohim revealed in His Son Yahushua the Messiah of Israel who redeemed us, we flee at the thought of spending large amounts of money for Him. Yet we are quite content to go out and get that £30,000 Mercedes to show our neighbours and friends; look at me how good I look. Not that it is wrong to buy an expensive car, but we as believers need to weigh things in the balance between luxury and work for YHWH. I am sure someone with £30,000 could consider spending £20,000 on a car and spend £10,000 for YHWH, but this is hardly considered, or even heard of in our society.

Back to the Garden. The term in Hebrew is "*gan*" and "Eden" the name of the place. It is not the same as our meaning of a garden, like in an English orchard. The Hebrew word "gan," is a derivative of words like "ganaan," meaning to "defend" and this can appropriately mean a plot of land. When Adam was cast out, he was thrown out of the garden and if you remember from the account in Genesis, there were four rivers mentioned in Genesis chapter 2.

> **Genesis 2: 10-15** Now a river went out of Eden to water the garden, and from there it parted and became four riverheads. **(11)** The name of the first is **Pishon**; it is the one which skirts the whole **land of Havilah**, where there is gold. And the gold of that land is good. Bdellium and the onyx stone are there. **(13)** The name of the second river is **Gihon**; it is the one, which goes around the whole **land of Cush**. **(14)** The name of the third river is **Hiddekel**; it is the one, which goes toward the **east of Assyria**. The fourth river is the **Euphrates**. Then the Master YHWH took the man and put him in the **Garden of Eden** to tend and keep it.

The one river that passes Eden is underground and it then splits into four heads or four rivers. Ezekiel also talks about a river (**Ezekiel 47:5**) that will gush forth in the Millennium and water will come forth when Yahweh enlarges the Temple Mount during the earthquake that will take place (**Ezekiel 38:20**). This flood will happen in the not too distant future Daniel 9:26 *and the end thereof shall be with a flood.* The first river Pishon is believed to be a dried up river, seen by LANDSAT Satellite images to be under Saudi territory. The Saudis and Kuwaitis know this as the Wadi Riniah and the Wadi Batin. This is also the land mentioned as having good gold, which was still mined during the 1950s. The Bible also says this region was rich in bdellium, an aromatic gum resin that can still be found in north Arabia.

The **land of Havilah** is believed to be South-Western Arabia (Genesis 10:7, 25:18). The name of the second river is "Gihon," according to the Jewish historian Josephus Flavius this is the name that the ancients called it, but we do know the only River that passes Cush (Sudan) is the Nile River. So this is the same river that was called "Gi-haan" by the Ethiopians of old, confirmed by Josephus. The name of the third River is Hiddekel; this is the River Tigris today. Now do you see the link and why s.a.tan is using Saudi Arabia and Jerusalem as the two key places of attack by the Muslims? If you mark the boundaries of all these rivers and stretch the Garden of Eden to fit this boundary, it is measured in distance of 1500 square miles. If you then looked at Jerusalem it is the centre of this region. The Jews believed Jerusalem is the centre of the Garden of Eden long ago.

The Bible tells us in Genesis 2:9 that the tree of life was in the midst of the garden, the word for midst in Hebrew is *"tokh"* which can translate as in the middle of the garden. So we could say the "**tree of life**" is in the middle centre of the garden.

> **Zechariah 2:10** Sing and rejoice, O daughter of Zion: for, lo, I come, and I will dwell in the midst (tokh) of thee, saith the LORD.

Zechariah was not wrong when he said that Yahushua would come and dwell in the middle of Jerusalem i.e. right there in His 3rd Temple that is the middle of Jerusalem.

There is a water source under the Temple Mount and no one knows where it originates from, but there is a certain type of catfish, which is found in the Sea of Galilee. This catfish is only found in the Nile River and it is believed that the Nile River connects with the Sea of Galilee. The Jews in Galilee believed that the Nile River runs underneath the Sea of Galilee connecting to the streams under the Temple Mount. This is more likely the source of Ezekiel's river that will come forth in the Millennium to create the huge flood to drown the Anti-Messiah's army (**Daniel 9:26**).

Now let us presuppose when Adam sinned, he was cast out by the east entrance, and YHWH placed the cherub there to protect the "tree of life." Remember the beautiful **Eastern Gate** that was shut by the Turkish Muslim King to prevent the Messiah walking through the "Eastern Gate." Have you ever wondered why we never hear of the tree of "knowledge and good" again in the Bible? This is because after eating its fruit, man is the one reproducing this tree with his seed because its seed is in all men and all men die, because this tree was to cause death. Only the "**tree of life**" can give us that eternal life back that we lost in the garden. That today is through Yahushua the Messiah, if you accept Him and obey Him. Otherwise it's futile to do any other human endeavour to restore that broken relationship, because it will only lead to damnation and hell.

Revelation 22:14 Blessed are those who do His commandments, that they may have the **right to the tree of life**, and may **enter through the gates into the city**.

Who shut the gate?
The "Golden Gate" was located in the Eastern wall of Jerusalem. It was one of eleven entrances into the city. It was sealed up in the 16th century A.D. A little background on the Eastern Gate of Jerusalem. The Eastern Gate was walled up by **Suleiman** the Magnificent, the Muslim conqueror (the Ottoman Turks) in 1530 A.D.

The golden era of Islam that no one remembers

[27] **Suleiman I** (modern Turkish: *Süleyman*; Arabic: سليمان *Sulaymān*) (November 6, 1494 – 5/6 September 1566), known in Europe as *the Magnificent* and in the Islamic world as *the Lawgiver* (in Turkish *Kanuni*; Arabic: القانونى, *al-Qānūnī*), was the tenth Osmanli sultan of the Ottoman Empire, and its longest-serving, reigning from 1520 to 1566. Under his leadership, the Ottoman Empire reached its zenith and became a **world power**, and Suleiman was considered one of the preeminent rulers of 16th Century Europe, a respected rival to Charles V, Holy Roman Emperor, Francis I of France, Henry VIII of England, and Sigismund II of Poland.

He personally led Ottoman armies to conquer Belgrade, Rhodes, and most of Hungary, besieged Vienna and annexed huge territories of North Africa as far west as Morocco and most of the Middle East. Briefly, the Ottomans achieved naval dominance in the Mediterranean Sea, Red Sea, and Persian Gulf, and the empire continued to expand for a century after his death.

Within the empire, Suleiman was known as a fair ruler and opponent of corruption. He was a great patron of artists and philosophers, and was noted as one of the greatest Islamic poets, as well as an accomplished goldsmith. He earned his nickname *the Lawgiver* from his complete reconstruction of the Ottoman legal system.

---

[27] http://en.wikipedia.org/wiki/Suleiman_the_Magnificent

Notice it was King Solomon who built the first Temple so that the glory of Yahweh can enter in and another Turkish King called Suleiman (equivalent of Solomon) who shut the Eastern Gate, so that he could stop the glory of the Master from coming in.

There is also a cemetery that has been planted in front of the gate and many Jews and Christians want to be buried there, so when the Messiah returns they can be resurrected first. It is well established that the Turkish King knew through the rabbis that the Messiah of Israel was to walk through the Eastern Gate. So his answer was to shut the gate permanently so the Messiah cannot walk through it. In affect he was defying the Elohim of Israel. But in his ignorance he did not realize that the Messiah Yahushua (The Elohim of Israel) had already walked through it and the gate was to be sealed as a prophecy for that very reason. The prophet who foretold the sealing was Ezekiel around 600BC that it would be shut "because the LORD (Yahweh), the Elohim of Israel, hath entered in by it, therefore it shall be shut."

Ezekiel 44:1-2 Then he brought me back the way of the **gate of the outward sanctuary** which looketh **toward the east**; and it *was* shut. (2) Then said the LORD unto me; **This gate shall be shut, it shall not be opened, and no man shall enter in by it;** because the LORD, the Elohim of Israel, hath entered in by it, therefore it shall be shut.

The Muslim king in actual fact helped fulfil the prophecy of Ezekiel. Praise YHWH that every word in the Bible is true and trustworthy.

There used to be a causeway that led from the peak of the Mount of Olives to the Eastern Gate, which was used in the Temple times as a processional for the red heifer to the altar in the sanctuary.

This is the path that Adam probably would have taken to walk out onto the Mount of Olives descending into the Judean wilderness into the sea of death (the Dead Sea). This is where there is an old city called the "city of Adam" near Jericho (**Joshua 3:16**). Jericho happens to be the oldest city in the world. Jericho in Hebrew is *"Yericho,"* which literally means the "moon city." The temple of the moon god 'Sin' was in Jericho in the old days. This was the stronghold of Sin/Allah, the false god, and Yahweh broke this stronghold after six days and the walls came crumbling down on the seventh day. YHWH says He gave Israel "His rest," symbolizing eternal life for those that believe in Him. He gives them "His rest," His Shalom (peace, blessings, protection and eternal life). This also symbolizes the six thousand years of humanity, when once again the stronghold of Allah will be brought down and we will enter His rest for 1000 years of Shabbat.

When Adam sinned he descended below sea level and vacated that area. This is significant because of what happens when we sin. We also descend in typology and are separated from YHWH's life. The Dead Sea is characteristic of death and decay, and is believed to be a sort of residing place, a habitation of demons and evil spirits. This is the Judean wilderness where John the baptiser preached repentance and baptism. This is also where Yahushua was tempted by s.a.tan, and now you know why that is, because as I explained it is the residing place of demons.

The Mount of Olives has been a special place of interest. It is a mountain east of Jerusalem across the Kidron Valley. I believe this is the proper site of the crucifixion where the Roman centurion saw the **Temple veil rent in two** (**Matthew 27:51-54**). The sites that most people believe for the crucifixion of Messiah do not fit the pattern of the centurion being able to see the Temple veil rent in two. Those sites are too low in elevation against the Temple Mount in order to see the curtain veil tear apart. You cannot see the Temple veil rent from either of the two traditional sites, plus one couldn't see the veil from the west, behind the wall of the Holy of Holies. If you ever go to Israel you will understand what I am saying.

> **Matthew 27:51-54** (51) And behold, the **veil of the temple was torn in two from top to bottom**; and the earth quaked, and the rocks were split, (52) and **the graves were opened**; and many **bodies of the saints who had fallen asleep were raised**; (53) and **coming out of the graves after His resurrection**, they went into the **holy city and appeared to many**. (54) Now when the **centurion and those with him**, who were guarding Yahushua, **saw the earthquake and the things that had happened**, they feared greatly, saying, "**Truly this was the Son of YHWH!**"

It is reasonable to assume this because a blasphemer had to be put to death facing the holy of holies and this was the charge that the Jews brought against Yahushua. Therefore, Yahushua was hung on a tree in the garden of Gethsemane **facing the Temple Mount** also fulfilling the appropriate qualifications for the Lamb of YHWH. On this mountain summit in the village of Bethpage just to the west is a very old altar, the Miphkad altar, where the Sanhedrin would have executed judgement on Yahushua for blasphemy. Here the Red Heifer was burned so that its ashes could purify the Temple. Do you see the connection with the Messiah and the Red Heifer? The word *"Miphkad"* means "numbering" or "counting," (and in this case it meant counting the heads of persons who were Israelites, firstborn ones, Levites, or Priests) so this is known as the "numbering" altar, this place was also known as the Golgolet area. "Golgolet" means head. This is the place where people were numbered, or counted, so it is known as "Golgotha" because it is the proper place of crucifixion.

The Mount of Olives is also where it is believed Yahushua cursed the fig tree, wept over Jerusalem, and made His triumphal Palm Sunday entrance in to the city. It is the forbidden hillside facing Jerusalem where no one was allowed to dwell, but which had from ancient times been a cemetery and a place of gardens. Many Christians and Jews are buried in the cemetery of the Mount of Olives in expectation of the Messiah returning there (**Zechariah 14:4**) for judgement, so that these people may be raised first. Yahushua the Messiah prayed at Gethsemane and His sweat was like blood (**Luke 22:44**). Gethsemane means an oil press for olives. In Temple days, the olives were pressed once for holy oil and if more then once, then they would not be used for the Temple because this would reduce the purity of the oil. This is significant for what happened to Yahushua in the garden. He was pressed for the sins of mankind, and gave forth the pure holy blood of Yahushua our Messiah.

Yahushua the Messiah cursed the fig tree in the gospels. Scholars are perplexed as to why Yahushua cursed the fig tree. They come with all sorts of explanations. The reason is simple that it is believed in traditions that this fig tree is the same one that Adam and Eve took fig leaves from to cover themselves for the sin they had committed. Yahushua recognized this tree in order to curse it, or else there is no reason just to curse a tree.

Remember YHWH put Adam in the garden, and most translators say he was there to tend the garden. The Hebrew word used in **Genesis 2:15** *"nuach"* is not the same as the

129

Hebrew word used *in **verse 8 "soom"*** and it means to **give rest** and **safety, comfort and to be in fellowship with YHWH**. This is what YHWH wanted. A family in humanity to be in fellowship with our Creator. Adam was not there just to tend the garden, but to be in fellowship with Yahweh. The primary factor was holiness within YHWH's ordained limits and protections offered by Yahweh.

This shows us the significance of the Temple Mount. The Muslims, do not worship Yahweh but Allah, who already possess the Temple Mount today and are ready to kill to keep it for reasons that I have illustrated briefly. s.a.tan is out to get this area, thinking he can somehow defeat YHWH. s.a.tan's idea is to steal YHWH's throne on earth, just like he tried to do in heaven. But this plan will not succeed, because this place has been ordained to become Yahweh's throne on the earth once again.

Slaughter of the Jews around the four rivers and its significance!

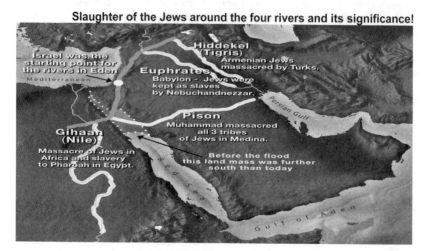

It should come as no surprise that rivers, or living water, are often symbolically used to denote YHWH's presence, or YHWH's redeeming work.

> **Jeremiah 2:13** "For My people have committed two evils: they have forsaken Me, **THE FOUNTAIN OF LIVING WATERS**, and hewn themselves cisterns, broken cisterns that can hold no water.
> **John 4:10** Yahushua answered and said to her, "If you knew the gift of YHWH, and who it is who says to you, `Give Me a drink,' you would have asked Him, **and He would have given you LIVING WATER**.

As you can see from the above picture of the four rivers that after the flood of Noah there is probably considerable land shifting that took place. These <u>four</u> rivers are significant historically because around these four rivers YHWH had His presence around the Hebrews, the nation of Israel in their times of distress. It's almost like He was feeding them and nurturing them. Let's look at what happened around these four rivers.

River Nile
The Hebrews were enslaved in Egypt and kept there under hard labour until YHWH raised up Moses and sent him to bring His people out of bondage.

River Hiddekel (Tigris)

Over 1.5 million Armenians were massacred here by the **Turks in 1915**. This is only ninety years ago. Some of your grandfathers will remember this event quite clearly because this is not so long ago. Who were the Armenians and also why the onslaught on the Bosnian Serbian people by the Turks and Muslims today?

1 Kings 14:15 "For the Master will strike Israel, as a reed is shaken in the water. He will uproot Israel from this **good land**, which He gave to their fathers, and **will scatter them beyond** the River [**Euphrates**], because they have made their wooden images, provoking the Master to anger.

In the Bible the Master gave a prophecy about the ten tribes being dispersed over the **Euphrates** because of their idolatry. That would mean these people would end up in Eastern Europe, Armenian regions, Yugoslavia and Bosnia. These people intermingled and became the Armenian Christians and Serbian people of today. The historian Josephus Flavius confirmed that parts of the ten tribes were driven to Armenia and also they were driven towards the east as far away as India and present day Pakistan. Again the River Tigris was a type of living water for the Hebrews, where YHWH nourished the children of Israel for a time.

River Euphrates
The 1st captivity of the Hebrews including Daniel the prophet were taken to Babylon around 604 BC (**Daniel 1:1-7**). The second captives taken around 597 BC (**2 Kings 24:12-14**), 3rd deportation of captives took place around about 581 BC (**Jeremiah 52:30**). The River Euphrates became a kind of symbolic picture of YHWH sustaining the Jews in Babylon.

River Pison
Muhammad forcefully removed ALL the three tribes of the Jews in Yathrib, or Medina that denotes a city, a name that is probably derived from the wealthy Jews that lived there.

All three tribes of the Jews were eliminated one by one.

Banu Qainuqa – Expelled.

Banu Nader – Expelled.

Banu Qurayza - All the men were beheaded, with women and children kept as booty.

In the battle of the Ditch (AD 627), Banu Qurayza was said to have sided with the Meccans against the Muslims, who were victorious (the Jews actually refused to help the Meccans because of what had happened to one of the other Jewish tribes, so this allegation is not true). As a result, the 400 to 600 hundred male Jews were beheaded, while their children and women became slaves of Muslims. The judgment was given by Sad, and Muhammad commended him for this judgment:

Here again took place the massacre of the Jews where there was a River representative of YHWH's sustenance for His people.

We also know about the holocaust that took place in Germany with six million Jews and five million Christians slaughtered by Hitler.

We know that the Messiah Yahushua is coming back to Jerusalem to save His people when they are besieged and being killed by the Muslim armies mentioned in Zechariah 12 and 14. Yahweh will establish His 3rd Temple in Jerusalem. That is extensively detailed in Ezekiel and that many people will stream to it to worship Yahushua, also mentioned by various prophets. So the Master is taking His people back to the "Garden of Eden," or Temple Mount area, where once again "the rivers of life" will flow. This is why these four rivers are significant in end-times eschatology. The river that will come out of the Temple Mount will give life to the Dead Sea.

> **Micah 4:2** Many **nations** shall come and say, **"Come, and let us go up to the mountain of the Master,** to the **house of the Elohim of Jacob;** He will teach us His ways,** and we shall walk in His paths. **For out of Zion the law shall go forth,** and **the word of the Master** from **Jerusalem."**

C.   Were the Philistines foreshadowing the Muslims to come?

The question could be why should Muslims <u>alone</u> fit this group of people?

Just like the Passover lamb was a foreshadowing of the Messiah, the ancient Philistines' hatred for the Hebrews was a foreshadowing of the real deal, which was and is **radical Islam today**. Fanatic Muslims today actively promote a global jihad policy both against the west for those that support the Jews e.g. the USA and against Israel. If you think the Philistines' were bad, or Hitler was bad, then you have seen nothing yet. The Islamists are even worse, and their violence is awful. The Philistines' killed the Jews, Hitler gassed them, but if you had seen the fate of the two soldiers in Ramallah, you would know that the fanatic Muslims literally **crushed** the soldiers (**Hebrew word is again shuwph, just like in Genesis 3:15. Yahweh's detail is 100% accurate**). They beat the Jews to a pulp and **ripped** their <u>brains out.</u> Some Muslims even bite the liver of their enemies literally as a sign of utter contempt. I am not going to put the pictures here, as they are too disturbing to show, but you can view them on many internet sites. Just type 'Ramallah soldiers lynching' in any web search engine.

This is what we are talking about here when we say they are a lot worse. In Syria as part of their training, the Muslims bite the cats and snakes' heads ripping them off the body to illustrate what they would do to their enemies the Jews. How many Germans in Hitler's army did their training this way? Muslim men in the past have captured Jewish people in the Palestinian territories and not only did they kill the Jews, but they literally removed the heart and/or liver from the body of the Jew. After having taken photographs of themselves with the organ(s), they tossed the organ(s) into a bag to proudly demonstrate what they do to their enemies.

Although this trait is part of the Arab culture, the contempt towards one's enemy is sometimes shown this way in extreme hostility. One case in point happened during the battle of Uhud in 625 AD, where Muhammad was fighting the Quraish: [28]

---

[28] http://ismaili.net/histoire/history03/history323.html

Among the slain, the **body of Hamza** was found **mutilated**, who had been **laid low by a spear thrust, which pierced him**. The fiend Hinda, **wife of Abu Sufian**, had cut open his body, and took a piece of his liver and gnawed it to quench her thirst for the vengeance of her father, Atba who was killed by Hamza in Badr. Because of this, **Muawiya, the son of Hinda was called the "son of the liver eater."**

Indeed, one could argue that this is a hard message to give. But this is the truth. And, we must be truthful with love. All those Muslims that **seek** the **Elohim of Israel** revealed in Yahushua of Nazareth will be **delivered** and saved upon repentance and acceptance of Yahushua the Messiah as their Savior after renouncing Islam. But all those that remain **obstinate** and **unrepentant** will be **marked for the wrath of Yahweh** and **will end up in hell permanently** for an **eternity that one cannot measure**, separated from the love of a holy YHWH to be under conscious torment in the lake of sulphur.

Ezekiel 35:5 Because **thou hast had a perpetual hatred**, and **hast shed the blood of the children of Israel** by the **force of the sword in the time of their calamity,** in the **time that their iniquity had an end.**

Revelation 9:11 And they had a **king over them, which is the angel of the bottomless pit**, whose name in the **Hebrew tongue is Abaddon,** but in the **Greek tongue hath his name as Apollyon.**

We can see that Allah is the only person that fits with **Revelation 9:11**, as the king over them [the Muslims] because he [Allah] does not value human life, beheading someone, cutting their hearts out are normal practices that radical Muslims do today. Allah asks his followers to sacrifice their sons for him in jihad. Allah has a trait of **pride** and we know that only s.a.tan has this attribute. We also know that s.a.tan has the attribute of having people killed in various deceptive ways. All these traits including the biblical Hebrew name "*Abaddon*" fits with Allah, considering the biggest clue to Allah's identity is in his 99 beautiful names that the Muslims will tell you about. The 62nd name of Allah in the Arabic language is **"the one who can destroy,"** or **"Al-Mumit."** One of Allah's other 99 beautiful names is "Al-Mutakbir," meaning "the proud one." This two attributes match exactly with s.a.tan, as described in **Revelation 9:11** as the **"destroyer"** who falls because of his **pride**.

Revelation 9:2 He opened the bottomless pit, and smoke went up out of the pit, like the smoke of a great furnace; and the sun and the air were darkened by the smoke of the pit.
This is also confirmed by **Isaiah 14:31**

"Howl, O gate; cry, O city; thou, whole **Palestina**, [art] **dissolved**: for there shall come from the **north a smoke**, and none [shall be] alone in his appointed times."

See here, "the north" is also confirmed by Isaiah, as well as this "smoke" which causes a regional catastrophe, in this instance in Isaiah the region of Israeli occupied regions by the Palestinians are hit with some type of warfare agents and are affected. Obviously, this "smoke" is symbolic of war and destruction caused by the Anti-Messiah. After all Abaddon/Apollyon in Revelation literally means The Destroyer and therefore his purpose is destruction. Have you not noticed the destruction that the fanatic Muslims bring when they invade or capture a region? Were not the Twin Towers in New York a sign of that destruction, or the Spanish train bombings, or the London bombs?

133

Why is the North Significant?

Biblically trouble comes from the North, but deliverance also comes from the North. Let me illustrate why s.a.tan and the **north** are significant.

s.a.tan attacks your mind. s.a.tan attacks the North **"the mind."** If he overcomes your mind, then that is it, game finished. Paul said to renew your mind (**Romans 12:2**), as he understood the battle is of the mind. Do you see how clever s.a.tan is with his tactics, as many people do not even know this yet? This is what is taking place in our societies.

What does the word s.a.tan mean? In **biblical Hebrew** it means **"To Divert!"**

Think about it; while most thought they had gotten the last world empire nailed down, they were wrong, because s.a.tan has diverted their attention to the wrong area, doing exactly what he is good at! To point you to Roman Catholicism, the USA, or the European Union, looking for the end time beast.

In Hebrew thinking, the NORTH is the area of the conscience and s.a.tan overpowers your conscience. This is even taught in the Bible. In **Isaiah 14:13-14** we are told a profound truth.

13. For thou hast said in thine heart, I will (1) ascend into heaven, I will (2) exalt my throne above the stars of YHWH: I will (3) sit also upon the mount of the congregation, in the sides of the north:
14. I will (4) ascend above the heights of the clouds; I will (5) be like the most High.

First there are the five "I wills." Here s.a.tan tries to be like YHWH by saying "I will." Where does he get this from and why the need for authority to be like YHWH? These are similar to when Yahweh made promises to Abraham where Yahweh also said "I will" five times in His promises to Abraham.

Yahweh spoke to Abraham and His five "I will's"

Genesis 12

(1) Now the Master had said to Abram: "Get out of your country, from your family and from your father's house, to a land that **I will (1)** show you. (2) **I will (2)** make you a great nation; **I will (3)** bless you and make your name great; and you shall be a blessing. (3) **I will (4)** bless those who bless you, and **I will (5)** curse him who curses you; and in you all the families of the earth shall be blessed."

Now we can clearly see here that s.a.tan wanted to have the same authority as Yahweh the Elohim of Abraham, Isaac and Jacob.

Tell me what happened to the **northern tribes** of Israel? They were scattered for disobedience. All invasions in Israel were also believed to have come from the north and the future anti-Messiah shall also take that route as well, since Ezekiel 38 confirms it.

Look at England; Islam has a stronghold in the north. Look at any nation and then look at its "north" region and you will find it spiritually lacking more so then the south. Look at the map of Israel and then look north what do you see on a world map?

134

The Middle East, Europe, Russia and Asia. What is the problem with these nations? The Middle East is into false monotheistic worship. Russia into atheism and communism. Europe into atheism and agnosticism. Asia Minor is also into false monotheistic worship. Hopefully, now you can see why s.a.tan attacks the "north," or your conscience, so that he may overcome it.

YHWH has allowed the Islamic nations to rise against Israel to show the Islamists who the true YHWH is. Also for the purpose of judgment and His severe wrath to be poured upon the Islamic nations that is written in the very first prophecy of the Bible and the prophets. This does not mean they are innocent in any way, but they are acting out their will in full to try and slaughter the children of Israel and kill and persecute Christians in the entire world which has been happening since Islam's inception. Islam has **never** been the **religion of peace** and never will be, because the very word **Islam** means submission. So it is every Christian's duty to bring the Good News of Yahushua to every Muslim, to try and save his or her soul for the glory of Yahweh.

D.   Ishmael - Abraham's First Son, or Is Isaac His <u>Only</u> Son?

Ishmael is Abraham's first son born through his Egyptian Slave Hagar. This is the first surrogate birth in the Bible, since Sarah could not conceive she gives Abraham her handmaid to have the conception though Ishmael. Ishmael could not claim a legitimate birthright (share in his estate), while Abraham's second son who was born through the legitimate wife Sarah had the birthright. Technically in the Torah the birthright means a <u>double</u> portion of a father's estate belonging to the eldest. In this case even though Ishmael is the eldest, because he is not from the natural wife, he cannot have this position. The Bible tells us that Abraham gave all he had to Isaac.

<u>Genesis 25:5</u> And Abraham gave ALL that he had to Isaac.

Ishmael had 12 sons; the Arabs are descendants of Ishmael. From Ishmael are descended the twelve tribes of the Arabs and from Jacob we get the twelve tribes of Israel.

This naturally leads to a grudge because Ishmael is seen as lesser, even though YHWH blessed him with much wealth and we can see his descendants are wealthy today and have plenty of oil and mineral wealth.

<u>Genesis 16:12</u> And he will be a <u>wild man</u>; his hand will be against every man, and every man's hand against him; and he shall dwell in the presence of all his brethren.

Ishmael is wild, rampant, cannot be in bondage to other men. The Assyrians, Medes, Persians and Romans, failed to tame his descendants. He is a hunter, and a wild man out of control, robbing and pillaging peoples and feeling he has a god given right to do so. This prophecy is literally true today, as the Arabs are involved in most of the world's conflicts and "his hand is against every man and every man's hand against him." The Muslims are involved in at least twenty-five out of the thirty ongoing conflicts in the world today indirectly funded by the Arabs.

The text in **Genesis 16** shows us that Ishmaelites [the Arabs] would be of a quarrelsome war like nature, wild, continually in hostility with their neighbors and in continuous defence of themselves. We see this prophecy literally fulfilled with Israel continually on the receiving end, trying to defend itself for its very survival. Now the west is beginning to realize the problems that Israel faces with the suicide bombings, because the suicide bombings have come to the west as I wrote back in 2003, when I predicted that they were coming to the UK also. Russia is already facing problems in Chechnya with suicide bombers and Iraq is seeing daily deaths as a result of actions by radical Muslims out to kill and destroy. Recently the riots in France that have continued for several days have been labelled by some as the intifada against France, where over 1,300 cars and several buildings have been burnt and many police injured. Which European city is next? Behind all of this violence are not simple demographics, poverty, or lack of opportunity as these do play a part, but more accurately and bluntly radical Islam is playing a major part. **But our politically correct news people and politicians cannot utter this truth due to the need for sensitivities.**

Let me tell you a golden truth that the poor people in Pakistan, India and China and that includes Muslims, do not go burning cars and buildings because of lack of opportunity. This rhetoric of poverty and depravation is a failure to recognize the underlying ideology that is at play here. The west does indeed need to deal with radical Islam, but in the meantime radical Islam is dealing with the west. Unless we are prepared to deal with radical Muslims and so-called terrorists, we will continue to suffer. When my family left India in 1947 and became homeless and penniless from a rich estate to nothing, my father and many other Muslims with him did not go rampaging and burning cars to show their discontent. So this nonsense needs to stop that poverty causes people to do these things.

In fact the poor people are the least likely people to do this, as they know that they have families struggling and if just one person in that family, who usually is the breadwinner, is incarcerated it does not help in the poverty cycle. Poor people simply need opportunity to develop themselves and only ask for a fair shot at life. This also shows many Muslims are not rioters and do respect limits and have been brought up respectably to obey the law. But when it comes to obeying the Qur'an and its decrees, then the lines become very blurred, because some Muslims follow it to the letter, while others do not. The ones who do follow it literally have enacted things against humanity i.e. bombings, suicide bombers etc. But we have to remember they are trying to be good Muslims, and unless the Muslim authorities can reform the Qur'an, the problem is difficult to resolve. The top Islamic universities like Al-Azhar in Egypt have qualified suicide bombings as appropriate in order to defeat the enemy who does not bow to Islam. So how is it possible that peace could ever be achieved between Muslim and non-Muslim nations?

The French have been here before and this is not new but old hat. Maybe they have forgotten their hero Charles in the year 732 AD during October. This is when Islam was on the march to conquer Europe and in October 732, the Moorish general Abdul Rahman and his army were within the reach of both Paris and England, if they had defeated the Frankish forces at St. Martin of Tours. Now you remember the battle of Tours or Poitiers. Here is where radical Islam put itself to the test against the Frankish forces and unlike Spain and other places, this force not only held its ground but also gave the Islamic army a humiliating defeat. They killed its commander Abdul Rahman and routed the army back to where it came from, never to return again.

Abdul Rahman led an infantry of 60,000 to 400,000 soldiers across the western Pyrenees toward the Loire River. They were met outside the city of Tours by Charles Martel, known as the Hammer and his much smaller force of around 15–75,000 men. [29]

Martel gathered his forces directly in the path of the oncoming Muslim army and prepared to defend themselves by using a phalanx style of combat. The invading Moslems rushed forward, relying on the slashing tactics and overwhelming number of horsemen that had brought them victories in the past. However, the French army, composed of foot soldiers armed only with swords, shields, axes, javelins, and daggers, was well trained. Despite the effectiveness of the Muslim army in previous battles, the terrain caused them a disadvantage. Their strength lied within their cavalry, armed with large swords and lances, which along with their baggage mules limited their mobility. The French army displayed great ardency in withstanding the ferocious attack. It was one of the rare times in the Middle Ages when infantry held its ground against a mounted attack. The exact length of the battle is undetermined. Arab sources claim that it was a two-day battle, whereas Christian sources hold that the fighting clamoured on for seven days. In either case, the battle ended when the French captured and killed Abd-er Rahman. The Muslim army withdrew peacefully overnight and even though Martel expected a surprise retaliation there was none. For the Moslems, the death of their leader caused a sharp setback and they had no choice but to retreat back across the Pyrenees, never to return again.

Whether we like it or not radical Islam is delivering blows to Europe and it is beginning to hurt. YHWH has allowed this judgement to come upon us due to our own lacklustre attitudes and lack of respect and zeal for YHWH and the intentional removal of YHWH from our society. The bottom line is this for Europe; repent and return to your first love, to the Master Yahushua the Messiah and stop appeasing radical Islam. Unless we are willing to defeat this aggression, we can fall and so some hard choices have to be made in order to defeat this ideology and survive.

Rabbi Onkelos calls Ishmael and his progeny, a WILD ASS among men.

Continually engaged in fighting with his neighbors, they with him in their own defence. And as such the Arabs his posterity always have been, and still are, given to raping and plunder, harassing their neighbors by continual excursions and robberies, and pillaging passengers of all nations, which they think they have a right to do; their father Ishmael being turned out into the plains and deserts.

The Arabs are **wild and fierce...** Muhammad built the religion of Islam through the power of the sword.

Sura 22:39 To those against whom war is made, permission is given (to fight), because they are wronged; - and verily, god is most powerful for their aid;

---

[29] A Dictionary of Battles, Eggenberger, David. Thomas Y. Crowell Company, 1967

[28] Battlefields of Europe, Edited by David Chandler. Hugh Evelyn Ltd,1965

Early Muslims were weak and only fought if they had to, until Muhammad migrated to Medina and built a small army of followers, who then started to rob and pillage wealthy Quraish caravans to quickly build up their wealth. The first raid is a well-remembered one that took place in Nakhla, where Muhammad's followers murdered the leader of the caravan taking the cargo for themselves. This became a regular pastime for Muslim bandidoes, who gave Muhammad 20% of the booty from each raid. This is recorded in the authentic biography of Muhammad by Ibn Ishaq.

Raid on Nakhla account in The Life of Muhammad by Ibn Ishaq by A. Guillaume Pgs. 286-287

The apostle sent Abdullah b. Jahsh, Ri'ab al-Asadi in Rajab on his return from the first badr. He sent with him eight emigrants without any of the ansar. He wrote for him a letter, and ordered him not to look at it until he had journeyed for two days, and to do what he was ordered to do, but not to put pressure on any of his companions. When Abdullah had travelled for two days he opened the letter looked into it, and this is what it said; 'When you have read this letter of mine proceed until you reach Nakhla between Mecca and Al-Taif, lie in wait there for Quraysh and find out for us what they are doing.

Having read the letter he said to hear is to obey. A caravan of Quraysh carrying dry raisins and leather and other merchandise of Quraysh passed by them, Amr b. Al-Hadrami (349), Uthman b. Abdullah b. Al-Mughira and his brother Naufal the Makhzumites, and Al-Hakam b. Kaysan, freedman of Hisham b. al-Mughira being among them. Then the caravan saw them they were afraid of them because they had camped near them. Ukkasha who had shaved his head, looked down on them and they saw him and felt safe, they are pilgrims, you have nothing to fear from them. The raiders took council amongst themselves, for this was the last day of Rajab, and they said, 'if you leave them alone tonight they will get into the sacred area and will be safe from you; and if you kill them, you will kill them in the sacred month,' so they were hesitant and feared to attack them. Then they encouraged each other, and decided to kill as many as they could of them and take what they have. Waqid shot 'Amr b. al-Hadrami with an arrow and killed him, and 'Uthman and Al-Hakam surrendered. Naufal escaped and eluded them. Abdullah and his companions took the caravan and the two prisoners and came to Medina with them. One of Abdullah's family mentioned that he said to his companions, 'A fifth of what we have belongs to the apostle.'

The following points are brought out.

❖   The Muslims pretended to be pilgrims.

❖   The Muslims tricked the Quraish into thinking they are religious.

❖   The Muslims attacked during a sacred month when it was forbidden to fight.

❖   Muhammad told them to only open the letter near the time for fear of dissension.

❖ This is exactly how the radical Muslims (aka Al-Qaeda and Co.) are avoiding authorities today. They are not told about missions until a couple of days before they happen. That way they do not know anything to gossip around, or if any get caught to confess about. Personally I believe this move by Muhammad was very smart.

Remember the Muslim nations attacked Israel during The Yom Kippur war while the Jews were fasting on their high holy day; this is a typical Islamic style of attack to hit their enemy while they are resting, or in prayer. Also you may not know that the Jews of Quraiza were attacked on a Sabbath, a holy day for the Jewish rest. The Muslims usually killed their own leaders while they were praying by stabbing them in the back or poisoning them.

Muslims quote this verse in complete contradiction, to allegedly say we do not want to argue with you. **Sura 109** "To you be your Way, and to me mine."

The actual verses are nothing to do with peace or separateness.

> **Sura 109:1-6** In the name of Allah, Most Gracious, Most Merciful, Say O ye that reject Faith! I worship not that which ye worship, nor will ye worship that which I worship. And I will not worship that which ye have been wont to worship, nor will ye worship that which I worship. **To you be your Way, and to me mine.**

The context determines the verse and it has nothing to do with peace. This Sura has to do with a dispute between the pagan Meccans and Muslims, and the Muslims simply rejected the pagans.

Syed Abu-Ala' Maududi gives a commentary on this verse and has this to say;

Syed Abu-Ala' Maududi, Chapter Introductions to the Qur'an.

> If the Surah is read with this background in mind, one finds that it was not revealed to preach **religious tolerance,** as some people of today seem to think. It was revealed in order to exonerate the Muslims from the **disbelievers religion**, their rites of worship, and their gods, and to express their total disgust and unconcern with them and to tell them that Islam and kufr (unbelief) had nothing in common and there was no possibility of their being **combined and mixed into one entity**. Although it was addressed in the beginning to the disbelieving Quraish in response to their proposals of compromise, yet it is not confined to them only, but having made it a part of the Qur'an, Allah gave the Muslims the eternal teaching that they should exonerate themselves by word and deed from the **creed of kufr** (oaths of unbelievers) wherever and in whatever form it be, and should declare without any reservation that they cannot make any compromise with the disbelievers in the matter of faith. (Emphasis mine)

In the early days of Islam in Mecca, the words were of peace and not confrontation: "there is no compulsion in Islam" (**Sura 2:256a**). This was a way of avoiding a fight. But later in Medina when Muhammad became stronger with his new followers, then it was no more appeasement and the local Arabs rallied to the war cry of **Allah hu Akbar** (Allah is great) with swords in their hands. All **earlier** peaceful Suras in the Qur'an were **abrogated** and replaced with newer ones to equip the Muslims to wage war on the infidels without feeling guilty about it. This continues to be a key principle of Islam!

Blaise Pascal had this to say about religious evil.
"Men never do evil so completely and cheerfully as when they do it from a **religious** conviction."

This is so true with Islam today. This can be seen all over the world with fanatic Muslims chanting the war cry of 'Allah hu Akbar,' blowing up bombs, shooting down planes, cutting people's throats and beheading them in the name of Allah. This is the biblical predicted **REVIVAL OF FANATIC ISLAM,** or **Revival of Global Jihad.** See it and recognize it if you have the eyes and ears to perceive it.

Revelation 13:11-15 Then I saw **another beast** coming up **out of the earth**, and he had **two horns like a lamb** and spoke like a dragon (12a) And he exercises all the authority of the **first** beast (15) He was granted power to give **breath to the image of the beast**, that the **image of the beast** should **both speak and cause as many as would not worship the image of the beast to be killed**.

Points to note:

❖ **Another beast** - Revival of radical Islamic religion/jihad.

❖ **Two horns** - Appears to offer salvation like the Messiah, but deceives instead; the two horns are probably Sunni plus Shiites the two major sects of Islam.

❖ **Has authority of the 1st beast** - The 7th King was the Islamic invasion.

❖ **Give breath to the image of the beast** – He will bring true global jihad/revival of Islamic countries.

❖ **Image of the beast should both speak** – The Muslim Empire will force people to convert or be killed.

Revelation 13:1 Then I stood on the **SAND OF THE SEA**. And I saw a beast rising up out of the **SEA**, having **seven heads** and **ten horns**, and on his horns ten crowns, and on his heads a blasphemous name.

Notice a few important points:

Context determines the passage.

❖ John is standing in the Middle East Desert near a Sea (Revelation 13:1).

❖ The 1st BEAST is rising out of the SAND OF THE SEA (reference to the sea or beach). This is NOT Europe. Can anyone deny that Saudi Arabia is a large Desert surrounded by literal seas?

❖ It immediately shows us that it literally rises out of the SEA. Saudi Arabia is surrounded by many oceans. Sea can be symbolic for different peoples and nations also, but the context here is "sand of the sea" i.e. sand, beach and water. Saudi Arabia is a much better fit then Rome.

❖ The 1st Beast has a blasphemous NAME. Could this be Islam and Submission to Allah? Most definitely that is what is taught here.

❖ The 2nd BEAST is REVIVED out of the earth, though we are not given exactly where, or which part of the earth. But the context is not only Saudi Arabia because Ha Eretz can be applied to the whole earth, or to single countries. It is Saudi Arabia that is reviving the 1st beast that was wounded and the 2nd Beast has the same authority of the first beast. In fact, when YHWH is telling us here the whole action is in the Middle East. Saudi Arabia has been spending billions of dollars for the last fifty years to revive true Islam globally and now we know they have succeeded to a large degree because we have an established critical mass of radical Islam in every country of the world.

❖ *Revelation 13:12 And he exercises all the authority of the first beast in his presence, and causes the earth and those who dwell in it to worship the first beast, whose deadly wound was healed.* The Bible tells us that the revival of Islam will succeed and the Islamists will be causing the people to worship the 1st beast and if you do not then you are to be executed.

Revelation 17:3 So he carried me away in the Spirit into the **wilderness** (desert). And I **saw a woman sitting on a scarlet beast**, which was full of names of blasphemy, having seven heads and ten horns. (Why would YHWH carry John to the desert if this were Rome, or the USA?)

Let me prove the point. In the above it can be seen that John was carried away in the **Spirit to the desert**. The Greek word used here is "eremos," meaning a **desert** and this is the clue that rules all European theories out. He saw the woman symbolic for a city and normally the Greek word **polis** is used. In Hebrew the word "eeyr" and in Arabic the word "medina" is used. But the more correct word in the Aramaic is the word "MDINTHA" and when used can also designate an area, or a district/province, range, or even a country. So this place is close to the sea and right in the desert and it fits Saudi Arabia perfectly. I believe this could correctly mean a country rather then just a city, because Saudi Arabia rides the beast, not just the city of Mecca. The "city" of Mecca is a better fit for the city by the seven mountains.

Although we do not have the Aramaic original, or a copy of the book of Revelation in the Aramaic language from 1st century Israel, I personally believe that the whole New Testament Scriptures were first written in the Aramaic/Hebrew square script, and later translated into Greek. We have enough evidence to know that this thesis is plausible and if you wish to know more, then please see my friend Andrew Gabriel Roth's book Ruach

Qadim at http://www.ruachqadim.com for evidence about this.

Here is some more is proof in the Aramaic;

John 4:44 Now Yahushua pointed out that a prophet has no honor in his COUNTRY (MDINTHA).

Acts 9:32 As Peter travelled throughout the COUNTRY (MDINTHA) he went to visit the saints in Lydda.

Acts 17:14 The brothers immediately sent Paul and the brothers to the COAST (MDINTHA).

People who say these things show they are looking for a COUNTRY (MDINTHA) of their own. **Hebrews 11:14** (the context here is clear from 11:13 and 15).

These though are the exceptions not the rule. Generally MDITHA is used as "town, hometown, or city." In fact, the Greek of Matthew, Mark and Luke's version of "prophet without honor" uses "hometown." John however means "country" for this same word. There are more precise terms for "nations" and "countries" in Aramaic, but yes, it can mean country. For one thing, Jerusalem is called the MDINTHA of the great King Yahushua (Matthew 5:35). But all Israel was under Roman domination, as a PROVINCE, in Judea. **Therefore, by the definitions of the time of the first century, all Israel can be a MDINTHA.** Even if someone disputed this, no one would dispute that Jerusalem, as an MDINTHA was the heart of Israel. The same could be said of Saudi Arabia in the first century. They were a province in the Persian Empire. [30]

Getting back to Islam let's see what else we can learn.

Sura 8:12 Remember thy Master inspired the angels (with the message): "I am with you: give **firmness to the believers**: I will **instil terror into the hearts of the unbelievers**: **smite ye above their necks** and **smite all their finger-tips off them**."

Here Allah gave a clear edict to strengthen the believing Muslims and that he would **instil terror** into those who did not believe, Muslims are instructed in the Qur'anic passage to explicitly **behead people** and even cut off ALL the fingers of the unbelievers.

Targum of Jonathan states this about Ishmael: Wild, fierce, untamed, not subject to a yoke, and impatient of it.

We find in **Genesis 25:12-16** that Ishmael had 12 sons:

Genesis 25:12-16 Now these are the generations of Ishmael, Abraham's son, whom Hagar the Egyptian, Sarah's handmaid, bare unto Abraham: And these

---

[30] Thanks to Andrew Gabriel Roth on the Aramaic sources of NT for the previous section.

are the names of the sons of Ishmael, by their names, according to their generations: the firstborn of Ishmael, Nebajoth; and Kedar, and Adbeel, and Mibsam, And Mishma, and Dumah, and Massa, Hadar, and Tema, Jetur, Naphish, and Kedemah: These are the sons of Ishmael, and these are their names, by their towns, and by their castles; twelve princes according to their nations.

We note that Ishmael was born to Hagar who was an <u>Egyptian</u>.

Later in **Genesis 21:21** we read: And he dwelt in the wilderness of Paran: and his mother took him a wife out of the <u>land of Egypt</u>.

So this links the Arabs directly with the Egyptians because of the mixed blood line both of Ishmael's mother who was an Egyptian and Ishmael's wife also being an Egyptian. This may explain the physical aspect of the hatred that the late Yasser Arafat and his merry men had towards the Jews, since he was also an Egyptian claiming to be a Palestinian and the spiritual hatred he showed was from being a Muslim. The cycle is now repeating with Mahmoud Abbas.

Genesis 25:18 And they dwelt from Havilah unto Shur; that is before Egypt, as thou goest toward Assyria: and he died in the presence of all his brethren.

The last portion of **Genesis 25:18** correctly read, "they" the "Ishmaelites" lived in "hostility" and "bloodshed" toward all his brethren the Jews. The living Bible brings points this out more clearly.

-Living Bible-
Genesis 25:18 These descendants of Ishmael were scattered across the country from Havilah to Shur (which is a little way to the northeast of the Egyptian border in the direction of Assyria). **And they were constantly at war with one another.**

Asshur/Assyria is modern day Iraq, Syria and parts of Turkey. They lived in hostility and are in hostility to this very day. Saddam Hussain fired scud missiles on Israel in the first Gulf War blaming Israel for the war, and then he fired scuds on Saudi Arabia. The Arabs even have a problem with each other and do not trust one another. In the past Muslims have killed their leaders through deception by either poisoning or stabbing them while they were praying. The only thing they all agree on is "**annihilation of Israel**" to drive the Jews into the sea. The rest is up for negotiation in the Islamic world and the highest bidder wins. Paul speaks about the spiritual aspect of this relationship:

Galatians 4:22-25 For it is written, that Abraham had two sons, the one by a bondmaid, the other by a freewoman. But he who was of the bondwoman [Ishmael] was <u>born after the flesh</u>; but he of the freewoman was by promise [Isaac]. Which things are allegories; for these are the **two covenants**; the one from the Mount Sinai, which **gendereth to bondage [Islam],** which is Hagar. For this Hagar is Mount Sinai in Arabia, and answers to Jerusalem, which now is, **and is in bondage with her children.**

143

Who is in bondage to comply with Islam today and their demands to give land for peace?

E.   Esau the disobedient son

Rebecca gave birth to Isaac.

Genesis 25:22-25 And the children struggled together within her; and she said, If it be so, why am I thus? And she went to enquire of YHWH. And YHWH said unto her, <u>two nations are in thy womb</u>, and <u>two manners of people shall be separated from thy bowels</u>; and the <u>one people shall be stronger than the other people</u>; and <u>the elder shall serve the younger</u>. And when her days to be delivered were fulfilled, behold, there were twins in her womb. And the first came out red, all over like a hairy garment; and they called his name Esau.

As a result, Esau would serve the younger brother Jacob, this is very similar to the condition Ishmael was in and this again leads to a type of jealousy and hatred.

In Genesis 25 we are told some key information about Esau who represents the **Mount of Esau,** which relates to Edom [present day Jordan]. But spiritually this is metaphoric of the entire Muslim world. YHWH also often refers to the "Mount of Esau" as the Temple Mount area where the Al-Aqsa Mosque is built.

Genesis 25:27 And the boys grew: and Esau was a cunning hunter, a man of the field; and **Jacob was a plain man**, dwelling in tents. And Isaac loved Esau, because he did eat of his venison: but Rebekah loved Jacob.

Jewish rabbis agree and I am in full agreement with them that the battle in the ends of days will be between the children of Jacob fighting with the children of Esav (Esau). Ishmaelites are included. It is even better to say the twelve tribes of Israel will be fighting for survival with the twelve tribes of Islam aka Ishmael who inter-mingled with Esau.

Esau was crafty and cunning while Jacob was a <u>simple man</u> and we can see this behavior in the Palestinians today. They like to deceive the world by portraying themselves as the victims, saying that Israel is hostile to us and occupying our land. In fact it is the Palestinians who occupy the Jewish land! Just as their ancestor Esau is described in the Bible long ago as cunning, the simplicity in Jacob [symbolic for Israel today, both spiritual and physical] is ready to concede portions of its own land for peace and expel the Jews from their homes as we witnessed in Gaza. The land they claim Israel is occupying does in actual fact <u>only</u> belong to the Hebrews, since they have had a presence in the land for the last 3,000 years, while the current day Palestinians have all arrived in Israel from the Arab world after 1917. The word "Palestinian" never existed before the 1967 war. You will not find a nation of people who were known as the Palestinians before that date. There are no coins, capital, or historical traces of any people who were called Palestinians. However there were a people called the Philistines and most of them are extinct today. These so-called Palestinians show the same level of hatred for Israel, but those Philistines were not Arabs.

Genesis 35:12 The land which I gave Abraham and Isaac I give to you; **[Jacob and his descendants the Hebrew nation]** and to your descendants after you I give this land.'

Arafat coined the word Palestinian in 1967 when the three Muslim states Syria, Egypt and Jordan took a crushing defeat by Israel. The term "Palestina" existed before, as set forth by the Romans to eradicate the name of Israel. This LATIN term only represented the Jews in the land of Israel and Judea. But Arafat particularly played on these words to make the Arab people into a separate group of people, who allegedly existed as a nation for thousand of years with a government and state. In order to give them legitimacy, the word they used literally reads "falastine" in Arabic, like the Hebrew word Plishte, and this was his way to give these people legitimacy.

The Arab people in the area used to be controlled by Jordan and were not controlled by Israel at all. These same people were quite happily living as Jordanians until the 1967 war. They even had Jordanian passports. Jordan began to revoke the passports in 1995.

So overnight the Jordanian people became Palestinian people. This was propaganda to oust Israel and occupy the Israeli land illegally once again. **The true Palestinian/Judean people, if the term could be qualified, would be the Hebrews themselves not Arabs with a new name.** Emperor Hadrian coined the term Palestine in 135 AD to blot out the name of Israel. The irony is that Jerusalem the capital of Israel has become a central issue on everyone's lips. Is YHWH trying to show people that Israel will never be blotted out?

Esau was also in close relationship with Ishmael as he married one of his daughters.

Genesis 28:8-9 And Esau seeing that the <u>daughters of Canaan</u> pleased not **Isaac his father**; Then went **Esau unto Ishmael**, and **took unto the wives which he had Mahalath** the daughter of <u>Ishmael Abraham's son</u>, the sister of Nebajoth, to be his wife.

Clearly, Esau was disobedient to his parents' will and authority knowing full well he was not to marry the Canaanite women, as they would persuade him into worshipping their false gods. And we also see that the bloodlines get mixed by Esau marrying Ishmael's daughter. The Edomites and Arabs got intermingled. Clearly Esau had no regard for his family's true faith, their relationship with Yahweh, or their customs. We even see this behavior today in Christians who go off marrying pagans, having no regard for their parents and the true faith in Messiah Yahushua that the parents honor. One sin leads to a multitude of sins, with backsliding and the denial of Yahushua as Master, which often will end having ones name blotted out of The Book of Life.

There are people that I know today who are from very devout Christian families, but sadly their children have dishonoured their parents and Yahweh by walking away marrying Muslims, Hindus, Sikhs or Atheists. This will only lead to an ultimate compromise for the sake of "love" that is only earthly and has <u>no</u> lasting value. A Christian person in such a situation can <u>never</u> be truly happy. I lost my marriage with my Muslim wife of seventeen years and my two children, my son is terminally ill. But how could I disgrace Yahushua's name and reject His love for me for the sake of earthly relations even though I do love my family?

For me death is better than to reject Yahweh. When my dad said to me return to your previous faith of Islam, I told him, "Dad it is better that you shoot me first, because my return is not possible." When you have known Yahushua as close as I have then rejection is not an option. People talk about being born again and being baptised in the Holy Spirit, but what good is our new birth if we are going to fall away and get hooked into family blackmail? The ultimate test of the new birth is our steadfastness and faith in Him to obey His commandments.

A few months ago it was on the news that Yousuf Yohanna a famous Pakistani cricketer who was from a Christian background family converted into Islam and his wife and children also. He was telling every other Christian in Pakistan to become Muslim. To me it shows that his falling away is exactly what the Bible predicted.

> **2 Thessalonians 2: 3** Let **no one deceive you** by any means; for that Day will not come **unless the falling away comes first**, and the man of sin is revealed, the son of perdition,

When I read this passage, I am encouraged that even though Christians may backslide and fall, but the Elohim of Israel is faithful and truthful. Some Christians will argue that Yousuf was not born again, or did not know the Bible. Either way the reality is that he has dishonoured our Master Yahushua the Messiah and his parents. He has <u>lost</u> his salvation and he simply fell away to be in league with s.a.tan. Being born again does not mean that you cannot fall away. In order to protect yourself from s.a.tan and his attack you have to be faithfully following Yahushua and be obedient to His words i.e. **His commandments**. To disobey Him and His commandments and to look for excuses to annul the Torah in ones life is rebellion to be used by s.a.tan. And he uses it to attack believers who are ready for a fall. The reality is there is no such thing as once saved and always saved. **It is a matter of the heart to consciously follow and obey YHWH through ongoing commitment and fidelity**. Salvation being a free gift does not mean people <u>cannot</u> backslide, or fall away, as we have seen many do. But Paul made it clear not to be haughty, because if YHWH can break the natural branches, then who are we (**Romans 11:21**)? The bottom line is to always **obey** Yahweh not men.

> **Ezekiel 18:24** "But when a **righteous man turns away** from his **righteousness and commits iniquity**, and does according to all the abominations that the wicked man does, shall he live? All the righteousness, which he has done, shall **not** be remembered; because of the **unfaithfulness of which he is guilty and the sin, which he has committed, because of them he shall die.**

We cannot contend with Scripture, when a person falls from his state of being in Messiah (His righteousness) then all his good deeds are worthless. Our righteousness lies in Messiah and if one chooses to deny that eternal life, can one really say 'we can go to heaven'?

> **2 Thessalonians 2: 12** If we endure, we shall also reign with Him. If **we deny Him, He also will deny us**.

It does not take a mathematical genius to realize that if we deny Yahushua the Messiah before men, then He will deny us before our Father in heaven, thereby meaning we have <u>no</u> salvation from the point of that denial.

146

Matthew 10:22 "And you **will be hated by all for My name's sake**. But **he who endures to the END will be saved.**

The truth of the matter is that any person who does not **endure** to the END of his life will be considered unfaithful and has fallen in the camp of s.a.tan. The real value we have is with Yahushua our Master and His faithfulness to carry out His eternal words. So repent and return, do "teshuvah," (In Hebrew that means to turn away or return) and ask forgiveness for your sins to our Master and stop disgracing His holy name.

Genesis 26:34-35 When Esau was forty years old, he took as wives Judith the daughter of Beeri the Hittite, and Basemath the daughter of Elon the Hittite. And they were a grief of mind to Isaac and Rebekah.

Further, Esau grieved his parents by marrying into the Hittites when he was told not to do this. Clearly Esau was in rebellion and did not show due regards to honoring his mother and father.

Genesis 25:29-33 And Jacob sod pottage: and Esau came from the field, and he was faint: And Esau said to Jacob, Feed me, I pray thee, with that same red pottage; for I am faint: therefore was his name called Edom. And Jacob said, Sell me this day **thy birthright**. And Esau said, Behold, I am at the point to die: and **what profit shall this birthright** do to me? And Jacob said, Swear to me this day; and he sware unto him: and he sold his birthright unto Jacob.

Many Bible teachers have wrongly called Jacob a deceiver when clearly he is a **tent dweller and a plain man**. Jacob was not the deceiver, but Esau was and this was fulfilled in his progeny. Christians would do well to stop perpetuating this error calling Jacob a deceiver, thus leading to the conclusion by the world that all Jews are deceivers. This is exactly what the Muslims play upon because of Christian error.

Genesis 25:27 And the boys grew: and Esau was a **cunning hunter**, a man of the field; and Jacob was a plain man, dwelling in tents.

"Jacob was a plain man in **Hebrew the word used is "tam."** one who lived in tents" (Genesis 25:27). Jacob was not an expert in all these things for his heart was his mouth. One who is not ingenious at deceiving people is called **TAM, PLAIN, PURE and SIMPLE**, or someone you can read like a book.

YHWH used Hebrew to convey the correct meaning in the biblical passages; this is why the rabbis call Hebrew "the language of YHWH," since some ideas cannot be conveyed in any other language. I am in full agreement with these rabbis that Hebrew is the language of Yahweh.

Rashi comments:

As long as they were little, they were indistinguishable by their deeds and no one could know their exact character. Once they turned thirteen, one [Yaakov] went his way to houses of study and the other went his way to worshipping idols. One became a "skilled trapper." In other words, he would deceive people, trapping them with his mouth. He had

147

no occupation. He used his bow to trap animals and birds. By contrast, Jacob was a scholarly man, who remained within the tents. He was one in word and thought. He was not a deceiver. Rather, he sat in the tents of Torah.

How dare we say Yahweh conducts business and cuts covenants with deceivers! Yahweh actually called Jacob "perfect" in this passage. See what Yahweh really calls deceivers:

Malachi 1:14 But cursed be the deceiver, which hath in his flock a male, and voweth, and sacrificeth unto YHWH a corrupt thing: for I am a great King, saith YHWH of hosts, and my Name is dreadful among the heathen.

By erroneously teaching that Jacob is a deceiver it makes all Jews today to seem like deceivers and hypocrites. This is the grave stereotypical error that many teach in churches of so called seminary scholars.

If you still insist that Jacob is a deceiver and I am wrong to say otherwise, then I suggest you take a close look at Job, because he is also described as *"TAM"* and here the word used in some Bibles is "perfect."

Job 1:1 There was a man in the land of Uz, whose name was Job; and that man was **PERFECT** (TAM), and upright, and one that feared God, and eschewed evil.

Yahweh calls Job "perfect-Tam." Some Bibles translate this as "blameless." Tam in both Job's case and also Jacob's case means:

1) Perfect.

2) Complete.

3) One who lacks nothing in physical strength, beauty, etc.

4) Sound, wholesome.

5) An ordinary, quiet sort of person.

6) Complete, morally innocent, having integrity.

7) One who is morally and ethically pure.

Moving on swiftly, YHWH knew before they were born that the older would serve the younger. Esau despised his birthright and sold it to his brother for a bowl of lentil soup. This means he sold his blessings to Jacob and his inheritance rights were forfeited. Esau did not value his birthright, he despised it. After this event Esau had no right to his inheritance by biblical law, or to blessings from his father, even though Esau was the elder son.

Is it not Esau who has possessed the **"Mount of Abraham"** (Temple Mount) and is referred to in the Bible as the **"Mountains of Esau" (Obadiah 1:9)**? His is the allegoric connection for the Islamic Empire that occupies the holy Temple Mount area by deception

148

today? Today, the Muslims claim that Abraham was somehow a Muslim and they have taken over the Temple Mount, claiming Muhammad ascended to heaven from there. The Qur'an does not mention Jerusalem even once. Who is the deceiver? Esau or Jacob? Clearly if we have any insight into YHWH's word and His pure language it is **Esau who is the deceiver not Jacob**.

YHWH uses very strong words against Esau [allegoric for Islam/Idolatry] to describe the relationship he had with Jacob [Israel/covenant people].

F.   YHWH's love and His curses

Malachi 1:2-3 "I have loved you," says YHWH. "Yet you say, "In what **way have You loved us**?' Was not Esau Jacob's brother?" Says YHWH. "**Yet Jacob I have loved**; But **Esau I have hated**, and **laid waste his mountains** [his kingdom, empire] and his heritage for the jackals of the wilderness."

YHWH's final judgment is set on Islam characterised by "Esau and his mountains." YHWH is going to destroy them because of the iniquity of Esau (Islam) for his brother Jacob/Israel and for his continuous hatred and violence towards them (Jews), e.g. All Muslim hatred for Israel is characterised by this. If we look and read the book of Genesis, a picture starts to emerge and we see what happened earlier and why things are happening today.

Genesis 37:28 Then there passed by Midianite merchantmen; and they drew and lifted up Joseph out of the pit, and sold Joseph to the Ishmaelites for twenty pieces of silver: and they brought Joseph into Egypt.

We read in Genesis chapter 37 where his brothers despised Joseph the son of Jacob, because he was loved by Jacob as his favorite son and sold into slavery to the Ishmaelites/Midianites (Arabs) by his own brothers.

Later the Arabs sold Joseph to the Egyptians, so we can make the clear connection here with the Arabs and Egyptians trading with each other. Is this not true today, where Jewish leaders themselves are selling their own brothers the Jews into the hands of the Arabs, by displacing them and pulling up settlements for "twenty pieces of silver?" This is symbolic of worldly gain and also of Joseph/Yisrael being brought into Egypt. In biblical terms it is symbolic for the world, or the Jewish leaders such as Yitzhak Rabin, Shimon Peres and Ariel Sharon selling their brothers to appease the world. Then mistakenly many of the Jewish people blame the USA, Europe, or Russia. The question is their own brothers are corrupt and should refuse to sell Israel (Joseph) to the Arabs (Midianites) for "twenty pieces of silver." They should stop blaming the rest of the world. Gaza was recently evacuated and given to the Palestinians by Ariel Sharon's government. So do you see that the above Scripture being fulfilled once again, where the Jews have sold their own brothers to terrorism?

Israel cannot keep blaming others by refusing to obey the Almighty Elohim of Israel. Did He not say that if you trust in me I would heal the land? And yet, these Israeli leaders refuse to trust their Elohim. This is indeed sad. In my opinion the best solution is to dismantle the Palestinian Authority, tell the Palestinians that they can live with Israel in peace or leave. I would refuse to allow a people to divide a land mandated by YHWH and whose only purpose is to destroy the Jews. I would obey my YHWH and not bring punishment upon myself, or calamity upon my people because of what other people think. Scripture teaches us that YHWH hates the division of Israel. Should we trust our living YHWH, or the people? Palestinians are even being used and killed by their own people who are not trustworthy.

> **Leviticus 25:23** The **land shall <u>not</u> be sold permanently**, for the land is Mine; for you are strangers and sojourners with Me.

If Israel refused to give land then no one can take it by force. That is the simple truth because YHWH said in **Amos 9:15** *"I will plant them in their land, and <u>no longer</u> shall <u>they be pulled up from the land I have given them</u>," says the Master your YHWH."* The bottom line is this; "trust your YHWH not the world" and 'stop dividing your land, oh people of Israel.' Have you forgotten how in the wilderness you were punished when you murmured against YHWH? He did not allow that generation to enter the land of milk and honey, and only Joshua and Caleb entered because of the people's lack of faithfulness to YHWH. Please be at least <u>faithful</u> to your YHWH and tell the world we are not going to divide our land because we <u>trust</u> our YHWH who is the "Rock" of salvation. Do not reap judgments upon yourself for disobedience.

> **Genesis 37:36** And the Midianites sold him into Egypt unto Potiphar, an officer of Pharaoh's, and captain of the guard.

Joseph was eventually made Prime Minister of Egypt, as he was wise and the Master was on his side.

> **Genesis 41:39-40** And Pharaoh said unto Joseph, Forasmuch as YHWH hath showed thee all this, there is none so **discreet and wise** as thou art: Thou shalt be over my house, and according unto thy word shall all my people be ruled: only in the throne will I be greater than thou.

When we accept the Master's provision and <u>bless His chosen people</u> we are blessed in turn. But when we turn away from Him and despise His chosen people then we also fall into calamities and the curse that is mentioned in **Genesis 12:3** is upon us and becomes real in or lives. Whoever despises the Hebrews today is in danger of being under a curse, based on the <u>written</u> word of YHWH. Pharaoh was a mighty King and showed wisdom by recognizing who Joseph was and blessed him, by making him the Prime Minister of Egypt. Likewise we should recognize that we should never hate the Jews, as they remain YHWH's covenant people. But we should recognize their worth by remembering they gave us the Bible, which is YHWH's oracles for mankind and foremost they gave us the Messiah Yahushua. The same Yahushua, who was born into a Jewish household, to a Jewish girl to redeem the world from sin. Without Yahushua none of us could be saved, YHWH's mercy and justice <u>met on the cross</u> when Yahushua took our punishment for our sins. What a great YHWH we have.

> **Genesis 12:3** And **I will bless them that bless thee**, and **curse him that curseth thee** and in thee shall all families of the earth be blessed/mixed.

The Hebrew word used is *'aw-rar'* in this sentence for curse and it is one that means that nations who oppose YHWH's chosen people will be brought to nothing and the curse will be a very painful one; a cutting down one. Guess who we see today cursing YHWH's chosen people?

None of the Islamic nations love Israel, but hate Israel to the core. Could it be that they do not worship the same YHWH and are in sync with the enemy of Israel who is s.a.tan? **Have you ever wondered why the richest Muslim nations are in squalor and chaos? The reason is the curse.**

Whereas the word used for bless is *'nivrechu* which entails not only spiritual blessings, but also physical blessings, plus more accurately is termed engrafted or mixing. The only nation to openly support Israel today is the USA and although she is a relatively young nation of just over 200 years old, yet the Master has brought her from nothing to a superpower. This proves YHWH's promises are real and tangible, not just arbitrary, or old fables.

Even Turkey that has a peace treaty with Israel has discord internally where the Islamists are intent on breaking off all their ties with Israel. The Islamists blew up the Neve Shalom synagogue on Saturday, November 15, 2003 just to prove their discontent with the Turks and the Jews in Turkey for supporting the Jews.

Is it not surprising that Ariel Sharon is almost repeating what happened with Joseph, uprooting the Jewish settlements in Gaza and giving the land of his brethren over to the Arabs, and in turn to appeasing the world? The Pharaoh showed wisdom and understanding with Joseph, but Ariel Sharon on the other hand did not show wisdom in dealing with his people.

Sometimes a Jew is his own worst enemy. There is a saying where there are two Jews there are <u>three</u> opinions. Is it not amazing that during the 2004 USA presidential election, Jews voted overwhelmingly for John Kerry? Yet he was the last person they should have voted for, since he was into Arab appeasement. But will the Jews ever learn from their mistakes?

Exodus 1:8-11 Now there arose up a <u>new king over Egypt</u>, which knew not Joseph. And he said unto his people, <u>Behold, the people of the children of Israel are more and mightier than we</u>: Come on, let us deal wisely with them; lest they multiply, and it come to pass, that, when there falleth out any war, they join also unto our enemies, and fight against us, and <u>so get them up out of the land</u>. Therefore they did set over them taskmasters to afflict them with their burdens. And they built for Pharaoh treasure cities, Pithom and Raamses.

Next, we see that a king in Egypt was afraid of the children of Israel for no apparent reason and brought the Hebrews under slavery to control them.

Later, after the Hebrews had been in heavy bondage, the Elohim of Israel freed the Hebrew people through Moses and then we see the first war of the Hebrews with the Midianites (Arabs).

151

Similarly, the same thing happened again with the King of Moab (Jordan), who was greatly afraid of the Hebrews for no reason and wanted to curse them because of what happened with the Amorites. However he did not know the reason for the battle with the Amorites.

As a good king, he should have sent emissaries to investigate the cause of this and would not have been afraid unnecessarily.

Balak did not show good leadership either. He did not represent his peoples' interests at all. Similarly, today we see Islamic nations attacking Israel for its little piece of land. The Islamic nations show lack of wisdom and that is not in their peoples' interests. But out of their own fear and prejudice they drive their people to such intense and wanton hatred.

> **Numbers 22:2-6** And <u>Balak the son of Zippor saw all that Israel had done to the Amorites</u>. And <u>Moab was sore afraid of the people</u>, because **they were many** and <u>Moab was distressed</u> because of the children of Israel. And Moab said unto the elders of Midian, Now shall this company lick up all that are round about us, as the ox licketh up the grass of the field. And <u>Balak the son of Zippor</u> was <u>king of the Moabites</u> at that time. He sent messengers therefore unto Balaam the son of Beor to Pethor, which is by the river of the land of the children of his people, to call him, saying, Behold, there is a people come out from Egypt: behold, they cover the face of the earth, and they abide over against me: <u>Come now therefore, I pray thee, curse me this people</u>; for they are too mighty for me: peradventure I shall prevail, that we may smite them, and that I may drive them out of the land: for I know that he whom thou blesses is blessed, and he whom thou curses is cursed.

After this event Balak tried to have Israel cursed by the seer Balaam and drive them out of the land. But the Elohim of Israel would not allow Balaam to curse Israel, but instead forced him to bless Israel. Since the curse option failed, they then used the daughters of Moab (Jordanians) to seduce the Israelites into worshipping their false gods, in order that the Elohim of Israel would be angry with the Jews for disobeying Him and would punish them. This shows that the enemy will stoop to any level to eradicate the Hebrews.

We can see throughout biblical history and secular history that the Islamists have been up in arms against the Jews in one way, or another, e.g. Muhammad in Arabia in the 7th century **ethnically cleansed** all the tribes from his land. Even to this day Jews are not allowed to go to Saudi Arabia. Today all the Muslim nations want to eradicate Israel from the face of the planet and drive the Jews to the sea; they want to possess the land of Israel for themselves.

In 1948 when Israel was created as a nation a major prophecy was fulfilled that Isaiah spoke about:

> **Isaiah 66:7-8** Before she travailed, <u>she gave birth</u> [Israel is born]; before her pain came, she delivered <u>a male child</u>. Who has heard such a thing? Who has seen such things? Shall the earth be made to <u>give birth in one day</u>? Or shall a <u>nation be born at once</u>? For as soon as Zion travailed, she gave birth to her children.

Israel was literally born in a day and upon its birth the Arabs started their onslaught to destroy Israel. The Arabs told the then-living Arabs in Israel to leave Israel so they could destroy the Jews and promised their brethren to give them Jewish land after they won the war. But things did not turn out as they had planned and Yahweh shamed them into a defeat, to uphold His promises to Israel. Yet the Arabs still did not learn that their fight is not with Israel, but with the Elohim of Israel.

No one forced the Arabs to leave Israel, yet they chose to go willingly because of their greed to acquire more land.

The Cairo paper had this to say

The Cairo daily - AKHBAR EL YOM (Oct 12th 1963):

'The 15th May, 1948, arrived...On that day the Mufti of Jerusalem appealed to the Arabs of Palestine to leave the country, because the Arab armies were about to enter and fight in their stead.'

The Jordanian paper had this to say;
The Jordanian daily newspaper FALASTIN (Feb 19th 1949):

'The Arab states which had encouraged the Palestine Arabs to leave their homes temporarily in order to be out of the way of the Arab invasion armies, have failed to keep their promise to help these refugees.'

It is estimated that about 600,000 Palestinians Arabs chose to leave during the first war with Israel and these were people who made their own mind up to leave, in response to the promises of their own brothers. The Jews never forced them out, or brutalized them. About 800,000 Jewish people were expelled, or those that were persecuted brutally in Arab countries left to go back to Israel. Israel a tiny nation absorbed their own people. But the Goliath Arabs on the other hand chose not to absorb their people and made these people into refugees to subsequently use them for their own game of cat and mouse with Israel, which sadly continues to this day.

The Lebanese paper reporting had this to say.
KUL-SHAY, Muslim weekly (Beirut, August 19,1951):

'Who brought the Palestinians to Lebanon as refugees, suffering now from the malign attitude of newspapers and communal leaders, who have neither honor nor conscience? Who brought them over in dire straits and penniless, after they lost their honor? The Arab states, and Lebanon amongst them, did it.'

The Jordanian daily reporting:

In 1953, April 9, the Jordanian daily newspaper AL URDUN:

'For the flight and fall of the other villages it is our leaders who are responsible because of their dissemination of rumors exaggerating Jewish crimes and describing them as atrocities in order to inflame the Arabs. By **spreading rumors** of Jewish atrocities, killings of women and children etc. They instilled fear and terror in the hearts of the Arabs in Palestine, until they fled leaving their homes and properties to the enemy.' "

Clearly, it can be seen that the Jews were shown to be evil and yet the Palestinian Arabs were promised much, but got nothing in return. What the Arab authorities did was to spread false rumors and lies to deceive their own people. Now that these refugees have quadrupled, Israel has been made to bear responsibility to take them back, which they refuse to do, since they did not create the refugee problem in the first place.

Israeli Jews who were themselves refugees all over the world for 2,000 years was a refugee problem that the world did not want to deal with. In fact, they compounded it by persecuting the Jews and it was only YHWH who through His promises gathered them back to their land in Israel as we see in prophecy.

> **Jeremiah 23:3-8** "But I will gather the remnant of My flock out of all countries where I have driven them, and bring them back to their folds; and they shall be fruitful and increase. I will set up shepherds over them who will feed them; and they shall fear no more, nor be dismayed, nor shall they be lacking," says the Master. Behold, the days are coming, says the Master, That I will raise to David a Branch of righteousness;

All the rabbis agree that the 'Branch of Righteousness' is no other than the prophesied Messiah, who will come to be King over them. Because Israel rejected her Messiah, she still suffers and is living in fear of constant attacks by the Islamists. When the Messiah returns He will settle the land issue once and for all times. At this point only the Nazarene Yisraelite and Messianic rabbis agree that Yahushua is the Messiah, who has redeemed us from our sins. But the orthodox rabbis remain in partial blindness.

> **Jeremiah 3:18** "In those days the **house of Judah** shall walk with **the house of Israel**, and **they shall come together out of the land of the north** to the land that I **have given as an inheritance** to your fathers.

It is YHWH who has given the land of Israel to the Jews and Ephraimites. They have not taken, or occupied this land by force, and it is theirs because of the promises to the fathers by inheritance.

> **Jeremiah 7:7** "then **I will cause you to dwell in this place, in the land** that I gave to your fathers **forever and ever**.

It is Yahweh the Elohim of Israel who causes the Hebrews to dwell in the land of Israel and it is not by some man's idea. Notice the land was given as an eternal possession and not for a few hundred years. The Hebrew word used is **Ha-Olam** for eternity, or "world without end." If people want to argue that it does not mean eternity, or that it is a conditional time period, then one could argue also that the verses that are used for our salvation are also conditional. The word/term "ha, or le olam" means our salvation is for eternity, or "without end," as are Israel's covenants with YHWH. We have to be consistent in our view.

In many of the schools in Cairo (Egypt), the Muslim youths recite daily petitions; one such typical curse upon Jews and Christians goes as follows: [31]

---

[31] Lane, E.W. *Modern Egyptians*, p. 575

"I seek refuge with god from s.a.tan the accursed. In the name of god, the Compassionate, the Merciful. O god, aid El-Islam, and exalt the word of truth, and the faith, by the preservation of thy servant and the son of thy servant, the Sultan of the two continents (Europe and Asia), and the Khakan (Emperor or monarch) of the two seas [the Mediterranean and Black Seas], the Sultan, son of the Sultan (Mahmood) Khan (the reigning Sultan when this prayer was composed). O god, assist him, and assist his armies, and all the forces of the Muslims: O Master of the beings of the whole world. *O god, destroy the infidels and polytheists, thine enemies, the enemies of the religion. O god, make their children orphans, and defile their abodes, and cause their feet to slip, and Give them and their families, and their households and their women and their children and their relations by marriage and their brothers and their friends and their possessions and their race and their wealth and their lands as booty to the Muslims*: O Master of the beings of the whole world."

Yet Yahweh's love and curses are real. Those that curse His chosen people will be cursed themselves and He will bless those that bless them. The blessing is not dependent on people believing in the Elohim of Israel, or being Christian as some people think. Even nations that do not worship Yahweh can receive physical blessings for their good treatment of the Hebrew people. The bottom line is this: "bless Israel and be blessed."

Chapter 6

Can We Be Certain That it is the Islamic Nations That s.a.tan is Using in the End Times to Attempt to Destroy His people?

It is clear that behind this hatred is s.a.tan himself. But it is the Muslim nations that are being used instrumentally by s.a.tan (**Genesis 3:15**) to attack the Jews and the western nations. I will show that the end-time wrath of YHWH is upon the Islamic nations for their grievous sins. These Islamic nations are going to come up against Israel to try and destroy Israel in the end-time scenario. There is a difference between the wrath of YHWH upon nations on the earth and the final judgment at the resurrection of the dead. All of mankind stands in sin and needs Yahushua the Messiah for their sins to be atoned. Indonesia woke up to severe judgement from Yahweh with the tsunami. Could it possibly be that their bitter persecution of the Christians for the last thirty years caused this reaction from the Elohim of Israel? Yahweh's patience ran out on that fateful day. Pakistan had a huge earthquake recently on its doorstep. This nation has been persecuting the Christians and other ethnic minorities for decades under its blasphemy law of 295c. How ridiculous it is to deify Muhammad and to believe that mere words could blaspheme the Muslim prophet. Yahweh is beginning to pour His wrath on Islamic nations and judging the so-called Christian nations also for their behavior towards Israel.

We can see s.a.tan's attempt once again to stop the return of the Messiah Yahushua. If there is no State of Israel then the Messiah Yahushua cannot return to fulfil the second coming prophecies of the Bible. This is history repeating itself. Remember the time of the Maccabees when Antiochus Epiphanies sacrificed a swine in the Temple in Jerusalem during 167 BC to desecrate the Temple? That was s.a.tan's attempt to stop Yahushua the Messiah's first coming. If the Temple was desecrated, then how could the Messiah fulfil the prophecies of His first coming to the Temple? Easy! YHWH made the way through the Maccabees, who although being outnumbered, still defeated the large Greek army to re-establish and re-dedicate (Chanukah) the Temple to the Master Elohim of Israel. The reason why the Jews and also we too should celebrate Chanukah, the Festival of Lights of the re-dedication, is that it shows us who the true Light of the world is-Yahushua of Nazareth of course!

They will even hate those nations that decide to stand with Israel and here we can see the USA is a clear example. Islamists attacked it many times severely in their on-going war against the USA for its firm stand with Israel. *"The second nation that is in line to get Islam's fury poured out is Great Britain."* I wrote these words in the first edition text of Islam Peace or Beast back in 2004. Then in 2005 we did indeed see the Islamists pour out their fury on July, 7th 2005, blowing up trains and a bus on the London transport system. I will devote a whole chapter later to this once "great nation" and its demise and resurrection back to glory in the end-times and how YHWH will use it to fight the Anti-Messiah.

It is quite easy to know if the nations that are going to come up against Israel are Islamic or not. Let us look at **Psalm 83**, which is still unfulfilled.

A   **Psalm 83 – Are these European or Islamic nations?**

Psalm 83 names the confederacy of nations that will come up against Israel and guess what! They are ALL Islamic today. Every one of them, you will not find even one European nation amongst this confederacy. I adjure you to prove it for yourself.

> **Psalm 83:5** "they have consulted together with one consent: they are **confederate** against thee."

They will come together as a joint force to target Israel, but are not fighting the Jews. In reality they are fighting the Elohim of Israel. Who can win against Yahweh? Islamists need to learn, or else a terrible fate lies ahead for them when they will get crushed on the mountains of Israel.

> Psalm 83: 1. Do not keep silent, O YHWH! Do not hold your peace, and do not be still, O YHWH!

"Do not hold your peace" is a cry to YHWH not to remain silent on this issue, or just sweep it under the carpet. The reverse of holding His peace is to outpour His fury on these nations.
> 2. For behold, your enemies make a tumult; and those who hate you have lifted up their head.

The hatred is not for the Jews alone but of the Elohim of Israel directly. This is s.a.tan mustering his forces who wanted to be like YHWH and to sit on His throne.

> 3. They have taken crafty counsel **against your people**, and consulted together against your **sheltered ones.**

All the Islamic nations have raised their voice against Israel.

> 4. They have said, "Come, and let us cut them off from being a nation, that the name of Israel may be remembered no more."

This was literally fulfilled by the Muslim nations as they did say these very exact words.

In order to "cut off" meaning to kill every living Jew from the land of Israel there had to be a land resurrected back after the Diaspora. For 1,878 years we did not see a land that the Jews could call home (Israel). Also we did not see the Muslim nations come into existence until Muhammad proclaimed the religion of Islam as supreme in the 7th century AD. So this prophecy cannot apply to the Roman Empire, or revived Roman Empire, or the USA theory, but only applies to the beast mentioned in Revelation 13. This beast is distinct from the others and is a collation of these three Empires, **Lion** (Babylon), **Bear** (Persia) and **Leopard** (Grecian), which are all Islamic regions today.

> 5. For they have consulted together with one consent; they form a confederacy against you: [all Muslims have joined ranks to try and destroy Israel, but in affect are fighting the Elohim of Israel]
> 6. The **tents of Edom** and the **Ishmaelites**; **Moab** and the **Hagarites**; [nations defined and these are ALL Middle Eastern]

7. **Gebal**, **Ammon**, and **Amalek**; **Philistia** with the inhabitants of **Tyre**;

8. Assyria also has joined with them; they have helped the **children of Lot**. Selah

9. Deal with them as with **Midian**, As with Sisera, as with Jabin at the Brook Kishon,

What happened at Brook Kishon? Let us investigate and understand this matter.

> **1 Kings 18:40** And Elijah said to them, "**Seize the prophets of Baal!**" Do not let one of them escape! So they seized them; and Elijah brought them down to the Brook Kishon and executed them there.

The prophets of Baal were killed here; so the prophets of [Allah who is Baal or Ba'il] will also be destroyed in the same way. This area has major prophetic significance for the future.

Brook Kishon is the area between Mount Tabor and Mount Gilboa and flows westward through the plains of Esdraelon and the Jezreel Valley and it was here that the encounter of Elijah took place. Mount Tabor is also the place where Yahweh routed Sisera and all his chariots and all his army before Barak (**Judges 4:13-15**).

The Jordan Valley marks the joint of a great tectonic-plate fault **awaiting a massive earthquake**. Geologists know about this region and study it. It runs straight up through the Red Sea, through the entire land of Israel under the Jordan River, and beyond. This is where the huge earthquake that Zechariah, Ezekiel and Revelation describe will take place, that will split the Mount of Olives making a valley for the Jews to escape and **drown the armies of the Anti-Messiah completely** *Daniel 9:26 ...the end of it shall be with a flood.*

Not one of these will escape just like with Sisera. *Judges 4:16 ...and all the army of Sisera fell by the edge of the sword; not a man was left.*

10. Who perished at Endor, Who became as refuse on the earth?

11. Make their nobles like **Oreb** and like **Zeeb**, yes, all their princes like Zebah and Zalmunna,

Oreb and Zeeb were Arab princes who were killed by Gideon's army.

12. Who said, "Let us take for ourselves the pastures of YHWH for a possession."

The reasons are obvious because they wanted to destroy the Jews and take their land, but Yahweh did not allow that to happen. Gideon used a tiny army of 300 men to route the Midianites who could not be numbered. This story can be read in the book of **Judges 7:1-7**.

In **Judges 7:12** the English word used for this army is either locusts or grasshoppers, but in the Hebrew we can understand another truth that Yahweh is trying to teach us allegorically using drash. The word used by the rabbis for locust is '**arbeh**,' which they refer to the 'desert creature' and use also synonymously for Arabs."

The Hebrew word used is "**arbeh**" and one can understand why the rabbis used this for the Arabs as **the desert-roaming creatures**. It is a foregone conclusion that the Arabs will come up in the end-times to try and destroy Israel with other Islamic nations and that Yahweh will crush them on the mountains of Israel. It is our job to warn them so that some may repent. However the last battle is not only a battle that will wake up Israel, but also save Muslims who are left. Ultimately it involves redemption of both peoples, the Arabs and the Jews, since both in their present state without the Messiah are lost.

Let me show you another understanding in the **Aramaic** in **Daniel 2:43** where he describes the fourth kingdom. Daniel shows us that this kingdom will be strong yet divided and we see this fracture in the Islamic Empire today. But they will unite to destroy Israel as a confederacy, just as Scripture dictates. One thing is 100% certain; that Yahweh is trustworthy and everything He said has so far come to pass and the rest will be fulfilled in its due course.

Daniel 2:43 "As you saw iron **mixed** with ceramic clay, they will **mingle with the seed of men**; but they will not adhere to one another, just as iron does not mix with clay.

The Aramaic word for "mix" is "**Arab**." Do you see how Yahweh is trying to show us that it is the Arabs who will mix with the seed of men, i.e. intermarriages, plus the spread of Islam globally, that will produce the end-time empire, although "arbah" can also mean the number four (4). **So another allegoric (drash) reading of this could be that the four beasts mix in the Middle East in this SAME region to produce this last empire, since this is the SAME geographic region for all these 4 beast empires, as both Daniel 7 and Revelation 13:2 clearly dictate.**

Psalm 83:13-16 O my YHWH; make them like the whirling dust, like the chaff before the wind! (14) As the fire burns the woods, And as the flame sets the mountains on fire, (15) So pursue them with your tempest, and frighten them with Your storm. (16) Fill their faces with shame, that they may seek **YOUR NAME** [Yahweh], O Master.

It is quite obvious that they would only SEEK THE NAME of YHWH because Muslims do not worship the true Elohim, but worship a false deity called Allah, who originated in Babylon (Iraq).

Who says the NAME is not important?

17. Let them be confounded and dismayed forever; yes, let them be put to shame and perish,

18. That men may know that You; whose **NAME** alone is the **Yahweh**, are the Most High over all the earth.

One day a 1/3 remnant of Muslims will know that the Elohim of Israel is Yahweh (Isaiah 19: 18-25) and that He is the only true Elohim; but then it maybe too late for many of them.

The table of nations in the war list are.

Now let us take a look and name the countries:

Edom	Southern Jordan.
Ishmaelite	Ishmael was the father of all the Arabs.
Moab	Central Jordan.
Hagarenes	Egypt.
Gebal	Lebanon.
Ammon	Northern Jordan.
Amalek	Esau's descendants who are Jordanians and Arabs.
Philistia	The Gaza Strip.
Assyria	Syria and Iraq.
Tyre	Phoenicia – Southern Lebanon.
Assur	Assyrians.
Children of Lot	Plains of Jordan – Genesis 13:11.
Zebah and Zalmunnah	Both Kings of Midianites, these were Arabs in Judges 8:5.
Oreb and Zeeb	Princes of Midians - Judges 8:3.

Do any of these countries resemble Western Europe? Think! Some prophecy teachers out of deliberate ignorance, or lack of knowledge want to fit Edom with and into Europe. It is surprising how any prophecy teacher can see Europe or the USA in this picture, when in fact none resemble any European people!

Many prophets of the Tanach (Torah and prophets) have prophesied concerning the people of this confederacy. The prophecies are far too complex and numerous to discuss exhaustively for the purposes of this book. However, I will discuss the most prominent passages of the Bible to examine in sufficient depth in order to show the nature of this confederacy. They are all Islamic nations without a shadow of a doubt and they fit like a glove on a hand. If I really wanted to go into the Hebrew and Aramaic of the words then I would have to write ten books to explain the significance of each passage of Scripture because the detail is in the words used for these people. Yahweh gives precise detail and therefore I have made a few pointers in this book because this book is already increasing in weight.

Two key elements in **Psalm 83:11** "Make their nobles like Oreb, and like **Zeeb**: yea, all their princes as Zebah, and as Zalmunna."

The question is, what happened in the account of Oreb, Zeeb, Zebah and Zalmunna and who were they?

We can see in **Judges 7:25** And they captured **two princes of the Midianites**, [two Arab princes] Oreb and Zeeb. They killed Oreb at the rock of Oreb, and Zeeb they killed at the winepress of Zeeb.

160

Zeev meaning a wolf is a picture of the Arabs today, who do not want to make true peace with Israel. They are primarily deceiving the world by making a false and insincere pseudo-peace with the State of Israel. We can see why this fits with Zeev. Wolves in sheep's clothing!

Also in **Judges 8:21** we find what happened to **Zebah** and **Zalmunnah the two Arab kings**.

"Then Zebah and Zalmunna said, "Rise yourself, and fall upon us; for as the man is, so is his strength." And Gideon arose and slew Zebah and Zalmunna; and **he took the crescents** that were on the necks of their camels [these were worshippers of the moon-elohim in that region of the world back then]."

Zebah and Zalmunnah were pursued by Gideon and also killed, for they had killed Gideon's brothers on Mount Tabor (**Judges 8:18-19**).

All of these people were Midianites [Arabs]; likewise the end-times confederacy is largely comprised of the Arabs at the head of the invasion, followed by the other Muslim nations at the rear.

In the same way, instead of Messiah taking away the crosses as predicted by the Islamic prophecy, we have the opposite to be true - all the **crescents** on the highest places (minarets of mosques) will be taken away. Just like the times of old when Israel had to remove Ashera (the female goddess) from the high places, since the Jews often fell into the false worship of false gods and goddesses and were rebuked by the Elohim of Israel. Here the word used in the Hebrew language for the crescent in **Judges 8:21** is "saharon," which means the crescent moon. This is a play on the word **Shachar** used for the name of s.a.tan in **Isaiah 14:12** regarding the name of s.a.tan (**Hilal ben Shachar – Son of the morning or dawn**). So we can see that the worship of the crescent moon god stems from the distant past. In fact it was Nabonidus who exported Allah from Babylon (Iraq) to Saudi Arabia in the 6th century BCE. When s.a.tan is cast down to the lower heavens, this is what Isaiah 14 describes. Namely that s.a.tan will possess a body, namely the Anti-Messiah.

Interestingly the Qur'an speaks of the dawn, when the angelic host came down from heaven described in the Qur'an:

Sura 97:1-5 Al-Qadr (The night vision) "We have sent it to thee in the Night of Vision, what do you know of this night of Vision. The Night of Vision is better then a thousand months. The angelic hosts descend [to earth] in it with the Spirit by command of their Master. Peace shall it be until the rising of the Dawn (Morning star)."

Isaiah 14:12a How you are fallen from heaven, O Lucifer, son of the morning!

This event apparently occurred on the 27th day of the month of Ramadan, when Muhammad had his encounter with the angel who revealed the Qur'an. This is the same month during which Muslims fast from dawn to dusk, basing the fasting season on the appearance of the moon. When we were young we were taught that we should stay up praying and we would get anything we asked for on this night from Allah. Some kids used to put bricks in cloth and pray that they would become gold. This is why they call it the **night of power**; needless to say the bricks never changed.

161

The words parallel Scripture regarding s.a.tan (dawn) being cast out of heaven, and the fallen angels.

It is essential to point out that the Hebrew word "Lucifer" in Isaiah 14:12 is "Ben Shachar":

Hilal is a Hebrew word, which means "The brightness" and in Aramaic/Arabic means **crescent moon**. s.a.tan is also an angel of light (**2 Corinthians 11:14**), so you can guess which Angel Muhammad saw.

Shachar in Hebrew means dawn, or morning star.

Add the two together and you get his symbol – "crescent moon" and "the star," and in Islam there is a great significance placed on this in the chapter of the night vision in the Qur'an as described above:

The words in **Isaiah 14** come right out of Scripture regarding s.a.tan (the dawn, the spirit, and their master) cast out of heaven, and the fallen angels. These verses should alert believers, for those who know the Bible should pay due attention. These verses came down regarding Ramadan, when Muslims fast at the appearing of the crescent moon with Venus (the morning star), which is the symbol of s.a.tan as written by Isaiah. Muslims usually wait until the late hours of the night gazing at the sky waiting to see the sky open and the angelic host descend. Many Muslims would go up on the roof with their families during the "Night Vision" and gaze at the sky in hopes for this night to happen.

The most well known Islamic song, which came from its founders:

ARABIC
Tala'al-Badru 'alayna,
min thaniyyatil-Wada'
wajaba al-shukru 'alayna,
ma da'a lillahi da'

ENGLISH
O' the White Moon rose over us
From the Valley of Wada'
And we owe it to show gratefulness
Where the call is to Allah

Isaiah 14 is not about the Babylonian king Nebuchadnezzar as most people think, or any other ruler, of ancient Babylon. Isaiah 14 verse one all the way to verse 23 is about s.a.tan, and then suddenly verses 24 and 25 consist of the following end-times terminology:

"As I have purposed, it shall rise; **to break Assyria in My land**, and on **My Mountains I will trample him**...this is the purpose that is purposed on all the earth, and this is the hand that is stretched out on all the nations."

The text suddenly goes from describing the Anti-Messiah's ultimate destruction to describing the destruction of "Assyria" without any apparent break in the subject. This shows us that this is end-time Assyria in the future not in the past.

In Isaiah the king of Assyria spoken of is very descriptive of the Anti-Messiah. **Isaiah chapter 30** proves the conclusion quite clearly:

Isaiah 30:30-31 "YHWH will make the majesty of His voice heard; the lowering of His arm He will show, with raging anger, and a consuming flame; with cloudburst and storm and hailstones. **For by the voice of YHWH, Assyria is crushed."**

It's that same unmistakable terminology signifying the Day of YHWH, where "His arm" is, as is the case throughout Isaiah (e.g. Isaiah 53:1), referring to Yahushua the Messiah of Israel. This is not the Assyria of that day, but an end-times revived "Assyria," which is destroyed by the fiery coming of Yahushua on dark and tempestuous clouds, when He destroys s.a.tan by the **"breath of His mouth"** and by the **"sword out of His mouth."**

Micah 5:5-6 And this **One shall be peace**. When The Assyrian comes into our land, and when he treads in our palaces, then we will raise against him **seven shepherds** and **eight princely men. They shall waste with the sword the land of Assyria, and the land of Nimrod at its entrances**; thus He shall deliver us from The Assyrian, when he comes into our land and when he treads within our borders.

This is a prophecy concerning the Messiah Yahushua's second return to this earth, to the holy hill, or Mount Zion in Jerusalem. The Messiah will be **the peace**, in Hebrew *"ha shalom."* He will be the **tower of refuge** and strength in the last days against The Assyrian and therefore The "Assyrian" is clearly another title for the Anti-Messiah.

Also, in Isaiah 31 the text emphasis on Assyria and that *"The Master will come down to fight for Mount Zion" (31:4)*, is literal. And in 31: 8 directly as a result of His coming, we again see that *"Assyria shall fall by a sword, not of man."* Yahushua clearly never fought battles against Assyria in His first coming and therefore this must be referring to Messiah's Second Advent.

Then we have the passages in **Isaiah 10:5, 6, 20, 21; 11:1, 4**:

"Woe to Assyria, the rod of My anger! And My fury is the staff in their hand. I will send Him against an ungodly nation, and against the people of My wrath. I will command Him to plunder, and to strip off spoil and to trample them like the mud in the streets. And it shall be in that day that the remnant of Israel shall not any more lean on him who struck him. But **they will truly lean on YHWH, the Holy One of Israel** [yet to be fulfilled]. The remnant shall return, the remnant of Jacob, to the Mighty Elohim. And a shoot [David] goes out from the stump of Jesse, and a Branch [**Yahushua**] will bear fruit out of his roots and He shall strike the earth with the rod of His mouth and the wolf shall live with the lamb."

It is quite clear that this passage is referring to the future end-time Assyria not past, when the wolf will lay with the lamb, which signifies peace on earth with Jerusalem being at the forefront of this spiritual and political renewal. This is when the promises of YHWH to Abraham will be fulfilled, when there is true peace on earth and the full blessings/engrafting of YHWH upon "all the families of the earth" (**Genesis 12:3b**). The city of Jerusalem is at the heart of controversy in global affairs, such as at the United Nations and so forth. In fact, it has been burnt to cinders three times in history. Ironically, the name comprises of two aspects, in Hebrew **"yira"** means "to see," or make manifest i.e. in biblical Hebrew this is a personal form, a reality such as seen in Yahushua of Nazareth, and "**shalem**" which means "peace, or fullness." And we shall see it lives up to its name, when the Messiah returns and defeats the dark forces that ravage His creation.

The Millennial restoration of Israel is a direct result of the defeat of "**Mystery Babylon**" and "**Assyria**." The Anti-Messiah has many guises and many titles such as: "King of Babylon" and "The Assyrian" (Babylon was a part of the Assyrian Empire), "King of Tyre" and "Cedar of Lebanon" to name a few. At the end of the day, we must comprehend and contend with the title of "Islam," which means to submit, or be "in submission to." Remember this too started in Babylon with the idol of the Moon-god. Men in their vain imaginations and reasoning's ascribed greatness to one, other than the true YHWH, an idol of stone that became an idol in their hearts and "Allah hu akbar" (Arabic: Allah is the greatest) became their battle cry, even unto death.

This is what Encyclopaedia Britannica says about this person:
> Also spelled Nabu-Na'id ("Reverer of Nabu") king of Babylonia from 556 until 539 BC, when Babylon fell to Cyrus, king of Persia. After a popular rising led by the priests of Marduk, chief god of the city, **Nabonidus**, who **favored the moon god Sin** [Allah's origin], made his son Belshazzar co-regent and **spent much of his reign in Arabia**. Returning to Babylon in 539 BC, he was captured by Cyrus's general Gobryas and exiled. (Emphasis mine)

Take a look at any mosque today and you will see a crescent symbol on the top. You will also find the crescent symbol and star on many Islamic national flags. The star comes from the Venus sign attributed to the worship of "Menat," the daughter of Allah in Mecca, who was the goddess of fate and destiny personified by the evening star. She was worshipped as a black stone situated between Mecca and Arabia. Today you can find that black stone in the Ka'ba revered by all Muslims, who circum-ambulate the Ka'ba seven times and kiss the black stone thinking it, purges their sins (Tawaf). The concept itself is unreasonable and illogical that a stone can take away anything, let alone sin.

Simply put the stone in the Ka'ba is enough to signify this to be pagan styled worship. To bow is to worship, and all Muslims bow to the Ka'ba, though they insist they do not worship the Ka'ba. However the definition of "bowing" to something, or someone, means to worship i.e. usually to the true Elohim, or a false god. We can see the evidence here, that they offer worship to a false god.

B.   Psalm 74 – A plea to YHWH to stop the Islamic onslaught

I will show how this Psalm applies to Islam word by word.

1 O' YHWH, why hast thou cast us off forever? Why doth thine anger smoke against the sheep of thy pasture?

Israel has been cast off for its sins and the Jews believe YHWH has neglected them.

2 Remember thy congregation, which thou hast purchased of old; the rod of thine inheritance, which thou hast redeemed; this Mount Zion, wherein thou hast dwelt.

The Master YHWH ordained Israel to proclaim the truth to the nations and called Israel His very own heritage.

3 Lift up thy feet unto the perpetual desolations; even all that <u>the enemy</u> <u>hath done wickedly in the sanctuary</u>.

Who has done wickedly in YHWH's sanctuary? None other then the present occupiers, the Islamic hordes, who daily pollute the sanctuary with their abominations. The Muslim Waqf of Jerusalem recently tried to destroy the artefacts that they dug up by dumping them on rubbish heaps, so that no Jew could claim the Temple Mount as the site of their ancient Temple. The Muslims even lie by saying Solomon was a Muslim and the Temple there was build by the Canaanite people, who they claim are the ancestors of the Palestinian people. We quote:

> "Bulldozers have been carting away huge mounds of earth from underneath the Temple Mount in Jerusalem, one of the most revered sacred sites in the world, drawing the ire of Israeli archaeologists who say Muslim authorities are damaging the inside of the Mount's eastern retaining wall and destroying possibly priceless historical information in the process.
> The furor stems from a construction project undertaken by the Waqf, the Muslim religious authority that controls the Temple Mount, to create a second entrance to the Al-Marawani mosque, located under the south-eastern quadrant of the Mount in an area popularly, but mistakenly, known as Solomon's Stables.
>
> The huge underground mosque at times attracts thousands of worshipers, so there was no question that a second entry way was needed for safety reasons. But the Waqf's decision to simply haul material from the area and to dump it, in the dead of night, in the nearby Kidron Valley has been attacked as irresponsible destruction of an archaeological site. Israeli archaeologists say the area should first have been subjected to a controlled excavation. Now personnel from the Israel Antiquities Authority (IAA) can only sift through the dump in the Kidron Valley in hopes of gaining some raw, but context less, data about ancient Jerusalem.[32]

Please note that many synagogues have been attacked not just in Israel, but also around the world, such as in Turkey and Tunisia in particular, as well as other Israeli targets. The Roman Catholic Church, the EU and the USA do not burn synagogues, or attack the religious shrines of Judaism today. In fact, the Muslims have gone as far as to destroy Abraham, Sarah, Rachel and Joseph's tomb in Israel, yet they falsely claim that they were all Muslims. Well it begs the question; if this was so, then why destroy the tombs?

4 Thine enemies roar in the midst of thy congregations; they set up their ensigns for signs.

The Muslims roar and rumble and throw stones on the Jews on the Temple wall below.

July 30, 2001- "Israeli police stormed the Temple Mount in Jerusalem's walled Old City on Sunday to quell a riot by Muslims. The clashes began after Muslim

---

[32] http://www.har-habayt.org/bar0.html

rioters began throwing stones at Jews praying below them at the adjoining Western Wall. Israeli police rushed onto the Temple Mount, site of the Jewish Temples in biblical times, and fired stun grenades at Muslim rioters. The clash took place in the most sensitive area in the Israeli-Arab conflict. The Temple Mount is the site of the holy Temples in biblical times, and is regarded as the most sacred place in the Jewish world. Since the Muslim conquest of Jerusalem in the 7th century AD, the area has also been home to the Dome of the Rock and Al-Aqsa Mosque. Muslims claim the site as the third holiest site in Islam, after Mecca and Medina in Saudi Arabia. Fifteen policemen and 20 Palestinians were injured in the clashes, which continued intermittently throughout the afternoon. Palestinians threw shoes on police trying to storm the Temple Mount to stop the riot." [33]

5 A man was famous according as he had lifted up axes upon the thick trees.

This refers to the men that cut down the trees to build YHWH's holy sanctuary.

6 But now they break down the carved work thereof at once with axes and hammers.
Who are these people breaking this place down? Are they perhaps the Islamists?

7 They have cast fire into thy sanctuary, they have defiled by casting down the dwelling place of thy Name to the ground.

They hate the Jews and hate the Elohim of Israel by denying that there was ever a Temple there to worship the Elohim of Israel. They proclaim and put up ensigns/emblems to say only "Allah is god and Muhammad his last prophet" and deny the one true Elohim of Israel.
8 They said in their hearts, <u>Let us destroy them together</u>: they have <u>burned up all the synagogues of YHWH</u> in the land.

They literally destroyed all the synagogues in the West Bank fulfilling the above verses prophetically spoken.

They conspire together with other Islamic nations to destroy the Jews, their plan is to destroy the 'Saturday people' first (Jews) and then the 'Sunday people' (Christians). Is it not ironic that Muhammad chose Friday as a day of worship, seemingly to pre-empt Saturday and Sunday by trying to make himself look first in the race to qualify for the truth?

Joseph's tomb destroyed by a Palestinian Muslim mob.

Look at pictures on the link below: http://www.shechem.org/kyos/engkyos.html
They were even dancing on Joseph's grave; pictures of this can be seen on the above website.

Joseph's tomb was destroyed and burned literally by Muslim mobs. Over 16 synagogues were desecrated on the West Bank, which are all of the synagogues in

---

[33] http://www.telegraph.co.uk/news/main.jhtml?xml=/news/2001/07/30/wmid30.xml By Inigo Gilmore

Judea. This is literally fulfilled just as the Psalm dictates. **Psalm 74:8b** they have burned up all the synagogues of YHWH in the land [literally destroyed by these heathens].

Excerpts from sermons delivered live over Palestinian television on the 13th of October 2000 by Dr. Ahmad Abu Halabiya: "Wherever you are, kill the Jews, the Americans, who are like them, and those who stand by them. They are all in one accord against the Muslims. It is forbidden to befriend Israelis in anyway. Do not love them, or enter into agreement with them, do not help them, or sign accords with them. Anyone who does this is one of them. This is the word of Allah for which various Suras are cited from the Qur'an e.g. Sura 9:5.

Sura 9:5 So when the sacred months have passed away, then slay the idolaters wherever you find them, and take them captives and besiege them and lie in wait for them in every ambush; then if they repent and keep up prayer and pay the poor-rate, leave their way free to them; surely Allah is Forgiving, Merciful.

Also Sura 9:29 includes Jews and Christians.
Fight those who believe not in Allah [all NON MUSLIMS] nor the Last Day, nor hold that forbidden which hath been forbidden by Allah and His Messenger, [things forbidden by Muhammad] nor acknowledge the Religion of Truth [Islam], from among the People of the Book [both Christians and Jews], until they pay the Jizzya [tax to live] with willing submission [the Jews and Christians are to submit to Muslims] and feel themselves subdued [humiliated by Muslims until they change, or become Muslims].

If you as a humanist, animist, polytheist, atheist, agnostic, or Hindu yet do not believe Muhammad is a messenger of Allah, then you are to be killed. There are no exceptions given. The only exception that is given is for the Christians, or the Jews (people of the book), is charging them Jizzya tax, and treating them like a 'dhimmi' (a protected person, but treated like a second class citizen, paying high taxes in order to live in Islamic lands), subjugating them to humiliation. Later, we will look at the Umar Edict that tells the Muslims how to treat non-Muslims.
The Ayatollah Khomeini of Iran expressed one of his purposes was to eradicate Israel.

Osama bin Laden repeated these purposes in 1998 and urged jihad against Americans and Jews. He ruled that it is obligatory for all Muslims to kill the infidels in Muslim lands and to drive them out. He considers them as those plundering Muslim resources i.e. oil, gas and minerals.

He has stated to kill the Americans and their allies i.e. the British and cited this; This is in accordance with the words of Almighty god, "and fight the pagans all together as they fight you all together," and "fight them until there is no more tumult, or oppression, and there prevails justice and faith in god."

The purposes are simply to free Palestine and get rid of all infidels; these include all Jews and Christians including pagans who do not believe in Allah as their god.

In a sermon, of all things, Sheikh Ibrahim Mahdi issued a warning over Palestinian television on June 8 2001:

"Allah is willing for the unjust State of Israel to be erased. The unjust state, the United States will be erased. The unjust state, Britain, will be erased."

167

Recently Ahmadinejad (October of 2005) stated as the imam said, Israel must be wiped off the map, referring to Iran's revolutionary leader Ayatullah Khomeini.
9 We see not our signs: there is no more any prophet: neither is there among us any that knoweth how long.

All the Jews are perplexed as to how long this can continue; surely it must end.

10 O' YHWH, how long shall the adversary reproach? Shall the enemy blaspheme thy Name forever?

They continuously ask YHWH how long these [Muslims] will blaspheme His holy Name.

11 Why withdrawest thou thy hand, even thy right hand? Take it out of Your bosom and destroy them.

YHWH's right hand signifies judgment to judge these nations.

12 For YHWH is my King of old, working salvation in the midst of the earth.

The Master YHWH is the one, who can work our salvation, and we are not worthy to work out our own salvation. We accept what the Master provides through His mercy upon us by the blood of the Lamb.

13 Thou didst divide the sea by thy strength: thou brakest the heads of the dragons in the waters.

This is referring to YHWH's division of the Red Sea during the exodus from Egypt.

14 Thou brakest the heads of leviathan in pieces, and gavest him to be meat to the people inhabiting the wilderness.

The dinosaur is such a huge beast, yet the Master gave this as meat to the people.

15 Thou didst cleave the fountain and the flood: thou driest up mighty rivers.

16 The day is thine, the night also is thine: thou hast prepared the light and the sun.

17 Thou hast set all the borders of the earth: thou hast made summer and winter.

18 Remember this, that the enemy hath reproached, O YHWH, and that the foolish people have blasphemed thy Name.

Again mention is made of the Master's glories and his Name is being blasphemed by these idolaters.

19 O deliver not the soul of thy turtledove unto the multitude of the wicked: forget not the congregation of thy poor forever.

168

20 Have respect unto the covenant: for the dark places of the earth are full of the habitations of cruelty.
They make a plea to the Elohim of Israel not to forget his covenant with them.
21 O let not the oppressed return ashamed: let the poor and needy praise thy name.

22 Arise, O YHWH, plead thine own cause: remember how the foolish man reproacheth thee daily.

23 Forget not the voice of thine enemies: the tumult of those that rise up against thee increaseth continually.

Things seem to be getting worse by the day so the Jewish people plead for the Elohim of Israel to intervene and cast justice on their behalf, as it seems the world is slowly turning against them. The reason for this is simple. The Arab Muslims control a lot of oil so they swing the balance of world opinion in their favor and even the European nations who rely heavily on Arab oil hold the Jews in contempt and favor the Muslims. The situation increases in sadness each day.

Clearly, these things are not going to remain as they are. YHWH is going to uphold His covenant people Israel and cast judgement soon.

It is quite clear for all to see that the Islamic nations are mentioned by their locations, since Islam did not exist prior to the 6th century AD. We must pay attention to the old biblical names and translate them into our modern countries, in order to know that these are indeed all-Islamic nations e.g. as the following table shows.

Edom	Southern Jordan.
Ishmaelite	Ishmael was the father of all the Arabs.
Mitzrayim	Egypt.
Moab	Central Jordan.
Hagarenes	Egyptians.
Gebal	Lebanon.
Ammon	Northern Jordan.
Amalek	Esau's descendants who are Jordanians and Arabs.
Philistia	The Gaza Strip.
Assyria	Syria and Iraq.
Tyre	Phoenicia – Southern Lebanon.
Assur	Assyrians.
Children of Lot	Plains of Jordan – Genesis 13:11.
Zebah and Zalmunnah	Both Kings of Midianites, these were Arabs in **Judges 8:5**.
Oreb and Zeeb	Princes of Midians - **Judges 8:3**.
Babylon	Iraq and parts of Syria and Turkey.
Lud	Lydia Modern Eastern Turkey.

Now if any "scholar" tries to tell you that Babylon is the USA, the EU, or the Vatican, then you have a sound biblical basis to show them that YHWH does not see it that way. This is the imagination and error of many scholars. s.a.tan quite happily does his job, keeping many looking in the wrong place, which is exactly his plan of deception. **YHWH is not in the business of confusing people, or concealing key end time truths!** YHWH did not send His only unique Son Yahushua the Messiah to save the world through blood atonement on the cross, yet point us to Muhammad as His last prophet, with the idea of good deeds earning our salvation. Yet this is the absurdity that many want to believe. Friends, this is of s.a.tan and this is his deception so be warned.

Chapter 7

Who Are the Heathens and Why Are There Judgments Against Them in The End Times?

Although it appears that the word "heathen" can be applied to just any godless person or people, the Bible has a very specific application to a specific end-time people. Historically it was used to describe the enemy of the Jews in biblical days and is also now applied the same way in the end-times. The historical heathen were the foreshadowing of the 'real beef to come,' that is Islam and the Muslims.

The Muslims worship their god Allah who is not the Elohim of Israel and their sermons are full of hatred against the very people whose land they occupy, also known as the Palestinian regions in Israel. These are the heathens that YHWH has spoken against time and time again. No they are not Europeans, or Americans, because at least the Europeans and Americans have Christian populations and even the godless there do not go around beheading, or cutting limbs off of people in the name of Allah.

> **Deuteronomy 4:27** And the Master shall scatter you among the nations, and **ye shall be left few in number among the heathen** [Islamic nations], whither the Master shall lead you.

Note that for the backsliding of the Jews the Master scattered them. Here particular mention is made of them being few in number among the heathens. Note in Islamic lands today there are very few Jews or Ephraimites, while this cannot be literally applied to the west, which has plenty of Jewish and Ephraimite populations, seeing that Scripture even says the end time nations are full of Yisraelites from both houses (Genesis 48:19). The only heathen nations that have almost no Israelite populations in these last days are those Islamic nations and those governed by Islamic Law!

866,000 Jews were living in around Arab lands, that mostly later left due to fear of their lives, as it was quite common in Muslim lands to lynch Jews. After Israel's birth very few Jews are now left in and around the Middle Eastern Muslim dominated areas. See these numbers:

Jewish Populations of Arab Countries: 1948 and 2001

(In 2006 no doubt there are less than 6,500 left) [34]

1948	2001
Aden 8,000	0
Algeria 140,000	0
Egypt 75,000 - 80,000	100
Iraq 135,000 -140,000	200
Lebanon 5,000	100
Libya 35,000 - 38,000	0
Morocco 250,000-265,000	5,230
Syria 15,000 - 30,000	100
Tunisia 50,000-105,000	1,000
Yemen 45,000 - 55,000	200
Total 758,000	**6,500**

In 2006 this figure may well be under 1,000 Jews in Muslim lands.

Now lets look at Ephraimite, or non-Jewish believers mostly from the 10 tribes living in Muslim lands. As one can see the numbers are small and yet greater than their Jewish brothers. These figures below highlight the need for Christians to "come our of her My people," sooner rather than later.

Revelation 18:4 And I heard another voice from heaven, saying, Come out of her, my people, that ye be not partakers of her sins, and that ye receive not of her plagues.

Christians in Muslim lands-not necessarily born again believers

Afghanistan	100,000	
Bahrain	61000	Expats
Bangladesh	1,050,000	
Egypt	3,500,000	Mainly Coptic.
Iran	136,000	
Iraq	750,000	The oldest Christian population is in this nation
Lebanon	1,500,000	
Libya	172,968	Expats
Morocco	35,000	
S. Arabia	95,000	Most of these are expatriates and again not necessarily born again.
Syria	1,844,876	
Turkey	139,000	
UAE	76,000	
Yemen	103,635	
Pakistan	3,000,00	Out of these only 1/3 are true born again.
Jordan	345,600	
Qatar	70,000	Mainly Expats

---

[34] http://en.wikipedia.org/wiki/Jewish_exodus_from_Arab_lands

When the plagues come about then many of these people will suffer also being in these regions where YHWH's wrath will pour. Some of these will deserve judgement because they have mixed with the Muslims and are only Christian by name.

While admittedly there are unbelievers in the west, the literal prophecy is only fulfilled through the Islamic lands that have decimated Jews and Ephraimites, driving them out, persecuting and killing them. Some might argue that the west has heathens, but this still applies to the Islamic hordes, more then any other people. There are plenty of Israelites in the west in increasing numbers. But apply this Scripture and others like it to any Muslim land and see how this can only be fulfilled in those lands.

> **Nehemiah 6:16** And it came to pass, that when all our enemies heard thereof, and **all the heathen** [**all the Arabs round about**] that were about us [**round about Israel just like the Muslim nations today**] saw these things, they were much cast down in their own eyes: for they perceived that this work was wrought of our YHWH.

These heathens who opposed them in rebuilding Israel were clearly Arabs and the text mentions "round about us." Now do you seriously think that Europeans, or the USA are 'round about Israel' and this somehow can be applied to them? Europeans had a very strong Christian witness and they have simply backslid from the truth and fallen away. Now most churches in Europe do not preach the gospel of Messiah, but a social gospel instead, to gather the dwindling masses. Those Arabs who were "round about" them worshipped the moon deity back then. They had crescent symbols on their camel's necks, just as stated in **Judges 8:21**. So these "heathens" never had the truth. Or should we say they never desired to embrace the truth shared by Nehemiah and Ezra!

> So Zebah and Zalmunna said, "Rise yourself, and kill us; for as a man is, so is his strength." So Gideon arose and killed Zebah and Zalmunna, and took the crescent ornaments that were on their camels' necks.

Note these were Midianites [Arab Kings]. Gideon is a picture of Messiah who on His return will also tear down the crescent symbols of the mosques and throw down these places of idolatry.

> **Isaiah 45:23** I have sworn by Myself; the word has gone out of My mouth in righteousness, and shall not return, that to Me every knee shall bow, every tongue shall take an oath.

The language is unmistakable and can never apply to Rome but to Islam only, who bow to a foreign elohim and one day will realize their folly.

> **Isaiah 46:1-2** Bel bows down, Nebo stoops; their idols were on the beasts and on the cattle. Your carriages were heavily loaded, a burden to the weary beast. (2) They stoop, they bow down together; they could not deliver the burden, but have themselves gone into captivity.

Read carefully that even Bel the idol namely (Allah) bows down. This is the name of the deity that came out of Iraq. Even their carriages carry the Islamic crescent symbols. Look today at any Muslim car and you will find Islamic signs such as hanging CDs with Qur'anic verses, or a tasbih (**rosary beads**) with Allah embedded on every bead along with other Islamic symbols. The verse is clear; these statues will bow down i.e. they will be broken

172

and smashed and made to bow down to YHWH. Despite so much evidence pinpointing Islam, why are many still saying it must be the Pope, the USA, the EU, or Roman Catholicism?

Psalms 2:1-3 Why do the **heathen rage** [Muslim nations], and the people imagine a vain thing? The kings of the earth [Islamic leaders] set themselves, and the rulers take counsel together [to destroy Israel], against the Master [against Yahweh the true Elohim], and against His anointed [Yahushua of Nazareth and all those that follow Him], saying, Let us break their bands asunder, and cast away their cords [refers to complete castigation of the anointed people i.e. complete and utter annihilation] from us.

Do not Muslims want to keep Christians and Jews in an ongoing 'dhimmitude' state of utter subjugation by killing them as history has shown us? Why do you think the edict in Islam is that the testimony of a non-Muslim has half the value of a Muslim? This means a non-Muslim, even though his rights may be violated, cannot bring a case against a Muslim because of insufficient evidence.

No Western nation plots to destroy Israel, but the Islamic ones certainly want to destroy Israel. Given half a chance they will remove every Jew from Israel and hang them on gallows. We also find plenty of Muslims travelling to Israel from the west to become suicide bombers. This shows that the true "heathen" analogy only fits these nations. There are many godless nations in the west, but the wording in these verses is not used for them nor intended for them.

Yahushua rightly warned about these people time after time...

Matthew 6:7 But when you pray, do not use vain repetitions as the **heathen** do. For they think that they will be heard for **their many words**.

Note another thing; people apply the word **heathen** to godless people generally. But this is not the correct usage here, as Yahushua clearly shows that these **heathen** people actually make prayers to a "god." Therefore this is not a broad definition as some apply it. Generally godless people do not make prayers to any elohim. This verse cannot be applied to an atheist who does not care to believe in any elohim, or let alone repeat a prayer. The only ones who repeat prayers daily are Muslims and what Yahushua was teaching was about things to come, not things, as they existed.

Do not the Muslims use vain repetitions praying the same prayer five times a day, even repeating it in their 'tayyad' prayer after midnight? They recite on the **rosary beads** the same thing 'Allah hu Akbar' (Allah is greater) and 'Bism Allah' (in the name of Allah), many hundreds of times after each prayer. Also in their homes they take the date fruit, dry out their seeds and use these to read Sura 36 (Yasin) from the Qur'an 72 times, as a special veneration to their deity. This is what Yahushua was warning about. Endless repetitions to please a deity who cannot forgive, and then attributing these readings as good works. This is typical of man trying to reach YHWH and it is futile. Whereas Yahushua of Nazareth is Almighty YHWH, who reached down into humanity. The only faith that has this attribute is biblical Judaism, or biblical Christianity. In all other religions people try to reach YHWH, but will not succeed because their gods are nothing more then wood and stone made by hands, or images of their vain imaginations.

Leviticus 25:44 Both thy bondmen, and thy bondmaids, which thou shalt have, shall be of the **heathen that are round about you**; of them shall you buy bondmen and bondmaids.

Looks like the Master was trying to teach a lesson to the Israelite nation and Yahushua simply reaffirmed the earlier teaching. Even though the words are so clear and so accurate still people fail to realize that these people are already "**roundabout**" Israel. Which Western nations are "**roundabout**" Israel? NONE!

Leviticus 26:33 And I will **scatter you among the heathen**, and will draw out a sword after you: and your land shall be desolate, and your cities waste.

One could argue that the Jews in Europe are also scattered amongst heathens, but here the context clearly is not Europe, but surrounding nations. The same nations that in the old times practiced false worship and even today do the same. They are all Islamic. The "drawing of the sword" against Israel has been literally fulfilled in all Islamic lands, where the Jews have been treated as a 'dhimmi' and subjugated, brought low to humiliation, often followed by death with the sword.

Although, some might argue that the Jews were also killed in Russia and in Europe during the Holocaust, they forget one thing. These nations are not "**roundabout**" Israel and so the application is not to these nations. If we look in the western nations, the Jews live in adequate luxury and states of well being in prominent positions.

Now take a hard look and see if you can find even one Jew in the same position in any Islamic country?

Leviticus 26:38 And **ye shall perish among the heathen**, and the land of your enemies shall eat you up.

Can one argue that the Jews are still living in the lands of their worst enemy the Muslims? The verse is clear in that this place is not an allegorical far away western civilisation, but the "land of their enemy." Israel's worst enemies historically were the Philistines "**roundabout**" them, followed by the Midianites also "**roundabout**" them. In a majority of Muslims countries the Jews were killed and it was very hard for them to leave these places. They lived in ghettos and still do. Usually entire Jewish communities perished under false charges. It was only in the USA, Europe and some North and Latin American countries, where Jews flourished after many set backs. But even today in Muslim lands they cannot live in peace. The Islamists even dig Jewish graves up not to let the dead rest in dignity. Only in Muslim lands do Jews perish, whereas in other lands, they are persecuted, but still survive. The surrounding heathen nations then are clearly Islamic and not western.

Leviticus 26:45 But I will for their sakes remember the covenant of their ancestors, whom I brought forth out of the land of Egypt in the sight of the heathen, [all of Egypt looked and surrounding nations when Moses rescued the Jews out of Egypt] that I might be their YHWH: [Moses was YHWH's agent on earth] I am the Master [YHWH is Elohim].

This was not only true for Israel coming out of Egypt but out of Islamic lands also. The largest exodus of the Jews occurred out of Islamic lands, about 800,000 Jews left to go back to Israel. Why is this if Islam was or is allegedly peaceful?

174

A.   **Psalm 79 fits Islam like a glove**

Psalms 79
1. O YHWH, the heathen are come into thine inheritance; Thy holy temple have they defiled; they have laid Jerusalem on heaps.

They have taken Jewish land and called it their own; they defiled the Temple Mount region by building several mosques on it and practicing worship to a false elohim chanting Allah hu Akbar and still defile that holy place.

2. The dead bodies of thy servants have they given to be meat unto the fowls of the heaven, the flesh of thy saints unto the beasts of the earth.

More hard times yet to come when the Jews and Christians will be killed in Israel. In the past, they have killed both Jews and Christians and left their bodies to rot in the streets as an example to others. We see this again in Revelation chapter 11 as Islam kills the two Israelite witnesses and parades their bodies through Jerusalem's streets.

3. Their blood have they shed like water **round about** Jerusalem; and there was none to bury them.

The Jews would be killed and no one would bury them in the Islamic areas. They will let the dead bodies lie in the streets and dance over them. Look what happened to the two soldiers in Ramallah, beaten and brutally killed and then their dead bodies put in the street as an example. There is that phrase again "**round about.**" Can you see why YHWH wants us to pay attention?

4. We are become a **reproach to our neighbors**, a scorn and derision to them **that are round about us**.

Clearly, the people "**roundabout**" the Jews today are not Europeans but Muslims. Could you please tell me who their **neighbors** are? Did I hear you say Islamic nations, who are ALL Muslims? Now you are also seeing what I see for the end times.

5. How long, Master? Wilt thou be angry forever? Shall thy jealousy burn like fire?

The Jews cry out for Justice to the Master. When will this come to an end?

6. Pour out **thy wrath** upon **the heathen that have not known thee**, and upon **the kingdoms** that have not called upon thy Name.

They call judgment upon these Islamic peoples; clearly "kingdoms" is a reference to all Islamic nations, who do not know the one true YHWH. Even though the west may be generally godless, there are Christians who know the true YHWH and worship Him. So there is always a faithful witness for the Master. Look at the USA. It has the largest population of born again believers estimated to be around eighty million. Yahweh's wrath is now beginning to be poured out on Islamic nations. First the Tsunami in Indonesia, the biggest Islamic nation, and now the earthquake in Pakistan, killing several hundred thousand and making millions homeless.

175

This is round one for Yahweh and there is much more to come.

7. For they have devoured Jacob, and laid waste his dwelling place.

Who is trying to devour Jacob [Israel] and lay waste his places, in the land of Israel? Should I dare to call them Islamists perhaps?

8. O remember not against us former iniquities: let thy tender mercies speedily prevent us: for we are brought very low.

The Jewish people are being humiliated daily.

9. Help us, O YHWH of our salvation, for the glory of **thy Name**: and deliver us, and **purge away our sins**, for **thy name's sake**.

They want deliverance of their sin, yet there is no Temple so that atonement can take place. Why ask for purging of sin if there is a Temple and sin can be atoned? Simple, this was speaking about a future time when there would be no Temple. The Jews have been without a Temple for almost 2000 years. They cry for their Moshiach and their Temple. Yahweh will preserve them for His NAME sake. Yahushua has come in the flesh and done the atonement but most Jews do not see it.

10. Wherefore should the **heathen say, where is their YHWH**? Let him be known **among the heathen in our sight** [Islamic neighbors] by the revenging of the blood of thy servants, which is shed.

The Muslims say the Jews are accursed by Allah and so they reason that 'we can do whatever we want with them.' Now even the Muslims claim to be the new chosen people and that the Jews have no one named YHWH to save them, so they say, "Where is their YHWH."

11. Let the sighing of the prisoner come before thee; according to the greatness of thy power preserve thou those that are appointed to die;

Those Jews that get caught and are massacred in Islamic areas in Israel. The Jews pray for a graceful death and a resurrection in the hereafter.

12. And render **unto our neighbors** [heathen Muslim neighbors] sevenfold into their bosom their reproach, wherewith they have reproached thee, O Master.

They cry out for judgment because these heathens are not up against the Jews only, but the Elohim of Israel Himself.

13. So we thy people and sheep of thy pasture will give thee thanks forever; we will shew forth thy praise to all generations.

The Jews, the chosen people, look towards YHWH for salvation and will be saved when the Messiah returns as He gathers His sheep back to Himself and His land. This will truly happen after their salvation, when they will truly once again know and praise Yahushua knowing that Yahweh revealed Himself in this Man.

Jeremiah 10:25 Pour out **thy fury upon the heathen** that **know thee not**, and upon **the families that call not on thy Name**: for **they have eaten up Jacob**, and **devoured him**, and **consumed him**, and **have made his habitation desolate**.

The "heathen" do not know YHWH's true NAME and do not worship the Elohim of Israel, for they worship Allah a foreign god. These are the ones trying to kill, maim and destroy the Jews. YHWH's end-time fury is going to pour upon all these Islamic nations foretold by the Hebrew prophets and is already starting to pour.

All the nations mentioned in the end-times wrath happen to be Islamic not Western, and in fact not one western nation is mentioned explicitly or implicitly.

Jeremiah 49:14 I have heard a rumour from the Master, and an ambassador is **sent unto the heathen**, saying, Gather ye together [all the Islamic nations], and come against her [Israel], and rise up to the battle.

YHWH is doing the gathering to show who is the true Elohim amongst the heathen; the gathering of the Islamic confederate nations is mentioned in Psalm 83, as well as the final war to come.

Ezekiel 11:12 And **ye shall know that I am the Master**: for ye have **not walked in my statutes**, neither **executed my judgments**, but have done after the **manners of the heathen that are round about** you.

Even Ezekiel mentions that the Jewish people had strayed from the truth and not known their true YHWH and have done wrong as the "heathen" "**roundabout**" them who today are all Muslims.

B.   Why these heathens?

YHWH chose these heathens simply because the heathens worshipped a false god and Israel also has gone after false gods and left their true YHWH. This is the current picture of Israel. The majority are in sin and do not know the Father, or their Messiah, Yahushua, who came and died for their sins and was raised from the dead. Yahushua was the perfect sacrifice, yet the Jews rejected Him to follow their own heart's desires. One should ask if Israel saved in its present condition? Clearly, the answer is no. Although there is a remnant in Israel (both houses) that do believe that Yahushua is their Messiah and that YHWH has not lost His witness in Israel. But a day will come when all those that remain in Israel after the revealing of the Anti-Messiah, will be saved. Presently there are only about 7,000 true believers in the State of Israel out of their five million Jewish population. What does that tell us about Israel's moral condition? Not much better then the rest of the world.

Until that happens, the Jews live in the error of many rabbinic traditions. Perhaps many do have zeal for YHWH but in the wrong way. One only has to go to Israel today to see the filthiness going on with nude beaches, open gay marches, and one wonders are these really the chosen people of YHWH, whom He chose to be a "light" unto the gentile nations? They have clearly fallen away and are living in sin. One could also reason that it is through their blindness that the offer of salvation was going to be made to the gentiles. This does not mean however that the Jews are not responsible for their sins, or that they can somehow enter heaven through a backdoor, although many teach this error. They say that the Jews are automatically saved through the Law/Torah (through their heartfelt love for the Jews), though no such biblical case exists. After the death and resurrection of Yahushua, there is only one way to the Father and that is through Yahushua the Messiah. The blindness was for the corporate guilt of national Israel rejecting their Messiah. But individual responsibility still rests on the Jewish person to receive atonement for their sins, or be eternally separated from a holy YHWH. Without the Messiah a Jew is as lost as a Muslim without atonement. YHWH NEVER cancelled the atonement for sin through blood and Yahushua is the only one who offers it today since there is no Temple. This must grieve YHWH greatly, that His chosen people are living blindly in sin and not recognizing their Messiah.

There is a small trickling in of Jews who come to faith in Yahushua (Yahushua Messiah) to enter the kingdom of YHWH. Out of the five million Jews in the State of Israel there are only about 7,000 Jews who are saved, does that sound like a remnant? It sure does, just like when Elijah was alive, he said they have all gone astray and want to kill me. But YHWH said that there were 7,000 in Israel who had not bowed their knees to Baal. This can be seen as an end time prophecy as well.

Ezekiel 28:25 Thus saith the Master YHWH; when I shall have gathered the house of Israel from the people among whom they are scattered, and **shall be sanctified in them in the sight of the heathen**, then shall they dwell in their land that **I have given** to My servant Jacob.

Clearly then, we cannot deny that YHWH loves Israel, His chosen people and will bring them back into their own land of Israel which has been partially fulfilled in 1948. Their first return was in unbelief and their second return would be in belief yet to be fulfilled. The rest of the land that presently the Muslims occupy including the illegal state of Jordan will be given back to the Jews upon Yahushua's return. The "House of Israel/Ephraim, or non Jewish Israelites" will also be in the land and "sanctified." YHWH makes mention that it is He "Himself" who has given the land back to Jacob (Israel).

We, who are alive today, are rather fortunate to have seen this happen in our lifetime, to know that YHWH's promises are true and YHWH is faithful in His words.

Ezekiel 34:28 And they shall no more be a prey to the **heathen**, neither shall **the beast of the land** [Middle East not Europe] devour them; but they shall dwell safely, and **none shall make them afraid**.

This has not happened yet, this is yet future.

Ezekiel 36:5 Therefore thus saith the Master YHWH; surely in the fire of my jealousy have I spoken against the residue of the heathen, and **against all Idumea**, which have **appointed my land into their possession** with the joy of all their heart, with despiteful minds, to cast it out for a prey.

YHWH is extremely angry with what the Arabs roundabout Israel are doing, and the term Idumea covers Southern Jordan and Northern Arabia. We are told that they want to take YHWH's land from His people and are happy in their hearts. Their intention is not simply the land, but to destroy His people the Hebrews.

Ezekiel 36:36 Then the heathen that are left round about you shall know that I the Master rebuilt the ruined places, and planted that which was desolate: I the Master have spoken it, and I will do it.

Here is a direct prophecy again talking about the "Heathens "**roundabout**" Israel." All these are Islamic nations.

> **Ezekiel 38:15-16** And thou shalt come from thy place out of the **north parts**, thou, and many people with thee, all of them riding upon horses, a great company, and a mighty army: And thou shalt come up against My people of Israel, as a cloud to cover the land; it shall be in **the latter days**, and I will bring thee against **My land**, **that the heathen may know me**, when **I shall be sanctified in thee, O Gog, before their eyes**.

This "Gog" is the Anti-Messiah that will come from the North. This is the prophecy of the Anti-Messiah, who will very likely come from Turkey and will be of the Turkic people. The northern quarters refers to Southern Russia, which today are all Islamic nations and are mostly Turkic people. This person will have an alliance with the Islamic nations as described in **Psalm 83**. As one believer appropriately put it Turkey is the 'black horse' that many have failed to recognize.

> **Joel 2:17** **Let the priests** [we are the priests, the true believers], the ministers of the Master [true Christians], weep between the porch and the altar, and let them say, Spare thy people [Jewish nation], **O Master, and give not thine heritage to reproach**, that the heathen [Islamic hordes] should rule over them: wherefore should they say among the people, **Where is their YHWH**?

A very emphatic prophecy, that we the priests of YHWH will pray for the salvation and protection of the Jews from the Islamic onslaught. These people are described as the "**heathen**." Who are these? They are all the Islamic nations, today the corporate alliance.

> **Joel 3:11-12** Assemble yourselves, **and come, all ye heathen**, and **gather yourselves together round about**: thither cause thy mighty ones to come down, O Master. Let the heathen be wakened, and **come up to the Valley of Jehoshaphat**: for **there will I sit to judge all the heathen round about**.

Does this sound like the whole world against Israel? No, this is the Islamists (Muslim world) that are being gathered "**roundabout**" and the context is clear from **Ezekiel 38** and **Psalm 83.** They desire to destroy Israel, but the Master will show Himself great amongst these people, to show them that the true Elohim is not Allah, but Yahweh instead. Amen.

Chapter 8

Israel's Prophets Cast Their Judgments on the Islamic Nations

Will this happen in our lifetime?

The possibilities are very high that the Messiah's return is very soon. My own personal opinion is that the Messiah could come in the next one or two generations. I cannot be certain of the timing as we do not know for certain and are not given a date. But certain events in Scripture indicate to us where we are in history and YHWH's timing. According to Nebuchadnezzar's dream of the great statue, we are at the feet, or the last stage. The Arabs/Islamic armies that are going to come up against Israel have to come during their peak strength. The Arabs have the oil and are now fast building and acquiring powerful weapons. It is estimated that the Arabs have a supply of oil that will last about 65 years. Going by this figure, one could argue that the peak strength of the Arabs could climax in the next fifteen years and then they will be in a prime position to attack Israel to literally fulfil **Psalm 83:4** "Come let us cut them off."

One thing people fail to realize is that not all Arab nations need nuclear weapons to strike Israel. The Bible indicates they will attack as a multitude i.e. a huge army in numbers. Remember the two hundred million-man army out of the Euphrates in Iraq. They need sufficient military strength and one thing they would really like to see is the USA backing off from helping Israel, so they can then have their way. Osama bin Laden warned the USA in his speech before the 2004 USA elections to back off Israel, so the Muslims can have their way and eradicate the Jews. **In our scenario Pakistan is already nuclear capable and has supplied Saudi Arabia with nuclear warheads pointing towards Israel**. Pakistan will play a crucial role in the end-time scenario, as it also hates Israel and helps its Arab brethren. Pakistan's leadership is untrustworthy. In fact, General Parvez Musharraf, contrary to popular opinion, is a very smart guy working to establish a 'caliphate' in league with many extremist Islamic organizations. He helps them through his undercover network, using all forms of deception to deceive the west.

He knows that open aggression is best avoided until the key people are established in the different parts of the world. Iran will become the next major strength in the Middle East, as the Bible reveals to us. While the USA is busy with Iraq and Israel is wrangling with the Palestinians to uproot its Jewish settlements, Iran will sneak in to become nuclear capable. And guess what? While the world wrestles with what to do, Pakistan is secretly helping Iran go nuclear. Also Iran is helping the likes of Osama bin Laden and his comrades to relax in Iran with full Iranian guard protection. Osama's sons have been spotted in Iran doing exactly this. Even if the USA were to warn their people of the need to stop Iran, after the recent Gulf War with Iraq and with no weapons of mass destruction found, the USA is not going to be able to convince their public to stop Iran. The weapons of mass destruction did exist, but were shipped to Syria secretly before the US led invasion into Iraq.

Jeremiah 49:35 Thus says the Master YHWH: Behold, I will break the bow of Elam, **the foremost of their might**. [the strength of the Anti-Messiah]

YHWH has used the USA (George W. Bush), the UK, plus other coalition partners as His weapons of indignation in Iraq (**Isaiah chapter 13**). He will do so again in the near future to come. As far as Iran is concerned, they are set to go critical and will become the strength of the Anti-Messiah sooner rather than later. Recognize it if you have the eyes to see it.

A.   The Prophet Obadiah speaks against the Islamists...

Obadiah-
> 1. The vision of Obadiah. Thus says the Master YHWH concerning Edom (We have heard a report from the Master, and a messenger has been sent among the nations, saying, "Arise, and let us rise up against her for battle"):

This is yet future for the sins of the Edomites and Ishmaelites for their judgment is set.

> 2. "Behold, I will make you small among the nations; you shall be greatly despised.

They have done something very wrong and judgement is set.

> 3. The pride of your heart has deceived you, **you who dwell in the clefts of the rock**, whose habitation is high; you who say in your heart, `who will bring me down to the ground**?'

Ah, that age old issue of "pride" and how all these Muslims are deceived by it and think they are a perfect people with a perfect faith of submission/Islam. They despise the true Elohim and say, "who can bring us down." Esau mingled with the Arabs, and we have our double whammy of pride. This is the most terrible sins one can have. s.a.tan was cast down from his position of authority for it. YHWH calls this one of the abominations that He hates. These are very strong words to use. You will find that these Islamic nations fit these sins, to a tee! The word "heathen" is not just a generalization for unbelievers, but solely directed in the end-times to Muslims alone and anyone else that joins them. Just look at the unmistakable wrath that has begun to be poured out on Islamic nations.

> **Proverbs 6:16-19** These six things the Master hates, yes, seven are an abomination to Him: **A proud look**, a **lying** tongue, **hands that shed innocent blood**, **a heart that devises wicked plans**, **feet that are swift in running to evil**, **a false witness** who speaks lies, and one who **sows discord** among brethren.

1. **Pride.**
2. **Lying tongue.**
3. **Shedding innocent blood.**
4. **Devise wicked plans.**
5. **Causing evil.**
6. **Bearing a false witness.**
7. **Sowing discord.**

The Arab Islamic nations are proud of their status and wealth that comes from oil. They lie against each other, while sitting at the same table. They shed innocent blood by funding Islamic terrorism around the world. Remember the petrodollar used in promoting violence and bloodshed in the Middle East. This is self-created evil. They bear false witness against their own brothers the Jews, to usurp their land, and they sow discord. The Palestinian problem is one that is self-created for sowing discord and it causes all of the seven sins above.

4. **Though you exalt yourself as high as the eagle**, and though you **set your nest among the stars**, from **there I will bring you down**," says the Master.

This is unmistakable language for s.a.tan, who exalts himself amongst the stars and wants to be "like" YHWH. This is described here for these Islamic nations who follow their god (Allah), or s.a.tan, disguised declaring 'who can defeat us, as we are god's chosen people and Israel has been cast off for their sins.' The language is very similar to **Ezekiel 28:5**.

5. "If thieves had come to you, if robbers by night Oh, how you will be cut off! Would they not have stolen till they had enough? If grape-gatherers had come to you, would they not have left some gleanings?

They troubled Israel day and night and stole their land, but are still not content.

YHWH called Esau a profane person. **Hebrews 12:16** Lest there be any fornicator or profane person like Esau.

These people are driven by greed and cannot be fulfilled by what they already have.

6. "Oh, how Esau shall be searched out! How his hidden treasures shall be sought after!

Divine retribution is set for the sins of these nations. "**Jacob I loved**; and **Esau I hated** (**Malachi 3:1**). This is what the Master said about these people, because of their continuous sins day and night, the never-ending hatred. On this day Islam will be fully exposed and eradicated.

7. All the men in your confederacy shall force you to the border; the men at peace with you shall deceive you and prevail against you. Those **who eat your bread shall lay a trap for you**. No one is aware of it.

This is the same confederacy as seen in Psalm 83 of Islamic nations coming up against Israel. It talks about the Muslim leaders who will deceive each other, even though they sit at the same table, eat and proclaim friendship, but plot against each other. This is the **clay with the Iron** (**Daniel 2:41**), the kingdom/Empire is divided from within, yet it has the strength of iron in it and it does not mix well. Not only that, but Edom is itself deceived, why? Essentially they follow a false god and are deceived by Muhammad into believing Allah is god and Muhammad his prophet. These people will learn the hard way and that is unfortunate because they do not reason and seek after the true YHWH.

8. "Will I not in that day," says the Master, "Even destroy the wise men from Edom, and understanding from the mountains of Esau?

Here it not only talks about their wise men that are warriors and leaders, but mountains are representative of the Kingdom/Empire of all Islamic nations that YHWH will destroy.

182

Those who ultimately trusted in themselves and their might. Their faulty understanding of proclaiming a false god to be the true Elohim will come to nothing.

Their reasoning that Israel is cast off by YHWH will be futile reasoning on that day when the Master Himself judges these nations for their arrogance against the Master YHWH.

9. Then your mighty men, O Teman, shall be dismayed, to the end that everyone from the **mountains of Esau** may be cut off by slaughter.

Teman is Arab lands together with other Islamic nations. These nations are going to be cut down by **death** through slaughter and this is the judgment that the Master has set for them. Here mountains of Esau not only refers to these nations figuratively, but also Jerusalem is in view, specifically the Temple Mount (mountains of Moriah) area where the Al-Aqsa Mosque and the Dome of the Rock are, that will be destroyed at Yahushua's return. Presently these are the "Mountains of Esau," trying to replace the "Mountains of Abraham/Moriah, in the land of Moriah, where YHWH and not Allah does the teaching!"

10. "For **your violence** against **your brother Jacob**, shame shall cover you, and you shall **be cut off forever**. [cast off into Hell]

There is a play on words-Here the Hebrew word used for violence is "**Hamas.**" Interesting that a prophet would speak of this group to come in Israel, whose sole purpose would be to terrorize and kill the Jews to capture their lands. The late Yasser Arafat funded the Hamas faction of terrorism and we know for certain that the prophet Obadiah does not speak about the Roman Empire, or the USA. Rather he speaks specially about the Islamic end-time empire that is going to be extremely violent against the Jews. YHWH is going to judge it for its pride, arrogance and bloodshed that it has caused to its brother Israel. The rest of the world is not safe either, as it too faces this type of **violence/hamas** in their lives if they make any kind of a stand with Israel, or for the Elohim of Israel. That means Christians, who believe in Yahweh Elohim, will also face the same problems of bloodshed and violence by the Islamists.

This kingdom/nations/empire's sin is characterized by simply the violence they do day in and day out against the Jews killing innocent babies, killing innocent Jews to appease their god. This is not one group of isolated individuals with a grudge towards the Jews, but this is a concerted effort by the Muslims in the world who support their Palestinian brothers. The continuous violence is hurled at Israel daily and for this reason they will face severe judgement. That judgment is going to be death on this earth and death spiritually in the second life with no salvation (second death).

11. In the day that you stood on the other side in the day that strangers carried captive his forces, when foreigners entered his gates and cast lots for Jerusalem **even you were as one of them**.

YHWH cites the charge sheet like a judge in court and explains why the judgment is set and what Edom (Islamic nations) failed to do. The Arabs are cousins to the Jews in bloodline Ishmael/Isaac and Esau was Jacob's brother. But instead of being the helper in his (Jacob's) hour of greatest need, these people became their worst enemies, cursing the Jews and then laughing about it. YHWH strictly commanded the Jews not to harm their brother Esau **(Deuteronomy 2:4-5),** but look what Esau has done to his brother Israel!

183

Deuteronomy 2:4-5 `And command the people, saying, "You are about to pass through the territory of your brethren, **the descendants of Esau, who live in Seir [not Jerusalem]**; and they will be afraid of you. **Therefore watch yourselves carefully**. (5) "Do not meddle with them, for **I will not give you any of their land**, no, not so much as one footstep, because **I have given Mount Seir to Esau as a possession**.

This is a triple whammy prophecy repeated more then once in history, referring to the Babylonians, Romans and Muslims. The Babylonians who captured Jerusalem took the Jews as captives and the Edomites were busy casting lots for the land, even though they had blood ties to the Jews. They did not care for their cousins the Jews. This also looks forward to this century, when the Muslims laughed and divided the land of Israel for themselves thinking that they could get away with it. The Jews were prevented from entering their own land by the league between the Muslims and Nazis and many died during the Holocaust.

Today, any Jew who dares to wander into Palestinian regions will not come back alive. The foreigners in verse 11 could also be England and France, who split Israel when they controlled the land. Jordan was created out of the 75% of the land that England occupied and Israel out of the other 25%. Remember the Sykes-Picot Agreement? France was in disagreement as to what it should do with the land. Muslims on the other hand, wanted the whole land for themselves, causing them to go to war with Israel in 1948. This prophecy will be repeated again in the future when Muslims trample Jerusalem and capture half of the city as prophesied by **Zechariah 14:2**.

> 12. **But you should not have gazed on the day of your brother in the day of his captivity; nor should you have rejoiced over the children of Judah in the day of their destruction; nor should you have spoken proudly in the day of distress.**

Again this is a repeated prophecy in the past and again in the present and future referring to Babylon. This continues up to the present situation with the Muslims, because whenever the Jews are suffering persecution, Muslims are happy and overjoyed. **Remember you cannot say it was fulfilled in the Babylonians, as they were not the brothers of the Jews. It is and will yet be fulfilled in the Islamic Arab people who are the brothers of the Jews.** They even praised Hitler and were on his side saying that Hitler did not finish the job. Whenever the Jews were and are in trouble, the Muslims were out celebrating and passing candy to their neighbors rejoicing.

> 13. **You should not have entered the gate of My people in the day of their calamity. Indeed, you should not have gazed on their affliction in the day of their calamity, nor laid hands on their substance in the day of their calamity.**

This is a very stern warning from the Master, as these are multiple prophecies where YHWH looks at both the past and future. These people should not have entered the land of Israel and proclaimed it as their own. Israel was going through a tough time and we have these people looting the land. **Remember the riots of 1920 instigated by Hajji Amin Al-Hussaini.**

184

14. **You should not have stood at the crossroads to cut off those among them who escaped; nor should you have delivered up those among them who remained in the day of distress.**

When the Holocaust came, the Muslims even killed Jews and did not want them to return to their land. They made every effort so the Jews would be annihilated. Hajji Amin Al Hussaini the grand Mufti of Jerusalem, met with Hitler to devise the Final Solution against the Jews. They were cooperating with Hitler to make sure every Jew was killed and those that escaped from Hitler to Judea, they would personally murder. YHWH condemned **Edom eight times** in parallel terminology because of his brutal violence in verses12-14.

YHWH says:
1. You should not gaze on your brother (The Jews).
2. You should not rejoice over the children of Israel.
3. You should not speak proudly.
4. You should not enter the gate of the Jews (They already have)
5. You should not gaze on their affliction (The Arabs make it worse).
6. You should not lay hands on their substance (The Arabs claim it as their own).
7. You should not stand at the crossroads (Ambushes to kill Jews and even shoot babies at close range).
8. You should not deliver them up (The record speaks for itself, look at what happened to the Ramallah soldiers).

In verse 11 YHWH cites the **charge sheet** against them laying out precisely what this kingdom/empire should not have done.

When Hitler was persecuting the Jews Muslims did all of the above and more. But there is no sign of repentance. Is YHWH wrong to punish these Islamic people?

15. For the day of YHWH is near upon **all the heathen** [Islamic nations round about]: as thou hast done, it shall be done unto thee: thy reward shall return **upon thine own head**.

YHWH warns that He will judge them, with the same judgment as they used against the Jews. Obviously they killed the Jews and took away their land. YHWH will do likewise and utterly destroy them. All these "heathen" are those that are "round about" Israel and are the Muslim of today. In fact as I am writing this book we have had the Tsunami and the big earthquake in Pakistan, both Muslim nations. YHWH has actively intervened and judged these nations and this has displaced millions of people. Now do you see how millions of Jews were displaced during the Holocaust? Likewise, these same people getting their deeds paid back to them with divine interest are fulfilling the prophecy of Obadiah. If only the Muslim nations had eyes to see it! Yahweh's wrath is beginning to pour out and more is to follow.

16. For as **you drank on my holy mountain**, so shall **all the nations** drink continually; yes, they shall drink, and swallow, and they shall be as though they had never been.

YHWH charges "you," but tells them judgement is on "all" nations. Well it is quite easy to know who "all" these nations are because they are "all" only Islamic. Who has mosques on the Temple Mount today on YHWH's Holy Mountain and are spiritually drunk in their false idolatrous worship? Who are "all" the nations? These nations are not western but eastern and are only Islamic. In light of history and prophecy, who will get these well deserved awards of YHWH's wrath?

Is this Europe or Islam? Islam continually blasphemes the Name of the one true YHWH Elohim. Islam is a perversion of the truth. Yahweh will defeat Islam for its blasphemies trying to replace the true YHWH with a false god.

17. "But on Mount Zion there shall be **deliverance**, and there shall be holiness; the house of Jacob shall possess their [Edom's] possessions.

This speaks about future return of Yahushua the Messiah when He returns the second time. A time when the Jews will be in control of the Temple Mount and the Master will reign here on earth. He will deliver us and the world from the Islamic occupation of the Temple-Mount for good and from the false religion of Islam. Even for those Muslims who repent and return to the true Elohim of Israel there will be deliverance on Mount Zion in Jerusalem.

18. The house of Jacob shall be a fire, and the house of Joseph a flame; but the house of Esau shall be stubble; they shall kindle them and **devour them**, and **no survivor shall remain of the house of Esau**," for the **Master has spoken**.

The Master has marked these nations, the confederacy of Islam, for destruction on the mountains of Israel; the same mountains that Islam so desperately seeks. It will be through Jacob and Joseph as this refers to both Judah and the northern tribes through whom YHWH will carry out His plans. This is not Simon Altaf's idea that the Islamic nations will be destroyed. Yahweh has spoken it and Simon has acknowledged by saying "Amen" (let it be done). Remarkable words indeed: "**Esau shall be stubble**," the same term used in **Psalm 83:13**, "as stubble before the wind." Now we know whom the Master is referring to with clarity.

19. The **inhabitants of the South** shall possess the **mountains of Esau**, and the inhabitants of the Philistine lowland. They **shall possess the fields of Ephraim** and the fields of Samaria. Benjamin shall possess Gilead.

The inhabitants of the south the house of Judah will possess the "mountains of Esau." The lowlands that are occupied by the Palestinians today did originally belong to the tribe of Judah also.

20. And the captives of this host of the children of Israel shall possess the land of the Canaanites as far as **Zarephath**. The captives of Jerusalem who are in **Sepharad** shall possess the cities of the South.

These people who are the captives in Zarephath and Sepharad are the Jewish people i.e. the tribe of Judah who are in France, Portugal and Spain today. Yahweh is calling them back to Israel and these people will possess the land and spoil Islam. Recently my friend Ariel heard the audible voice of our Master Yahushua telling him to take a shofar/ram's horn and go to the Negev to a particular place and blow the shofar and consecrate the ground because He is bringing the captives back. My friend was scared at first because He had not heard the Master's voice in such clarity and such awe. He prayed with his friends and then with his friends they not only found the two green trees (two

186

houses) that he saw in the vision that accompanied the voice, but also consecrated the ground and blew the shofar. The Master also told him to go to Spain and France and blow the shofar there, because he was told that Yahushua is bringing His people back to their land. A similar thing happened in Mount Gerazim where another Jewish person was asked to go and blow the shofar and consecrate the ground, because again he was told that the Master is bringing His people back.

21.Then <u>saviors shall come to Mount Zion</u> to judge the <u>mountains of Esau</u>, and <u>the kingdom shall be the Master's</u>.

This refers to the two houses of Judah/Ephraim possessing all the areas that are presently occupied by the Jordanians, Palestinians, Iraqis, and Arabs. Edom is referred to as a paradigm of all the "Islamic nations" characterised as Edom. The **"Mount of Esau"** is the Temple area with the Muslim mosques, which will soon come to destruction, as the Jews will once again possess their holy Temple Mount area.

The "saviors" who will come to judge the "Mountains of Esau" (figurative Islamic Kingdom's) and the literal Temple Mount area occupied by the Muslims are Israelites, since the judgement is seen in "Mount Zion." This is in clear reference to Jerusalem where the **"Mount of Esau"** the current Temple Mount mosques will be destroyed. The believers who put their faith in Yahushua as the Messiah are no doubt the Gentile nations, whom YHWH will muster **at the end of days**. Two of these nations stand prominent in YHWH's eyes, Great Britain and the USA, which we will look at later. YHWH literally calls Great Britain and the USA "great nations." These will be the saviors in Jerusalem, who will come up for those that have noticed who the saviors really are.

The rabbis well knew that the Messiah would come and defeat Israel's ultimate enemies the Arabs, characterised as Mount Seir, Mountains of Esau, and Edom. Rashi quoted Edom (signifies not just Jordan but the entire Arab nations) as the perpetual enemy of Israel, and the Messiah will ultimately defeat Edom. (Obadiah Yoma 10a Midrash Tehillim 6:2 and Tanchuma, Bo. 4). Interestingly the Midrash (Jewish commentary) on Tehillim (Psalm) 2:6 and 83:3 says that Edom and the Ishmaelites have intermingled exactly as I stated. Beresheeth Rabba 99:2 states that Edom shall fall by the "Meshuach Milchamah," (the one anointed for battle) who will be descended from Joseph. This is the Messiah coming for His final battle for Israel, as the Holy One of Israel.

The Jews says **Ben Achorono Shel Olam** – (the one who will be at the end of the world's time)- According to this "Meshuach Milchamah" (the one anointed for battle) will descend from Joseph. This is the title of the Messiah. Sota 42a. The battle of Gog and Magog is identified with the Messiah, Son of Joseph, who suffered for our sins, like Joseph suffered for the sins of his own brothers.

B.   The Prophet Ezekiel confirms the end is with Islamists...

Ezekiel 27:3a "And say unto Tyrus, O thou that art situated at the **entry of the sea**."

This is future Tyre (Mystery Babylon) and also used for literal Tyre. Saudi Arabia is located between many seas as illustrated in the diagram in this book, Red Sea, Gulf of Aden, and Arabian Sea etc; see the diagram for more:

Ezekiel 38 map

Ezekiel 27:4 "Thy borders [are] in the midst of the seas, thy builders have perfected thy beauty."

Saudi Arabia literally sits midst many waters, many seas. This matches Revelation 17:1. Ask any Muslim and they will tell you that Saudi Arabia is beautiful. Mecca is the perfect place that god made for his house etc. etc. which is what is meant by "thy builders have perfected thy beauty."

It appears Islam is trading with Tyre (Mystery Babylon), which in effect is a reference to the Islamic kingdom of Saudi Arabia along with other Islamic nations such as Lebanon, Turkey, Jordan, Syria etc. that trade with many Muslim partners. They trade with her thus fulfilling this verse.

> **Ezekiel 27:36** "The merchants among the people shall hiss at thee; thou shalt be a terror, and never shalt be any more."

This country is marked for destruction and all the merchants shall see this just like it states in Revelation 18.

Ezekiel Chapter 27 clearly shows us the destruction of ancient Tyre and the destruction of future Tyre (the harlot of Babylon - Saudi Arabia).

In Ezekiel 27
Verse 13: Ivory, ebony and slaves.
Verse 15: Gemstones and fine clothes.
Verse 16: Oil and balm.
Verse 17: Wine.
Verse 18: Iron and Cassia wood.
Verse 19: Cedar.
Verse 24: Animals.

All the merchandise here matches perfectly with Revelation 18, as this is the same harlot of Babylon who also said:

> **Ezekiel 28:2** "Because thine heart [is] lifted up, and thou hast said, I [am] an elohim, **I sit [in] the seat of YHWH**, in the midst of the seas; yet thou [art] a man, and not YHWH, though thou set thine heart as the heart of YHWH:"

188

Here the reference to YHWH is mentioned e.g. he equals himself with YHWH, not that he is YHWH Elohim of heaven or earth. He equates himself with the supreme YHWH; he sits in the Temple of YHWH just as the Anti-Messiah is meant to do. The Arab nations occupying the Temple Mount is enough to satisfy this requirement all alone because the Temple Mount area is where YHWH's shekinah glory dwelt to deal with mankind and where the two Temples were and also the third one to come.

Ezekiel 28:7 "Behold, therefore I will bring strangers upon thee, the terrible of the nations: and they shall draw their swords against the beauty of thy wisdom, and they shall defile thy brightness"

It is here that the "one-world government" theorists have to face reality when YHWH raises **many different nations** to fight against the Anti-Messiah. If there is a "one-world government," is it not strange that these many nations are not part of it, and have somehow gotten themselves loose from s.a.tan's grip to attack the whore of Babylon (Saudi Arabia)? According to them Anti-Messiah is supposed to be the leader of this phoney "one-world government." **But how can he lead them, when many nations are fighting him?** The answer is simple! There is no such thing as a "one-world government." Which "one world government" would Islam join? The USA or the Hindus?

Ezekiel 29:3 "Speak, and say, `Thus says the Master YHWH: "Behold, I am against you, O Pharaoh king of Egypt, O great monster who lies in the midst of his rivers, who has said, `My river is my own; I have made it for myself.'

This is not the king of Egypt, the old pharaoh, but a title for the Anti-Messiah. This depicts the future king, when the Anti-Messiah will conquer Egypt for a time. The 'midst of rivers' is the flow of nations round about her.

Ezekiel 30:3 For the day is near, even the day of the Master is near, a cloudy day; it shall be the "time of the heathen."

This is judgement time "the day of the Master" for these "heathens," Muslims who do not know YHWH. No doubt the Islamists time is up.

Ezekiel 29:5 I will leave you in the wilderness, you and all the fish of your rivers; [all his allies who cling to Egypt] you shall fall on the open field; you shall not be picked up or gathered. I have given you as food to the beasts of the field and to the birds of the heavens.

This is biblical symbolism where YHWH tells us that all the men who will come up with the "King of Babylon" will be killed by the Master on the mountains of Israel by the earthquake which is depicted in **Ezekiel 38:20.**

Ezekiel 29:10-11 Indeed, therefore, I am against you and against your rivers, and I will make the land of Egypt utterly waste and desolate, from Migdol to Syene, as far as the border of Ethiopia. Neither foot of man shall pass through it nor foot of beast pass through it, and it shall be uninhabited forty years.

YHWH will waste Egypt and scatter them for forty years, this has never happened yet.

Ezekiel 29:11-15 Neither foot of man shall pass through it nor foot of beast pass through it, and it shall be uninhabited forty years. I will make the land of Egypt

189

desolate in the midst of the countries that are desolate; and among the cities that are laid waste, her cities shall be desolate forty years; and I will scatter the Egyptians among the nations and disperse them throughout the countries. Yet, thus says the Master YHWH: "At the end of forty years I will gather the Egyptians from the peoples among whom they were scattered. I will bring back the captives of Egypt and cause them to return to the land of Pathros, to the land of their origin, and there they shall be a lowly kingdom. It shall be the lowliest of kingdoms; it shall never again exalt itself above the nations, for I will diminish them so that they will not rule over the nations anymore.

The Egyptians shall be desolate for forty years so peace with them and YHWH will come after forty years. After YHWH brings Egypt back they will never rule any nations again and will be a lowly kingdom.

Isaiah 19:22-25 And the Master will strike Egypt, He will strike and heal it; they will return to the Master, and He will be entreated by them and heal them. In that day there will be a highway from Egypt to Assyria, and the Assyrian will come into Egypt and the Egyptian into Assyria, and the Egyptians will serve with the Assyrians. In that day Israel will be one of three with Egypt and Assyria, even a blessing in the midst of the land, whom YHWH of hosts shall bless, saying, blessed is Egypt My people, and Assyria the work of My hands, and Israel My inheritance.

After this time the Egyptians that are left will worship the true Elohim of Israel and no longer worship their present false god. It says "in that day" there shall be a highway and YHWH will save them alongside the Assyrians.

Ezekiel 28:9 "Wilt thou yet say before him that slayeth thee, I [am] YHWH? But thou [shalt be] a man, and no elohim, in the hand of him that slayeth thee."

If we look carefully at the wording it is very similar to **Isaiah 14**. s.a.tan depicted as a man who wanted to sit in the seat of YHWH. This is the same person again who we know to be the Anti-Messiah.

There are those that still doubt if these words are really speaking of s.a.tan, or someone else. You can hear them already saying surely this cannot be s.a.tan.

Ezekiel 28 clears up all the confusion for those in doubt.

Ezekiel 28:12 "Thou sealest up the sum, full of wisdom, and **perfect in beauty.**"

s.a.tan was an angel created in perfect beauty i.e. not the two-horned TV character depicted on screen, which is an inaccurate description of him. In fact, YHWH created him very handsome, but because of pride he fell. A friend of mine saw s.a.tan in a vision because YHWH showed her the edge of hell and the edge of heaven and I asked her to describe what he looks like. She said he looked very princely, but very dark, obviously with time his sins have made him this way. Then she saw him transform into a bulldog coming at her almost to bite her and she screamed at his transformation. For Yahushua she saw the figure of a glowing man from the edge of heaven with lots of people around Him and she felt this figure oozing with love and felt drawn to Him.

Ezekiel 28:13 "Thou hast been in Eden The Garden of YHWH."

We know that this king of Tyre has never been to the Garden of Eden. Well there were only four people present in Eden. YHWH, Adam, Eve and s.a.tan, **so which one is the king of Tyre?**

The King of Tyre is no other but the depiction of Anti-Messiah powered by s.a.tan himself. So the titles "King of Babylon," "Prince of Tyre" and "Pharaoh of Egypt," are of the same person THE ANTI-MESSIAH in an end time application.

Ezekiel 34:6 My sheep wandered through all the <u>mountains</u>, and upon every high hill: yea, my flock was scattered upon all the face of the earth, and none did search or seek [after them].

This is referring to Israel that was scattered and for 2,000 years. They had no home and were like wandering nomads. No one cared for them to offer them a home, or land until the Master brought them back with His own strength. Here the "Mountain" is symbolic of the nations where Israel wondered from nation to nation. They had the inquisitions in Spain, pogroms in Russia, the Holocaust in Germany, anti-Semitism in France and England.

Ezekiel 35:6-7 Therefore, as I live, saith the Master YHWH, I will prepare thee unto blood, and <u>blood shall pursue thee</u>: since thou hast not hated blood, even blood shall pursue thee. Thus will I make **Mount Seir most desolate**, and cut off from it him that passeth out and him that returneth.

Interesting play on words, the Hebrew word "dam" means blood. YHWH is saying that Edom, which means "red" in color, will be full of blood, i.e. this is the slaughter of these nations when the Messiah returns.

Ezekiel 35:15 "As **thou didst rejoice at the inheritance of the house of Israel**, because it was desolate, so will I do unto thee: thou shalt be desolate, O Mount Seir, and all Idumea, [even] all of it: and they shall know that I [am] YHWH."

Here again all Idumean (Southern Jordan, Bosrah and Idumea being the descendants of Esau including Northern Arabia) and Mount Seir are all the nations of Muslims, who have aligned themselves together to fight Israel. Edom was the one who had squabbles with Israel over the land issue from times past. And YHWH set judgement once and for all on Edom, along with all those nations that align themselves with Edom today.

Ezekiel 39:7 So will I make <u>my holy Name known</u> in the midst of My people Israel; and I will not let them pollute My holy name any more: and the heathen shall know that I am the Master [Yahweh], the Holy One **"IN"** Israel.

Messiah will come down in person to destroy the Islamic confederacy that will come up to destroy Jerusalem. This time the text says that the Holy One is "IN" Israel rather then being The Holy one "OF" Israel. Usually YHWH describes Himself as Holy One "of" Israel, but here the text shows us that the Messiah is down here in person and ready to finish His business.

Ezekiel 38:19-20 For in my jealousy and in the fire of my wrath have I spoken, surely **in that day [Day of YHWH] there shall be a great shaking [big earthquake] in the land of Israel**. So that the fishes of the sea, and the fowls of

191

the heaven, and the beasts of the field, and all creeping things that creep upon the earth, and all the men that are upon the face of the earth, shall shake at My presence, and the mountains shall be thrown down, and the steep places shall fall, and every wall shall fall to the ground.

This is the time for the destruction of the Anti-Messiah's army mostly by drowning and by the ground swallowing them up as prophesied. This is the time to have the Temple Mount region cleared of those abominable mosques that utter blasphemy day and night. The Muslims will have to pay for their sins for the destruction of churches and synagogues, massacring of Christians and non-Christians alike, and hatred of the Jews. The only trouble is they will have no one to intercede on their behalf and it will be right to the Lake of Fire for all these Islamic armies that came up against Israel. However those who repent and turn even at the last minute will have a chance to save their souls. Life is not just lived in the physical world, but also the non-physical, what we cannot see and the Muslims are well aware of that.

The **earthquake** of Ezekiel perfectly matches the **earthquake** of **Zechariah 14.** The earthquake is in Israel, but the nations will feel the impact so to speak, not just physically but spiritually. The news will spread very quickly especially now that we have TV/Satellite and the internet.

Zechariah 14:4-5 And his feet shall stand in that day upon the mount of Olives, which is before Jerusalem on the east, and the mount of Olives shall cleave in the midst thereof toward the east and toward the west, and there shall be a very great valley; and half of the mountain shall remove toward the north, and half of it toward the south. And ye shall flee to the valley of the mountains; for the valley of the mountains shall reach unto Azal: yea, ye shall flee, like as ye fled from before the earthquake in the days of Uzziah king of Judah: and YHWH my Master shall come, and all the saints with thee.

Its quite logical to assume that if "**HIS FEET**" shall stand on the mount of olives, then the rest of His body will also. This is the Messiah Yahushua back to take control of things. The Islamists, who are now bordering on destroying Israel, have done enough damage. YHWH is not going to sit silently and watch His "covenant people" destroyed. **This is the start Armageddon: a huge earthquake with the splitting of the mountains, leading to the final end time face-off between Jacob and Esau!**

The earthquake also perfectly matches that of Revelation 16.

Revelation 16:18-19 And there were voices, and thunders, and lightnings; **and there was a great earthquake, such as was not since men were upon the earth, so mighty an earthquake, and so great**. And the great city was divided **into three parts**, and the cities of the nations fell: and great Babylon came up in remembrance before YHWH, to give unto her the cup of the wine of the fierceness of His wrath.

Note this earthquake is going to be so huge that it will cause the city of Jerusalem to divide into three portions. It also mentions the "city of the nations fell." How can one deduce that Europe will fall from this? These "cities of the nations" that will fall are the cities round about Israel, or all of the Islamic nations that will be obliterated through this supernatural disaster. Jerusalem will be protected while the surrounding nations will be annihilated causing much damage.

192

The verses in Zechariah link with **Revelation 19:11** that speak of Messiah's second coming for war. So those Christians who are strictly pacifist, better wake up because a war is looming in the near future.

Revelation 19:11 And **I saw heaven opened, and behold a white horse**; and He that sat upon it was called Faithful and True, and in righteousness He doth judge and make war.

Yahushua's triumphant entry will be on a white horse that flies. Does that mean that heaven could have other animals and other horses that fly? The answer is absolutely yes! The picture is not symbolic, but literal/pashat and He is sitting on this white horse. Heaven has the most beautiful things that we cannot imagine, so be ready all ye faithful ones. Our Master is coming.

Isaiah 29:6-7 Thou shalt be visited of YHWH of hosts with thunder, and with earthquake, and great noise, with storm and tempest, and the flame of devouring fire. And the multitude of all the nations [confederacy of Islamic nations] that fight against Ariel, even all that fight against her and her munition, and that distress her, shall be as a dream of a night vision.

This again speaks about the coming back of the Messiah to fight, the same multitude that is out to annihilate Israel. The Hebrew word "*Ariel*" in the above passage refers to **Jerusalem** and is in parallel with the passages in **Zechariah 12**. The word "*Ariel*" means the "Lion of EL" or Lioness of EL.

Zechariah 12:8a In that day shall the Master defend the inhabitants of Jerusalem.

The Master Yahushua the Messiah is on the ground and doing the fighting personally and remembers that He is no longer a lowly Servant who came to suffer two thousand years ago. Now He is a warring King who will come to defend His people.

Zechariah 9:13 When **I have bent Judah for me**, filled the bow with Ephraim, and **raised up thy sons, O Zion**, against **thy sons, O Greece, [Yavan]** and made thee as the sword of a mighty man.

This passage has partial fulfilment in the Maccabees revolt. However it has a future fulfilment with the Islamists depicted as the Grecian Empire, because ancient Greece ruled all throughout the Middle East all the way to Pakistan. YHWH will use Israel to break His enemies. This is why this is a revived Grecian Empire not Roman as believed. You would not be far wrong if you said an Assyrian mix because YHWH does call the Anti-Messiah by the title "The Assyrian." Where is Rome in all this? Only in comic books perhaps.

The word for "Greece" is "Yavan," or the Ionians in the Hebrew and Josephus the historian tells us that these people belong to the western portions of Turkey. Guess what they are today? Muslims not Grecians. Another interesting thing is that this is the meeting of the twelve tribes of Israel. You have Judah, Levi and Benjamin as one house of Israel and then you have the EU/Western Alliance the biological and spiritual Ephraim, or non Jewish-Israel, the sons of Joseph, who became a "multitude," or "company, or fullness of nations" (Genesis 48:19). They are reunited at long last by a common enemy and to battle the end time Islamic beast!

Jeremiah 51:20 "You are **My battle-axe** and **weapons of war**: for with you I will **break the nation in pieces**; with you I will destroy kingdoms;

Zechariah 9:13 also ties in with this verse where Yahweh is going to use both houses of Israel as His battle axe. Which nation is He going to break in pieces? Only the Islamists my friends and any other nation that joins with them will be broken up.

When did YHWH use Israel as His battle-axe to break the nations in the past? The answer is never, and this is why this is yet future and only meant for all Islamic nations. One could claim partial fulfilment in this with the five wars Israel has had with the Arabs, but in reality these nations still stand and their kingdom was not destroyed, and so this remains to be fulfilled.

Zechariah 9:14-17 And the Master YHWH shall be seen over them, and his arrow shall go forth as the lightning: and the **Master YHWH shall blow the trumpet**, and shall go with whirlwinds of the south. The Master YHWH shall defend them; and they shall devour, and subdue with sling stones; and they shall drink, and make a noise as through wine; and they shall be filled like bowls, and as the corners of the altar. And the Master their Elohim shall save them in that day as the flock of His people: for they shall be as the stones of a crown, lifted up as an ensign upon his land.

Note that the Master is here seen over them, and watching over the Jewish people, the trumpet is blown just like in **Matthew Chapter 24** and all the Jews and Ephraimites in that time will get saved as Romans 11 states. These verses have never been fulfilled in the past. If Yahweh is blowing the trumpet/shofar, then surely He needs a mouth, and hands to hold the shofar, legs to stand on and so forth. This is the Master Yahushua of Nazareth, the very King who was depicted in **Jeremiah 23:6 as the physical Branch of King David**.

Jeremiah 23:6 In His days Judah will be saved, and Israel will dwell safely; now this is His name by which He will be called: YHWH OUR RIGHTEOUSNESS.

Jeremiah 51:24-25 And I will render unto Babylon and to all the inhabitants of Chaldea all their evil that they have done in Zion in your sight, saith the Master. Behold, I am against thee, O destroying mountain, saith the Master, which destroyest all the earth: and I will stretch out mine hand upon thee, and roll thee down from the rocks, and will make thee a burnt mountain.

If this was just talking about Iraq, Iraq never destroyed the whole earth in any way in the past. This is symbolic, as the mountain is the kingdom of the Anti-Messiah, who is from Islam and who destroys the earth with their corrupt false religion.

This is yet future when the Islamists will face their most humiliating defeat. This will be the final blow to this false religion and its false god when it will be brought to an end.

Isaiah 29:8 It shall even be as when a **hungry man dreameth**, and, behold, he eateth; **but he awaketh, and his soul is empty**: or as when a thirsty man dreameth, and, behold, he drinketh; but he awaketh, and, behold, he is faint, and

194

his soul hath appetite: **so shall the multitude of all the nations be, that fight against mount Zion.**

The Islamic dream is to devour Israel and take their land, but the Elohim of Israel has other plans. We are shown in the verse above that these people may dream, but it will turn out to be a nightmare, as these people fight the Elohim of Israel not mere flesh on the ground. Their battle is not with the Jews alone, but with their Maker. When the Muslims wake up from their dream they will realize they were following a false and utterly useless god all along and that Allah will prove to be impotent to defend them and unable to help them when reality hits them. Even though most of Israel fails to see YHWH's purposes, YHWH will defend Israel in the day of calamity.

The Master personally goes to fight the aggressors this time and Israel's enemies are annihilated once and for all time.

Where is the revival?

A lot of Christians are looking for that great elusive revival. The Bible says that instead of a big revival there will be a big falling away from faith and that the Anti-Messiah will not be revealed until the falling away happens. In other words there is no revival until the Master Himself returns.

> **2 Thessalonians 2: 3** Let no man deceive you by any means: for that day shall not come, except **there come a falling away first**, and that man of sin be revealed, the son of perdition;

If you do not believe me then at least believe the Scriptures. If not the Scriptures, then just look at the churches breaking up, or the backsliding Christians all around us. Does that look like a revival or survival? Christianity is fighting for its survival not revival. Europe is under attack from hostile Muslims with their ideology to crush Europe. The USA is being indoctrinated within with corrupt doctrines in the church and outside the Islamists attack with their ideology. Schools are teaching Islam. What in the world is going on? This is Bible prophecy coming to play friends and be prepared for more things to come. The beast is in all our institutions that we now treasure. The faithful will separate and carefully watch the times for the return of the Messiah, while the herd will head for their destruction in their current path. Remember the majority is usually wrong and the minority usually holds the truth. Torah/the Law warns us not to follow a large multitude to pursue evil, corruption, or even false eschatological doctrine!

> **1 Timothy 4:1** Now the Spirit speaketh expressly, that in the **latter times some shall depart from the faith**, giving heed to seducing spirits, and **doctrines of devils**;

However there is a promised revival coming and it happens on the mountains of Israel. Yes that is correct, it happens on the mountains of Israel in the end.

> **Ezekiel 39:2** And I will turn thee back, and **leave but the sixth part of thee**, and will cause thee to come up from the north parts, and will bring thee upon the mountains of Israel:

When the Muslim hoards come they will try to destroy Israel with their two hundred million-man army in the Armageddon battle. However YHWH has His own plan and will crush this army and only allow **one sixth** to be left who will most likely get saved. Imagine the numbers; one sixth of two hundred million is 16.6% that is just over 33 million Muslims. This is revival right on the mountains of Israel. As for a "one-world government," that will be when Yahushua the Messiah returns. Then He will rule and reign the world from Jerusalem, the only "one world government" coming to this sin cursed planet. Amen.

C.   The Prophet Joel confirms the end is with Islamists...

Joel 2:1 Blow ye the trumpet in Zion, and sound an alarm in my holy mountain: let all the inhabitants of the land tremble: for the day of YHWH cometh, for it is nigh at hand;

YHWH's holy mountain is in Jerusalem, and the sound cry of battle is heard in Israel. The Master is going to <u>descend</u> with a shout. This is the time for a showdown with the haters of the Master who pretend submission.

Psalm 81:15 The haters of the Master would **pretend submission** to Him, but their fate would endure forever.

Although the Muslims pretend submission to Yahweh, they actually submit to Allah a foreign god. They hate Yahweh by definition, because they hate His chosen people. The word for "submission" in Arabic is "Islam" and correctly depicts these people.

Joel 2:2 "A day of darkness and of gloominess, a day of clouds and of thick darkness, as the morning spread upon the mountains: <u>a great people</u> and a <u>strong</u>; there hath not been ever the like, neither shall be any more after it, even to the years of many generations."

This is the big battle and guess what? YHWH will raise up His army in response to the Northern Army. This is the Christian response to the Islamist Jihad.

Joel 1:6 For a **nation has come up against My land**, strong, and without number; his teeth are the **teeth of a lion**, and he **has the fangs of a fierce lion**.

Can anyone deny that the Arabs are not a strong people? They come marching along folks with all the Islamic nations, against Israel to cut her off. But YHWH will raise His own army. The depiction of lions has to do with the fact that biological Babylonians are part of the army whose symbol is the lion.

Joel 2:3 A <u>fire devoureth before them</u>; and <u>behind them</u> a <u>flame burneth</u>: <u>the land</u> is as the <u>Garden of Eden</u> before them, and <u>behind them a desolate wilderness</u>; yea, and <u>nothing shall escape them</u>.

Make no mistake these are the saints, the Master's own army marching for counter-attack. Many prophecy writers have a problem with this being a Christian army and come up with excuses that these are not believers. However the text speaks against them, as I shall prove in a minute.

196

Joel 1:5 Awake, you drunkards, and weep; and wail, all you drinkers of wine [Arab oil], because of the new wine [Holy Spirit and salvation], for it has been cut off from your mouth.

The church is asleep, the Master warns them to wake up the drunkards and warn the people of the impending disaster on hand.

Joel 2:4-5 The appearance of them is as the appearance of horses; and as horsemen, so shall they run. Like the noise of chariots on the tops of mountains shall they leap, like the noise of a flame of fire that devoureth the stubble, as a strong people set in battle array.

This is the unmistakable language of war with the same people mentioned in Revelation for war with their armaments, tanks, guns and planes. Yet the evangelical world waits for the Pope as the Anti-Messiah. The army that marches for war is the Master's own army verses the Northern army. About time we saw a proper response to all the killings, beheadings and torture exercised by the Islamists. YHWH has let them run their course and is now ready to show them who Yahweh really is. Who can stand against Him? The Islamist confederacy is intent on the destruction and overthrow of Israel. Yahweh the Elohim of Israel will not remain silent. Exodus 15 reminds us that YHWH IS A MAN OF WAR!

Joel 2:20 "But I will remove far from you the northern army, and will drive him away into a barren and desolate land, with his face toward the eastern sea and his back toward the western sea; his stench will come up, and his foul odor will rise, because he has done monstrous things."

There are two armies here one is the Master's personal army and the other is the northern army of Islamic nations that has come to destroy Israel. Friends this is the catching up, learn it if you do not know. The Master is returning with the saints, who are going to meet Him in the air by resurrection from the grave and then descend to fight in Israel. Now you can clearly see the errors in the idea of pre and mid-tribulation raptures. Why have YHWH's army fight on the ground if there was a pre-tribulation rapture? It simply does not exist. Messiah will come to end the Great Tribulation and destroy those who cause Jacob the trouble in Jacob's Trouble!

Revelation 9:2 And he opened the bottomless pit; and there arose a smoke out of the pit, as the smoke of a great furnace; and the sun and the air were darkened by reason of the smoke of the pit.

The "**smoke**" is unquestionably the symbol of war. This is the battle that was to come and is the biggest in history. It is World War III! It will make World War II look like a tiny war. The Islamist army is two hundred million alone, but we are not given the number of the Master's army.

Revelation 9:3 And there came out of the smoke **locusts** [in Hebrew Arbeh] upon the earth: and unto them was given power, as the **scorpions** of the earth have power.

When s.a.tan is released then it is war with the saints and the world. Signs are given before this happens. The sign of locusts is the Hebrew play on words "*Arabeh*" meaning locusts and the character of the Arabs is that of the locusts i.e. desert roaming things. So the word for "Arab" is used in this verse and is the Hebrew word "*Arabee*" for the Arabians. This is a play on words to mean the Arabs. Arbah on the other hand in Hebrew also means the number 4. So here the only thing that can correspond to that number is the geographic nature of the beast such as in **Revelation 13:2**. Thus the end time beast is a geo-composite of the Leopard (Grecian), Bear (Medo-Persian), Lion (Babylonian) and of course the Eastern leg of the Roman Empire. Arbah also signifies the global influence of the end time beast, covering the 4 corners of the globe!

Also the Arabian Desert is teeming with locusts because of its favourable climate. This is a befitting imagery. Here we can see a drash of these passages. As well as locusts, the Arabian climate also sustains scorpions and it is interesting that the zoology depicted in Revelation 9 fits both the Arabs and the Arab climate perfectly.

Islam also, does not permit the destruction of trees or green things. The "locusts" will not be allowed to "hurt the grass, or green things etc." (Revelation 9:4). **The Saracen Muslim (first Beast/7th head) Ottoman armies were under orders that match this verse exactly**.

When Yazid was marching with his army to invade Syria, Abu Bakar, the first Muslim Caliph after Muhammad charged him with this, among other orders, *"Destroy no palm trees, nor burn any fields of corn; cut down no fruit trees, nor do any mischief to cattle, only such as you kill to eat" (Thomas Newton).*

The "locusts" will attack idolatrous Christians who "do not have the seal of YHWH on their forehead and who dishonor the commandments/Torah." This also applies to all those who do not have the mark, or seal of the true Name of YHWH on their hearts and in their minds to protect them from radical Islam in the time of Jacob's Trouble.

Historically the Saracens (Arab Muslims referred to as Saracen by the Europeans) worked mainly in those countries where corruption of Christianity prevailed, i.e. the Greek Orthodox and Roman Catholic churches. Verses 7-9 describe the Saracens outfit. They were renowned for their horsemanship.

These are the ones who are going to bring trouble to the earth and make war. They are the ones who are gathering the Muslim nations. This is the Saudi Arabian style of Islam that is intolerant of any other faith on the face of this planet. The start was with the Arabs, then the Ottomans and ends up with the rest of the Islamic world ready for war once again.

As early as 766 AD, a Christian clergyman writing in Syriac spoke of the "locust swarm" of unconverted barbarians, Sindhis, Alans, Khazars, and others, who served in the Caliph's army, and by the ninth century slave locust armies appeared all over the Islamic empire. *Bernard Lewis, Race and Slavery in the Middle East, Oxford University Press, 1994.*

Revelation 9:7-9 And the shapes of the locusts *were* like unto horses prepared unto battle; and on their heads *were* as it were crowns like gold [wearing turbans], and their faces *were* as the faces of men [are men]. And they had hair as the hair of women, and their teeth were as *the teeth* of lions [fierce teeth]. And they had breastplates, as it were breastplates of iron [description of tanks]; and the sound of their wings [sound of engines] *was* as the sound of chariots of many horses running to battle [description of war planes].

Here the locusts are described exactly like the Ottoman army. The Ottomans had long hair, golden turbans, fierce teeth and even their horses were wearing armour of breastplates and this essentially it describes the rise of Islam.

Symbols of The Ottoman Empire-

* Hair of men: These are men with long hair.
* Faces of men: Description of battle ready men.
* Teeth of lions: Very fierce fighters.
* Breastplates: Description of tanks (modern warfare).
* Sound of wings: Engine noises.
* Sound of chariots: Warplanes, choppers, helicopter gun ships.

Revelation 9:10 And they had tails like unto scorpions, and there were stings in their tails: and their power *was* to hurt men five months.

Fighter planes carrying missiles with stings/payload in the tails of the missiles. This Islamic army from the east is ready for war and coming for battle.

Joel 2:10 "The earth shall quake before them; the heavens shall tremble: the sun and the moon shall be dark, and the stars shall withdraw their shining"

This only happens when lots of bullets, missiles and bombs are fired. Could this be the time of Armageddon? Most definitely the language leaves us in no doubt. It is the same language used in **Matthew 24:29**.

"Immediately after the tribulation of those days the sun will be darkened, and the moon will not give its light; the stars will fall from heaven, and the powers of the heavens will be shaken. In Revelation we also have these verses that fit:

Revelation 9:2 And he opened the bottomless pit, and smoke arose out of the pit like the smoke of a great furnace. And the sun and the air were darkened because of the smoke of the pit.

This speaks in the same language as **Ezekiel 38**. Heavenly signs accompany the day of the Master's return.

Joel 2:11 And YHWH shall utter His voice before His army: for His camp is very great: for He is strong that executeth His word: for the day of YHWH is great and very terrible; and who can abide it?

The Master Yahushua is here on earth leading His army. This indicates that we will physically fight with Him in the end of days. The battle will then be in the physical realm and not just the spiritual. There is no such thing as pacifist Christianity. This is the end-time big battle. YHWH will raise His army that will fight in the physical realm and will be undefeatable.

199

Joel 2:8 They do not push one another; every one marches in his own column. And when they lunge between the weapons, **they are not cut down**.

Scholars be warned who say it is not a Christian army because how come these people are not able to die? This is because they are 'resurrected glorified believers,' who can fight and lunge between the weapons and not die. Can we really deny the plain text above that **"they are not cut down"** e.g. killed?

Joel 2:12 Therefore also now, saith YHWH, turn ye even to Me with all your heart, and with **fasting**, and with **weeping**, and with **mourning**:"

The remaining Jewish people weep for their Messiah to come back, "hosheeanu," Master come save us."

This is also prophesied in **Psalm 118:26** and **Matthew 23:39** where they cry "Baruch Haba B'Shem YHWH" (blessed is He who comes in the name of the Master YHWH).

Joel 2:15 Blow the trumpet in Zion, sanctify a fast, call a solemn assembly (16) **Gather the people, sanctify the congregation, assemble the elders, gather the children**, and those that suck the breasts: **let the bridegroom go forth from his chamber**, and **the bride out of her closet**.

Zion/Jerusalem is ready for war. Gather the saints (believers), the bridegroom is the Messiah Yahushua, who is ready to take His bride and to redeem Israel. However before this takes place one final battle is still at hand.
We are going to battle.

Psalm 144:1 Blessed be the Master my Rock, Who **trains my hands for war**, and my **fingers for battle**.

It is YHWH who trains us for war, as we have a responsibility to the Master and His chosen people.

Joel 2:17-18 Let the priests, the ministers of YHWH, weep between the porch and the altar, and let them say, Spare thy people, O YHWH, and give not thine heritage [Israel] to reproach, that the <u>**heathen should rule over them**</u>: [these are Muslims] wherefore should they say among the people, Where is their Elohim? **Then will YHWH be jealous for His land, and pity His people.**

The "priests" of Yahweh are the believers (**Revelation 1:5-6**) who will pray to the Master to let His covenant people (physical Israel) be saved and not be annihilated by the enemy. This is both physical and spiritual that they may know their Messiah. The Islamic nations have gathered to wipe them off the face of the earth. The same word "heathen" is used here for these Islamic people.

Joel 2:20 But I will remove far off from you the <u>**northern *army***</u>, and will drive him into a land barren and desolate, with his face toward the east sea, and his hinder part toward the utmost sea, and his stink shall come up, and his ill savour shall come up, because he hath done great things.

200

The **northern army** matches both **Ezekiel 38** and **Revelation 2**, as we are shown even the terms 'the death and the stink'. These same words are used to describe the end of this army. It is apparent from this alone that the invading armies will be destroyed completely who come from the north.

> **Revelation 2:12-13** And to the angel of the church in **Pergamos** [Turkey] write; These things saith he which hath the sharp sword with two edges; I know thy works, and where thou dwellest, *even* where s.a.tan's seat *is*: and thou holdest fast my name, and hast not denied my faith, even in those days wherein Antipas *was* my faithful martyr, who was slain among you, where s.a.tan dwells.

Pergamos is in Turkey and falls <u>north of Israel</u> and Turkey will be the place from where the Anti-Messiah will most likely arise. Turkey will be the major power, part of the Anti-Messiah's confederacy, the same place where the Ottoman Empire originated from and where the last bastion of Christianity was destroyed. The emperor Constantine was the last Roman emperor killed in Constantinople (present day Istanbul) and now Turkey is penned to join Europe. Let's pray that the Master helps us, with seventy two million Muslims now politically poised to cross over into Europe without a fight and cause havoc.

Although the Arabs have 650 times more land mass than Israel they still want the land of Israel but YHWH is not going to give it to them. This is not a mere land battle, but a battle for the survival of the Jewish nation. At this point, the Jewish state will have exhausted its effort to save itself and through sheer anxiety would be calling out for their Messiah.

In a recent report by AIPAC, it states the following:

> Terrorists from over 40 terrorist organizations assembled in Tehran last week for a 10-day summit designated the "Ten Days of Dawn." The summit, attended by Hamas, Hezbollah, Islamic Jihad and allies of al-Qaeda was held to discuss a new strategy aimed at driving America out of the Middle East, **destroying Israel** and replacing all Arab governments with fundamentalist Islamic regimes.

The intent is clear. Islam marks Israel for destruction, just as Islam is marked by YHWH for the same!

D.   The Prophet Isaiah declares the end is with Islamists...

> **Isaiah 14:4-7**- That you will take up this proverb against the king of Babylon, and say: "How the oppressor has ceased, the golden city ceased! The Master has broken the staff of the wicked, the sceptre of the rulers; he who struck the people in wrath with a continual stroke, he who ruled the nations in anger, is persecuted and no one hinders. The whole earth is at rest and quiet; they break forth into singing.

We are told king of Babylon will be brought down, so this is not Nebuchadnezzar, but the future king i.e. the Anti-Messiah who will rule this region of the world.

201

Isaiah 14:9 "Hell from beneath is excited about you, to meet you at your coming; it stirs up the dead for you, all the chief ones of the earth; it has raised up from their thrones all the kings of the nations.

The Hebrew word *"Goy"* means "heathen," or "nations" and is used here for "all the kings of these nations." So it would be "kings of the heathens." This indicates that these are all "the heathens" (Islamic kings) whom YHWH will judge and set His wrath against their wickedness. The word for "earth" is eretz, which more correctly relates to the countries surrounding Israel and not the whole world, as assumed by many, since the context is Babylon and the fight is with Israel.

The King of Babylon (future) who will be sent to hell, and all the kings of the "heathens." YHWH uses these words for Islamic nations "around and about" Israel, but it covers the whole Islamic world in general.

Isaiah 14:12 How art thou fallen from heaven, O Lucifer, son of the morning! How art thou cut down to the ground, which didst weaken the nations!

YHWH starts to describe this individual as s.a.tan. The Hebrew word Hilal Ben Shachar is used for son of the morning, which literally means in Aramaic **son of the crescent moon**. Does this ring a bell with Islam and their global crescent symbol, under which early morning prayers are uttered?

Isaiah 14:13 For thou hast said in thine heart, I will ascend into heaven, I will exalt my throne above the stars of YHWH: I will sit also upon the mount of the congregation, in the sides of the north:

The language here starts to describe s.a.tan but the play on words describes the Anti-Messiah; "the sides of the north" (Temple Mount and Holy of Holies) are mentioned.

14. I will ascend above the heights of the clouds; I will be like the most High.

We know it was s.a.tan who wanted to be like YHWH.

15. Yet thou shalt be brought down to hell, to the sides of the pit.

Judgement is set for s.a.tan and cannot change. It is only a matter of time now before he is cast into hell. You can see his five "I wills" in **Isaiah 14:13**, all s.a.tan's proclamations to be like YHWH.

16. They that see thee shall narrowly look upon thee, and consider thee, saying, **Is this the man** that made the earth to tremble, that did **shake kingdoms**;

Here comes the switch where now s.a.tan is being described as a man. This play on words shows that this talk is of the Anti-Messiah who is like s.a.tan. Isaiah 14 starts by judging s.a.tan and the reasons for his judgment are obvious, then switching to this person that we know to be the Anti-Messiah, **who is described as the son of the moon crescent (Hilal ben Shachar)**. The text also tells us he does "shake kingdoms." This is not loose talk, but he will cause grief in many nations in the world. This person is out to destroy and cause mischief and mayhem. Just take a look at present day Islam and how people are troubled by fanatic Islam with many people dead, or wounded already. How about the riots in France, the suicide bombings in Israel, Iraq and proliferation in

Afghanistan. But perhaps you're thinking about the alleged peace in Afghanistan. What peace? Have you ever been to Afghanistan? Well when you go there you can come and tell me about the peace. The Islamic tribalism and warlords in Afghanistan can never usher in true peace. Only government's change but the tribes remain at war.

Recently a woman author was beaten to death by her husband for the simple fact that she wrote an ordinary novel that angered him. Another woman who stood for free elections was killed because she is a woman. Now if this is a definition of peace then perhaps my definition of peace is inaccurate.

17. That made the world as a wilderness, and destroyed the cities thereof; that opened not the house of his prisoners?

This person's principle sign is not government like most people predict an alleged "one-world government." His principle sign is **destruction** as that is what he brings to the cities of the world. Look around the world! Who is blowing up bombs and becoming suicide bombers?

18. All the kings of the nations, even all of them, lie in glory, every one in his own house.

It describes the kings as having graves and lying in wait for the resurrection.
19. But thou art cast out of thy grave like an **abominable branch**, and as the raiment of those that are slain, thrust through with a sword, that go down to the stones of the pit; as a carcase trodden under feet.
This person is not s.a.tan but the Anti-Messiah who has no grave. Here he is described as "an abominable branch," yet the true Messiah is described as "The Branch" also (Isaiah 11:1).

20. Thou shalt not be joined with them in burial, because thou hast destroyed thy land, and slain thy people: the seed of evildoers shall never be renowned.

It describes the fact that this person will not be buried in the grave and his body will just disappear after his death, so that no one can go to his grave and try to exalt him, or make a shrine for him like the Muslims do. His end signifies extreme judgement and "his seed" signifies both his children and his followers, who will not be known, i.e. made famous due to their lack of righteousness.

Isaiah 14:25 That I will break The **Assyrian in my land**, and upon my mountains tread him under foot: then shall his yoke depart from off them, and his burden departs from off their shoulders.

The identity is revealed again. We are told this is The "Assyrian," this is the same person called the "Gog" in Ezekiel 38. He will be destroyed on the mountains of Israel. Now ask yourself; where was biblical Assyria? New York? Washington DC? I think not! The region of Turkey, Iraq, Syria and Lebanon is the answer.

Isaiah 14:29-31 Rejoice not thou, whole Palestina [all the Palestinians], because the rod of him that smote thee is broken [the prime minister is suddenly killed or removed]: for out of the serpent's root shall come forth a cockatrice, and his fruit shall be a fiery flying serpent [description of missiles]. And the firstborn of the poor shall feed, and the needy shall lie down in safety: and I will kill thy root with

203

<u>famine</u>, and <u>he shall slay thy remnant</u> [YHWH sends his famine and kills the Palestinians by his hand, this could be supernatural]. Howl, O gate; cry, O city; thou, whole Palestina, **art dissolved**: for there shall come from the <u>north a smoke</u>, and none shall be alone in his appointed times. [big trouble to come from the north]

This appears to be a warning to the Palestinian people not to rejoice so soon or start giving out candy as they did when it was 9/11. It appears likely that the king of Israel is killed or removed. We are not told if it is by assassination, but this is a possibility. Could this be for a future prime minister, who is suddenly removed whereby the Palestinians rejoice? But then another Israeli prime minister will come who is even fiercer, or more determined than the one before him to deal with the Palestinian terrorists. He kills them by firing missiles "fiery flying serpent." Literally this can read burning flying snake (represents missiles). We know Ariel Sharon had been executing terrorists in this fashion, so this could have an application for him, or for another prime minister to come. It talks about there being famine sent by YHWH in the Palestinian territories and the war ascending out of the north e.g. Turkey/Iraq/Syria/Lebanese regions, with all these nations getting involved in some serious action. Whether it is some sort of biological accident, or missile strike, there appears to be much trouble in the Palestinian regions, probably caused by one of their own leaders. The language used for this is "art dissolved." This seems some type of biological hazard and is extreme.

Burden of the desert-
Isaiah 21:1 The burden of the <u>desert of the sea</u>. As whirlwinds in the south pass through; so it cometh from the desert, from a terrible land.

Saudi Arabia is literally 'the desert of the sea,' i.e. nations around about it, and seas around about it. Look at the Middle East map in this book.

In Jeremiah YHWH gives us another indication that this is the nation with many seas:

Jeremiah 51:13 O you who dwell **by many waters**, abundant in treasures, your end has come, the measure of your covetousness.

These many waters are literal and not symbolic of nations and peoples, for if it were, it would say "you who dwell **with** many waters not **by many waters**."

Burden against the Sea (Saudi Arabia)-
Isaiah 21:1-10 The burden against the <u>Wilderness of the Sea</u>. As whirlwinds in the South pass through, so it comes from the desert, from a terrible land. A distressing vision is declared to me; the treacherous dealer deals treacherously, and <u>the plunderer plunders</u>. Go up, **O Elam! Besiege, O Media!** All its sighing I have made to cease. Therefore my loins are filled with pain; pangs have taken hold of me, like the pangs of a woman in labor. I was distressed when I heard it; I was dismayed when I saw it. My heart wavered, fearfulness frightened me; the night for which I longed He turned into fear for me. Prepare the table, set a watchman in the tower, eat and drink. Arise, you princes, anoint the shield! For thus has the Master said to me: "Go, set a watchman, let him declare what he sees." And he saw a chariot with a pair of horsemen, a chariot of donkeys, and a chariot of camels, and he listened diligently with great care. Then he cried, "A lion, my Master! I stand continually on the watchtower in the daytime; I have sat at my post every night. And look, here comes a chariot of men with a pair of

204

horsemen!" and he answered and said, "Babylon is fallen, is fallen! And all the carved images of her gods he has broken to the ground." Oh, my threshing and the grain of my floor! That which I have heard from YHWH of hosts, the Elohim of Israel, I have declared to you.

Note it comes from the desert not Europe.

It is imperative for Iran to join this confederacy. Is it any wonder Iran wants to destroy and wipe away Israel and is exactly what the present leader of Iran (January 2006) Mahmoud Ahamdinejad has declared recently.

Burden of Dumah (Arabia)-
Isaiah 21:11-12 "The burden of **Dumah**. He calleth to me out of Seir, Watchman, what of the night? Watchman, what of the night? The watchman said, he morning cometh, and also the night: if ye will enquire, enquire ye: return, come."

Dumat el-Jandal is in Saudi Arabia mentioned here by Isaiah.

Burden against Arabia-
Isaiah 21:13-17 "The burden upon Arabia. In the forest in Arabia shall ye lodge, O ye travelling companies of **Dedanim**. He inhabitants of the land of **Tema** brought water to him that was thirsty, they prevented with their bread him that fled. For they fled from the swords, from the drawn sword, and from the bent bow, and from the grievousness of war. For thus hath the Master said unto me, Within a year, according to the years of an hireling, and all the glory of Kedar shall fail: And the residue of the number of archers, the mighty men of the children of Kedar, shall be diminished: for YHWH Elohim of Israel hath spoken [it]."

Saudi Arabia is going to be judged, as many of its mighty men are going to be killed in the war that will be started by the radical Islamic nations. Tema, Kedar, Dedanim and Dhumah are all references to this nation. Dhumah and Kedar were the sons of Ishmael and Dhumah's location is near Medina in Saudi Arabia today. Three times the Master has pronounced judgment on Saudi Arabia, since after all this is the nation that exports its false religion to the entire world. The mention of "glory of Kedar shall fail" could be a reference to Mecca and Ka'ba that will be destroyed. Note, here clear reference is made that this speech is uttered from the mouth of the "Elohim of Israel."

The "glory of Kedar" failing symbolizes the destruction of Saudi Arabia. [35]

Dumah is mentioned in the biblical records as a city in Canaan (Joshua 15:52). It is also associated with Edom and Seir in Isaiah 21:11.

Dumah is generally identified by historians with the Addyrian Adummatu people. Esarhaddon related how, in his attempt to subdue the Arabs, his father, Sennacherib struck against their capital, Adummatu, which he called the stronghold of the Arabs. Sennacherib captured their king, Haza'il, who is called, King of the Arabs. Haza'il is also referred to in one inscription of Ashurbanipal as King of the Kedarites.

From a geographical standpoint, Adummatu is often associated with the medieval Arabic Dumat el-Jandal, which was in ancient times a very important and strategic junction on the major trade route between Syria, Babylon, Najd and the Hijaz area. Dumat el Jandal is at the south-eastern end of Al Jawf, which is a desert basin. It often denotes the whole lower region of Wadi as Sirhan; the famous depression situated half way between Syria and Mesopotamia. This area has water, and was a stopping place for caravan traders coming from Tayma, before proceeding on to Syria or Babylonia.

This strategic location effectively made Dumah the entrance to north Arabia. This oasis was the centre of rule for many north Arabian kings and queens, as related to us in Assyrian records.

We can conclude that this mention of "Babylon is fallen" in **Isaiah 21:9** is not related to Iraq, but Saudi Arabia only, as no mention is made of any of the cities of Babylon proper such as Erech, Accad, Sumer, Assur and Calneh etc. The clear references to Saudi Arabia above forces us to conclude that the harlot of Babylon is none other but Mecca in Saudi Arabia. We cannot force and portray the harlot as the Vatican, or New York, or any other city in the world, as there is no biblical data to support this. The majority of scholars who have built up a premise on one verse of the Bible, which is not even taken in its proper context e.g. the woman arrayed in purple and scarlet in **Revelation 17:4**, cannot continually twist Scripture and get away with it. Only sound theology can stand close scrutiny.

There is another prophecy of this works related religion that we find both in Genesis and in Revelation.

E.   Is Genesis pointing to the big battle to come?

Genesis 3:27 And the eyes of them both were opened, and they knew that they *were* naked; and they sewed **FIG LEAVES** together, and made themselves aprons [partial coverings].

They were doing works to cover themselves to save them from YHWH. Interestingly the covering is of "fig leaves" and as we know fig leaves are green and represent good deeds in Judaism. The color green is also associated with death. In short, if you are doing works to get to YHWH, then you are not doing what YHWH ordained for reconciliation back to Himself. Namely, to atone for your soul through blood atonement, by slaughtering an animal through the high priest as seen in Leviticus 17:11. Instead if one is religious but doing their own good works, that person is heading for spiritual death.

Leviticus 17:11 For the life of the flesh is in the blood: and I have given it to you upon the altar to make an atonement for your souls: **for it is the blood that maketh an atonement for the soul.**

There is something else taught in Genesis 3:27 regarding the Anti-Messiah. These people will do works and deeds of the flesh. The color green signifies all those (Muslims) that follow this method and who will die spiritually i.e. not enter heaven. This is also associated with the fig leaves matching the Book of Revelation as follows:

206

Do you remember the green mosque of Muhammad in Medina? Muslims go there every year as a symbol of good works to be saved. They also consider the green color holy and do not use it for flooring, or anything domestic in the home, so it may not be denigrated. They also teach the same good works to all others they preach to and try and annul YHWH's true method of salvation which is/was the blood atonement now found in the Master Yahushua the Messiah, through His blood on the cross.

Yet, The Master is teaching us something bigger.

Here, the Master is trying to disclose a deeper meaning.

This is also a sign of the end Beast/4th Empire of Daniel the prophet.

> **Revelation 6:7-8** And when he had opened the fourth seal, I heard the voice of the fourth beast say, come and see. And I looked and behold a pale [green] horse; and his name that sat on him was death, and hell followed with him. And power was given unto them over the fourth part of the earth, to kill with sword, and with hunger, and with death, and with the beasts of the earth.

Chloros, is the same root word from where we get the word chlorophyll (the substance which helps make leafy plants green – remember the fig leaves). Biblically this color is the color of disease, pestilence and death, because that is where good works without blood salvation leads us. That does not mean you should not do good works because that is a sign unto being saved since we are created for good works.

> **Ephesians 2:10** For we are His workmanship, **created in Messiah Yahushua for good works**, which YHWH prepared beforehand that we should walk in them. .

The beast rising out of the sea is the Islamic Empire. The pale [green] horse has a rider who is called death; the **pale (green) horse** is the **revival of fundamentalist Islam**. Anybody following this person will end up in hell. The word is not "pale" but "green" (Greek *Chloros*). So we are going to see a push in the world of Islamists saying to people not to worry about blood atonement, since you only need to do good works before Allah to be saved.

This is also the tool that s.a.tan will use to deceive the people through Islam, as it seems to have a solid structure of established monotheistic belief. People get all worked up about the trinity, but they are quite happy to accept a god that is not YHWH at all and is just a monad. Allah has no will, or purpose in eternity, he creates only if he feels like it, he forgives sins on a Thursday, his penalty for sin is pouring boiling liquids down peoples throats and many other demonic attributes. This is all fear mongering to deceive normal and simple people, who do not know otherwise. Revelation 6:7-8 says that the "riders" name is "Death," i.e. he rides a horse, but kills people, taking their souls because "hell" follows him everywhere his culture is established.

Islam holds the green color sacred and it is revered and put on domes of Mosques. The Muslim saints have the green shawls over their graves. **The Green Mosque** of Muhammad in Mecca is a huge symbol that the Bible reveals. So we can see the Master did not use the green color simply as a general guideline, but specifically to point out how to recognize this person (Mohammed) who teaches these things and how these doctrines

207

of submission/works will lead to eternal <u>spiritual death</u>. **He who has ears to hear, let him hear," "whoso readeth, let him understand."** Well we all have ears, but do we all listen and understand? After years of false eschatology with our senses now dulled are we still teachable?

That is the million-dollar question; now that the Master has used me to reveal to you what there is to understand, so there need not be any more confusion. Our YHWH is not an Elohim of confusion, but a YHWH of understanding, full of wisdom and truth. We need to pay heed to what He has to say to us.

F.   The Prophet Zechariah confirms the end-time battle is with Islamists-

> **Zechariah 2:5**-For I, says the Master will be a wall of fire all around her, and I will be the glory in her midst.

The Master intends to protect Israel supernaturally against her enemy; this is yet future.

> 6. Up, up! Flee from the **land of the north**, says the Master; for I have spread you abroad like the four winds of heaven, says the Master.

Turkey map [36]

Why flee from the north? This is because these nations are joining together for the attack on Israel. The Hebrew word *"tsaw-fone"* is translated north/north sides.

This incorporates Turkey with Iraq/Iran and CIS nations (look at the Turkey map above). Ironically Israel is most comfortable right now with Turkey as a Muslim nation and the armies are gathering from that direction to take Israel out. The lives of the Jews will not be safe in Turkey and the other lands adjoining Turkey in the near future. YHWH is warning them to leave these places now, but will the Jews listen? History teaches us probably not until they are slaughtered again and again like chickens. And yet, they cannot complain that Yahweh did not warn them about it in Scripture.

---

[36] www.prophecymaps.com

7. "Up, Zion! Escape, you who dwell with the daughter of Babylon."

YHWH warns Israel not to dwell with the "daughter of Babylon" (Saudi Arabia), who intends to do peace deals with Israel on certain pre-conditions, as this is the "harlot of Babylon." Also part of Zion as explained in this book are born again Christians, or Ephraimites who are told to leave Babylon.

8. For thus says YHWH of hosts: "He sent Me [Yahushua the Messiah] after glory, to the nations [the only nations who want to plunder Israel are Islamic] which plunder you; for he who touches you touches the apple of His eye.

So YHWH is warning about Islamic nations who will plunder Israel. The "Me" in this verse is the Master Yahushua the Messiah, who will come at His second coming and the nations in plural are all Islamic.

9. "For surely I will shake My hand against them, and they shall become spoil for their servants. Then you will know that the Master of hosts has sent Me.

This time the Jews will recognize the Messiah Yahushua who comes to fight those nations gathered against Israel.

10. "Sing and rejoice, **O daughter of Zion!** For behold, I am coming and I will dwell in your midst," says the Master.

Make no mistake; Yahushua of Nazareth will soon be here on earth in full glory amidst the Jews in Jerusalem that is referred to here as "daughter of Zion."

11. "Many nations shall be joined to the Master in that day, and they shall become My people. And I will dwell in your midst. Then you will know that the Master of hosts has sent Me to you.

This reference to "in that day" is to the great day of the Master that is coming upon the world. Twice mention is made of the fact that "they would know that YHWH of hosts has sent Me." This is Messianic talk about Messiah returning to Jerusalem and the Jews recognizing Him finally. It also talks about the fact that at this time many other nations will also recognize Him as Master and Savior and become His people. Clearly many nations did not recognize Yahushua of Nazareth as Master before, but in this end-time prophecy they will do so. It is quite possible that part of these nations would be some Islamic nations, who might rebel and turn against the confederacy of Islam. The reason is because brother turns against brothers, as the Muslims will kill their own, as prophesied by Ezekiel.

This also fits with Zechariah's prophecy of an end-times revival out of Islam. Zechariah is given a fantastic prophecy of the future and an end-time scenario of the same people. Let us look at this:

In Zechariah 5 we are told ...

1. Then I turned, and lifted up mine eyes, and looked, and behold a flying roll.

This is no ordinary scroll. This is the LAW of YHWH that Zechariah saw, or the Law that Moses penned down on scrolls.

2. And he said unto me, what seest thou? And I answered, I see a flying roll; the length thereof is twenty cubits, and the breadth thereof ten cubits.

He is asked what does he see, to which the prophet replies a flying book, or scroll, as in ancient times when the Law/Torah was written on scrolls. Writings bound in books is a later invention. This is a flying scroll i.e. it would be known throughout the world. Whether people believe in the Elohim of Israel or not, they all know the famous Ten Commandments, or the Decalogue.

Remember Yahushua also read from Isaiah's scroll in the Temple. People in those days did carry scrolls, and if you go to a Jewish synagogue today you will see scrolls that they reverently keep. The prophet is told that the scroll is 30 feet by 15 feet, and this is enough paper to fit the Law/Torah of Moses easily. I have used the standard length of a cubit, roughly half a meter equalling 1 cubit. There is writing on both sides of the scroll as mentioned in the next passage.

3. Then said he unto me, This is **the curse** that goeth forth over the face of the whole earth: for every one that stealeth shall be cut off as on this side according to it; and every one that sweareth shall be cut off as on that side according to it.

Two important aspects of this, the Law is written on both sides of the scrolls that are revealed here in the text. The Hebrew word used for whole earth is *V'kol Ha Eretz* that can refer to the "whole world" or a region of the world such as a single country. This is what we would call a synecdoche, or a figure of speech and the Bible does use this in a lot of the passages. However, here the usage only refers to Eretz Israel, i.e. the "whole land of Israel" not the "whole world." The NASB Bible translates it correctly as the "whole land." The Law of Moses would become like a double edge sword written on both sides of the scrolls.

YHWH is setting forth judgement for all those that try to steal the "land of Israel," or heave it away. YHWH is setting forth a precedent by the Law that He gave to Moses, hence the reference to "this side" and "that side," or both sides of the tablets.

Remember that the law if not obeyed can become a curse for us, or it can become a blessing to us when obeyed. It shows us our sin, and it is our tutor to lead us to the Messiah as our Savior. If this passage is referring to the "whole world," then is YHWH saying I will judge you if you steal my land i.e. from the "whole world?" The place that is in view here is not the land of the "whole world," but only Israel. YHWH is particularly concerned about this nation that He established His covenants with. Both the promises and this curse you could say are an expounding of **Genesis 12:3**, revealed again in Deuteronomy 28. However the application as I will show lateron, is to one specific group of people only, who have come to steal the land. These are all Islamic nations today, but technically it could be wider, yet YHWH is narrowing it down to "**this land**" for the people of Israel and those that are "round about" them (Muslims). YHWH starts with a wider

210

group and then narrows things down to a people, and to a land, just like He did with Ishmael and Isaac where the blessings were given to both. The covenant however was narrowed down to Isaac only. This was to indicate that YHWH did not recognize Ishmael as Abraham's legitimate heir for the land, or covenant. Many today would argue that Ishmael being the older son should somehow have the right as an heir, but YHWH said the older shall serve the younger.

4. I will bring it forth, saith YHWH of hosts, and it shall enter into the house of the thief, and into the house of him that sweareth falsely by My Name: and it shall remain in the midst of his house, and shall consume it with the timber thereof and the stones thereof.

All those that swear falsely by the Torah shall be killed, or cut off by it. All those that falsely claim Israel as their own land, shall suffer and bring a curse upon themselves and their children, as seen in Zechariah 5:3. The text "remain in their house," is a reference to a **generational curse**. Have you not noticed how though Arab Muslim nations are rich and wealthy, they still cannot prosper in real practical terms for the man on the street. Why is this? The reason is given above, that these are the ones who make the false claims on the land of Israel. The curse that they brought upon themselves and is a **generational curse. No ones children can ever escape Islam without the blood of Yahushua liberating them and breaking the curse.** The only way to break this curse is through the Messiah Yahushua by repentance and by acknowledging the promises of the Elohim of Israel to His chosen people Israel.

Zachariah-5: 5: Then the angel that talked with me went forth, and said unto me, lift up now thine eyes, and see what is this that goeth forth.

6. And I said, what is it? And he said, this is an **ephah that goeth forth**. He said moreover, this is **their resemblance through all the earth.**

Now the Master is really identifying these people. The word "ephah" can be used for either gallons of liquid, or dry things, but here liquid is in view and we are talking about barrels, what barrels? Barrels of oil my friends. YHWH is identifying a people with "gallons of oil" an economical wealth that affects the whole earth and the people identified are in the Middle East, confirmed by other references in the Bible such as Psalm 83, Ezekiel 35, Obadiah 1.

7. And, behold, there was lifted up a talent of lead: and this is **a woman that sitteth in the midst of the ephah**.

This woman (city, or a range of location) sits in the middle of the oil! The talent is presented as the city that is controlling the economic cycles of the nations. And who do you think this could be? The nations who control the economic cycles are the Arab nations with their oil. This woman, symbolic for a city is in the midst of this entire black liquid (oil). Note the talent Hebrew word "*kikkar*" also describes a round about area near Jordan. Now we may understand the symbols in this passage.

8. And he said, **this is wickedness**. And he cast it into the midst of the ephah; and **he cast the weight of lead upon the mouth thereof.**

211

The Master describes this city as wickedness reserved for judgment with the lead weight i.e. its sins being very heavy and not cast out. Casting the lead weight is also symbolic of war and guess what we already have? War going on in Iraq. When the Fallujah Muslims attacked some US civilians during the end of March 2004, they killed four Americans with grenades and burned their bodies. Then they were beating the charred bodies with metal bars, later hanging the pieces of the charred corpses on a bridge. Is this not wickedness? Saddam Hussain tortured his victims to death, some by burning, and others by cutting hands and feet, breaking of bones, and the ripping of skin off of the body. This is what sort of atrocities took place in the Iraqi cities. This is the sort of wickedness that is in view here also.

9. Then lifted I up mine eyes, and looked, and, **behold, there came out two women, and the wind was in their wings; for they had wings like the wings of a stork: and they lifted up the ephah between the earth and the heaven.**

First there was one woman (city) now there are two women (two cities). These women (propagating false faith) are spreading false religion through their political clout i.e. through the barrel of oil, and the petrodollar. They have a lot of economical power to move nations. The picture of the stork is an unclean animal that spreads something foul. This is why the wings indicate spreading abroad through the wind. Have we seen a revival of Islam since 9/11? I would say absolutely "yes," as we are strangely finding more people becoming Muslims rather then less. **Basically we are told this is the revival of Islam, and the two cities in view are Babylon in Iraq and Mecca in Saudi Arabia.**

Remember the TV stations continually telling people about the holy city of Najjaf, where there is the shrine of Imam Ali, the first martyr of Islam? It is correct to say this is the revival of the old into the new, or the old Islam into the new Islam. Just as the old was fundamentalist, so the new must be fundamentalist also.

Let us not forget that the false religion of Islam came from Babylonia and Allah already existed before Muhammad proclaimed his own prophet hood. He was formerly a statue, but Muhammad proclaimed him to be the unseen god in heaven. So this monotheism was his invention and we have both cities in view propagating the same evil to lead people astray. Muqtada al-Sadr was willing to sacrifice himself and his Mahdi army to fight the USA forces. The name Mahdi is taken from the person who will herald the coming of Dajjal, the Muslim version of the Anti-Messiah.

10. Then said I to the angel that talked with me, whither do these bear the ephah?

The prophet enquires about where is this going with this liquid black gold?

11. And he said unto me, to **build it a house in the land of Shinar: and it shall be established**, and set there upon her own base.

Bingo! In order to build a house of economic significance, we have both British and American forces fighting the war in Iraq involved in entrenched battles with local and foreign Muslim fighters for control of the cities. Iraq is intrinsically linked to Bible prophecy, as this is where we get our "daughter of Babylon," or Saudi Arabia from. They are the modern power bases that originated out of Iraq. Where are the pundits saying that we will establish western democracy next? Iraq is the place of the real struggle, since it is also the place housing the world's second largest reserves of oil. Already we are told that democracy will come to Iraq. I would urge you to look at Northern Iraq in the Kurdish regions, as they are now established as the most democratic regions in all of the Middle East.

Revelation 18:7-8 "In the measure that she glorified herself and lived luxuriously, in the same measure give her torment and sorrow; for she says in her heart, `I sit as queen, and am no widow, and will not see sorrow.' "Therefore her plagues will come in one day, death and mourning and famine. And she will be utterly burned with fire, for strong is the Master YHWH who judges her.

Still, the destruction of Mecca is also presented in the Bible. The harlot of Babylon will be ravaged. Muslims themselves will destroy it and ravage Mecca, since this is what the Master has proposed and it will be fulfilled.

Furthermore, in one of the Islamic books "Yawmul-Ghadhab hal-Bada'a be-Intifadat Rajab," by Sheikh Safar Al-Hwaly: "The Day of Wrath, did it start with the Month of the Rajab Uprising?" Selecting the "Yawmul-Ghadab," for a name alludes to the Day of YHWH's wrath.

"The final battle will be waged by Muslim faithful coming on the backs of horses, carrying black banners. They will stand on the east side of the Jordan River and will wage war that the earth has never seen before. The true Messiah who is the Islamic Madhi, who will kill the pig and will break the cross and will defeat Europe, will lead this army of **Seljuk's. He will preside over the world from Jerusalem because Mecca would have been destroyed,"**

The Seljuk Empire was a Turkic Empire that preceded the Ottomans who arose from the division of the Empire. It covered the region of Anatolia (Turkey), Northern Iran, Syria, Iraq, Southern Caucasus, and Azerbaijan. It is fascinating that even Islamic scholars believe that the Islamic Mahdi (the one who is to precede the coming of the Islamic Messiah) will lead an army of Seljuk's who were clearly Turkic people in history. And they are also ascribing the last battle to these people. **It is fascinating that Muslim scholars believe that Mecca, the spiritual headquarters of Islam, will be destroyed and this is exactly what the Bible foretells based on the analysis of the Scriptures as outlined in this book**. It would not be accurate for me to say that Muhammad was not a prophet. He's just not a prophet of Yahweh. However **he was prophet of Allah**, those who worship Yahweh belong to the camp of the righteous, while those who belong to Allah belong to the camp of the unrighteous. Likewise we had Baal and his prophets and Yahweh and His prophets. There is no argument as to Muhammad's prophet hood to Allah, but then Allah is not Yahweh.

The Turks and Arabs have had a feudal past and from the above it can be seen that the Turks will not hesitate to go to war with their pseudo brothers to settle old scores given half the chance.

Saudi Arabia glorifies herself and lives **luxuriously** today more then any city in the world with gold, silver, expensive cars, expensive sports, expensive Jewellery and sins in

213

secret. They think they are the custodians of a true faith, while propagating a wicked religion that asks people to murder others and to kill themselves as martyrs for Allah.

Revelation 17:4 The woman was arrayed in **purple** and **scarlet**, and adorned with gold and precious stones and pearls, having in her hand a golden cup full of abominations and **the filthiness of her fornication**.

The great scholars play on these words to make this into a Roman Catholic Empire. Unfortunately the context and connection of this particular passage has nothing to do with Roman Catholicism. The woman is somehow made to look like a priest wearing these robes holding a golden cup. They build whole theories around this passage and it has led many people into error.

Using proper biblical interpretation the woman in this passage refers to a city, or a country that is very rich. This is why she is arrayed in purple, adorned with gold and precious stones. Let me give you an idea of how rich we are looking at. In the old days producing the color purple, or blue was a very expensive process. The Hebrews were commanded to wear tzitzits on the four corners of their garments that we read about in Numbers 15:37-41.

Numbers 15:37-41 And YHWH spake unto Moses, saying, Speak unto the children of Israel, and bid them that they make them **fringes** in the **borders of their garments** throughout their generations, and that **they put upon the fringe of the borders a ribbon of blue**: And it shall be unto you for a fringe, that ye may **look upon it**, and **remember all the commandments of YHWH**, and do them; and that ye seek not after your own heart and your own eyes, after which ye use to go a whoring: That ye may remember, and do all my commandments, and be holy unto your Elohim.

The **word translated, hem**, is actually referring to the fringes, or tassels (called *tzitziyot,* in Hebrew), required to be on the four corners of all clothing of Hebrew men, in accordance with Yahweh's instructions.

In ancient days, at the time of Yahushua and even before, the Hebrews wore the four tzitzits and of course Yahushua did too. Today the modern Jews take a 'tallit' that is an outer garment like a shawl. This garment is always worn in public. Why? So that when you would see the tzitzits you would remember YHWH's mitzvoth/commands and perform them all the time. If you go to Israel today you will see the Jews wearing this garment as they are going to the synagogues or the Temple Mount area. There is another garment that is called a 'kataan' that some Jews wear underneath their top clothing. This is a four-cornered garment that especially allows the attaching of tzitzits and is specially designed for this use.

This garment is speaking of the mantle, or cloak that is worn as an outer garment. The Hebrew word for mantle, cloak, or robe is **"meiyl."** However, it was later that it became known as the tallit. The tallit is a rectangular garment that is draped over the shoulders. Today it's often called a **prayer shawl**.

Before synthetic dyes were invented, the only source for these was a small gland in the murex snail. It took 12,000 snails to fill up a thimble of blue dye. In 200 BC, one pound of cloth, dyed blue, cost the equivalent of £23,000 British Pounds Sterling. By AD 300, this same pound of blue cloth would cost £60,000 British Pounds Sterling. Let me relate to you an interesting biblical account that Lydia of Thyatira, a merchant who was an early convert to Christianity, sold purple cloth, and was one of the wealthiest women in the empire (Acts 16:14). Imagine the excitement it would have generated knowing that a person such as this was saved. She was very godly and helped the early church with her money.

> **Acts 16:14** And a certain woman named Lydia, a seller of purple [cloth], of the city of Thyatira, which worshipped YHWH, heard us: whose heart the Master opened, that she attended unto the things which were spoken of Paul.

This shows us that when the Bible describes the woman in Revelation we are talking about huge wealth. You can just imagine the amount of money required to make a dress of this type of purple clothing. YHWH is using these symbols to indicate the wealth of this city. Now let us travel to Rome in Italy and do we see this type of wealth? Clearly we do not, in fact I know of at least two Catholic dioceses in the USA who have filed for bankruptcy. By the time all the lawsuits are over the Catholic Church will struggle to survive.

Let us travel to the Middle East to Mecca and do we see this wealth? The answer is yes. Do we see Saudi Arabians filthy rich with oil? The answer is yes. Oil prices after the 2nd Gulf War almost doubled, while many people struggle to make ends meet, the Arabs sit and bathe in luxury. The Arabs have got it made and it is all YHWH given, but not appreciated, as they continue to ascribe their worship to a foreign god.

Every second they make around £60,000 pounds UK Sterling. This is how rich we are talking about. Every second that we breathe the Arabs get richer because of the black gold that gushes out of the ground. Do you know why it is cheap to get oil from the Arabs? Because it literally gushes out of the ground. They do not even have to drill for it. Next time you buy your gas, think about all the money that you are filling into their coffers. And do not forget that a lot of this money today goes into militant Islamic terrorism. This is what we call state sponsored terrorism, if you know what I mean. In fact we ignorantly sponsor terrorism, but we are not given a choice to use alternate fuels and so the cycle continues.

Look at how difficult it was to put out the fires that were started in the oil fields of Iraq during the first Gulf War. In the west you have to spend lots of money to drill oil. YHWH really did bless Ishmael and his progeny based on the wealth they have, described here in Revelation 17. Try using whatever artistic license of scholarly subterfuge and you just cannot fit this to the Vatican, its impossible.

G.   Zechariah on Islam in chapter 6

Zechariah 6

1. Then I turned and raised my eyes and looked, and behold, four chariots were coming from between two mountains, and the mountains were mountains of bronze.

Four chariots, a sign of judgment and war coming out of two mountains. We are seeing two kingdoms with the mountain being a symbol for Kingdom/Empire/nations. This is the old and new Islam [two mountains], a revival of Islam. The chariots and horses represent war. The Ottoman Empire faded and was wounded but now the revival of Islam is rampant and the wound that was is healing. It does not mean that the Ottoman Empire will come back. It means Islam, as a whole will revive worldwide with all Islamic nations taking active part. Even Muslims in the west will take part, and this is the conglomerate empire that will dominate the world scene.

This is the battle of Gog and Magog.

These are bronze mountains; this is referring to the revived Grecian Empire. The entire Middle East region was once part of the Grecian Empire (now all Islamic), the place of the Anti-Messiah, as the "little horn" comes out from one of the divisions of the Alexandrian kingdom. Here he joins forces with his comrades to form his confederacy.

2. With the first chariot were red horses, with the second chariot black horses,

We see horses; these are strong sturdy animals very graceful. Here this speaks about the war, bloodshed and violence with the color of red that is to come from Islam. The black horse signifying death is also an Islamic color and destruction which will accompany these people. You have seen the Palestinians wearing black and Muslim women wearing black.

> **Revelation 6:4** And another horse, **fiery red**, went out. And it was granted to the one who sat on it to take **peace** from the earth, and that people should **kill** one another; and there was given to him a **great sword**.

> The word for peace is "**lambano**."
> The word for kill in the Greek language is "**sfad-zo**" to kill violently.

The red horse in Revelation matches Zechariah's red horse going out killing people as the sign of bloodshed and violence. The Greek word used for kill is *"sfad-zo"* which means not just to kill, but also to "kill with violence." This resembles the tactics of the Islamic armies and matches what the radical Islamists do today. The Greek word for "to take" is "lambano," which means to take by force. So they will take by force and destroy any concept of peace, even if the world likes it or not. We can see this behavior in Iraq. A lot of Islamists are fighting there from foreign nations even if they have no business there. So they take hold of people by force killing anyone and shatter the peace. This passage is figurative of the Anti-Messiah and his forces having victory for a time. These are the armies of the Anti-Messiah from the Islamic nations.

3. With the third chariot white horses, and with the fourth chariot dappled horses strong steeds.

The white horse indicates that these people proclaim a sort of godliness, righteousness through outward works and salvation through their false peace and false prophet. They will even win wars for a time as the Bible suggests. He will overcome the saints. They think that they are the armies of heaven fighting for their god Allah. The dappled horse signifies the disease and decay that is about to come to the world through these people so be warned.

> **Revelation 6:2** And I looked, and behold, a white horse. And he who sat on it had a bow; and a crown was given to him, and he went out conquering and to conquer.

The white horse in Revelation matches with Zechariah who goes out and wins wars. This is the sign of the Anti-Messiah king who will go and win battles. The crown signifies that he is a king and the bow and arrow is the sign of him making war. The white horse also signifies him offering a false peace and a false salvation.

Revelation 6:8 And I looked, and behold, a pale horse. And the name of him who sat on it was Death, and Hades followed with him. And power was given to them over a fourth of the earth, to kill with sword, with hunger, with death, and by the beasts of the earth.

The one who sits on the pale horse is not pale but green (Greek word *chloros*) horse and he wages war and death on the earth. The green color signifies death and pestilence. Is it any wonder that after the green horse is released that there is much death and destruction; the Islamic rider causes this:

Revelation 6:9 When He opened the fifth seal, I saw under the altar the souls of those who had been slain for the word of YHWH and for the testimony, which they held.

Many believers will be killed during this time for the testimony of Yahweh.

Revelation 6:5 When He opened the third seal, I heard the third living creature say, "Come and see." And I looked, and behold, a black horse, and he who sat on it had a pair of scales in his hand.

This rider is shown to have a pair of scales, but in actual fact this is not translated accurately as the Greek word used is "**dzoo-gos**" meaning yoke. He has a yoke in his hand to put people to servitude, or more correctly to bring people to servitude through this black gold.

This has to do with the oil economy, which controls the world. Here it is time for it to come to an end and judgment is set for these. This will bring trouble to the world. The same is seen in Revelation 18.

4. Then I answered and said to the angel who talked with me, "What are these, my lord?"

5. And the angel answered and said to me, "These are four spirits of heaven, who go out from their station before the Master of all the earth.

These will be released from the Master both for judgment and for destruction that is to come.

6. "The one with the black horses is going to the north country, the white are going after them, and the dappled are going toward the south country."
Death and destruction comes from the north country. That is Turkey where the Anti-Messiah will rise out of and they are going to attack the south (Egypt) just as prophet Daniel prophesied and the Anti-Messiah will overcome them. The dappled horses bring death and destruction to the south i.e. through possible biological warfare.

Daniel 11:40 "And at the time of the end shall the king of the south **[Egypt]** push at him **[Anti-Messiah]** and the king of the north (**Anti-Messiah**) shall come

217

against him (**king of the south/Egypt**) like a whirlwind, with chariots, and with horsemen [**with his mighty armies**], and with many ships; and he shall enter into the countries, and shall overflow and pass over [**complete victory**]."

Some people think there are three parties in Daniel 11:40, but in affect there are only two kings one from the north and one from the south. The king of the south is Egypt and the King of the North is the Turkic Anti-Messiah. He will attack Egypt, which will fall to him, Libya (Phut) and Sudan (Cush), which is mentioned in Daniel 11:43 are also following in the steps of the Anti-Messiah.

Daniel proves and concludes with Isaiah that Egypt is going to be won over. Remember the white horse above in Zechariah; this also signifies some victories before the Anti-Messiah is brought down.

Daniel 11:25 And he shall stir up his power and his courage against the king of the south [Egypt] with a great army; and the king of the south shall be stirred up to battle with a very great and mighty army; but he shall not stand [defeat awaits Egypt] for they shall forecast devices against him.

Egypt shall be brought down for its arrogance.

Isaiah 19:4 And the Egyptians will I give over into **the hand of a cruel lord**; and **a fierce king** [this is the Anti-Messiah] shall rule over them, saith the Master, YHWH of hosts.

Isaiah concurs with what I said above. He is to be given over to the fierce northern king who is the Anti-Messiah. This has never happened before in the past. The Egyptians will be ruled by this king by force whether they like it or not.

7.Then the strong steeds went out, eager to go, that they might walk to and fro throughout the earth. And He said, "**Go, walk to and fro throughout the earth.**" **So they walked to and fro throughout the earth.**

These people are upon the earth executing vengeance. Do the Muslims do this today? Yes and it will get worse. Do not be fooled by the politician's statements that things will become better. It is their business to give you the feel good factor so you can spend, spend, spend. But tomorrow brings much trouble. I tell you beware of the danger ahead and prepare today not tomorrow.

8. And He called to me, and spoke to me, saying, "See, those who go toward the North Country have given rest to My Spirit in the North Country."

These go to the north country [Turkey] from where the whole thing started, executing their form of judgement on the earth. The Master allowed them to execute this judgement in order to show and reveal His glory. This does not excuse these people from guilt, but it shows their evil nature.

H.   The Prophet Zephaniah established that the end is with Islamists...

Zephaniah Chapter 2

4. For Gaza shall be forsaken, and Ashkelon a desolation; they shall drive out Ashdod at the noonday, and Ekron shall be rooted up.

Israel gave up Gaza and the Palestinians have taken over that region. YHWH will act, or more correctly respond. This is only a matter of time.

This is talking about the judgment to come on the Palestinian regions of Israel. We know this is the day of the Master as the context is given in **Zephaniah 1:14a**. "The great day of the Master is near, it is near," **It also tells us this is the day of wrath in Zephaniah 1:15a.** "That day is a day of wrath, a day of trouble and distress."

5. Woe unto the inhabitants of the seacoast, the nation of the Cherethites! The word of the Master is against you; O Canaan, the land of the Philistines, I will even destroy thee, that there shall be no inhabitant.

This is a past, present and future use of these words. The destruction on the Palestinians is yet future and could possibly come through either a hurricane, or Tsunami like event.

8. I have heard the reproach of Moab, and the reviling of the children of Ammon, whereby they have reproached My people, and magnified themselves against their border.

Are we surprised that YHWH is saying that even He has heard the slanderous speech of the Jordanians also known as the Palestinians and others around with them against His covenant people? Wait a minute! Does not Christendom teach that YHWH is done away with Israel? You better not believe that because Yahweh is very much interested in Israel's affairs. These Arab people magnify themselves and say Israel is cast off and has no Elohim. They slander the Jewish nation so much so, that world opinion is against Israel.

9. Therefore as I live, saith the Master of hosts, the Elohim of Israel, Surely Moab shall be as Sodom, and the children of Ammon as Gomorrah, even the breeding of nettles, and saltpits, and a perpetual desolation: the residue of My people shall spoil them, and the remnant of My people shall possess them.

Note Israel is going to destroy these people as it says "residue of My people" i.e. the remnant of Israel is going to destroy these violators and hate mongers.

10. This shall they have for their pride, because they have reproached and magnified themselves against the people of YHWH of hosts.

Notice the clear-cut injunction here that they have pridefully reviled the covenant people (Hebrews) of the one true YHWH, who is not pleased.

219

11. The Master will be terrible unto them: for **He will famish all the gods** of the earth; and men shall worship Him, every one from his place, even all **the isles of the heathen**.

How is Yahweh going to starve the false gods? Easy. Allah demands that you send your son or daughter for jihad. Muslims are lining up to go on suicide missions as human bombs, as these are the sacrifices that this god Allah demands. Yahweh is going to put an end to it.

Here is that magic word again in verses 11. All the "Isles of the heathens," or countries of heathens who are Muslim today will come to know that the true Elohim is not Allah, but YHWH. A redeemed remnant will come to worship Him one day who is revealed in the person of Yahushua of Nazareth. The "Isles of heathen" include countries like Indonesia.

Those that do not acknowledge Him as YHWH will die spiritually; they will die physically and also be cut off from the world hereafter (spiritual death).

This is what this new magazine had to say in a recent article;
AL-QA'EDA WOMEN'S MAGAZINE: "WOMEN MUST PARTICIPATE IN JIHAD"

The first edition of the new online magazine Al-Khansaa features an editorial calling on women to participate in jihad. The magazine is published by Al Qaeda's "Arabian Peninsula Women's Information Bureau."

The editorial is titled: 'Our Goal Is Paradise.' It states: ..." We love Allah and his Messenger. We march in a single path, the path of jihad for the sake of Allah, and our goal is shahada [martyrdom] for the sake of Allah, and our goal is [to gain] the pleasure of Allah and his Paradise.

"We will stand covered by our veils and wrapped in our robes, weapons in hand, our children in our laps, with the Qur'an and the Sunna of the Prophet of Allah directing and guiding us. **The blood of our husbands and the body parts of our children are the sacrifice by means of which we draw closer to Allah**."

What kind of a god requires sacrifices of children?

Notice below particular emphasis on child martyrdom. This is child sacrifice, no different than the false worship and child sacrifice in the days of old.

CHILD MARTYRDOM PROMOTION CLIP RETURNS TO PA TV AFTER YEAR'S ABSENCE

A broadcast clip titled "Farewell Letter," that had been removed from Palestinian Authority TV after it was exposed at a USA Senate hearing in October 2003, and was subsequently harshly criticized by USA senators, has returned to Yasser Arafat's Palestinian Authority TV station after nearly a year's absence.

"Farewell Letter" has been broadcast at least three times in the last 2 weeks. On August 23, 26, and 31, 2004, the clip was replayed on PA TV.

In the broadcast, a child sings a farewell letter he has written to his parents, glorifying his desire to die, and then he goes out to the combat zone, where he is shot and achieves his death wish. As he falls in death, the words of his letter are sung twice: "How sweet is shahada (death for Allah) when I embrace you my land."

In the farewell letter sung during the clip, the "martyred" boy says: "My beloved, my mother, my most dear, be joyous over my blood and do not cry for me."

This is Baal in action that requires ongoing child sacrifices. The clip can be seen at www.pmw.org.il

12. Ye Ethiopians also, ye shall be slain by my sword.

This is not Ethiopia of today but Cush, which is Sudan, south of Egypt in biblical days. Is it any wonder that there is currently slaughter going on there of innocent Christians (estimates are over 400,000 already massacred) and animists by the Muslim Arabs, trying to drive them out of the oil rich regions of the South? This will also be part of the end-time confederacy and that is why we are seeing a merging of this region with the Islamic regions.

13. And he will stretch out his hand against the north, and destroy Assyria; and will make Nineveh desolation, and dry like a wilderness.

The Master is going to destroy Nineveh in the north which is still pretty much thriving; again mention is made of Assyria as this is another reference to the Anti-Messiah who will come from the north (not the west).

One might ask why Nineveh? Is that not in Iraq and if I claim the Anti-Messiah comes from the north (Turkey) then why Nineveh?

We have to understand that Turkey is not the only nation in the end-time confederacy, but it has other CIS (Common Independent States, Southern Russian) states with it. Turkey will be leading the confederacy including the Southern Russian Turkic nations. Nineveh fits in nicely in this picture because it is north of Iraq in present day Mosul, which was Israel's enemy during the Assyrian Empire. Nineveh was established as a capital of the Assyrians in 705 BC.

In order to fit the "type" of Antiochus Epiphanes the Anti-Messiah will have a strong link with this region. Interestingly Turkey hates the Kurds who reside in this region today. If they are given half a chance, then they will kill all the Kurds and overtake this region.

Parts of Turkey were part of the Assyrian Empire. It was in Syria that Antiochus ruled and this is important in end-time typology for the end-time Anti-Messiah has a strong link to this same region. Meshech and Tubal mentioned in Ezekiel 38 alongside northern Syria and northern Iraq are important aspects of the end-times prophecy.

Zephaniah 2:15 This is the rejoicing city that dwelt carelessly, that said in her heart, **I am**, [equals itself to YHWH] and there is none beside me: how is she become desolation, **a place for beasts to lie down in!** Every one that passeth by her shall hiss, and wag his hand.

221

This is Saudi Arabia that is **penned** to be destroyed, she said in her heart "I am" (only YHWH says I AM) and no one can touch me, she sins in secret and Isaiah also predicted her destruction the same way.

> **Isaiah 21:16-17** For thus hath the Master said unto me, Within a year, according to the years of an hireling, and **all the glory of Kedar shall fail**: And the **residue of the number of archers**, the **mighty men of the children of Kedar**, shall be diminished: for **the Master YHWH the Elohim of Israel hath spoken it**.

We can see that many prophets of Israel spoke about these nations and each one confirms that the end-time wrath is on Islamic nations who will join together as a confederacy. Could the "glory of Kedar" failing be the end of Mecca? This is a likely scenario and the "mighty archers" diminishing will be through warfare.

Here is a likely scenario of possible events

Syria has enough biological weapons to be a serious threat to Israel. Syria could strike Israel with a biological weapon which could cause Israel to retaliate by striking Damascus with a <u>nuclear</u> strike thus fulfilling **Isaiah 17:1**. There are at least two, or possibly three nuclear strikes in the Bible and one is on Damascus.

> The burden of Damascus. Behold, Damascus is taken away from being a city, and it shall be **a ruinous heap**.

If this were to happen then this would allow the Islamic nations to come together very quickly to try and destroy Israel. This would also mean that a lot of western governments would distance themselves and condemn Israel leaving Israel all open to a big heavy attack by the Anti-Messiah's forces. The enemy would know that Israel is not going to get international supported during a war. What would happen if Israel did strike in retaliation to an Arab missile strike coming in to strike Israel that had nuclear, or biological capabilities?

It is my personal opinion and knowledge that Israel has drawn plans to keep nuclear ambiguity until such time as it becomes absolutely necessary to openly declare what they have in their arsenal. In an attack on the sovereign state of Israel by bio or nuclear weapons Israel is prepared to strike at least 15 targets of hostile Islamic nations and in this event Israel hopes to do enough damage to put at least 15 of them out of business.

On the face of it this seems like a good strategy but the problem is that there are more then 15 Islamic nations e.g. 52 at present count and increasing. Many could acquire certain strategic power in which case they will attack Israel together with all hostility and fury. This is exactly what the Bible teaches us. That they will attack Israel and prosper to a certain extent i.e. to the extent that even half of Jerusalem is taken away captive (Zechariah 14:2). This in itself means there will be an invasion from the North by a large force. This would also mean that open combat, street fighting and in the end, what we will see is that half of Jerusalem, most probably East Jerusalem will fall. This is obvious, because if you go to Jerusalem today, it is likely that east Jerusalem which is moarly Islamic, along with other Muslim states will rise and attack Israel, thus causing the Jews to take cover in west Jerusalem and prevent it from falling.

Interestingly before the return of the Messiah it is the European/western nations that will come to Israel's rescue with their ships and armament. We will discuss this in a later chapter; our interest is in two key nations the UK and the USA, to see how they fit in end-times prophecy. I will also add that in the final destruction of the Babylonian Empire, the USA and UK are fully involved and behind Israel. They will participate in striking down Iraq and Saudi Arabia. The USA/UK Alliance will also be behind the attack on Iran when that war comes and of course Syria.

How is it that I can conclude such a bold scenario?

Response: I make my conclusion from Bible prophecy and not just conjecture alone. The situation is already all built in the Middle East for this to take place.

Here are verses to support this conclusion:

Jeremiah 50:41 "Behold, a people shall come from the north, and a **great nation** and **many kings shall be raised up from the ends of the earth.**

The "GREAT NATION" in the North is the country of the United Kingdom and it will lead the battle, and the USA will follow it. Yahweh will raise these nations for His wrath on the Islamic Empire.

Jeremiah 50:42 They shall hold the **bow and the lance**; they are cruel and shall not show mercy. Their voice shall roar like the sea; they shall ride on horses, set in array, like a man for the battle, **against you, O daughter of Babylon.**

Here clearly in view is not only Babylon, but Iraq plus Saudi Arabia, the "**daughter of Babylon,**" since Saudi Arabia worships the god that came out of Iraq via Nabonidus.

What causes the USA/UK to suddenly come out of slumber?

Scenario 1-The reason could be oil. If Iraq or Saudi Arabia are either taken over by hostile Islamic radicals and Iran will be a key player in this all, then that could pose a major problem for the west. Let us assume that Saudi is taken over by a group such as Al-Qaeda, or one that is linked to Al-Qaeda. The Bible teaches Iran will attack Saudi and Iraq. If taken over Saudi would stop the oil exports to the west and in retaliation in order to protect their interests the USA/UK would attack. Of course, the attack in the first place would be equal to the Kuwait invasion that is to support and reinstate the local government that has been ousted. When the attack takes place, the hostile regime would respond by blowing up the oil wells and in return the allied alliance will strike with missiles and all fury to remove this hostile regime. In the end things will become so ugly that Saudi Arabia will be up in smoke and Iraq will be up in smoke, Iran will get attacked by all four sides and end up in smoke but not completely destroyed as Iraq and Arabia.

Scenario 2- Lets assume the Anti-Messiah is revealed. Yet most will fail to recognize him according to Scripture, as their heads are turned westward. Then his first point of contact is he will take over Iraq. Why take over Iraq one may ask?

223

His point of entry is Turkey and the northern regions of Iraq. Guess where? Kurdistan! Why Kurdistan? Because this is an area of Iraq rich in oil. The major oil areas here are:

* ❖ Oil was first discovered near Kirkuk in 1927.
* ❖ Discoveries at Mosul and Basra followed.
* ❖ Although the northern fields, notably Kirkuk, Jambur, and Sasan, have produced the most oil, the south also has oil.
* ❖ The southern oil fields have the largest reserves.
* ❖ Iraq has large reserves of natural gas.

FACTS-

* ❖ More than half of the Kurds live in south-eastern Turkey.
* ❖ 25 % reside in northern western Iran, and about 17 % live in northeastern Iraq.
* ❖ Kurdistan is a wealthy region with deposits of petroleum and other minerals as explained above.
* ❖ A large part of Iraq's oil resources are in Kurdistan, in the regions around Kirkuk and Hanikin.
* ❖ A part of the important oil resources of Iran is also in Kurdistan, in the region around Kirmanshah.
* ❖ Turkey's oil resources are almost exclusively in Kurdistan (in the regions around Batman, Diyarbakir, and Adiyaman).
* ❖ Syria's oil resources are also mainly in Kurdistan, in the region around Cezire.

There are logistical and financial gains in taking this area. The Bible even tells us that this will happen in that he is called the 'King of Babylon.' Next, he will attack and take over Egypt. He could stop the oil supplies to the west in retaliation by stopping the oil supplies to Western European nations by cutting off traffic in the Suez Canal. Then what would Europe do? Their only choice of survival is to fight back. So this is how the lack lustre European sleeping giant will spring into action because their very survival will depend on it. Then they will no longer be able to take an anti-Israeli position, or a neutral one vis-à-vis the Muslim-Israeli conflict.

World oil choke points

How do you kill someone? You do not have to fire even one missile, but you could choke them to death. This strategy does indeed exist and it's a dangerous one too.

Did you know that **five of the six major oil entry points in the world are controlled by Islamic nations?** So in order to control terrorism, or radical Islam the western leaders must involve Islamic leaders, or else they are going to fail and fall flat on their faces. Something needs to be done about this, or else one day, not too far in the distant future, we will have a problem that we have no answer for. Imagine any one of the world 'choke points' going over to any radical Islamic regime. Then what can the west do? They can do little else but fight.

1. **Bab el- Mandab**
2. **Bosporus- Turkish Straits**
3. **Panama Canal**

224

4. **Strait of Hormuz**
5. **Strait of Malacca**
6. **Suez Canal**

1- Bab el-Mandab-

Location: Djibouti/Eritrea/Yemen; connects the Red Sea with the Gulf of Aden and the Arabian Sea Oil Flows (2000): 3.2-3.3 million bbl/d
Destination of Oil Exports: Europe, United States, and Asia.

Concerns/Background: Closure of the Bab el-Mandab could keep tankers from the Persian Gulf from reaching the Suez Canal, diverting them around the southern tip of Africa (the Cape of Good Hope).

This would add greatly to transit time and cost, and effectively tie up spare tanker capacity. In addition, closure of the Bab el-Mandab would effectively block **non-oil shipping** from using the Suez Canal.

Security remains a major concern particularly after the French-flagged tanker Limburg was attacked off the coast of Yemen by terrorists in October 2002.

2-Bosporus/Turkish Straits

Location: Turkey; this 17-mile long waterway divides Asia from Europe and connects the Black Sea with the Mediterranean Sea
Oil Flows: (2001E): 2.0 million bbl/d (nearly all southbound; mostly crude oil with several hundred thousand barrels per day of products as well).
Destination of Oil Exports: Western and Southern Europe;
Concerns/Background: Only half a mile wide at its narrowest point, the Turkish Straits are one of the world's busiest (50,000 vessels annually, including 5,500 oil tankers), and most difficult-to-navigate waterways. Many of the proposed export routes for forthcoming production from the Caspian Sea region pass westwards through the Black Sea and the Turkish Straits en route to the Mediterranean Sea and world markets. The ports of the Black Sea, along with those in the Baltic Sea, were the primary oil export routes of the former Soviet Union, and the Black Sea remains the largest outlet for Russian oil exports.

Under the Montreux Convention of 1936, commercial shipping has the right of free passage through the Bosporus and Turkish Straits in peacetime, **although Turkey claims the right to impose regulations for safety and environmental purposes**. In October 2002, for instance, Turkey placed new restrictions on oil tanker transit through the Bosporus, including: a ban on nigh time transit for ships longer than 200 meters; a requirement that ships carrying dangerous cargo (including oil) request permission to transit 48 hours in advance; and a one-way traffic regulation on ships more than 250-300 meters long or carrying liquefied natural gas (LNG) or liquefied petroleum gas (LPG). The regulations reportedly have slowed tanker transit by as much as 3 1/2 days.

3-Panama Canal and Trans-Panama Pipeline

Location: Panama; connects the Pacific Ocean with the Caribbean Sea and Atlantic Ocean.
Oil Flows (2001E): 613,000 bbl/d.
Concerns/Background: The Panama Canal extends approximately 50 miles from Panama City on the Pacific Ocean to Colon on the Caribbean Sea. In fiscal year (FY) 2001, petroleum and petroleum products was the largest commodity (by tonnage) shipped through the Canal, accounting for 16% of total canal shipments. Around 64% of total oil shipments went south from the Atlantic to the Pacific, with oil products dominating southbound traffic. Chemicals (including petrochemicals) and coal are shipped through the canal as well, accounting for 5% and 3%, respectively, of total Canal traffic. The largest vessel that can transit the Panama Canal is known as a PANAMAX-size vessel. A long-term program is underway to widen the narrow, eight-mile stretch of Gaillard Cut to allow unrestricted two-way traffic of PANAMAX-size vessels.

If transit were halted through the Canal, the Trans-Panama pipeline (Petroterminal de Panama, S.A.) could be re-opened to carry oil in either direction. This pipeline is located outside the former Canal Zone near the Costa Rican border, and runs from the port of Charco Azul on the Pacific Coast (near Puerto Armuelles, southwest of David) to the port of Chiriqui Grande, Bocas del Toro on the Caribbean. It was opened in October 1982 as an economical alternative to the Panama Canal for transporting Alaskan oil across Panama en route to Gulf Coast ports. Transit time from Alaska to the U.S. Gulf Coast via Panama is about 16 days, whereas a tanker would take 40 days to reach the Gulf Coast from Alaska if rerouted around Cape Horn (the southern tip of South America). To date, more than 2.2 billion barrels of Alaskan crude oil has been transported through the 81-mile pipeline.

However, the 860,000-bbl/d pipeline was closed in April 1996 after Alaskan oil shipments to the Gulf Coast declined with falling Alaskan oil production (Alaska now produces about 1 million bbl/d) and increased oil consumption on the west coast of the United States, especially in California. In addition, the decision to allow Alaskan oil to be exported outside the United States reduced the incentives to ship Alaskan oil to the Gulf Coast. There has been some discussion of reversing the direction of the pipeline to allow Caribbean oil producers a less expensive outlet to Pacific destinations.

4-Strait of Hormuz

Location: Oman/Iran; connects the Persian Gulf with the Gulf of Oman and the Arabian Sea.
Oil Flows (2002E): 13 million bbl/d
Destination of Oil Exports: Japan, United States, Western Europe
Concerns/Background: By far the world's most important oil chokepoint, the Strait consists of 2-mile wide channels for inbound and outbound tanker traffic, as well as a 2-mile wide buffer zone. Closure of the Strait of Hormuz would require use of longer alternate routes (if available) at increased transportation costs. Such routes include the 5 million-bbl/d capacity Petroline (East-West Pipeline) and the 290,000-bbl/d Abqaiq-Yanbu natural gas liquids line across Saudi Arabia to the Red Sea. Theoretically, the 1.65-million bbl/d Iraqi Pipeline

across Saudi Arabia (IPSA) also could be utilized, more oil could be pumped north to Ceyhan (Turkey), and the 0.5 million-bbl/d Tapline to Lebanon could be reactivated.

5-Strait of Malacca

Location: Malaysia/Singapore; connects the Indian Ocean with the South China Sea and the Pacific Ocean.
Oil Flows (2002E): 10.3 million bbl/d
Destination of Oil Exports: Japan, South Korea, China, other Pacific Rim countries.
Concerns/Background: The Strait of Malacca, linking the Indian and Pacific Oceans, is the shortest sea route between three of the world's most populous countries -- India, China, and Indonesia -- and therefore is considered to be the key choke point in Asia. The narrowest point of this shipping lane is the Phillips Channel in the Singapore Strait, which is only 1.5 miles wide at its narrowest point. This creates a natural bottleneck, with the potential for a collision, grounding, or oil spill (in addition, piracy is a regular occurrence in the Singapore Strait). If the strait were closed, nearly half of the world's fleet would be required to sail further, generating a substantial increase in the requirement for vessel capacity. All excess capacity of the world fleet might be absorbed, with the effect strongest for crude oil shipments and dry bulk such as coal. Closure of the Strait of Malacca would immediately raise freight rates worldwide. More than 50,000 vessels per year transit the Strait of Malacca. With Chinese oil imports from the Middle East increasing steadily, the Strait of Malacca is likely to grow in strategic importance in coming years.

The bombing in October 2002 of a nightclub on the Indonesian island of Bali raised concerns throughout the region that other targets - including oil transit "chokepoints" like the Strait of Malacca - could be targeted by terrorists as well. As of early November 2002, insurance rates had not been affected for tankers travelling through the Straits, but insurance companies did place a "war-risk" designation on Indonesian ports. That means that ships docking at those ports forfeit their insurance coverage. Reportedly, Singapore and Malaysia have begun escorting oil tankers and increasing naval patrols in their waters, but this has not eliminated the threat of terrorism in the region's shipping channels.

In short if the terrorists were to control or block any of these ports then the world would face a very difficult time to reconcile the shortage of oil. Out of these only one, the Panama Canal currently belongs to the west and the rest, like it or not, all belong to the Muslims. They could choke the oil supply today if they wanted to by cutting off any one of these supply points and we would have a big global problem on our hands.

6-Suez Canal and Sumed Pipeline

Location: Egypt; connects the Red Sea and Gulf of Suez with the Mediterranean Sea.
Oil Flows (2001E/2002E): 3.8 million bbl/d. Of this total, the Sumed Pipeline transported 2.5 million bbl/d of oil northbound (nearly all from Saudi Arabia) and the Suez Canal around 1.3 million bbl/d total.
Destination of Sumed Oil Exports: Predominantly Europe; also United States.

Concerns/Background: Closure of the Suez Canal and/or Sumed Pipeline would divert tankers around the southern tip of Africa (the Cape of Good Hope), adding greatly to transit time and effectively tying up tanker capacity.

The Suez Canal transported around 1.3 million bbl/d of petroleum in 2001. Southbound trade consisted of about 300,000 bbl/d of petroleum, over 80% of which was refined products and the rest crude oil. Northbound trade consisted of about 955,000 bbl/d of petroleum, around 60% of which was crude oil. For the first eight months of 2001, an average of about 238 oil tankers passed through the Suez Canal each month, 20% of the total, and significantly below the canal's capacity. Currently, the Suez Canal can accommodate ships with drafts of up to 58 feet, which means that very large crude carriers (VLCCs) and ultra large crude carriers (ULCCs) cannot pass through the Canal. The Egyptian government plans to widen and deepen the Suez Canal, so that by 2010 it can accommodate VLCCs and ULCCs. In 2001, the Suez Canal Authority (SCA) launched a 5-year program to reduce tanker transit times (from 14 hours to 11 hours) through the Canal. The SCA also is moving ahead with a project to widen and deepened the Canal to allow for transit of larger ships than the 200,000-dead-weight-ton maximum now.

The Sumed pipeline, with capacity of around 2.5 million bbl/d, links the Ain Sukhna terminal on the Gulf of Suez with Sidi Kerir on the Mediterranean. Sumed consists of two parallel 42-inch lines, and is owned by Arab Petroleum Pipeline Co., a joint venture of EGPC, Saudi Aramco, Abu Dhabi's ADNOC, three Kuwaiti companies, and Qatar's QGPC.

Jeremiah 50:26 Come against **her from the farthest border**; [this nation is the USA] open her storehouses; cast her up as heaps of ruins, and destroy her utterly; let nothing of her be left.

Coming against Babylon from the "farthest border" is no other nation, but the United States of America.

How do we know this to be true? The prophesies in the book of Numbers 24:24 and Daniel 11:30 (Ships of Chittim) make the connection for us absolutely crystal clear.

Number 24:24 And ships shall come from **the coast of Chittim**, and shall afflict Asshur, and shall afflict Eber, and he also shall perish forever.

The coast of Chittim is not Cyprus alone, but coasts far west of Israel. That includes the USA and it also includes the coasts of Spain and Italy. However the nation that fits the "farthest border, or widest border" is the USA.

Jeremiah 50:25 The Master has opened His armory, and has brought out the **weapons of His indignation**; For this is the work of the Master YHWH of hosts in the **land of the Chaldeans**. [Iraq]

This is 100% conclusive proof that it is the USA and the UK that are at war with Assyria, because the only nations that YHWH called "WEAPONS OF HIS INDIGNATION" are none

228

other than the USA and UK, specified in Isaiah 13:1-5. These are the two nations that came to fight Iraq in the two gulf wars along with their partner nations.

Isaiah 13:5 They come from **a far country**, from the **end of heaven**, even the Master, and the **weapons of His indignation**, to destroy the whole land.

Points to note:

❖ They are from a **far country**; the USA is the one who came with the UK for two gulf wars. The USA is the one from the farthest border and we also have Australia as part of this.

❖ It mentions the nation from the ends of heaven, i.e. "from the end of the earth" from Israel's point of view, which is far west, taking the prophecy of Numbers 24:24 to the door of the USA, way west of Cyprus. Australia is included and so is New Zealand.

❖ YHWH called these "weapons of His indignation" just like in Jeremiah 50:25.

Jeremiah 50:21 "Go up against the **land of Merathaim**, against it, and against **the inhabitants of Pekod**. Waste and utterly destroy them," says the Master, "And do according to all that I have commanded you."

The word "land of Merathaim" means the land of double rebellion. These are the areas of Mesopotamia, modern Iraq including Syria. The word Pekod means "punishment," so punishment is coming upon these lands from the Master Himself. The question is are you ready?

I. The Prophet Nahum prophesies the end is with the Islamists...

Nahum 3:4 "Because of the **multitude of the whoredoms** of the **well favoured harlot**, the **mistress of witchcrafts**, that **selleth nations** through **her whoredoms**, and **families through her witchcrafts**."

Nahum is not a prophecy of the past but a prophecy of the future Islamic Empire to fall. It has only a type/shadow with the Assyrian Empire of old. The scholars have mistakenly concluded it is all about the past. If it were, then many verses in Nahum would make no sense whatsoever. There are too many to list here, but one such example that is 100% applicable to Yahushua the Messiah who yet to return is in **Nahum 1:15**. We know Yahushua did not appear to Israel as the Messiah during 612 BC, the time ascribed to the writing by the prophet Nahum.

Nahum 1:15 Behold, **on the mountains the feet of him who brings good tidings**, who proclaims peace! O Judah, keep your appointed feasts, perform your vows. For the wicked one shall no more pass through you; he is utterly cut off.

This prophecy is coupled with **Isaiah 52:7** who wrote in approximately 740 BC. Judah is told to keep her feasts and if we are tied to Judah, then so are we to keep them. Are the Christians keeping the Master's feasts?

How beautiful **upon the mountains are the feet of him who brings good news**, who proclaims peace, who brings glad tidings of good things, who proclaims salvation-Yahushua, who says to Zion, "Your YHWH reigns!"

Rightly ascribed by Paul of Tarsus, one of the great theologians and Pharisees of his day, to have been fulfilled in the person of Yahushua the Messiah;

Romans 10:15 And how shall they preach unless they are sent? As it is written: "How beautiful are the feet of those who preach the gospel of peace, who bring glad tidings of good things!"

With this thought then let's continue, the same words used in **Revelation 17:5**

And upon her forehead was a name written, MYSTERY, BABYLON THE GREAT; THE MOTHER OF HARLOTS AND ABOMINATIONS OF THE EARTH.

This is the "**whore of Babylon**," mystery Babylon (Saudi Arabia) who sells nations oil and through this sells and exports the false religion of Islam as truth. This is referred to as witchcrafts in Nahum 3:4. It is no longer a mystery once you know it is Islamists on the attack. **The mystery existed only as long as Islam had not been birthed and was not revealed**. The titles for this harlot are given in Revelation 17:5.

Nahum 3:15 There shall the **fire devour thee**; **the sword shall cut thee off**, it shall **eat thee up like the cankerworm**: make thyself many as the cankerworm; make thyself many as the **locusts** (Arabs/Aravim).

We also note the same language as in **Revelation 9:3** for locusts (Arabs) in **Nahum 3:15**. It says these shall be killed and devoured by fire, that will likely be the oil burning and by the sword through warfare.

Nahum 3:13 Surely, your people in your midst are women! The gates of your land are wide open for your enemies; fire shall devour the bars of your gates.

Since these are desert regions no wonder the allegory YHWH has chosen is of gates wide open.

Nahum 3:16 You have multiplied your merchants more than the stars of heaven. The locust plunders and flies away.

The reason being that Babylon (Iraq) also has lots of oil, the second largest reserve, so they also have plenty of merchants they sell their black gold to.

Nahum 3:19 Your **injury has no healing**, your **wound** is severe. All who hear news of you will **clap their hands over you**, for upon **whom has not your wickedness passed continually**?

Look at Iraq today, shootings, bombs going off and homicide bombers. The constant onslaught of suicide bombers, terrorism, shootings and blowing up innocent civilians affected the whole world not just one region of Iraq. This is why the whole world will clap their hands when this Empire goes down to the ground.

The old king of Assyria did not inflict the whole world but this one certainly does as the Islamic Empire and the same Assyrian king are in view who is also mentioned In **Micah 5:5**.

And this **One shall be peace.** [Yahushua the Messiah] When **the Assyrian** [The Anti-Messiah] **comes into our land**, and when he treads in our palaces, then we will raise against him **seven shepherds** and **eight princely men**.

The Assyrian (Anti-Messiah) comes into the land. If the Assyrian was King Sannacherib, then he did not come into the land (house of Judah, or Jerusalem) so the prophecy was not fulfilled in him, because he is only a shadow of the real thing to come. You want proof then the Bible answers that question for us.

Isaiah 37:33-37 "Therefore thus says the Master concerning the **king of Assyria**: `He shall not come into this city**, nor shoot an arrow there, nor come before it with shield, nor build a siege mound against it. (34) By the way that he came, by the same shall he return; and **he shall not come into this city**,' says the Master. (35) `For **I will defend this city**, to save it for My own sake and for My servant David's sake.' " (36) Then the angel of the Master went out, and **killed in the camp of the Assyrians one hundred and eighty-five thousand**; and when people arose early in the morning, there were the corpses all dead. (37) **So Sennacherib king of Assyria departed** and went away, returned home, and remained at Nineveh.

King Sannacherib came with a large army and the Angel of the Master (Yahushua the Messiah) brought a plague into the army killing 185,000 soldiers during the night. The Hebrew word "*nakah*" "smite" implies a pestilence of some sort. So King Sannacherib had to go home with a sad face because he was fighting the Elohim of Israel (Yahweh) and not just flesh and blood.

YHWH will raise against him (The Anti-Messiah) seven shepherds and eight princely men. Who are these seven shepherds and eight princely men? This refers to the Allied Alliance of seven leader nations and seven kings. The eighth princely man is none other than Yahushua the Messiah Himself. Please take note that the prophecy is not just against Nineveh, but the whole Islamic kingdom, as YHWH used interchangeable language. At times this points to only the city and at other times its application is to the whole end time Assyrian Empire.

J.   Will Mecca be destroyed and the other Islamic holy places?

Yes there is ample evidence in the Bible for this event; we shall look at this briefly.

Revelation 17:16 "And the ten horns which you saw on the beast, **these will hate the harlot, make her desolate** and **naked, eat her flesh and burn her with fire.**

231

This event is the actual destruction of Saudi Arabia, more specifically Mecca that sits near seven mountains. The Bible is clear that the destruction will be by the ten horns (The Islamic nations).

> **Revelation 17:17** "For YHWH has put it into their hearts to fulfil His purpose, to be of one mind, and to give their kingdom to the beast, until the words of YHWH are fulfilled.

The Bible makes it clear that it is YHWH who has put it into their hearts that they will destroy the harlot. Most Muslims hate Saudi Arabia and its secular leaders who they think are appeasing the west. Osama bin Laden has attacked Saudi Arabia a few times and it appears that when the ten horns come together they will succeed in burning Saudi Arabia, since this is the method of her destruction. It will burn, since there is ample oil and it has to burn before the oil runs out. That means there has to be enough oil there for this event to occur. The experts predict the oil to run out in about sixty-five years. So the promised destruction one can conclude is less then 65 years away. We have to remember this all happens when there is still plenty of oil around for it to burn, not when the oil fields are empty.

It is rumoured that the House of Saud has booby-trapped all their oil fields with very high-grade explosives and radioactive devices. The king did this so as to prevent terrorists, or western governments from taking over the oil fields. They have decided that when they feel threatened, or are about to be overtaken, then they will hit that switch and all the oil fields will explode in smoke. The fires that will rage will burn for a very long time and with the radioactive material, it will be very difficult to revive the oil fields and extinguish the fires. We do not really know if this information is true regarding to the Semtex explosives being there. Plus Semtex has a shelf life of around twenty years and that means it needs to be replaced at some point. Whether they have the oil fields wired or not, will become apparent in the not too distant future.

The Bible says it like this:

> **Isaiah 21:15** For **they fled from the swords,** from the drawn sword, from the **bent bow, and from the distress of war.** (16) For thus the Master has said to me: "**Within a yea**r, according to the year of a hired man, **all the glory of Kedar will fail**;

Kedar was Ishmael's son. It is likely that there will be war as Isaiah tells us and within one year of that Saudi Arabia will be a ruinous heap with oil burning and smoke ascending up. The "**glory of Kedar**" is not only the oil, but also Mecca the prestigious place of Islamic worship that will also go up in smoke, just as the Bible has foretold long ago.

> **Micah 5:10-11** "And it shall be in that day," says the Master, "That I will cut off your horses from your midst and destroy your chariots. (11) I will **cut off THE CITIES of your LAND and throw down ALL your STRONGHOLDS**'.

The timeline given is when the Anti-Messiah comes into the land (Micah 5:5b) of Israel that will be the time that the Master will go into action and destroy ALL the **STRONGHOLDS** of the Islamic Empire. The Hebrew word "eretz" can apply to a piece of land i.e. a country such as Israel and also to other parts of the world, or the whole world. This means no more Mecca, no more Iraq with its Islamic holy sites. The rest of the Islamic world will suffer the same fate facing extreme wrath from YHWH for how they despised His chosen people Israel. Many did not recognize them as a legitimate country.

The prophecy applies to the Anti-Messiah nations and **THE CITIES** they occupy. YHWH will bring His wrath against them. The Muslims have taken the curse of Genesis 12:3 (*Genesis 12:3a I will bless those who bless you, and I will curse him who curses you*) upon themselves. The reason why the Islamic nations (general populace) can never prosper is because of their denial of Israel and for cursing the Jews.

Remember the Tsunami in December 2004, which was a judgement on Indonesia for their persecution and killing of innocent Christians for the last twenty years. Though the world may remain silent and the church in denial that this was judgement upon the corrupt Islamic nation, YHWH will not remain silent when the enemy is slaughtering His people. The same regarding Pakistan another Muslim nation that has been persecuting Christians since the blasphemy law 295c introduced by General Zia. Well an earthquake just hit home (October 2005) killing hundreds of thousands to wake this nation up from its gross idolatry and false worship to Allah. The times of the birth pains of the Islamic nations have started and Yahweh is now actively involved in mankind's affairs.

Micah 5:11-15 I will **cut off the cities of your land** and throw **down all your strongholds**. (12) I will cut off sorceries from your hand, and you shall have no soothsayers. (13) Your **carved images I will also cut off**, and your **sacred pillars from your midst**; you shall **no more worship the work of your hands**; (14) I will pluck your **wooden images from your midst**; thus I will destroy your cities. (15) And I will execute vengeance in anger and fury on the nations that have not heard."

This is the time YHWH will cut off all their sorceries, their lies i.e. The Imams and firebrand clerics will no longer be selling their religion that espouses suicide bombings, killing for Allah for a reward of virgins that have big curves in heaven with lush wine and beautiful gardens. Their carved images, their holy places like Mecca and Karbala will become mush on the ground.

Qur'an Sura 78:31 As for the righteous, they shall surely triumph. Theirs shall be **gardens and vineyards**, and **high-bosomed virgins for companions**: a truly overflowing cup.

Judgement is long due on the Islamic world and now Yahweh is delivering as He promised. He is flattening their cities and this will continue. Expect some more major earthquakes and a few more Tsunami like events to change the Islamic landscape. The only hope for the Islamic world is to repent and turn to Yahweh and the Master Yahushua the Messiah His Son and give up their false worship.

Chapter 9

Beheading - Is This A New Phenomenon, or A Revival of True Islam?

The culture of beheadings is not something the Islamists have invented in the 21st century, as most people like to believe. The general opinion is that this is something the fringe element in Islam would carry out due to an incorrect extremist outlook (i.e. they are nice people otherwise). Again this is far from the truth as I will show later in this work. The problem is the political correctness that is plaguing the west and stifling free speech to deal with the issue at hand. Unless we are honest we cannot deal with the issue at all. We need to be sensitive and truthful about the issues we are facing. Our aim is not to isolate, or separate Muslims into groups, but to raise awareness of what is happening in our world and how best to deal with it.

If we take a look around ourselves can we honestly name one serious conflict where the Islamists are not involved? Is our war a war on terror, or a war against Islamic terrorists? How many Hindu, Jewish and Buddhist terrorists are we fighting? Lets take a brief snapshot of the world as it stands today:

- Chechnya — Muslims active in that region of Russia.
- Philippines — Muslims active in fighting against the government.
- Iraq — Muslims active in beheading, bombing and killing.
- Saudi Arabia — Muslims active in bombings and terrorist acts.
- Israel — Daily suicide bombings, firing of Qassam rockets into Jewish settlements such as Gush Katif; over 6000 rockets fired so far.
- Afghanistan — Muslims active in bitter conflict with the USA coalition forces.
- Egypt — Muslim uprising against the Coptic Christians.
- Turkey — Muslim suicide bombings on Western and Jewish targets.
- Pakistan — Muslims active in the borders of Pakistan fighting with the government troops.
- Sudan — Muslims active against the Sudanese Christians, forceful conversions and murder of innocent civilians both Christians and non-Christians.
- Indonesia — Muslim insurgents forcing the Christians to convert or face death.
- Algeria — Muslims insurgents fighting the government.
- Nigeria — Muslims fighting the Christians and destroying churches along the north south divide.
- Bosnia — Muslims fighting and killing the Serbian villagers and desecrating churches.
- Eritrea — Muslims waging war against the Christians.
- Lebanon — Muslims active against the Lebanese Christian massacres.
- India — Muslims insurgents fighting in Kashmir breaking out into the street of India.

The list is endless and we can see that everywhere you look the Islamists are active. Do you still want to paint a picture of Islam being peaceful? Or, a "great religion that some have sadly hijacked?" Thing again! If you want to walk in the dark and bury your head in the sand and pretend it is not happening and that Islam is not the enemy that would still not turn Islam into a peaceful faith. It remains a religion of submission and

234

brutal ghastly violence against the most vulnerable peoples in our society, along with their equally vulnerable governments.

First of all Islam as a religion is very much stuck in the past so to say. It just does not move on. The rhetoric of peace will just not work. Sure you can fool the people some of the time, but you cannot fool all peoples all of the time. What does this mean? Islam wants to force people into a 7th century paradigm. This means you cannot re-interpret the Qur'an according to your whims and desires. No matter how peaceful a Muslim wants to become, he has to accept the Qur'an as a de-facto standard in his life. The teachings of the beheadings are taken out of the pages of the Qur'an, also elaborated upon by the Hadiths (sayings and deeds of Muhammad). The Qur'an cannot be interpreted without the Hadiths and you cannot separate one from the other. They are intertwined and used in all aspects of Islamic jurisprudence. The Hadiths are held to an exalted status by the dominant sects of Islam i.e. Sunni and Shiites. The Hadiths are considered part of the faith of Islam. Rejection of the Hadiths is seen as a rejection of Islam. Muslims believe one MUST adhere to them in order to live out a life as a good Muslim.

Anything the Muslims do must be seen through Islamic lenses, which most people rarely do today. Have you ever wondered why Muslims get so incensed when you call them terrorists? This is because they are trying to be good Muslims NOT terrorists, or extremists. What the west defines as terrorism, Islam sees as the legal code for jihad and Muslim conversions for the spread of Islam.

Also many people incorrectly say Wahabbism is a sect of Islam that has extremist views. Again the Muslims see this as a false view. Muhammad Ibn Abd al-Wahab (18th century) simply should be considered a puritan for Islam, who asked people to go back to the truth of Muhammad and his teachings. It is akin to the reformations in Christianity to go back to the truth of the Bible. The truths of the Bible teach peace and harmony and the truths of the Qur'an teach Jihad against the infidels.

Oh, by the way since you are thinking perhaps we can co-exist with Islam and Islam after all does call both houses of Israel the 'people of the book,' keep in mind they also call you pagans and idolaters if you ever call upon Yahushua the Son of YHWH.

Sura 5:17 **Pagans indeed are those** who say that **GOD is the Messiah**, the son of Mary. Say, "who could oppose GOD if He willed to annihilate the Messiah, son of Mary, and his mother, and everyone on earth?" To GOD belongs the sovereignty of the heavens and the earth, and everything between them. He creates whatever He wills. GOD is Omnipotent.

Only one person has a stake in the denial of the deity of Messiah and His Sonship and that person is s.a.tan the one who diverts.

In the Judeo/Christian worldview YHWH is personal who wants to have a relationship with His creation loving all of mankind. He wants all of mankind to turn away from sin and be reconciled through the person of Yahushua the Messiah. Yahushua the Messiah thus elaborated the need for all to repent, and gave us two 'golden rules' of Hebraic conduct.

1. Love the Master YHWH with all your hearts, soul and mind.

2. Love your neighbors as yourself i.e. love all mankind, treating them as we would like to be treated recognizing that we are all created in the image of YHWH.

In the Islamic world we also have two interesting concepts; that Allah (the Islamic deity) is the Supreme Being and Muhammad is his last and final prophet being the supreme authority on earth. Anything that Muhammad says goes and you cannot question that authority. This is why when we read Islamic history we see that no one ever questioned Muhammad's authority and if anyone dared to challenge his authority, then they were swiftly dealt with and permanently ended up six feet under.

A. The Jihad on Infidels

It is a widely held belief that in Islam it is incumbent on all Muslims to go for jihad for Allah and establish the caliphate i.e. the Islamic state. Jihad is the greatest thing a Muslim can do, to outwardly convert others to Islam by preaching first. If they do not listen, then one is to use all means possible e.g. setting up mosques, madrassas (Islamic schools and centres of worship) and lastly force i.e. to convert, or to kill any and all unbelievers. Do you see that Muslims in Europe are already actively setting up mosques, and Islamic centres? Force, the final step in this perverted evangelism, will follow later, given the right circumstances. Just take a look at Egypt, Indonesia, Lebanon, and Nigeria etc? Are we seeing the promised Islamic utopia in these countries? Not likely!

According to Imam Al-Qastalani (Shaafi), Imam Al-Mawardi (Shaafi), Imam Al-Taftazani (Hanafi) and Imam Jirjani (Hanafi) schools of thought, the condition to fight the Infidels is to give victory to Islam. That victory has as its aim and intention to make Allah's (the Islamic god) name the highest. The Muslim aim is to make Allah's faith the highest and the struggle is real. It always ends with fighting and the fighting has to be started by Muslims, after offering someone Islam. Their non-acceptance of Islam can start this violence.

Let us look at the first cases of how Muhammad dealt with people living in Saudi Arabia.

> **Sura 47:4** Therefore, when ye meet the unbelievers (in fight), smite at their necks [i.e. **behead them**]; at length, when ye have thoroughly subdued them [humiliated them], bind a bond firmly (on them): thereafter (is the time for) either generosity or ransom [can be released for a sum of money]: until the war lays down its burdens. Thus (are ye commanded): but if it had been Allah's will, he could certainly have exacted retribution from them (himself); but (he lets you fight) in order to test you, some with others. But those who are slain in the way of Allah, he will never let their deeds be lost.

The Qur'an is clear that this is to instil fear in the people's hearts who are unbelievers [non-Muslims].

> **Sura 8:12-13** Remember thy Master inspired the angels (with the message): "I am with you: give firmness to the Believers [Muslims]: I will instil terror into the hearts of the Unbelievers [all non-Muslims]: **smite ye above their necks [cut off their heads] and smite all their finger tips off them**." This because they contended against Allah and His Messenger [Muhammad]: if any contend against Allah and His Messenger, Allah is strict in punishment. [no mercy]

236

Again the Qur'an makes mention here that this is ordained by Allah himself to cut people's heads and fingers off. This is not allegory, but the real deal of Islam that most people are in denial about. For those who want to deny them, these Suras are in force today and have not been abrogated.

We are told by the ignorant masses not to judge Islam based on the actions of a few Muslims. So then what are we to judge Islam on?

There is only one answer, look at Muhammad and his actions. Would you not judge Christianity and Nazarene Yisraelite faith by the actions of Yahushua of Nazareth? Of course you would! This is the right thing to do, since the followers must never do things not advocated by the founder. Did Yahushua tell the Catholic Church to do the inquisitions against the Jews? Did Yahushua tell the Puritans to do the witch trials? No. Did Muhammad tell his followers to behead people? Yes. Did Muhammad tell his followers to wage a holy jihad against infidels? Yes.

In Islamic history these kinds of things are clearly established. In fact the Pact of Umar is one clear one, where Jews and Christians were treated very badly as 'dhimmis' (under a kind of protection where they had to pay severe taxes to live).

The Umar Pact - Coexistence with the Christians

Let us see what edict Umar Ibn Khattab laid down. He was the second caliph after Muhammad's death. This is known as the Umar Pact for all non-Muslims.

We heard from 'Abd al-Rahman ibn Ghanam (died 7/8/697 AD) as follows: When Umar ibn al-Khattab, may Allah be pleased with him, accorded a peace to the Christians of Syria, we wrote to him as follows:

In the name of god, the Merciful and Compassionate, this is a letter to the servant of god Umar (Ibn al-Khattab), Commander of the Faithful, from the Christians of such-and-such a city. When you came against us, we asked you for safe-conduct (ayman) for ourselves, our descendants, our property, and the people of our community, and we undertook the following obligations toward you:

❖ We shall not build, in our cities or in their neighbourhood, new monasteries, churches, convents, or monks' cells, nor shall we repair, by day or by night, such of them as fall in ruins or are situated in the quarters of the Muslims.

❖ We shall keep our gates wide open for passers by and travellers. We shall give board and lodging to all Muslims who pass our way for three days.

❖ We shall not give shelter in our churches or in our dwellings to any spy, nor hide him from the Muslims.

❖ We shall not teach the Qur'an to our children.

❖ We shall not manifest our religion publicly nor convert anyone to it. We shall not prevent any of our kin from entering Islam if they wish it.

237

❖ We shall show respect toward the Muslims, and we shall rise from our seats when they wish to sit.

❖ We shall not seek to resemble the Muslims by imitating any of their garments, the qalansuwa, the turban, footwear, or the parting of the hair. We shall not speak as they do, nor shall we adopt their kunyas.

❖ We shall not mount on saddles, nor shall we gird swords nor bear any kind of arms nor carry them on our- persons.
❖ We shall not engrave Arabic inscriptions on our seals.

❖ We shall not sell fermented drinks.

❖ We shall clip the fronts of our heads.

❖ We shall always dress in the same way wherever we may be, and we shall bind the zunar round our waists

❖ We shall not display our crosses or our books in the roads or markets of the Muslims.

❖ We shall use only clappers in our churches very softly. We shall not raise our voices when following our dead. We shall not show lights on any of the roads of the Muslims or in their markets. We shall not bury our dead near the Muslims.

❖ We shall not take slaves who have been allotted to Muslims.

❖ We shall not build houses overtopping the houses of the Muslims.
❖ (When I brought the letter to Umar, may Allah be pleased with him, he added, "We shall not strike a Muslim.")

❖ We accept these conditions for ourselves and for the people of our community, and in return we receive safe-conduct.

❖ If we in any way violate these undertakings for which we ourselves stand surety, we forfeit our covenant (dhimma), and we become liable to the penalties for contumacy and sedition.

❖ Umar Ibn al-Khattab replied: Sign what they ask, but add two clauses and impose them in addition to those, which they have undertaken. They are: "They shall not buy anyone made prisoner by the Muslims," and "Whoever strikes a Muslim with deliberate intent shall forfeit the protection of this pact."

From Al-Turtushi, Siraj al-Muluk, pp. 229-230.

As can be seen from this edict it was a very hard life for Christians and Jews in Islamic lands. In fact on his deathbed Muhammad cursed the Jews and told his followers to expel all pagans from Arabia. Based on this Umar cited that no two religions can co-exist in Saudi Arabia.

B. The Slaughtering of the Jews by beheading

Let's see the evidence...

The life of Muhammad by ibn Ishaq Sirat Rasul Allah by A. Guillaume p 464 and 465

Even a Jewish woman was **beheaded** whose only crime was that she was a Jewess.

Aisha said; 'Only one of their woman was killed. She was actually with me and was talking with me and laughing immoderately as the apostle was killing her men in the market when suddenly an unseen voice called her name. 'Good heavens,' I cried, 'what is the matter?' 'I am to be killed,' she replied. 'What for?' I asked. 'Because of something I did,' she answered. She was taken away and **beheaded**. End quote – emphasis mine.

The beheading of Kab bin Ashraf

BUKHARI, VOLUME 5, #369

Narrated Jabir Abdullah:

Allah's messenger said "Who is willing to kill Ka`b bin al-Ashraf who has hurt Allah and His apostle?" Thereupon Maslama got up saying, "O Allah's messenger! Would you like that I kill him?" The prophet said, "Yes." Maslama said, **"Then allow me to say a (false) thing (i.e. to deceive Ka`b). The prophet said, "You may say it."**

Maslama went to Ka`b and said, "That man (i.e. Muhammad) demands Sadaqa (i.e. Zakat) [taxes] from us, and he has troubled us, and I have come to borrow something from you." On that, Ka`b said, "By Allah, you will get tired of him!" Maslama said, "Now as we have followed him, we do not want to leave him unless and until we see how his end is going to be. Now we want you to lend us a camel load or two of food." Ka`b said, "Yes, but you should mortgage something to me." Maslama and his companion said, "What do you want?" Ka`b replied, "Mortgage your women to me." They said, "How can we mortgage our women to you and you are the most handsome of the Arabs?" Ka`b said, "Then mortgage your sons to me." They said, "How can we mortgage our sons to you? Later they would be abused by the people's saying that so and so has been mortgaged for a camel load of food. That would cause us great disgrace, but we will mortgage our arms to you."

Maslama and his companion promised Ka`b that Maslama would return to him. He came to Ka`b at night along with Ka`b's foster brother, Abu Na'ila. Ka`b invited them to come into his fort and then he went down to them. His wife asked him, "Where are you going at this time?" Ka`b replied, none but Maslama and my (foster) brother Abu Na'ila have come." His wife said, "I hear a voice as if blood is dropping from him." Ka`b said, "They are none by my brother Maslama and my foster brother Abu Na'ila. A generous man should respond to a call at night even if invited to be killed."

Maslama went with two men. So Maslama went in together with two men, and said to them, "When Ka`b comes, I will touch his hair and smell it, and when you see that I have got hold of his head, strike him. I will let you smell his head."

Ka`b bin al-Ashraf came down to them wrapped in his clothes, and diffusing perfume. Maslama said, "I have never smelt a better scent than this." Ka`b replied, "I have got the best Arab women who know how to use the high class of perfume." Maslama requested Ka`b "will you allow me to smell your head?" Ka`b said "yes." Maslama smelt it and made his companions smell it as well. Then he requested Ka`b again, "will you let me (smell your head)?" Ka`b said, "Yes." When Maslama got a strong hold of him, he said (to his companions) "get at him!" So they killed him and went to the prophet and informed him."

Ibn Sa'd's Kitab al-Tabaqat al-Kabir adds another interesting feature to this story.

From the Tabaqat, Vol. 2, page 37:

"Then they **cut his head** and took it with them. ..... they cast his head before him [Muhammad]. He (the prophet) praised Allah on his being slain."

The beheading of Kab bin Ashraf took place simply because he wrote some slanderous poems against the Muslim women and exposed Muhammad as a false prophet. Muhammad not able to withstand this criticism took swift action through his followers. That act laid the foundation for today that if anyone criticises Islam, it is not to be tolerated in any way shape, or form and swift action must be taken against such a person. This is why today if you debate with a Muslim they can get so offended at you labelling Muhammad as a false prophet, that they are ready to kill you for it. You will often find Muslims cannot behave well in a discussion about religion and get abusive very quick. In short this spirit of anger is the manifested spirit of s.a.tan, not of the one true YHWH and the Master Yahushua the Messiah. It is s.a.tan who is a liar and was a murderer from the beginning, therefore whoever is under s.a.tan will do likewise. The Spirit of Yahweh on the other hand is love and compassion, understanding and forgiveness. YHWH can defend Himself, so there is no need for any individual to defend YHWH. He is bigger then all of us and vengeance is His.

The second big event that happened was with the tribe of Quraiza. This was a well-known slaughter of many innocent Jews.

Their fate recorded in the Hadiths goes something like this...

Volume 5, Book 59, Number 448:
Narrated 'Aisha:

When the Prophet returned from the (battle) of Al-Khandaq (i.e. Trench) and laid down his arms and took a bath Gabriel came to him while he (i.e. Gabriel) was shaking the dust off his head, and said, "You have laid down the arms?" By Allah, I have not laid them down. Go out to them (to attack them)." The Prophet said, "Where?" Gabriel pointed towards Bani Quraiza. So Allah's Apostle went to them (i.e. Banu Quraiza) (i.e. besieged them). They then surrendered to the Prophet's judgment but he directed them to Sad to give his verdict concerning them. Sad said, "I give my judgment that their warriors should be killed, their women and children should be taken as captives, and their properties distributed."

In this event Muhammad ordered the beheadings of between 400 to 600 men, the women and children were taken as reward for the battle and split between the Muslims involved in the fighting.

Another account in the life of Muhammad book Ibn Ishaq Sirat Rasul Allah by A. Guillaume p 461-464 and 465 states;

Asad said to them; 'O Jews, you can see what has happened to you; I offer you three alternatives. Take which you please. (I) We will follow this man [Muhammad] and accept him as true, for by god it has become plain to you that he is a prophet who has been sent and that it is he that you find mentioned in your Scripture; and then your lives, your property, your women and children will be saved. They [the Jews] said, 'We will never abandon the laws of the Torah and never change it for another.' [p. 463] Al-Aus leapt up and said O' Apostle they [Jews] are our allies not allies of Khazraj, and you know how you recently treated the allies of our brethren.' Now the apostle had besieged B. Qanuqa who were allies of Al Khazrah. [p.464] Then the apostle went out to the market in Medina (which is still its market today) and dug trenches in it. Then he sent for them and struck off their heads in those trenches as they were brought out to him in batches. Among them was the enemy of Allah Huyayy b. Akhtab and Ka'b b. Asad their chief. There were 600 or 700 in all, though some put the figure as high as 800 or 900. End quote. Emphasis mine [my comments in square brackets]

The men were lined up against huge dug up trenches and were brought out five or six at a time and **beheaded**. These are not the only cases of beheadings, but they do tell us some of the things that Muhammad was personally involved in. It begins to paint a picture of why Muslims today who follow Islam strictly want to carry out the **same things** of their Islamic past. It leaves us in no doubt that the events on our screens today of the beheadings, the barbarism, the bombs are a by-product of an Islamic era that is being revived by Muslims all over the world. I predict things will get worse and suicide bombings, though common in Israel, are now happening in Iraq, Russia the USA and Europe, as I predicated in my first edition of the book Islam, Peace or Beast. These things will increase and government measures need to be taken to put these insidious crimes to a halt.

The Bible talks about these things happening in end of days.

Revelation 13:2 And **the beast** which I saw was like unto a **leopard**, and his **feet were as the feet of a bear**, and **his mouth as the mouth of a lion** and the **dragon gave him his power**, and his seat, and great authority.

Points to note:

❖ Beast = Empire/kingdom/nations.
❖ Leopard = Grecian Empire (ruled throughout the Middle East, today all Islamic).
❖ Feet of a Bear = Medo/Persian Empire, today all Islamic.
❖ Mouth of a Lion = Babylon (Iraq), today all Islamic.
❖ The Dragon = s.a.tan the one who diverts and opposes, this is the meaning of ha s.a.tan.

It goes on to tell us that there is a huge revival of Islam, the empire that everyone thought had died. Yet is actually going to come back and is even now being brought back. The larger part of this growth is organic, because Muslim households do have many children, at least six to eight children per family. And the smaller part of this growth is through proselytizing. Many Muslims feel that they have come to the west to get back at the west for ruling their lands. A case in point is the raj in India by the British. Some Muslims often say in private quite honestly that they (the west) plundered our lands. Now we have come to plunder them by making false claims. This often occurs with false social security claims and false immigration claims, such as a brother and sister claiming to be husband and wife, in order to obtain entry into the west.

At this point their religion plays no part in their thinking and their morality goes out of the window. So much for those five prayers and false outward righteousness. However having said that, I can vouch for some Muslims, who are very honest and upright in their morality. They will often put many Christians to shame. Muslims stick to the doctrines taught to them and do not argue over certain principles such as homosexuality, abortion, and food laws. Yet most of these things are taken from the Bible. Nazarene Yisraelites and Christians should agree upon the Bible, especially the clear directives. But sadly amongst Christians the arguments are never ending. The Bible stands proof against all those who want to deny His holy laws/Torah. Here I must say I have respect for the Jews, because they do not argue over the basic Torah principles of daily living. This is where Islam gets morality from, as it was the Jews who Muhammad saw practicing these things and it drew him close to monotheism. I myself firmly agree with all the Torah principles being eternal and unchanging and you will find this to be the case amongst many Muslim converts.

Revelation 13:3 - And I saw one of his heads as it were **wounded** to death; and his **deadly wound** was **healed**: and all the world wondered after the beast. **Points:**

❖ Wounded head = Islam wounded; Islamic Empire brought to a close in 1924 when the Islamic Ottoman Empire ceased.
❖ Wound healed = Current day - People proclaiming Islam's resurrection that allows it to wage war against the powerful west. It is growing in influence and in winning converts.

The Bible also warns us that Christians would be beheaded for the witness of Yahushua the Messiah in the last days by this empire and the followers of Islam [see the classic case of Kim Sun Il who was an evangelical Christian in Iraq brutally beheaded]. Nick Berg had the same fate in Iraq, as the Muslims also beheaded him.

Is this a new tactic? Not so. Are more people going to be beheaded this way? Unfortunately yes. The Bible has proved to be true in the past, so this is the likely scenario to be followed as described in Revelation 20:4 as we enter Jacob's Trouble. In Bosnia the Serbs suffered the same fate. Why should it be different for other people? Islamists do not care about boundaries, or different views in acting out their violence on the non-Muslims, or against what it terms the Islamic push against the infidels.

Below- A joyful Muslim fighter in Bosnia, holding the head of a Serbian Boogie Blogojevic as his trophy of victory. [37]

Above-Slaughtered by Islamic Mujahideens – Blagoje Blagojevic, Nenad Petkovic and Brano Duric, beheaded and shown as trophies rolled on the ground with contempt.

---

[37] Chronicles of an announced death page 55.
[38] http://www.slobodnasrpska.org/en/mudzahedini/7muslimanaska.html

What was the fault of these Serbs seen above? They were Christians and were in the wrong place and at the wrong time. They were beheaded because they tried to stop the Islamists from pillaging and looting their villages and desecrating their churches. Most in the west sit idly and do nothing, thus many more similar people will yet come to the same fate. Recently in Indonesia-Poso three young girls were beheaded. Their fault was that they were Christians. They were asked to deny Yahushua the Messiah, but they refused and paid with their lives. In YHWH's eyes these are His people who He will avenge very soon. The western response remains lacklustre and we continue to do business with murderers; for such reasons YHWH's judgement is also upon us and His baton is swinging and hitting us as well. Too many of us are too ignorant to realize this because we do not want to hear about impending judgement, but only about the love of YHWH. Yet we forget the justice of the Holy One.

> **Revelation 20:4** And I saw thrones, and they sat upon them, and judgment was given unto them: and I <u>saw the souls of them</u> that were **beheaded** for the **witness of Yahushua**, [believers] and for the <u>word of YHWH [either believers, or Torah keeping Jews]</u>. Both houses of Israel are the beats main targets.

This is not new and has been happening for a while now, however we were just not told by the mainstream media machine. A good case in point happened in 1996 when Chechen Muslim fanatics murdered Evgeny Rodionov on the 23rd of May 1996 in the Chechen settlement of Bamut. The Muslims asked him to convert to Islam, join them and take his cross from off his neck. He refused, upon which they beheaded him, as he stood firm. This was his witness for Messiah. He refused to give up his faith, even to the point of death by decapitation, a most brutal way to die. He will stand amongst the righteous and inherit a heavenly throne as promised. The young lad was only 19 years old. He certainly showed bravery and refused to take the mark of the beast. His mother had to re-mortgage her house to find his body. His father died five days after his funeral because he was devastated by his loss. This young lad's sacrifice will not be forgotten by Yahweh to stand firm for His name.

Today, the Muslims actively wage war everywhere against Christians and Jews and say proudly and loudly that they are fighting the Crusaders and the Jews. It is not a big secret, yet our governments are bent on keeping this secret.

Yahushua gave us a very clear warning of the future of a people who would do these atrocities and they are the Islamists. The words of Yahushua should come home to those who have not recognized the end-time beast. Many believers are still stuck with Rome, the Vatican, or various USA end time theories.

> **John 16:2-3** They shall put you out of the synagogues [congregations] yea, the time cometh [a time will come which is here now], that whosoever killeth you will think **that he doeth elohim service**. And these things will they do unto you, because they have **not known the Father, nor Me**.

Why did Yahushua mention those words "**not known by the Father nor Me?**" This is where the clue lies; He was not talking about the Roman Armies because they never professed the Master Yahushua, nor was He speaking about the Greeks. He was actually talking about Muslims who claim to worship YHWH as Allah, but reject the fact that Allah is the Father of anyone. Muslims claim to know Isa as a prophet only, yet deny the deity of Yahushua, because they replace Yahushua the true Master YHWH, with Isa who is a <u>false mere human</u> Messiah. Essentially they know <u>neither the Father nor the Son denying both</u>. Yet we still have many Christians who are falling heads over heals, still trying to prove that Isa is the same person as Yahushua. This in itself is a lie, because Isa is not the Son of Yahweh according to the Qur'an. This is why Yahushua is particular about His last proclamation in verses 2 and 3. **These are the only people who think they do YHWH a service.**

Muslims would kill both Christians and Jews and think they are doing YHWH a service. Actually it is Allah that they serve. And they do not discriminate whether you are a Catholic, Presbyterian, Pentecostal, Baptist, or whatever. The time has come to deal with Islam decisively. Either the Muslims governments need to deal with their errant peoples, or the west will have to take punitive action to deal a deathblow to fanatical Islam. Until this happens it will not only increase, but will thrive in the current environment helped by pro Arab politicians and the liberals in the west.

Photo Above-Sadik Cufjala and his son (on the right of the first picture), today a colonel in the Protection Corps of Kosovo, which is the only UCK terrorists converted by the United Nations into a civilian corps.[39]

---

[39] http://www.pogledi.co.yu/english/index.php

Chapter 10

Why Should the Western World Support Israel?

There are many reasons why the western world should support Israel, a tiny nation, and the only democracy in the Middle East.

When Yahushua comes back He does an interesting thing which we see in **Matthew Chapter 25:46:**

> When the **Son of Man comes in His glory**, and **all the holy angels with Him**, then **He will sit on the throne of His glory**. **All the nations will be gathered before Him**, and **He will separate them one from another**, as a shepherd divides his sheep from the goats. And **He will set the sheep on His right hand, but the goats on the left**. Then the King will say to those **on His right hand**, come, **you blessed of My Father, inherit the kingdom prepared for you** from the foundation of the world: for I was hungry and **you gave Me food**; I was thirsty and **you gave Me drink**; I was a stranger and you took Me in; **I was naked and you clothed Me**; I was sick and you visited Me; I was in prison and **you came to Me.**' "Then the righteous will answer Him, saying, **Master, when did we see You hungry and feed You**, or **thirsty and give You drink**? When did we **see You a stranger** and **take You in, or naked and clothe You**? Or when **did we see You sick**, or in **prison**, and come to You?
>
> And **the King** will answer and say to them, Assuredly, I say to you, **inasmuch as you did it to one of the least of these My brethren, you did it to Me**. Then He will also say to those on the left hand, `Depart from Me, **you cursed**, into the **everlasting fire prepared for the devil and his angels**: for **I was hungry** and **you gave Me no food**; **I was thirsty** and **you gave Me no drink**; **I was a stranger** and **you did not take Me in**, naked and you **did not clothe Me**, sick and in prison and **you did not visit Me**. Then they also will answer Him, saying, `Master, when did we see You hungry or thirsty or a stranger or naked or sick or in prison, and did not minister to You? Then He will answer them, saying, **Assuredly, I say to you, inasmuch as you did not do it to one of the least of these, you did not do it to Me**. And these will go away into **everlasting punishment**, but the **righteous into eternal life.**

Points to note:

* The Master Yahushua is back sitting on His throne as the King in Jerusalem on the Temple Mount.
* All the nations are gathered by the angels before Him to be judged.
* He separates them, goats on the left, sheep on the right.
* There is a **third** group of people he calls "**My brethren**," how interesting.
* He judges all nations on account of the third group of people He calls "**My brethren.**"
* Who are the "**My brethren?** These are the Jews who were hungry, thirsty, in prisons, deprived, and cursed by the world, those to whom many turned a blind eye. But there were some good Christians who did help them.
* He sends the believers (sheep nations) into heaven the kingdom of YHWH.

❖ He casts the unbelievers (goat nations) into hell because of their mishandling of the Jews.
❖ The reason is they did not **clothe Him, feed Him, visit Him** and **help Him** in sickness, figurative for the Jews.

A lot of people in the Christian world have wrongly interpreted the phrase "**My brethren**" in this passage as speaking of Christians and not Jews. But Yahushua calls them "My brethren," and this third group of people are none other but the Jews. The manner in which we treat the Jews and the State of Israel is linked to our judgement also. Many people will stand condemned because of their ill treatment of the Jews. Some are confused as to why the term "all nations" does not incorporate Israel? These nations are in the Hebrew language called "goyim" i.e. gentile nations and Israel is not a latter day "goy," or a latter day gentile nation, so it is excluded.

We are told in **Genesis 12:3** that YHWH will bless those who bless the Hebrew nation and curse those who curse the Hebrews. When the King Messiah casts the goat nations into hell, look at the word he uses for them. "Depart from me you cursed," i.e. they are cursed because they cursed Israel and this is the primary reason given here for their judgement. Yahushua describes the fact that in their time of trouble, if you help the Jews, whom He calls "My brethren," then that is like helping Yahushua. And if you hated them and cursed them, then that is taken against you on judgement day. So be warned because even though the Jews are in unbelief they are still loved by the Father.

Romans 11:28 Concerning the gospel they are enemies for your sake, but **concerning the election they are beloved** for the sake of the fathers.

Yahushua would not put the sheep on His right and then say to the goats I am judging you on account of these sheep/gentile Christians, because clearly He is referring to a third group of people. The bottom line is if you are a believer you cannot hate the Jews. If those Christians who want to take the passages for "my brethren" to be Christians, then you better be very careful because you fall right into the argument of the Muslims. If you believe that "my brethren" are Christians, then you would also have to say the same for Moses. He wrote under the inspiration of YHWH in **Deuteronomy 18:18**: "I will raise up for them a Prophet like you from among **their brethren**," in order to be consistent we'd have to say that 'their brethren' in the Torah are also gentile Christians. Do you see how that argument is fallacious?

That misinterpretation creates another problem. This then can be easily misapplied to Muhammad, because Muslims believe this passage applies to their prophet Muhammad, as he is a cousin of the Jews. According to this warped logic, Muhammad has more right to be 'a brethren' then do gentile Christians! This is how absurd the argument can get. We cannot be inconsistent in our approach. The problem with some Christians is that they are not consistent. Take the Passion of The Christ film made by a Roman Catholic with Roman Catholic dogma.

On the one hand they tell you Catholics are not Christians and yet on the other hand they encourage you to watch this movie made by a Catholic. So which one is it?

We cannot say that the **Deuteronomy 18:18** passage applies to the Jews in that particular verse and then turn around and say that in **Matthew 25:40** the "**My brethren**" applies to Gentile Christians in order to fit our narrow worldview. Clearly in Matthew 25 there are three groups of people, "the sheep," "the goats," and "my brethren." Both "My brethren" and the sheep grouping cannot both be Christians. The reality is that in both passages the "brethren" only applies to Jewish Israel. With this understanding we should be warned of any inappropriate behavior towards the Jews. Jewish Israel is not perfect, but we are not called to hate them either, but to pray for their salvation, as they are YHWH's covenant nation living in error by the rejection of their Messiah. This is why I am warning you not to deny this truth, or else you could put your very salvation in jeopardy. To hate the Jews is akin to hating Yahweh and if you hate Yahweh then you can forget about salvation! Have you ever wondered why Yahushua in the Book of Matthew chapter 7:21 says this;

> **Matthew 7:22-23** "Many will say to Me in that day, Master, Master, have we not prophesied in Your name, cast out demons in Your name, and done many wonders in Your name? (23) And then I will declare to them, I never knew you; depart from Me, you who practice lawlessness!"

Are these Muslims? Of course not then are they Hindus? No way my friend. When did we see Hindus casting out demons in Yahushua's Name and prophesying in His name since they have millions of idols to worship; then who are they? These are people casting out demons and prophesying in His name. Contrary to popular error that these people are not Christians in fact these are. These are lawless ones, or Christians who do not practice true Torah and thus are open to be deceived regarding their obligation to stand with and support Jewish Israel, along with the Jewish State of Israel! Also they either do not know or use YHWH's true Name!

Here are some other compelling reasons to support Israel:

❖ It is the "only" democratic state in the Middle East and our only true friend.

❖ It is Yahweh's chosen miracle nation who gave us our Bible and our Messiah Yahushua of Nazareth.

❖ The Messiah Yahushua is Jewish, and we owe that to the Jews. If there was no Israel, then there would not be a Messiah either. YHWH used the Jews to save the world from sin and death.

❖ The Messiah is coming back to Israel and will come back to help Israel in the end-time as this book will illustrate. All glory is to the Messiah of Israel who is our Master and Savior. He is the living Word, revealed out of the bosom of the Father (John 1:18).

❖ The third Temple will be rebuilt in Jerusalem; for out of Zion shall go forth the Law/Torah, and the word of the Master [Yahweh] from Jerusalem (Isaiah 2:3b).

❖ YHWH loves Israel, so should we not if we claim to follow a Jewish Messiah?
❖ The true church/kehilla are both saved Jews and the Gentiles. The end-time, 144,000 Israelites are sealed for salvation from the 12 tribes of Israel.
❖ The olive tree is Israel and gentiles are the wild branches grafted in.

❖ All nations will offer sacrifices in the third Temple in Jerusalem during the millennial reign at the Feast of Tabernacles (Zechariah 14:16).

❖ Glorious is the nation whose YHWH is the Elohim of Israel-Yahushua the King Messiah. When we obey and walk with Him, He blesses us, whether we are individuals, or nations, such as the USA and the UK. But when we offend our holy YHWH by doing harm to His covenant people, He chastises us. Remember hurricanes Charley, Frances, Ivan, Jeanne, Katrina and Wilma? These are not freaks of nature, but the very hand of YHWH.

Chapter 11

A Revelation

Now that I have described some of the attributes of the beast/Empire/Kingdom in this book, I would like to touch on a few other things. Let us talk about 666 so called code in the Bible, which is referred to as the "mark of the beast." Most people believe this to be some kind of chip implant in the skin that would allow the Anti-Messiah to impose some kind of monetary control on us.

Many books are written on this one verse of the Bible without any due thought, or process by ignoring the hundreds of other prophecies that contradict the theory of most proponents.

Many people ask me what is the mark and what is meant by "allegiance to the beast?" Let us first recognize that the beast is both one man and a group of nations, not just one man alone. The end time beast is a **confederacy of nations** all under the same banner of Islam. It will however be controlled by this one individual who will be revealed in latter times, who we recognize as the Anti-Messiah. Muslims will declare him as the supreme Caliph. He is against all those things that the Messiah Yahushua is for i.e. salvation, peace, the well being of individuals etc.

The Bible itself indicates three elements to what we can call allegiance to this confederacy or beast system.

> <u>Revelation 13:16-18</u> "And he causeth <u>all</u>, both small and great, rich and poor, free and bond, to receive <u>a mark in their right hand</u>, or <u>on their foreheads</u>: And that no man might buy or sell, **save he that had the mark**, or the **name of the beast,** or **the number of his name**. <u>Here is wisdom</u>. Let <u>him that hath understanding</u> **count the number of the beast**: for it is the number of a man; and his number is <u>Six hundred threescore and six</u>."

On casual reading we notice three elements:

❖ The beast has a Mark.
❖ The beast has a Name.
❖ Number or better translated the beast has a "multitude."
❖ Also a challenge is made that "here is wisdom," let him that has understanding recognize this.

Men do not have a "number," but they have a "**name.**" If you notice it also says "**name of the beast,**" so one must ask why is it written the "number of his name." Because the context is not a "number" at all, but a "**multitude.**" My name is Simon not number 7467 if you understand what I mean.

Perhaps the best explanation of the mark of the beast with a literal and correct understanding is found in the Restoration Scriptures True Name Edition (3rd edition)-www.restorationscriptures.org, which reads as follows:

Revelation 13:
16 And he causes all, both small and great, rich and poor, free and bond, to receive a mark in their right hand, or in their foreheads:

Mohammed's religion brings people to his god Allah.

17 And that no man might buy, or sell, except he that had the mark, or the name of the beast, even the multitudes who have his name.

The mark of the beast, or the name of Allah is for those who conform to the one-world political and religious order of Islam, both emanating from Mecca in the last generation. That beast system has as its mark the rejection of Yahushua as YHWH's Savior/Son, the changing of the everlasting covenant from Shabbat to Friday, YHWH's Name to Allah, and YHWH's Torah to Qur'an superceding and changing the laws. The name and destruction in the name of Allah is the single most overriding and defining mark of the beast, in addition to its Torah-less-ness. Anyone who has not sold out to their intoxicating "wine of oil" (ideology) and thus not given allegiance to the revived end time beast cannot buy or sell energy elsewhere, as all the earth's economies are fully dependant upon black gold, or oil. Think of this, if Rome, or the USA were the end time beast, what commodity do they sell that would destroy the global economy were it to be withheld? Rome has nothing that any business man would want to buy and as for the US well unless you want to buy sophisticated missiles and bombs they don't exactly fit everyone's need and staple diet.

18 Here is chochmah [wisdom]. Let him that has binah [understanding] consider the multitude of the beast: for it is the multitude of a man;

The multitudes, or number of Mohammed's followers. Not a literal number but the marker or identification.

and his multitude is encoded in 'chi, xi, sigma.'

The three Greek letters are a code, which portrays a message to John and through John to us, in order to identify the end time beast. This is not a literal number, as no man has a number in place of a name. All men have real names, as does the end time beast.

Some manuscripts say 614, some 646, some 665, so lets understand 666 is just one reading of a variant of readings. Moreover, one cannot use Greek words, or letters to figure Gematria, or the numerical value of letters, since that only applies to the Hebrew language. Additionally, the last Greek letter is an accent not a letter. The first Greek letter 'chi' looks like two crossed swords, the very symbol of Islam seen by John before Islam was even invented by Mohammed. The next letter in Greek, 'xi' is written vertically and is the exact name of Allah when written horizontally in Arabic. Thus the symbol of the crossed swords, along with the name of Allah is the mark with the final letter more of an accent mark, known as a 'sigma

250

score' and not a 'sigma' itself. The letter sigma does not even exist in Modern Greek. The verse when translated in its correct reading would look like this.

"Here is wisdom. Let him that has understanding decide who the multitude of the beast is, for it is the multitudes of a man (Mohammed) and (the same multitudes) are all involved with the mark, the name of Allah. The Greek word number is more accurately translated as multitudes, or the great number/multitude of those who worship the end time beast day and night.

The identity of Anti-Messiah will be hidden and kept secret until the last of the last days when a previous empire is revived. But it will not be the Roman Empire that's revived, but the world's last and only Islamic empire the Ottoman Empire that declined in 1920. According to many hundreds of Scriptures such as First John 2:22, those who deny the Father and, or the Son (as does Islam) are types of the Anti-Messiah, but The Anti-Messiah Beast System is clearly dictated as the Assyrian in Micah 5:6 and many other verses. All Christians and even Catholics believe in the Father and Son, another indicator that this system is based in Mecca not Rome.

> **Revelation 14:11** "And the smoke of their torment ascendeth up for ever and ever: and they have no rest day nor night, who worship the beast and his image, and whosoever receiveth the **mark of his name.**"

Did you know that this is literally true in a Muslims life? He/she has no real rest; he must pray 5 times a day and pray after midnight at about 1 AM and then again starting at 5 AM in the morning. This is apart from the other prayers needed as an around the clock tribute to Allah to save them from hell-fire and please Allah. Could one argue if prayer was enough to atone for sin then many Sadus or Gurus would be more forgiven who spend their entire life in trances of one type or another but **all these false systems forget that without the shedding of blood there is no atonement of sin!**

Thus without a sacrifice one could never be saved no matter how much he prayed unless it was done in the prescribed way as dictated by Yahweh in the Bible. The only one who fulfilled that criterion fully for substitutionary atonement was Yahushua of Nazareth and without Him we can forget about any possibility of salvation. Sin must be punished by a just Elohim but at the same time He is merciful to forgive but He cannot forgive in isolation of His holy requirements that a sinner will die thus mercy and justice met at the cross. While for Islam mercy never met anywhere and as for justice I am still searching if I can find true justice in Islam so far I have been unsuccessful to locate any cases of true justice in the Islamic theology. I was speaking to my Arab friend from Saudi Arabia and he told me forget about mercy and justice in Islam even in Saudi Arabia the so called bastion of Sha'ria law there is no form of mercy or justice but only oppression. I was shocked to learn that there are poor people in Saudi the oil rich country of the world.

Swiftly moving on let us try and understand the meaning of the "mark of his name" and here is another clue.

> **Revelation 17:5** And upon her forehead [was] a name written, **MYSTERY, BABYLON THE GREAT, THE MOTHER OF HARLOTS** and **ABOMINATIONS OF THE EARTH**.

The above text indicates that this system of worship has the following Titles-Attributes:

251

❖ Mystery Babylon the Great.
❖ Mother of Harlots.
❖ Abominations of the Earth.

One thing is obvious. The Master is trying to show us something significant. That this is the same thing described by these three different titles and interestingly it is also called the "**abominations of the earth**." The same way the true Messiah has titles such as Immanuel "YHWH with us," the "Word of YHWH," "The Branch," and others, they are all titles of the true Elohim.

For YHWH to call this "the abominations of the earth" is highly significant, as this is not just some system of worship where followers are minding their own business. Rather it is a type of active worship being an ongoing abomination before the Master i.e. they are blaspheming His Name day and night. Look at the Muslims; they pray 5 times a day; some even do six prayers, even one after midnight called the 'tayyad salat' (prayer). In each prayer they say the following:

Allah hu Akbar at least 6 times, which means Allah, is greater. They recite other formulas as well. There is no mention of Yahweh the true Elohim at all and then they replace the true Messiah Savoir with a mere man, an alleged prophet of Allah. Don't you think this causes great sadness to Yahweh, who created these people in His love, and yet they have been led astray like this? Today they do not even recognize the one true YHWH, since they have taken the ultimate lie and accepted it as truth. **The ultimate lie is that Allah is just another name for YHWH, or merely the Arabic name for Yahweh! Look at this:**

2 Thessalonians 2:11 And for this cause YHWH shall send them strong delusion, that they should believe THE LIE [not a lie, but THE lie]:

One of my cousins said to me that he almost had an accident once driving his car because he fell asleep, but Allah made him aware so that his eyes opened and he was saved. This demonstrates he has believed the lie and anything else you say to him, or any other Muslim does not matter, because he/she will always tell you that whatever alleged miracle happened it was due to Allah.

This is blasphemy to say that "Allah is greater," when we know Allah is not Yahweh, but in reality only Yahweh is great and the greatest. So should it not be 'Yahweh Akbar?' Who is Allah then? s.a.tan disguised as Allah deceiving the Muslim people.

A. Why the abomination?

In the Bible Baal is also called Beelzebub, or Baalzebub, ONE OF THE FALLEN ANGELS OF SATAN. Beelzebub is the patron god of the Philistines in ancient Israel. He is also identified with the god of Ekron, Baal-Zebub. The term is a deliberate mocking perversion of the Canaanite deity Baal-Zebul ("Prince Baal"), one of the standard titles of the god Baal. In the Bible, Beelzebub is the prince of evil spirits and in Milton's 'Paradise Lost' he is s.a.tan's chief lieutenant. He is also called 'Master of the Flies', derived from the Hebrew "Baal-Zevuv." (Hefner, Alan G., Encyclopaedia Mystica – Baal Article)

This shows us again that Baal, with its IL or AN root did not come from Arabia but from earlier cultures.

Interesting is the name **HU-BAL** (in Arabic and Hebrew script the vowels were not noted). This shows a very suspicious connection to the Hebrew **HA-BAAL** (The Baal). As we all know this was an idol mentioned in the Bible (Numbers. 25:3, Hosea 9:10, Deut. 4:3, Josh. 22:17 and Ps. 106:28-29). Where was Baal worshipped? In Moab, It was the "god of fertility." **Amr ibn Luhaiy brought Hubal from Moab to Arabia.**

Let us identify Baal. First we remove the definite article from BA'IL and AL-Ilah, remove the suffix from Al-ILAH which has been added for gender and then we are left with "IL" found in Babylon. Now we know what this deity is stripped to its core. The only culture to use **IL** was Babylon since this is where this was deity exported from to Saudi Arabia. Hubal or Ha-bal was Master of the Ka'ba in Arabia in Mecca. Remember the god of the Sumerians was Lil and from there in its short form it became known as IL, add the suffix and prefix and you get Ba'il, or Baal. In Arabic the suffix was added and it became Hallah, these inscriptions were found in Arabia.

Hitti wrote about this. He shows that the Arabs of Saba in South Arabia inscribed **HLH** in some of their inscriptions for the high god. With the vowels supplied this becomes Hallah, and later, Allah. Hitti reports that this inscription was also found in the Lihyan inscriptions in North Arabia, and he says that its origin were from Assyria (Hitti Philip, History of The Arabs, London, 1950 pg.100-101).

Allah's root is LIL, shortened to IL from Enlil. So Allah really evolved from Enlil to Lil and then IL. Remember the name used in the Bible Baal, is the Hebrew Ba'il meaning "the god," in Arabic. It would be Al-Ilah and in Aramaic Alaha.

There are inscriptions that were found in stone from Al-Ula in Northern Arabia, circa 500 BC, at least one 1,000 years before Muhammad was born. In the same Semitic language dialect, and in the same time frame, are two other names of the gods- Mar-Allah, meaning Master-god, and Adar'IL. This is a Sardonic contraction using the root form of the name for god from Sumer LIL. This once again shows us the sinister connections back to the god of the Sumerians.

We also noted that:

The Quraish ADOPTED Baal as Allah, and added the goddesses to his cult the same way as Baal had **three daughters in the Fertile Crescent**. They venerated him and his three female companions in his new house, the Kaaba at Mecca. (Bergsson, Snorri G., Goddesses and Wica Worship, 'Neo-paganism at its most deceptive form, Islam and Goddess Worship Chpt. IV, pg. 15, 1998-2000).

What does this mean? It means that Baal was worshipped as Allah by the Quraish tribal clans and by Muhammad later and that the Muslim prophet Muhammad used his monotheism to subjugate the people roundabout.

Now let us see if Scripture indicates titles.

253

Revelation 19:13 "And He [was] clothed with a vesture dipped in blood: and His Name is called **The Word of YHWH**."

Yahushua is the true Name of the western European Jesus Christ, but He has the title; "The Word of YHWH."

Revelation 19:16 "And He hath on [His] vesture and on His thigh a name written, KING OF KINGS, AND LORD OF LORDS."

Yahushua (Yahushua) also has titles of "King of Kings" and "Master of Masters."

Clearly we can see that the "names of blasphemy" are not only titles, but may be **attributes** also of the Anti-Messiah system. The Islamic creed of the Shahadah (the profession of faith) "La Ilah ha il Allah Muhammad rasul Allah," means there is no elohim but Allah and Muhammad is his prophet." That would correspond to a "**name of blasphemy**," or a title of blasphemy as explained above. The one true YHWH never ordained Muhammad as a prophet, as there was no need for further revelation. Yahushua finished the work on the cross and said "**it is finished**" (**John 19:30**) meaning the end of the sacrificial system to atone for the sins of all those that come to Yahushua the Messiah. There was no need for any more prophets or seers after this.

This beast empire literally rises out of the desert "sand of the sea" and the sea. This again is the very area of the Middle East where Muhammad proclaimed his prophethood. Just take a look at the map of Saudi Arabia as it is literally surrounded by seas.

This shows us that the above are titles and personal attributes of the Anti-Messiah system and not actual names.

1 John 2:22 "Who is a liar but he that denieth that Yahushua is the Messiah? He is Anti-Messiah, that denieth **the Father and the Son**"

We can also see from the above verse that these people deny the Father and His Son. The Muslims categorically deny the Father and His Son Yahushua the Messiah. In the Qur'an, their religious texts show that Yahushua is not even the same Yahushua as seen in the gospels and they make it a point to teach this to their followers. In fact the Yahushua of the Qur'an is a Yahushua far removed from Israel and was some person who has been created by Allah the same way as Adam was.

Sura 4:171 "The **Messiah, Isa [Yahushua] the son of Mary, was no more than god's apostle** . . . god is but one god. Allah FORBID **that he should have a son!**"

Of course the statement is quite true, Allah is not god and he does not have any Son.

Sura 9:88-93 "And they say, The All-merciful has taken unto Himself a son. **You have indeed advanced something hideous**. As if the skies are about to burst, the earth to split asunder and its mountain to fall down in the utter ruin **for that they have attributed to the All-merciful a son**; and it **behaves [behooves] not the All-merciful to take a son.** None are there in the heavens and earth but comes to the All-merciful, as a servant"

Who do you think would have a stake in denying the truth of the cross? s.a.tan? s.a.tan has to pervert the truth and he has to deceive the people to prevent them from knowing the truth! That is why he is behind this whole charade.

The verse in **1 John 2:22** is not a "type" that can be applied to any group, as it only matches one group of people and these are the Muslims who religiously deny that Yahushua is YHWH, or that YHWH came in the flesh. All other groups of people could not care less about Yahushua and do not include active denial of both the Father and the Son as part of their mantra. Have you seen how even some Hindus accept Yahushua as a deity in their pantheon and worship Him! The Muslims are the only group of people obsessed with denying the deity of Yahushua and obsessed with the Bible allegedly being corrupt. You can go and debate with the Muslims anytime and they are quite happy to take up the challenge to disprove the Bible, but without success of course.

In addition, many people believe it is the Roman Catholic Church, or perhaps one of the Popes that will be the Anti-Messiah. Unfortunately, far too many try to fit certain readings of Scripture to fit their preconceived notions and come to the wrong conclusion. The Bible says the ones who profess the Father and Son are not the Anti-Messiah! Yet these writers would have you believe that the Roman Catholic Church somehow does not believe in the same YHWH, which is a plain lie. In fact to be fair to Roman Catholics if it came to devotion many are more devout than evangelicals. There are at least 10% among Catholics who can be fully called born again believers and those are 100% saved in my opinion. Do you think the Master Yahushua would throw Catholics into hell who have stood firm for His Name, or those lukewarm bible believing Christians who denied His Name to save themselves? The Roman Catholics do profess both the Father and the Son so it rules them out. The Catholics have at times stood up for many biblical principles, often more so than mainstream Christians, on such key moral issues as divorce, abortion and homosexuality. Those people who say that works have nothing to do with our faith well you are wrong. YHWH states CLEARLY in His word that He will judge every work we did for Him. Works are manifestations of a willingness to give our obedience to His written words. If we are not obedient to His commandments then being born again is a meaningless term. We are born again in order to have a heart to follow Him and His Torah fully.

The very term so misunderstood in Christendom is not just that you are born of the Holy Spirit, but that you are born from above by YHWH's Word/Yahushua. So then, how can one turn around and disobey portions of that same word. If you are truly born from above, failing to obey His commandments is tantamount to denying your spiritual conception.

The proof of the pudding lies in the fact that if you are born of above then it means you will obey the words of Him who came from above, now start looking around you and tell me how many Christians today obey His words? Salvation is made in to cheap grace without any understanding of obeying YHWH's eternal words.

Ecclesiastes 12:13-14 Let us hear the conclusion of the whole matter: **Fear YHWH and keep His commandments**, for this is **the whole duty of man**. (14) For YHWH will bring every work into judgment, including every secret thing, whether it is good or whether it is evil.

If you do not understand this then take a look at the Jewish people who do understand what obeying YHWH means. The Rabbis have built fences around the commandments in order to protect people from breaking them. Yet they ended up going too far, so that they

255

couldn't recognize their Messiah, as he did not resemble the fences obscuring the Torah. The second group to look at are the Muslims, who also built religious fences such as the Hadith and ended up going too far entirely missing YHWH and even their false Allah. Since this book is not about faith and the meaning of faith, we need to obey YHWH's word that proceeds out of His mouth and stop arguing like little children about things He never said and focus instead on obeying what He did say.

In addition, many Catholics hold to papal (men's doctrines) essentially denying the gospel of Messiah. They claim to believe in the Master Yahushua in words yet fail in other tests of the Bible by calling Mary another Advocate, Helper, Benefactress, Co-Mediatory and Queen of Heaven. They set up statues of Mary for worship, which is plain Idolatry. One could argue, as does rabbinical Judaism, these were papal fences in order to proclaim the deity of Yahushua and protect it from heretics in the early 2nd and 3rd century church. Yet the Bible makes it clear that titles such as advocate and intermediary only belong to Yahushua the Messiah and our way to the Father is only through Him. The worship to Mary is never mentioned, or given to her because she was also a sinner who needed blood atonement like the rest of us. Scripture never called Mary/Miriam sinless. The late Pope John Paul II by kissing the Qur'an only legitimized what is an idolatrous false religion. It is fair to say that there are now some 10% of Catholics who have left the doctrines of Rome/men and do believe in YHWH's promises for Israel and do not fall into the same Roman group. Whenever we need to correct error we must look at written Scripture and return to the Master Yahushua the Messiah.

Many Jews and Christians also worship with their words but not their deeds. Yet we know that YHWH created us for good works (**Ephesians 2:10**). They talk the talk without walking the walk.

Only one religion on earth is set for a showdown with Jews and Christians and that is ISLAM. Whether you agree or not that is the reality. It is better we face reality then to live in la la land. Many Christians running around proclaiming the gift of tongues that somehow make them more spiritual than others, is not going to help them resist the reality of the beast coming to kill them daily as seen daily on TV.

B. **The Mark of the Beast Identified-**

Let us remember this Beast/Empire/Kingdom kills in the name of Allah, which is the mark.

❖ In the name of Allah - Kenya USA Embassy bombings 1998.
❖ In the name of Allah - First World Trade Center bombings 1993.
❖ In the name of Allah - Australian Embassy blown up in Indonesia 9/2004.
❖ In the name of Allah - Crashing planes into twin towers in N.Y. 9/2001.
❖ In the name of Allah - The naval ship USS Cole bombed in Yemen 2000.
❖ In the name of Allah - Saudi Arabia Muslims slaughtered 9 people in Khobar and wounded several others.
❖ In the name of Allah - In the Philippines kidnapped American missionary Martin Burnham killed.
❖ In the name of Allah - French oil tanker attacked 2002.
❖ In the name of Allah - Bali nightclub blown up.
❖ In the name of Allah - Beheading of Daniel Pearl.
❖ In the name of Allah - Beheading of Paul Johnson.
❖ In the name of Allah - Beheading of interpreter/missionary Kim Sun II in Iraq and the beheading of Kenneth Bigley.

256

- ❖ In the name of Allah - Muslim terrorists in Saudi Arabia kidnapped and beheaded American engineer Paul Johnson.
- ❖ In the name of Allah - The Ghriba Synagogue in Tunisia bombed in 1982.
- ❖ In the name of Allah - Beheading of Nick Berg.
- ❖ In the name of Allah - Italian security guard Fabrizio Quattrocchi executed.
- ❖ In the name of Allah - Four Spanish trains blown up.
- ❖ In the name of Allah - Countless suicide terrorist attacks in Israel.
- ❖ In the name of Allah - Countless suicide bombings in Iraq.
- ❖ In the name of Allah - Morocco suicide bombing in Casablanca.
- ❖ In the name of Allah - In Turkey bombed two synagogues, the British consulate plus a British bank.
- ❖ In the name of Allah - Babies and Kids shot and killed in Chechnya/Russia.
- ❖ In the name of Allah - Chechen Muslim terrorists tried to detonate a dirty bomb in 1996 in Moscow but failed.
- ❖ In the name of Allah – Suicide attacks on the London transport system 7th July 2005.
- ❖ In the name of Allah – Jordanian American hotels blown up by two would be suicide bombers with the woman's device failing.
- ❖ Countless other daily atrocities visited on civilization by Islam in the name of Allah.

These are some of the incidents "in the name of Allah," the mark of the beast [Islam] with countless others. Recognise it if you have the eyes to see this. Do you think it would be unreasonable to ask Muslims to recognise and apologise for these things, if it does not hurt their ego than at least for unity?

Revelation 13:17 And that no man might buy or sell, save he that had the mark, or the name of the beast, or the number of his name.

Note the "number" in Greek is the word "**arithmos**."

Notice the beast has a NAME. The word "arithmos" in Greek can also be translated as "multitude," which has been often translated as **number** in the above verse. With the translation of "multitude" it would read, or the "multitude of/in his name." Men have names, and no man has a number and also the multitude rally under a banner, or emblem, not "numbers." It is absurd to assume that people rally under some "number."

A lot of people simply believe the computer chip theory, that the Anti-Messiah will insert a chip in our skin and when this happens we will know Anti-Messiah has arrived. Yet this can happen today through many USA or European companies, but that does not make the USA, President George W. Bush, or the European Union any more the Anti-Messiah, then Santa Claus is actually Father Christmas.

We have to tie the whole Bible together and not just jump to a conclusion based on one verse of the Bible.

"**No man may buy or sell**" can indeed mean that if you are in the dominion of the beast/empire/kingdom that he, the Anti-Messiah, can impose his will on you, so that you cannot buy, or sell unless you accept what he commands. He may ask you to convert to Islam, or he may ask you to pledge allegiance to his kingdom or cause (or forsake your spiritual, or political support for Israel/the Jews, or the "Crusaders the derogatory Muslim

257

term for Christians), and that would be enough to satisfy the mark. There are three "ors" given in Revelation 13 verse 17. Basically the mark is a submission to his will.

- ❖ He that had the mark (*The Shahadah* [Muslim creed of faith], or ANY form of real allegiance to Islam).
- ❖ Name of the beast (Titles of blasphemy, Allah is god, Muhammad is his prophet etc.)
- ❖ Multitude of his name [many people following in the name of Allah).

If we look at the following verse in **Revelation 13:18**, which has been the most contested verse in history, one sees the problem associated with trying to find the Anti-Messiah in just one verse and forgetting the rest of Scripture as a cohesive unit.

Here is wisdom. Let him that hath <u>understanding count the number of the beast</u>: for it is the <u>number of a man</u>; and his number is Six hundred threescore and six.

The above verse has caused a lot of people to use Gematria to equate this number to a man e.g. Hitler, Kissinger, Prince Charles and so many others in history that have proved to be wrong. The New Testament is written in street language (Koine Greek), and we at times need to see all the variant readings to come to a correct fuller understanding. The Master does tell us "Here is wisdom," "he that had understanding," e.g. if you have wisdom and understanding then know what it means. It is a kind of challenge to test your end time prophetic wisdom and knowledge.

The theory of the chip is just not tenable and far too exaggerated for our study. Now we know there are clubs and bars in Spain utilizing the chip for its customer base. Does this mean the prime minister of Spain is the Anti-Messiah, or perhaps even the bar owner? You may say that is ridiculous and really it is.

We need to be aware of a few things.

The Bible is a collection of books, 66 to be exact, divinely inspired by YHWH and written by men. Some prophets spoke more about the Anti-Messiah, while others may have spoken none, or very little about him. However, we need to take the Bible as a whole and look at all the evidence in the Bible to come to a correct understanding, or else we could be barking up the wrong tree.

International law even if used to enforce the chip theory cannot accommodate such activity and is not enforceable on sovereign states. We would potentially have to go to war with each nation and defeat them in order to implement this solution and even then, we know it would not work. Take a look at Iraq and see how many casualties occur on a daily basis, to the USA and British soldiers in order to maintain law and order in one country. How then can one nation, or person impose their will on EVERY person and culture in the world? Bullets and ballots would both fall short.

The chip theory is simply not tenable and a diversion tactic created by the Illuminists and many sincere people are falling for it. They should snap out of it. Did not Yahushua tell us "Do not be deceived?" Why did He say that? The answer is that Christians are also prone to deception by the world, thus, the reason for Yahushua's warning.

In Scripture we have to examine the language, context and idioms to know what YHWH is trying to teach us. For example the word "earth" does not always mean the whole world, yet most people will think this somehow applies to the whole world. Let me illustrate by an example, Eretz is the Hebrew word for land, but it does not always mean the whole world. Eretz Israel is often applied to the land of Israel, sometimes eretz is used in the context of the locality of a land e.g. the Middle East, but not necessarily whole world. Or this can even be applied to a country and at other times it can be applied to the whole population of one country, so that usually the context determines scope. This is what we would call a synecdoche, a figure of speech. Let us analyze this:

In Daniel 8:5a we see a reading that says: "And as I was considering, suddenly a male goat came from the west, across the surface of the whole earth."

Now on casual reading it might appear that this goat, who we know is Alexander the Great, came upon the face of the "whole earth." But in history we know that he never conquered the whole world, e.g. he never touched Western Europe, and he never conquered China, or even Australia. The Bible's method of describing this is simply to show that he could have had the strength to conquer the whole earth, but in principle he did not. Alexander the Great conquered all the way from Assyria to Pakistan. YHWH was only looking at the Middle East, while the majority of prophecy scholars want to stretch this to the whole world and it will not work. Remember Yahweh is always right.

Here is another example, when John was baptizing in the province of Judea, the biblical text says in **Mark 1:5:**

> **Mark 1:5** And there went out unto him **ALL the land of Judea**, and they of Jerusalem, and were **ALL** baptized of him in the river of Jordan, confessing their sins.

Now looking at the text of Mark, could we say that every man was baptized in ALL of Judea and Jerusalem? Clearly not! This simply refers to the group of people that turned up to be baptised and that was not every man. A large number of people perhaps, but not everyone. In like manner we must be very careful how we interpret Scripture to see whether it is talking about a whole region, or part of a region.

Here are some examples:

> **1 Kings 10:24** And all the earth sought to Solomon, to hear his wisdom, which YHWH had put in his heart.

We can see that in context we have to pay attention to the language and the Hebrew words used to describe the event in **1 Kings 10:24** (Hebrew "Vkol Ha' Eretz") i.e. the "whole world."

We just need to ask a simple question, did the "whole world" come to King Solomon to hear his wisdom? The answer is no.

> **Ezra 1:2** Thus saith Cyrus king of Persia, The Master YHWH of heaven hath given me **ALL the kingdoms of the earth**.

Did King Cyrus rule the entire world? Clearly, he never touched Western Europe, China, Indonesia, or Japan, but only the Middle Eastern portions. I can cite many other examples, but this is enough to prove my point.

Now if Pakistan decided to use Arab Dinaars, would it be reasonable to expect that India a separate nation also has to use Arab Dinaars? Of course not. If Pakistan has dominion only in its present land, then that is where it can apply this new law. The Bible reads the same way. The Anti-Messiah will apply the buying and selling to his area of dominion only, not the "whole world." ALL in his dominion will be under his influence! The problem is some people stretch things out to see their own preconceived views and do not reason with the Scriptures. They end up with inaccurate conclusions. They then in turn just become the blind leading the blind.

> **Revelation 13:17** And that <u>no man might buy or sell</u>, save he that had **the mark**, or **the name** of the beast, or **the number of his name**.

Applying proper interpretation criteria we can conclude that no man in the Islamic kingdom may buy or sell unless they give allegiance to the beast/empire. This is why I warn Christians and Jews to get out of Muslim lands, because one day, this jihad/force will be applied to you, even as YHWH has said, *"Come out of her My people (Revelation 18:4).*

The church has done the exact opposite of what YHWH required. They have been consistently breaking His commandments for 1,970 years, by saying the 'Old Testament does not apply to us, only the New Testament applies to us'. This is far from the truth and in fact it is out and out error and rebellion against YHWH. Our Messiah Yahushua quoted from the Old Testament time and time again validating YHWH's word as holy truth. He was not carrying a New Testament with Him in Israel. In fact, He recited from the Torah scrolls and prophets. The disciples were also quoting from the Old Testament and it was the Tanach (Hebrew Bible) they quoted from many times. The foundation of all biblical books are the five books of Moses known as the Torah.

We are born into a very fortunate generation where not only do we have so much technology at our disposal, but we have seen prophecies fulfilled in the Bible. People only have read about these prophecies in the past and dreamed to see them fulfilled. The prophets of the Bible would have desired to see these fulfilled, but it is our generation that has this privilege.
Therefore we can arrive at some firm conclusions: YHWH tells us:

> **Isaiah 45:19** **I have not spoken in secret**, in a dark place of the earth: I said not unto the seed of Jacob, Seek ye me in vain: I YHWH speak righteousness, I declare things that are right.

Many scholars today may agree with some sort of hidden code in the Bible, or try to fit the number 666 in **Revelation 13:18** using Jewish Gematria (letters possessing numerical values) to some person in the world. They have tried this in the past to fit this to Hitler, Henry Kissinger, President Putin, and the Roman Catholic Pope with no success. YHWH clearly tells us "I do not speak in secret," yet these individuals will not believe YHWH. They make vain attempts try to fit some codes to the Bible to prove that they are somehow more clever to understand YHWH's word. Revelation and Daniel were written to reveal not to conceal end time truths.

Let us look at the verse in question briefly:

Revelation 13:18 Here is wisdom. Let him that hath understanding count the number of the beast: for it is the number of a man; and his number is **Six hundred threescore and six [666]**.

Or have we missed the boat and did not get on Noah's ark?

Another more appropriate rendering of **Revelation 13:18** is

"Here is wisdom. Let him that hath understanding (decide) [who] (the multitude) of the beast [is], for it is the (multitude) of (a man i.e. Muhammad) and (the same) (multitude) [are] "In the Name of Allah." Explanation of this text follows below.

Failed End Time prophecies- [40]

1978: Chuck Smith, Pastor of Calvary Chapel in Cost Mesa, CA, predicted the rapture in 1981.
1982: Pat Robertson predicted a few years previously that the world would end in the fall of 1982.
1988: Hal Lindsey had predicted in his book "The Late, Great Planet Earth" that the Rapture was coming in 1988 - one generation or 40 years after the creation of the state of Israel. This failed prophecy did not appear to damage his reputation. He continues to write books of prophecy, which sell very well indeed.

All these people were dead wrong and countless others with them, but I cannot recall if any of these people have apologized for their error; in fact they continue to sell their books without any apology.

Remember Noah was preaching the upcoming flood for 120 years and no one believed him because they had never seen rain. They all thought that they were right and that Noah was a religious nut. Obviously they were all wrong by their standards. Guess what friends! Noah was right and they were all wrong. That is right, THEY WERE ALL WRONG. There are some stubborn Christians who even if you tell them that these guys are wrong will not listen. I sincerely hope you are not one of these. By the very fact that you read this book with an open mind, shows you have a mind for investigation. So do not miss the boat relying on teachers who have little insight.

Read this book and do the research and see why all the prophets in the Bible are saying the wrath to come is **on Islamic nations** and its followers, and not on Europe and not on the USA. Then why would YHWH mislead us by giving us a number that the church has been trying to decipher for two millennia? IT DOES NOT MAKE SENSE. The simple reason is that it was NEVER given as a number, but as a **symbolic** text that the early church thought was applicable to Nero. This symbol could likely be a piece of Arabic text. It is remarkable how YHWH has chosen Muslims to see this truth and bring them to His light. It takes an ex-Muslim to connect all the dots and cross the t's and praise YHWH that He chosen us to fulfil His will.

Many Christians have fallen into many false theories to try and fit 666 to one individual or another; but YHWH was not showing us a number at all. You will be startled to know

---

[40] http://www.religioustolerance.org/end_wrl2.htm

that this is not a number as believed by most, but a piece of writing representing a very "key event" which is here now.

We also note that scholars have not been entirely consistent in their translations of each word in Scripture. In order to read into the correct translation of a word, we really have to look at the old manuscripts that we have in the Hebrew/Greek and Aramaic languages. We need to see for ourselves what translation the word can be given within the context of the passage.

We do have manuscripts in our possession with variant readings of the Scripture for **Revelation 13:18** e.g. in one codex we find the number to be **616**, in another it is **646** and one contains **665**, so logically the question is which one is right?

The Oxyrhynchus Papyrion below shows 616 rather then 666.

41

The Oxyrhynchus Papyrus is one of the oldest manuscripts that we have in our possession and we can look at this number in this text because it is not 666.

The honest answer is none of the above are correct, not even 666 is a correct rendering of the word, as this is not how the early church saw this verse.

A scholar **Edward L. Pothier** had this to say against the 666 **representation**. [42]

Of particular interest to us are a set of manuscripts, which are recorded as affirming the reading for the number included in the critical text. These are the manuscripts, which, instead of writing out the words for the number, use the Greek alphabetic notation, i.e. the three Greek letters *(chi)(xi)(sigma)*. The manuscripts so listed are P47 (a papyrus manuscript, hence the P in the name, from the third century, known as Chester Beatty III), a tenth century manuscript known as 051, and the "Majority-Text" symbol (which indicates many late Byzantine manuscripts). Here is the P47 text: **The Book of Revelation c. AD 250**

Greek text on papyrus-Egypt-Chester Beatty Biblical Papyri III f.7 [43]

[41] http://www.csad.ox.ac.uk/POxy/beast616.htm
[42] http://answering-islam.org.uk/Religions/Numerics/six.html
[43] http://www.cbl.ie/imagegallery/gallery.asp?sec=3&order=2

WW 3-Unmasking The End Time Beast-Simon Altaf

P47 is from the third century and is the oldest manuscript of the Book of Revelation in existence. It contains parts of Revelation chapters 9-17. We will consider its readings for the "number" in **Revelation 13:18** and neighboring verses in the next section.

Because, as listed above, **the majority of the manuscripts** (mostly late Byzantine miniscule manuscripts) include the representation of the number six hundred sixty-six **by the three letters** (*chi)(xi)(sigma)*.

The text presented in another modern (but non-standard) edition called not surprisingly THE GREEK NEW TESTAMENT ACCORDING TO THE MAJORITY TEXT, does so also. Note that there is a major disagreement in presuppositions about the value of various manuscripts and manuscript groups between the editors of this edition and those of the standard editions.

The so-called Textus Receptus, which acted as the standard from the 16th century (the actual term first being used in the 17th) until well into the 19th century when modern critical editions started to displace it, was an evolution of earlier printed editions of the Greek NT. **Its printed text also used the** (*chi)(xi)(sigma)*) **notation**. The main textual basis of this edition was only a handful of fairly late manuscripts, a subset of the majority text.

In summary he states this study has attempted to argue against using the anachronistic (later usage being placed in greater importance than the prior, or original usage) numerical representation 666 for the number of the beast in **Revelation 13:18. Such a poor representation of these Greek letters could not have been made for many centuries after the Book of Revelation was written. Any interpretation based on this exact representation (666 as an actual number) would have to be <u>highly</u> suspect.** Zane Hodges and Arthur L. Farstad (eds),The Greek New Testament According To The Majority Text 2nd Ed. (Nashville: Thomas Nelson Publishers, 1985).

D.A. Carson, The King James Version Debate: A Plea For Realism (Grand Rapids: Baker Book House, 1979) contains a sane discussion on the subject. The title indicates that the topic of the book is broader than just the majority text vs. other critical editions. The King James Version was translated from a Textus Receptus type text which has similarities to, but is not identical to, the Majority text as compiled today.

What I believe is this, that the apostle John saw something amazing. He was revealed an Arabic text to tell him who these beast people are and the text is **BISM ALLAH [in the name of Allah]** with two cross swords beside it. That is the Islamic symbol John had revealed before the religion was even born. This is amazing! I believe we have a lost original manuscript of Revelation out there somewhere that was not written in Greek, but in Aramaic/Hebrew script, as many scholars now believe. These Aramaic/Hebrew letters in Aramaic are very similar to Arabic. So until we find this manuscript we have to rely on the only manuscripts that we have in Greek. Why would John, who perhaps had very little knowledge of Greek and was more than likely fluent in Hebrew/Aramaic, wrote a book of immense future significance to the Diaspora from the exiles of Yisrael in Greek? Even Josephus the historian tells us that he was not at all an expert in the Greek language, but more so in his own language. Until we can recover new manuscript evidence, we will have to wait on Yahweh to reveal more to us. However when we study the verses for the Islamic Empire in the Hebrew Bible we have no doubt that Islam is the end time beast.

Image 1   Image 2   Image 3

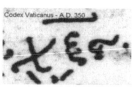

Compare image 3 with the text of Allah in image 2 and cross swords above with the Islamic cross swords in Image 1!

Image 3 is an Old Text (**Revelation 13:18**) in glass display at Bob Jones University Library - Greenville, S.C.

Let me show you something interesting with Allah in Arabic sideways, as it is easier to see this:

Image 4

Now look at the above image 3 and Allah in Image 4, they look identical. Let's make it even clearer.

Image 5   Image 6

Do you see it? That is what YHWH was showing John (the first to receive the mind of wisdom and end time understanding), the Islamic invasion to come, with the words were "Bism Allah" (in the name of Allah), that is in **whose name this multitude will belong to**!

Let us look at another one:

Image 7   The Greek text showing **Revelation 13:18**.

Hinds & Noble - 1897 - Rev. 13:18
Interlinear New Testament

Image 9   [is]   υ6ϭ.

John put down in exact writing what he saw! The scholars have been wrestling with this text for a long time, looking for the wrong thing. John saw the coming Islamic fighters/suicide bombers with the text written on their arms, waists and foreheads. He saw the text of Allah written sideways with the Arabic text Bism meaning (in the name of). John

264

faithfully penned down what he saw, it is clear that he saw **BISM Allah**⎯الله رسم [in the name of Allah] in calligraphy style Arabic, which we can see in many Islamic writings and John faithfully penned it down. These people who are to come would be fighting in Allah's name.

THE TRUE/MARK and NAME of the Beast.

In Hebrew culture the name [ha Shem] is important. This is why we have ha-Shem (the blessed name) in the Bible, attributed to the one true Elohim of Israel. YHWH was trying to tell us, that it is Islam that will come to try and destroy Israel and conquer the world in the name of the beast. Yet many have failed to recognize this. The scholars thought this was a Greek letter digamma, which no longer exists by the way.

The Greek letters in 666 are chi, xi, sigma but the last letter does not exist in the Modern Greek language. Some experts in old Greek even argue that it is not sigma but sigma score. The translators of the Bible no doubt took the words at face value. With their limited knowledge, they ascribed interpretations that made sense to them. It is interesting to note that the number translation of 666 is a late sixteenth century phenomena. This was not the understanding of the early church as also stated by Edward Pothier.

Revelation 13:18

Text	Strongs reference	Greek
Here	[5602]	Hode
Is	[2076]	esti
wisdom.	[4678]	Sophia
Let him that hath	[2192]	echo
understanding	[3563]	nous
count	[5585]	psephizo
the number	[706]	Arithmos
of the beast:	[2342]	Therion
for	[1063]	gar
it is	[2076]	Esti
the number	[706]	Arithmos
of a man;	[444]	anthropos
and	[2532]	kai
his	[846]	Autos
number	[706]	Arithmos
[is] six hundred threescore [and] six	[5516]	chi xi sigma

After careful analysis the only plausible conclusion I can come to is that these are not numerals but the **Arabic language which John saw, fitting today's "Bism Allah" in Arabic meaning "in the name of Allah." He understood that this multitude is "in the name of Allah." This is the god that the coming Empire is to follow and worship.**

265

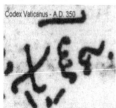

Fig 10 [44]

The X in figure 10 is the Islamic symbol of the swords. Compare the swords to the actual text in Figure 10. Today Islam comes with its crossed swords to steal, kill and destroy. The sword of Allah is a devilish counterfeit for the two edged metaphoric sword of Yahushua's pure holy Word.

Fig 11 [45]

In 1961 the Saudi civil symbol was a green equilateral triangle bearing the two swords. This is the same symbol seen in **Revelation 13:18** as the mark identifying these people and this **harlot of Babylon** is Mecca in Saudi Arabia known in the Bible as the literal Mystery Babylon! How many of you had the chance to go and watch the movie Kingdom of Heaven? In there the man who plays Salah din Ayubi, has this symbol above on both his arms.

Fig 12 [46]

The Royal standard Saudi flag. Note the two swords crossed in the top right hand corner of Fig 12.

In light of this understanding Revelation 13:18 uses the Greek word **psephizo** (count/consider), which can also mean, 'to decide,' or 'to vote.' Arithmos (number) can also mean simply, a 'multitude.' YHWH is in essence saying, 'now its time for you to consider/vote on the identity of the beast and his multitude, since you claim the mind of spiritual wisdom and understanding!'

Considering the above alternative reading of this translation we can come to this text in **Revelation 13:18** with an alternative reading that is a high possibility and with a probability of at least 99.99%.

---

[44] Bob Jones University or Bible College at Greenville, S.C
[45] by *António Martins- http://flagspot.net/flags/sa.html*
[46] by *António Martins & Ivan Sarajcic*

266

"Here is wisdom. Let him that hath **understanding** (decide) [who] (the **multitude) of the beast** [is], **for it is the** (multitude) of (a man i.e. Muhammad) and (the same) **(multitude)** [are coming] in the Name of Allah."

For another reference to the appropriateness of this interpretation see the following passage:

Revelation 17:15 "And he saith unto me, the waters which thou sawest, where the whore sitteth, **are peoples**, and **multitudes**, and **nations, and tongues**."

This whore (Saudi Arabia) sits on many waters between many nations and controls "multitudes" of people with and by the mark of the beast.

Revelation 13:16-18 And he causeth all, both small and great, rich and poor, free and bond, to receive a mark in their right hand, or in their foreheads: And that no man might buy or sell, save he that had the mark, or **the name of the beast**, or the **number of his name**.

It is interesting to note that the words "**name of the beast**" is mentioned in **Revelation 13:17** above. This **name** is the one that all Muslims already carry and in order to have this mark there are three things given for those people who will join this beast/kingdom/empire.

1. Allah is the only god.
2. Muhammad is his prophet.
3. Join with other Muslims to fight for their cause.

Any Christian who joins this cause will be considered having the mark and can consider himself blotted out of the book of life. This can even be a political, or economic reliance (filling your car with gas would not qualify as taking the mark, as would outright business dealings). In light of this one ought to consider the crucial discernment you will need to unlearn error and see who this prophesied beast truly is.

This is what having the mark means. There were quite a few young Pakistani men who went to fight against the USA and Great Britain in the war in Afghanistan for the Taliban and in Iraq for Saddam demonstrating that they have the "mark" and would even fight against the country where they live to uphold Islam. There were even English people who have been brainwashed into Islam ready to fight their own country of birth. We saw the same thing in the USA. Britain with its lenient laws does not enact the penalty for treason anymore, but this is what these people would get under normal circumstances. However due to the current lax UK laws they can get away with it.

In **Revelation 14:11**, the **"mark of his name"** is probably a title just as the title for Messiah being the "**word of YHWH**" as in **Revelation 19:13** and "**King of Kings**" in **Revelation 19:16**.

The mark can be relating to anything to do with Islam. Revelation does give us indications of what it could be with its alternative reading. So if you are in an Islamic state they can prohibit you from buying, or selling, unless your give your allegiance to Islam. It is as simple as that, and there's no fancy computer chip required. This is why it is imperative that all Christians get out of Muslim lands for their own safety, or be forced to be submitted to Islam. Furthermore, it is imperative that the Book of Revelation conform to the Hebrew

267

Bible not stand on its own, with people trying to use Gematria with Greek letters, turning Greek letters into numbers which can't be done in Gematria.

This is the ongoing problem with prophecy teachers that they try to interpret the book in isolation and this interpretation is not only highly suspect, but will end up being inaccurate, even endangering believers everywhere in Muslim, or Islamic influenced societies.
The following are some examples of the words **BISM Allah**, which are currently used, in almost every type of Muslim communication.

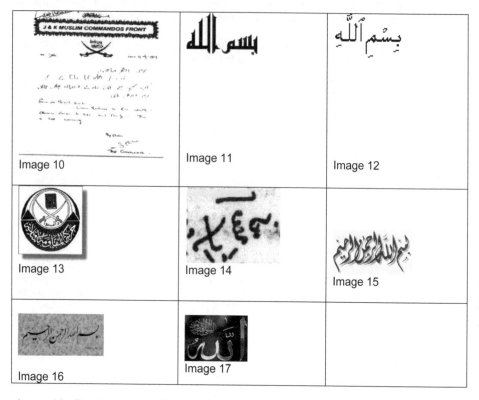

Image 10 - The two swords of Islam on a note with "Bismillah Alrahman Alraheem" on the header. This is common on every stationary used throughout the Islamic world and it means "In the name of Allah who is merciful."
Image 11 - "Bismillah" in the Arabic calligraphy style.
Image 12 - Smaller version of bismillah.
Image 13 - The crescent moon, the Qur'an and the two swords as an emblem of the Islamic resistance movement shown above.
Image 14 – One of the manuscripts of the NT [47] (Bible College at Greenville) - Bismillah (In the name of Allah) is clearly visible. The word "Allah" is at an angle upwards and the two swords are clear as well.
Image 15 - Bismillah Alrahman Alraheem. The first two words are the same as what John had. Again, the "Allah" is vertical in the Codex.

---

[47] Bob Jones University or Bible College at Greenville, S.C

Image 16 - Similar to image 6.
Image 17 – This is the word "Allah" in Arabic, exactly as depicted in image 5 with the vertical "Allah." Here "Allah" is horizontal.

Muslims continue make all sorts of baseless claims that they worship the same elohim as Christians and Jews as does the mainstream media. But when you examine the Qur'an you will find Islam is only a monotheistic religion with a clear pagan wrapping. Calling Abraham the first Muslim does not make him a Muslim. Calling Yahushua a Muslim also does not make Him a Muslim, especially when the Qur'an describes Him as a created being. The Yahushua of the Bible is uncreated and eternal. Allah denies Yahushua is the Son of YHWH. Who would have a stake in the denial of the cross and the denial of Yahushua being uncreated? The only person that has a stake is s.a.tan that deceiver of old, the one whose very name means, "to divert."

> **Sura 4:171** "The Messiah, Isa the son of Mary, was no more than Allah's apostle; Allah is but one Allah. GOD FORBID THAT <u>he</u> SHOULD HAVE A SON!"

When did Yahweh ever instruct to cut off the hands and feet of thieves? When did Yahushua say to hate your enemy, or pillage innocent people? Or that it was ordained for people to 'lie in wait' in order to kill others? Yet this is what Muhammad's god teaches. All the things that s.a.tan wants people to do Allah teaches and condones. He has a lustful filthy heaven full of orgies around him with Muslims having 72 times 70 virgins who remain a virgin upon sexual intercourse, carrying perpetual erections. This is a morally dirty home for any deity, don't you think? Does that sound like a holy god? To some misguided people it just might be.

The Shiites Muslims even beat themselves up to punish themselves with knives attached to chains in order to cut and bleed for their sin of killing Imam Hussain in Iraq. He was Muhammad's grandson. The actual day of Ashura that used to be celebrated by Muslims to mimic the Jewish Yom Kippur was later revoked by Muhammad when the Jews rejected his prophethood.

Does this not sound like Baal's prophets?

> **1 Kings 18:27-28** And so it was, at noon, that Elijah mocked them and said, "<u>Cry aloud, for he is a god</u>; either he is meditating, or he is busy, or he is on a journey, or perhaps he is sleeping and must be awakened." **So they cried aloud**, and **cut themselves**, as **was their custom**, **with knives and lances, until the blood gushed out on them.**

The Muslims do almost the same thing by cutting themselves, shouting 'Allah hu Akbar' and wailing. The pattern is very similar because these people also follow after Baal. There is no question about what we are seeing today. If you look at the Shiites they pierce themselves with knives, their bodies bleeding, every year on the religious festival of Ashura (Muharram) by chanting and crying over the death of Hussain. Is it any surprise that this incident of Imam Hussain happened near the River Euphrates where we will get the two hundred million-man army? Since when is the Euphrates River in China, or near China as prophecy teachers would have you believe? These are jihadist Muslims, not china men.

What is Ashura? [48]

In the month of <u>Muharram</u> 61 <u>AH</u> (approx. 20 October 680 AD), an event took place in **Iraq** at a place known as Kerbala **on the bank of the river Euphrates**. It seemed in those days insignificant from the historical point of view. A large army which had been mobilized by the Umayyad regime besieged a group of persons numbering less than a hundred and put them under pressure to pay allegiance to the Caliph of the time and submit to his authority. The small group resisted and a severe battle took place in which they were all killed.

It appeared at that time that like hundreds of similar events, this battle would be recorded in history and forgotten in time. However, the events that occurred on the 10th day of Muharram in Kerbala were to become a beacon and an inspiration for future generations. Let us examine briefly the principal adversaries.

Who is Husain?

The leader of the small band of men who were martyred in Kerbala was none other than Husain, son of Ali bin Abi Talib and grandson of the Holy Prophet. Who was Husain? He was the son of Fatima for whom the Holy Prophet said, *"Husain is from me and I am from Husain. May Allah love whoever loves Husain."* Ibn Majah: Sunan, Hadith 144 [49]

The most visual of these celebrations is the flagellation by male Shi'is. Whips, often with sharp ends, or even small knives are used to make their backs bleed. The reason for this ritual is that only physical pain can truly reflect the pain of the Muslim world when Husayn died, and the family of Ali's fight for leading the Muslim world came to an end. This flagellation ritual is however just a part of a complex ritual where the Shiites commemorate every stage of the preparation to the battle, and the battle itself.

According to Muslim traditions, Ashura can be traced back to ancient Arab times and Ibrahim/Abraham. Muhammad allegedly brought the tradition back to its old purity and correct practice.

You may be interested to know that Muslims are already set up by s.a.tan to believe that Isa (Jesus) of the Qur'an, is going to come back to kill the Jews and pigs (derogatory term for Christians) and break their crosses. When this happens, Muslims will supposedly know that their 'Messiah' is here and the truth of the matter is that at that time we will all know that our Anti-Messiah is here. This Muslim Jesus, or Isa is going to kill Dajjal (Anti-Messiah) and then get married, and live on earth for forty years and die like a mortal, only

---

[48] http://www.ashura.com/home.html

[49] http://i-cias.com/e.o/ashura.htm

to be buried in an empty grave in Medina! This is what the Muslims believe and are waiting for.

One Muslim apologist writes about this like this: **From Ibn Khaldun's al-Maqqadima:**

"There will come forth a man from my nation who will talk according to my Sunnah, god will send upon him rain from heaven, and the earth will sprout forth for him its blessing. The earth will be filled through him with equity and justice, as it his been filled with injustice and crime. **He will direct the affairs of this nation for seven years, and he will settle in Jerusalem."**

The Mahdi of Islam has many descriptions to set up the Muslims for the greatest deceiver. This is remarkable considering Daniel wrote prophecies to show the covenant will be confirmed with Israel for seven years.

Below, the map shows the four divisions of the Grecian Empire and the rise of the little horn (Anti-Messiah) from this area. Map of Alexander's Empire with its four divisions:

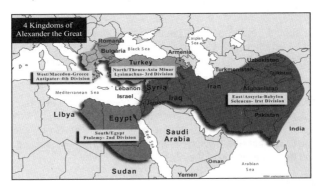

Note that Pakistan is included in the Grecian Empire, but not in present day India, as Pakistan split from India in 1947. Is it any wonder that Pakistan denies Israel as a sovereign state and hates the Jews? The only Muslim nation with a nuclear bomb and these are likely to supply the Arabs with technology and nuclear arms against Israel in the near future, if they haven't already. You could say this is an Assyrian/Grecian Empire, but if you said Roman as well, then we have to qualify that by saying that the Revived Roman Empire theory is only true for the former eastern leg of the Roman Empire and not the western leg. You could say Revived Eastern Romano/Greco/Assyrian/Babylonian Empire if you like, even though the Anti-Messiah comes out of the Grecian division of the Empire. Strictly speaking this area was also shared by the Roman Empire. If you have noticed **Revelation 13** makes it clear that the final beast empire is a combination of all the previous Middle Eastern Empires.

Chapter 12

The Second Coming of Yahushua of Nazareth – The Chronology of Events

Many Christians are taught to believe that they should not worry about the Great Tribulation to come because it will not affect them since they are going to be taken out of the world before this happens; this event is described as the rapture.

A lot of Christians are taught that Yahushua will return briefly during the rapture in the sky and take believers into heaven before His proper second coming, i.e. before the Great Tribulation begins. They affirm that the second coming will be the rapture when only the true Christians will see Yahushua the Messiah and be taken away. The true Christians will allegedly meet Yahushua the Messiah in the air during the rapture and then are whisked away to heaven without any judgement. And the third coming will be when the whole world will see Him, which they call the second coming.

Confused? You should be and so am I because this view breaks Scripture left right and centre? This is the problem with Christian scholars today as they create more confusion then clarity. First of all, there is only a Great Tribulation of three and a half years and not seven years.

Yahushua the Messiah will certainly come back for judgement and there is no support in the Bible for a rapture type event, separate from His return to earth. We must note that the Bible does not mention the word "rapture" even once. The Greek word used in First Thessalonians 4:17 is "harpazo," which means to be caught up or plucked up. Plucked up from the grave in the resurrection of the righteous.

The Bible only talks about TWO comings of Yahushua the Messiah. The first as a suffering servant as seen in **Isaiah 42** and the second coming for what is generally, but wrongly understood to be the rapture to set up the one thousand year millennial reign. There is no mention of three comings (or a partial second coming) in the Bible. That is a misconception and not supported by Scripture, as there is no such thing. There is only one second coming of Messiah and the Bible says that "**all the world**" will see Him.

The word used for Yahushua the Messiah's return is "parousia" in **1 Thessalonians 4:15,** which in essence talks about His 2nd coming and nothing more. Christian scholars use this text to allege the rapture.

The same word is described in **Matthew 24:27-31**

> For as the lightning cometh out of the east, and shineth even unto the west; so shall also the **coming of the Son of man be**. For wheresoever the carcase is, there will the eagles be gathered together. **Immediately after the tribulation** of those days shall the sun be darkened, and the moon shall not give her light, and the stars shall fall from heaven, and the powers of the heavens shall be shaken: And then shall appear the sign of the **Son of man in heaven: and then shall all the tribes of the earth** mourn, and **they shall see the Son of man coming** [this magnificent event will not be missed or kept secret] (parousia) in the clouds of heaven with power and great glory. And he shall send his angels with

a great sound of a trumpet, (same trumpet as in 1 Thessalonians 4:16) and **they shall gather together his elect [believers]** from the four winds, from one end of heaven to the other.

Note: All the tribes of the earth mourn and all see Yahushua the Messiah. It is not a hidden, or secret event for just Christians. That is most absurd to say that only Christians will see the Master and no one else will. This is the erroneous theology of the pre-tribulation theorists. Also note this event happens after the Great Tribulation is over (the text says "**immediately after**") and all the Christians are gathered together from around the world! I think after this reading we should stop playing games with the Bible to make it fit into a pre-tribulation rapture position, because YHWH did not teach any such thing.

People who want to make the word "elect" In Matthew 24:27-31 apply here for the Jews only, especially dispensationalists take heed. This is not the Jews alone, but all future believers. Jews and gentiles together who accept Messiah as Savior. When Yahushua was speaking, He used the term "elect" synonymously with "you," when addressing disciples. Obviously if it is only the disciples in Yahushua's own day, remember that the abomination of desolation had not occurred back then, and neither had the promised signs appeared, but were yet future. Matthew 24:9 reads "then shall they deliver you up to be afflicted, and shall kill you: and ye shall be hated of all nations for My name's sake," it is quite clear these are believers in the future who are hated for Yahushua's name. Let us take a look, at who hates believers the most; the Muslims of course! They say we commit "*shirk*" [idolatry] when we say Yahushua is Master and for that reason alone they must kill us. In fact many Christians have been killed by the Islamists because of this hatred alone. They only want to accept the view that Yahushua is just a prophet, but not YHWH incarnate.

With **POWER** and **GLORY** means this is one **HUGE** event that cannot be missed, as it is more spectacular than the Red Sea parting in the Exodus. This is the grand finale! Every believing and unbelieving eye will behold the true second coming. Wow.

What other links do we see in these passages?

> **Matthew 24:27 Coming (Parousia).**
> **Matthew 24:31 Sound of the trumpet/shofar heard.**
> **Matthew 24:31 Angels present.**
> **Matthew 24:30 Yahushua descends from heaven to earth.**

> **1 Thessalonians 4:15 Coming (Parousia).**
> **1 Thessalonians 4:16 Sound of the trumpet/shofar heard.**
> **1 Thessalonians 4:16 Archangel present.**
> **1 Thessalonians 4:16 Yahushua descends from heaven.**

If we compare the above Scriptures we can quite clearly see that this is the same event described in both passages, NOT a so-called rapture as popularly believed but simply "**the coming of Messiah**." The second coming of Messiah as we should know it.

<u>**Revelation 13:7**</u> And it was given unto him to make **war with the saints** [believers in Yahushua Messiah], and to overcome them: and power was given him over all kindreds, and tongues, and nations.

273

It all happens after the Great Tribulation not before. If you look at the above passage, the saints are being killed by the Anti-Messiah. Well if we have all been raptured before the seven-year period started, then who are the believers that are being killed by the Anti-Messiah? Some believe these are the people who will come to faith after the Great Tribulation has begun, but unfortunately this is a far stretch of scholars' imagination playing tricks on peoples' minds.

Note: Many of the churches teach that those Christians who are not strong enough to endure the 7-year period will be raised to heaven. Those who are strong enough to endure it will be left here to evangelize unbelievers who are then willing to listen. And also that YHWH will not let you suffer more than you can handle. This is not what YHWH teaches throughout the Bible.

Daniel 7:21-22 I beheld, and the same horn made war with the saints, and prevailed against them; Until the Ancient of days came, [the Master Yahushua Messiah] and judgment was given to the saints of the most High; and the time came that the saints possessed the kingdom [millennial reign].

Amazing! This is the same event as Revelation 13:7 and it talks about the "ancient of days" coming for judgment and it links with Matthew 24 of Yahushua the Messiah's second coming.

If you read carefully in these passages, the beast is revived **Revelation 13:3** that is ISLAM REVIVED, the beast that people thought had died. Then immediately after it's strengthening, this beast [Islam] is actively warring with the saints, killing them everywhere it has control. The birth pangs of the Great Tribulation believers have already started.

Radical Islam teaches that Islam is at war in a worldwide conflict with Jews/Zionists and Christians/crusaders and that blood must flow for the glory of Allah. This proclamation is about the only truth that Islam factually states, as all its theology is anti-messiah to the core. The so-called war on terror is merely the politically correct term for the World War of Islam against the Judeo Christian world, with Islam gaining the victory until Messiah Yahushua Himself returns to put an end to the beast. Those are the facts and we had better prepare our lives accordingly.

One cannot claim to be Jacob from either of Israel's two houses and then turn right around and not be able to identify exactly whom it is, or who the people are that cause Jacob this Great Tribulation! If we cannot identify the beast from Scripture, we will get blindsided. Now is the time for both houses to see not only their previously hidden identity as Israel, but also the revelation of just who it is that is causing us this end time tribulation. And surprise, surprise, it is the same enemy Israel has had from the get go. Esau is now being fully revived, and remain the people YHWH says are the people of His indignation until the END OF TIME (See and study Malachi 1:2-4).

If theologians are going to substitute the Catholics, or Rome, or the USA for Esau/Islam in the books of Daniel and Revelation, even though YHWH says Edom is Israel's eternal enemy, then that is equivalent to changing the Shabbat/Sabbath to Sunday, when Shabbat is the day of rest for all eternity. **The bride Israel and the enemy of Israel, both remain the same till the end of the age!**

274

Now back to the Anti-Messiah!

When does he war? Easy, the war is active throughout time, but gets really worse after the three and a half years. Then he will become better known as more political and spiritual power is granted to the Anti-Messiah in order to overcome the saints. The true tribulation is only three and a half years, not seven as popularised. The Anti-Messiah confirms the hudna (peace deal), so that really the first three and a half years are relatively peaceful with no trouble in Israel.

> **Revelation 6:11** And white robes were given <u>unto every one of them</u>; and it was said unto them, that they should rest yet for a little season, until **their fellow servants also and their brethren**, that <u>should be killed as they</u> *were*, should be fulfilled.

The important thing in the above passage is that in the early church believers were martyred and we should consider this a shadow, or promise of the future end time persecution. The verse is very clear that believers will be killed during the Great Tribulation. The question one should ask is why will believers be killed if they are not on this earth anymore?

> **Revelation 6:12** And I beheld when he had opened the sixth seal, and, lo, there was a <u>great earthquake</u>; and <u>the sun became black</u> as sackcloth of hair, and the moon became as blood;

Note also the "earthquake," "the blackening of the sun" and "moon" matches Matthew 24 and this passage follows after the saints are killed not before meaning the resurrection of the dead has not happened yet.

We note something very interesting in Revelation 14.

> **Revelation 14:6-12** And I saw another angel fly in the midst of heaven, having the <u>everlasting gospel</u> to preach unto them <u>that dwell on the earth</u>, and to <u>every nation</u>, and <u>kindred</u>, and <u>tongue, and people</u>,
>
> 7 Saying with a loud voice, Fear YHWH, and give glory to him; for the <u>hour of his judgment</u> is come: and worship Him that made heaven, and earth, and the sea, and the fountains of waters.
>
> 8 And there followed another angel, saying, <u>Babylon is fallen</u>, is fallen, **that great city**, because she made all nations drink of the wine of the wrath of her fornication.
>
> 9 And the third angel followed them, saying with a loud voice, If <u>any man</u> **worship the beast** <u>and his image</u>, and <u>receive *his* mark in his forehead</u>, or <u>in his hand</u>,

If people at this point still think the angel is saying do not take the computer chip, he has got to be kidding. He is warning against false worship ascribed to a false god/deity condemning them to hell. Is it not amazing that YHWH has made a provision to preach the gospel finally through angels and not men? There will be absolutely no doubt left as to

275

who is in real control and what is the fate of men if they do not listen. The onus is on man to choose correctly as no one is forced into truth, and this is the justice of our true YHWH and the Master Yahushua the Messiah; hallelu-Yah to the Lamb.

10 The same shall drink of the <u>wine of the wrath of YHWH</u>, which is poured out without mixture into the cup of his indignation; and he shall be tormented with fire and brimstone in the presence of the holy angels, and in the presence of the Lamb:

11 And the smoke of their torment ascendeth up forever and ever: and they have no rest day nor night, who worship the beast and his image, and whosoever receiveth the mark of his name.

12 Here is the <u>patience of the saints</u>: **here are they that keep the commandments of YHWH, <u>and the faith of Yahushua</u>**.

* ❖ In **Revelation 14:6-7** we see the first angel preaching the everlasting gospel of Messiah to all nations and tongues.
* ❖ The second angel proclaims Babylon is fallen, i.e. the destruction of Saudi Arabia, the "harlot of Babylon," the one which causes kings to fornicate with her because of her oil wealth including Iraq.
* ❖ The third angel warning that those who take the "mark of the beast" i.e. become Muslims, or stand with them, or giving allegiance to Islam and Muhammad, or reciting the Shahadah (Muslim creed), will be judged for eternal condemnation in front of the angels and the 'Lamb of YHWH,' that is the Master Yahushua our Messiah.
* ❖ These (Muslims) will be in **everlasting punishment** because of their hard heartedness and not believing in the one true YHWH for faith in Messiah as their Savior.
* ❖ Verse 12 states: "here is the patience of the saints" meaning those Christians that were patient and came out of the tribulation, willing to die but not accept Islam and its false god even unto death.

Look at Bible eschatology; the Anti-Messiah does not reveal himself until three and a half years after the false treaty, i.e. when he comes initially pretending to be a nice guy who has come to make peace with the Jews, but deep down he is deceiving them and the world.

<u>Daniel 9:27</u> Then he shall confirm a covenant with many for one week [**7 years**]; but in the middle of the week [**3.5 years**] He shall bring an end to sacrifice and offering.

Now we must be very careful. The believers that are being killed are killed three and a half years into the 7-year period. If they have been raptured then they cannot be killed. So it breaks the case for a pre-tribulation rapture. This discredits (or disproves) the pre-tribulation teaching disclosing its error!

<u>2 Thessalonians 2: 1-3</u> Now we beseech you, brethren, by the coming of our Master Yahushua the Messiah, and **by our gathering together** [we are gathered together after the tribulation] unto him, That ye be **not** soon shaken in mind, or be

troubled, neither by spirit, nor by word, nor by letter as from us, as that **the day of Messiah is at hand**. **Let no man deceive** you by **any means** [includes erroneous teaching of pre-tribulation rapture]: for *that day shall not come*, except there come a **falling away first**, [those teaching revival are in error] and **that man of sin be revealed**, the son of perdition [no more so-called revivals, but in fact a massive falling away of the church becoming more apostate by the day, this is happening today];

Not a crucial thing that no pre-tribulation person will tell you, read very carefully between the lines. We are **ALL GATHERED TOGETHER** "by our **gathering together**" thus no separate gatherings.

Luke 21:36 Watch ye therefore, and pray always [**pray for protection**], that ye may be accounted worthy to <u>escape all these things</u> [tribulation to come] that shall come to pass [tribulation is upon all to go through including Christians], and to stand before the Son of man. [pray not for a pre-tribulation rapture, but that YHWH will give us the strength to endure it].

Why would the Master warn us to **pray always** if we will escape the Great Tribulation? Many are teaching that we are not going through the tribulation, so people sit comfortably thinking, 'well since I am not going to face the hard time during tribulation period, therefore, I can sit and relax.' This is the error that churches are teaching believers today that our Master continuously warned us about. We are to pray that we escape this horrendous and evil time that is to come through divine preservation. The context is already given in Luke 21:26-27.

Luke 21:26-27 Men's hearts failing them for fear, and for looking after those things, which are coming on the earth [this is all during tribulation]: for the powers of heaven shall be shaken. And then shall they see the Son of man coming in a cloud with power and great glory.

Revelation 13:10 He that <u>leadeth into captivity</u> shall go into captivity: he <u>that killeth with the sword</u> must be killed with the sword. Here is <u>the patience and the faith of the saints</u>.

This is the patience of the saints (believers in Yahushua Messiah). They are being killed for their faith and are upholding the words of Messiah as they refuse the words of Allah and his false prophet. These are not "name it and claim it" believers, but strong believers in the Master who do not care even if their life is lost for Him.

Matthew 24:15 When ye [the believers] therefore shall see the abomination of desolation, spoken of by Daniel the prophet, stand in the holy place **(whoso readeth, let him understand)**,.........

Who will see this? The Christians (you) will see this and this is yet future when the Islamists pollute the sanctuary so we can know that the end time is here. If the Jews have not even rebuilt their altar on Mt. Moriah how can this have happened already? Well the "abomination of desolation" is there today with the Al-Aqsa Mosque with the Arabic text saying, "Allah is god and Muhammad is his last prophet and Allah does not have a son" on their dome. What the Anti-Messiah will do is in the future, is enter the rebuilt Temple, and then commit the abomination of desolation and spread it to the wing or southwest corner of the temple mount as promised in Daniel 9:27 where he stands in the Al Aqsa Mosque deceiving the world as a deity, yet he himself worships Allah the god of brute forces/jihad. See Daniel 11:38!

Yahushua made it clear this is still in the future **in Matthew 24:15** "**When ye [the believers] therefore shall see** the abomination of desolation, spoken of by Daniel the prophet..." If believers have been raptured already before the Great Tribulation, then how can they see this? This is the absurdity that some Christians want to live with, that we are all raptured up. But when the time comes they will be disappointed and this may also lead Christians to backslide since their expectations were not met and Yahushua constantly warns about being deceived by end time events. Why would Yahushua warn us if we could not be deceived?

> **Matthew 24:31** And He shall send his angels with a great sound of a trumpet, and they shall gather together his elect [gather the believers after the tribulation after the abomination of desolation has occurred] from the four winds [all parts of the world], from one end of heaven to the other.

This leaves absolutely no room for further argument or manoeuvring for the pre-tribulation house of cards.

> **Revelation 7:9-14** After this I beheld, and, lo, a great multitude, which no man could number, of all nations, and **kindreds**, and **people**, and **tongues**, stood before the throne, and before the Lamb, clothed with white robes, and **palms** in their hands; And cried with a loud voice, saying, **Salvation to our YHWH which sitteth upon the throne**, and **unto the Lamb**. And **all the angels stood round about the throne**, and **about the elders and the four beasts**, and fell before the throne on their faces, and worshipped YHWH, Saying, Amen: **Blessing, and glory, and wisdom, and thanksgiving, and honor, and power, and might, be unto our YHWH for ever and ever**. Amen. And one of the elders answered, saying unto me, What are these, which are arrayed, in white robes? And **whence came they**? And I said unto him, Sir, thou knowest. And he said to me, **These are they which came out of Great Tribulation**, and have washed their robes, and **made them white in the blood of the Lamb**.

This is a nail in the coffin passage for those that teach pre, or mid-tribulation rapture as these verses in **Revelation 7:9-14** are clear. They are answered in the positive that "these are they which came out of the great tribulation." How come they wash their robes if they were already saved? This is simple; these Christians are those believers who remained faithful to Yahushua of Nazareth and His words. They did not sway with the wind and deny Yahushua at the point of death.

The coming of Messiah takes place **before the first resurrection**:

> **Revelation 20:4-5** And I saw thrones, and they sat upon them, and judgment was given unto them: and I saw the souls of them that were **beheaded for the witness of Yahushua**, and for the word of YHWH, [Muslims slaughtering Christians happening today] and which had not worshipped the beast [not submitted to Islam], neither his image, neither had received his mark upon their foreheads, or in their hands; **and they lived and reigned with Messiah a thousand years.** But the rest of the dead lived not again until the thousand years were finished. **This is the first resurrection.**

278

If we examine this carefully we can see this event happens after the tribulation and it is simply the second coming of Messiah which causes the first resurrection (I Thessalonians 4:15) that happens after Yahushua descends to earth to reign on earth. The first resurrection has 2 parts. Part A is the raising of the believing dead and Part B is the changing of the living believers. One event in 2 stages.

The true Christians meet Yahushua the Messiah in the air, but what happens after that? Many Christians are taught that they will be whisked to heaven for the great feast.

I cannot find any verse in Scripture that says that after the resurrection people are going to be **lifted up into heaven**. In fact Rev. 20:5 tells us **"it is the first resurrection**." Let us analyze these events further:

What happens after?
Zechariah 14:3 Then shall the Master go forth, and fight against those nations, as when he fought in the day of battle.

Which nations? The Islamic nations described in Psalm 83.

Revelation 19:13 "And He was clothed with a garment sprinkled with blood; and his Name is called The Word of YHWH."

The Master Himself correctly defined as the word of YHWH comes for judgement.

Revelation 19:14-16 "And the armies that were in heaven [the aerial heaven or sky] followed him upon white horses, clothed in fine linen, white and clean. And **out of his mouth goeth a sharp sword, that with it he should smite the nations**, and he shall rule them with a rod of iron; and He treadeth the winepress of the fierceness and wrath of Almighty YHWH. And he hath on his vesture and on his thigh a name written, **KING OF KINGS, AND LORD OF LORDS.**"

Notice, the armies are "clothed in fine linen, white and clean." According to **Revelation 19:7-8**, this is the attire of the bride of Messiah [the true people of Messiah ready for battle].

This is not a sword coming out of the Messiah's mouth to kill the enemy. This is biblical symbolism not black magic; the Messiah will not have a big metal blade protruding, or being wielded by an invisible hand. The symbol of the sword protruding from the mouth represents the Messiah's judgement upon the nations and the crimson, or scarlet color represents sin (Isaiah 1:18).

Isaiah 63:1-6 "Who is this that comes from Edom, from Bozrah in garments stained crimson? Who is this so splendidly robed, marching in his great might?" "It is I, announcing vindication, mighty to save." "Why are your robes red, and your garments like theirs who tread the wine press?" "I have trodden the wine press alone, and from the peoples no one was with me; I trod them in my anger and trampled them in my wrath; their juice spattered on my garments, and stained all my robes. For the day of vengeance was in My heart, and the year for My redeeming work had come. I looked, but there was no helper; I stared, but there was no one to sustain Me; so my own arm brought Me victory, and My wrath sustained me. I trampled down peoples in my anger, I crushed them in My wrath, and I poured out their lifeblood on the earth."

279

Yahushua the Messiah of Israel is back in His glory and in His anger He will crush and kill the hostile foes i.e. the fanatic Muslims. He will tread upon them and take their life, and their blood will be on His clothes. Some may think this is symbolism, but this is both literal and symbolic. He crushes the final Islamic Empire because no one else was able to do so and so He does the job Himself. These are the fanatics who were killing and destroying the innocent lives of other peoples. Edom here is the symbol of not just Jordan, but the whole kingdom of Islam, which will fall like a house of cards.

> **Amos 1:11-12** "I (the Master) will send a fire into Teman: and it shall devour the **houses of Bozrah.**"

> **Zechariah 14:4** states that the **Messiah will stand on the Mount of Olives** with an earthquake as He comes for the **battle in Jerusalem**. [this is war on those who were out to destroy the Jews. Only one end time group of people are bent on Jewish destruction and these are **ALL** fanatic Muslims].

The nation of Israel was punished for 2,000 years of Diaspora for not paying attention to "the time of thy visitation" (Luke 19:44). I guarantee the same problem of ignorance will happen again at His second coming. The problem was caused by ignorance: *"My people are destroyed from lack of knowledge" (Hosea 4:6a)*. And of course with today's attitude of most people that "we will find out when He comes," or "we'll know the truth when we die," is simply closing your eyes and sticking your head in the sand.

The reason why they did not recognize His first coming is that they did not care "how" He was to come. They simply followed the main line of interpretation by famous rabbis who said that Messiah would defeat Rome militarily and politically.

Noah preached for 120 years and not one person outside his family listened to him. The moral of Noah's account is, do not miss the boat. If you are looking at the wrong place and wrong area for Jacob's enemy, then your situation will be that of the Jews in Yahushua's day, when they did <u>not</u> pay attention to the time or direction of their visitation.

> **2 Peter 2:5** And spared not the old world, but saved Noah the eighth person, a <u>preacher of righteousness</u>, bringing in the flood upon the world of the ungodly;

Every word regarding Messiah's second coming is crucial. How else will people distinguish between the Anti-Messiah, who performs signs and wonders and the true Messiah who performs signs and wonders? Most Christians' regard for Israel is lukewarm and must meditate on the written word of YHWH to realize that the Messiah is coming back for Israel His eternal and only bride. He will fight for her and for you, since you are Israel as a believer, so we ought to decide right now which camp we are in. Do we sit by while Jewish Israel's enemies try to crush her and say "YHWH will take care of it," or do we do something about it now? What can we do? Warn both houses and sound the shofar that the beast is none other than our old friend Easu/Islam.

Today, the church depends on the rapture, yet there is not one single verse that supports a pre-tribulation rapture. Worse still, the word nor the concept, is even mentioned in the Bible. It all happens at the end. Indeed, all of church history up until the last hundred years or so all supported the resurrection at the end of the tribulation. This pre-tribulation teaching is a recent idea, in order to stir up discord and anti-Semitic doctrine within the church. The catching up is to be in the air to meet the Master as **He is coming down to** the Mount of Olives so we can be changed to immortality off of the sin cursed earth, in a clean environment in the air.

That is what the text below actually says when you link the New Covenant writings with the prophets of Israel, so that then we really get to know what it means.

1 Thessalonians 4:17a "Then we which are alive [and] remain shall be caught up together with them in the clouds, to meet the Master in the air...."

The Master is waiting in the clouds to descend on earth to fight for Israel in the battle of Armageddon.

1 Thessalonians 4:16 "For the Master Himself shall descend from heaven with a shout, with the voice of the archangel, and with the trump/shofar of YHWH: and the dead in Messiah shall rise first."

The Bible says that we ought to focus on His second coming and meeting Him and being with Him. Yet we have movies and books all over two verses, which clearly do not support a pre-tribulation rapture. Therefore, we should get the idea Messiah is coming for Israel to save His people (the Jewish nation and Ephraim-Israel) with His saints (us). These saints are none other than the true Christians who rise up to meet Him in the air, and then descend down to fight the enemy on the ground in Jerusalem.

Zechariah 1:14 So the angel that communed with me said unto me, Cry thou, saying, Thus saith the Master of hosts; <u>I am jealous for Jerusalem</u> and for Zion **[Israel]** with a great jealousy.

The Master is greatly concerned for Jerusalem, His holy city and his people of Israel to the point where he is jealous for his people and will fight for them in the last days.

Zechariah 1:15 And I am very sore displeased with the <u>heathen</u> that are at ease: for I was but a little displeased, and they helped forward the affliction.

The word "heathen" is a very strong reference to those people who think they are saved but are in affect <u>still dead in their sins</u> e.g. Muslims. These Muslims have furthered the affliction of His "people of Israel" i.e. slaughtered them with suicide bombs, killed them with Kassam rockets and shot them dead openly. Yet the world says that Israel has no right to defend itself. This is a popular theory proposed by the Arabs using the petrodollar to influence the world to propagate it's own opinions.

Note, some people may apply the word "heathen" to any unsaved person, but this is not the Master's application of this word. The Master is very angry that the people "round about" (Muslims) who have made the lives of Jewish people very hard and bitter. Other nations did not do anything about it either sitting by idly.

- ❖ **The Muslim nations round about want to destroy Israel and drive them out into the sea.**
- ❖ **Most Western nations sit at ease trying to either negotiate false peace deals, or put sanctions on Israel through the UN.**
- ❖ **Christians are lukewarm and do not really care. The church is in a state of pathetic disquiet inaugurating gay and lesbian bishops and proclaiming a**

social gospel, rather then the gospel of Yahushua for repentance and faith in the One who died on the cross and is alive. He will come back to judge these corrupt Christians and the rest of the world.

❖ Many of these Christians are into replacement theology i.e. the church replaces Jewish Israel and the Jews are simply not YHWH's concern anymore.

❖ Only a few Christians have a true understanding and stand in the gap for the Jewish nation, by being zealous for YHWH's chosen people, and His commandments by voicing a concern for Jewish Israel's safety.

Evils of replacement theology:
➢ Israel is not Israel anymore.
➢ Jerusalem is no longer holy.
➢ The gospel is conceptualized into some four steps/laws. Did the thief on the cross know the four laws/steps of salvation? We forget the daily relationship with the Master is not about the four laws, but a consistent pattern of repentance and walking in faith. The fruits (works) of the Spirit are to reflect our believing life. Yahushua emphasizes that we obey His commandments. Replacement theology advocates usually do not want to look at the commandments already given on Mount Sinai, yet abide by their own rules of believing conduct.
➢ The commandments are replaced with gentile ones.
➢ Yahushua is a western European as seen in many churches with blonde hair and nice blue eyes. The Jewish Yahushua is replaced with a Western Jesus.
➢ The Christian church has somehow replaced Jewish Israel and the future Temple.
➢ Some of the Catholics into Replacement theology say it like this: 'Mary is the ark of the new covenant.'
➢ Muslims on the other hand, the Palestinian ones, make Yahushua a Palestinian freedom fighter, who like themselves hated Jews.
➢ Muslims also engage in many forms of Replacement theology, teaching that the real Yahushua was simply created, was not YHWH, and never died on Golgotha.

Is it any wonder Yahushua said:

Matthew 7:13-14 "Enter by the narrow gate; for WIDE is the GATE [false prophets and teachers proclaim a social gospel] and **broad is the way [ALL ROADS LEAD TO GOD]** that **leads to destruction [TO HELL]**, and there are many [**MAJORITY OF THE WORLD**] who go in by it. Because NARROW [they way of Messiah] is the gate and difficult is the way which leads to life [**Yahushua the Messiah's way is not easy, as it leads to social problems at home, and persecution and hatred by the world, all because you have to live a holy life for YHWH**], and there are few who find it [**very few are willing to give up worldly things to live for YHWH**].

Hell is a real place and the torment and shame there is real. Many people who do not know the Master Yahushua will end up there and then it will be too late to come out. That punishment is permanent and everlasting and in my book, everlasting means just that, so that, that state is unchangeable. Just like Yahushua our Master is everlasting, so is Hell and so is Heaven. No one wants to talk about hell, as it is a depressing place with torment, so why bog down with the real deal.

Zechariah 1:16 Therefore thus saith the Master; I am returned to Jerusalem with mercies: my house shall be built in it, [literally the third Temple] saith the Master YHWH hosts, and a line shall be stretched forth upon Jerusalem.

The Master is going to return where? Did you say Europe? Excuse me? **No it is JERUSALEM! Why? Because that is where the Anti-Messiah and his Islamic confederacy will be gathering all the surrounding heathen nations.**

What house is going to be built? The third Temple of Jerusalem is going to be built in Israel on the Temple Mount.

Now we truly understand that the Messiah Yahushua descends to Jerusalem in London, right? No, **Jerusalem in Israel!** YHWH's covenant nation is still Israel and all true Christians are part of the true Israel of Yahweh.

Zechariah 14:3 Then shall the Master go forth, and fight against those nations, as when he fought in the day of battle.

The Master fights those nations [all Islamic and all mentioned in the Bible] that come up against Israel to destroy it to possess its land, so that they will be no more, i.e. the end of Islam.

Zechariah 14:12 And this shall be the plague wherewith the Master will smite all the people that have fought against Jerusalem [these are all mentioned in Psalm 83 and are all Islamic]; Their flesh shall consume away while they stand upon their feet, and their eyes shall consume away in their holes, and their tongue shall consume away in their mouth.

This is not an atomic bomb strike, as some incorrectly believe but rather a supernatural judgment from YHWH. He does not need to use nuclear missiles to do this type of damage. People forget that a nuclear strike on the mountains of Israel has the potential of killing many millions of Jews in Israel and rendering the land useless. The Master will not allow this to happen.

Zechariah 14:14 A supernatural plague will kill the people who come up to fight Israel and take Jerusalem. The only people who want to take Jerusalem for a possession are the Islamic nations. They are none other than the countries round about...and the wealth of **all the heathens round about** shall be gathered together;

Who are the heathens 'around about?'

It is the 52 nations containing the 1.5 billion Muslims ready to destroy Israel. YHWH calls them heathen because of their idolatrous practices, sorcery, often chanting the same words over and over again like pagans, being into all sorts of weird things, cutting off hands and feet, and beheading people etc, etc.

Those that survive will go to Jerusalem to pay their homage to the Elohim of Israel in His Temple:

Micah 4:2 And many nations shall come, and say, Come, and let us go up to the mountain of YHWH, and to the house of the Elohim of Jacob; and he will teach us of his ways, and we will walk in his paths: **for the law shall go forth of Zion, and the word of the Master YHWH from Jerusalem.**

The Law, YHWH's holy commandments, shall go forth from Zion i.e. greater Israel in Jerusalem where YHWH's holy mountain is, and where His third holy Temple will be rebuilt. There Messiah will rule forever with his people. So here the mountain is the center of His kingdom/Israel (the land and nation), the literal capital of YHWH's chosen holy city Jerusalem Our Creator wants to dwell with us, and tabernacle with us there.

Zechariah 2:10 Sing and rejoice, O **daughter of Zion** [Jerusalem]: for, lo, I come, and I will dwell in the midst of thee, saith the Master.

YHWH dwells in our midst i.e. our Master Yahushua the Messiah on earth amongst us once again in Jerusalem, while the daughter of Babylon/Mecca is completely destroyed.

Psalm 9:13-14 "Have mercy upon me, O Master; consider my trouble which I suffer of them that hate me [the Muslims hate the Jews day and night continuously plotting against them]. Thou that liftest me up from the gates of death: That I may show forth all Thy praise in the gates of the daughter of Zion: I will rejoice in Thy salvation."

The Master will have mercy upon His people who are hated for having His witness.

Zechariah 2:11 And many nations shall be joined to the Master in that day, and shall be My people: and I will dwell in the midst of thee, and thou shalt know that the Master of hosts hath sent me unto thee.

Many countries that confess Yahushua, as their Savior will be amongst YHWH's people, called His people, and will all personally know the Master Yahushua the Messiah.

Quite clearly, this is not allegoric but YHWH amongst us who is revealed in the person of Yahushua the Messiah sent by our Father in heaven.

Zechariah 2:12 And the Master shall inherit Judah his portion in the holy land, and shall choose Jerusalem again.

Jerusalem, YHWH's holy capital will once again be used for His purposes, where all people will flow for supplications and blessings.

2 Chronicles 6:6a; 7:16b :33:7b But I [YHWH] have chosen Jerusalem; that My Name may be there for ever: and mine eyes and mine heart shall be there perpetually...In this house, and in Jerusalem, which I have chosen before all the tribes of Israel, will I put my name for ever;

Why would YHWH give so many instructions in the Bible for an alleged rapture to occur before the tribulation, if it was not meant for us to endure it? It is important to realize that the reason for His instructions are precisely so that we prepare ourselves for this event and not be in any confusion so as to what to do when this day comes upon us. We should be building provisions for three and a half years to endure this event.

Those that are taught to believe that they will get taken out will not only be disappointed, but will face a lot more hardship then is necessary. The reason is simply because they did not prepare. They will be like those foolish virgins who did not recognize the coming of the bridegroom and did not put oil in their lamps. They were too busy with things in the world and thinking that we will just be taken out so why worry.

The Bible indicates that every person will be resurrected together and will all come out of the Great Tribulation one by one.

> **Revelation 7:14** And I said to him, "Sir, you know." So he said to me, "These are the ones who **come** out <u>of the great tribulation</u>, and washed their robes and made them white in the blood of the Lamb.

The Greek word "*erchomai*" **come** is a verb in the statement of **Revelation 7:14.** "These are they who "come" out of the great tribulation." The verb is in the <u>present tense</u>, which normally indicates <u>continuous</u> action. The people of the great multitude come out of the great Tribulation one-by-one through death, or preservation, not all at once as in the alleged rapture of the church.

The pre-wrath view is not accurate either, as it answers some questions, but still leaves us with problems. The early church fathers believed in a full tribulation and catching up/resurrection at the end of YHWH's wrath, not before, or during the 6th or 7th seal.

The angel reveals in Daniel 12:7 that the period is three and a half years and not 6.5 years of tribulation. Essentially the tribulation is **3.5-years** from the time the Anti-Messiah is revealed and it will run its entire course without any pre-wrath type rapture. That is not taught in Scripture.

Early in the third century Hippolytus wrote;

> 'Now concerning the tribulation of the persecution which is to fall on the church from the enemy (he has been speaking about the Antichrist and about the Antichrist's persecution of the saints and continues in the same vein). That refers to the 1,260 days (the half of the week) during which the tyrant is to reign and persecute the church (Treatise on Messiah and the Antichrist 60-61).'

One of the pre-wrath teachings is that the great multitude of Revelation 7:9-17 is the church which has just been raptured to Heaven between the sixth and seventh seals. The only problem with this view is that this must be a partial rapture of the church and not a full rapture.

> **Revelation 16:15** Behold, I come as a thief. <u>Blessed is he that watcheth</u>, and <u>keepeth his garments</u>, lest he walk naked, and they see his shame.

If no one is saved after the pre-wrath rapture, why does the 6th bowl imply that there are those on earth who are blessed, staying awake and keeping their garments?

> **Revelation 16:6** For they have shed the blood of saints and prophets, and thou hast given them blood to drink; for they are worthy.

The pre-wrath view is problematic and has many problems with it; if some are saved after the pre-wrath rapture then will they suffer the wrath of YHWH? Or are protected from it? If the pre-wrath people believe that they will suffer then they should explain why.

The seals, vials and trumpets are not successive, but occur simultaneously e.g. run parallel, look at the following table.

Event	6th Seal Rev. 6:12-17	7th Trumpet Rev. 11:18-19	7th Vial Rev. 16:18-19	Gog-MaGog Ezekiel 38:19-20
Earthquake	(verse 12) Great Earthquake	(verse 19) An Earthquake	(verse 18) Great Earthquake	(verse 20) Earthquake
YHWH's wrath	(verse 17) Great day of His wrath	(verse 18) Thy Wrath	(verse 19) His wrath	(verse 19) YHWH's wrath

The above are the same events described in different passages. If the pre-wrath people believe these are separate events, then we have four earthquakes and four wraths. We know that this is not true. **This indicates that the Book of Revelation is not in any chronological sequential order, as some have been led to believe. Also the judgements are not on the entire world, but are clearly restricted geographically.** It would take me another book to explain exactly what I mean by this, but you can research it for yourselves.

Now we understand the true meaning of what the catching up/resurrection is really about, do not just sit there please. Prepare for these things and you will be most wise to make some preparation to store some food that may help you in the hard times to come upon the world. You would be wise to secure your family by saving some dry food, grains, rice and some other foods that will not perish easily and will have a long shelf life.

Brief chronology of events-

- **The Islamic nations will gather around Israel to destroy it.**
- **Israel will be crushed to the point where half of Jerusalem is taken, women are raped, men are killed, children slaughtered.**
- **Israel's strength will be spent and now they cannot rely on their strength anymore.**
- **The remaining Jews cry out for the Moshiach (Hebrew for Messiah) realizing Yahushua is the Messiah. Baruch Ha ba B'Shem YHWH. (In Hebrew, blessed is he who comes in the Name of YHWH)**
- **The last trumpet, sound of the loud Shofar will be heard.**
- **Yahushua will descend to save his covenant people**

- **He will come with the angels, the elect (Those that are dead are raised to meet the Master in the air first, followed by Christians and Jewish believers in Yahushua, both gathered together, from all four corners of the world).**

- **The Master takes his flock, his bride, to Jerusalem and we will land in Jerusalem where the big battle is at hand.**

- Some of us will be fighting on the ground.

- The tribe of Judah is also fighting the enemy.

- The Anti-Messiah forces are defeated.

- The remnant of Jews that are left in Israel put their faith in Messiah and all of Israel is saved.

- The Third Temple is rebuilt by YHWH on the Temple Mount after its fascia enlarges to 8 miles by 3 miles as mentioned in Ezekiel 45.

- s.a.tan is bound in the abyss for 1000 years.

- 1,000 year reign.
- After the 1,000 years s.a.tan is once again released.

- s.a.tan goes out again and gathers another army of people described as the Gog and Magog second time round to deceive the nations, i.e. this is the second and last battle.

- This Master Yahushua will defeat this army.

- s.a.tan is now captured and thrown into the Lake of Fire.

- The world is renewed; we go into the eternal state.

Chapter 13

What Role Will the USA And the UK Play in the End Times?

Many prophecy students ask if the USA and the UK would be for or against the Anti-Messiah. Many scholars do not see either of these nations in the Scriptures, so they just write them off as insignificant. They think just because the UK is now having issues within the church (such as empty church pews, and bishops who have backslidden in the Master e.g. like the Bishop of Durham who does not believe Yahushua was born of a virgin), with things such as the inauguration of homosexual bishops and other key issues, that the UK is no longer significant. It may look as if this nation has gone bananas, but actually this is prophecy being fulfilled in front of our eyes, that is if we have the ability to see. This morning on radio an archbishop was asked a blunt question if homosexuals are born with their condition and the archbishop only gave a political answer. He did not state the truth that homosexuals are not born with their condition, but choose a lifestyle to live the unnatural way.

Friends this is not the end of England or the USA. This is prophecy being fulfilled in front of our eyes, but many cannot even see this.

In fact as these things are happening we are told to be strong in spirit.

2 Thessalonians 2: 1-2 Now we beseech you, brethren, by the coming of our Master Yahushua the Messiah, and by our **gathering together** unto him, That ye be **not soon shaken in mind**, or **be troubled**, neither **by spirit, nor by word**, nor by letter as from us, as that the **day of Messiah** is at hand.

Do not be troubled in spirit, mind, body, or by what you see out there. In fact rejoice that the time of our Master Yahushua the Messiah is very close at hand. He is coming soon... The good news is that Yahushua the Messiah is coming back soon, Hallelu-Yah to the Lamb of YHWH and our mighty King.

2 Thessalonians 2: 2-3 Let no man deceive you by any means: **for that day** shall not come, except there come a falling away first, and that man of sin be revealed, the son of perdition;

Some Key things in the passage above:

❖ Let no man, that means any man or woman deceive you in anyway even if he is a priest, pastor, deacon, or whoever does not matter.
❖ Or by any means that includes signs and wonders and false doctrine.
❖ For that day "descriptive of the day of the Master" will not come.
❖ Until the falling away has come e.g. many will become cold in their faith and leave Messiah, or deny Him altogether.

Note these things must come to pass. Hallelu-Yah, we know our YHWH is truthful. What we see should not discourage us but encourage us. You might think this is insane, but the Master knows all things beforehand and He wants us to be "switched on" and be encouraged.

288

So we know these things must come to pass. Many though will use this wrongly to teach the end of the church, as we know it and some will say that Christianity does not have the truth. But this is the exact opposite of what the Master is warning us about. We have the truth written down in the Bible and we must be vigilant, as these people who are the negativists will cause further falling.

As to the UK and the USA, unfortunately those who teach that both of these nations have no part in end time prophecy are very short sighted and do not fully appreciate Scripture. YHWH would not allow His once faithful servants the United Kingdom and the Unites States to just whither away. We need to be on course and not be living in la la land as most of Christendom is.

It is true that these nations are facing judgement for their wrong actions; the USA has just gone through a terrible hurricane Katrina. Why is this happening? This is judgement to correct them from error, because they wanted to divide the land of Israel and asked Israel to follow the road map to give the settlements in Israel away to the Muslims affectively rewarding them for terror. YHWH does not sit there like a hawk waiting for us to make one wrong move and pounce on us, but He has built His whole scenario around Israel. And woe to those who mess with the apple of His eye!

Imagine a computer program that is able to take predictive action based on certain user actions. Well guess what? This is how YHWH has designed the world. YHWH said I will bless those who bless you/Israel and curse those who curse you/Israel meaning the judgements will fall automatically as a result of our wrong actions. His end-time wrath will be different, as He will be fully involved and is now starting to show this.

❖ **Indonesia** was hit by a Tsunami in 2004– A Muslim nation lost over 370,000 people; no clear estimates as to how many died.
❖ **Pakistan** hit by a huge earthquake (2005) of biblical proportions – Hundreds of thousands died, the place is levelled.
❖ **Iran** – Hit by earthquake.

Notice now the time has come for active judgement not passive. All three of these nations are Islamic and have been persecuting the Christians; in my opinion other Islamic nations will be facing similar consequences soon. Yahweh is shaking the Muslim world a bit and showing who is in control. Unless the Muslims repent of their sins and their bloodshed, they will be facing a lot more earthquakes and calamities.

YHWH was not wrong when He said you shall not divide His land.

Leviticus 25:23 The land shall not be sold permanently, for the land is Mine; for you are strangers and sojourners with Me.

He will punish those that do divide His land because it has been given to His chosen people the Hebrews.

Joel 3:2 I will also gather all nations, and bring them down to the Valley of Jehoshaphat; and **I will enter into judgment** with them there on account of **My people, My heritage Israel**, whom they have scattered among the nations; **they have also divided up My land [Israel]**.

289

YHWH makes it very clear that He will judge those that divide His land. The passage also clarifies that His people here are the Jews and the land is Israel, so no one can misapply this passage.

YHWH is trying to show them what happens to people who are displaced from their land as many had to flee the Florida coastlines to save their lives during Hurricane Charley. YHWH in his utmost love is correcting these nations with these judgments, because YHWH will not destroy these nations as long as we have ten righteous men. This was the standard that YHWH used to judge Sodom and Gomorrah. Why would an eternal unchangeable YHWH change His standard of judgement for the USA or the UK, especially since these Israelite nations have a righteous and redeemed remnant of faithful bible believers? The same of course cannot be said for most Islamic nations, which hardly have a remnant of bible believers.

Was their not more corruption in Sodom and Gomorrah than in the USA and UK today? Was it not that YHWH could not find ten righteous men in Sodom and Gomorrah to spare judgement? I am sure if you look up and down in the USA you will find more then 10 men amongst the 80 million born again Christians made righteous by the blood of the Lamb that praise and worship the true YHWH. HalleluYah to the Lamb of YHWH, and the Master Yahushua the Messiah.

A loving father must correct his children when they are wrong, but that does not mean he stops loving them. In like manner these nations are having selective (not massive) judgments poured out upon them and YHWH is cleansing the rebels from these nations. The correct question should be how long will these judgments last?

We cannot be certain how long the judgments will last but we can make some intelligent calculations based on past performance e.g. how did YHWH judge Israel and for how long?

The same way when Israel sinned against the Master, and after warnings by the prophets, YHWH gave them over to the Babylonians as slaves and they served 70 years for the judgment of breaking His holy ordinances.

When the Jews rejected Yahushua their Messiah, once again YHWH judged them and took away their most precious possessions, including the land of Israel and the Temple as a prelude to their scattering. Forty years after their rejection of Yahushua without a cause came the judgment and then the worldwide dispersion.

When Israel disobeyed YHWH in the wilderness and murmured against Him, YHWH judged the Israelites. They wandered in the wilderness for forty-years as they were not allowed to enter the Promised Land. Only Joshua and Caleb were allowed to enter the land of milk and honey. Do you see the significance of this? Joshua was an Ephraimite and Caleb was a Jew who was worthy of his faith. Joshua and Caleb was a picture of the remnant of Israel's two houses that will be victorious over Islam at the end of the age. Joshua gives Hebron (Joshua 14:13) as an inheritance to Caleb as Joshua inherits parts of Mt Ephraim. A remnant of a nation spares the seed of that nation. Let's recall:

When Moses (Numbers 13) sent out the twelve to spy the land the ten spies came back disheartened and told the people that the walls were high and the people were giants too mighty to be defeated. Let us follow this story a bit.

Numbers 13:3-33 (3) So Moses sent them from the Wilderness of Paran according to the command of the Master, **all of them men who were heads of the children of Israel**. (17) So Moses sent them to spy out the land of Canaan, and said to them, "Go up this way into the South, and go up to the mountains, (18) "and see **what the land is like**: whether the people who dwell in it are strong or weak, few or many; (23) Then they came to the Valley of School, and there <u>cut</u> down a branch with one cluster of grapes; they **carried it between two of them on a pole**. They also brought some of the pomegranates and figs. (27) Then they told him, and said: "We went to the land where you sent us. It **truly flows with milk and honey**, and this is its fruit. (28) "Nevertheless the people who dwell in the land are strong; the **cities are fortified and very large**; moreover we saw the **descendants of Ana** there. (30) Then **Caleb** quieted the people before Moses, and said, **"Let us go up at once and take possession**, for we are well able to overcome it." (31) But the men who had gone up with him said, "We are not able to go up against the people, for they are stronger than we." (32) And they gave the children of Israel a bad report of the land which they had spied out, saying, "The land through which we have gone as spies is a land that devours its inhabitants, and all the people whom we saw in it are men of great stature. (33) "There we saw the giants (the descendants of Ana came from the giants); and we were like grasshoppers in our own sight, and so we were in their sight."

Numbers 14:6-10 (6) And Joshua the son of Nun and Caleb the son of Jephunneh, who were among those who had spied out the land, **tore their clothes**; (8) "If the Master delights in us, then He will bring us into this land and give it to us, `a land which flows with milk and honey.' (9) "Only do **not** rebel against the Master, nor **fear the people of the land**, for they are our bread; their protection has departed from them, and the Master is with us. Do not fear them." (10) And all the congregation said to **stone them with stones**. Now the glory of the Master appeared in the tabernacle of meeting before all the children of Israel. (24) "But My servant **Caleb, because he has a different spirit in him and has followed Me fully**, I will bring into the land where he went, and **his descendants shall inherit it**. (30) `Except for Caleb the son of Jephunneh and Joshua the son of Nun, you shall by no means enter the land which I swore I would make you dwell in. (33) `And your sons shall be shepherds in the wilderness **forty years**, and **bear the brunt of your infidelity**, until your carcasses are consumed in the wilderness. (34) `According to the number of the days in which you spied out the land, **forty days**, for each day you shall bear **your guilt one year, namely forty years**, and you shall know My rejection. (35) `I the Master have spoken this; I will surely do so to all this evil congregation who are gathered together against Me. In this wilderness they shall be consumed, and there they shall die.' "

Points to note;

❖ Twelve spies sent, each was the head of an Israelite tribe.
❖ They spied the land for forty days (Numbers 14:34).
❖ They cut down the "branch of grapes" that is so fruitful that it takes two men to carry one back, I believe this "branch of grapes" is still the symbol of the department for tourism in Israel signifying the land that is very fruitful, symbolic also of the Messiah Yahushua.
❖ The ten spies i.e. the majority is against the minority going into the land because they are afraid, they do not trust Yahweh.

291

❖ They see the Anakim who are described in verse 33 as giants.
❖ Caleb is ready to go in (Verse 30) as he is not afraid and says **let us go at once**. We must remember the minority is usually right.
❖ The congregation is ready to stone Caleb and Joshua because these two trusted in the Yahweh and wanted to "obey" Him, but the Master intervenes to protect them.
❖ Caleb trusted the Elohim of Israel "fully" (Numbers 14:24), no question about it.
❖ Yahweh punished Israel for their unbelief for forty years.

Caleb with his family defeated the land of the giants e.g. Hebron known as Kiriath-Arba and the lower plains. It was named after a giant called **Arba** who was Anak's father and his sons who were Ahiman, Sheshai, and Talmai. Arba was considered to be a great mighty man (Joshua 14:15). The Arabs are also considered to be great mighty people; the Hebrew word for Arab is "*Arabee*" the Hebrew word for locust is **Arbeh**. Rabbis use this for the Arabs, a fitting description for the Arabs.

Now the connection is this that these were not only Anak and his three sons, but they controlled Southern portions of the land of Israel. They were considered a **confederacy** that **Caleb** had to defeat and these were known as the mighty men of that area. When the 12 spies were sent into the land by Moses, it was these giants that put fear into Israel because they had a reputation.

> **Deuteronomy 9:2** A people great and tall, the descendants of the Anakim, whom you know, and of whom you heard it said, who can stand before the descendants of Anak?

Now recognize this that it was Caleb with his men who defeated these mighty giants, and many of them in quantities like the locusts [Arabs of today]. Now try applying this to our time. It will be those non-Jews like Caleb's family who joined Judah, who will once again defeat the (confederacy) giants, or the Arab nations gathered with other Muslim nations. Israel's enemies will be driven out of the land, and this is how Yahweh is going to use the USA and the UK as His mighty weapons. This is really amazing. This also rules out any notion of an alleged pre-tribulation rapture.

This is what the Master Yahushua said about the Centurion another righteous non-Jew/Roman.

> **Matthew 8:10-13** When Yahushua heard it, He marvelled, and said to those who followed, Assuredly, I say to you, **I have not found such great faith, not even in Israel!** And I say to you that **many will come from east and west, and sit down with Abraham, Isaac, and Jacob in the kingdom of heaven.** But the **sons of the kingdom** will be cast out into outer darkness. There will be weeping and gnashing of teeth.

This shows that many Gentiles will be joined to the Elohim of Israel and will show great faith in Him while some of the true covenant people and inheritors of the covenants are lost without Yahushua. Jews today face eternal death if they are not careful. It is very sad to read a passage like this and looking at the current state of Israel, it shows you that Ephraimites, non-Jews from the 10 northern tribes, have a big responsibility and part to play in Israel's future and the land. This is one of the reasons why we should pray for the Jewish people for them to recognize their Messiah Yahushua. To give them the gospel of Yahushua is so imperative for their eternity. We must take an active role in helping our

292

Jewish brethren. Some of us are biological Ephraimites and some are grafted into Israel, but largely the church is made up of Ephraimites, or the lost son of Luke 16, who went prostituting and is still in prostitution refusing to obey Yahweh and His commandments.

Going by the pattern of judgments for Israel, generally it usually seems to be a period of 40 to 70 years. The Diaspora of the Jews lasted almost 1,878 years, if we calculate the dispersion from 70 AD until their arrival back in their land in 1948 when Israel was recreated.

We can see two things. Firstly, that YHWH warns His people to stop doing the wrong things, if they do not listen, then He brings judgement in some form of calamity. Secondly, if they still refuse to listen, then He usually brings a foreign nation to invade them. In Jewish Israel's case Babylon took them captive and made them slaves, where as the Assyrians scattered the ten northern tribes of Israel earlier. The Grecians on the other hand tried to destroy their religion by desecrating the Temple, banning Judaism and forcing them to adopt Hellenistic culture by assimilation.

Let me show you some interesting points:

❖ Babylon changed the names of the Jews (Daniel 1:7); Name change means nature change. YHWH changed the name of Abram to Abraham and Sarai to Sarah so a name change means a nature change in Middle Eastern culture.
❖ Assyria assimilated the ten tribes (2 Kings 17:6,24).
❖ Greece banned Judaism.

Let's look at Islam:
❖ Converts change names, even Caucasian converts change names.
❖ They assimilate wearing Arab clothes thus Arabisation and learn Arabic.
❖ Islam bans them worshipping in any other religion, or even accepting other gods that includes the Elohim of Israel.

Do you see the three traits they are ALL present in Islam.

In the same way, the reason is obvious as to why Israel was judged harshly because they knew the Master **personally**, but still ignored His message. Is it any wonder they were making a golden calf after seeing so many wonders? This illustrates another good point that **signs** and **wonders** are not what we need, but rather we need faith in the Master Yahushua our Messiah, a living faith, in fact a **LIFE STYLE** not mere worship on Sunday alone. Those that focus on signs and wonders alone will at some point face disappointment. The Master can make signs and wonders if He wills, but that is not a standard for salvation, or something that we should be chasing after all the time. The standard for salvation is the **blood of the Lamb** "Yahushua the Messiah" and repentance and faith in Him.

These two nations (UK and USA) are also under limited judgment for not listening to YHWH. The judgment is proceeding because first they refused to listen and second they tried to divide YHWH's covenant people out of their land in Israel by trying to give it to the Muslim fanatic terrorists. YHWH first brought supernatural calamities and now the second portion, which is to bring a heathen nation [Muslims and the fanaticism] in to cause chaos and confusion. That of course is already happening. Does YHWH hate the Muslims? No, in fact, He is also desires to reach them to show them the truth of Messiah Yahushua, so they can be with Him in eternity. The question is will they listen?

293

European nations have like the USA have also sided with the Muslim people, whom YHWH calls heathens. He is using this heathen Empire to judge these western nations both from afar and from within. Those fanatic Muslims that live there are trying to destroy the true faith of the Master Yahushua the Messiah by trying to deceive the people into their false religion. They proclaim it as the only truth. They evangelize their faith by acting out in aggression and violence against these people. Europe is becoming more of Eurabia and this is the plan of the Arabs to turn these nations into Islamic nations. Great Britain will **never** become an Islamic nation because YHWH will never allow this to happen. Prophesy demands that both the USA and the UK are going to be used as the weapons of the Master's indignation upon the Middle East and the Anti-Messiah forces. The Anti-Messiah forces will be routed by these two nations in alliance in Israel's hour of need.

The Bible says a cord of three will not be broken.

Ecclesiastes 4:12 Though one may be overpowered by another, two can withstand him and a **threefold cord** is not quickly broken.
We certainly cannot pinpoint a date as to when this judgment will finish, but we can make somewhat of an educated calculation based on current events. A 40 or years 70 year time cycle can be expected taking into consideration the start of the judgment. There will be disagreement as to when the actual judgements started. Only YHWH knows when these will come to an end. But we can pray for an end sooner. My opinion is this that we are looking at a forty-year time span; we can see this pattern of judgement continuing for perhaps another 15 years based on the first major attack on the USA by the Islamists in 1979. For Britain it would be another 20 years based on the first policewoman shot by the Libyans in 1984 followed by the BSE crisis in 1986. This is by no means a measure of accuracy, but only an educated guess. You can do your own calculations, which perhaps may be more accurate than mine. This is at least what I see for the future of UK and the USA.

Do not expect to see things just turn in an instant. We will see things getting worse, but pray for these two nations so that the Master will have mercy on both the British and American peoples. Petition YHWH that they do not forget that blessings come from our sovereign YHWH only and not by appeasing the Islamic world or the UN. It is apparent that these were the two nations that were the driving power of Christianity to the rest of the world sending out missionaries. Though one cannot really call these Christian nations today, they still have the stump of the tree, i.e. the faith that they once showed the world and YHWH is perfectly capable of using them in His own time.

A. Is there evidence for UK and the USA in Bible Prophecy?

Isaiah 13:1-6 The burden against Babylon which Isaiah the son of Amoz saw. "Lift up a banner on the high mountain, raise your voice to them; wave your hand, that they may enter the gates of the nobles. I have commanded **My sanctified ones**; I have also **called My mighty ones** for **My anger those who rejoice in My exaltation.**" The **noise of a multitude** in the mountains [kingdoms, nations], like that of many people! A tumultuous noise of the **kingdoms of nations gathered together!** The Master of hosts **musters the army for battle. They come from a far country, from the end of heaven, even the Master and His weapons of indignation,** to **destroy the whole land.**

Wail, for the **day of the Master is at hand! It will come as destruction from the Almighty.**

The Master has mustered His armies from the far country the USA and the UK. They have come for the Master's "sanctified ones" the Jews and the Master calls these three nations His "mighty ones." Remember the cord of three cannot be broken easily in life or politics. This pattern has been repeated twice in the Gulf where the USA in coalition with the UK has gone to war with Iraq. However the last war to come with this same coalition will be more severe as Iraq will be completely destroyed and Saudi Arabia will lie in ruins. Do not forget Australia and New Zealand will be part of this alliance, seeing that both of these nations have British blood. Actually most of this alliance against the Islamic Anti-Messiah has Israelite blood and are English speaking, thus forming the "great company" of a great nation spoken of in Ezekiel 38 and Jeremiah 51.

The following symbols are used in Isaiah 13:1-6:

- ❖ **The High Mountain:** This is the symbol of the Temple-Mount, one day it will be an extremely high mountain.
- ❖ **My sanctified ones:** YHWH's chosen people, the root word here is Kadosh which means "set apart ones," He set Israel apart to be His covenant people.
- ❖ **My mighty ones:** YHWH's called out nations from Europe and the USA plus others with them as a coalition. There is no such thing as a "one-world government" in the Master's eyes. The only "one-world government" will come to pass only when the Messiah rules the earth upon His return.
- ❖ **Noise of a multitude:** The noise of a large army.
- ❖ **Kingdom of nations gathered together:** The Islamic confederacy out to destroy Israel.
- ❖ **Far country and end of heaven:** This is England, Italy, USA, Australia and Northern Russia, far points from Jerusalem.
- ❖ **Weapons of His indignation:** They have come for YHWH's Judgment and wrath on the Islamic invaders.
- ❖ **Destroy the whole land:** Iraq and Saudi Arabia part of ancient Iraq will be destroyed.
- ❖ **Day of the Master:** This signifies judgement on the people that hate Israel.

Jeremiah 50:2 "Declare among the nations, Proclaim, and set up a standard; proclaim, and do not conceal it Say, `Babylon is taken, Bel is shamed. Merodach is broken in pieces; her idols are humiliated, her images are broken in pieces.'

YHWH is declaring something amazing here; this is the end of Islam. Allah who was Bel of Babylon is finished and put to shame and all their idols are broken, i.e. no more Saudi Arabia or Mecca, no more Al-Aqsa Mosque and the Mosque of The Dome of the Rock. Remember that all of ancient Babylon today has been divided into several Muslin states and all these states are consumed, not merely Iraq. Bad news indeed for Mecca, the center of every unclean and HATEFUL bird according to Revelation 18:2.

Jeremiah 50:3 For **out of the north a nation** comes **up against her,** which **shall make her land desolate,** and **no one shall dwell therein.** They shall move, they shall depart, **both man (Mohammed) and beast (Islamic Empire revived).** [50]

Who is this nation out of the North? Great Britain the "**great nation**" that YHWH has called out, as I shall demonstrate in this book. See the European map above to see that the north country, or northern nation from Israel pointed to as the "**great nation**" is none other but Great Britain.

> **Jeremiah 50:4** "In **those days and in that time**," [future] says the Master, "The **children of Israel shall come**, [Ephraim] they and the **children of Judah together**; [Judah the Southern nation] with continual weeping they shall come, and **seek the Master YHWH their Elohim**.

This is yet future when the children of Israel [Ephraim/non Jewish Israel] and children of Judah [Judeans] will repent of their sins seeking their Messiah together; this is the second gathering of the Jewish nation from the Diaspora and the return of Ephraim, the other son of YHWH's two chosen families.

In **Jeremiah 50:9-11** we read this passage: **For, lo**, **I will raise** and cause to **come up against Babylon** an **assembly of great nations** from the **north country**: and **they shall set themselves in array against her**; from **thence she shall be taken**: **their arrows shall be as of a mighty expert man**; **none shall return in vain**. And **Chaldea shall be a spoil**: **all that spoil her shall be satisfied, saith the Master**. Because ye were glad, because ye rejoiced, **O ye destroyers of mine heritage**, because **ye are grown fat as the heifer at grass, and bellow as bulls**;

This is yet future when YHWH does these things...

- ❖ "**I will raise**" YHWH will <u>raise</u> these nations with good leadership to use them for His purposes.

❖ **"Come up against Babylon"** YHWH will call them up to Iraq; this has happened <u>twice</u> already in two Gulf Wars, but will happen again as a repeated pattern, as also mentioned in Isaiah 13.

❖ **"Assembly of great nations"** This can be none other but the UK and the USA with other partners from Europe. Italy would be a key ally also. The "ships of Chattim" incorporate lands all the way to Italy including Spain.

❖ **"From the north country"** This can only apply to the UK that is in the North Country, there is no other nation of this description in the "north country" that matches with its history or genre.

UK/USA Northern Alliance map

The UK has key bases at Cyprus that are visible in the UK/USA Alliance map above. In addition, the USA has bases in Europe including the United Kingdom. These bases will prove to be very favorable on the day these forces muster for an attack on the Anti-Messiah's Islamic forces to come through the straits of Gibraltar into the Mediterranean Sea, which poses a lot less risk than coming through the Gulf.

Their superior sea power and air power will be key in destroying the forces they are up against because **Jeremiah 50:9** says their arrows (precision bombs) shall not miss on that day.

> **Jeremiah 50:41** "Behold, <u>a people shall come from the north</u>, and a "<u>great nation</u>" [Great Britain] and <u>many</u> kings shall be raised up from the <u>ends of the earth</u> [USA with other nations].

This tiny nation (UK) whom YHWH calls a "**great nation**," is great for obvious reasons, as it had many blessings of YHWH upon it. The UK practically ruled the world once, yet when you look at its size now, it is much smaller than Texas. Was it not this "great nation" that decimated the large and best Armada Spain had to offer at a time when Spain ruled the ocean waves. Yet YHWH proved them wrong, by using a small nation to judge the mighty Spanish, whose Armada was sunk by British ships that were few in number.

This was Spain's judgement for cursing YHWH's covenant people (the Jews), by expelling them in 1492 and forcing them to convert to Roman Catholicism, or face death.

---

[51] www.prophecymaps.com

YHWH used the British Navy in 1588 as the weapons of **His indignation** to eradicate and sink Spain's great Armada under Queen Elizabeth I putting Spain out of business for good. Yahweh said in Genesis 12:3a I will curse those that curse thee, and this is literally fulfilled in that nation. Nevertheless YHWH will give Spain another chance to show themselves worthy.

To go to war with the Jews on the wrong pretext, is to go to war with Yahweh and inevitably one will face certain defeat. This is not because Israel is great, but because the Elohim of Israel, Yahweh Elohim revealed in Yahushua the Messiah, is a great YHWH. He will protect His own, even though at times He has given them over to judgment for their sins. Yet not all His people deserve judgement, and thus YHWH always protects His remnant.

The UK decimated the Argentinean air force with only 20 untested battle ready sea Harrier Jets that turned the war in their favor. Many at that time were saying the Harrier as a fighter is unworthy, clumsy, and overweight. But look what YHWH can do when He wants this "great nation" to win. He will turn the tide and the scoffers can scoff all they can.

> **Jeremiah 50:42** They shall hold the bow and the lance; they are cruel and shall not show mercy. Their voice shall **roar like the sea**; they shall **ride on horses, set in array**, like a man for the battle, against you, O **daughter of Babylon**.

This is it. Saudi Arabia will be history, the "daughter of Babylon." Finally the USA and the UK in alliance are upon it to destroy it for the evils it has done on the world and to the Jews for so long. They come with their ships fully equipped with warplanes, missiles and command great firepower. What does this tell those that scoff at the USA or the UK? It says that both these nations will be strong for the end time to play the role that YHWH has ordained.

There is no reason for YHWH to call the nation of the Anti-Messiah "great," as it is evil and has come to plunder and destroy Jerusalem. **Jeremiah 50:43** "**The king of Babylon has heard the report about them**, and **his hands grow feeble**; anguish has taken hold of him, pangs as of a woman in childbirth.

The end time King of Babylon (future king/leader of Iraq) is no other figure but the Anti-Messiah, who has heard the report and is not happy, but is rather afraid at this alliance that is mustered against him.

> **Jeremiah 50:44** "Behold, **he shall come up like a lion** from the flooding of the Jordan against the **habitation of the strong**; but I will make **them suddenly run away from her**. And who is a chosen man that I may appoint over her? For who is like Me? Who will arraign Me? And who is that shepherd who will withstand Me?"

- ❖ Who is like Yahweh?
- ❖ Who will accuse Yahweh?
- ❖ Which leader can withstand Him?

Rhetorical questions perhaps, but the answer is no one can withstand when Yahweh fights for both houses of Israel. The king of Babylon here is the figurative name for the Anti-Messiah who comes to fight. Instead of prevailing, he runs away as he faces defeat from the Master who has made it certain. Even s.a.tan cannot help him here because the

298

Master is on the side of the alliance of the USA and the UK coming together. Most probably Italy will be with them. The route to this war is Jordan and as I have explained the ships coming from the Mediterranean the "**ships of Chattim**" (Daniel 11:30) are the crucial link.

<u>Obadiah 1:21</u> Then saviors [USA and the UK together] shall come to Mount Zion to judge the <u>mountains of Esau</u>, and the **kingdom shall be the Master's. The point is made clear that saviors will come up to judge the "Mount of Esau"** (the Temple Mount now belonging to the Muslims) and these saviors are none other than YHWH's ordained nations, of which the UK and the USA are two of the most important ones listed here. Look at the following map below called the "**Final Battle Map**."

52

The Hebrew word for saviors "*Yaw-Shaw*" can also be translated as **deliverers**. These are YHWH's mighty weapons of indignation; the nations that He has mustered here include the Great nations of the USA and the UK together as an alliance. We know from history that although at one time these nations were bitter enemies, all that has changed. Since the friendship created between these nations from the days of the early Puritans, who were British settlers in the USA, these two have always stuck together like brothers. Other European nations like France and Germany have backed off any UK-USA alliance. They own a poor record of not supporting a coalition against terror, especially now that they are considered appeasers of the Arabs. They are not all out fighters of terror. We can see also how Italy has stuck together with the coalition, even though other nations around it refused to stand together. We will see the same alignment throughout the end-times as is seen today. Still many people see Rome as the Anti-Messiah nation, but this is not true, not by any biblical standard.

> **Micah 5:5** And this man shall be the peace, when <u>the Assyrian</u> shall come into our land: and when he shall tread in our palaces, then shall we raise against him **seven shepherds**, and **eight principal men**.

This is the Anti-Messiah's humiliating defeat to come. He is called the Assyrian here, so this text rings out in its simplicity that the Anti-Messiah is not Roman or American. If there is a "one-world government" then YHWH has and will yet raise His shepherds. He said He is going to raise **seven shepherds** and **eight principle men**. Hang on a minute! Is it not taught by many that there will be <u>no</u> righteous leaders in the world who will not be part of

---

the alleged one world government? If all the world is corrupted, everyone would then be under the control of s.a.tan. Try asking the "one-world government" theorists how is it that YHWH has managed to raise these **seven** shepherds and eight principle men out of a corrupt "one world government," especially if the whole world is supposedly locked under s.a.tan's control? The "one-world government" theory is erroneous leading people into error and causing many to look at the wrong things. This wild and unbiblical theory does not fit with the words of Yahweh.

The seven shepherds of Micah 5 in my opinion are these:

- ❖ **USA**
- ❖ **UK**
- ❖ **Italy**
- ❖ **Spain**
- ❖ **Australia**
- ❖ **Northern Russia**
- ❖ **South Korea**

The seven principle men are the leaders of these nations and the eighth is none other than the Messiah Yahushua Himself. The clue of the 8th principle man is in the verse where it says, "**this one shall be peace**," the Hebrew word for this is "*shalom,*" which is literally applied to the Messiah of Israel. He will bring true peace to Israel by crushing Her enemies, led by **the Assyrian** in this passage who is the Anti-Messiah. Look at the ships of Chattim (Daniel 11:30). These incorporate some of these nations with other references in the Bible supporting this view. Pacifist Christians unfortunately do not understand the Bible to realize that peace never comes without a struggle or war for it. The Bible shows that the final peace will also come when a war is fought against evil and evil will be defeated. Those Christians who want to waste time in Iraq trying to establish peace will fail because Babylon is the place of severe wickedness. Wars sadly sometimes must be fought, or else we would have evil reigning instead. Kind David and King Solomon knew this all too well. The Torah even gives much instruction to the Commonwealth of Israel on how to wage war fairly, with mercy and justice. In the final battle of Armageddon, the end time redemption of a remnant of both Muslims and Israel is tied to YHWH manifesting His power over evil. He does that as the Warrior on the white horse in the Book of Revelation, who unlike the Muslim Anti-Messiah, wars to deliver and not to destroy. Both houses must repent as ordained by Scripture and see Messiah defeat the Muslims. Most likely about 1/6 of the Islamic army will be saved from the two hundred million army crossing the Euphrates in the Islamic attack against Jerusalem (Ezekiel 39:2).

> **Daniel 11:30** For "**ships from Cyprus/Kittim**" shall come against **him**; [the Anti-Messiah] therefore he shall be grieved, and return in rage against the holy covenant, and do damage. So he shall return and show regard for those who forsake the holy covenant.

Holman Bible Dictionary describes "Kittim" as follows:

(Kit' tihm)[53]-Tribal name for the island of Cyprus, sometimes spelled Chittim. This name was derived from Kition, a city-state on the southeastern side of the island. Long associated with maritime lore, the island was ruled first by Greece, **then**

---

[53] http://www.studylight.org/dic/hbd/view.cgi?word=kittim&action=Lookup

the **Assyrians**, and finally, Rome. Genesis 10:4 traces the people's roots to Noah's son Japheth. Jeremiah and Ezekiel both mention it in their prophecies (Jeremiah 2:10; Ezekiel 27:6; compare Isaiah 23:1,Isaiah 23:12).

Kittim is used in intertestamental writings as denoting **all of the land west of Cyprus**. 1 Maccabees credits it as being the land of Alexander the Great (1 Maccabees 1:1; 1 Maccabees 8:5). The writer of Daniel understood it to be a part of the Roman Empire (Daniel 11:30) used to threaten Antiochus Epiphanes. The Dead Sea Scrolls contain several references to Kittim, the most notable being the defeat of her people (Romans) at the hands of YHWH's people.

Lands west of Cyprus are all considered part of Kittim, this is also why we know for sure that the USA is part of this western alliance, but we are given other Scriptures to be certain.

-- New Jerusalem with Apocrypha

Daniel 11:30 "The [war] ships of the Kittim will oppose him," and he will be **worstened**. He will retire and take furious action **against the holy covenant** [both houses] and, as before, will favor those who forsake that holy covenant [Islam].

Interesting how the New Jerusalem phrases it, not only will "war ships" oppose him (The Anti-Messiah), they are far more than ordinary ships. This will be a turning point in the war that he has against Israel. This will show those who actually truly stand for Israel and those who do not care for Israel. **The Bible tells us that these Kittim nations are for Israel and are the shepherds of Israel at this most difficult time.** This is why we have to be careful when we say the whole world is against Israel! We must qualify what we mean by "whole world" because theologically this is impossible. When the Anti-Messiah is defeated in this battle, he will even become angrier because the agreement he had made was that Israel had a political right to exist. But in reality he wanted to destroy Israel in his timing. Therefore these nations that will oppose him actually shamed him in front of everyone else. Who do you think will lead this coalition of Kittim nations? It will most likely be the USA closely followed by the UK forces plus the others I have described above who the Master calls part of a coalition, or company of great nations.

Jeremiah 51:25 Behold, I am against thee, **O destroying mountain**, saith the Master, **which destroyest all the earth**: and I will stretch out mine hand upon thee, and **roll thee down from the rocks**, and will **make thee a burnt mountain**.

Points to note:

- ❖ The allegory of the "destroying Mountain" is the kingdom of Islam.
- ❖ She destroys the whole world by her corrupt false religion.
- ❖ Yahweh will destroy her and He will do it through His sanctified ones.

THE WHOLE WAR IS ABOUT THE PROMISED INHERITANCE!

Jerusalem is a Hebrew word and if you ask many Christian pastors you'll find that most of them translate it as "city of peace." This is what is commonly taught in churches and is the accepted translation. In the Hebrew it reads Yahrushalayim, or Yah's "**inheritance of peace**," not "city of peace" as is erroneously taught in many churches. The word to inherit is the Hebrew word "yarash." This is one of the root words in the word "Jerusalem," apart from "rosh" that means "head." It does not contain the Hebrew word for city, which is eer, thus it cannot mean city of shalom. Moreover it has mostly been the city of wars and desolations in its history. This inheritance is what the Muslims are fighting for and clearly we can see this in the name of this place, the very thing these people fight for. An illegal and illegitimate inheritance at that! According to Yahweh, this inheritance belongs to the children of Israel. Of course these heirs cannot be Arab Muslims, since they never accepted Yahweh as LORD, but they worship the god of the desert, namely Allah.

> **Numbers 34:2** Command the children of Israel, and say unto them, When ye come into the land of Canaan; (this is the land that shall fall unto you for an inheritance, even the land of Canaan with the coasts thereof:)

Yahweh gave them their inheritance. Ultimately the children of Israel themselves are an "inheritance" on to Yahweh.

> **Deuteronomy 4:20** But the Master hath taken you, and brought you forth out of the iron furnace, even out of Egypt, to be unto Him a **people of inheritance**, as ye are this day.

Now it should make sense that a "**people of inheritance**" e.g. Israel will receive a "**city of inheritance**" e.g. **Jerusalem**. The only person who would hate this idea is s.a.tan and this is why he is deceiving Muslims to remove that inheritance.

The "inheritance" was not simply Jerusalem but the whole land of Canaan that is today called Israel.

> **Deuteronomy 32:8-9** When the most high divided to the nations their inheritance, when he separated the sons of Adam, he set the bounds of the people according to the number of the children of Israel. (9) For the Master's portion is His people; Jacob is the **lot of His inheritance**.

> **Genesis 15:7** And he said unto him, I am the Master that brought thee [Abraham] out of Ur of the Chaldees, to give thee this land to inherit it.

The "children of Israel" simply inherited what was given to their forefathers as an everlasting promise. Abraham sent all his other children away to the east only leaving the inheritance for Isaac from whom the Israelite nation has descended.

> **Genesis 25:6** But unto the sons of the concubines, which Abraham had, Abraham gave gifts, and sent them away from Isaac his son, while he yet lived, **eastward, unto the east country [from where Islam will attack Jerusalem, seeking to gain the inheritance by bloodshed]**.

Muslims would do well to read these passages and should stop fighting with the inheritance that is given to B'nai Israel. s.a.tan himself is going to the "pit" (hell) so he wants to take the Muslims with him to the "pit" (hell).

The only reason I believe the USA/UK are significant is that Bible prophecy agrees with this seen in such key end time passages as Jeremiah 51:27/Isaiah 13.

302

These nations are intrinsically, historically as well as prophetically linked to the freedom of Jerusalem. Let us not forget that it was the British General Allenby Walker who **freed Jerusalem from the Turks** and England who mandated the land of Palestine to create the new State of Israel. General Allenby Walker had the Welsh Regiment with him. It has been the USA that has stood firmly beside Israel to help her in her time of need and today the only country that openly supports Israel. When Osama bin Laden threatened the USA just before the 2004 elections, he made mention of the USA helping Israel and warned the USA to distance itself from Israel, or to expect even more attacks.

What about the Australian connection?

Historically, the Light Horse division [54] also played a major role in the battle and freedom of Jerusalem. These were the mounted soldiers of Australia; This Aussie connection is not much remembered, but nevertheless they played a key role in the past liberation of Jerusalem. In fact the 10th Light Horse division were the first mounted troops to enter the city. http://www.lighthorse.org.au/military/msa.htm And I quote:

The Master of Armageddon

At Beersheba, the Light Horse had shown themselves to be superb cavalrymen. Now, at their own request, nine regiments were armed with swords and rushed through cavalry training. Then they waited, hidden among coastal orange and olive groves, while Allenby - like a brilliant chess player - prepared for his winning move.

Everything told the **Turks** he was getting ready to attack in the east. Empty camps and long lines of dummy horses were laid out in the Jordan Valley. Infantry marched down into the valley each day - and marched out again each night. A Jerusalem hotel was taken over and set up as a fake headquarters.

Then, in September 1918, Allenby struck near the coast. He pounded the **Turks** with an artillery bombardment; broke their line with the infantry, and Chauvel sent his huge mounted force through the gap to sweep around behind the enemy.

The **retreating Turks** were further battered by aerial attacks. Dazed, bewildered, they streamed down from the Samarian Hills in their thousands. In three days 15,000 prisoners were taken. Within the fortnight, three complete armies were smashed and there were 75,000 prisoners.

"Banjo" Paterson had brought horses up for the great drive. He described how **captured Turkish soldiers** who hadn't eaten for three days, sat down silently to accept their fate. He commented: "Neither English nor Australian troops had any grudge against the Turks, and the captured 'Jackos' were given more food and more cigarettes than they had enjoyed during the whole war."

The Turkish commander had refused to eat until his troops were fed. Said Paterson: "Even in his worn and shabby uniform he could have walked into any officer's mess in the world and they would have stood up to make room for him."

---

[54] http://www.lighthorse.org.au/military/msa.htm

This crippling defeat was centred on the plain of Megiddo - the biblical Armageddon where a last terrible battle would be fought on the Day of Judgement. This will be the Turkish Anti-Messiah against the UK-USA alliance, as history once again is seen to repeat itself, as Jerusalem is liberated for a final time!

When Allenby was made a Master, he took as his title **Viscount Allenby of Megiddo. He was, literally, the Master of Armageddon.** The great drive continued against the Turks' last remaining bastion, Damascus in Syria. Covering 700 kilometres in 12 days, the Desert Mounted Corps thrust at the ancient city.

After a terrible massacre of retreating Turks in the Barada Gorge, Damascus fell on 1 October, almost without a fight. The 3rd Brigade, which had been shot to pieces at The Nek three years before, rode straight through the city, pausing only to receive its surrender. A single squadron of the 4th Regiment took 10,000 prisoners with only a few shots fired and an officer and three men wounded.

Damascus was a crowded, unhealthy place and epidemics of influenza and malaria swept through the Desert Mounted Corps. Dozens of men who had survived Anzac and the desert campaigns, died in hospital beds.

But the great move to the north continued - almost to the Turkish border. The Turks saw that further resistance was hopeless and signed an armistice. On October 31 the war in the east was over, 11 days before the armistice on the Western Front.

Before the Light Horse left for Australia, Allenby wrote a remarkable tribute to them. It concluded: "The Australian light horseman combines with a splendid physique a restless activity of mind. This mental quality renders him somewhat impatient of rigid and formal discipline, but it confers upon him the gift of adaptability, and this is the secret of much of his success mounted, or on foot. In this dual role, the Australian light horseman has proved himself equal to the best. He has earned the gratitude of the Empire and the admiration of the world."

Eventually, late in 1919, the last of the Light Horse were back in Australia. The regiments broke up. The men returned to homes and families and farms and jobs.

This should leave us in no doubt as to why Australia will once again be part of the end-time coalition to fight the Anti-Messiah's forces. This should include our good friends the New Zealanders with them. It was in 1770 that an Englishman by the name of Captain James Cook, aboard the Endeavour, extended a scientific voyage to the South Pacific in order to further chart the east coast of Australia and claim it for the British Crown. The same person was also involved in colonizing New Zealand. Both Australia and New Zealand have British blood, so why would they not be part of the coalition.

Jeremiah 50:46 At the noise of the taking of Babylon the earth trembles, and the cry is heard among the nations.

304

Babylon is destroyed by these nations and the world gets to hear about it and is surprised at how can this be. The Anti-Messiah forces taste a big defeat here.

> **Jeremiah 50:23** How the **hammer of the whole earth** has been cut apart and broken! How <u>Babylon has become a desolation</u> among the nations! I have laid a snare for you;

How the "**hammer of the whole world**" is broken is a reference to the fact that this false religion of Islam and its fanatic adherents has made the whole world a troublesome place with suicide bombings, terrorism, plane hijackings, and blowing up buildings. But now this hammer <u>literally</u> is broken, as it was hitting different parts of the world, as Yahweh will judge it, eventually breaking it apart. Not only they controlled the nations e.g. politically with the oil they sold, but also they sold them the false religion of Islam and put people into spiritual bondage, thus also a kind of slavery to sin. Finally the hammer has been broken. Yahweh has allowed this "hammer" to strike the different nations in times past, simply because these nations betrayed Him and the people backslid into idolatries.

For the Islamic nations it is **Yah's way, or NO WAY, and** certainly not Allah's way, as that heads to hell and damnation. Scripture stares us straight in the face. If Islam was the truth, then why the need for the Muslims to head deep under the earth into the pit!

Judgment on the Islamic nations and their DESTINY in Hell

(Note these Scriptures speak of the multitudes, but we know because of Yahweh's mercy a remnant of Muslims will inherit the kingdom as seen in such places as Isaiah 19 and elsewhere.)

Egypt is thrown into hell.

> **Ezekiel 32:18 18.**Son of man, wail for the multitude of Egypt, and cast them down, even her, and the daughters of the famous nations, unto the **nether parts of the earth**, with them that **go down into the pit**.

Assyrian is thrown into hell; this includes modern day Iraq/Syria, Lebanon and parts of Turkey.

> **Ezekiel 32:22** Asshur is there and all her company: **his graves are about him**: all of them slain, fallen by the sword:

Iran is thrown into hell.

> **Ezekiel 32:24** There is Elam [Iran] and all her multitude round about her grave, all of them slain, fallen by the sword, which are gone down uncircumcised [in heart] into the nether parts of the earth, which caused their terror in the land of the living; yet have they borne their shame with them that go down to the pit.

Turkey and Southern Russia are thrown into hell.

> **Ezekiel 32:26** There is Meshech, Tubal, and all her multitude: her graves are round about him: all of them uncircumcised [in heart], slain by the sword, though **they caused their terror** in the land of the living.

Jordanians are thrown into hell.

Ezekiel 32:29 There is Edom, **her kings**, and all her princes, which with their might are laid by them that were slain by the sword: they shall lie with the uncircumcised [in heart], and with them that go down to the pit.

Lebanon is thrown into hell.

Ezekiel 32:30 There be the princes of the north, all of them, and all the **Zidonians**, which are gone down with the slain; with their terror they are ashamed of their might; and they lie uncircumcised [in heart] with them that are slain by the sword, and bear their shame with them that go down to the pit.

Can anyone argue with Scripture that these manifold judgements are not on Islamic nations? The failure of Muslims to repent means that the eternal destiny that awaits them is hell. All the talk of a Muslim revival, or a sudden mass conversion of Muslim nations to fill up churches is merely an illusion of the mind. I have no doubt that Muslims will come to faith individually, though few in numbers. But there will be no such mass conversions in entire nations.

The Bible is clear that Armageddon requires Islamic nations to be active on the attack. If there is a large shift in Islamic countries to Christianity, then where o where is the prophesied Islamic army that will come up, whom the Bible clearly labels as Islamic as the revived Ottoman Empire? Surely many have gotten their math wrong, as the two hundred million-man army of Muslim fighters crossing through Iraq, indicate that the majority of the world's 1.5 billion Muslims will not be saved. There will be a revival, but that will be on the mountains of Israel, when Yahweh smites them and leaves just one sixth out of the two hundred million physically alive that in my rough estimation is 33 million Muslims. These 33 million may in fact have the chance to receive and or proclaim Messiah as their Savior. The rest will end up in hell. This is may be hard to swallow, but this is Scripture my friends, so we had all better believe it. Those who join with the Muslims [the mark and name and worship of the beast] will also go to hell. Armageddon is not just about a war, but in it is tied the redemption plan of YHWH for many million Muslims and Jews who are lost without the Messiah. At this battle many hearts and eyes will be opened.

Ezekiel 39:7 So will **I make My [kadosh] holy Name** known **IN** the midst of My people Israel; and I will not let them pollute My holy Name any more: and the heathen [surrounding heathen] shall know that I am the Master, the Holy One **IN** Israel.

A few important things in the above verse.
Yahushua the Messiah is on the ground in Israel and in the middle of Israel, or more accurately the Temple Mount region from where He will rule and reign. He calls the Jews and Ephraimites MY people. Well these are ghastly words for those teaching replacement theology both in the Muslim and Christian worlds. It is apparent that the both houses are presently polluting His holy NAME. Thus this promised ending of spiritual pollution will not occur again until after His return. They will know that He is YHWH **IN** Israel i.e. He has finally landed on the Mount of Olives as promised.

Jeremiah 49:21 The earth is moved at the noise of their fall, at the cry the noise thereof was heard in the "**RED SEA**."

The earth is moved at the noise of their fall, and guess where the cry is heard? Oh see, it is the Vatican in Europe! See I told you so (smile). **No my friend this is in the "Red Sea," right in the heart of the Middle East, on the BORDER OF MECCA! See any world map for this proximity.**

The judgement is active on the Islamic nations. Is this near Saudi Arabia, New York, Washington, or Europe? The Master has made it <u>absolutely</u> clear that the judgement is set and the destruction of Saudi Arabia is in sight and not Europe or the USA! Those who teach full scale national end time judgement on Europe, or the USA, or that the end time Anti-Messiah will be coming from Europe, are not only interpreting prophecy incorrectly, but are misguiding others. To be fair to them maybe they do not deceive deliberately, as this is what they have been taught to believe.

The problem is most people in the west have been brought up with a Hellenistic worldview and look at prophecy with a western mindset and this is a huge drawback. Look and be sure that the Master Himself is not misleading us by telling us that it is the "**Red Sea**" which is near MECCA in Saudi Arabia. Yet most prophecy teachers want us to believe that this is Rome, Brussels, or New York, which remains an untenable and unrealistic position. The judgement in the Middle East is not just on Saudi Arabia the **harlot daughter of Babylon,** but also on other Islamic nations as far as Pakistan and Indonesia, as they are part of the religious system and part of those who oppose the covenant with both houses of Israel.

All those that teach that the Anti-Messiah alliance will be from Europe, should show us from Scripture even just one nation that YHWH will judge in Europe in the promised end-time WW III. The problem with their argument is that they have no evidence to back up their claims. When asked they cannot show even "one" nation mentioned by name that is European, or western, when all along YHWH's wrath is on the Islamic nations that are ALL mentioned by name and by region and by city by the prophets of Israel! We cannot be mistaken as to their identity, if we choose not to be mistaken.

These preachers should read what the Bible has to say and be good shepherds to their flock. I know there maybe a certain amount of pride involved with some of these Bible teachers. They might think that they have written several books on the European or the USA view and that it would be embarrassing and near impossible to change. This should not be a problem, as it is very easy to say 'sorry I was wrong and apologize.' That is the sign of a humble and godly man. Just recently I saw this with my own eyes and heard it with both my ears. A pastor in a church, who was teaching the European view, after my discussion with him and after his searching the Scriptures, saw his serious error. He apologized to his congregation by saying "I am sorry I was wrong." May YHWH bless him for being forthright with his flock. It is interesting to know that the Master YHWH gave us two ears and not one so that we can listen more intently. The inner ear contains balance and equilibrium and these help us to stay upright. The Bible says in **Judges 5:3**:

"**Hear, O kings! Give ear**, O princes! I, even I, will sing to the Master; I will **sing praise to the Master Elohim of Israel**.

It is very clear that the Master is asking the **kings of the earth** to listen carefully, to pay heed to the Master's words, so they can make wise decisions and have balance in their life. And not only in their lives, but they will also be affecting the lives of many other people whom they rule or influence.

307

B.   A Further look into the ships of Kittim. Are they really Western powers?

> **Daniel 11:30** For the **ships of Chittim** [UK and the USA forces] shall come against him [the Anti-Messiah]: therefore he shall be grieved, and return, and have indignation against the holy covenant: so shall he do; he shall even return, and have intelligence [unity] with them that forsake the holy covenant.

The ships of Kittim will include other EU nations such as Italy & Spain.

> **Numbers 24:24** And **ships shall come from the coast of Chittim** [from Cyprus to Italy, UK and USA plus Spain], and **shall afflict Asshur** [Syria, Iraq and parts of Turkey], and shall afflict Eber, and he also shall perish forever.

More likely France will come to its senses and will be an ally including Belgium, Germany, Denmark and Holland. This will be a fight for Europe's very survival and will have nothing to do with these nations suddenly choosing Christianity as a religion. YHWH is actively and yet only PARTIALLY judging these western nations now for their gross idolatries. Guess through whom? Islam is delivering the blows; recognize it if you can. The only trouble with people is they do not want to hear the word judgement but judgement it is. I can safely say we will see at least two nuclear strikes in the Middle East prophesied in the Bible. I can also tell you that Al-Qaeda is planning to blow up cities in Europe and a heavy attack on the USA is in the pipeline, with dirty bombs that Al-Qaeda is known to have purchased through their Chechen contacts.

Here is a likely scenario: Al-Qaeda, or similar affiliated groups strike the mainland USA with one, or several dirty bombs and end up killing thousands perhaps millions. The most likely target is New York and Washington. New York also has a large liberalist godless population that will be affected. The people who would then survive will end up being dismayed and will then choose a radical president that will be ready to fight Al-Qaeda and will declare the Islamist ideology as evil, as opposed to the politically correct term used now "the war on terror." We can start to see how the USA could be brought into large-scale action. As for Europe, once a major city is hit with some serious bombings that will begin to wake up Europe, such as the riots in France have woken up the lack lustre French. Yet I do see a bigger strike yet to come. Sources close to me inform me that an attack is being planned for 2,007, though now a days it is very difficult to know which country and city. This information is not given until only a few days before the attack. The only ones who know what they are planning are very close top Al-Qaeda lieutenants.

My premise is built on Scripture illustrating verses such as **Daniel 11:30** and **Numbers 24:24**. Do not also forget the verses in Jeremiah and Ezekiel, which point to western nations coming to Israel's rescue before the coming of our Master. These northern nations only fit the USA and the UK. Praise YHWH that He will use these nations as the weapons of **His indignation** against Babylon.

The Jewish/Roman historian Josephus Flavius identifies Chittim [Kittim] as Cyprus whose ancient capital was called Kition by the Greeks.[55] **This extended all the way to lands west of Syria, all of Greece including Illyricum and Italy. None of these lands today are Islamic.**

[55] New International Standard Bible Encyclopedia

The name Kittim was used for the Phoenician port of Citium in Cyprus mentioned in the Dead Sea Scrolls. This term "Kittim" was used for the Romans in Daniel 11:30 although it also has future application, because we all know that the Romans had their western capital in Italy. If we conclude that the Anti-Messiah is a western Roman from Italy, then I am afraid he is fighting himself, as a kingdom divided will not stand. This poses many problems for those that believe the Anti-Messiah must come from Rome, but not for us, as we know he is not a Roman but a Grecian, a land that was shared by the eastern leg of the Roman Empire and encompassed the whole Middle East.

Interestingly the "people of the prince" who destroyed the Jewish Temple in 70 AD were all from the Middle East region from the following group of eastern Roman legions, specifically legion X, that destroyed the Temple in the Roman army. This further points us to east not the west as the forces of the future Anti-Messiah assemble.

- ❖ **Thracum Syriaca E.**
- ❖ **IV Cohort Thracia.**
- ❖ **Syria Ulpia Petraeorum.**
- ❖ **IV Cohort Arabia.**

The ones who destroyed the Temple in 70 AD are the very ancestors of the Anti-Messiah to come, as we see the evidence for this in Daniel 9:27. The word "he" is mentioned who will "confirm the covenant." Titus did <u>not</u> confirm any covenant; neither is "he" coming back from the dead to do this, although some would like this to help in their prophecy fulfilment. Thus the "he" in verse 27 has to be the same person in verse 26 "**the prince that shall come,**" If it was fulfilled in Titus alone, then the prophecy fails because Titus did not make a covenant with Israel because there is no text breaks between verses 26 and 27. The "he" has yet to make the covenant and there are no time gaps so we cannot say that this involves a time gap of 2000 years. In the Hebrew text this will not hold and it reads as a continuous verse. We should remember the numbering was put in the Bible later to help us read the Bible, but it was not there in the beginning.

Daniel 9:27 "And **he shall confirm** the covenant with many for one week." This "he" is referring to the same person in verse 26 "the prince that shall come."

It is a stretch of the imagination of prophecy writers to fit this to Titus; again the same rules apply to **Daniel 11**.

Daniel 11:37 "He shall regard **neither <u>the gods</u>** of his fathers nor the <u>desire of women</u>, nor regard any god; for he shall magnify himself above them all.

He does not worship the "gods" (plural) of his fathers, or forefathers simply because he will worship Allah who was instituted by Muhammad as a singular god. Remember the Arab fathers worshipped many deities in the Ka'ba; at least 360 idols. Muhammad had those idols smashed for them to worship Allah alone as an unseen god.

"The <u>Elohai of his fathers</u>, or <u>gods</u> of his fathers"

The Hebrew word in **Daniel 11:37** for God is in the plural "*Elohai,*" meaning "gods." **The Anti-Messiah does not worship the many idols of his forefathers in the Kaba before Muhammad**. But like Muhammad, as Muhammad's end time spokesman, he is supernaturally empowered by the Dragon/s.a.tan to make the beast's teachings come alive. He worships the same demon-god that Muhammad proclaimed as truth. We know him as Allah, the god of jihad (war on non-Muslims), referred to in **Daniel 11:38** as the "god of fortress/jihad and sheer brutality."

This is not the same as Yahweh, who is called the ROCK and FORTRESS OF DEFENCE for the righteous who willingly forsake evil.

> **Psalm 31:2** Bow down Your ear to me, Deliver me speedily; Be my Rock of refuge, **a fortress of defence** to save me.

Here Yahweh is described as a fortress. The Hebrew word is "mets-oo-daw" which is more akin to a defence like a castle or tower where you can take refuge and roam around freely, fully safe from your enemies. So if you are abiding in Yahushua, then you are safe from your enemies. You should have no fear because Yahushua the Messiah has driven that fear out through His perfect love.

> **1 John 4:18** There is **no** fear in love; but **perfect love casts out fear**, because fear involves torment. But he who fears has not been made perfect in love.

The word used in **Daniel 11:38** for the god of fortress is the Hebrew "maw'oze" that more appropriately means a "stronghold" i.e. a supernatural negative stronghold. This bondage is where a person is imprisoned in chains, and is certainly <u>not</u> the fortress we need and should avoid altogether. The New American translation describes it most accurately.

> New American with Apocrypha:
> **Daniel 11:38** Instead, he shall give glory to the **god of strongholds**; a god **unknown to his fathers he shall glorify with gold, silver, precious stones, and other treasures.**

Paul described this god in the following verse:

> **2 Corinthians 4:3-4** (3) But even if our gospel is veiled, it is **veiled to those who are perishing,** (4) whose minds **the god of this age has blinded**, who do not believe, lest the light of the gospel of the glory of Messiah, who is the image of YHWH, should shine on them.

The gospel is veiled for the Muslims and without it they will end up in hell permanently. Their minds have been blinded by s.a.tan, but we **must** try and reach them through prayer and giving them the gospel of Yahushua of Nazareth. **Could this "god of strongholds" of <u>Daniel 11:38</u> be the same creature described by Paul of Tarsus as the god of this age s.a.tan?**

Many scholars think that the Anti-Messiah has to be Jewish by translating this word into a singular Eloah, rather than Elohai. They did not realize that <u>no</u> Jew would proclaim this kind of polytheism to be the one true Elohim of Israel, as this would be the most serious offence in Judaism. Is this not this the perceived offence of Yahushua of Nazareth? They incorrectly think that He was teaching 3 gods, rather than three manifestations of YHWH. The Anti-Messiah cannot be Jewish and no Jew would follow this kind of blatant polytheism. The real Anti-Messiah's religion is polytheistic to the core, when stripped of its false monotheistic veneer!

Matthew 26:64-65 Yahushua said to him, "**It is as you said**." [admits He is the Son of YHWH but there is more] Nevertheless, I say to you, hereafter you will see the **Son of Man** [In His human nature] sitting at the **right hand of the Power**, [bingo, declaration of being YHWH on high] and **coming on the clouds of heaven**. Then **the high priest tore his clothes**, saying, **He has spoken blasphemy**! What further need do we have of witnesses? Look, now you have heard His blasphemy!

The blasphemy was that Yahushua the Messiah of Israel declared He is the very "Elohim of Israel" and shares the very nature/substance of our Father in heaven.

"Nor the desire of women"

The Anti-Messiah does not care about women in his kingdom (or the desire of women). He does not regard **their opinions or matters**, and this is what happens in Islamic societies where women do not have political roles other then to be the typically submitted silent housewives. The religious clergy has shunned even those women who have stood up in Islamic countries for political goals.

Daniel 11:38 "But in their place he shall honor a god of fortresses; [god of Jihad] and a god which his fathers did not know **he shall honor with gold and silver, with precious stones and pleasant things.**

He shall honor a "god of jihad" i.e. Allah and honor him with silver and gold, Muslims do this today by adorning their shrines with gold and silver. I know a shrine in Lahore Pakistan which has a golden door placed there as a tribute.

Daniel 11:39 "Thus he shall act against the strongest fortresses with **a foreign god**, which he shall acknowledge, and advance its glory; and he shall cause them to rule over many, and divide the land for gain.

Did I read that correctly "**with a foreign god**?" That means not the true "Elohim of Israel." When Muslims have won battles in the past they honor Allah as the one who did it not themselves, the exact same way that the Anti-Messiah will likewise glorify Allah for his triumphs. The end time beast has already come to divide the land and gain it for their foreign/ non-Hebraic deity by seeking the division of Jerusalem! Most nations are already in agreement (dividing the land in a two state solution) and thus have already begun to ride this ferocious beast.

Here is something even more interesting about the "abomination of desolation" in Jerusalem.

Daniel 9:27 Then **he shall confirm a covenant with many for one week**; but in the middle of the week He shall bring an end to sacrifice and offering and **on the wing of abominations** shall be one who makes desolate, even until the consummation, which is determined, is poured out on the desolate."

He (The Anti-Messiah) confirms the covenant (peace treaty already in place re-established) with many i.e. many Muslim nations and Israel so that they all agree not to attack the Jews for seven years. In Islam this is called a *hudna* (a temporary treaty that allows Muhammad's forces a time to strengthen). After three and a half years he ends the *hudna*. A careful reading shows that something happens "on the **wing of abominations** shall be one who makes desolate." What does this mean? The Anti-Messiah himself will be the abomination that sits there in the shrine and proclaim himself as the authority on earth, or **the final Caliph**. He is the instigator of the final global jihad upon the world.

Daniel is saying that the "abomination" will be in place on the "*kanaph*," in Hebrew, which means "corner," or "edge," or wing of the Temple Mount. While he is in power the word "desolate" means that he would not allow the gospel to go out and will suppress this as much as possible. This means that believers will have literally no open preaching in any lands that he has control of. Even today it is very difficult to live in Islamic countries, as they do not like people doing open air preaching of the gospel or giving out Bibles. In some Muslim countries you can get arrested for this, while in others like Saudi Arabia they will behead you.

The Hebrew word "*kanaph*" means: Wing, extremity, edge, winged, border, or corner of a shirt-

If you look at the Al-Aqsa Mosque today you will realize that the abomination is already there right on **the corner *(kanaph)*** just as Daniel told us. You will find the Mosque right on the "edge" of the Temple Mount. This is why Daniel said "*kanaph*" and not just anywhere on the Temple Mount. He was not talking about the 'Dome of the Rock' as most believe. See photos of the Temple Mount below. Daniel is telling us that the abomination will remain there where idolatry takes place daily until it is destroyed after The Tribulation. I took the pictures below while in Israel during September 2004 so you can see the evidence for yourself.

Photo 1-Above-South-Western wall of the Temple-Mount with the Al-Aqsa minaret at the top.

Photo 2-Above-Simon in Jerusalem - pictured with the Dome of the Rock, Al-Aqsa Mosque and the Eastern Gate. Note Al-Aqsa Mosque (the current abomination of desolations) is on the corner (kanaph) of the Temple-Mount exactly as Daniel predicted, and will remain there until Armageddon. The Anti-Messiah is also the abomination to occur in the Al-Aqsa Mosque and the rebuilt Temple in the near future, as he proclaims himself as having all authority on earth for the Muslim *umma* (community), after stopping the Torah sacrifices a few yards away. This is referred to in Daniel 9:27 as the spreading of abominations, from the current the Al-Aqsa Mosque, to the future rebuilt Moriah Temple.

Photo 3-Below-Close up picture of the Al-Aqsa mosque right on the edge of the Temple Mount just as the prophet Daniel said regarding the Kanaph.

Diagram 4 –Below-The kanaph of the abomination that will spread to the area now occupied by the Dome of The Rock as the Temple is rebuilt and the Anti-Messiah enters that as well. Theoretically these proclamations of deity can take place in both locations within a matter of hours.

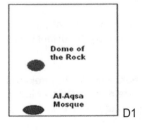

313

The prophet Daniel shows us that the "king of the north" [Turkey or a leader arising in Northern Iraq] is the one who sets up the 'abomination of desolation' and puts an end to the sacrifices (**Daniel 11:31**). The abomination of desolation is there already right on the corner as Daniel prophesied. Today on the Temple Mount it says in Arabic letters "*Allah does not have a son and Muhammad is his final prophet*." **This is the message that Anti-Messiah comes with and takes to the world. He proclaims what is already inscribed there! These are the biblical facts. No speculation is involved.**

This is the emblem of the Anti-Messiah that people bow down to, and it will be here, that the Anti-Messiah will proclaim himself as the ultimate authority on earth when he arrives. The Great Tribulation is not seven years, but three and a half years only, as written in Scripture. It commences when the Anti-Messiah will appear on the world stage with this same basic message.

This perfectly ties up with Yahushua telling His disciples to watch out for this same event described in Matthew 24:15, **as the event** to begin the countdown to His second coming. YHWH does not play games, but is very descriptive. Who do you think will come from the 'coasts of Chittim' (from Cyprus all the way to Italy)? How about Great Britain and the USA as explained earlier? This great coalition of western nations will muster their forces and come to attack the Anti-Messiah, as the two British bases currently at Cyprus will come in handy with 3,500 soldiers stationed there now.

When Cyprus became an independent country in 1960, the British Government kept ownership of 250 square kilometres of land on the southern coast. This is effectively sovereign British land. This is where British military planes fly and land to keep an eye on the Middle East. Is it not amazing that Great Britain is already lined up prophetically for this?

Jeremiah 50:9: For, lo, I will raise and cause to come up against Babylon **an assembly of great nations from the north country**: and **they shall set themselves in array against her**; from thence she shall be taken: **their arrows shall be as of a mighty expert man**; none shall return in vain. (10) **And Chaldea shall be a spoil**: all that spoil her shall be satisfied, saith YHWH. (11) **Because ye were glad, because ye rejoiced, O ye destroyers of mine heritage**, because ye are grown fat as the heifer at grass, and bellow as bulls;

- ❖ **"They shall set themselves as an array"** - They will come up as a coalition; the UK has the North Atlantic Treaty with North America, so it will participate without any problem with European federal laws.

- ❖ **"Their arrows shall be as of a mighty expert man"** - This is talking about precision bombing, none shall fail and all will hit their target precisely.

- ❖ **"Chaldea shall be a spoil"** - Iraq will be plundered; this is during the end-time, when both Iraq and Saudi Arabia will be destroyed together by the alliance with the USA.

- ❖ **"Because ye rejoiced, O ye destroyers of mine heritage"** - They rejoiced whenever something happened to Israel, when Jews were massacred by Muslim suicide bombers; these people rejoice by singing, giving out candy and dancing

314

for joy in the streets. We have seen this often even when they kill Americans they do the same. But rest assured wickedness will not last forever.

If you look at the map below (Cyprus map), you can see Cyprus is not far from Israel.

Cyprus map

C. Who is Ararat, Minni and Ashkenaz in Jeremiah 51:27?

Jeremiah 51:27 Set up a banner in the land, blow the trumpet among the nations! Prepare the nations against her, **call the kingdoms together against her**: Ararat, **Minni, and Ashchenaz**. Appoint a marshal against her; cause the horses to come up like the bristling locusts.

Is it not amazing in this supposed fictional "one-world government" that YHWH is able to muster kingdoms from the western nations to fight Islam?

Ararat, Minni and Ashkenaz will come up against Babylon and these are European nations as explained before. England, the USA, Australia and Italy are going to be part of this coalition.

The prominent city of Van, on the eastern lakeshore of beautiful, scenic and sacred Lake Van in the **heart of Armenia**, was the capital of the exalted and powerful Araratian Kingdom.[56]

The land or the kingdom of Ararat (9th-7th cent B.C.), called in Assyrian Urartu, was situated between the river Araks and the lakes Van and Rezaiyeh. **It included all the land later called Armenia.[57] (This is not to confuse "Mount Ararat" (Turkey) with the Kingdom of Ararat (Armenia)).**

The Armenians were the only people to cooperate and aid the crusaders to rid Jerusalem of Muslims. Is this why s.a.tan hated them the most? The crusaders went to Jerusalem with good intentions, but tragically some saw this as an opportunity to kill, loot and pillage. Let us not forget that the purpose of the crusades was a noble one, to open the roads and protect the pilgrims travelling to Jerusalem from Islam. These often levelled

---

[56] http://www.armenianhighland.com/van/chronicle240.html
[57] Columbia Electronic Encyclopedia, sixth edition

charges of "western crusaders against the Muslims" is absurd in the sense that it was Islam that initially went crusading against the nations in order to plunder loot and pillage their pilgrims. Therefore, the initial purpose of the crusades was against the original crusaders, who were the Muslims themselves. The crusaders purpose was not wrong and most of what they wanted to achieve they did achieve. However, like any army there are always "joy riders," or those whose sole purpose and motivation is greed. And, it is these that give the majority a bad name. So if say 100 crusaders went pillaging and rampaging, then naturally all of them will get a bad name no matter what. So let us keep things in their proper historical perspective. They did achieve their initial objective, but later things did not go according to plan. And we cannot deny that innocent people were killed both amongst the Jews, Muslims and Christians. In essence let the truth be told that the crusades were a very weak response from Europe against a very strong Islamic force.

In fact far worse atrocities did happen after the crusaders withdrew from these areas. Why does no one write about these, or do they get amnesia? Armenia was invaded by the Caliphs of Baghdad (Muslims), the Sultans of Egypt (Muslims), the Khans of Tartar (Muslims), and the Shahs of Persia (Muslims) and let us not forget that the worst of all their enemies, the Ottomans of Turkey (Muslims). Why does no one write about the atrocities that the Muslims committed against the non-Muslims, or do you not have the boldness to write about the events that the radical Muslims have perpetrated and how they killed, beheaded, raped and pillaged lands? Could it be that you are afraid of Islam today?

It was the Ottomans (Muslims) who massacred what is believed to be, though no exact numbers are known, over 1.5 million Armenians during 16th September 1915 under Tal'at Pasha. This happened under our very noses, yet today Turkey still does not acknowledge the massacre. Now the same thing has been repeated in Sudan where 2 million Christians and animists have been killed and 50,000 people are now displaced from their homes in Darfur (southern Sudan). Why is it that no one questions that Arab Muslims are doing wholesale slaughter, rape and pillaging of the innocent families there? Is it because an "ill spoken word" against Islam would cause the oil supply to be shut off, thus causing untold disasters to the west?

Does the world get amnesia when it comes to the Muslims or has no one got the courage to expose these people for their wickedness? Why do all the Western news outlets have to use words like militants, radicals, freedom fighters, and separatists, or a generic war on terror when it comes to reporting? Why do they not tell the world that they have made little kids drink their urine? They raped women. Is that not trying to humiliate Christians and degrading the women as objects of lust? Where is the objectivity of the west when it comes to Islam? It is an outcry when Israel builds a wall to protect its citizens and of course the puppets in Hague have to hold a special court to condemn Israel. Why have they not held court for Sudan? Why did they not hold court for Beslan? What about the court for the Bosnian Serbs who were massacred by the Kosovo Liberation Army headed by Osama Bin Laden at one time? **Where is justice for these murderers? Thankfully one day soon, Yahushua our Savoir will hold open court at the Great White Throne Judgement and will bring all these atrocities to a "no holds barred" eternal reckoning, away from the corruption of man's jurisprudence!**

Professor Edmond Paris, "Genocide in Satellite Croatia, 1941- 1945," Chicago, 1961, The American Institute for Balkan Affairs, from the introduction of the book.

Quote: The greatest genocide during World War II, in proportion to a nation's population, took place, not in Nazi Germany but in the Nazi-created puppet state of Croatia. There, in the years 1941-1945, some 750,000 Serbs, 60,000 Jews and 26,000 Gypsies - men, women and children - perished in a gigantic holocaust. These are the figures used by most foreign authors, especially Germans, who were in the best position to know. The magnitude and the bestial nature of these atrocities make it difficult to believe that such a thing could have happened in an allegedly civilized part of the world.

Now which is worse, the crusaders, or the radical Muslims, whose violence is not merely historical, but is current and ongoing? When the Muslims were brutally killing the Serbians in World War II, even the Nazis were horrified at their actions and yet we know that the Nazis were not nice people.

D. Who are the two thirds of people that will be killed? Is it the whole world, a single country or a single geographic location?

Some prophecy scholars see the entire world perishing in the end of days. This end time view sees two thirds of the world, or about two billion being slaughtered. The problem is that much of the book of Revelation is symbolic. We have gone through how to interpret certain symbols, yet we still must be careful of that tricky word "ALL." All is often a synecdoche and not every man woman, or child is destined to perish.

> **Zechariah 13:8** And it shall come to pass, that in **ALL THE LAND**, saith the Master, **two parts therein shall be cut off and die**; but the third shall be left therein.

This is usually referred to by many as Jacob's trouble. What land are these two thirds being destroyed in? Anyone will tell you that the two thirds are clearly in "The Land" Ha Aretz and this is only the land of Israel.

Zechariah 13:1: In that day there shall be a fountain opened **to the house of David** and **to the inhabitants of Jerusalem** for sin and for uncleanness.
It is quite clear that the reference in context is to Israel and in fact Jerusalem is mentioned. We cannot mistake this as a reference to the entire planet; this fountain of forgiveness and grace to both houses of Israel will open when the Messiah returns.

> **Zechariah 13:7** Awake, O sword, against **My shepherd**, and against the man that is my fellow, saith the Master of hosts: smite the shepherd, and the sheep shall be scattered: and I will turn mine hand upon the little ones.

This is a fulfilled prophecy of Jerusalem when Yahushua (Jesus) the Messiah was killed and resurrected. Judgement was then set on Israel for her rejection of the Messiah. **We can see that in history the Romans came and besieged Jerusalem and killed two thirds of the people at that time. So contrary to popular belief that this is yet to happen this prophecy has already been fulfilled.** Zechariah 13:7 is clear that this is because the Shepherd of Israel is killed (Yahushua the Messiah) and verse 9 shows that Israel had to go through a refining process before they were going to be gathered back.

317

Zechariah 13:9 is yet future and will be fulfilled when the Jews cry out for their Messiah and get saved.

Most evangelicals believe that Jacob's trouble will occur during the time of the Anti-Messiah. Unfortunately you cannot mix the day of the Master (Tribulation) i.e. during Anti-Messiah's (future) reign, with Jacob's trouble (past), which are two separate events. One is future the other past.

Only problem is someone forgot to tell them that Jacob's Trouble has already been fulfilled in the past. They incorrectly base their whole theory on just one verse in **Zechariah 13:8**. Let's see what the Scripture has to say:

First of all it is estimated that during the invasion of Titus in AD 70 in Jerusalem there were about 3 million Jews in Israel and of these two thirds were killed i.e. about 2 million. This would render this prophecy to have been fulfilled in the past e.g. AD 70 not in the future. Although the prophecy was given in Zechariah's time (6 BC) to be fulfilled in 70 AD it was clearly still future from Zechariah's perspective.

In fact this has nothing to do with Jacob's Trouble in the future, or in the latter times of the Tribulation. Let's analyze this and look at some noted commentaries:

> **Zechariah 13:8** And it shall come to pass, **that in all the land,** saith the Master, two parts therein shall be cut off and die; but the third shall be left therein.

Commentary of Matthew Henry - Zechariah 13:8-

It shall come to pass that in all the land of Israel two parts shall be cut off and die. **The Roman army laid the country waste, and slew at least two-thirds of the Jews**.

Commentary of John Wesley - Zechariah 13:8-

Two parts - Not precisely two, but the greater part shall die a temporal death, **by the sword of Titus**, or in eternal death under unbelief.

Commentary of Jamieson, Faussett - Zechariah 13:8-

Two-thirds of the Jewish nation was to perish in the **Roman wars**, and a third will survive.

Clearly the earlier commentators also did not believe this had anything to do with Jacob's Trouble in the future. I am not in the minority; well perhaps I am nowadays. The majority echo the pastor's microphone and believe in something that has already taken place. Now where did the evangelicals get this idea? It is difficult to say for sure, but I know this has been around for at least this century.

Now let's turn to Yahushua's own words-

Matthew 26:31 Then saith Yahushua unto them, All ye shall be offended because of me this night: <u>for it is written,</u> I will **SMITE THE SHEPHERD**, and the <u>sheep of the flock shall be scattered abroad.</u>

Bingo... We have the evidence; the gun that was fired and we find the empty bullet shells.

This sums it up; Yahushua tells us that the Shepherd (Yahushua) was going to be crucified and the flock (the Jewish people) IMMEDIATELY scattered abroad, subsequent to the execution stake. From the time the Jewish people rejected their Messiah, the judgment was set to occur within forty years. This scattering was to happen as a judgment that was to come upon Jewish Israel for the rejection of their Messiah (the destruction of the Temple and dispersion of the Jews, or the scattering of the flock). You may well ask why forty years? This has significance in Scripture, as a generation is represented by forty years. So this generation i.e. Yahushua's generation was under judgment for the rejection of their Messiah. This is very similar to when YHWH brought out the children of Israel from Egypt and they sinned against Him by murmuring in the wilderness, as He punished that generation for forty years also. Yahushua was in fact quoting the prophet Zechariah.

Zechariah 13:7 Awake, O sword, against my shepherd, and against the man that is my fellow, saith the Master of hosts: smite the shepherd, and the sheep shall be scattered: and I will turn mine hand upon the little ones.

The shepherd (Yahushua) crucified and the sheep (Jews) scattered for unbelief. The little ones here are those who believed in Yahushua as Messiah in the time of Yahushua.

Then we see the following verse which is yet future, and is even now being partly fulfilled in Zechariah 13:9.

Zechariah 13:9 And I will bring **the third part through the fire**, and will refine them as silver is refined, and will try them as gold is tried: **they shall call on my Name [YHWH]**, and I will hear them: I will say, <u>It is my people</u>: and they shall say, <u>The Master YHWH is my Elohim.</u>

This is very interesting. This tells us that the Jews are still YHWH's people and are being refined through trials. This and many verses like this, at least gets rid of the idea that Israel has been, or is being replaced by the church (this kind of doctrinal anti-Semitism in churches along with replacement theology is rife and is simply evil).

The Elohim of Israel is testing Israel. Eventually YHWH says I will hear them and I will say these are **MY PEOPLE** and they shall also call upon Yahweh their Elohim. This is yet to happen as most Jews are still in unbelief regarding Yahushua being their Messiah and have not called upon Yahweh or His true Name. Just take a look at the state of Israel and you will understand what I mean.

Revelation 9:15 And the four angels were loosed, which were prepared for an hour, and a day, and a month, and a year, for to slay the third part of men.

Now we can ask this same question again, this time looking into the book of Revelation. Who are the one-third people group who will be killed? Is it two billion people in the entire world, or simply the people living in a specific geographic location e.g. the Middle East? We can see that in Revelation 9 there is an army that is preparing to fight and as they fight with Israel, the four angels will be loosed in the Euphrates River. This is in the Middle East.

Revelation 9:18-21 By these three was the **third part of men killed**, by the **fire**, and by the **smoke**, and by the **brimstone**, which issued out of their mouths. (19) For their power is in their mouth, and in their tails: for their tails were like unto serpents, and had heads, and with them they do hurt. (20) And the rest of the men which were not killed by these **plagues** yet repented not of the works of their hands, that they should not worship devils, and idols of gold, and silver, and brass, and stone, and of wood: which neither can see, nor hear, nor walk: (21) Neither repented they of their murders, nor of their sorceries, nor of their fornication, nor of their thefts.

Revelation 9:18 makes it abundantly clear that these third part of men are killed by wars generated by the eastern Muslims themselves e.g. symbols of war are "fire," "smoke" and "brimstone." It is evident that since the angels are loosed in the Euphrates River and the two hundred million man army is gathered in the Middle East marching towards Jerusalem Israel to destroy Israel, then we can conclude that this third part of men that will die as a result of this huge war will be amongst the residents of the Middle East. This completely rules out 2 billion people who supposedly will die, as a figure that cannot be justified by Scripture. This death clearly comes as a result of Armageddon and is limited to 1/3 of the Middle Eastern population.

In order to clarify and use correct hermeneutics, we cannot just simply take one verse from the apostolic writings and give our conclusion on it without understanding what the rest of the Bible says. Remember we must illustrate this in principle from the Tanach (Hebrew Bible) and we certainly can do that.

Ezekiel 38:9 Thou shalt **ascend and come like a storm**, thou shalt be like a **cloud to cover the land**, thou, and all thy bands, and many people with thee.

Many nations are gathered and these are Asia minor/CIS nations, they are all Muslim; this confirms Revelation chapter 9.

Zechariah 12:2 Behold, I will make Jerusalem a cup of trembling unto **ALL THE PEOPLE ROUND ABOUT**, when they shall be **in the siege** both against **Judah and against Jerusalem**.

We see the same pattern in Zechariah, similar to that in Ezekiel and Revelation and so we have a reliable witness that all these Islamic nations will come up against Israel.

Zephaniah 2:9 Therefore as I live, saith the Master of hosts, the Elohim of Israel, **Surely Moab shall be as Sodom**, and the children of **Ammon as Gomorrah**, even the breeding of nettles, and saltpits, and a **perpetual desolation**: the residue of my people shall spoil them, and the **remnant of my people shall possess them.**

Different prophets have made mention of these events linking different nations. But the end result is that they are all Islamic. We cannot even find one mention of any EU nation forming an alliance with these nations. This is troubling considering that almost every prophecy writer out there thinks that the Anti-Messiah will come out of Europe. Sadly as always, unless we move away from this rather late traditional view, we are in danger of being misled.

Ezekiel 38:17 Thus saith the Master YHWH; **Art thou he of whom I have spoken in old time by my servants the prophets of Israel**, which prophesied in those days many years that I would bring thee against them?

We can see that YHWH did not use the same name Gog to speak to the different prophets of Israel about the same person. He was addressed as **The Assyrian, Pharaoh, Gog, King of Babylon, and Prince of Tyrus** and other names as well to address this evil individual. The Bible is a book that we must read cover-to-cover to determine a truth and a person's identity. We cannot dissect the Bible and reject the Tanach (Hebrew Bible) as irrelevant for us and merely rely on the apostolic writings for our doctrines. The whole Bible has to serve us as our witness, not just one or two verses. It is clear that the pattern of Israel's latter day redemption is incredibly similar to the redemption in Egypt. In fact, it is even a bigger event, considering that the plagues similarly match.

2 Timothy 3:16-17 All Scripture is given by inspiration of YHWH, and is profitable for doctrine, for reproof, for correction, for instruction in righteousness: (17) That the man of YHWH may be perfect, thoroughly furnished unto all good works.

Paul warned Timothy that he needs the entire Bible and guess what? At the time this warning came, the apostolic writings were not even written by the disciples of Yahushua, or compiled into a single book. Here Paul clearly gives testimony and value to the Tanach as the book that was around to teach us all necessary doctrines. The Apostolic writings simply help us fill the gaps.

Chapter 14

Further Insights

__Question__-Is there any literal mention of Mecca in the Bible?

__Answer__-In Revelation 17:9 the woman (city) is allegorically described to be <u>near</u> seven mountains.

A tight fit is already present in Genesis where Mecca is referred to by its ancient name e.g. Mesha.

Genesis 10:30 And their dwelling was from **Mesha**, as thou goest unto Sephar a mount of the east. In the Arabic tongue a "ch" could be a "k," so we would say "Metcha" for Mecca. The "K" is pronounced differently.

Here is what the commentator Gill says on this subject

Perhaps nearer the truth may be the Arabic paraphrase of Saadiah {r}, which is "from Mecca till you come to the city of the eastern mountain, or (as in a manuscript) to **the eastern city,"meaning perhaps Medina**, situate to the east; so that the sense is, according to this paraphrase, that the **sons of Joktan had their dwelling from Mecca to Medina**; and so R. Zacuth {s} says, **Mesha in the Arabic tongue is called Mecca**; and it is a point **agreed upon by the Arabs that Mesha was one of the most ancient names of Mecca**; they believe that all the mountainous part of the region producing frankincense went in the earliest times by the name of Sephar; from whence Golius concludes this tract to be the Mount Zephar of Moses, a strong presumption of the truth of which is that Dhafar, the same with the modern Arabs as the ancient Saphar, is the name of a town in Shihr, the only province in Arabia bearing frankincense on the coast of the Indian ocean {t}.

Here is what one writer writes:

Sixty Centuries of Human Progress published in New York and Chicago. The frontispiece states the contents were reviewed, verified, and endorsed by the professors of history in five American universities by Moses Coit Tyler, A.M., L.H.D., professor of American History in Cornell University. Some top writers contributed to the series of 12 volumes including President Theodore Roosevelt. It provides an interesting view of the subject. [volume 5, pages 1352 to 1356]:

"The Arabs believe that Mecca was founded by Adam, and that its temple, the Kaaba, was built by Abraham. They ascribe the early prosperity of the city to Ishmael, who established his residence there, because, as the Arabian traditions assert, the brackish well of Zemzem was the one to which the angel directed Hagar. Mecca must have been a very ancient city, if, as the commentators believe, it was the Mesha mentioned by Moses as inhabited by Joktans posterity. Medina called Yatreb before the appearance of Mohammed possesses more natural advantages than Mecca; but it is not situated so conveniently for traffic. The people of Medina seem always to have been jealous of the supremacy claimed by the Meccans, and this was probably the reason why they espoused the cause of Mohammed when he was banished by their rivals."

Strongs Concordance says "Mesha (perhaps Mesha "retreat," the boundries of Joctanite Arabia").

Interesting that this is called a **retreat**. Why a retreat? Arabs retreated there for Hajj. It's exactly as it is today, the Hajj (pilgrimage) ceremony is not one started by Muhammad in the 7th century AD but has been well in place before Muhammad's birth.

So Mecca is also mentioned by its ancient name in the book of Genesis thus pointing us back to why the start of the Bible is so important.

322

Question- Here is an interesting question that can refute this whole theory that it is Islam, in *Revelation 16:6*. *For they have shed the blood of saints and prophets, and thou hast given them blood to drink; for they are worthy.* Clearly Islam could only qualify for killing the saints, but not prophets, since Islam was not around until at least six hundred years after Yahushua's resurrection so it fails this test?

Answer- This is indeed interesting and the good thing is that coming from an Islamic background it helps me to have known history and our tribal backgrounds. We need to see how Scripture speaks, rather than how one should fit it. On the surface, the questioner seems to have won the argument. But he has failed to take into consideration the corpus of Scripture that details that we cannot avoid or deny the Islamic regions that the Bible clearly mentions. But here is the answer to this peculiar dilemma. Radical Islam indeed killed many saints and prophets yes and I mean prophets. **Here is the evidence that it shall indeed kill Old Testament prophets.**

Revelation 11:3 And I will give power unto my two witnesses, and they shall prophesy a thousand two hundred and threescore days, clothed in sackcloth.

And in verse 7 we read *And when they shall have finished their testimony, **the beast** that ascendeth out of the bottomless pit **shall make war against them, and shall overcome them, and kill them.**

Amazing indeed that the Muslims are going to kill the prophets. Therefore whether you believe me, or not that it is Elijah and Zerubbabel, or as some others say Moses and Enoch, the beast will kill these people. Thus this is sufficient to satisfy the verses in **Revelation 16:6**. This is not all. As Paul even said in ***Ephesians 4:11-12*** *And He gave some, **apostles**; and some, **prophets**; and some, evangelists; and some, pastors and teachers;* Rabbi Shaul of Tarsus, or Paul concurs that Yahushua gave for the perfecting of the saints on this earth five offices and one of these included **prophets**. Now the question is how many of these prophets have already, or will soon be killed by the beast? You can decide for yourself, but the verses in **Revelation 11:7** alone perfectly fit with the Islamists slaying prophets (the two witnesses) thus fulfilling **Revelation 16:6** once again proves you cannot get away from the fact that the Beast of Revelation and Daniel are no other than Islamic kingdoms! Now let me turn it around and ask you, when did the Roman Catholic church slay OT prophets? The verses in Revelation 17/18 talk about the Middle-East not Europe as believed by many.

For a refutation of why the US cannot be Babylon please go to my website www.abrahamic-faith.com and see 100 points refuting why American cannot be Babylon.

Question- Why cannot the "Great Sea" spoken of by **Daniel 7:2** be Rome where the 4th beast arises out of to make it a revived Roman Empire?

Daniel 7:2 Daniel spoke, saying, "I saw in my vision by night, and behold, the four winds of heaven were stirring up **the Great Sea**.

Answer-The answer is right there in the very next verse that states all four beasts will arise out of the Middle Eastern region and not Europe, or some far away obscure land.

Daniel 7:3 And **four great beasts** came up **from the sea**, each different from the other.

- ❖ The Lion = Babylon
- ❖ The Bear = Medo-Persia
- ❖ The Leopard = Grecia
- ❖ Ottoman-Islam Revived

If the three beasts were from the Middle East then why is it that the 4th has to waltz out of Europe or the USA? By what hermeneutic right can we make that conclusion? Some people make this to be only peoples, nations and tongues, but if this was the case in order to be consistent then why is the wind stirring up in the "Great Sea," or the Mediterranean Ocean and not over the entire world. This would break Scripture and the interpretation would not stand. Let me illustrate a point.

YHWH tells Joshua that He has divided the land of Israel by lot to be given to the tribes of Israel and He mentions that allotment as far as the **"Great Sea."** This is the Western portion of the Mediterranean as YHWH's sees it.

Joshua 1:4 "From the wilderness and this Lebanon as far as the great river, the **River Euphrates**, all the land of the Hittites, and to the **Great Sea** toward the going down of the sun, shall be your territory.

Read the Scriptures carefully and tell me does it look like YHWH has given Israel land all the way from Israel to Italy? Israel has trouble convincing the world that its present borders belong to her. Can she ever conclude that all the lands up to Italy are hers? That claim would also include all of Eastern Europe. Why is it that these prophecy writers have made this blunder? Could it be that they have not paid attention to detail and in their zeal have simply followed one person? The answer is yes and we can find that person was Clarence Larkins, who made different conclusions based on what was happening at his time. Today's writers have picked up on his thread and concluded their theories with no scriptural justification whatsoever not realizing that their theory breaks Scripture.

Joshua 23:4 "See, I have divided to you by lot these nations that remain, to be an inheritance for your tribes, from the Jordan, with all the nations that I have cut off, as far as the **Great Sea** westward.

Joshua 15:12 The **west border was the coastline of the Great Sea**. This is the boundary of the children of Judah all around according to their families.

YHWH describes the boundary for us also so the buck stops here. It is abundantly clear that the "Great Sea" spoken of here and in Daniel is the Mediterranean and the part or coast that connects to Israel, not to Rome in Italy.

Question- Who is the army of 200 million?

Answer- An interesting army is mentioned in Revelation 9, which most people think is China. Unfortunately this is not realistic and there is no biblical qualifier for this to be

China. What made the biblical scholars choose China? Here is what this could be. If we add up the 15% fundamentalist radical Muslims in the world today, then that is more than enough to exceed the 200 million man army. Could this be the army of radical Islam?

Revelation 12:12 And the sixth angel poured out his vial upon the great <u>River Euphrates</u>; and the water thereof was dried up, that the way of the **kings of the east** might be prepared.

The verse states an army of 200 million. Where do people get the idea of China? This does not talk about China at all. This army is released from the **Middle East,** more likely crossing from Iraq and is entirely Muslim. The sixth angel poured out the vial on the **"River Euphrates,"** this is Iraq. Furthermore, the Magi <u>from the east</u> at Yahushua's birth came to give gifts to Messiah Yahushua (Matthew 2:1-2) also came <u>from the east</u>. So it is reasonable to conclude that these kings and the armies are both from the Middle East and not China. China has no part to play in end time battle with Israel and she has nothing to gain by capturing a land so far away that is no bigger than the landmass of New Jersey. Prophecy writers have once again arrived at a conclusion without providing one single verse for their justification.

Daniel 2:48 Then the king made <u>Daniel a great man</u>, and gave him many great gifts, and made him <u>ruler over the whole province of Babylon</u>, and chief of the governors over all the wise *men* of Babylon.

The Magi were watching the stars for the sign of the King to come; we should ask why were they watching these signs?

Daniel 2:2 Then the king commanded to call the magicians, and the <u>astrologers, and the sorcerers, and the Chaldeans</u>, for to show the king his dreams. So they came and stood before the king.

It is quite plausible to believe that the expectation of the King (Moshiach) is something the Prophet Daniel would have talked about and he also wrote about it. You have to go back to the book of Daniel to understand that he was the chief of all the <u>magicians and wise men of the East</u> as he was in Babylon (Iraq). We can conclude from this that the army is from Babylonia, just as the angel mentions the Babylonian River Euphrates; there is no need for us to run to China to find this army there.

Revelation 9:16-21 And the number of the army of the horsemen were two hundred thousand thousand and I heard the number of them.

Interestingly the end of verse 16 is "and I heard the number of them?" Question is heard what? You cannot hear a number, a number of what? It does not say a number of people. However you can hear a multitude of people shouting though. This word in the Greek is "*arithmos*" and can here be best translated from a "number" to "a multitude." This is yet another possibility that is highly likely "and I heard the multitude of them," probably most likely chanting 'Allah hu Akbar' (Allah is greater). The context is people, so this is a large multitude marching for war in the name of Allah heading west to Jerusalem for the final battle of this age. An army always marches for war under a banner and this banner is no doubt Islam, as Scripture confirms and elaborates on this confederacy both in Psalm 83 and Ezekiel 38. These are clearly Islamic nations.

Isaiah 14:25 That **I will** break **the Assyrian** in **My land** and upon **My mountains** [Israel] tread him under foot: then shall his yoke depart from off them, and his burden departs from off their shoulders.

This is the same "Gog" army mentioned in **Ezekiel 38** described as **the Assyrian**. This is why this army is described as locusts, not only the Arabs are involved, but there are many millions of these people marching for holy war - jihad. Here are some Muslim populations today:

Nations	Count
Arabs	300 million
Pakistan	140 million
India	144 million
Indonesia	201 million
China	75 million
Bangladesh	108 million
Egypt	65 million
Turkey	66 million
Syria	14 million
Somalia	9.6 million
Sudan	26 million

This could easily form into an army of well over 200 million out of these nations alone. There are still many other Muslim nations with large populations as well. Therefore, the figure of 200 million seen in Revelation 9:16 should be easily achievable from these Islamic nations alone.

Revelation 9:17 And thus I saw the horses in the vision, and them that sat on them, having breastplates of fire, and of jacinth, and brimstone: and the heads of the horses were as the heads of lions; and out of their mouths issued fire and smoke and brimstone.

"Heads of lions" these are tanks. **"Smoke and brimstone"** tank rounds. The description of the soldiers is Islamic, and so this is talking about tanks and armoured vehicles here.

Revelation 9:18 By these three was **the third part of men killed, by the fire,** and **by the smoke**, and by the brimstone, which issued out of their mouths.

A third of men are going to die by this army, which is the damage that Islam will do. The "fire" and "smoke" represent war. **Since the action takes place in the Middle East, therefore one could conclude that the one third killed will be in the Middle East and not the whole world.**

326

Revelation 9:19 For their power is in their mouth, and in their tails for their tails *were* like unto serpents, and had heads, and with them they do hurt. **"In their tails"** carrying payload of missiles. This is army talk of missiles carrying warheads perhaps nuclear, or strategic missiles.

Revelation 9:20 And the rest of the men which were not killed by these plagues yet <u>repented</u> not of the <u>works of their hands</u>, that they should not worship devils, and idols of gold, and silver, and brass, and stone, and of wood: which neither can see, nor hear, nor walk:

The firing of these missiles and all this warfare will result in disease and destruction upon men. The men that remain will still refuse to repent and will carry on with the natural course of events and refuse to recognize Yahushua as YHWH, or repent of their sins.

Revelation 9:21 Neither repented they of their murders, nor of their sorceries nor of their fornication, nor of their thefts. **"Their murders"** Radical Muslims killing other people like westerners. **"Nor of their sorceries"** spreading and believing in the false religion of Islam. **"Nor of their thefts"** plundering and looting people.

This is talking about pure Idolatrous Islam. Radical Muslims killing by beheadings, torture, forcing people to convert, just like we saw in the Second Gulf War. The worst is yet to come. Make sure you have provisions for the future. This is not as far away now as some think. The return of our Master is soon. But even more importantly we will go through the Tribulation, so we need to prepare for it. Those misguided Christians who cannot heed YHWH's word, and who want to go for peace projects in Iraq (Babylon) beware you will lose your life. The Islamists will persecute and kill you and you also by your faulty logic have failed to recognize the times and heed YHWH's words and will have put your life in danger out of ignorance.

Revelation 18:4 And I heard another voice from heaven, saying, Come out of her, My people, that ye be not partakers of her sins, and that ye receive not of her plagues.

Jeremiah 51:45 **My people, go ye out of the midst of her**, and deliver you every man his soul from the fierce anger of the Master.

The beast <u>must</u> kill as this is prophesied, yet many will be beheaded and yet fail to heed the warnings. We are witnessing this in Iraq, as sadly many Christians are failing to see the times and by going to Iraq they put their earthly lives at risk.

Revelation 20:4 And I saw thrones, and they sat upon them, and judgment was given unto them: and I saw the souls of them that **were beheaded for the witness of Yahushua**, and for the **word of YHWH**, and which had not worshipped the beast, neither his image, neither had received his mark upon their foreheads, or in their hands; and they lived and reigned with Messiah a thousand years.

<u>Question</u>- Are <u>not</u> the "ships of Tarshish" from the European Union?

Answer- Many prophecy teachers claim that the European Union is the Anti-Messiah's dominion by pointing to Tarshish being a candidate for Europe in the Bible. They speculate that it is a reference being Spain, or Britain without any biblical or historic support. They even claim that the "merchants of Tarshish and all the young lions thereof" (Ezekiel 38:13) refers to other European countries. In the Bible, we find many references to Tarshish, all of which point to Lebanon as Tyre is in Lebanon. One such verse is in Isaiah:

> **Isaiah 23:1 The burden of Tyre.** Howl, **ye ships of Tarshish**; for it is laid waste, so that there is no house, no entering in: from the **land of Chittim** it is revealed to them.

Many writers have used **Ezekiel 27:12** to propose that only Britain manufactured tin, since "**Tarshish** [was] thy merchant by reason of the multitude of all [kind of] riches; with **silver, iron, tin, and lead**, they traded in thy fairs." And since Britain manufactures tin, then it must be Tarshish. This is a very poor argument because for this to be true, Britain must also manufacture silver, lead and iron as well which we know they do not.

The next attempt is to use Jonah who in attempting to flee to Tarshish from Israel boarded a ship at the port of Joppa (on the Mediterranean coast) Jonah 1:3. This would indicate that Tarshish lies west. This is true, but the ships could also sail to Turkey and Lebanon westwards also. In fact, historically, Turkey is renowned for its silver, iron, and lead. Even so, many modern authors are divided between Tartessos in Iberia and Tarsus in Cilicia (Turkey). Cilicia, was the ancient name of Southern Turkey. Göltepe was associated with tin mining; Kestel, located in the central Taurus Mountains of Turkey also produced tin. Turkey also mined iron and silver:

> "Tharsus to the Tharsians, for so was Cilicia of old called; the sign of which is this, that the nobelest city they have and a metropolis also is Tarsus."[58] Josephus, citing from the Hebrew Bible, notes that Tarshish is a descendant of Japheth (Greek Iapetos/Japetus) and Javan (Hebrew Iawan), associated with the Greek Ionia, a province in modern Western Turkey. The ancient Greek historian Athendorus, a citizen of Tarsus, gives a descent from Japetus, the ancestor of Javan, for Tarsus:

> "Athendorus, the Tarsian, said that the city was originally called Parthenia, from Parthenius, son of Cydnus, the grandson of Anchiale, daughter of Japetus."[59]

Ancient Anatolia was famous for its metals, which were carried in Phoenician ships as trade items to other parts of the ancient near eastern world. Phoenician inscriptions have been found at Karatepe, in Cilicia."[60] Silver heads the list of precious metals associated with Tarshish, and ancient Assyrian sources noted that the Taurus Mountains above Tarsus were referred to as the Silver

---

[58] Josephus: *Antiquities of the Jews.* 6.1.127
[59] p.686, Vol.4, "Tarsus," James Hastings. *A Dictionary of the Bible.* Peabody, Mass.
[60] cf. p. 336 "Karatepe," Charles F. Pfeiffer. The Biblical World, A Dictionary of Biblical Archaeology. Nashville, Tennessee. Broadman Press. 1966

Mountains. In fact, modern metallurgy maps indicate that every single metal associated with Tarshish, can be found in the Taurus Mountains.[61]

Jeremiah 10:9 Silver beaten into plates is brought from Tarshish.

"Tarsus, the capital of Cilicia. The city was built on the banks of the swift Cydnus River, 10 miles from the Mediterranean and 30 miles south of the Taurus ("Silver") mountains, which were veined with lead and silver."[62]

Archaeologists found evidence of smelters in the vicinity of Tarsus in antiquity, as noted by MacQueen:

> *"The final shaping into tools and weapons was done locally, and areas devoted to this have been found at Bogazkoy and Tarsus marked by the presence of large quantities of slag. Tarsus also produced a clay crucible with bronze adhering to it."[63]*

It is obvious that bronze is an alloy of tin and copper. Obviously, the natives of ancient Tarsus had access to Tin in order to make the bronze.

Hodges notes that the Assyrians were interested in controlling the tin resources of Eastern Anatolia (Turkey):

> "There can be little doubt that Sargon's chief concern in this enterprise was to attempt to control the sources of supply of his raw materials, and one is tempted, therefore, to suppose that much of the tin required for bronze making came from the mountains of Syria and Turkey..."[64]

No later than Early Bronze Age times, Anatolian bronze objects were utilizing tin.

> It seems certain that bronze and bronze working originated in the Middle East, where Anatolia and Armenia were mining regions...between 2,300-2,000 BC...the quantity of the bronze with an already remarkably high tin content is impressive." (Pp.166-175,"The Appearance and Spread of Metal) [65]

Aslihan Yener discovered an Early Bronze Age Tin mine, 60 miles north of Tarsus:

> "Aslihan Yener, assistant professor at the university of Chicago's Oriental Institute, believes that a mine and ancient mining village she has found in the central Taurus mountains of Turkey shows that TIN MINING was a well developed industry in the area as early as 2870 BC. The mine at a site called Kestel some 60 miles north of Tarsus, on the Mediterranean coast- has two miles

---

[61] cf. minerals map titled *Turkey Maden Zuhurlari*. Maden Tetkik Arama Enstitusu Yayinlarindan. Haziran. 1960

[62] p.727, "Tarsus," Madeleine S. Miller, *The New Harper's Bible Dictionary*. New York. Harper & Row. 1973

[63] p. 78, J.G. MacQueen, *The Hittites and Their Contemporaries in Asia Minor*. Boulder, Colorado. Westview Press. 1975

[64] p.108, Henry Hodges, *Technology in the Ancient World*. Baltimore, Maryland. Penguin Books. 1971

[65] *The Larousse Encyclopaedia of Prehistoric and Ancient Art*. London. Hamlyn Publishers. 1970)

of tunnels. Nearby stands the mining village of Goltepe, which was probably occupied by 500 to 1,000 persons more or less continuously between 3,290 and 1,840 BC...the site contains no evidence of copper metallurgy...it did not produce bronze; instead it **produced tin for export**...Yener and her colleagues have analyzed tin-rich slag from 50 crucibles discovered at Goltepe. Within the total one metric ton of metallurgical debris in the form of crucible and vitrified materials, she has excavated some **that have 30 percent tin content** (a high percentage) still intact in the crucible."[66]

If the people of Cilicia were capable of mining tin in the Early Bronze Age, they certainly did not need to sail to Tartessos in Spain to get tin to make bronze!

Ezekiel 38:13 Sheba and Dedan and the merchants of Tarshish with all its villages will say to you, 'Have you come to capture spoil? Have you assembled your company to seize plunder, to carry away silver and gold, to take away cattle and goods, to capture great spoil?'

While this statement does not conclude which side Sheba, Dedan, and the Merchants of Tarshish are on; it could be obvious that booty and plunder is an Islamic trait in which these nations could likely join in. The Bible however sheds light as to the judgement of the ships of Tarshish from the following verse:

Isaiah 23:1-2 The **burden of Tyre**. **Howl, ye ships of Tarshish**; for it is laid waste, so that there is no house, no entering in: from the **land of Chittim it is revealed to them**. Be still, ye inhabitants of the isle; thou whom the merchants of Zidon, that pass over the sea, have replenished.

To end all the arguments, the Bible concludes that the merchants/ships of Tarshish is a reference to Lebanon because the burden is for Tyre (Lebanon). There is more confirmation; **Isaiah 23** calls Tyre/Lebanon the **"daughter" of Tarshish**:

Isaiah 23:10 Pass through thy land as a river, O daughter of Tarshish: [there is] no more strength.

Isaiah 23:6 Pass ye over to Tarshish; howl, ye inhabitants of the isle."

This place is somewhat related to Tarshish and is in close proximity to her in order to "pass over" to her. If Tarshish is Spain or England, how is Tyre able to pass over to such a far off place into the distance?

Then we have others who make Tarshish out to be Europe cite Isaiah 60:9 for the simple fact that it was western ships which carried immigrant Jews to Israel.

Isaiah 60:9 Surely the isles shall wait for me, and the ships of Tarshish first, to bring thy sons from far, their silver and their gold with them, unto the name of the

[66] pp.16-17, "Bronze Age Source of Tin Found in Turkey ?" *Biblical Archaeology Review*, Vol.20 No.3, May-June, 1994

LORD [Yahweh] thy Elohim, and to the Holy One of Israel, because He hath glorified thee.

A closer glance at the whole chapter reveals that this is fulfilled in the Messianic Kingdom, since all the nations that hated Israel will participate:

Isaiah 60:6-7 The multitude of camels shall cover thee, the dromedaries of **Midian** and **Ephah**; all they from Sheba shall come: they shall bring gold and incense; and they shall shew forth the praises of YHWH. All the flocks of Kedar shall be gathered together unto thee, the rams of Nebaioth shall minister unto thee: they shall come up with acceptance on mine altar, and I will glorify the House of My glory.

It is obvious that the Arabs will participate as well. If today Europe is the only candidate for the "ships of Tarshish" which carry Jews back to their homeland, then when did the Arabs (Midian, Kedar, Sheba) ever do such a thing? Today the Arabs would rather drown the Jews into the sea, than to extend assistance to carry them to the land of Israel.

The Bible is our best witness with other verses to clarify this issue:

Isaiah 66:19 And **I will set a sign among them**, and I will send those that escape of them unto the nations, [to] **Tarshish, Pul, and Lud, that draw the bow, [to] Tubal, and Javan**, [to] the **isles afar off, that have not heard My fame, neither have seen My glory**; and they shall declare My glory among the Gentiles.

Here, Tarshish, Pul, Tubal, and Lud are all lumped together as the ones who "draw the bow." All these areas are in close proximity to Turkey. Why should Tarshish then be in Spain or England?

Question-How can you say that Turkey is <u>included</u> in the rise of the Islamic Empire, even though the Ottoman Empire no longer exists?

Answer-The Ottoman Empire might have died away, but as illustrated above I do not predict a rise of the Ottoman Empire, but a rise of the Islamic Empire. Turkey was a part of the last Islamic empire, so the question should be would Turkey the seat of the eastern Roman Empire and also part of the Grecian Empire rise to power with Islam again? I believe it will play a major role as indicated by Daniel the prophet.

This book illustrates that you can choose to believe YHWH or ignore YHWH. The choice is yours but one thing is certain. We in Europe are being 'Islamised' slowly with our leaders' trying to tell us that Islam is a peaceful religion. That is just a lie, as western European civilization will learn the hard way. The following article appeared recently in the London Telegraph proving my theory that this is happening already. Whether Turkey is allowed to join Europe or not, this is a significant step towards what I am saying will happen. Whichever way Turkey goes, either east or west, it will become the base for the coming Anti-Messiah, as indicated by the prophets aligning itself with Southern Russia who are in fact all Turks with different flavors of Turkic dialects. We should expect persecution of Christians and Jews to increase in these lands and expect an increased activity of suicide bombings and attacks. We are beginning to see signs of these things already.

Turkey's Muslim millions threaten EU values, says commissioner

By Ambrose Evans-Pritchard in Brussels (Filed: 08/09/2004)-A European commissioner set off a furious row yesterday after warning that Europe's Christian civilization risked being overrun by Islam. If Turkey is allowed to join then we are going to open up a Pandora's box. We will see trouble ahead and things will move very rapidly for the Islamization of Europe. The enemy within will get stronger and parts of Europe will sway to Muslim feelings isolating key member states. **Parts of Sweden have already gone Islamic. From** http://www.jihadwatch.org/dhimmiwatch/

An exclusive series of translations from the Swedish press, made for Jihad **Watch by Ali Dashti, who writes:** Sweden is one of the worst hit countries in Europe of Muslim immigration and political correctness. Now, the police themselves have publicly admitted that they no longer control one of Sweden's major cities. I have made some exclusive translations from the Swedish media. They show the future of Eurabia unless Europeans wake up.

I have seen the future of Eurabia, and it's called 'Sweden.' Malm is Sweden's third largest city, after Stockholm and Gothenburg. Once-peaceful Sweden, home of ABBA, IKEA and the Nobel Prize, is increasingly looking like the Middle East on a bad day.

All the following links to major Swedish newspapers, with a brief translation; http://www.aftonbladet.se/vss/nyheter/story/0,2789,529910,00.html

Malm, Sweden. The police now publicly admit what many Scandinavians have known for a long time: They no longer control the situation in the nation's third largest city because it is effectively ruled by violent gangs of Muslim immigrants. Some of the Muslims have lived in the area of Roseng rd, Malm, for twenty years, and still don't know how to read or write Swedish. Ambulance personnel are attacked by stones or weapons and refuse to help anybody in the area without police escort.

The immigrants also spit at them when they come to help. Recently, an Albanian youth was stabbed by an Arab and was left bleeding to death on the ground while the ambulance waited for the police to arrive. The police themselves hesitate to enter parts of their own city unless they have several patrols and need to have guards to watch their cars, otherwise they will be vandalized. "Something drastic has to be done, or much more blood will be spilled" says one of the locals.

Question- How can Islam be the "one-world government" spoken of in the Bible?

Answer- The Bible does not speak about a "one-world government." It speaks about a united single **confederacy of end time Islamic nations**. The Islamic nations do not need to be a "one-world government," or world dominating power. They have enough influence on the world right now. YHWH is going to make His own confederacy to combat those nations who come up against Israel to fight and try to destroy Israel as mentioned in **Psalm 83**.

> In **Micah 5:5-6** we read: And this **Man** shall be the peace, when **the Assyrian [the Anti-Messiah]** shall come into our land: and when he shall tread in our palaces, **[Temple Mount] then shall we raise against him seven shepherds, and eight principal men**.

YHWH will call out seven **Sheep nations** **with eight principle men to fight this Islamic confederacy**. The whole world is not locked together and there is no real conspiracy theory out there. That exists only in fiction! We need to stop being sensationalists and start looking at Bible prophecy with a serious eye. The mighty USA army is having enough trouble bringing order to Iraq, so then how could anyone seriously hope that by some magic the whole world will be brought under an alleged "one-world government" through one man. These sorts of theories do not give serious considerations to world politics, cultural behaviors, or Bible prophecy.

On a prophecy level alone this is untenable. YHWH is mustering nations and in Genesis YHWH gave a prophecy for Ishmael's progeny that no one can control. Islamists are the seed of Esau. That means no "one-world government" nonsense that somehow can rein Esau in. **If Esau is not involved in a "one-world government," then by definition there is no "one-world government."**

> **Genesis 16:12 He shall be a wild man**; his hand shall be against every man, and **every man's hand against him**. And he shall dwell in the presence of all his brethren."

Historically speaking no nation has ruled the Arabs, they have been exactly as the Bible suggests. This one prophecy alone is enough to break any "one-world government" idea, or theory invented by men who for the most part, cannot even believe YHWH's word, when He tells them that Babylon is Babylon and not New York, or Washington! The only "one-world government" in history will form when Yahushua the Messiah returns and forms that "one-world government" to rule the world. Until then we have several governments ruling regions of the world. We can either believe Yahweh, or believe man. I choose to believe Yahweh. By saying and proclaiming a coming "one-world Anti-Messiah government," we call YHWH a liar. The end time action will take place in the region of the Middle East and like it or not, nations will be drawn to battle there.

> **Micah 5:8** And the remnant of Jacob shall be among the Gentiles [Gentile nations supporting Israel] in the midst of many people as a lion among the beasts of the forest, as a young lion among the flocks of sheep: who, if he go through, both treadeth down, and teareth in pieces, and none can deliver ["one-world government" idea is utterly false].

Jacob's descendants are very powerful and no one can deliver out of their hands. This has never happened before and no "one-world government" is in view either.

333

Micah 5:9 Thine hand shall be lifted up upon <u>thine adversaries, and ALL thine enemies</u> shall be <u>cut off</u>.

If the <u>whole-world</u> [led by an alleged "one-world government"] is against Israel, then the whole world will be cut-off (killed) and <u>none</u> left, since all YHWH's foes will be destroyed. But this is not what Scripture teaches. It is absurd and cannot be reconciled with Scripture. Israel's primary enemies are the Muslims and it is them [all of them] that will be annihilated and anyone else that is with them when Armageddon starts.

Micah 5:12 And I will cut off witchcrafts [false religion of Islam] out of thine hand; and thou shalt have no more soothsayers.

At the end of the age the false religion of Islam also is destroyed, its clerics also removed.

Micah 5:13 Thy **graven images also will I cut off**, and *thy standing images* [AL-AQSA Mosque will be demolished, Mecca and the standing Kabba will be destroyed] out of the midst of thee; and thou shalt no more worship the work of thine hands.

Since there are no more **graven images** left, then one could safely reason that there are no more people going to the Hajj pilgrimage to Mecca, or visiting the Iraqi Muslim holy sites.

Micah 5:15 And I will execute vengeance in anger and fury upon the <u>heathen</u> [YHWH calls them heathen because of their vile practices], such as they have not heard.

Who are these Muslims? These are heathens who do not know the one true YHWH, but follow after the false god Allah.

The prophecy writers have created confusion by calling end-times Babylon a "one-world government" and then placing this fictitious government in Europe or in the USA. When Islamic nations join together and become one confederacy, then they will have sufficient strength to accomplish Psalm 83 in principle. But we know that YHWH will not allow them to defeat Israel and take over the land that YHWH gave to the Jewish people. Look at the following chart to understand the number of Muslims in the world today. They are truly spread globally and can create enough havoc to destabilize the whole world. This could in itself form the so-called "one-world government" [more accurately 'one world havoc, since this beast breaks down the rule of justice wherever it is established], but suffice is to say I do not advocate any such theories, neither does the Bible, so I refrain from writing about it. [67]

---

[67] http://www.iiie.net/Intl/PopStats.html The number of the total population has been taken from <u>The CIA's World Fact Book</u> which can be found at: http://www.cia.gov/cia/publications/factbookhttp://members.tripod.com/arabicpaper/country.html Percentages are calculated on an estimated basis from the sites above with adjustments made for the total population for each nation.

Country	Total Population	Muslim Percentage	Number Of Muslims
Total	6,281,727,918	24%	1,537,986,663
Afghanistan	26,813,057	99%	26,544,926
Albania	3,510,484	70%	2,457,339
Algeria	31,736,053	99%	31,418,692
Angola	10,366,031	25%	2,591,508
Antigua Barbuda	66,970	?	?
Argentina	37,384,816	2.1%	785,081
Armenia	3,336,100	1%	33,361
Aruba	70,007	5%	3,500
Australia	19,357,594	2%	387,152
Austria	8,150,835	4.2%	342,335
Azerbaijan	7,771,092	93.4%	7,258,200
Bahamas, The	297,852	?	?
Bahrain	645,361	100%	645,361
Bangladesh	141,340,476	83%	117,312,595
Barbados	275,330	?	?
Belarus	10,350,194	5%	517,510
Belgium	10,258,762	4%	410,350
Belize	256,062	?	?
Benin	6,590,782	20%	1,318,156
Bhutan	2,049,412	5%	102,471
Bolivia	8,300,463	?	?
Bosnia-Herzegovina	3,922,205	40%	1,568,882
Botswana	1,586,119	5%	79,306
Brazil	174,468,575	1.1%	1,919,154
Brunei	343,653	67%	230,248
Bulgaria	7,707,495	13%	1,001,974
Burkina-Faso	12,272,289	50%	6,136,145
Burma	41,994,678	4%	4,597,563
Burundi	6,223,897	20%	1,244,779
Cambodia	12,491,501	1%	124,915
Cameroon	15,803,220	55%	8,691,771
Canada	31,592,805	1.5%	473,892

335

Cape Verde	405,163	?	?
Central African Republic	3,576,884	55%	1,967,286
Chad	8,707,078	85%	7,401,016
Chile	15,328,467	?	?
China	1,306,313,812	5%	65,315,691
Christmas Island	2,771	10%	277
Cocos (Keeling) Island	633	57%	361
Colombia	40,349,388	?	?
Comoros	596,202	98%	584,278
Congo, Dem. Rep. of the	53,624,718	10%	5,362,472
Congo, Republic of the	2,894,336	15%	434,150
Costa Rica	3,773,057	?	?
Cote d'Ivoire	14,762,445	60%	8,857,467
Croatia	4,496,869	1.3%	58,459
Cuba	11,184,023	0%	550
Cyprus	775,927	18%	139,667
Czech Republic	10,264,212	2%	205,284
Denmark	5,352,815	2%	107,056
Djibouti	427,642	94%	401,983
Dominican Republic	8,581,477	?	?
Ecuador	13,183,978	?	?
Egypt	76,117,421	94%	71,550,376
El Salvador	6,237,662	?	?
Equatorial Guinea	523,051	20%	104,610
Eritrea	4,561,599	50%	2,280,800
Estonia	1,423,316	?	?
Ethiopia	67,851,281	55%	37,318,205
Fiji	880,874	8%	70,470
Finland	5,175,783	1%	51,758
France	59,551,227	7.5%	4,466,342
Gabon	1,172,798	1%	11,728
Gambia	1,546,848	90%	1,392,163
Gaza Strip	1,324,991	98.7%	1,307,766
Georgia	4,693,892	11%	516,328
Germany	83,536,115	3.7%	3,090,836
Ghana	20,757,032	16%	3,321,125

Gibraltar	27,884	4%	1,115
Greece	10,668,354	1.3%	138,689
Guatemala	14,655,189	?	?
Guinea	9,467,866	85%	8,047,686
Guinea Bissau	1,416,027	45%	637,212
Guyana	765,283	10%	76,528
Haiti	8,121,622	?	?
Honduras	6,975,204	?	?
Hong Kong	6,898,686	1%	68,987
Hungary	10,006,835	2%	200,137
Iceland	296,737	?	?
India	1,080,264,388	14%	151,237,014
Indonesia	241,973,879	88%	212,937,014
Iran	68,017,860	98%	66,657,503
Iraq	26,074,906	97%	25,292,659
Ireland	4,015,676	2%	80,314
Israel	6,276,883	16%	1,004,301
Italy	58,103,033	1%	581,030
Jamaica	2,665,636	?	?
Japan	125,449,703	1%	1,254,497
Jordan	4,212,152	95%	4,001,544
Kazakstan	16,916,463	51.2%	8,661,229
Kenya	28,176,686	29.5%	8,312,122
Korea, North	21,968,228	?	?
Korea, South	47,904,370	1%	479,044
Kuwait	1,950,047	89%	1,735,542
Kyrgyzstan	4,529,648	76.1%	3,447,062
Laos	5,635,967	2%	112,719
Latvia	2,385,231	?	?
Lebanon	3,776,317	70%	2,643,422
Lesotho	1,970,781	10%	197,078
Liberia	2,109,789	30%	632,937
Libya	5,445,436	100%	5,445,436
Lithuania	3,610,535	1%	36,105
Macedonia	2,104,035	30%	631,211
Madagascar	13,670,507	20%	2,734,101

337

Malawi	9,452,844	35%	3,308,495
Malaysia	23,522,482	52%	12,231,691
Maldives	270,758	100%	270,758
Mali	11,956,788	90%	10,761,109
Malta	375,576	14%	52,581
Mauritania	2,336,048	100%	2,336,048
Mauritius	1,140,256	19.5%	222,350
Mayotte	100,838	99%	99,830
Mexico	101,879,171	?	?
Moldova	4,431,570	?	?
Mongolia	2,496,617	4%	99,865
Morocco	29,779,156	98.7%	29,392,027
Mozambique	17,877,927	29%	5,184,599
Namibia	1,677,243	5%	83,862
Nepal	22,094,033	4%	883,761
Netherlands	16,318,199	6%	979,092
New Zealand	3,864,129	1%	38,641
Nicaragua	4,918,393	?	?
Niger	9,113,001	91%	8,292,831
Nigeria	137,253,133	60%	82,351,880
Norway	4,438,547	1.5%	66,578
Oman	2,186,548	100%	2,186,548
Pakistan	159,196,336	97%	154,420,446
Panama	2,655,094	4%	106,204
Paraguay	5,734,139	?	?
Papua New Guinea	5,049,055	?	?
Peru	27,483,864	?	?
Philippines	86,241,697	5%	4,312,085
Poland	38,633,912	2%	772,678
Portugal	10,066,253	?	?
Puerto Rico	3,937,316	?	?
Qatar	547,761	100%	547,761
Reunion	679,198	20%	135,840
Romania	22,329,977	0.8%	178,640
Russia	145,470,197	9%	13,092,318
Rwanda	7,312,756	14%	1,023,786

338

Saudi Arabia	19,409,058	100%	19,409,058
Senegal	9,092,749	95%	8,638,112
Serbia and Montenegro	10,677,290	19%	2,028,685
Sierra Leone	4,793,121	65%	3,115,529
Singapore	4,353,893	17%	740,162
Slovakia	5,414,937	2%	108,299
Slovenia	1,951,443	1%	19,514
Somalia	9,639,151	100%	9,639,151
South Africa	41,743,459	2%	834,869
Spain	40,037,995	?	?
Sri Lanka	18,553,074	9%	1,669,777
Sudan	39,148,162	80%	31,318,530
Suriname	436,418	25%	109,105
Swaziland	998,730	10%	99,873
Sweden	9,800,000	3.6%	320,000
Switzerland	7,283,274	?	?
Syria	15,608,648	90%	14,047,783
Taiwan	22,370,461	?	?
Tajikistan	5,916,373	85%	5,028,917
Tanzania	29,058,470	65%	18,888,006
Thailand	58,851,357	14%	8,239,190
Togo	4,570,530	55%	2,513,792
Trinidad and Tobago	1,272,385	12%	152,686
Tunisia	9,019,687	98%	8,839,293
Turkey	66,493,970	99.8%	66,360,982
Turkmenistan	4,149,283	87%	3,609,876
Uganda	20,158,176	36%	7,256,943
Ukraine	48,760,474	?	?
United Arab Emirates	3,057,337	96%	2,935,044
United Kingdom	58,489,975	2.7%	1,579,229
United States	293,027,571	3%	8,790,827
Uruguay	3,360,105	?	?
Uzbekistan	23,418,381	88%	20,608,175
Venezuela	23,916,810	?	?
Vietnam	79,939,014	1%	799,390
West Bank	2,090,713	75%	1,568,035

339

Western Sahara	222,631	100%	222,631
Yemen	13,483,178	99%	13,348,346
Zambia	10,462,436	25%	2,615,609
Zimbabwe	12,671,860	1%	126,719

There are a total of 52 official Islamic nations and over 1.5 billion Muslim followers who are increasing by the day. The question marks (?) in the chart above, indicates that we do not know what percentage of the population in these nations are truly Muslims.

Question- How can "Gog" be both a person and the Anti-Messiah?

Answer- I understand your dilemma, but since YHWH does not have a problem with calling Gog both a person and a confederacy of many peoples, then likewise I do not have a problem either.

> **Ezekiel 38:2** Son of man, set thy face against Gog, the land of Magog; Here the Master is separating the two, but in other passages the usage is combined.

In **Ezekiel 38:16** *"You will come up against My people Israel like a cloud, to cover the land. **It will be in the latter days** that I will bring **you** against My land, so that the nations may know Me, when I am hallowed in **you**, O Gog, before their eyes."* Note that YHWH addresses Gog as a singular person "you," applying it to the individual and also many other nations with him. But we do know that it represents a group of nations that are coming up to attack Israel which are all mentioned in Ezekiel 38:2. This is both an individual name given to the Anti-Messiah and it also incorporates the conglomerate nations of the Anti-Messiah's beast/Empire. Let us not forget that the bride of Messiah, singular is used to identify a group of believers. So how can it be a group of people, as well as a single bride? The answer is the same. This is YHWH's way of describing the body of believers, His only wife.

> **Revelation 19:20** **Then the beast was captured**, and **with him the false prophet** who worked signs in his presence, by which he deceived those who received the mark of the beast and those who worshiped his image. **These two were cast alive** into the lake of fire burning with brimstone.

Although most people think that the beast is just one individual, but no it is a group of nations judged together and thrown in the lake of fire along with Anti-Messiah and the false prophet.

Question-Why do you say that the Anti-Messiah has to come from Turkey?

Answer-All the biblical references are to a place, which is today called Turkey. If you look at **Ezekiel 38** it says this person is Gog, the prince of Rosh, Meshech, and Tubal. This person who is mentioned as Meshech is a Turkic leader. This is coupled with lots of references in the Bible and the other reference in Revelation 2:13. We are also told that Turkic nations will form part of the attack on Israel. In Zechariah 9:13 we are told in no uncertain terms that the battle is with the Grecians. In Hebrew the word is Yavan, Turkic,

340

not modern Greece. Daniel gives it away by saying the Anti-Messiah comes out of the historical division of the Grecian Empire from one of the four divisions, and the "little horn" is from the Seleucid kingdom, or the quarter north of Israel, the same place that Aniochus Epiphanes came from. See Daniel 8:9. **The Macmillan Bible Atlas, Oxford Bible Atlas, The Moody Atlas of Bible Lands, and others, locate Magog, Meshech, Tubal, Gomer and Beth Togarmah in Asia Minor, not Russia as a whole.** But southern Russia will also be part of the Magog nations, while northern Russians are Slavic peoples historically speaking and will not be involved in the attack on Israel. This region of Asia Minor includes the following locations:

-Turkey
-Uzbekistan
-Kyrgyzstan
-Tajikistan
-Girgestan
-Uzbekistan
-Dagestan
-Azerbaijan
-Turkmenistan

Hesiod the contemporary of Ezekiel has already indicated in historical writings that the Magogians were Scythians and Southern Russians in the 7th century BC. Today these nations form the CIS nations and are all Muslim with the majority being racially Turkic. Even the languages they speak are all different dialects of the Turkic language. Those teachers that deny that the Anti-Messiah is Turkic, or place him in Europe, or Washington are not only calling Daniel, Micah and Zechariah false witnesses, but also deny the written word of YHWH. By definition calling Yahweh a liar is blasphemy and is classified as bearing false witness. They will have to answer to Yahweh on the day of judgement for the reasons that they denied His plain words. The Master Yahushua said that by the mouth of two, or three credible witnesses, a matter shall be established (Matthew 18:16). And, we have more than three witnesses one of whom is the Master Himself.

Question-Are you saying that all the Muslims are bad, when my neighbors are good Muslims and are not into terrorism?

Answer-No. I did not say all the Muslims are bad. On the contrary, there are many good Muslims. Those that we generally consider Muslims are not considered Muslims by Islamist standards. Most so called good Muslims are not working for and toward an outward jihad. However if they really followed the Qur'an and the Hadith fully and literally, then there is only one way for them and that is to subjugate Christians and Jews by conversion, or by the killing of the infidels. There are many good secular Muslims in the world, but the Islamists do not consider them Muslims at all, because they are considered to be on the side of the west. By not partaking in jihad, they are automatically seen as collaborators with Israel and, or the USA. Did we not see the beheading of "secular Muslims" working in Iraq for Americans and non-American companies? Why were they beheaded if they are Muslims? The reason is simple and fully agrees with my conclusion. They are not considered to be following true Islam. In history, the sword always propagated Islam. A famous case in Islam was that of Abu Sufyan who was against Muhammad. When Muhammad had him captured, he was offered a choice to either to embrace Islam, or face the sword. He chose Islam, not because Islam was the truth, but simply to remain live. The true final question is not should we condemn all Muslims as evil, but do they all carry the mark of the beast or not? The answer is sadly yes. Muslims whether good, or bad, practicing their religion or not, all carry the <u>mark</u> and are most likely to follow their leaders in the end time battle against the west and Israel. That remains the reality of the situation whether we like it or not.

Those Muslims that oppose their crazed recognized leaders will be killed and labelled as apostates. Is YHWH going to automatically forgive those Muslims who remain in Islam without repentance, even if they are secularists? Again the answer is no! It is not up to me to decide the fate of 1.5 billion Muslims, as that is a decision for them to make whether to choose eternity in hell, or eternity in heaven. But the bottom line is this; without repentance in and to King Yahushua, they are in the wrong camp and are not headed for eternity into heaven. Like me coming from a Muslim background, it was a harsh reality from my old religion that I could not claim to be heading for the kingdom of YHWH without the blood of the Lamb. That changed with my repenting of all my sins to the Master Yahushua the Messiah. He said it beautifully; that eternity is not merely a future promise, but is available right now, but only if one believes in Him. If Muslims continue in their present course and die in their sins, they, like all others who reject Yahushua's deity and atonement end up in hell. **John 8:24** "Therefore I said to you that **you will die in your sins**; for **if you do not believe that I AM [I AM THAT I AM]** He, you will die in your sins." **John 10:28** "And I [Yahushua the Messiah] give them eternal life [the right to be in heaven] and they shall never perish**; neither shall anyone snatch them out of My hand.

Question- Are "All the nations" of <u>**Zechariah 12:9**</u> that will come up against Jerusalem the whole world?

Answer- No, this is the most misapplied reading of this passage and others like it. The context is very clear, as it tells us in **Zechariah 12:2** that these are ALL the '**surrounding nations**' but I have heard many respectable prophecy writers read the whole world into it, which is not true at all.

> <u>Zechariah 12:2</u> "Behold, I will make Jerusalem a cup of drunkenness to **all the surrounding peoples**, when they lay siege against Judah and Jerusalem.

This verse and others like it also destroys the credibility of the ones who propagate the alleged "one-world government" theory, which is why they will never mention **Zechariah 12:2**. It makes it abundantly clear that "ALL" the surrounding nations are ALL Islamic nations/heathens when THEY (the Muslims) lay the SIEGE against Jerusalem. Is it not incredible that people do not pay attention to this text, even though it spells it out for us? In this book I have explained the meaning of the term "all" in order to get rid of the confusion. All does not mean the "whole world," as explained earlier. **It needs to be qualified and we can see that Zechariah 12:2 does qualify this ALL for us, as it is ALL the 'surrounding nations'**.

> <u>Zechariah 14:14</u> Judah also will fight at [for] Jerusalem. And the wealth of **ALL the surrounding nations shall be gathered together**: gold, silver, and apparel in great abundance. There is no mention of any western nations against Israel. In fact, Judah is fighting on the ground. If the Messiah is going to kill and remove the enemy by His words alone, then why is Judah fighting with Him?

Joel 3:12 "Let the nations be wakened, and come up to the Valley of Jehoshaphat; for there I will sit to judge **ALL the surrounding [Islamic] nations**.

Even Joel confirms that **all the "surrounding nations"** will be judged for the division of Israel. We know that these are ALL Islamic. There can be no mistake about this, yet many want to argue in favor of impending judgement on the whole word for the division of Israel. Would it be fair for a Holy and Just YHWH to judge Japan who has nothing to do with the division? How about South Korea or Canada? There are many problems with the view that the whole world lies in judgement, due to Israel's impotent leadership giving away land usurped by the Islamic nations. Let me give you another example, in the book of **Matthew Chapter 2:3** we are told: When Herod the king had heard these things, he was troubled, **and ALL Jerusalem with him**. Now ask yourself this question; was ALL of Jerusalem troubled? That would mean every man, woman and child was troubled by the announcement of The King being born? Were the atheists and agnostics troubled? The answer is No. Moreover many people rejoiced at his birth. The "ALL" in the above passage is in context ALL the people who were in King Herod's Palace close to him. These are the people who were troubled, not the whole of Jerusalem. The reason is simple, as they were troubled because their jobs were threatened, including Herod's kingdom. So the ALL is a synecdoche, or a figure of speech.

Question-What is the significance of Sudan in the end times?

Answer-Just like Pakistan that is part of the former Grecian Empire and split from India to join forces with Islam, the same way Sudan is "Cush," south of the river Egypt, that will join forces with Islam to fight Israel. **Habakkuk 3:7-**I saw the tents of Cushan in affliction; the curtains of the land of Midian trembled. The tents of Sudan are under judgement at the return of Messiah because of the part they play within Islam. The Midians (Arabs) are trembling also; it mentions their land trembling with fear. Sudan has had a genocide going on for the past twenty plus years and so far very few nations have spoken of the affliction of the Sudanese people other than the USA. The genocide is orchestrated by the fiends that rule Saudi Arabia, against Sudan's Christians.

1 Chronicles 1:10 And Cush begat Nimrod: he began to be mighty upon the earth. It is interesting that Cush begat Nimrod. **Genesis 10:8-9** Cush begot Nimrod; he began to be a mighty one on the earth. He **was a mighty hunter before the Master**; therefore it is said, "Like Nimrod the mighty hunter before the Master."

Nimrod means – We shall rebel. He was neither, a hunter of deer, or fox but rather a rebel, a type of dictator. We can call him the first dictator of the world who started out of Iraq. This is not surprising given the current situation of Iraq and its place in Bible prophecy. **Genesis 10:10** And the beginning of his kingdom [Cush, Nimrod] was Babel, Erech, Accad, and Calneh, in **the land of Shinar**. [Iraq]. He had the first kingdom in open rebellion against YHWH. That's where the Sudanese come from. The Hebrew word "pawnaeem" here in verse 9 more appropriately is translated "against the Master," rather than "before" the Master. He was not before the Master as a good man, but against the Master as a wicked man. One commentary of the Jewish Talmud on this passage reads "a hunter of the souls of men." He was a rebel against YHWH and sought to turn those he ruled away from YHWH as well.

We have to ask, just who is committing the atrocities in Sudan today? You and I both know it is one group of people in Sudan, **the Islamists from Saudi Arabia**, who are backing this group that is wrongly called the militia. Saudi Arabia's real agenda is to take Southern Sudan, which is rich in oil. No oil exists in northern Sudan, or one could argue none has been found, because of its rocky terrain. Many Muslims are located in northern Sudan; however, Christians are in the South. Now the agenda becomes clear; to kill, pillage and drive Christians out of this area. This is called ethnic cleansing, just so we get our bearings straight. This agenda and genocide is government based and permits Muslims/the beast, to drill for oil in the south, thereby claiming all of the wealth for themselves. **Sudan is referred to as Cush in the Bible and many people make the mistake of thinking that it is present day Ethiopia**. It is not Ethiopia. But is it not interesting that this nation is also part of the end time confederacy of Muslim nations and is now an Islamic country?

What is the west doing about Sudan? The answer is other then a few protests by Christian groups and a USA backed resolution not much else. The UN passed a resolution against the Sudanese government to bring the persecution and suffering of the Christian citizens to an end. The deadline has passed and nothing has happened. This shows the power of the UN, which is able to do nothing because it is a puppet of Islamic nations that largely make up the UN. It was the Arab League of Nations within the UN that had the wording of the resolution changed so as not to penalize the Sudanese government. The UN has been proven to be corrupt in the oil for food program, where Saddam Hussain was rewarding them to protect his interests. Many believe that its time to disband the UN and form another more stable organization. The significance of Sudan is simply that it will join forces with the Anti-Messiah's forces and that is why we are seeing the redefining of their borders.

Question- Who are the two witnesses of Revelation?

Answer- I prayed and asked the Master to reveal this and He revealed that the one witness is Elijah and he will come just like the Jews expect him to, the other witness is Zerubbabel. **Malachi 4:5-6** Behold, I will send you Elijah the prophet **before the coming of the great and dreadful day of the Master**. And he will **turn the hearts of the fathers to the children**, and the **hearts of the children to their fathers**, lest I come and strike the earth with a curse." YHWH is absolutely clear that He will send the prophet Elijah before the day of the Master and he will turn the hearts of the Jewish people back to the faith of their fathers. **Matthew 11:14** "And if you are willing to receive it, he is Elijah who is to come. Yahushua did not say that John was Elijah, but that John was *"like"* Elijah, if they accepted him. But most of the Jewish leadership did not accept him. **Luke 1:17** "He will also go before Him in the spirit and power of Elijah, `to turn the hearts of the fathers to the children,' and the disobedient to the wisdom of the just, to make ready a people prepared for the Master." We are told that John the Baptiser was coming in the spirit of Elijah to turn the hearts of men to the Elohim of Israel. **Matthew 17:10-11** And His disciples asked Him, saying, "Why then do the scribes say that Elijah must come first?" Then Yahushua answered and said to them, "Elijah truly is coming first and will restore all things. Yahushua confirms that Elijah is truly coming to restore all things.

What about the scholars who say Elijah cannot come and die because now he has a new resurrected body and how can he come and die given this situation? The scholars who believe in this have built a straw man for themselves; the Bible does not say Elijah has gone to YHWH's third heaven or that he is now in his new resurrected body. Elijah was taken up in a cloud to the first heaven i.e. the sky and even after Elijah was taken up by YHWH, he somehow managed to write a letter from heaven three years after his ascension. So where did this letter come from if Elijah is no longer on the earth? **2 Chronicles 21:12** And a letter came to him from Elijah the prophet, saying, thus says the Master YHWH of your father David: "Because you have not walked in the ways of Jehoshaphat your father, or in the ways of Asa king of Judah. Those scholars that want to proclaim Elijah has gone to heaven have to distort YHWH's word by saying this verse is perhaps a scribal error because how could Elijah write a letter if he was no longer on the earth? **2 Kings 2:11** Then it happened, as they continued on and talked, that suddenly a chariot of fire appeared with horses of fire, and separated the two of them; and **Elijah went up by a whirlwind into heaven.** The Hebrew word for heaven used in this passage is "*shaw-mah-yim*," the same one used in Genesis 1:1, and in this context it could very well refer to the arterial sky not YHWH's personal dwelling place. **Revelation 11:6** These have power to shut **heaven**, so that no rain falls in the days of their prophecy; and <u>they have power over waters to turn them to blood</u>, and to strike the earth with all plagues, as often as they desire.

The two witnesses have the power to shut heaven i.e. they can stop the rain as it says in Revelation 11:6. We know that Elijah did have this power in the past and he will use this to demonstrate YHWH's authority on the earth in the future. The First Covenant was brought with mighty signs and wonders, and the New/Renewed Covenant was brought with mighty signs and wonders. The end of the age will also be brought with mighty signs and wonders. The two witnesses (one from Judah and one from Ephraim) will come and witness throughout the three and a half years of the Great Tribulation period and will be killed by the Islamic beast at the end. Their dead bodies are left in the streets of Jerusalem for three days. The trait of leaving dead bodies in the streets without proper burial to serve as object warnings to other "infidels" is an Islamic one. They do this to make this a lesson for other people. Today no European country would allow this to happen, neither would the Jews allow a corpse to rot in the streets of Jerusalem. Muslims have demonstrated that they can and will allow this to happen, as we saw in Iraq, where people who were killed by the Islamists, had their dead corpses rotting in the streets for days.

Revelation 11:7-12 Now when they finish their testimony, the beast that ascends out of the bottomless pit will **make war against them**, overcome them, and **kill them**. And their <u>dead bodies will lie in the street</u> of the great city, **which spiritually is called Sodom and Egypt [because much of it is made up of Muslims and their pagan shrines]**, where also our Master is crucified. Then those from the peoples, tribes, tongues, and nations will see their dead bodies <u>three and a half days [years?]</u>, and <u>not allow</u> their dead bodies to be put into graves. And those who **dwell on the earth will rejoice** over them, **make merry**, and **send gifts** to one another, because these two [Israelite] prophets tormented those who dwell on the earth [or in the land]. Now after the three and a half days [years] the <u>breath of life</u> from YHWH entered them, and they stood on their feet, and <u>great fear fell</u> on those who saw them. And they heard a loud voice from heaven saying to them, "<u>Come up here.</u>" And they <u>ascended to heaven in a cloud</u>, and their enemies saw them. Notice these things:

❖ Their ministry will last three and a half years of the tribulation (Revelation 11:3) – Tribulation is 3.5 years, not seven years, as most believe.

❖ The Islamic beast kills the Israelite witnesses after their ministry when YHWH allows it.
❖ Their dead bodies lie in the street for **three** and a **half** days.
❖ Their dead bodies are deliberately not given a burial to make an example of them by the Islamists, this is an Islamic trait also seen in Iraq.
❖ The people in this **region**, the Greek word "*ghay*" *is* used to represent a region of the world. These people are happy and send candy to celebrate the death of the two witnesses. Muslims also do this when Israelites are murdered in case you have not noticed.
❖ Three and a half days later they are resurrected.
❖ People are greatly afraid in that region after seeing these witnesses resurrected back to life.

The witnesses are then taken back to the arterial heaven. The only people who do this are Islamic. They make examples with dead corpses; they send candy to celebrate death and murder, just like they did when Osama bin Laden struck the twin towers. The same holds true in Iraq, when Americans soldiers were killed. These traits are completely Islamic. During the Twin Towers destruction, on exit 50 (Brentwood) of the Long Island Expressway, Muslims were seen dancing in the streets praising Allah. In the USA in the Cape Cod Massachusetts area a Muslim doctor working in a hospital at the time, upon hearing the news of the Twin Towers collapsing, started to rejoice and dance praising Allah. FBI agents swiftly removed him. Does this not show that even the Muslim intellectuals are deceived and though this doctor's job was to save lives, yet he was literally celebrating death? This is evil acted out by the people of the beast.

The language used to indicate that Zerubbabel is the second witness is very clear. Here is why he has been chosen:

> **Zechariah 4:7-13** Who are you, **O Great Mountain**? Before Zerubbabel you shall become a plain! And he shall bring forth the capstone with shouts of "**Grace, grace to it**! Moreover the word of the Master came to me, saying: "The hands of Zerubbabel have laid the foundation of this Temple; **his hands shall also finish it**. Then you will know that the Master of hosts has sent me to you. For who has despised the day of small things? For **these seven rejoice** to see **the plumb line in the hand of Zerubbabel**. They are the eyes of the Master, which scan to and fro throughout the whole earth. Then I answered and said to him, what are these two olive trees, one at the right of the lampstand and the other at its left?' And I further answered and said to him, what are these two olive branches that drip into the receptacles of the two gold pipes from which the golden oil drains?' Then he answered me and said, do you not know what these are? And I said, No, my lord. So he said, "These are the two anointed ones, who stand beside the Master of the whole earth."

Note these things: Zerubbabel laid the foundation of the Temple and he shall finish it.

He says "**who are you O Great Mountain**," this reference is to the Islamic Empire, or the beast/kingdom to tell them that they have no control over us. The Mountain (kingdom) still stands and is not destroyed. This prophecy has had only a partial fulfilment and in proper order it will only be fully fulfilled in the latter days.

The Master tells us that these two olive trees are the witnesses of the Master. The clincher is the passage in **Revelation 11:4.** These are the two olive trees and the two lamp stands standing before the Elohim YHWH of the earth. The same is repeated earlier in **Zechariah 4:14** where YHWH said, "These are the two anointed ones, who stand beside the Master of the whole earth."

Moreover, Haggai gives us a tremendous prophecy about Zerubbabel and the end times.

> **Haggai 2:20-23** And again the word of the Master came unto Haggai in the four and twentieth day of the month, saying, Speak to Zerubbabel, governor of Judah, saying, **I will shake the heavens and the earth**; [end times] and I will overthrow **the throne of kingdoms**, [confederacy of nations] and **I will destroy the strength of the kingdoms of the heathen** [the Islamic empire that comes up against Israel]; and I will overthrow the chariots, and those that ride in them; and the horses and their riders shall come down, every one by the sword of his brother. **In that day,** [Day of the Master] saith the Master of hosts, will I take thee, O **Zerubbabel, my servant**, the **son of Shealtiel**, saith the Master, **and will make thee as a signet: [chosen to come back as a witness] for I have chosen thee [again]**, saith the Master of hosts.

This is amazing! Haggai is told that the Master will destroy the "**throne [Turkey/Pergamos/Beth Togarmah] of these kingdoms.**" They are the Islamic confederacy with 10 heads/kings as seen in Psalm 83, Ezekiel 38, Zechariah chapters 12 and 14. This is the prophesied Islamic coalition, of surrounding heathens. They are killed by confusion and by their own brothers. The reference to **"in that day,"** is none other than the "Day of the Master" yet future. The Master reveals **HE HAS CHOSEN** Zerubbabel for a divine mission and given him a special ring as a sign that he has been selected to fulfil YHWH's future purpose. This is why Zerubbabel will come back with Elijah and do great signs and wonders, before being subdued by the beast and then being resurrected.

Zerubbabel and Elijah both typify the Messiah Yahushua who came and was killed on the cross then was resurrected after three days. He will surely come back again with great glory and power. Both of these witnesses herald the coming of the Messiah with signs and wonders. When they come we know that this is during the 3.5 years of great tribulation, as their ministry will last three and a half years as specified by Revelation 11:3. They will turn many Jews and Ephraimites back to the Messiah. These Jews and Ephraimites in turn will pray for their Messiah Yahushua to return and save them from the enemy who wants to destroy them. The idea of a seven-year tribulation is not correct because the tribulation is really three and a half years when the Anti-Messiah is revealed, which many might refer to as mid-tribulation. It is clear from these passages in Zechariah, Malachi, Haggai and Revelation, why Elijah and Zerubbabel are the ones chosen as the two witnesses.

Question-When will Israel burn the weapons for seven years, is this not before the Tribulation?

Answer-First of all tribulation is really three and a half years and not seven as most are led to believe. The first three and a half years are to be relatively peaceful during the confirmation of the treaty. Where does Scripture dictate the timing of this event before, or during the tribulation? This event can only occur once the armies of Gog are destroyed on the mountains of Israel. In my opinion this event is linked into the Millennium reign. Logically this would happen in the first seven years of the Millennium. Since Israel will be so decimated by wars, floods, and earthquakes, YHWH could just click his fingers and recreate all the vegetation, trees and plants that have been destroyed. It makes sense that they will have to burn the weapons and other things left from the war for fuel, until new vegetation and trees have grown up. This is why this will happen during the first seven years of the millennial reign. When Israel was left as a barren land for many centuries it was the Jews who came back and irrigated the land to build and plant and the same will happen again.

> **Ezekiel 39:9** "Then those who live in the towns of Israel will go out and use the weapons for fuel and burn them-the small and large shields, the bows and arrows, the war clubs and spears." For seven years they will use them for fuel. Just like the text says they will burn these for fuel most probably in the first seven years of the Millennium.

> **Isaiah 9:5** For every **boot of the tramping warrior** in battle tumult and every garment rolled in blood will be burned as fuel for the fire.

> Here is a clue, it would be more correct to use the word "trampler" in **Isaiah 9:5**, instead of "tramping," this is another name for the Anti-Messiah called "**the trampler**" and this indicates burning of their weapons and even their clothes for fuel after Armageddon. Since the end of Armageddon is towards the end of the tribulation, or before the time Messiah comes back, it leaves us no room to assume the burning is before the Millennium period and His return. After the Trampler (Anti-Messiah is killed) we have Yahushua the Messiah's eternal government. This government is real just like the Master is real and physical and not just spiritual. We who are alive will be in our new glorified bodies and those that were dead will also be raised first in the resurrection and will also have glorified bodies.

> **Isaiah 9:6-7** For unto us a Child is born, unto us a Son is given; and the government will be upon His shoulder. And His name will be called Wonderful, Counsellor, **Mighty EL**, Everlasting Father, **Prince of Peace**. Of the increase of His government and peace there will be no end, upon the throne of David and over His kingdom, to order it and establish it with judgment and justice from that time forward, even forever. The zeal of the Master of hosts will perform this.

We know this prophecy is played out in two parts. The birth has happened, but the government is to be established in the future when the Messiah returns to reign with us on earth for 1,000 years. He is Almighty YHWH that is in Hebrew "El Gibbor." This title only applies to Yahweh and no one else, and this Yahushua our YHWH, will rule and reign from Jerusalem.

Question- What message would you like to share with the Muslims?

Answer- I was once there myself and dead in my sins. As long as you think Allah is god and Muhammad is his prophet you remain lost in eternity. You are nothing but a walking zombie. Your soul is destined to be separated from the loving true YHWH. I am not

348

Mother Teresa and I do not want to send you to hell with love. I am Simon Altaf and I am pleading with you to save your souls, leave Islam, follow that which is good, the Master Yahushua Messiah, who is the Savior of sinners made clean. You need blood atonement to fulfil YHWH's requirements; Yahushua of Nazareth is the <u>only</u> one who offers it in holiness. Some Jews today take chickens and swing it around their heads, thinking that that blood saves their soul. This is foolishness and contradicts His Holy requirement for the penalty of sin.

> <u>**Leviticus 17:11**</u> `For the **life of the flesh is in the blood,** and I have given it to you **upon the altar to make atonement for your souls; for it is the blood that makes atonement for the soul.**'

Was YHWH lying when He said <u>without</u> the blood there is no atonement of sin?

> <u>**Leviticus 1:1-3**</u> Now the **Master YHWH spoke to Moses,** saying, (2) "Speak to the children of Israel, saying: `If a person sins unintentionally against any of the commandments of the Master in anything which ought not to be done, and does any of them, (3) `if the anointed priest sins, bringing guilt on the people, then **let him offer to the Master for his sin which he has sinned a young bull** without blemish as a sin offering.

> <u>**Leviticus 1:10-14**</u> `And if his offering is of **the flocks of the sheep or of the goats** as a burnt sacrifice, he shall bring a male without blemish. (14) `And if the burnt sacrifice of his offering to the Master is of birds, then he shall bring his offering of **turtledoves or young pigeons**.

YHWH never allowed chickens for atonement even for the poorest of people. It was a turtledove or young pigeons but never chickens. See how foolish some of the Jewish Rabbis have become? So likewise, do not become foolish in your thinking like the Imams who falsely teach that good Muslim works can open a door to heaven for you, because they cannot. You <u>must</u> meet Yahweh's Holy requirements and that can only be met through the Master Yahushua in the absence of the Holy Temple in Jerusalem. There is no other way other than the one that YHWH Himself has provided. **Isaiah 64:6** tells us: "But we are all like **an unclean thing,** and **all our righteousness are like filthy rags**; we all fade as a leaf, and our iniquities, like the wind, have taken us away."

YHWH loves the Muslims because they are created in His image. Yahushua died for your sins if you will accept it. On the other hand if you will not listen, then you will have to pay the penalty of your sins all alone, which of course you cannot. The end result of that attempt is eternity is eternity without the Creator and eternal torment in Hell. I can assure you Hell is a real place, as most Muslims are taught and it is not a nice place to be. Seek the Master YHWH with all your heart and He will reveal Himself to you, like He did to me. His name is not Allah but Yahweh; so seek Him who is revealed in Yahushua of Nazareth and keep His commandments and that means all of them.

I say to you as our Yahweh Elohim said to our Israelite forefathers: <u>**Deuteronomy 30:19**</u> "I call heaven and earth **as witnesses today against you,** that I have set before **you life and death**, blessing and cursing; **therefore choose life**, that **both you and your**

descendants may live; May prayer is that you choose life for yourselves and avoid death.

Question-Did not the Crusaders kill the Muslims?

Answer-The crusades were against **Islam.** No, I would say that the Crusaders stated intention was not to pillage and kill Christians and Jews, but rather they undertook a crusade against the "original crusaders" who were the Muslims. Muslims had blocked trade routes, raped women, killed and pillaged pilgrims who were heading to Jerusalem. That is why the crusaders initially went to Jerusalem. The reasons were right, but the result was not the desired one. Let us not become confused and blame everything on the Roman Catholic Church. Yes, there was religious rhetoric, but the intention was not all wrong. In fact this was a very weak response from Europe and in my opinion the response should have been a lot earlier. In the recent second Gulf war the coalition forces freed Iraq from the grips of Saddam Hussain and there were some bad soldiers who mistreated Iraqi prisoners in Abu Gharaib prison. But are we now to say that the entire coalition force is bad? The Arabs invaded other people's lands and killed millions. It is estimated that in India alone millions of Hindus were slaughtered in the name of Allah. Sixty thousand people were slaughtered in a short period of time in the Hindu Kush Mountains, when Islam was forced on the populace. The words "Hindu Kush" are taken from the literal reading that Hindus were crushed there and there was blood flowing through the mountains. Interestingly this is the place where Osama bin Laden trained with his comrades too. Also the World Trade Center bombings were planned there. Could he be remembering old times to act out the same violence on the Americans? If you want to know what the Muslims did during that time then I suggest you read about a character by the name of Saladin Ayubi and then you may get to learn what the Islamists were like. Meanwhile here are some things that he is known to have done.

✦ Saladin stoned and blinded a Jewish doctor who dared to ride a horse (remember Umar's pact), please read "Saladin and the Jews," by E. Ashtor-Strauss.

✦ He cut the bodies of fellow Muslims who were Shiites since he himself was a Sunni Muslim and hated Shiites.

✦ He personally had many Christian Crusaders beheaded and watched his soldiers cut up their bodies.

✦ The Muslim jihadists in Spain killed and abased the Sephardic Jews including many Christians during this time. Rambam (Maimonides the Jewish scholar) even wrote about how bad the killings were, even though the Jews wanted peace.

Question- Was not Islam peaceful during its inception and culturally advanced?

Answer- I am sorry it wasn't. Islam was NEVER peaceful and never culturally advanced. Unfortunately this dream is conjured up in the minds of Muslims not Christians. For Christians it was nothing short of a nightmare living amongst Muslims being treated like dogs. Well actually that would be wrong for me to say because dogs get very good treatment in the west; but alas in the east they kick dogs and throw stones at them and even drive their cars on top of them. Do you call beheadings peaceful? Cutting off arms and feet peaceful? This was the order of the day in Islam, and many Christians lost their lives upon the inception of Islam along with many Jews who were decapitated. Oh yes, some may argue that the Muslims were only getting rid of those pesky rightwing activists, so that the Islamists could bring peace with the leftists. Sadly this was only the beginning of Jewish and Christian sorrows and whether they were on the right, center or left did not matter. Fundamentalist Christians and Jews were such a headache for the Muslims, that they decided rather than offer them an aspirin, that they would rather take their head off for a more permanent solution.

How would they be culturally advanced? In fact the Arab Bedouins were running around pillaging trade caravans of the Quraish tribe on Muhammad's orders. The same Quraish tribe that Muhammad himself once belonged to and was ejected from. He did not even forgive them, or let them live in peace until he subdued them. However, before Muhammad's time, they were quite happy to live in peace with each other, every man having his own deity until Muhammad came and changed the idea of personal deity to the one in the Ka'ba. Muhammad was a very unforgiving man and did not forgive his enemies. He allowed the Jews and Christians to live as Dhimmis (2nd class citizens) by paying Jizzya tax but he did not allow his own fellow countrymen to live, their only choice was to convert or die. In Islam the idea is either you are submit or make them submit, there is no such thing as living peacefully by you worship your God and we worship ours. This only happened during Islamic weakness not during its strength. The West does not understand that a radical Muslim lives this mentality day in day out thus it is impossible to make peace in such situations. The only way the radicals will give you respect is if they are subdued and defeated utterly! However the moderate Muslims, many are kind people and will quite happily let you live and live themselves but the severe jurists in Islam will not let that happen and will thus kill the moderate Muslims for dissension and apostasy because they did not follow the strict commandments of the Qur'an.

Question- The Spanish Inquisitions (Anti-Messiah?) persecuted both genuine Christians and Jews in great numbers?

Answer- Where is the biblical reference for calling the Spanish Inquisitors the Anti-Messiah nation? These men went astray killing people as heretics and forcing Jews to convert. Mind you these were not Orthodox Christians, but Roman Catholics that did believe in the Father and Son, but did not act according to the commandments. That is outright false Churchianity, not Anti-Messiah. Big difference! Please see **1 John 2:22** for reference to the Anti-Messiah below:

> **1 John 2:22** Who is a **liar** but he [all Muslims] that denieth that Yahushua is the Messiah? **He is Anti-Messiah,** [one to come from Islam] that **denieth the Father and the Son** [all of Islam denies the Father and the Son, as it is a religious denial repeated and reinforced 5 times daily!].

Do Roman Catholics deny the Father and Son? The simple answer is no. This verse does not say anything about adding to the word of YHWH, or removing from it. It simply states that this is the "mark," of the Anti-Messiah doctrine! Now unless you can prove that the RC Church denies the Father and the Son they cannot birth the Anti-Messiah. The Bible places these people who deny both the Father and Son firmly in the Middle East region. So mankind would have to break Scripture to try and force their own interpretation here, to somehow prove it is the Roman Catholic Church. Can they be classified as the Antichrist nation? No, not by the above biblical reference. And moreover, it would be a scholarly stretch to do so based on some loose Scriptures taken out of a Middle Eastern context that do not point to them. However, all readings of the Bible concur that it is the

Islamic nations that are Anti-Messiah. Don't forget when they come against Jerusalem, and they will, they will equally kill Roman Catholics because to them these people are Christians, whether they are born again or not. This is not a vague reference but a concrete reference to the Anti-Messiah's nation by John. And, let us not forget that John also wrote the book of Revelation.

Now let us analyze the Muslim view using the same reference. Do Muslims deny the Father and the Son? Yes. The Qur'an teaches: "The Messiah Isa, the son of Mary, was no more than Allah's apostle. Allah is but one god. GOD FORBID THAT HE SHOULD HAVE A SON!"(Sura 4:171) Is this a religious or personal denial? This is a **religious** denial found in the holy book of Islam (the Qur'an). Is John talking about these Muslims to come, who would deny the Father and the Son and be the Anti-Messiah nation giving us the person of the Anti-Messiah. Let us not forget that it was John who saw the "mark" of the beast the "name" <u>not</u> 666 but "**in the name of Allah**" as explained earlier.

Question-Babylon clearly relates to modern day Iraq as you identify in your in-depth analysis, but then you also refer to 'Babylon' and 'Spiritual Babylon' as being Mecca in Saudi Arabia. Why do you assign one name to two different regions?

Answer-The reference is to the root of the origins of the beast i.e. Iraq (Babylon). But YHWH also refers to a place as the "daughter of Babylon" and spiritual Babylon. In **Isaiah 21:9** we read: And, behold, here cometh a chariot of men, *with* a couple of horsemen. And he answered and said, <u>Babylon is fallen, is fallen</u>; and all the graven images of her gods he hath broken unto the ground. Do you think this is talking about Iraq? Clearly the context of Isaiah is the **desert of Arabia,** which is Saudi Arabia, as stated in the passages so this is why we interpret it this way.

We are not assigning one name to two regions, but the root of all false religions is Iraq. And modern day Islam is centred in Saudi Arabia where the entire Muslim world goes for pilgrimages every year to Mecca. However, Iraq is the place where the deity of Islam came from. It was in Iraq that Nabonidus exported the deity to Arabia in the 6th century BC. Therefore, the extension is now in Saudi Arabia the spiritual capital of Islam. So this is in view here as the "daughter of Babylon" and at other times YHWH does indeed view Saudi Arabia as Babylon for leading the whole corrupt Anti-Messiah system. We are dealing with biblical idioms here. In the east when someone would refer to me, they would not say Simon, but they would say Simon the son of so and so, e.g. **they would use my father's name to describe me.** In like manner we can see this in the Bible, where Saudi Arabia is the "daughter of Babylon." So we have to deduce with spiritual discernment just when the Bible describes Iraq (Babylon proper) and where the reference is to Saudi Arabia. Other Islamic nations sometimes are called Babylon as well, but we must never forget the source of these countries being Nimrod's religion in Iraq, now flourishing elsewhere. When the people will soon cry out "**Babylon is fallen,**" Isaiah was referring to Saudi Arabia being destroyed. However at the same time intrinsically Iraq is also Islamic and linked with Saudi Arabia. **This is common knowledge, as even the secularist Saddam Hussein viewed Saudi Arabia as a province of Iraq. Geographically and spiritually he was correct! This explains why when the false system of Islam is destroyed; it will collectively be destroyed in both the place of its roots (Iraq) as well as its spiritual headquarters (Saudi Arabia).**

352

Question-A friend asked this pertinent question: s.a.tan's throne in Pergamum (referred to in **Revelation 2:13**) is located in Turkey as you say and this place also had the Altar to Zeus during the Hellenistic period of the Roman Empire (301 B.C). It lasted for 150 years, but fell into decay and its altar was finally carried away to Germany in 1871. Before that Pergamum was also a treasure storehouse for Alexandra the Great (the shaggy goat mentioned in the prophecies of Daniel). It can therefore be considered to be the former seat of s.a.tan (in Yahushua's Asia Minor prophecy to the 7 churches), but not necessarily the contemporary, or future one. Correct?

Answer-YHWH does not see this seat/throne as a former seat/throne alone, but also sees it as a future seat/throne as well. We must understand YHWH's language does not always involve time, since time is outside eternity. If this only applied to the church in Pergamum, then it was not even built in Yahushua' day. This would make the prophecy meaningless to apply in John's time. When John was given this prophecy the Roman Empire was present and active and at the height of its power. YHWH was pointing to the future; the 7 churches were all future nothing past, At future times, the churches were destined to face some of the worst persecutions and Yahushua our Messiah exhorted them, warned them and prepared them for what was to come. To assume that this seat/throne has moved to Berlin would not have a strong case at all. The question has to be asked; was Germany a part of the Roman Empire? The answer is it was not part of the Roman Empire. In fact, the Germanic tribes fought against Rome. Those people who link it to Germany only do so in thinking that somehow Germany was part of the Roman Empire, so it has to be revived as a capital. s.a.tan is a spiritual being; can he move his **spiritual seat** somewhere else physically? The verse used to allegedly identify that s.a.tan's seat/throne might have moved is 1 Peter 5:8. **1 Peter 5:8** Be sober, be vigilant; because your adversary the devil walks about like a roaring lion, seeking whom he may devour.

Nowhere does this verse describe s.a.tan's throne being moved! Yes, s.a.tan as a being moves around. Perhaps he flies, perhaps he floats, but you and I walk and use transportation. But where do you or I come back at the end of our day? Where do we come back after visiting abroad for a holiday? We have one place of permanent residence. The same way Yahushua the Messiah pointed at s.a.tan having a throne in Asia Minor. **Is it not both ironic and factual that this became the seat of the Eastern Roman Empire and also the seat of power for the later Islamic Empire History reminds us that Christians suffered the worst persecutions here under both Empires!** This tells us something significant. In the end of days, once again, we will see a repeat of earlier events and the Asia Minor region will once again be active in doing what it once did. That is what Yahushua the Messiah was warning us about, by declaring that all seven churches will be involved in being persecuted. Even though some are clearly shown to be corrupt, that does not exempt them from the persecution to come through Islam. To Islam all Christians and all Jews are corrupt regardless of doctrinal differences.

My friend further states, "but his seat/throne can change course, just like the nation states. Why not?" There is no need. Turkey is only one cog in the puzzle, and there are plenty of other nations with Turkey that will play a part in the end time scenario. So we should not concentrate on any of the wrong areas, but I do say Turkey for good reasons.

Several prophets mention it and that cannot be refuted. Not only this, but Southern Russia comes up too and these are not only Islamic, but Turkic peoples who migrated and today live in those regions. The Anti-Messiah is referred to as "Gog" from the land of

Magog (Ezekiel 38:2) and this is in Turkey today. We cannot deny Daniel the prophet providing us irrefutable evidence in Daniel 8:9 by pinpointing to the physical region. Yet many still want to argue for Europe, or the USA when we cannot find one shred of evidence in the Bible for it. This only leaves such a person in the terrible position to deny that Daniel the prophet is a reliable witness and thus by extension that YHWH is not trustworthy. This is a position I will not adopt to please the masses.

Below are the languages in Southern Russia and they are all Turkic tribes. Altai, Azerbaijani, Balkar, Bashkir, Chagatay, Chuvash, Cuman, Crimean Tatar, Gagauz, Karachay, Karaim, Kazakh, Khakas, Kumyk, Kyrgyz, Nogay, Old Uyghur, Orkhon, Ottoman, Shor, Tatar, Tofa, Turkish, Turkmen, Tuvan, Uyghur, Uzbek, Yakut, Yellow Uyghur. Knowing Turkish, you only have to make a relatively small effort to understand other Turkic languages such as Azeri, Turkmen, Tatar, Uzbek, Kazakh and Kyrgyz. [68]

> **Daniel 9:27** Then he [Anti-Messiah] **shall confirm** [re-affirm] a covenant **with many** [several Muslim nations involved]; for one week [it will last seven years] but in the middle of the week he shall bring **an end to sacrifice and offering** and **on the wing of abominations shall be one who makes desolate**, even until the consummation, which is determined, is poured out on the desolate.

Note the above word "many" is very interesting and it is given for a reason. Not only will the Anti-Messiah confirm a covenant with Israel, but also other nations will be involved. Who do you think they are? These will likely be Islamic nations and that is why YHWH chose to use the word "many." They will agree to the peace treaty that he introduces and Israel will accept it to end the daily bloodshed that is happening in Israel. However the Anti-Messiah's intent is deception and his Islamic partners know it too as this will be a classic "hudna" (Arabic for a temporary treaty until strength is restored). He will break the hudna in the middle of the seven-year treaty and then start advancing to capture Jerusalem. **Turkey Egypt and now Jordan are the only three Muslim nations that have a treaty with Israel**, this is very important for Bible prophecy as he (the Anti-Messiah) will "confirm the covenant" exactly as Dan 9:27 tells us, i.e. the renewal of some peace treaty that is already in place and **we know this is true for Turkey**.

He (the Turkic Anti-Messiah) has no Sha'ria (Islamic law) at present, but again this is important for prophecy. He (the Anti-Messiah from Turkey) will change this law at a future time. **It will surely be a switch from Gregorian to Islamic Sha'ria law.** Turkey is already making rounds to do this. (Daniel 7:25 shows that Gog will change the calendar of the west in a secondary application, though admittedly the primary reading sees him breaking and mocking the written Torah/instructions that YHWH gave Israel turning many to the false celebrations of Islam. Both applications fit best with the understanding that Islam and not Rome, or Washington is the prophesied end time beast empire.) Turkey is also acting as the peace broker between Hamas and Israel and between Israel and Pakistan, both trying to establish diplomatic relations with Israel in a clandestine manner. Daniel 9:27 is all about a covenant that is already in place being confirmed with **many. And as I suggested that this is the agreement with many Muslim nations who presently do not talk directly with Israel and so Turkey is definitely playing the "peace" card while many people do not even know about this. Moreover, as you may have heard**

[68] Turkic languages in Southern Russia
http://users.pandora.be/orientaal/turkcestan.html

Turkey may soon join the European Union thus even satisfying those who claim there is a European Union link with the Anti-Messiah. Even on that angle, Turkey alone perfectly fits the bill!

We do need to discern what YHWH is saying; just because it does not fit our favorite theory that has been repeated by many scholars does not mean it is invalid. In fact this has more biblical basis than any other theory making the prophetic rounds. In Islam it is taught that they will capture Jerusalem and rape the women there, because even rape is a legitimate act when it is captured women from booty. The Imams justify this because Allah has allegedly given the enemy into their hands and the Qur'an endorses this. This is not new, as all you just have to do is look at Islamic history to know Muhammad already did this with his followers in Arabia, allowing this when they massacred the Jews. The women were taken and raped forcefully and married or kept as slaves.

Daniel 12:4 But thou, O Daniel, shut up the words, and seal the book, even to the time of the end: many shall run to and fro, and **knowledge shall be increased.** One thing is for sure that the knowledge of the end times has increased as we near the end. I do believe this is speaking about end-time knowledge of events, not science because the context is the end-time battles.

Question-You say that the Anti-Messiah is of Gentile origin, not Jewish origin. You speak of dialogue with the Anti-Messiah by the Jewish authorities as evidence of his Gentile credentials. How can this be? For the Jews are expecting a Jewish Messiah, not a Gentile Messiah, for how else could they possibly accept him as their leader?

Answer-This person is a charismatic leader, not a Messiah as Yahushua was. The hypothesis of a false Messiah like figure has been built up by Churchianity, teaching that this person will call himself a Messiah. If we assume this person is of great importance, or carries an anointing to end the Middle East problem, then even that could allow him to be called a great Messiah of some sort. The Bible tells us plainly, he is a leader who will come in peace and deceive the Jews and the nations who accept him as a good leader. The Bible does not state they will hail him as the Messiah, or the "anointed of YHWH." The "anointed" of YHWH will come when their Muslim cousins are slaughtering the Jews in the name of Allah and the Anti-Messiah forces take half of Jerusalem. Even YHWH called King Cyrus "anointed," yet he was worshipping Marduk a false god. Now can we say he was THE Messiah of Israel? No! Yet we know he was a good man and a Messiah of sorts for the Jewish nation, anointed to allow them to return to Israel.

The Jews have been under hostilities with the Muslims for so long that they would love to make a peace deal with them. Just take a look at Yesha (Judea and Samaria); Ariel Sharon is willingly ready now to give up settlements to the Palestinians so it is not a problem. Gaza has already been given away and more land is in progress to be given. **They do know and consider the Muslim Arabs their cousins/brothers. He does not need to tell them I am the Messiah to save your sins, which is not stated in the Scriptures as a qualification for the Anti-Messiah.** Remember the text says he will come in peacefully and deceive them. This is the <u>only</u> requirement of this person. **Daniel 11:21** "And in his place shall arise a **vile** person, to whom they will not give the honor of royalty [not be the Messiah, or a Messiah figure]; but he shall **come in peaceably** [political manuvering], and **seize the kingdom by intrigue** [e.g. deception]. The Hebrew for "intrigue" is *"khal-ak-lak-kaw,"* meaning treacherously or by deception. If I was to take the bogus Messiahship argument I could even win on that but to be honest this is not the case in this scenario. You are saying the Jews cannot possibly accept a Messiah figure that is a non-Jew. Let us examine this hypothesis and see if it is possible.

Did not the Jews proclaim Simon Bar Kochba as the Messiah? He was killed and he performed no miracles and made no peace treaties. Did not the Jews proclaim Shabbatai Zvi as the Messiah? By the way he became a Muslim. Did not the Jews proclaim Napoleon as the Messiah (gentile)?

Now this is what the Jews, or some of them claim regarding the recognition of Messiah:

1. He must be a father-to-son descendant of King David. Therefore, a Kohein, Levi, or a convert (and his children) cannot be Moshiach.
2. He must be completely immersed in the study of Torah, just like his ancestor David.
3. He must follow the entire Torah, both the Written and the Oral.
4. He must lead all the Jews back to the Torah, so that they follow all its laws.[69]

Some have proclaimed Schneerson as the Messiah - only problem is he died and did not rise from the dead either, but they are still waiting for him to come back. Now if I claim I am the son of David, immersed in the Torah and will lead many back to the Torah, can I proclaim Messiahship? The answer is YES. BUT the question is how can this claim be possible? The unsaved Jewish people have set themselves up a straw man in this matter.

He must be the descendant of David they claim. There is no way to validate this as there is no Temple in Jerusalem and all the records have been destroyed that were once kept in the Temple. Based on this, it is mere conjecture, as any Tom, Dick or Harry can stand up and claim to be a descendant of David. I know many Jews in Israel who do not have any proof of being Jewish other than having certain names that run in their family. Yet they have claimed aliya [immigration to Israel] as their right and the government has had to accept their verbal testimony. In fact a person of my background has more validity considering there are scattered tribes in the east and I may well have a legitimate Hebrew ancestry.

Here is the 2nd straw man going by their argument. "The second stage is completed when the presumed Moshiach succeeds in rebuilding the Holy Temple in Jerusalem and gathering all the Jewish people back to the land of Israel. At that point we know that he is certainly Moshiach."

Now if a Muslim stands up tomorrow and says he follows the true Torah contained in the Qur'an and does not believe in the Son of YHWH, does not believe that YHWH came in the flesh and grants the Jewish people the freedom to build an altar on the Temple Mount, he qualifies automatically. No birth certificate needed! Think about this one. There is no real need to destroy the Al-Aqsa Mosque, or the dome. He would agree that the

---

[69] http://members.aol.com/LazerA/moshiach.htm

Jewish Torah is valid, as most Muslims do today (although they believe the Jews have corrupted and changed it to anger Allah), so that they only have a problem with Yahushua being YHWH as do the majority of Jewish people.

Any Muslim person can agree with the following straw man set up by the Jewish people themselves:

Please note the expectation of the Jewish Messiah is no longer a biblical one, but a rabbinical one (meaning seen in the light of rabbinical commentary taking precedence over prophetic declaration). They have set themselves up for a fall again.[70] _What Moshiach Is "Not"_? *This is what the unsaved Jewish people generally (the majority) believe about the Messiah today:*

Moshiach will be a normal human being born from human parents. He will not be divine, or a "Son of the Most High."

Moshiach will be mortal. He will not live forever. When he dies he will be succeeded by his son, like any normal king.

Moshiach will not atone for our sins. Every person must atone for his own sins; no one else can do it for you.

Moshiach will not change the laws of the Torah in any way. If he attempts to do so then we know that he is a false messiah.

If a man comes who fulfils all of these conditions, then we can *assume* that he is the Moshiach. This is the first stage of the identification of Moshiach. (End quote) Maybe you get the picture now, as a Muslim leader will agree with all of the above points by deception. I never said that he is going to be a Messiah figure, like Yahushua Messiah.

That is not necessary because he can qualify quite easily with flying colors based on the above rabbinical expectations, with which most Muslims agree in principal regarding the validity of the Torah and its laws. Do you know that some Afghanis are from the tribe of Judah/Jewish, yet they are all Muslim in faith? Some of them can trace their lineage back to the tribe of Judah. What about a Jew from Afghanistan practicing Islam and living in Turkey. See how it fits?

Question- A usurper and deceiver to the House of David must represent it, in-order to be successful. In relation to the above, the Bible states that the Anti-Messiah will enter the third (and final) Jewish temple, violating it as his throne as occurred with pre Anti-Messiah Titus in the 2nd Temple (see works of Josephus). How do you envisage the removal of the Dome of the Rock, the third holiest site to Islam and the rebuilding of the third Temple without triggering a third world war? The gentiles have indeed trampled this site for the biblically stated number of days. Yet the Bible clearly indicates that there will be a third Temple **before** final conflict occurs and Messiah's return?

---

[70] http://members.aol.com/LazerA/moshiach.htm

Answer- First let me state that the Bible does not say a complete third Temple is a requirement before the appearance of the Anti-Messiah. The complete third Temple will only be built upon the return of Yahushua of Nazareth, as seen in Ezekiel 43, which discusses things to happen after the final battle. All the Jewish people need is **an altar** to perform the sacrifices to Yahweh their Elohim. The requirement is perfectly satisfied **in Revelation 11 as the Book of Revelation dictates that at the time of the altar the area of gentiles i.e. the heathen mosques are still there.** Many Christians are expecting a completed 3rd Temple before the return of the Messiah, but unfortunately once again, we find that many have simply not paid attention to detail. **Revelation 11:1-2** Then I was given a reed like a measuring rod. And the angel stood, saying, "Rise and measure the Temple of YHWH, **the altar,** and those who worship there. "But leave out the court, which is outside the Temple, and do not **measure it, for it has been given to the Gentiles. And they will tread the holy city under foot for forty-two months.**

Note that Revelation 11 states that Israel will get an area for an altar to start their sacrifices, <u>not</u> a Third Temple. Moreover the instructions are given to leave the "court of the gentiles" alone, do NOT measure it. This is the area of the Mosques to be left alone. The Jewish people will be quite happy if given a spot on the Temple Mount to start their sacrifices, because right now they are not even allowed to ascend the mount as it is closed to them. If you ever get a chance, look at the Jewish people who pray and wail at the Wailing Wall down below the Temple Mount and see how much they long to ascend to their Holy Place, but are told that it is illegal.

The Palestinians claim the second Intifada started because of Ariel Sharon entered their holy mosque on the Temple Mount but that is not true. He did not go inside the mosque. The point is this; if an Israeli leader can cause a wave of suicide bombings to start just because he went to the Temple Mount area, then how much more of a problem do you think it will create if the Jews forcefully want to start sacrifices in the Temple area? This is why the Jewish people will be happy to have a place as an altar to begin the sacrifices to the Master YHWH in agreement with the Palestinians and this charismatic leader, the Anti-Messiah, will form this agreement.

Question- Why do you say that in Ezekiel 38 it is mentioned that Israel will be attacked by an army from the north when it says this land lives in unwalled villages, but we have a wall now dividing Israel, so how could this be Israel since Israel does have a wall?

Answer- The verse in question is this **Ezekiel 38:10-12;** Thus says the Master YHWH: "On that day it shall come to pass that <u>thoughts</u> will arise in your mind, and you will make an evil plan: "You will say, I will go up against a land of <u>unwalled villages</u>; I will go to a peaceful people, who dwell safely, all of them dwelling without walls, and having neither bars nor gates' "to <u>take plunder</u> and <u>to take booty,</u> to stretch out your hand against the waste places that are again inhabited, and against a people <u>gathered from the nations,</u> who have acquired livestock and goods, who dwell in the midst of the land. If we read the verse carefully above, it says "thoughts will arise in his mind" and "you will say" i.e. the Anti-Messiah is thinking to himself, I will go to Israel and attack it and capture it, as it is hardly defensible.

The Hebrew word that is used above for the unwalled village is *"per-aw-zaw,"* which can also mean just a town or a village. You need to visit Israel to see that Israel has many unwalled beautiful villages all on the outskirts of Jerusalem. The recent wall that Israel has put up is hardly a wall circling Israel. It is only placed in certain strategic locations outside Jerusalem. Do not think that this wall is like the wall of China as it is not. This wall is no defence barrier against an army and if you look at the wall you will realize it is patchy. In some parts you may see a wall, while in other places you might see a fence or nothing at all. The other strong possibility is that Israel is willing to take the wall down if a peace agreement can be reached. However all it takes is two shells from a tank to make a hole in such a wall if the enemy attacked Jerusalem. Note the verse in **Ezekiel 38:12 says he comes to take a "plunder" and "booty."** Muslim armies historically do this. This is how Muhammad behaved in his time when he looted the Quraish (his own tribe) caravans for plunder and booty. The reference is for Israel, as it indicates the Master has gathered these people out of many nations and it is abundantly clear these are the Jewish people and Ephraimites as well. In **Ezekiel 38:8b** it is clear that this is the nation of Israel. In the latter years you will come into the land of those brought back from the sword and **gathered from many people** on the **mountains of Israel**.

Question- What do you say about America being labelled as the end times beast? There have been many Christian books written saying nuclear bombs will destroy America because it is the end time beast/Babylon. I know they are pro-Israel. The Scripture also talks about the end time Babylon being totally destroyed, namely the "daughter of Babylon." It cannot be Iraq can it? The nation that attacks her is from the North. The following Scripture references are applied: **Jeremiah 50:3, 9, 41.** Who is the daughter of Babylon if not America in **Jeremiah 50:42**? We are also told this is the **hammer of the whole earth** in **Jeremiah 50:23** and **Jeremiah 50:46** says, that the whole earth will tremble with its fall. I cannot think that nations would tremble if Iraq was destroyed, but it could be a possibility with USA. Many people claim to have seen visions and dreams about America being destroyed, could this be true?

Answer- This is not just one question, but about nine questions, so I will break them down into a, b, c responses.

a) Can the USA be labelled as Babylon?

The reasons are given in this book why the USA cannot be Babylon. Babylon is always referred to Iraq in its proper context, but the greater Babylon combines all the Islamic nations together. Just because many Christians have written books on America being Babylon does not make it so. Christians have also been saying that Babylon is the Vatican in Rome for years now; does that make the Pope the Anti-Messiah? We have to read what YHWH writes about America and He certainly does not call it Babylon at any time.

b) Is the Daughter of Babylon USA? No, I have demonstrated in this book that the "daughter of Babylon" is only applied to Saudi Arabia not USA. Yes, Saudi Arabia will be totally destroyed as you mention rightly. This is in reference to the extension of Babylon, which is Saudi Arabia, or the "daughter of Babylon." The nation that comes out of the north is none other than Great Britain in alliance with the USA to fight Babylon in the end of days (currently called the War on Terror). We must remember if Iraq is Babylon then the daughter has to be close by in geography not 10,000 miles away. Spiritually they are one and the same as well, proclaiming the doctrines of Nimrod.

c) <u>Who is the hammer of the whole earth?</u> This is Babylon Iraq with Saudi Arabia that exports Islamic terrorism, suicide bombings, hijacking planes, and blowing up buildings. These "hammers" are Islamic traits of aggression, so when YHWH says the "hammer of the whole earth is broken," He means it. This is literally applied to these Islamic nations, especially Saudi Arabia as it exports, underwrites and aids in terrorism. Islam believes that Qur'an based evangelism involves hammering the opponent into submission to Allah. Now the new tactic of Saudi Arabia is to give millions to top American universities to brainwash their young people to promote Islam and then recruit them into Islam. One needs to ask why is Saudi Arabia and people such as prince Al-Walid bin Talal not allowing churches to be built in Saudi Arabia to show the alleged tolerance of Islam? Talk about crass hypocrisy. He has given money to spread Islam to American universities to indoctrinate American youth to Islam. This money is given to very good universities such as Harvard, so that Islam can buy into the cream of the crop of young students. Think about it; you can win converts from rich influential families in the USA and then it makes it easier to change policy decisions in the government because of associations with the political elite. These are the future leaders of America, being bought with Mecca's wine of fornication, so that these students will be drunk with Mecca's power and wealth when they grow older! In England there are 14,000 known Muslim converts among the elite, the sons and daughters of lords and ladies, including Prince Charles. It just shows how Islam can penetrate at the political level and influence key decisions in their favor.

d) <u>Why would nations tremble?</u> This reference is not to the USA, in context it applies to Babylon (Iraq) and the daughter of Babylon (Saudi Arabia). The nations tremble at Babylon and all the extensions of Babylon, namely Saudi Arabia and other Islamic oil producing nations. This is enough to send shudders to all peoples, when these nations are destroyed, because when Saudi Arabia is destroyed, the consequences of no oil being exported will cause jitters in the whole planet, sending petrol prices sky high. Nations will be worried about their very survival. We have already seen the second Gulf War in Iraq, causing gas to reach over $60 a barrel and people worldwide have paniced. Now try and apply this to Saudi Arabia being destroyed, then what would happen? It will lead to chaos in ALL the world markets making the nations tremble, with Saudi Arabia, Iran and Iraq up in smoke. We will soon be looking at losing over 52% of the world's oil supplies. Recently in Hemel Hempstead in England in December 2005 an oil depot accidentally exploded and for many days the fire fighters were trying to bring the blaze under control. This caused panic buying by motorists throughout the UK. Now this is only a storage place with no source of continued oil to burn, yet the sky around the area was dark for days. Try applying these principles to about 150 oil refineries in the Gulf with oil going up in smoke for months perhaps, and then you will really see the day sky being dark like night. Then the fire and smoke of the Book of Revelation will literally be seen, as all the world trembles.

e) <u>Many visions are written about the destruction of the USA?</u> I am afraid these are false visions not true by any biblical standard. YHWH is not going to destroy the very people who have helped spread the gospel of Messiah in the world and who have the largest believing population. The USA remains the only nation in the world to openly support Israel. There are plenty of false prophets and false teachers in Christendom and we need to be careful of what we accept as truth from these people. Without a single supported verse supporting them from the Bible, we can write these folks off as a fringe element. Moreover, Edom/Islam remains the perpetual enemy of Israel and prophecy writers, or dreamers have no authority to exchange Islam for the USA. If they can be allowed to do that, then they should be allowed to change the Shabbat/Sabbath (7th day) to Sunday. If you don't let them get away with that, neither should you let these dreamers dictate, or supersede the revealed word of YHWH.

Question- Where do you get the idea that **Daniel 9:27** speaks of a period of 7 years and not any other length of time?

Answer- In order to work the time-line of Daniel we have to work out the biblical days and years. We can use an example from Genesis to work our timeline, or you may choose to use other verses in the Bible. **Genesis 7:11** In the six hundredth year of Noah's life, in the second month, the seventeenth day of the month, on that day all the fountains of the great deep were broken up, and the windows of heaven were opened. From **Genesis 7:11** we get the 17th day of the second month as the start of the flood. **Genesis 8:4** And the ark rested in the seventh month, on the seventeenth day of the month, upon the mountains of Ararat. We are told in Genesis 8:4 that the flood stopped on the 7th month of the 17th day. **Genesis 7:24** "the waters prevailed upon the earth an hundred and fifty days." In **Genesis 7:24** we get the number of days the water was on the earth, which is a total of 150 days. We can take this figure of 150 days and divide by 30, which gives us five months-150/30=5. We know that a biblical year is 360 days (12 X 30 = 360) and if the flood lasted 150 days then we have our 5-month period (150/30=5). In the book of **Revelation 12:6** we are given similar details when we are told that the woman (Israel) fled into the wilderness for 1,260 days. So 1,260 days divided by 360 days per biblical year gives us three and a half biblical years (1260/30=3.5). To calculate the period of Daniel's vision for the Messiah's coming we go to: **Daniel 9:25-26** Know therefore and understand, that from the going forth of the commandment to restore and to build Jerusalem unto the Messiah the Prince shall be **seven weeks, and threescore and two weeks**: the street shall be built again, and the wall, even in troublous times. And after threescore and two weeks shall Messiah be cut off, but not for himself: and the people of the prince that shall come shall destroy the city and the sanctuary; and the end thereof shall be with a flood, and unto the end of the war desolations are determined. Daniel prophesied the coming of Messiah as follows: 7 weeks + three score (60) + 2 weeks = 69 weeks. So we take 69 sevens which is equal to 69 X 7 = 483 years since a prophetic day can also represent a year in prophecy depending on the context. Now we multiply 483 x 360 = 173,880 days in prophetic years. We then convert this data to our solar years 173,880 divided by 365.25 = 476 solar years for the arrival of Messiah to be killed. Since we know that Yahushua the Messiah came and fulfilled all the prophecies in the past and the above timeline is based on the decree going forth from Artaxerxes in Nehemiah chapter 2, we therefore have our timeline already established.

> **Daniel 9:27** And he shall confirm the covenant with many **for one week**: and **in the midst of the week** he shall cause the sacrifice and the oblation to cease, and for the overspreading of abominations he shall make it desolate, even until the consummation, and that determined shall be poured upon the desolate.

Now we can work out the data confidently. In **Daniel 9:27** seven weeks is seven years, divided it into two portions (7/2=3.5 years). The covenant/peace treaty, which we know is already existent with Turkey and Israel, needs to merely be confirmed through added details when the Anti-Messiah shows up in the future. The word used in the Hebrew language is shuvah that means the number **seven**. This will be for a full seven year period with other Muslim nations involved in the agreement, as it says in the biblical text; that it is with "**many**." This attack will occur so that the Muslims do not attack Israel and let them

361

have a portion of the Temple-Mount to perform their sacrifices. In **Daniel 9:26**, the prophet said that a future ruler over the land of Israel would destroy Jerusalem and the Temple. Daniel said this would happen after an anointed one (Messiah) is "cut off," which means, "killed." We know that a few centuries after Daniel, the Romans had taken control of the land of Israel. Yahushua announced Himself as the Messiah, and the Romans crucified Him. Forty years after Yahushua was crucified, the Romans came and destroyed Jerusalem and the Temple so we can conclude that Daniel 9:26 is partially fulfilled. **Daniel 9:26** "And after the sixty-two weeks Messiah shall be cut off, but not for Himself; and the people of the prince who is to come shall destroy the city and the sanctuary. The end of it shall be with a flood, until the end of the war desolations are determined.

Why do you think it is partially fulfilled? Let me explain the text says that after Messiah was to be killed that the end was to be with a "flood." Many people believe this is a type of flood of an army like the Roman army that came, unfortunately this is not so. This flood that is to happen is a literal flood and not a type, or a metaphor of an army. The flood is yet to happen and I believe this will happen when the mountains split during the great earthquake as specified by Ezekiel. This flood will be the cause of the drowning of much of the Anti-Messiah's future army. **Daniel 9:26** "**and the end thereof shall be with a flood."** **This flood in all likelihood is a literal flood, as there is nothing in Daniel 9 regarding the seventy weeks that we can consider to be symbolic. Not a single thing.**

Zechariah 14:5 "and there shall be a very great valley; and half of the **mountain shall remove toward the north**, and **half of it toward the south**. And ye shall flee to the valley of the mountains; for the valley of the mountains shall reach unto Azal; yea, ye shall flee, like as ye fled from before the **earthquake in the days of Uzziah king of Judah**: and YHWH my Elohim shall come, and all the saints with thee." A great earthquake will divide the area and the enemy will not know how to escape. Those big tanks and army vehicles will smash like tin. **Zechariah 14:8-** "And it shall be in that day, **that living waters shall go out from Jerusalem; half of them toward the former sea, and half of them toward the hinder sea: in summer and in winter shall it be.**" The mountain will part, allowing the Jews to flee, and then drown the enemies. Exactly what happened with the Red Sea! This whole process was shadowed by what happened in the escape in the Exodus from Egypt. Like the ten plagues, these events are very similar, with the plagues followed by the flood. **Nahum 1:8-But with an overrunning flood, He will make an utter end of the place thereof, and __darkness__ [choshech] shall pursue his enemies**. The Hebrew word for "darkness," **choshech**, can literally here mean "destruction" and not darkness, as in a light going out. And this is exactly what is set to happen in Jerusalem.

Nahum 2:6- The gates of the rivers shall be opened, and the palace shall be dissolved. This living water is not allegoric, but literal and will gush through the Temple Mount and literally cleanse it from its defilement. Yahweh's toilet flushes the enemy once and for all time like dung being cleansed from a hill. **Isaiah 14:19-20**- But thou art cast out of **thy grave like an abominable branch**, and as the raiment of those that are slain, thrust through with a sword, that go down to the stones of the pit; as a carcase trodden under feet. (20) Thou shalt **not be joined with them in burial**, because thou hast destroyed thy land, and slain thy people: the seed of evildoers shall never be renowned. The Anti-Messiah will not have a grave, or a burial place so that people cannot lay wreaths for him. This is what Yahweh has spoken and it shall come to pass. We must not forget the events of Pharaoh and the Exodus that took place, along with the final climax of that event, which was the drowning of the Egyptian army. And here once again the super

362

climax will be the drowning of the Anti-Messiah's army. Who can fight Yahweh and live? Baruch HaShem Yahweh (Praise be the Name of Yahweh).

Question- It is not Islam, but the Arab culture that is violent. Correct?

Answer- Some misguided Muslims and other people believe that Islam is a peaceful way of life. But the Arab culture is violent and all the violence we see stems from the Arab culture and not Islam. First, not all Arabs are Muslims. Do we see violence in the Arab Christians? Arab culture is not at fault, as it is like most other cultures. The primary difference is that men have a lot bigger role to play in Arab societies, which can lead to attitude issues. But that does not mean that all Arab men are violent. Far from it. Most Arab people are friendly and congenial. The ones who want to blame the Arab culture are misguided completely. At the heart of the violence that comes out of fanatical Islam is not that they are Arabs, but that they are Muslims and support the ideology of radical Islam. Their radical view is hatred towards all non-Muslims. Have you ever wondered why Indonesian Muslims are violent? What about Pakistani Muslims? In fact, any Muslim in the world that fully supports and commits himself to the ideology of Islam, will lean towards what the west calls terrorist activity. The Arabs before Muhammad's time were generally peaceful people. Yes they did have feuds between themselves, but that does not mean they went around beheading people. In fact the Jews prospered in the 6th century in (Saudi) Arabia before Muhammad turned up proclaiming his prophethood and he went on his crusade to eradicate them completely.

Question- How can the Jews accept a Muslim proclaiming himself as the Messiah? Will he not imitate Yahushua as the Messiah and sit in the Temple of YHWH proclaiming himself as YHWH?

Answer- Why is it that these error prone teachers confuse and bewilder Christians so easily? The reason is simple because many Christians did not read their Bibles carefully enough and should not take everything as gospel. I would encourage you to check everything I have written, for you to know that what I have written is what the Bible teaches and is sure to come to pass. Test every spirit brethren because many false prophets have gone out into the world. That is what the Bible teaches and I encourage you fully to do just that. To answer the question about the Anti-Messiah calling himself god the verse that is used for this is **2 Thessalonians 2: 4** Who opposes and exalts himself above all that is called YHWH or that is worshiped, so that he sits as YHWH sits in the temple of YHWH, showing himself that he is YHWH.

The Anti-Messiah does not say "I am god worship me," nor does he say I am your Master Yahushua the Messiah of Israel." This is the error made by many writers brought about by misreading the text. Let us take a close look at the verse above and let us see how it should read using the Greek. First of all the Bible does not say that the Anti-Messiah proclaims himself as the Messiah. You will not find one passage supporting this claim. Secondly, the issue of him sitting and exalting himself as YHWH needs to be examined. I did not build my case on one verse of the Bible, but I used the entire Bible to show the end time Islamic confederacy.

Let us now go back to the Greek language to get some more insight. The very first words in 2 Thessalonians 2:4 say, "who opposes." There lies the first clue, and we have to ask the question, opposes what? The Greek word used here is *"antikeimai"* which means **opposite, contrary, or against**. He opposes, or is against the teachings of Yahushua the Messiah by proclaiming himself as the way to YHWH by **good works**. While the Bible teaches blood atonement for salvation, Muslims teach good works to gain paradise, so this leader will do likewise. Furthermore, the text says, "He sits as YHWH." Yet many rulers have proclaimed themselves "as" YHWH, but died later, because they were "only" human. In like manner this individual proclaims "himself" like YHWH by saying in essence, 'if you follow me and take the mark i.e. acceptance of Allah, then you will go to heaven.' So this displays power over men's souls like YHWH, but not the true power of YHWH.

When Muhammad the Muslim prophet was around, he had on many occasions equalled himself with Allah. He was recorded as saying things that made him on par with Allah e.g. that on the day of judgement he would have the right of committing people to heaven or hell. To prove that Muhammad was the seal of the prophets, Muslims even claim that he was created from light, he had no shadow, his body did not rot in the grave etc. Allah set 50 prayers a day for the Muslims, but Muhammad allegedly persuaded Allah to set them to 5. Who has the authority in this religion, Allah or Muhammad?

Pakistan has a law 295c that puts Christians behind bars on the basis of the blaspheming of Muhammad. Yet can one really blaspheme a mere man unless he is co-equal to YHWH. The second clue in **2 Thessalonians 2: 4** is in the Greek word *apodeiknumi* "**showing himself**" which means to "prove." He is trying to "prove" to himself that he is YHWH, because he controls the destiny of all the people who follow him. This person, the Anti-Messiah, is possessed by s.a.tan and we have to remember that s.a.tan wanted to sit in the seat of YHWH in heaven. So when the Anti-Messiah sits in the seat of YHWH i.e. in the Temple Mount, he sits in the Muslim shrine of Al Aqsa and thinks to himself that he is god. It is clear that this person is not saying to the world "I am YHWH Almighty" because the text in **Daniel 11:38** must be reconciled; But in their place he [the Anti-Messiah] **shall honor a god of fortresses**; [Allah] and a god which **his fathers did not know** he shall honor with **gold and silver**, with **precious stones** and pleasant things. Daniel's text shows us that the Anti-Messiah worships a god of Jihad behind closed doors! He is merely trying to fool the world including Christians, who have been wrongly taught that he must declare deity. **The Anti-Messiah will not proclaim himself as YHWH of heaven and earth. That's way too obvious**. He is simply saying look at me, I am cool and I am like YHWH, as I can control the destiny of masses of people e.g. "like" YHWH here on earth. At my command I can have someone killed, or give someone life. A human knows he will not live forever, so he cannot claim to be eternal in any way. Plus we know that **2 Thessalonians 2: 4** cannot contradict what Daniel already told us. Scripture cannot be broken and the apostolic writings must be interpreted in light of the Tanach (Hebrew Bible). Why would he show "lying wonders" as stated in **2 Thessalonians 2:9** if he believes he is YHWH. A desire for divinity is only a thought in his sick mind. The New Jerusalem Bible with Apocrypha reads more clearly. **2 Thessalonians 2: 4** states "the enemy, who raises himself above every so-called elohim, or object of worship to enthrone himself in YHWH's sanctuary **and flaunts the claim that he is YHWH**. This text is closer to the actual meaning. This person hates all other forms of worship and claims that his false way is the only right way. The text saying he sits in the sanctuary is also clear. The Greek word for Sanctuary is "**naos***" and* can be equally translated as a "heathen shrine," just as it can be referring to YHWH's shrine. This is where this guy is sitting, in the Al-Aqsa Mosque, very abomination of desolation. Yahushua said in **John 10:34** that "you are gods." Now are we to take this literally to mean that the men He was speaking to were gods? This is Bible's way of making a point about a person. In the same way a lying Anti-

Messiah cannot literally say, "he is YHWH," as it breaks Scripture. Daniel shows he actually worships a god of fortresses, or "jihad."

Question-Who is The Restrainer in **2 Thessalonians 2:7?** Who will be taken out of the way before the Anti-Messiah comes?

Answer-This is one question many have tried to answer. Many say it is the Holy Spirit that will leave this world and now there is a new theory on the block that it is the Angel Michael who stands back and let's Israel suffer until the time determined. Unfortunately both fail to take into consideration that the premise is built up on one verse of the Bible. Paul the Pharisee has written this letter to the Thessalonians because of their confusion and Paul was pointing them back to the Hebrew Bible (Tanach) for the answer. Without the Tanach we cannot arrive at a satisfactory answer. Simply to teach that the Holy Spirit has been taken away is not enough as it breaks Scripture. This problem lies with the idea of a pre-tribulation rapture, because those that teach this mainly vouch for the pre-tribulation position and the removing of the Holy Spirit, thus leaving the wrath for the ungodly. Some teachers in Christian circles have used the word "in the Greek **"apostasia"** for "departure" to mean, "escape," so as to suggest that Christians have left the earth. But nothing could be further from the truth. In reality, this is talking about falling from something that was once held as <u>truth</u> and no longer is. The Greek word **"apostasia"** means **defection** from truth (properly the state), ("apostasy"), or falling away to **forsake**. Do we see the falling away today? It is self evident that there are many denominations of Christians who argue with each other on different doctrines of the Bible. You will not find denominations in the Bible. This itself causes contention between the different groups of people. We have cases such as the Anglican clergy ordaining gay bishops that causes much division in the church. So we can see that the apostasia can mean falling away from the truth to something that is not truthful. These people do not have to become something else, like converts to Islam, but they simply leave the once truthful position to one not truthful. And, yes that is happening on a big scale today in the churches.

> **Leviticus 18:22** You shall not lie with a male as with a woman. It is an abomination. The Master commands us to love one another (believers) and also to love our neighbor. That means we have to also treat homosexuals with the same respect i.e. we are all made in the image of YHWH. But that does not mean that we have to agree with their lifestyle, because it leads to eternal death. It is a sin before our holy YHWH and is rebellion before YHWH and we have to warn them with love and concern.

> **2 Thessalonians 2** (1) Now, brethren, **concerning the coming of our Master Yahushua the Messiah** and **our gathering together to Him,** we ask you, (2) not to be soon **shaken in mind or troubled, either by spirit or by word or by letter**, as if from us, as though the day of Messiah had come. (3) Let **no one deceive you by any means;** for that Day will not come unless the **"falling away" [forsaking] comes first**, and the **man of sin is revealed**, the son of perdition. The apostasy was also taught in Paul's letter to Timothy. **1 Timothy 4:1** Now the Spirit expressly says that in **latter times** some will **depart from the faith, giving heed to deceiving spirits and doctrines of demons**. YHWH has always provided His protection to those that have followed Him. He only had to order Noah to build an ark to avoid the coming tribulation (flood) in the world. Let us look at a short exegesis of some of the second letter to the Thessalonians.

Paul was writing to the Thessalonians telling them not to be confused, or deceived by false teachings within the church that were saying that Yahushua is returning imminently. People were packing their bags waiting for the Master's imminent return. These were Christians teaching others into believing erroneous end time doctrines. Paul writes very firmly saying "let no one deceive you." Paul reassures them that certain things **must** take place **first** before Yahushua returns e.g. there will be a falling away from the truth and then the Anti-Messiah will be revealed. He even admonished lazy Christians (**2 Thessalonians 11-12**).

> **2 Thessalonians 2: 4** who opposes and exalts himself above all that is called YHWH, or that is worshiped, so that he sits as YHWH in the temple of YHWH, **showing himself** that he is YHWH.

As explained in my earlier answer the Anti-Messiah does not declare himself as YHWH to the world. That is a mis-reading, but the Anti-Messiah **"thinks to himself in his own heart"** that he is LIKE YHWH. He can control the affairs of people who are in his kingdom and make life, or death decisions for them, which is a function that YHWH alone can do. So he becomes "like" a self proclaimed elohim and does not declare his humanity to anyone else but **"HIMSELF."** That is the key because he himself worships the god of jihad. **Daniel 11:38** But in their place he shall honor a god of fortresses. **2 Thessalonians 2: 5** Do you not remember that when I was still with you I told you these things? Paul had told the followers of Yahushua something earlier and these were the things from the Torah and prophets e.g. prophesies of the dispersal of the Jews from the land as we shall see later. Paul had no "Apostolic writings" in his hands and had only the Tanach (Hebrew Bible). He was speaking about the Jews and their exile as a result of their sins that Yahweh would punish them for. **2 Thessalonians 2: 6** And now <u>you</u> know what is <u>restraining</u>, that he may be <u>revealed</u> in his <u>own</u> time. Where did the Hebrew Bible ever talk about the departure of the Holy Spirit? Nowhere. It is all about the judgement that will happen to the Hebrew nation as a result of rejecting YHWH's Holy word and His Son. The dispersal of the Jews from the land and thus their "forsaking" and expulsion would occur, leaving the place open to outside influence. What would happen if you left your house open and left the country? Do you think someone else may come in and take possession? This is exactly what happened with the Jewish people.

> **Deuteronomy 29:22-29** (22) so that the coming generation of your children who rise up after you, and the foreigner who comes from a far land, would say, when **they see the plagues of that land and the sicknesses which the Master has laid on it**: (23) The whole land is brimstone, salt, and burning; it is not sown, nor does it bear, nor does any grass grow there, **like the overthrow of Sodom and Gomorrah**, Admah, and Zeboim, which the Master overthrew in His anger and His wrath. [Israel was a forsaken land] (24) "All nations would say, `Why has the **Master done so to this land**? What does the heat of this great anger mean?' (25) "Then men would say: `Because they have <u>forsaken</u> the covenant of the Master YHWH of their fathers, which He made with them when He brought them out of the land of Egypt; (26) `for they went and <u>served other gods and worshiped them</u>, gods that they did not know and that He had not given to them. (27) `Then the anger of the Master was aroused against this land, to bring on it <u>every curse that is written in this book</u>. (28) `And the **Master uprooted them from their land in anger, in wrath**, and **in great indignation, and cast them into another land, as it is this day**.' (29) "The secret things belong to the Master our YHWH, but those things which are revealed belong to us and to our children forever, that

we may do all the words of this law. It is quite clear Paul was not referring to something new but something old, the "forsaking" was to occur because of the disobedience of the Hebrew nation against Yahweh. And, it was Yahweh who was going to cast them from the land of Israel and make the land desolate. So in other words it would involve both the falling away and the forsaking of truth. The judgment had come because they rejected their Messiah i.e. forsaking the Torah and prophets, that had quite clearly detailed the coming of the Messiah e.g. Isaiah chapters 42, 52 and 53.

Deuteronomy 31:17 "Then My anger shall be aroused against them in that day, and **I will forsake them**, and I will hide My face from them, and they shall be devoured. And **many evils and troubles shall befall them**, so that they will say in that day, `Have not these evils come upon us because our YHWH is not among us?'

2 Thessalonians 2: 7-8 (7) For the mystery of **lawlessness** [anomia] is already at work; only He [Yahweh] who now restrains will do so until He [the Jewish nation] is taken out of the way. (8) And **then the lawless** [anomos] **one will be revealed**, [Anti-Torah] whom the Master will consume with the breath of His mouth and destroy with the brightness of His coming.

"Anomos" means **violator of the Mosaic Torah**, Torah-less, one not following the Torah correctly and in violation of its ordinances. In order to fulfil this word you would have to be claiming to follow the Mosaic Torah, but not following it fully. This is exactly what Islam claims. That they follow the Mosaic Torah, but we know that they are in violation of the Torah, believing it to be corrupted, so that Allah sent Mohammed and fixed all the Jewish mistakes in the Qur'an. This is what Paul was saying. That a people and the Anti-Messiah would come who would be violators of the Torah, all the while claiming to uphold it. This could never be said about the Romans because they never made the religious claim to obey the Torah, as do Muslims. Paul tells us that they "the Muslims/the beast" will be revealed once the Jews [he, or Jacob] would be taken out of the land. This clearly happened in 637 A, when Jerusalem was handed over to the Muslim Caliph Omar without a fight, by the Patriarch of Jerusalem Sophronius. Sophronius was granted a writ of privileges that guaranteed certain rights to Christians for maintaining the holy places and the pursuit of their worship and customs in Omar's reign.

Yet others may still ask who is the "he" in **2 Thessalonians 2: 7**? Is he not a singular person? Let us look at some other verses to get an even better understanding.

2 Thessalonians 2: 7 The mystery of wickedness is already at work, but let him who is restraining it once be removed. -New Jerusalem with Apocrypha- YHWH sees Israel both as a singular person and a group of people. Did not YHWH often call Israel made up of many millions of people as "Jacob" the individual?

Ezekiel 39:25 Therefore thus says the Master YHWH: `Now I will bring back the **captives of Jacob**, and have mercy on the **whole house of Israel**; and I will be jealous for My holy name.

Malachi 1:2 "I have loved you," says the Master. "Yet you say, `In what way have You loved **us**?' "Was not Esau Jacob's brother?" says the Master. "Yet **Jacob** I have loved;

367

Note YHWH says, "**I have loved you**" again singular, but referring to many people within Israel. The same with Esau; not just Esau, but this refers to the conglomerate of nations that are biblically referred to as Mount Seir (Ezekiel 35:2); remember a mountain is a kingdom, not just a formation of rock. **Psalm 24:6** This is Jacob, **the generation** of those who seek Him; who seek Your face.

In biblical terminology YHWH sometimes views an individual to mean a whole group and a whole group can also be applied to an individual. Gog of Magog is seen as a singular being (Ezekiel 38:2), but is also seen as many nations (Ezekiel 38:16). "**You**" will come up against My people Israel like a cloud, to cover the land. It will be in the latter days that I will bring **you** against My land, so that the nations may know Me, when I am hallowed in **you**, O Gog, before their eyes.' The word "you" is not just referring to "Gog," but many other nations with him. So YHWH is applying a singular word to many people because they are both, the individual named "Gog," and the multiple of nations compromising Gog. Often the head of a group becomes interchangeable with the group he represents, just as Adam became the federal head of humanity! So YHWH when speaking to Adam can also be referring to all of humanity.

Islam's lawlessness is clear for those with discernment. Muslims have changed the ordinances e.g. camel meat is now considered clean in Islam and is allowed, but biblically it remains unclean.

> **Deuteronomy 14:6** "And you may eat every animal with cloven hooves, having the hoof split into two parts, and that chews the cud, among the animals.

> The same applies to Islam's sin in changing the eternal Shabbat to Friday. This is a deceptive spirit of lawlessness, all the while claiming that Muhammad fixed the errors in the Torah in order to liberate Muslims and to uphold the true Torah, free from alleged Jewish lies.

Let us see how **2 Thessalonians 2: 7-8** should read:

> **2 Thessalonians 2: 7-8** (7) For the mystery of **lawlessness** [anomia] is already at work; [now or at that very time] who [the Jewish Nation] now restrains will do so until [they come into existence or appear in history] in the midst. (8) And **then the lawless** [anomos - Torahless] **one will be revealed.**

In fact when we look at the Greek there is no word for "he" as this is simply interpreted and implied. It is clear that when the Jewish people would be taken out of the way, **removed from the land of Israel then a few things were to happen**. The lawless (Torahless) ones (Islamists) were to be revealed. This happened after the dispersal of the Jews in 70 AD from the land. It was the Jews that YHWH was going to remove from the land because of their sins. Then in 637 AD came the Muslims (the Torahless ones), and these claimed to follow the Torah, but were actually not following the Torah. They set up the sign/structure of the abomination of desolation on the Temple-Mount and all that is now left is for the Anti-Messiah to come and sit there and proclaim his Caliphate. As explained the Anti-Messiah does not have to sit in a built 3rd Temple because no such Temple will be rebuilt until the return of the Master. The only thing that will be built is an "altar" for the Jewish people to start their sacrificial system. So at some point in near future a part of the Temple Mount will be conceded to the Jews to start this system as Revelation 11 indicates. **Revelation 11:1**-Then I was given a reed like a measuring rod. And the angel stood, saying, "Rise and measure the temple of YHWH, **"the altar,"** and those who worship there.

After this is instituted, the Anti-Messiah will come and sit in the Temple i.e. in Greek this is "naos," but which Temple is this? The word "naos" is not only applied to the Holy of Holies, but it can be applied to the entire Temple Mount region. It can also be applied to a pagan shrine. The Anti-Messiah will sit in a pagan shrine, the Mosque of Omar, called the Al-Aqsa Mosque where he will say to **himself** that he is like YHWH. Privately however he will worship the god of jihad, that is Allah. The whole of the Temple Area is sacred to YHWH, not just the Holy of Holies. When YHWH is looking at things, He does not just see a small area. But the writers of the Bible told us that after this "abomination of desolation" is set up, there will be further desolation that spreads. <u>Daniel 9:27</u> Then he shall **confirm a covenant with many for one week**; but in the **middle of the week He shall bring an end to sacrifice and offering. And on the wing of abominations shall be one who makes desolate, even until the consummation, which is determined**, is **poured out on the desolate.** The Anti-Messiah comes, sets up the treaty for the seven years with both Israel and the many Muslim nations that are in agreement with it. The text in Daniel says on the "corner" in Hebrew "kanaph," where the abomination is set up that causes the desolation. The Hebrew word for **"desolation"** is shamem.[71] A primitive root; to *stun* (or intransitively *grow numb*), that is, *devastate* or (figuratively) *stupefy* (both usually in a passive sense): - make amazed, be astonished, (be an) astonish (-ment), (be, bring into, unto, lay, lie, make) desolate (-ion, places), be destitute, destroy (self), (lay, lie, make) waste, wonder.

So this word not only would mean to cause desolation in the land by confusion between people, but also a literal desolation where the gospel cannot be proclaimed. Islam will get an open and huge airing along with a stronghold, as the people will be confused over what is going on and which faith is the truth. If you went to East Jerusalem today and heard the many calls of the Muezzin (Islamic clerics calling Muslims to pray), you would think you are in the middle of an Islamic country. You would never think that you are in Israel. You can get confused. When I was woken up by the loud call of the Muezzin on my first day in Israel, I thought to myself, is this not supposed to be the land of the King of Israel, where shofars would blow at one time to call people to prayer? But now this? I was very saddened to hear this sound, as I might as well have been in Lahore Pakistan, hearing the same Islamic call for prayer. Unfortunately Israel has become a most unholy land today. So save yourselves and get out of the Babylonian system and do <u>not</u> have any spiritual association with the harlot of Babylon.

Question-Some may argue how I can paint a good picture of Europe, considering that Europe is generally considered to be godless and into liberalism?

Answer-First of all we should not say that all of Europe is corrupt because there are true Christians spread throughout Europe in both high and low places. People should remember that YHWH can use any nation whether godly, or ungodly. My painting a positive picture of Europe is not to show that one-day all Europeans will become Christians, or will become godly. It is simply to show that the wrath of YHWH is not on Europe and never was. Is it too hard to fathom that Jeremiah gave specific prophecies to show that YHWH will call certain nations out of Europe to attack the Anti-Messiah nations? When the Islamic nations muster forces and start to openly persecute and kill people,

---

[71] http://www.e-sword.net

whether the Europeans are Christians or not, the Europeans will help. Certainly not because they have suddenly decided to become Christians overnight, but because they will be posed by a potential threat. When Hitler attacked the European nations why did the allied forces get together against Germany? The reason is obvious. Hitler did not hide the fact that he wanted to conquer Europe. This is why his Nazi policies permeated Poland, Hungary and Austria etc. Why did Europe fight back? Was it because they were all Christians? No, it was because there was a threat to their national security and Hitler was growing stronger. Was the desire to fight and defend themselves because of their Christian values? No, the desire was for self-preservation, albeit some did empathize with the Jews. It may well be that in the future when Islam is becoming very strong in Europe, that Europe will fight back for the same principles, but not necessarily because they have a desire to follow the Elohim of Israel. When the Jews were being slaughtered by Hitler, did many in Europe help because the Jews were the covenant people? No, even then it was politically motivated by defending their various constitutions and lifestyles. Christians forget that YHWH does not need to muster Christian nations, because truly no such nation exists. YHWH musters leaders who will act out His will. Was King Cyrus a Christian? Yet YHWH used him to free His people and even called him His anointed; think about that one.

What should I do now? To start with you should be praying for yourself that if you are alive when this happens that the Master saves you from the trouble that is to come. In addition, you should also be praying that Muslims and others will get saved before this happens, as it is better to have Muslims as friends than as enemies. May their souls be saved for the glory of YHWH. You should get this book into as many hands as possible, so people know what is coming to pass, as time is short. We are not talking about hundreds of years anymore but maybe at most one or two generations or less. Remember that one Muslim saved by Yahushua's blood is one less terrorist or suicide bomber. You should prepare for yourself enough food to survive the crisis that will come, the three and a half year period of tribulation. You should be looking at storing some food and water, and I would recommend at least six months supply to be on the safe side, perhaps more if you can afford it and are able to do so. Tin packaged foods, dry foods, things that can last a long period of time are good to store. These days you can get dry foods that have a long life; you should look at having wheat, rice types of foods, also which can be stored. This website gives you simple techniques of securing and safe guarding water. See: http://www.thegoldenreport.com. This book's intention is not to scare you or make you panic, but to prepare you both spiritually and physically; this is the message that YHWH wants you to have.

Conclusion

I have shown enough data from the Bible to make certain that we are facing real dangers ahead. Some people may not want to believe this because they are sceptical, or have been led to believe different things. Please, I implore you to go through the Bible with a fine-toothed-comb. First of all the Bible translation that I would recommend for you to read is **the Restoration Scriptures True Name Edition** available at: www.restorationscriptures.org, which is the closest to the original translation.

I am not joking when I say this is serious stuff. If you are not convinced then you will be caught off guard and will be sorry that you did not pay attention. When all this comes upon you then it will be too late. All these things will happen suddenly as there will be no warning, but there will be plenty of tell tale signs, with some already appearing.

Fanatic Islam is the real danger to the world today and Islamic fanaticism is totally out of hand. Many innocent people have lost their lives and many more will die, either due to ignorance, or due to not knowing how to deal with Islamic fanatics. Do you realize that the USA with all its might has been unable to catch Osama bin Laden. They have been unable to apprehend Abu Musab al-Zarkawi in Iraq with their 140,000 troops. His henchmen are quite confidently beheading people. Remember s.a.tan protects his own nefarious people; computer technology will not help against spiritual forces, bullets and missiles do not shoot down spiritual entities, but only prayers and complete trust in YHWH do. We must defeat the aerial enemy by the power of prayer. Remember that s.a.tan the serpent of old protects his own.

Our governments' needs to tighten up their laws so no one can cause terrorism in the western world. Anyone who is into this type of fanaticism should be dealt with. The Muslims who are peaceful should be encouraged to see the truth of the Master Yahushua the Messiah by the Christians who honor YHWH. We should do our best to coexist in a peaceful way without violence against them. There is a funny quote "not all Muslims are terrorists, but unfortunately all terrorists today happen to be fanatic Muslims. The irony is that this is actually true. I would discourage any vigilante behavior, because it is not moral against any group of people. We should pray for our society and for our leaders that the Master gives us good wise leadership.

Our governments need to do a lot more to stop terrorism by fanatic Islam and I also know there are many terrorist elements in our society that are being given handouts. Something needs to be done about these people as they pose a threat to our societies existence. These are the ticking time bombs that can cause havoc and we will only have ourselves to blame because we did not pay attention to this.

The Bible is clear on this issue and YHWH is not silent either. He gave us enough signs through the prophets of Israel to show that we are not facing a makeshift army of rag tag soldiers. There is one real way to protect ourselves, which in my view is to come to personally know the Elohim of Israel, who revealed Himself in the person of Yahushua as our Messiah, Savior and Redeemer. He died on the cross to atone for our sins and cleanse man's hateful heart. This gives us a far higher level of protection and a perfect Advocate along with perfectly wise council. Remember the case of Thomas Hamill who was taken captive in Iraq on the 9th of April 2004. He would have been beheaded like most other hostages, and no government on this earth was be able to negotiate his release. But he trusted in the Master Yahushua the Messiah and knew that YHWH was going to save him and he was saved through our great and mighty Yahushua.

The only one that is on our side in situations of dire straits is the Elohim of Israel (Yahushua of Nazareth), YHWH who truly loves and cares for His children. No government can really help or protect us and we all know what happened to Margaret Hassan a charity worker. No negotiations helped her on that fateful day when they killed her. We face a very brutal enemy, but we should be glad that we have an almighty YHWH who is able to help us in any trouble as long as we remain faithful to Him.

Remember salvation is our need and YHWH's standard of salvation is 100% righteousness. **Proverbs 14:12**-There is a way that **seems right to a man**, but in the **end it leads to death**. We all think we can do it on our own, but the end result is <u>no life</u> after death i.e. eternal separation from a holy YHWH. This is what this verse is saying in light of the fact that all humans die physically. So this is talking about the 2nd death i.e. when you are judged and found to have no atonement for your sins. Then the end result is the "second death," or the casting off into the Lake of Fire for eternal conscious punishment.

You may still continue to do your own works to get to YHWH, or you may not even believe that YHWH exists. However all you need do is look at the Jewish nation of Israel as proof. After 2,000 years of dispersion, the Elohim of Israel gathered them to re-establish them back in the land of Israel. This could only have happened to this minority nation because of the **Creator** YHWH, who exists, along with His divine providence. What YHWH had promised to Abraham, Isaac and Jacob declared through the prophets of Israel in the Bible has surely come to pass. If YHWH does not exist, then the Jewish race would have been annihilated long ago. They would <u>not</u> have survived the constant onslaught by the different superpowers that arose against them in times past. The Jewish people are set as a sign for all other peoples whether they believe in YHWH, or not. YHWH has set apart the Jewish nation **as a witness** for all peoples.

> <u>Isaiah 43:10</u> "**You are My witnesses**," says the Master, "**And My servant whom I have chosen**, that you may know and believe Me, and understand that I am He. Before Me there was no El formed, nor shall there be after Me.

History is our witness that the Jewish people <u>did</u> survive every calamity that befell them. Many big name nations came and went e.g. the Egyptian, Assyrian, Babylonian, Persian, Grecian and the Roman Empires. Yet the Jews are still here and all the big name empires faded into mere history. All we have left of all these so-called great empires are the artefacts they have left behind. Other nations who have tried to deal harshly with the Jews, YHWH also dealt harshly with them. YHWH set one standard in the book of Genesis in the Bible **"I will bless those who bless MY people [Israel] and I will curse those who curse MY people" (Genesis 12:3a).** The curse is evident in all those nations who have dealt with the Jews harshly:

❖ Spain - a superpower in its history — no longer rules the seas; it started the inquisitions and forced conversions and the expulsion of the Jews.

❖ Russia - broken and divided into small pieces for its pogroms against the Jews; it also stopped the Jews from leaving Russia to go back to Israel. Today Russia is well on its way to becoming part of the Muslim end time confederacy to attack Israel.

❖ Germany - has no real power base today for what Hitler did to the Jewish people; but it certainly has many Christians today who recognize the past errors of their nation and pray that this is not repeated.

❖ England - used to rule the world and was mightily blessed by YHWH for its great acts. It birthed some of the great Christian hero's, Charles Haddon Spurgeon, FB Meyer, William Tidal, Charles Finney, and CS Lewis to name a few. This vast nation has now fallen by the wayside. After its mishandling of the Jewish affair in 1948, when Winston Churchill gave 75% of mandated Jewish land to Jordan, YHWH did not remain silent on this issue. This nation thus went through a trying time, and it no longer rules the world as it did before. Its once flourishing empire withdrew into decadence and into all sorts of false spirituality. There are a few Christians in this nation who have gone back to their first love (Yahushua the Messiah) and they also support Israel vehemently for its right to exist. YHWH certainly has a plan for this "great nation" in the end of days as I have illustrated most clearly in this book.

YHWH will again bless the UK and lead them in the right path with YHWH fearing and wise leaders.

❖ Muslim Nations - Though, some vastly rich Arab nations with oil and mineral wealth do exist, they remain powerless and impotent in world affairs. Yet these are the ones who will get their power for a short season, as allowed by YHWH, in order to cause end time terror and havoc in the world.

❖ USA – The only nation today who openly stands to defend and support Israel. A nation, which was born just over 200 years ago and still, uses the principle of Genesis 12:3a. YHWH blessed them exceedingly, now they are a superpower and control most of the world's affairs. We are told in the Bible that YHWH will use this nation once again in the end of days. May YHWH bless the USA and may it have wise leaders also.

This is the standard that YHWH uses for the entire world. He also said "**and in thee shall all families of the earth be blessed (Genesis 12:3b)**." This blessing was to come through the Messiah Yahushua and whoever accepted Him; YHWH would bless them both spiritually and physically. This is evident in the Western world that by and large accepted Yahushua the Messiah as their Savior. Now we see all sorts of false spirituality, invading the west and we need to return to our FIRST LOVE, our Master Yahushua the Messiah. YHWH calls us out as seen in **Revelation 18:4**: *"And I heard another voice from heaven, saying, **Come out of her, My People**, that you be not partakers of her sins, and that you receive not her plagues."* Unfortunately a lot of the western nations are involved in appeasing Babylon and simply will not heed the call to come out of these various beast alliances (spiritual, economic and/or physical), until judgement rains down from YHWH.

Europe is once again into the appeasement of the Arabs because of their oil. This does involve an associated cost that Europe will come to realize later. Need we be reminded of the past when the Islamic invaders took Spain and ruled it for 800 years? Europe was asleep back then, just like it is today, until Islamic forces pushed into Europe and were met by the brave Charles Martel (the Hammer) who stopped them in dead in their tracks in France. Without his brave actions, all of Europe would likely be Islamic today! Where are the Charles Martels of today that will stand firm against Islam's conduct and call it to account before they are consumed by the beast?

We see the same thing happening once again. The only difference is that now the radical Muslims want to conquer from within, by establishing communities, mosques, banks and Islamic schools. Saudi Arabia is at the forefront of this global movement to establish these things, whose hidden agenda is to literally Islamise Europe and break it from within. There is an explosion of Islamic culture in the west. If one were to go to certain areas in the west, you would think you are in the east. Mostly these communities are peaceful now, but when the Islamic call for jihad comes from the clerics in these same mosques, things may not be the same anymore. How difficult is an enemy fighting from within? We already know the answer when we look at Israel and the daily suicide bombings.

Suicide bombings have come to Europe. London has already been hit as I predicted earlier in February 2005. I have been warning about this for a while, but many people may have thought I was being over zealous. Looking back at the events that shook London on July 7th 2005, I myself was caught up in the bombings, as I was on the tube/subway at Baker Street, when it all started and I got off at Bond Street, where the tubes/subways were stopped. I then caught the number 55 bus from Oxford Circus a short walk away. That is when a friend phoned me telling me to get off the bus because in the direction that I was headed to was a bus that had been blown up by a suicide bomber. I stayed on the bus because the Master wanted me amongst the people and I had no fear. The Master brought me out of that experience unscathed. Praise Yahushua, who remains the best bullet and bombproof vest to have. My heartfelt condolences go to the dead people's families and the families of those injured on that fateful day. May our Master stretch out His hands of love and mercy for them, comfort them, heal their wounds and cure their broken hearts; it's a sad and senseless loss.

This is a warning for those that think that terror attacks are limited to Israel and the Middle East. We will see more suicide bombings in the west not less. I am going to predict again, that London will be hit again; the question is when, where and how? Our leaders think they can give money to the corrupt leadership of the Palestinian Authority and divide Israel and remain unscathed. However no such thing will stand in Yahweh's eyes because He will not remain silent. While Tony Blair was working out the three billion dollar plan for the corrupt PA authority and the division of Israel, Yahweh was working out His own plan as He lifted His protection from this nation. That allowed the radical Muslims to be unleashed in London, so much so, that Tony Blair had to leave his meeting. These people do not realize that they are not dealing with flesh and blood alone, but the fight is between s.a.tan and Yahweh. s.a.tan has already lost, but people need to realize this truth and deal with it accordingly. The only nation that is safe is a praying nation, who realizes that the only way to defeat evil forces is through a wall of prayer with true protection from Yahweh.

Europeans be warned and alert because this is just the start and not the end. Fanatic Islam, like it or not, is at war with the west and the war has just been officially and openly declared with Great Britain on Thursday 7th July 2005, with the bombings on the London transportation system. Unfortunately the enemy does not have a border, or a single nationality, and unless we tighten up our laws in Europe and the USA, we are just sitting ducks to be taken out one by one. Any such people who act out these types of crimes should be dealt with within the framework of the law. It may well be necessary that new laws will need to be enacted immediately, to accommodate for such massive and unprecedented crimes against humanity.

I know my life is on the line and anyone who leaves Islam faces possible death. It is difficult to understand this theology of Islam and it is also difficult to be on the receiving end of its brutality, but since Yahushua called me, and I answered that call literally, I am honored to serve Him. I love the Master Yahushua with all my heart and because of my love for Him I will continue to share His truth with the world. I have presented enough evidence to point people to the truth. For me death is a short trip to eternity with my Master and Savior Yahushua of Nazareth. My only prayer for the world is that they come to know the one true Savior who died for them and that people do not die in their sins and face eternity without receiving YHWH's love. That will be a human being's most painful experience and that pain will last for all eternity.

Today the top 21 most wanted terrorists on the USA list are ALL Muslims. You can visit the link below on the internet and examine it for yourself.

http://www.fbi.gov/mostwant/terrorists/fugitives.htm Fanatic Islam is the biggest threat we face in our history. Many thousands of innocent people are dead already and many more will die if we remain silent. Either the west has to do something about fanatic Islam and tell the people the real truth, or fanatic Islam will do something about the west. One day the west will have to deal with this issue decisively and it is written in the Bible that this will not be through dialogue alone. The beast has been unmasked on these pages. **World War Three has begun to play itself out**. Redeem these times, as these days are abundantly evil. As the prophet Elijah said and as that same Elijah spirit still calls out today saying: 'How long will you live between shifting opinions. If YHWH is elohim serve Him and prepare for the days ahead. If Allah/Baal is elohim serve him. The choice is yours. The time is at hand. WW 3 has begun. Blow the shofar with me in Zion!

Maps for our Understanding

Map 5 The evil triangle [72]

Map #5 seen above is the evil triangle, showing the rectangle, which is part of the 10/40 window of the world, containing some 90% of the un-reached peoples (mostly Muslims) of the world. Turkey, the area of the earthly throne of s.a.tan, is within the inner evil triangle shown in the map. Iraq is <u>the area</u> of extreme evil activity. Have you wondered why so many beheadings are occurring in Iraq? Remember that at one time the entire evil triangle including Saudi Arabia was ancient Babylon, so that Saudi Arabia and Mecca are in essence Babylon!

This is the same place where the four angels will be loosed and extreme trouble will be unleashed upon the world soon to come. **Revelation 9:14-15**- saying to the sixth angel who had the trumpet, "Release the four angels <u>who are bound at the great river Euphrates</u>." **So the four angels, who had been prepared for the hour and day and month and year**, were released **to kill a third of mankind**. These will kill a third of mankind and are released from the river Euphrates in Iraq. This is the center of all trouble, the center of all the false religions, the center of the religion and the morbid culture of Islam, **which is also unleashed from this area**. Once the Anti-Messiah is unleashed upon the world, Islam will cause unprecedented trouble. Those preachers that are looking at Europe, or the USA for the Anti-Messiah will be disappointed, as YHWH never meant Europe when He spoke of the Middle East. The one-third of the people that will be killed are only in the Middle East, not the whole world. If you still think Islam is basically peaceful, then wait and see because Islam is going to get stronger. This may cause some

---

[72] www.prophecymaps.com

with wisdom to question the very legitimacy of the religion of Islam, because of the amount of people that it will kill, as it spreads hatred and intolerance in the west and elsewhere. Expect at least two nuclear strikes in the Middle East that the Bible speaks about.

This is the future map of Israel [73] that YHWH is going to bring about through the power of Messiah Yahushua fighting for Israel as seen in Scripture- The view is that of the millennial kingdom.

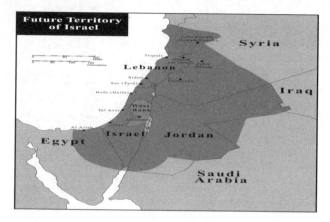

The Interlock Map

The 10 heads/kings of Psalm 83 are the same as the confederacy of the Islamic Gog and Magog nations. These are the surrounding heathens mentioned many times in Scripture.

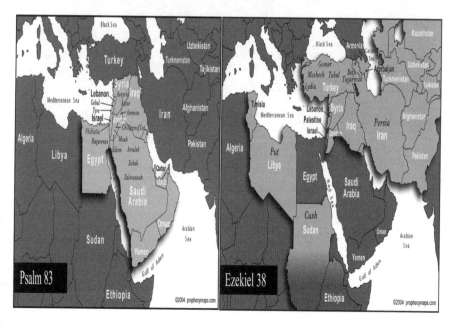

---

[73] www.prophecymaps.com

Other Titles

INDEX

I

I John 2
   22 ... denies the Father and the Son, 26
it broke in pieces the iron, the bronze, the clay, the silver, and the gold, 34

J

Jewish, 37, 42, 43, 53, 65, 66, 68, 78, 83, 84, 88, 90, 104, 105, 118, 123, 126, 131, 132, 139, 144, 148, 149, 150, 151, 153, 166, 169, 170, 174, 175, 176, 177, 179, 180, 186, 187, 194, 200, 201, 210, 214, 219, 234, 239, 248, 255, 260, 269, 280, 281, 282, 286, 290, 292, 296, 308, 309, 310, 334, 343, 344, 349, 350, 355, 356, 357, 366, 368, 371, 372
Jews driven from Saudi Arabia, 131
Jihad – Outward war, IV, 11, 13, 14, 56, 132, 133, 140, 167, 196, 201, 220, 235, 236, 311, 332, 364

K

Kanaph – Hebrew for wing, 312, 313, 368

L

Legion X composed of Arabs, 19
Light Horse, 303, 304
Living Water, 130

M

Mamra, 120
Mansookh - abrogated, 11
Mark of the Beast, 256
Medina, 11, 39, 55, 86, 88, 103, 131, 138, 139, 166, 205, 207, 241, 271
Medo-Persia, 32, 34, 76, 79, 324
Miphkad altar, 129
moon city, 128
Mount of Abraham, 148
Mount of Esau, 144, 187, 299
Mount Seir, 35, 36, 47, 51, 184, 187, 191, 367

N

Nebuchadnezzar, 31, 34, 51, 80, 162, 180, 201
Nivrechu – Grafted in, 42
North, 20, 39, 46, 47, 62, 77, 98, 127, 134, 179, 201, 208, 217, 218, 222, 223, 253, 296, 297, 314, 358, 359

O

Oros – A Mountain, 75

P

people of the prince – the ones to destroy Jerusalem, 17, 18, 19, 309, 361
Plucked, 32

R

Rapture, 261, 272
Revival – not so soon, IV, 79, 140, 141
Revival of radical Islam, IV, 32, 79, 140
Rosh - Head, 340

S

Saharon – Crescent symbols, 161
seed of men, 34, 35, 159
Seven mountains, 74, 75, 76, 93, 94, 232
Seven Mountains, 72, 93
Shachar – Morning star, 107, 124, 161, 162, 202
Ships of Kittim, 77
Shuwph - crushing, 132
Sir Robert Anderson, 79, 80
Smoke, 69, 70, 99, 100, 133, 164, 197, 199, 204, 223, 232, 251, 276, 326, 360
Son of God, 311
Submission, 11, 105, 107, 135, 164, 167, 196, 234, 258
Sunni, 50, 92, 235, 350
Sura 47
   4 – Beheading sanctioned in the Qur'an, 13, 236
Sura 9